11th Edition

RETAIL MERCHANDISING

CONSUMER GOODS & SERVICES

Harland E. Samson
Professor of Marketing Education
University of Wisconsin-Madison

Wayne G. Little
Professor of Marketing Education
St. Cloud State University
St. Cloud, Minnesota

SOUTH-WESTERN PUBLISHING CO.

Managing Editor: Robert E. Lewis
Developmental Editor: Nancy A. Long
Production Editor: Melanie A. Blair
Production Artist: Steven McMahon
Associate Photo Editor/Stylist: Linda Ellis
Marketing Manager: Donald H. Fox

ISBN: 0–538–61326–2

Library of Congress Catalog Card Number: 91–62552

4 5 6 7 8 9 D 99 98

Printed in the United States of America

PREFACE

Retailing includes all the activities associated with the marketing of goods and services to consumers. These activities involve obtaining products from manufacturers and suppliers from all over the world and selling these goods to people who will use them. The changing needs and wants of consumers, the wide varieties and sources of merchandise, the expansion of consumer services, and the increased use of technology are a few of the forces that make retail marketing an exciting and challenging career choice.

Retail businesses are found in every community. For those who want to work in retailing businesses, ability in basic academic skills—reading, writing, calculating, communicating—is very important. However, successful retail workers must also understand the modern methods of and trends in retailing as well as the application of critical thinking and problem solving to the tasks of retail marketing. Modern retail merchandising requires employees who can perform effectively and efficiently as well as have the potential to advance into management and even business ownership. This eleventh edition of *Retail Merchandising: Consumer Goods and Services* is designed to introduce students to the nature and scope of retail merchandising, to help them acquire the skill and knowledge essential to perform a variety of retail activities, and to understand what is required in retail management or retail business ownership.

Content and Organization

This edition of *Retail Merchandising: Consumer Goods and Services* emphasizes (1) the role of retail marketing within a free-enterprise society, (2) the retail concepts and practices necessary for successfully carrying out the retail functions, (3) the problem solving and critical thinking necessary for effective retail merchandising, and (4) the importance of each individual worker to the success of a retail enterprise.

The eleventh edition of *Retail Merchandising: Consumer Goods and Services* contains 55 chapters arranged into nine units:

- Unit 1 provides an overview of retailing and retail functions and introduces topics covered in the remainder of the textbook.
- Unit 2 explains the sources and channels of distribution used for consumer goods and services and the organization of retail businesses in a free-enterprise economy.

- Unit 3 examines the qualifications necessary for people entering the retailing field and explores the management of human resources in retailing, including selecting, supervising, and training workers.
- Unit 4 covers merchandise planning, selecting, buying, and pricing.
- Unit 5 introduces retail promotion, including advertising strategies and the development and use of displays.
- Unit 6 describes consumer behavior, the selling process, and the duties of retail salespeople.
- Unit 7 presents store operations, including space layout, maintenance, service and credit policies, and stock management.
- Unit 8 examines principles of financing a business and the use of business records and financial statements.
- Unit 9 explores retail research, changes in retailing technology, and career advancement in the retailing field.

Each of the 55 chapters within these nine units contains a list of learning outcomes, a chapter summary, and four types of learning activities:

1. **Review** requires students to answer questions that are correlated with the chapter's learning outcomes. If students have difficulty with these review questions, they should spend additional time reading and studying the chapter material before pursuing the other three activities.
2. **Terms** provides students with a convenient study list of the merchandising terminology appearing in boldface in the chapter.
3. **Discuss** encourages students to relate local retail practices and their own observations and opinions to topics in the chapter.
4. **Problem Solving** requires students to collect, analyze, and interpret data on subjects relevant to the chapter.

Each of the nine units opens with an overview and a set of learning outcomes that should result from reading the unit chapters and completing the chapter and unit activities. Ten types of learning activities in five categories appear at the end of each unit:

1. **Checking Key Points** uses a series of true-false questions to check students' understanding of the retailing fundamentals presented in the unit. Students who answer most of these questions correctly are ready to advance to the other learning activities. Students who have difficulty with these questions should review the chapters in the unit.
2. **Building Basic Skills** contains three different activities:

- **Calculations** asks students to perform computations similar to those shown in the various chapters of the unit.
- **Working with People** has students analyze "people problems" using the four-step DICE method.
- **Writing Skills** asks students to prepare various written communications about retailing projects.

3. **Applying Your Knowledge** contains two activities:
   - **Can You Do the Following?** poses questions that require application of the knowledge and skills presented in the chapters.
   - **Retail Decisions** asks students to make judgments about retail business situations using the information they have acquired.

4. **Developing Critical-Thinking Skills** contains two activities:
   - **Retail Projects** presents situations commonly faced by retailers. These situations involve students in problems that usually can be analyzed with school-based information.
   - **Field Projects** requires students to carry out small-scale investigations similar to those pursued by retailers. Some projects require students to conduct interviews with local businesspeople or consumers.

5. **Continuing Projects** involves two types of activities:
   - **Developing a Career Plan** leads students through a series of questions and activities designed to help them make tentative career decisions.
   - **Developing a Business Plan** guides students through the process of planning, developing, and operating their own retail businesses. By completing this activity at the end of each unit, students create portfolios of plans and ideas for retail businesses of their choice.

The units and chapters of *Retail Merchandising: Consumer Goods and Services,* Eleventh Edition, may be used in sequence or on a selective basis. In Unit 1, Chapter 1 is an overview of retail marketing and the retail functions. Chapters 2 through 8 each introduce a subsequent unit of the text. For example, a complete study of the promotion function is provided in Chapter 1, Chapter 5, and all the chapters in Unit 5 (Chapters 27–33).

The Complete Package

Retail Merchandising: Consumer Goods and Services is supported by a complete selection of ancillaries:

1. The *Teacher's Manual* provides unit outlines, discussion starters,

transparency masters, solutions to text questions and activities, test answers, and solutions to the student workbook.

2. The text-workbook *Retailing in Action* contains a series of simulation exercises correlated with each unit of *Retail Merchandising: Consumer Goods and Services.* This text-workbook contains 50 projects dealing with job activities in retailing. Suggested solutions are contained in a separate manual.

3. Printed and computerized *Achievement Tests* provide unit reviews and a final exam.

4. A *Student Supplement,* new this edition in response to teacher requests, provides additional objective questions for student review. This supplement can be used for reteaching or reinforcing key content areas.

Acknowledgments

The authors gratefully acknowledge the retail executives, store managers, and retail workers who so generously shared their perceptions and views on the theory and practice of modern retailing. Appreciation is also extended to the many marketing education and retail merchandising teachers and students who shared their views and made recommendations for the organization of material and learning activities. This edition of *Retail Merchandising: Consumer Goods and Services* is enriched to the extent that we have properly interpreted and incorporated these insights and suggestions.

Harland E. Samson
Wayne G. Little

CONTENTS

UNIT 1
Dynamics of Retailing   1

UNIT 2
Retailing Businesses   84

UNIT 3
Managing Human Resources　164

UNIT 4
Merchandising　224

UNIT 5
Promotion   304

UNIT 6
Selling   386

UNIT 7
Operations   452

UNIT 8
Business Control   532

UNIT 1
Dynamics of Retailing

Retail businesses provide the goods and services that consumers need and want. To bring these products to consumers in cities, towns, and villages across the country requires that retail businesses be well organized and able to perform a variety of functions. Retail workers have to be employed; goods have to be purchased, promoted, and sold. Records of all operations must be kept, and financial statements must be prepared for controlling and guiding the business.

The products made for consumer use continually change. New products are introduced and changes made in many others every year. In addition, consumer preferences, wants, and needs change. Thus, retailing is a dynamic, ever-changing field—from both consumers' and retailers' viewpoints.

Unit 1 introduces the main activities of retailing. Subsequent units develop this introductory information and present additional concepts and ideas about the business of retailing.

UNIT OUTCOMES

After studying this unit and completing the activities, you should be able to:

1. State the purposes and value of retailing to consumers and describe the types of retail marketing
2. Describe ways in which retail businesses are organized
3. List the characteristics of personnel needed to perform the retailing activities in various retail stores
4. List the four kinds of consumer goods and explain three policies that might be used in pricing these goods
5. Describe how retail sellers communicate information about stores and merchandise to prospective customers
6. List some qualifications of retail sales personnel and the techniques used in selling merchandise and services
7. List the activities carried out by the operations division and the control division of retail stores
8. Explain two factors affecting the future of retailing and briefly describe how to plan for a retailing career

CHAPTER 1

Retail Marketing

CHAPTER OUTCOMES

When you have mastered the information provided in this chapter, you should be able to:

1. Define the terms *marketing*, *retailing*, and *retailer*

2. Explain the purpose of retailing

3. Explain the value of retail marketing to consumers

4. Describe four types of retail marketing businesses

5. List the four main forms of retail business ownership

6. Describe the career opportunities available in retail marketing

7. List the characteristics of successful retail management

3

The movement and sale of merchandise and services to consumers and business users is called **marketing.** Marketing covers those activities necessary for the successful flow of goods and services from their place of production to the place where they are ultimately used. **Retail marketing** is marketing goods or services used by individual consumers.

A business that provides goods and services to individual consumers is called a **retail store.** The process of obtaining a variety of goods and making them easily available for sale to customers is called **retailing.** A person who manages or assists in the management of retail businesses is called a **retailer.** This chapter will introduce you to various types of retail marketing and the importance of retailing to our consumer-oriented society. The ideas introduced in this chapter are explained more fully in the seven chapters of Unit 2, Retailing Businesses.

THE PURPOSE OF RETAIL MARKETING

The main purpose of retail marketing is to provide consumers with a steady flow of the goods and services they desire. Retailers collect products from manufacturers or suppliers all over the world. They sell these goods to people who will use them. The retailer serves as an agent between manufacturers or other suppliers of goods and services and the consumer. The retailer informs manufacturers and suppliers of customers' needs and wants. The retailer also answers customers' questions about merchandise. Retail marketing businesses buy goods to fill the merchandise and service needs of people who are the ultimate users of the products. Many businesses buy goods for resale; some buy goods to use in manufacturing other goods. Only retail businesses buy merchandise for resale to the **ultimate consumer:** the person who finally uses the goods for personal benefit and satisfaction.

The terms **merchandise** and **goods** usually mean material items such as a pair of shoes, a sweater, or a gallon of milk. Many retailers also provide customer **services,** such as credit, alterations, and delivery. Some businesses, such as dry cleaners, travel agencies, or appliance repair shops, deal only in service. Many personal service businesses, such as barber and beauty shops, are considered service businesses rather than retail businesses.

Retailing is generally described as "having the right merchandise at the right place, at the right time, in the right quantities, and at the right price." Think about that statement: Each of these rights is an important part of retailing. (1) Having the right merchandise means knowing what customers want. (2) Having merchandise at the right place means having the goods where customers can see and examine them. (3) Having merchandise at the right time means having goods in stock during the season, month, or days when the cus-

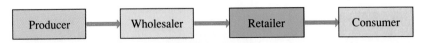

Illus. 1–1   Retail marketing is that part of marketing that provides goods and services to consumers.

Illus. 1–2   Retail businesses provide goods and services desired by consumers.

tomers expect to buy. (4) Having merchandise in the right quantities means being able to supply the smallest or largest order. (5) Having merchandise at the right price means having goods at the prices customers are willing to pay. The activities represented by these five rights constitute the main work in retail marketing.

VALUE TO CONSUMERS

Without retail marketing businesses, a consumer would have to search for desired merchandise from manufacturers or producers who may be thousands of miles away. Without retailers, consumers would find that local choices of goods were limited, less popular items were available only occasionally, and the price of most merchandise would be higher. Retailing provides every community with a selection of merchandise that would otherwise not be possible.

TYPES OF RETAIL MARKETING

Most people think of a retail business as a store where merchandise can be bought. This is true, but the retail store is only one of four major types or methods of retailing.

In-store Retailing

Most retail marketing is done through **in-store retailing,** which involves a conveniently located building supplied with a selection of merchandise. Customers may come to the store and personally examine, select, and purchase desired merchandise from the stock assembled by the retailer.

Mail-order Retailing

In **mail-order retailing,** customers examine a catalog or advertisement describing merchandise offered by a retailer. Customers mail or telephone their orders to the retailer. The retailer receives the orders and sends the merchandise to the customers by mail or some other delivery method. For many busy consumers, mail-order retailing offers an easy means of obtaining needed merchandise.

Direct Retailing

Door-to-door merchandising is an example of **direct retailing.** The retailer's salesperson comes to the home of the customer with either merchandise or samples. Orders are taken and the goods are delivered later. Some salespeople carry a supply of merchandise for immediate delivery and contact their customers on a regular basis.

Automatic Retailing

In **automatic retailing,** the customer puts money in a machine and immediately receives the merchandise selected. Introduced to sell candy, gum, and peanuts, these automatic vending machines are now used for many articles. Generally, convenience items such as soft drinks, hosiery, hot and cold food, and reading material are sold through automatic retailing. Even banking services are available from electronic machines.

Other Types of Retailing

Changes in retailing tend to follow the needs and desires of consumers. As new consumer demands develop, new types of retailing appear. Retailing cannot change consumer demand to any significant degree, but consumer demand has great influence on retailing. Auctions, warehouse retailing, and video merchandising are innovations that many consumers find attractive. A major challenge in retailing is making the changes desired by consumers.

KINDS OF RETAIL BUSINESSES

Retail businesses vary from small firms operated by just the owner and perhaps one or two other family members to large firms with thousands of employees. It is estimated that there are more than 2.4 million retail firms in the United States. About half of these businesses are small, having fewer than four employees.

Some retail businesses seldom sell more than $150 in goods in one day, while other firms have sales of more than $150,000 every business day. Some carry only one product, such as belts or flowers. Some businesses are new, while others have been in operation for many decades.

Retail businesses, such as grocery stores, clothing stores, toy stores, or furniture stores, may be classified by the products they carry. Some may carry a wide variety of merchandise and be called by a functional name such as *department store, discount store,* or *convenience store.* Others provide services such as dry cleaning, travel reservations, or dining.

Number of Retail Firms

The U.S. Bureau of the Census reports that, in 1987, there were more than 2.4 million retail business firms in the United States, as shown in Illustration 1–3. You

will note that the largest number of retail firms are food stores and eating and drinking establishments. The sole proprietorship and partnership type of ownership are used by 57 percent of the retail establishments.

Sales by Retail Firms

Sales by retail firms have increased dramatically over a 10-year period, as shown in Illustration 1–4. This increase is partially due to inflation, but, even more, it

NUMBER AND ORGANIZATION OF RETAIL ESTABLISHMENTS

Type of Firm	Type of Ownership			Total
	Sole Proprietorship	Partnership	Corporation	
Building materials and garden supplies	45,113	5,915	55,746	106,774
General merchandise	24,777	2,651	29,440	56,868
Food	152,937	19,706	117,602	290,245
Automotive	103,803	8,303	82,209	194,315
Gasoline	65,960	7,586	63,634	137,180
Apparel and accessory	65,589	11,277	120,545	197,411
Furniture and home furnishings	91,923	8,983	79,106	180,012
Eating and drinking	209,000	39,541	241,842	490,383
Drug and proprietary	11,427	1,769	42,759	55,955
Miscellaneous	472,259	39,212	199,027	710,498
Total	1,242,788	144,943	1,031,910	2,419,641

Source: U.S. Bureau of the Census, *Census of Retail Trade, 1987* (Washington, D.C.: Supt. of Documents, U.S. Government Printing Office, 1990).

Illus. 1–3 The total number of retail establishments in the United States continues to increase.

is due to a larger population. Illustration 1–4 also shows that the automotive group accounts for the greatest amount of retail sales. Food sales represent the next largest dollar amount of retail sales.

Employment in Retailing

The retailing field has always needed employees who have many different talents to buy, handle, promote, and sell consumer goods and services. Staffing and managing the more than 2.4 million retail firms requires more than 29 million workers (see Illustration 1–5). In the past 30 years, there has been an explosion in the kinds of merchandise, techniques, and knowledge necessary to keep retailing businesses operating effectively.

OWNERSHIP OF RETAIL BUSINESSES

Ownership of retail businesses may take one of three forms. When only one person owns the business, the arrangement is known as **sole proprietorship.** When two or more persons join together to own and manage a business, the arrangement is called a **partnership.** When several people want to share in the ownership, they may create a **corporation.** In a corporation, ownership is obtained by purchasing shares of stock.

About 51 percent of all retail stores are owned by individual proprietors. About 6 percent of the retail stores are partnerships. The rest, about 43 percent, have a corporate form of ownership (see Illustra-

SALES BY RETAIL BUSINESSES

Type of Firm	1987 Sales (in Billions)	1977 Sales (in Billions)
Automotive	$333.4	$150.1
Furniture and appliance	74.7	33.3
Building materials/garden supply	81.5	38.9
Apparel	77.4	37.2
Drug and proprietary	58.8	23.4
Eating and drinking	148.8	63.4
Food	301.8	158.4
Gasoline service	102.0	56.6
General merchandise	181.1	87.8
Catalog and mail order	20.3	7.5
Merchandise machines	5.7	3.0
Direct sales	7.9	2.9

Source: U.S. Bureau of the Census, *Statistical Abstract of the United States: 1990,* 110th ed. (Washington, D.C., 1990), 769.

Illus. 1–4   Retail sales for 1987 totaled almost $1,600 billion. About 93 percent of the total was accounted for by the types of retail businesses listed above.

TOTAL LABOR FORCE AND EMPLOYMENT IN RETAIL AND WHOLESALE TRADES

Year	Total Labor Force	Retail and Wholesale Trade Employees	Percentage of Total Labor Force
1970	81,664,000	15,041,000	18.4%
1980	102,019,000	20,310,000	19.9
1988	118,104,000	25,139,000	21.3
2000 (est.)	136,211,000	29,811,000	21.9

Source: U.S. Bureau of the Census, *Statistical Abstract of the United States: 1990*, 110th ed. (Washington, D.C., 1990), 395.

Illus. 1–5   Retail and wholesale trade employees are expected to total nearly 22 percent of the labor force by the year 2000.

tion 1–3). Proprietorships and partnerships are the most common forms of ownership for small retail businesses with sales of $250,000 or less per year. The number of corporations is increasing because the corporate form of ownership is best suited for large-scale retailing.

CAREERS IN RETAILING

Retailing is a dynamic, ever-changing field of business activity. People are attracted to retail employment for many reasons. Some are interested in working with the wide variety of exciting merchandise that retail firms provide to consumers. Some people are interested in working where they can interact with other people. Still others see in retailing the opportunity to become managers or owners of their own businesses.

Jobs in retailing involve a wide range of activities. Basic jobs include merchandise receiver-checker, stock clerk, display or advertising assistant, salesperson, and cashier-checker. Advanced jobs include

buyer, department manager, sales promotion or advertising manager, and fashion coordinator. They also involve management in other areas including personnel, operations, and accounting. While the special skills required for each job vary, the personal qualifications for all retail jobs are similar. In retailing, successful persons are usually friendly and outgoing, willing to work hard, and able to communicate effectively. They generally are of good character and honest, and they have a strong need to help others. Successful retailers have the ability to recognize changes taking place around them and to promptly adjust to those changes. Whatever the reasons people have for entering the field, retailing clearly needs many workers with various talents and interests.

SUCCESSFUL RETAIL MANAGEMENT

Success in retailing requires more than good character and enthusiasm. While these qualities are important, employees and managers also must have a sound knowledge of retail practices, products, consumer behavior, and the business economy. Experience and education are important qualities for success in retail management. Most people, even though they have experience as retail customers, know little about the business side of retailing. They know almost nothing about what it takes to make goods and services available to consumers.

A major objective of this text is to help you learn how retail businesses are started; how locations for retail stores are determined; how merchandise is selected, promoted, and sold; and how various management decisions in personnel, operations, and control affect business success. These skills should help you improve retail services for consumers.

Summary

Retail marketing provides the goods and services desired by consumers. Without retail marketing, consumers would have fewer goods to choose from and prices would be higher. Consumer goods are provided through more than 2.4 million retail stores, mail-order firms, and direct retail or automatic retail operations. About 51 percent of all retail stores are owned by individuals, about 6 percent are owned by two or more persons in a partnership, and about 43 percent are owned by corporations which, in turn, are owned by many stockholders. Careers in retail marketing are numerous and diverse. A sound background in retail marketing can prepare a person for a challenging retail career, including ownership of a business.

Review

1. Define *marketing, retailing,* and *retailer*.
2. What is the purpose of retailing?
3. Name the rights in the classic description of retailing.
4. Of what value is retailing to consumers?
5. List the four major types or methods of retailing.
6. What were the yearly retail sales of food products in 1987?
7. For what reasons are people attracted to retail work?
8. What two qualities are important for success in retail management?

Discuss

1. Which of the rights in the description of retailing do you consider to be the most important to consumers? Why? Which would be most important to the retailer? Why?
2. Which of the four main types or methods of retailing would be best for each of the following products or services: dress shoes, light bulbs, newspapers, travel service, bread, women's blouses, and gasoline?

3. Why do you think eating and drinking establishments are the most numerous retail businesses?
4. Of what value are retail businesses to you?
5. What characteristics do you observe in the successful retail managers in your community?

*T*erms

The following terms were introduced in this chapter. Write a separate sentence correctly using each new term.

automatic retailing	partnership
corporation	retailer
direct retailing	retailing
goods	retail marketing
in-store retailing	retail store
mail-order retailing	services
marketing	sole proprietorship
merchandise	ultimate consumer

*P*roblem *S*olving

1. Who is the ultimate consumer in each of the following cases? Explain your decision.
    a. A customer buys two frozen pizzas for a family dinner.
    b. A customer at a discount store buys a lamp for the family living room.
    c. A painter buys four liters of paint to be used to paint a lawyer's reception room.
    d. A customer in a department store buys a sweater as a gift for his Aunt Maggie.
    e. A hardware store customer buys six light bulbs to be used in her restaurant.
2. Using data provided in this chapter's illustrations, determine the number of retail stores per thousand people in the United States, the average sales per retail store, and the average number of people employed per retail store (in 1987, there were 237,000,000 people living in the United States). Hint: To find the last answer, divide the number of people employed in retailing by the number of retail firms.
3. Using the classified advertising section (want ads) of your local newspaper, prepare a list of available retail jobs. Determine the number of openings for each kind of job.

CHAPTER 2

Organization

When you have mastered the information provided in this chapter, you should be able to:

1. Apply the four steps of setting up a business organization

2. Explain the differences between formal and informal organization

3. Give examples of activities performed in each of the four retail functions

4. Explain how small business organization differs from large business organization

5. Describe how informal organization would operate in a large retail business

6. Distinguish between business organization and business policy

The way an owner or manager arranges the activities necessary for the successful operation of a retail business is called **organization.** Organization is found everywhere. It is found in homes where the work of maintaining a household is divided among the members of the family. Parents assign jobs to children and to themselves according to ability. If everyone does what is assigned, the home runs smoothly. There is organization in schools. The principal, teachers, counselors, and custodians all have distinct and important activities to perform. Retail businesses also must have good organization to operate effectively. When retailing activities are divided and arranged so that they can be performed efficiently and well by all employees, good organization is achieved.

BASIC BUSINESS ORGANIZATION

A retail business is made up of workers, and each worker has specific duties and responsibilities. In a well-organized business, workers and duties are combined to ensure that necessary activities are carried out effectively. In setting up any business, four major organizational steps must be taken:

1. Business activities must be grouped into related and manageable units.
2. People must be selected either to perform the work or to supervise.
3. The duties, responsibilities, and authority of each person must be specified and assigned.
4. Direction and evaluation of the individuals and their work must be provided.

The same four steps are necessary to organize any business. The ways they are taken may differ from one business to another. The size of the business, the type of merchandise or services offered, the form of ownership, and other factors affect the organization of a retail business.

The retail organization must be flexible enough to permit a shifting of responsibility and authority. A well-organized business responds quickly to changes in customer needs, the economy, and worker capabilities. When a business adds new goods, opens new departments or closes old ones, and adds or trains personnel, the business owner should consider changing the organization of the firm.

Formal Organization

Most retail employees agree that there are two types of organization in every retail business: formal and informal. The **formal organization** usually is shown in a chart that outlines the activities of the business. This organization chart provides a picture of how the work of the business is divided. It shows who is responsible for each type of work and who reports to whom. The chart also divides the work by departments, units, and other subgroups of the store.

For small firms, an organization chart may be a simple statement of what the manager does and what work has been assigned to each of the few employees. In larger firms, the organization chart may be a complex diagram supplemented by an organization manual.

An organization manual is a handbook that describes in detail the specific responsibilities of each subgroup and the personnel who are responsible for that work. For ex-

Illus. 2–1   Hundreds of informal interactions make a retail business operate.

ample, an organization manual would contain the job description of a stock person, such as "will check stock, pull new stock from store room, place price marks or tickets on goods or shelves, and arrange stock on counters or display areas."

Informal Organization

Informal organization covers the uncharted, undefined relationships of people and work. It explains how the company's work gets done on a day-to-day basis. An organization chart may show merchandising and promotion as separate functions. In practice, however, some activities may require the merchandise staff and the promotion staff to work together. For example, a salesperson in a shoe department and a display assistant may discuss what styles of shoes would be best for a spring shoe display. This type of interaction, repeated hundreds of times daily between workers from the various divisions of the formal organization, is what actually makes a retail business operate. Good managers agree that the informal organization is at least as important as the formal organization—maybe more important.

Retail Functions

Regardless of the size, type, or ownership of a retail business, there are certain functions to be performed. Traditional retail functions can be divided into four groups:

1. *Buying* includes locating, selecting, and acquiring an assortment or line of goods for sale.
2. *Selling* involves direct and indirect means of informing the public about the store or its merchandise.
3. *Operations* include locating and maintaining a building, handling merchandise, securing a store and its contents, recruiting and training employees, and providing employee and customer services.
4. *Control* includes keeping records, accounting, budgeting, and preparing financial reports.

These four functions are developed in considerable detail in this text. Material about buying is contained in Unit 4. Selling is covered in Unit 6, and material about promotion is presented in Unit 5. The operations function is also in two units: personnel in Unit 3 and other operations in Unit 7. Information about control is covered in Unit 8.

SMALL BUSINESS ORGANIZATION

Often, one person alone supervises all the activities of a small business, so an organizational plan may seem unnecessary. However, an organizational plan is necessary. Organization saves time, effort, and money. Without good organization, future business success is unlikely even for the very small business. The organization of a small retail business is described in the following situation.

Blair Gustina recently opened a bed-and-bath store. Mr. Gustina carries several lines of blankets, bedspreads, sheets, towels, and curtains. The business has been growing rapidly. He plans to hire a second and third employee soon. The current employee and the two new people will all be responsible for selling. One employee will handle the promotion activities. Another employee will handle all operations, except for personnel, which Mr. Gustina will oversee. The third employee will take care of all aspects of the control function except budgeting. Consequently, Mr. Gustina will have more time for budgeting, buying, personnel, and general supervision. Because this is a small company, all three employees and Mr. Gustina will sometimes need to help with receiving, stocking, taking inventory, displaying merchandise, and general store maintenance. Illustration 2–2 shows the main duties of each employee and Mr. Gustina.

If the bed-and-bath business continues to grow, other employees may be needed. Mr. Gustina may need to appoint one person as an assistant manager to make necessary decisions in his absence. One feature of small retail firms is that employees han-

GUSTINA'S BED-AND-BATH STORE

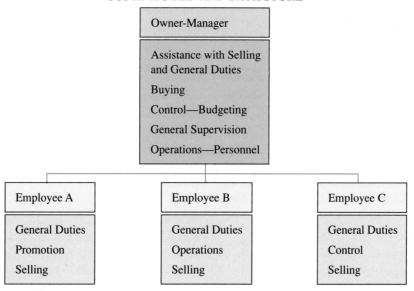

Illus. 2–2   In a small store, each employee has primary responsibility for certain retailing functions in addition to selling.

dle duties in several functional areas. A complete separation of functions is almost impossible, even for employee assignments in large retail firms.

LARGE BUSINESS ORGANIZATION

Large stores, for the purposes of this book, are those with annual sales of over $1 million and/or fifteen or more full-time employees. Large retail firms such as department stores and national chain stores can separate retail functions into subclusters and organize workers to specialize in one cluster (see Illustration 2–3). Large department stores come closer than other types and sizes of stores to having the four retail functions in specialized divisions.

Buying

Workers in the buying division do all that is required to select, negotiate the lowest cost for, and obtain merchandise for resale to customers. Buyers may be in charge of the departments selling the goods they buy, or buyers may work separately from the selling department. Much of the glamour associated with retailing is found in the buying function. However, buying is only one part of the retailing picture. Goods that are interesting and fun to buy must also be sold at a profit.

Selling

The majority of workers in the selling division are involved in personal selling to customers. Others are involved in nonpersonal selling duties such as advertising, interior and exterior displays, promotional events, and public relations. The manager of this division must work closely with the manager of the buying division to carry out promotion and publicity activities. The various merchandise departments (housewares, men's shoes, women's sportswear, gifts, and so on) are headed by managers who may also be the buyers for the goods carried in the department. The main duty of department managers is to supervise the salespeople who sell the merchandise.

Operations

The operations division conducts all the necessary activities that are not covered by the buying, selling, or control divisions. Thus, there is a wide range of duties performed in the operations division. The head of store operations is responsible for personnel matters (recruiting, hiring, and training) and employee services (compensation, health and accident insurance, and employee benefit programs). Also, the store operations manager is accountable for the maintenance of the building, receiving and handling of merchandise, customer services, store security, and special services such as store restaurants and parking.

Control

The main responsibility of those in the control division is to maintain records necessary for an effective business. They keep accurate accounting records, maintain proper insurance coverage, handle credit collections, establish systems for merchandise

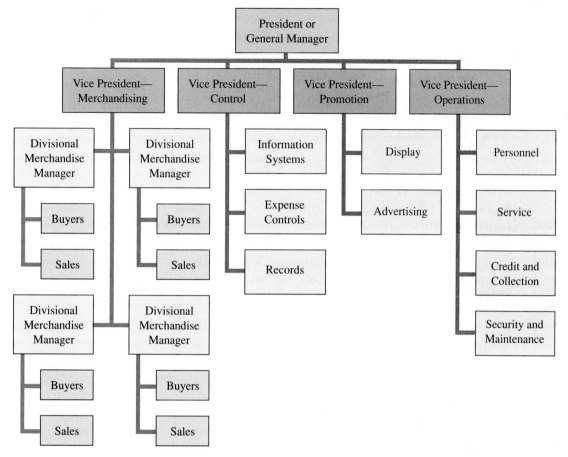

Illus. 2–3 A retail business's formal organization chart shows how the work of the firm is divided.

budgets and inventory, and prepare all the financial reports and statements that are needed by the store managers. The control division staff also maintains the records and reports required by local, state, and federal governments.

Central Organization

The organization of the four retail functions becomes even more complex when a firm has stores in several locations. Often, when several stores are involved, one or more of these functions are **centralized.** If a function is centralized, the major decisions are not made by personnel in the local store. For example, all the buying for a chain of stores can be handled by a staff of buyers located at the main office. Also, a chain of stores may have centralized promotion—all advertising is planned and supplied by the main office. Centralized organization of a group of stores generally is more efficient than separate organization. In a centralized setting, workers become specialized as they make decisions and perform tasks that otherwise would have to be performed by less experienced people at each store.

ORGANIZATION VERSUS POLICY

Business organization should not be confused with business policy. **Policy** is made up of the rules under which a retail business operates. Policies set forth definite and uniform rules for all workers. For example, a store policy may state that merchandise returns must be accompanied by the sales receipt or that no checks may be cashed for more than the purchase amount. All policies must be clear, workable, and easily understood by both customers and employees. Effective policies are vital to the smooth and successful operation of a store. Store managers need to think through the store policies carefully and consider their long-term effects. Only when store managers have established sound policies can the store employees work to bring about sales and profits.

Four types of retailing policies are covered in this book: personnel policies are discussed in Chapter 16; pricing policies, in Chapter 26; service policies, in Chapter 41; and credit and collection policies, in Chapter 42.

Summary   Profitable retail marketing requires good business organization. Business activities have to be planned and grouped into related units, workers selected, duties assigned, and employees supervised and evaluated. As needs change, work and responsibility within a business must be easily shifted to accommodate the functions of retailing—buying, selling, operations, and control. These four functions are performed in all businesses regardless of size. In smaller firms, the owner will perform more of this work; in larger stores, specialized personnel will be employed to deal with specific duties. Business organization should not be confused with business policy. Organization determines how the work of the business is arranged and assigned. Policy sets forth the rules under which a retail business operates.

Review
1. List four steps that must be taken by any retailer setting up a business organization.
2. State the purpose of an organization chart.
3. State how formal and informal organization differ.
4. Name the four groupings of traditional retail functions.
5. List four activities included in store operations.
6. List three activities included in store control.

7. Explain the difference between business organization and business policy.

Terms

The following terms were introduced in this chapter. Write a separate sentence correctly using each new term.

centralized   organization
formal organization   policy
informal organization

Discuss

1. Which retail functions might best be performed by a centralized staff of a chain of retail stores? Why?
2. What duties are performed by workers in the small retail stores in your community?
3. Which retail functions would most likely be kept directly under the store owner's control?
4. Why are clearly written store policies very important to store workers?

Problem Solving

1. Plan to open a retail business selling men's and women's hats. What decisions do you have to make in order to set up an effective organization for your business?
2. Blair Gustina's bed-and-bath store continues to be successful. He plans to add several new lines of curtains and a major line of draperies. Two additional people will be employed. Prepare a revised organization chart showing the duties assigned each of the five workers and Mr. Gustina.
3. Lianne Flin plans to open a dress shop for tall women. The store will handle a full line of sports and dress clothes plus accessories designed for women five feet nine inches tall or taller. Lianne plans to have three full-time and three part-time employees. Prepare a formal organization chart for her store. Also, describe what the informal organization of the store might be. How do the two organization plans differ?

CHAPTER 3

Retail Opportunities

CHAPTER OUTCOMES

When you have mastered the information provided in this chapter, you should be able to:

1. Describe the potential for employment in the retailing field

2. Name and describe the basic retailing activities

3. Identify major retail employers and the kinds of positions they offer

4. List recruitment techniques retailers use to locate potential employees

5. Describe the selection and training procedures followed by retail employers

6. State the opportunities for advancement available in retailing

Retailers have a continual need for qualified personnel. Currently, one in five persons in the labor force is employed in the retailing industry. More important, this number is expected to grow rapidly in the next several years. In fact, the United States Department of Labor predicts that the number of retail and wholesale workers will reach 30 million by the year 2000. This represents a tremendous increase over the number of retail personnel now employed.

For many people, a good job means (1) excitement, (2) rapid advancement, (3) good pay, (4) variety, and (5) security. Are really good jobs and chances for advancement possible in the retail field? The answer is a definite *yes*. Make no mistake, retailing is hard work. It does, however, have its attractions. Retailing can provide employment for those who are willing to put in the time and effort this field requires. For many people it provides a worthwhile career and personal satisfaction. This chapter explores the employment opportunities of retailing, where they are found, and the rewards they can offer.

BEGINNING A RETAILING CAREER

Knowing how to begin a career is important. But this knowledge is of little use unless you first know something about yourself. For example, how would you describe your personality, attitude, and motivation to work at home or school? Are your communication skills good or not so good? Can you work well with all types of people in a variety of situations? Are you a team player, or do you prefer to go it alone?

These are important questions that a potential employer might ask.

As you study retailing, you will probably notice that jobs vary greatly as do the abilities needed to perform them. When people talk about a career, they usually mean two or more related jobs held over a period of years. Careers in some fields often require years of in-school preparation before employment begins. Starting a career in retailing, however, requires neither special degrees nor years of hard study. It may begin with a part-time job in which you perform basic tasks within a certain area of a store. For example, receiving and marking merchandise, operating a sales register, and providing customer services, such as wrapping and packing merchandise, are some of a beginner's duties in a retail store. Opportunities for advancement increase as retailing skills are learned and perfected through on-the-job experiences and classroom instruction.

UNDERSTANDING BASIC RETAILING ACTIVITIES

Before you begin your search for a job in retailing, you should become familiar with four basic retailing activities: (1) buying, (2) selling, (3) store operations, and (4) control.

Buying

Some people believe that anyone can order merchandise for resale. The truth is, it takes know-how to order merchandise that customers will buy. The personal likes and dislikes of the retail buyer should not affect the decision. To do a good job of buying, retailers must study customer wants and needs carefully. This task can be difficult since the merchandise needs of the same types of customers may be quite different in two similar stores. In any case, retailers must know the kind, quality, brand, size, and quantity of merchandise wanted by customers. When the job of buying for a retail store is performed well, the results can produce satisfied customers and a profit.

Selling

Nothing worthwhile happens in retailing until goods or services are sold. All the planning and organizing in the world are of little value if store owners are unable to sell

A.   *Buying*

B.   *Selling*

C.   *Store Operations*

D.   *Control*

Illus. 3–1   Retailing jobs involve buying, selling, store operations, and control activities.

their merchandise. Successful merchants think selling is one of the most important duties their employees perform. Generally, *selling* is the means by which retailers provide customers with goods and services that best satisfy the customers' wants and needs. Selling can involve two kinds of activity. One, called *personal selling,* requires direct contact between the customer and the salesperson. The other, called *nonpersonal selling,* uses advertising, displaying, and sales promotion to attract customers and inform them about the store and its merchandise. Personal and nonpersonal selling are used in different combinations depending on the store and merchandise involved.

Store Operations

A major purpose of *store operations* is to provide good customer service. Store employees must have a desire to work with people. Merchandise has to be sold quickly. Store personnel must be hired, trained, paid, promoted, and sometimes replaced. Customer credit, adjustments, and returns must be handled politely. Constant store security, building care, and modernization must be conducted to help ensure a safe, pleasant atmosphere for customers and employees.

Control

Every retail store owner needs up-to-date information about the financial condition of the business. The record-keeping activities that produce this kind of information are the **control functions** of store management. Information related to stock control, sales, operations, and credit costs are important to making correct management decisions. The control functions of store management appeal to the individual who likes working with numbers and can do it accurately.

KINDS OF RETAIL CAREERS

Unlike many other employers, retailers offer their personnel a wide range of job choices and wages. The opportunities these jobs provide for career advancement also vary widely. For example, some large retailers pay high wages but offer few opportunities to gain broad experience in buying, selling, operations, or control. Instead, employees may gain an in-depth knowledge of one function because they may work exclusively in one department. Small retail store owners, on the other hand, often encourage their workers to learn all aspects of store operation. However, the small retailers may not pay wages comparable to those of large stores. Because of these and other variations in employment practices, a retailing career should be planned carefully. The following are examples of various retail employers and the positions such firms can provide career-oriented employees.

Department and Limited-line Stores

A **department store** consists of a large number of related merchandise departments. Merchandise offered for sale usually consists of many hard lines, such as tools and appliances; soft lines, such as sportswear and clothing; and home furnishings. Macy's in New York, Dayton-Hudson in

Minneapolis, Nordstroms in Seattle, and Sanger-Harris in Dallas are among the better known full-line department stores in the United States. Discount department stores include retailers such as Wal-Mart, K mart, and Target.

A **limited-line store** offers a wide selection of only one kind of goods. For example, Saks Fifth Avenue offers high-fashion clothing and jewelry. Sherwin Williams specializes in paint products and accessories. Limited-line stores may either be proprietorships or partnerships, or they may belong to a chain-store organization.

Beginning jobs in department and limited-line stores include such positions as stock assistant, sales trainee, display assistant, and merchandise wrapper. Individuals holding these positions are usually paid an hourly wage at the current minimum wage level. Some sales associates are paid a commission over and above the hourly rate. Experiences gained in these beginning jobs often pave the way for advancement to posi-

RETAIL STORE OCCUPATIONS

Job	Average Weekly Earnings	Average Yearly Earnings
Accounting Clerk	$260	$13,520
Barber	310	16,120
Building Custodian	225	11,700
Cashier	170	8,840
Chef/Cook	180	9,360
Computer Operator	300	15,600
Cosmetologist	205	10,660
Credit Manager	346	17,992
Jeweler	290	15,080
Meat Cutter	540	28,080
Receptionist	265	13,780
Retail Manager	525	27,300
Retail Sales Worker	288	14,976
Retail Store Laborer	160	8,320
Shipping and Receiving Clerk	280	14,560
Shoe Repairer	250	13,000
Travel Clerk	225	11,700
Waiter/Waitress (excluding tips)	180	9,360

Source: Department of Labor, Bureau of Labor Statistics, *Occupational Outlook Handbook*, April 1987.

Illus. 3–2   *Retail wages vary widely, depending on the kind of store, the location of the store (urban or rural), the status of the job (union or nonunion), and the job responsibilities.*

tions with more responsibility, such as assistant department manager, display specialist, and associate buyer. To take on management responsibilities, more retailing knowledge and experience is needed. Store managers, merchandise managers, and head buyers in department and limited-line stores are usually paid a yearly salary. In addition, the manager may receive **add-ons,** called commissions or bonuses, which are based on the individual's performance or on the store's sales for the year.

Chain Stores

Many beginners in retailing find employment with chain stores. A **chain store** is one of a number of similar stores under single ownership. *Chains* usually have a headquarters, or main store, that operates all the other stores in its system. The chain system of retailing can be found in almost every type of merchandising and service business. Food chains, variety store chains, and general merchandise chains are among the major operators in this field. Some of the best-known retail chain stores include Sears, Roebuck and Co.; J. C. Penney; Safeway Stores; Woolworth Corporations; and Melville Corporations.

Chain stores are always looking for salespeople, stockkeepers, supervisors, and security personnel. Advancement in chain stores leads to assistant manager, store manager, district supervisor, or chain executive positions. Salaries of management personnel vary widely, ranging from $16,000 to $150,000 a year, depending on the size of the organization, opportunities for advancement, and the worker's desire to succeed.

Retail Franchises

The retail franchise has been one of the great American success stories. In a franchise arrangement, a manufacturer or supplier (franchisor) and a retailer (franchisee) enter into an agreement. The franchisor agrees to provide one or more services, such as help with designing the store or training employees, and the franchisee agrees to sell the franchisor's product. Some typical franchise operations are McDonalds, Ramada Inn, Mr. Donut, Schwinn Bicycles, Kentucky Fried Chicken, Hertz, Dairy Queen, Rexall Drug, and Ben Franklin Stores.

Almost every beginning job that retailing offers can be found within the huge number of franchises operating in the United States today. The goal of many who

Illus. 3–3   Franchise operations are big business. They are especially attractive to people who want to operate businesses but cannot raise enough capital.

seek a job with a retail franchise is to become a franchise owner. Reaching this goal requires a strong desire to be the boss. Owning a franchise can also mean long hours, few days off, and irregular vacations. Many franchise owners believe that they earn more than they would as retail employees; therefore, they make the sacrifices necessary to being franchisees.

EMPLOYING RETAIL PERSONNEL

Most retailers use recruitment techniques that they believe identify potential employees. Typical recruitment techniques are (1) help-wanted signs; (2) newspaper, television, and radio advertisements; (3) employment agencies; and (4) school career planning and placement offices. Increasing numbers of retail employers are finding school-sponsored internships or cooperative part-time programs to be excellent sources of well-qualified employees. The Marketing Education program, for example, allows students to combine classroom instruction with on-the-job retailing experience.

Selecting Retail Personnel

Once a sufficient number of job candidates has been recruited, the employer must select those best suited for the available jobs. Generally, this task is begun by asking each applicant to complete a job application. Applications contain a series of questions designed to provide information

Illus. 3–4   After reviewing job applications, employers interview only qualified individuals.

Illus. 3–5   Many varied methods are used to train new employees. The purpose, however, is always the same—to develop competent employees who can deal with customers effectively.

about the educational background, personal qualifications, and occupational experience of the applicant. In addition, some employers require job candidates to provide a letter of application and a personal résumé. These documents usually contain information similar to that found on an application form, but they are written in the potential worker's own words.

After the applicant's employment file (job application, letter of application, résumé) has been reviewed, those individuals most qualified are interviewed. The purpose of an interview is to confirm information in the employment file and to judge the potential employee's personal qualifications. Appearance, dress, poise, communication skills, and attitude are important areas examined during a job interview. The employee selection process is completed when successful candidates are offered jobs.

Training Retail Personnel

The amount of time devoted to the training of new retail employees depends on several factors. Among the factors are the new employee's previous work experience and personal skills, as well as the demands of the new job and the importance the employer places on employee training. Wide variations exist in the methods retailers use to train employees. Some employers emphasize classroom instruction, while others prefer on-the-job training conducted by experienced employees. Regardless of the method or methods used, the main objective of an initial training program is to give each new employee a proper start.

Beginning training usually involves instruction in the retailer's methods of operation. Supervisors generally include in the

initial training program such topics as greeting customers, knowing where merchandise
is located, and handling cash and charge-
card purchases. Instruction may also include a review of company policies as they
relate to such areas as job advancement,
wages, insurance, and sick leave. Over a
period of several months, on-the-job instruction may be conducted in one or more
departments of the store. At this later stage
of a training program, emphasis is most often placed on such areas as effective selling
methods, customer relations, and merchandise information. As time passes, advanced
training may be offered in merchandising
and ordering techniques, management
skills, sales promotion, and general store
operations. Advancement to middle management and executive management positions within the firm depends on the
individual's potential to manage operations
and employees in a manner that brings a
profit to the store.

CAREER ADVANCEMENT IN RETAILING

Earlier in this chapter, it was mentioned that managers of retail businesses

can earn from $16,000 to $150,000 a year,
depending on the size of the store and the
amount of responsibility involved. Some
beginning salaries may be low, but the potential to earn a high salary in retailing is
excellent. Many jobs in retailing make it
possible to determine quickly an employee's worth to the company. Factors such as
a worker's sales volume and customer reaction to the service they receive provide
some indication of the quality of work.
Such quick assessment can mean rapid advancement for those individuals who show
interest in and work hard at their jobs.

Retailing is a highly competitive field.
As a result, it can also be physically and
mentally demanding. In addition to the possibility of long hours, dealing with a variety
of customer personalities under the pressure
of time can be stressful. Therefore, good
physical, mental, and emotional health are
prerequisites of a successful retailing career. Retailing is exciting and rewarding—
both financially and personally. Those who
like a challenge, constant change, and a
chance to be creative may be interested in
the retailing field. To fully understand the
personnel policies that are followed by retail
merchants, study carefully the chapters contained in Unit 3, Managing Human Resources.

Summary

Many persons start their careers in retailing with part-time jobs
in one of the four basic retailing activities—buying, selling, operations, and control. Job choices among these four functions are extensive and can be found in a variety of retail firms; among them,
department stores, limited-line stores, chain stores, and franchised

businesses. Employers attract retail personnel with help-wanted signs and advertisements and through employment agencies and school placement offices. Persons applying for retail employment are expected to prepare a letter of application and a résumé and to be interviewed. Most employers are interested in a potential worker's appearance, poise, communication skills, and attitude.

Training programs involving classroom instruction, on-the-job training, or both are designed to give new employees a chance at success. Employees who learn rapidly and perform well often advance quickly to management levels.

Review

1. Name four basic kinds of retailing activities.
2. Identify the major types of retail employers. Give an example of each in your area.
3. Identify four recruitment techniques retailers use to locate potential employees.
4. Describe the potential for job opportunities in the retailing field.
5. List three kinds of information that can be obtained from a job application.
6. Explain the relationship between a job application, letter of application, and résumé.
7. State the purpose of a job interview.
8. Identify four factors that affect the amount of time an employer will devote to training new employees.
9. List two methods used by retailers to train employees.
10. Name two key prerequisites for a successful career in retailing.

Terms

The following terms were introduced in this chapter. Write a separate sentence correctly using each new term.

add-ons   department store
chain store   limited-line store
control functions

Discuss

1. Explain why it is important to understand yourself before you begin identifying possible careers in retailing.
2. Identify and describe what you believe is the most important basic retailing activity. Explain why you believe this activity is most important.

3. Name three kinds of beginning job opportunities that are available in most department, limited-line, chain, and retail-franchise stores.
4. State two reasons why good initial training is important for new retail employees.
5. State two reasons why you agree or disagree with this statement: Retailing is relatively dull and unrewarding.

Problem Solving

1. Ramona has been employed part-time in your department for three months. As her supervisor, you recognize that she does not seem to enjoy her work. In an informal discussion, Ramona indicates that she can't find a job she really likes. Offer suggestions to help Ramona select a fulfilling job and to start building a career.
2. Your employer decided to open another store in a new shopping center. Hard work and enthusiasm result in your promotion to manager of the new store. Outline a series of steps to follow in finding, selecting, and training your new employees.
3. A classmate says, "I'm not interested in retailing because chances for advancement are slim." Prepare a response to your classmate. Be sure to explain why you respond as you do.

CHAPTER 4

Merchandising

The anticipated needs of customers in a retailer's market indicate what merchandise or services should be offered by the business. The merchandise or service offered by a business usually has more power to attract customers than does any other single feature of the firm's operation. Key considerations are the types and levels of quality of merchandise that customers are most likely to purchase. Do customers want the latest styles, large assortments, national brands, low prices, luxurious goods, shopping convenience, or customer services? The objectives of the business, its competition, characteristics of the community, and the manager's business philosophy or beliefs will all have a bearing on the merchandise policies and practices of the business.

KINDS OF MERCHANDISE

Retailers classify the entire range of consumer goods into four categories: staple or regular goods, fashion goods, seasonal goods, and convenience goods.

Staple or **regular goods** are the core of a store's merchandise offering. Staple goods are carried year round and make up a substantial portion of annual sales. **Fashion goods** are items that are new or the latest or most popular styles. **Seasonal goods,** such as Halloween costumes or garden hoses, are those that are sold only during certain periods of the year. **Convenience goods** are those that are bought frequently, perhaps even daily, such as newspapers, candy, and gum.

MERCHANDISE MIX

The merchandise carried by a store depends primarily on the merchandise policies selected by the retailer. **Merchandise mix** is the variety of merchandise lines carried and the breadth and depth with which these lines are stocked (see Illustration 4–1). The merchandise mix may vary considerably from one store to another of the same type. The mix will depend on the store's size, location, and customers and on the owner's financial resources, retailing ability, and experience. For example, one men's store may carry all types of men's clothing—dress, sport, and work. Another men's store may carry only a few selected lines of sportswear.

Merchandise Breadth

Merchandise breadth refers to the number of merchandise lines carried by a store. Some retail firms, such as department stores, carry many lines of merchandise and have a wide assortment of goods within each line. Other stores carry only one or two lines, each with a limited selection. A shoe store, for example, may choose to sell only men's shoes, while another will sell men's, women's, and children's footwear.

When a store chooses to carry a large number of lines, some of which have little or no relationship to the regular goods of the store, it is said to be practicing scrambled merchandising. Thus, a drugstore that carries antifreeze, furnace filters, grocery items, and children's clothing has *scrambled* its merchandise lines. Its merchandise breadth has gone beyond related drugstore

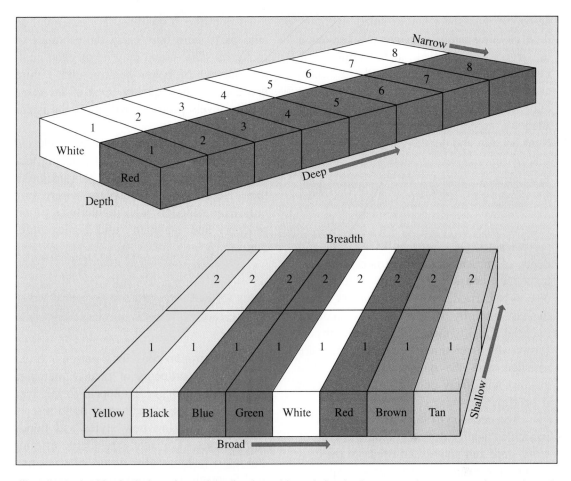

Illus. 4–1 In this depiction of merchandise breadth and depth, the numerals represent the number of units stocked in each color.

lines. Stores that go into scrambled merchandising do so to increase merchandise breadth and to gain additional sales of goods not carried in normal lines.

Merchandise Depth

Merchandise depth refers to the quantity of a line of goods offered in various colors, sizes, styles, and price ranges. One merchant may carry only a few items of each color and size, expecting to be able to quickly replace the stock that is sold. Another merchant, handling the same merchandise, may carry extensive stocks of certain sizes, colors, or prices to ensure that popular items are always available.

Small store merchants have a better chance at success by offering a few merchandise lines in some depth, rather than carrying many lines with limited stock. If the owner of a specialty clothing store has limited financial resources or limited space, he or she may specialize in small-size day-time clothing rather than carry a few each of large-size, half-size, and evening-wear items. A safe rule for the small store merchant is to add a new line of merchandise only when there is enough store space and adequate money to provide stock in sufficient breadth and depth.

QUALITY OF MERCHANDISE

Besides the questions of breadth and depth of merchandise assortments, the retailer must consider the quality of merchandise to be carried. A **quality product** is one that is carefully constructed of excellent material. Quality merchandise wears or performs well over time. Customers who are satisfied with the quality and price of a product will likely purchase the item again if needed.

The decision to stock merchandise of a particular quality depends upon the type of retail store and anticipated needs of the customers. For example, a retailer who specializes in discount merchandise should not attempt to carry the finest quality products available. In many cases, customers' needs can be filled with medium quality products. Price, then, may be a more important consideration than material or craftsmanship. Merchants usually identify the quality that most customers select and offer the deepest assortment of merchandise of that quality. This becomes the retailer's **middle line.** Merchandise of higher and lower quality is carried but in lesser assortment.

The retailer may offer assortments with multiple quality levels of popular merchandise in which customers may be interested in different qualities. For example, an auto parts store may carry three brands of motor oil. One brand may be of good quality, another of better quality, and a third brand of the best quality. One of the three quality levels probably will meet the needs of most customers.

Many retail firms, such as Sears and Macy's, have their own quality testing laboratories for goods that will be sold under their labels. Smaller retailers wisely buy only from suppliers who regularly test their products and maintain rigid quality standards.

STYLE OF MERCHANDISE

For fashion-conscious patrons, broad and deep assortments of quality merchandise are not enough. To appeal to this type of customer, the retailer must build a reputation for stocking new styles and trendy merchandise. For many retailers, offering the latest fashions also means offering limited assortments in some lines. Keeping up with the latest fashions and stocking such items requires a store to be in close contact with manufacturers in major fashion centers such as New York, Los Angeles, and Dallas.

PRICING MERCHANDISE

Price is the amount of money asked for something. Price is a measure of the value or worth of a good or service. In retailing, price is the amount of money that a

Illus. 4–2   Merchants usually offer the deepest assortment of merchandise of the quality that most customers select.

retailer will take in exchange for an item of merchandise. The price a retailer sets for merchandise must be enough to cover the cost of the goods and business expenses as well as generate a profit.

Price Competition

Pricing considerations are a major part of merchandising. Most store owners try to keep their prices competitive by setting their prices in relation to prices at other stores of the same type in the area. Some retailers watch competitors' prices and meet all prices on key items that are lower than their own. Some specialty stores stock exclusive merchandise and pay little attention to competitors' prices. Specialty retailers justify higher prices by the unusual nature of their merchandise and their extra services.

A merchant may decide (1) to price merchandise below the price of competitors, (2) to price merchandise at the same level as competitors, or (3) to price merchandise above competition and appeal to customers on some basis other than price.

One question underlies all price competition: "Who *is* my competitor?" Competition for a large department store or a discount store may be all other stores in the same market area. On the other hand, a small store owner might consider only other stores of about the same size as competitors. Small store retailers find greater advantage in offering merchandise and service tailored to customer needs than in attempting to compete on price. Few small stores, unless they are affiliated with other independent stores, have the buying power to compete on a low-price basis with larger stores or with chain stores.

One-price Policy

Today almost every reputable store has a **one-price policy.** This means that on any given day all customers will be charged the same amount for a certain article. Thus, a store that advertises or offers an item for $2.49 will sell the item only at that price. With a one-price policy, it is still possible to lower or raise a price as long as the goods are made available at that price to everyone. Automobile and appliance dealerships may have a one-price policy. By accepting trade-ins or allowing terms of sale to be negotiated, however, the retailer's actual price may differ from one customer to another.

Price-line Policy

Many stores have a **price-line policy;** that is, only a few prices, or price lines, are set and then applied to many different items. For example, all men's jackets in a particular store may be priced at $27.95, $45.95, or $67.95. Three price lines for one category of merchandise is a common policy. Although the merchandise may be bought at various costs, the merchant will offer these goods at one of the predetermined price lines. Sorting goods into a few specific price lines reduces the customer confusion that comes from having many small price differences. Price lines also eliminate confusion for salespeople selling and stocking merchandise.

Other Price Policies

Stores may also have policies about price endings and image pricing. Some merchants decide that all goods will be marked with an odd-cent ending, such as $5.79. The odd price, they believe, implies that the article is a bargain. Other retailers use even prices, such as $6.50 or $10.00, because they believe even prices give an impression of quality.

Price policies, generally, help convey a certain image of a store and retail mix. If a store strives for an exclusive image, the retailer may deliberately set prices higher than competitors' prices on the same merchandise and use even price endings. To maintain a bargain or discount image, a retailer may set prices low and use odd-price endings to strengthen the bargain image and encourage high-volume sales.

Within a store, price policies should be uniform. A retailer should use either odd- or even-price endings but not both in one store. Likewise, it is best to maintain a consistent price image. In any case, price policies should be simple so that they confuse neither customers nor employees.

MERCHANDISE PLANNING

Merchandise planning is essential to the success of a retail business. Once key decisions have been made about a store's merchandising activities, the decisions must be put into the form of a **merchandising plan.** The plan should reflect the various merchandise policies set for the store and

Illus. 4–3 Odd-cent prices are believed to imply a bargain.

describe how these policies are to be carried out. Goals should be set in terms of dollars to be spent on merchandise, sales expected, and costs associated with merchandising activities. Thus, a merchandise plan is most often expressed as a budget. General plans should be made for at least a year ahead and specific plans set for at least six months ahead. Merchandise plans can be made for each merchandise item, for classifications of items, for merchandise departments or divisions, or for the entire store. For multiple stores or chain store organizations, goals and budgets may be developed by central management and assigned to individual stores or departments.

Because a merchandise plan is essential for success in retailing, the chapters in Unit 4 focus on planning, selecting, buying, pricing, and budgeting merchandise.

Summary

Merchandising deals with the types, qualities, and quantities of goods the retailer carries in a retail store. There are four kinds of merchandise: staple or regular goods, fashion goods, seasonal goods, and convenience goods. The amount and variety of each kind of goods to be carried (the breadth and depth of the merchandise mix) as well as the quality must be decided by a retailer. The pricing policy of a store is also important. Price is the amount of money a retailer will accept in exchange for a product. Most retailers operate with a one-price policy; that is, all customers pay the same price for a specific item of merchandise. Sometimes only a few prices, or price lines, are applied to many different items in a store. The pricing policies that merchants establish help form the business image and operating procedures. Retailers put the main decisions about their merchandising activities in the form of a merchandise plan.

Review

1. Define *seasonal goods*. Give three examples of seasonal merchandise.
2. Define *scrambled merchandising*. Identify two stores in your area that practice scrambled merchandising.
3. Describe how a line of women's purses might be stocked if the merchant wanted to stress merchandise breadth.
4. Why do retailers attempt to identify the quality of merchandise customers most often select and buy?
5. Define *price*. Explain the relationship between price and cost of goods.
6. State two reasons why a store might use odd-price endings.
7. For what periods of time should merchandising plans be developed?

Terms

The following terms were introduced in this chapter. Write a separate sentence correctly using each new term.

convenience goods   one-price policy
fashion goods   price
merchandise breadth   price-line policy
merchandise depth   quality product
merchandise mix   seasonal goods
merchandising plan   staple or regular goods
middle line

Discuss

1. For what two conditions would a store manager most likely choose to carry a broad merchandise mix with little depth?
2. For what reasons would a retailer carry products that are not of the very best quality?
3. What store in your community appears to follow a competitive-price policy? In your judgment, why does it do this?
4. Under what circumstances would a merchant carry only one quality of a merchandise line?

Problem Solving

1. Identify four different retail stores in your community. Identify the major merchandise lines and describe the merchandise mix of each store. Do your classmates agree with your conclusions?
2. Describe what you believe to be the price competition policy of each store identified above. Do your classmates agree with your conclusions?
3. Assume that you are the owner-manager of a women's specialty clothing store. You are contacted by a vendor who is promoting a new line of fabric-and-leather luggage. Develop a list of factors you would consider before deciding to add or not add this line of merchandise to your store.
4. If you were an independent retailer handling only three items—pocket knives, kitchen knives, and hunting knives—describe two ways in which merchandising plans might be developed.

CHAPTER 5
Promotion

CHAPTER OUTCOMES

When you have mastered the information provided in this chapter you should be able to:

1. Define *promotion* and explain how store policies affect its use

2. Identify models that explain how communication takes place between sellers and buyers

3. Explain what motivates customers to make buying decisions

4. Identify appeals merchants can use to motivate customers to buy

5. List the promotional methods used by retailers

6. Define *promotional mix* and identify the primary purpose of promotion

Merchants know that their success depends on effective communication with customers. Efforts to organize an attractive store, plan the right merchandise, and assemble fine assortments of goods are meaningless if customers do not know the merchant exists. The buying public must know (1) the merchant's location, (2) the store hours, (3) the products and services available, and (4) the merchandise prices. The process of communicating this information to the public in order to increase sales is called **promotion.** Methods of promoting retail goods, services, and store image include (1) advertising, (2) visual merchandising, (3) sales promotion, (4) public relations, and (5) personal selling. When these methods are carefully blended, the retailer can expect to increase store traffic and profits. Chapter 6 outlines the use of personal selling in the promotion of a retail store. This chapter deals with other methods of promotion.

STORE PROMOTION POLICIES

The promotion policies of a retail firm establish the basis for all sales promotion efforts. The first major decision that a merchant must make about promotion is the type of store he or she will operate. Store managers may choose from among three types of promotion policies. They may choose to operate a **promotional store,** which stresses sales, bargains, and price reductions. Another choice is a **nonpromotional store,** which stresses assortments of goods, leadership in fashion, or customer services. The third choice is a **semipromotional store,** which features merchandise assortments at regular prices with infrequent special sales or reduced prices. By choosing one of these broad policies, a merchant determines the nature and extent of a store's promotion efforts.

COMMUNICATION MODELS

To choose effective promotion methods, retailers must know how communication between sellers and potential buyers occurs. The most basic communication system involves a retailer talking directly with a potential customer. The retailer informs the customer about the product or service, and the customer, in turn, communicates needs and wants and asks questions about the product or service. In other words, there is an easy two-way interaction that continues between the buyer and the seller until they understand or agree with each other. This basic communication model can be illustrated as follows:

seller (retailer) ◄────────────► buyer (customer)

To start communication, the seller must have a product or service that interests the buyer. If the customer has no need or desire for the product or service, the communication will be of little value. Likewise, a potential buyer's communication will have little impact on a retailer unless the retailer has or is able to get the product or service that the buyer requires. In other words, seller-buyer communication is based upon mutual interest in a particular product or service.

Most seller-buyer communication is more complex than the basic communica-

Illus. 5–1   A customer's impression of a store is often the result of the merchant's promotion policies.

tion model. When a retailer wishes to let people know about a line of goods or a new store service, he or she may not be able to personally inform all potential customers. To let many people know about the goods or services available, the retailer may use the media: radio, television, and newspapers. In the basic communication model, an activity called *advertising* comes between the seller and buyer. A customer who is interested in the advertised merchandise may go to the store to see the product display or demonstration. The display or demonstration adds to the customer's understanding, so it, too, is part of the communication process. The following is the seller-media-buyer communication model:

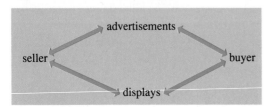

A third communication model involves the use of publicity by the retailer. *Publicity* is information about a store or its merchandise that is provided by public media, such as radio, television, and newspapers, at no cost to the retailer. In practice, publicity resembles advertising in seller-buyer communication. However, publicity information usually is not about specific products. Information about a store's participation in community affairs is an example of publicity. What follows is the publicity model of retailer-customer communication:

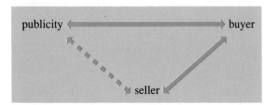

The broken line indicates that the seller is not wholly responsible for the contents of the publicity and does not pay for it.

There are, of course, many variations of these models, but most seller-to-buyer and buyer-to-seller communication can be described by one of these three.

CUSTOMER MOTIVATION

Communication models help the retailer understand *how* information is exchanged between sellers and buyers. Just as important is knowing *why* consumers react in various ways to certain advertisements, displays, product samples, and publicity stories. Why do people behave as they do? Why do some people look for the best bargains from promotional stores and other people of the same social and economic status buy only nationally known brands from nonpromotional stores? What causes a person to start shopping seriously for a product or a service?

Needs and Wants

All persons have a great many **needs**—goods and services necessary for their survival or well-being. They also have **wants**—products or services that fulfill a function other than that of satisfying a need. Only when a person becomes aware of a need or want does he or she take action. The action taken to satisfy a need or to fulfill a want is called **motivated behavior.** The need or want that leads to the action is called a **motive.**

Behavior may be motivated by individual motives or by social motives.

Illus. 5-2 Consumer buying decisions are influenced by a variety of motives.

Individual motives are those that originate within the person, such as hunger, thirst, comfort, curiosity, and freedom from fear and danger. **Social motives** are those that arise from a person's relationships with other people and objects in the environment. The need to be accepted and recognized by others and to feel good about oneself are social motives. Thus, when a person is cold and *needs* clothing to keep warm, the motive is individual and basic to survival. When the individual *wants* additional high-fashion clothing to impress friends, the motive is social. The difference in the motive generally makes a difference in the motivated behavior—in the type of clothing purchased, in this case.

Retailers constantly face this question: What will prompt people to buy my goods? Marketers know that several reasons usually underlie a customer's choice of a particular product. Also, not all consumer choices are of the same importance. Some purchases are minor and repetitive—dish soap or garbage bags. Some are important but not critical—a topcoat, a garden tool, or a bicycle. Other purchases are of great importance and involve complex judgments and values—a new car, a house, or an insurance plan. The differences can be illustrated simply: If you buy a bran cereal this week, you can easily decide to buy a wheat cereal next week. However, if you buy a sports car this week, you probably won't purchase a subcompact or another car for months if not years.

Most people constantly attempt to satisfy their various needs and wants. Retailers should not forget, however, that many people have needs that have not yet reached a conscious level and wants that have not yet taken a definite form. Promotion requires retailers to answer two questions: (1) What communication will make customers aware of their needs and wants? (2) How can I show people that my merchandise will satisfy those needs and wants? The purpose of promotion is to develop consumers' awareness of their needs and wants and to appeal to the appropriate motives.

Rational and Emotional Appeals

Appeals to consumers' motives can either be classified as rational appeals or emotional appeals. **Rational appeals** stress the good features of a product—its fair price, its quality, and its dependability. **Emotional appeals** stress the security, safety, love, beauty, social acceptance, or power that may be derived from use of a product. Some people react more favorably to rational appeals. They tend to consider the real value of a product and weigh carefully the pros and cons of a particular purchase. Other people respond better to emotional appeals. They select a product because of its beauty or because it makes them feel safe or socially accepted.

However, no one responds strictly to one appeal. Those people who generally respond to rational appeals may, for some products, respond to emotional appeals. For example, an individual who shops for bargains may be persuaded to buy the higher-priced item because a famous person recommends its use. Similarly, those persons who generally respond to emotional appeals may make a buying decision based on a factual, rational appeal. For instance, a customer may occasionally buy a little-known brand when it is very clearly presented as being equal to the better-known product. In that situation, the influence of the factual appeal is stronger than that of the emotional appeal.

Purpose of Promotion

With thousands of products available—often dozens in the same category—a consumer is faced with the difficult task of sorting through the features and benefits of each in terms of his or her needs. Through promotion, retailers help consumers with this task by providing information about goods and services. This important information includes features, price, and availability. Unfortunately, the promotional information provided by some businesses is not reliable. Sometimes promotional information is factual, but the selling skills of store employees make buying from a particular merchant an unpleasant experience. Clearly, the promotional efforts and business practices of a firm must be complementary for either to be effective.

PROMOTIONAL METHODS

The first part of this chapter identified methods of promoting goods, services, and store image. These included advertising, visual merchandising, sales promotion, public relations, and personal selling. To plan effective promotions, retailers must be aware of the purposes, advantages, and disadvantages of each promotional method.

Retail Advertising

There are a number of advertising methods that retailers use to attract consumers to their stores. **Printed media** include newspapers, magazines, direct mail, and billboards. Radio and television are examples of **electronic media.** The purpose of most retail advertising is to increase store traffic and sales volume during a certain period of time. For example, a retailer may decide to emphasize through advertisements a holiday such as the Fourth of July when business is slow. Special sales such as "Back to School" or "Bargain Days" are often heavily advertised.

A major advantage of advertising is that it attracts large audiences at a relatively low cost per reader or viewer. In the case of newspapers and direct mail, consumers can read and reread advertisements at their leisure. Television and radio are attractive advertising media because the advertisements are often accompanied by entertainment. However, electronic media, particularly television, is considerably more expensive than printed media. Such advertising may be wasteful if it is broadcast beyond the specific market that retailers wish to reach.

In general, however, retail advertising has proven to be a most effective means of promoting retail goods and services.

Visual Merchandising

Visual merchandising refers to efforts that make a store inviting and thereby persuade the public to purchase the retailer's goods and services. Such merchandising could involve store design and layout, lights, signs, fixtures, and merchandise displays. To be truly effective, visual merchandising techniques must be coordinated with the store's overall promotional plan. Merchandise displays, particularly, should complement advertisements placed in the printed and electronic media. A major advantage of merchandise displays is that they enable customers to personally inspect the advertised products.

Among the most common displays are **window displays.** These displays are designed to be viewed by potential customers outside the store. Window displays are used for various types of promotions, including special-event sales and storewide sales. **Interior displays** are located on the sales floor of a retail store. This visual merchandising technique is effective because it gives merchandise high visibility and customers an opportunity to inspect goods or services firsthand. *Point-of-purchase displays* are an especially effective means of presenting goods and services. These displays usually are tied in with a manufacturer's advertising or sales promotional efforts for a particular product. Point-of-purchase displays are generally located near checkout counters or store exits. Department stores, discount stores, supermarkets, and most other self-service operations rely heavily

this kind of visual merchandising. Normally, point-of-purchase displays are provided by the manufacturer and are easy for a retailer to set up and maintain. In recent years, point-of-purchase displays have become a popular means of promoting fast-selling merchandise in all types of retail sales.

To maintain their effectiveness, window and interior displays must be continually restocked, replaced, or relocated. Although these tasks require much time and effort, keeping displays up-to-date is important. Displays are a retailer's best means of bringing consumers in direct contact with promoted goods.

Sales Promotion

Sales promotion is another effective means of presenting goods for sale. Sales promotion techniques are specifically designed to increase sales volume. They are particularly helpful when used to attract new customers, increase the size of individual purchases, and introduce new goods and services. Typical examples of sales promotion techniques include (1) product sampling, (2) premiums, ___ons, (4) special prices, (5) reb___ ___s, and (7) trading stamps ___ ___les promotion activi___ nificantly whe___ of promotin___

Publi___

of maintaining a positive image, some firms employ specialists who perform public relations duties on a full-time basis. Good public relations is also the responsibility of all retail employees. Maintaining positive relationships with customers is foremost, but active participation in various community affairs also generates an important positive image.

Another aspect of a good public relations program is publicity. **Publicity** is the nonpaid promotion of a business or its product and services by the public media. Most publicity occurs when a retailer has an event that captures public interest and when that event is reported as a news story. Fashion shows, community service projects, and donations of time and money to charities are typical publicity events. While the retailer rarely decides just what the media reports, publicity can create a favorable public image and promote a store's merchandise, usually at no cost to the retailer.

Personal Selling

A key component of any store promotion program is personal selling. This promotional method provides a means by which sales personnel promote merchandise directly to their customers; unlike most promotional techniques, the salesperson's ability to interact in a positive way with store clientele will often be the deciding factor in whether a sale is completed. To be effective, the salesperson must be able to deter the customers' needs and meet those effective and efficient manner. in detail those skills and mastered in order to of a retail

PROMOTIONAL MIX

Promotional mix is the combination of messages and media that a retailer uses to communicate information about merchandise to prospective buyers. For example, a retailer of men's clothing may decide that a combination of personalized customer service, newspaper advertising, a charity fashion show, direct mail to a selected list of regular customers, and in-store displays is the best promotional mix. A hardware store operator may rely on radio commercials, newspaper advertisements, direct mail, and in-store product demonstrations. Radio commercials may be used for a few items, newspaper advertisements for a larger number of items considered specials, direct mail for a comprehensive list of available goods, and weekend product demonstrations to highlight one or two leaders among the regular high-quality merchandise. Carefully planned messages used in the right media direct communication to people most likely to buy. Getting the greatest results from each promotional dollar spent is the goal of every merchant.

Among the primary purposes of promotion are letting consumers know what the retailer has for sale, what he or she expects to sell at a given time, and what price has been assigned to the goods. Through their promotional efforts, retailers also attempt to establish their merchandising personality. They choose promotional methods and media to appeal to the motives of particular types of consumers. Retailers also tell how their merchandise offerings differ from other retailers' offerings. Unit 5 provides more information about promotional methods and strategies that retailers use to gain a competitive edge.

Illus. 5–3   Retailers use a mix of promotional techniques to communicate with their customers about goods and services they offer for sale.

Summary

    Communicating information to the public about a store or merchandise is called *promotion*. Retailers may choose different promotional policies depending upon the image they wish to convey and the needs and wants of their customers. Good promotion requires that a retailer know something about the individual and social motives that motivate, or cause, customers to buy. Promotions may appeal to consumers' logic or to their emotions. Promotion may be accomplished by various means: printed or electronic advertising, window or interior displays, personal selling by store staff, and publicity. The combination of these promotional methods is called the *promotional mix*. The main purpose of all promotions is telling likely consumers what merchandise is available at what prices.

Review

1. Name four kinds of merchant information that promotion communicates to the buying public.
2. List five methods of promoting retail goods and services.
3. Define *promotional store, nonpromotional store*, and *semipromotional store*.
4. Describe the basic communication model.
5. Explain the difference between wants and needs.
6. Define *rational appeal* and *emotional appeal*.
7. Explain the similarities and differences among window displays, interior displays, and point-of-purchase displays.
8. Define *publicity*.
9. State the purpose of a carefully selected promotional mix.

Terms

The following terms were introduced in this chapter. Write a separate sentence correctly using each new term.

electronic media   promotional mix
emotional appeals   promotional store
individual motives   publicity
interior displays   public relations
motivated behavior   rational appeals
motive   semipromotional store
needs   social motives
nonpromotional store   wants
printed media   window displays
promotion

Discuss

1. Why is it important for a new retail store operator to have a promotional policy?
2. Explain the roles of advertising, visual merchandising, and publicity in the seller-buyer communications model.
3. What are the effects of individual motives and social motives on the types of goods and services consumers purchase?
4. For what goods would emotional appeals likely influence consumer buying decisions?
5. Compare retail advertising with visual merchandising and publicity.
6. What is meant by the statement "Retailers, through their promotional efforts, try to establish a merchandising personality"?

*Problem
Solving*

1. Margarita and Hector Rivera have decided their dry cleaning business will rely on promotional methods to attract business. What kind of buyer-seller communication model will you suggest they use? Why?
2. For two years, Sylvia has ordered all merchandise sold in the women's sportswear department of your store. Her goal is to become a buyer. While discussing career plans, she indicates that she is not always sure what motivates customers to buy. How will you help her solve this problem?
3. As the new owner of a greeting card shop, your promotion plans are to stress wide merchandise assortments. Describe the promotional mix you will use. Give reasons for your choices.

CHAPTER 6

Selling

CHAPTER OUTCOMES

When you have mastered the information provided in this chapter, you should be able to:

1. Explain the importance of selling in retailing

2. Identify the qualifications of an effective salesperson

3. Describe the various types of retail selling careers

4. Describe a selling process that can be used effectively in most retail stores

5. List various special selling skills and support skills needed by a retail store salesperson

"Creative advertising, well-designed displays, and pleasant surroundings are all that is needed to sell merchandise." True? No, not really! Each strategy is an important ingredient in the success of a retail store. None, however, has replaced the salesperson who can use effective sales methods when assisting customers. Even self-service retailers recognize the importance of personal selling—responding to customer questions about product features, uses, prices, and location. *Personal selling* means having face-to-face encounters with the customers in order to present them with the products and services they want or need. To make these encounters successful, retail salespeople must possess strong human relations skills. They must also know their merchandise and be able to apply a variety of selling techniques to dealing with customers.

QUALIFICATIONS OF SUCCESSFUL SALES PERSONNEL

Most employers agree that success in retail selling requires a high level of job knowledge and skill. They also agree that there are certain personal traits that distinguish successful from unsuccessful sales personnel. Traits that employers look for include dependability, enthusiasm, courtesy, cooperation, honesty, and ambition. Employers also expect sales personnel to be neat in appearance, punctual, and loyal to the store.

No doubt having these characteristics is important for a successful career in retail-ing; but personal traits alone are not enough. Salespeople must be able to speak, write, and listen effectively. Also, salespeople need arithmetic skills and good memory for names, faces, facts, and figures. Accuracy—a willingness and ability to do every part of the job right—is a valuable personal quality for all sales personnel.

The qualifications mentioned above may sound as though they could be difficult to meet. Keep in mind, however, that many of these skills can be learned or developed with training and experience. Few occupations offer as many opportunities for advancement as does selling. A wide variety of sales positions are available in retail stores.

TYPES OF RETAIL SALES JOBS

Retail selling jobs can be classified into several categories on the basis of (1) the merchandise sold, (2) the services performed, and (3) the level of responsibility of the sales position. Selling positions that can be included in this list are the salesclerk, sales demonstrator, salesperson, and sales representative.

Salesclerk

The key responsibilities of **salesclerks** include greeting customers, operating sales registers, and wrapping merchandise. Stores that sell convenience goods are major employers of salesclerks. New workers are often employed as salesclerks and paid the minimum wage.

Sales Demonstrator

As the name implies, the job of the **sales demonstrator** is to show customers how to use a product or service. Good human relations skills and the ability to communicate effectively are essential qualifications for this work. The position requires limited sales techniques such as answering questions and asking the customer to buy. Food and small appliances are the typical kinds of merchandise demonstrated. Sales demonstrators are paid an hourly rate that is often higher than the minimum wage.

Salesperson

A **salesperson** performs the functions of both salesclerk and sales demonstrator. In addition, salespeople determine customer wants and needs, handle customer objections, close sales, and suggest additional purchases. Salespeople, or sales associates as they are often called, must be merchandise experts. They also must use a variety of selling techniques when assisting customers. These retail personnel are paid on either an hourly or weekly basis. Sometimes retailers provide bonus pay to salespeople who attain certain sales volumes.

Sales Representative

At times, retail **sales representatives** may be called on to complete tasks usually performed by salesclerks, sales demonstrators, and salespeople. A retail sales representative's primary responsibility, however, is to sell higher priced items, such as major appliances, tires, home building supplies and repairs, and auto insurance. In some cases, a retail sales representative must go to the customer rather than having the customer come to the store. For example, a sales representative who assists a customer wishing to buy new drapes performs many sales tasks at the customer's home or place of business. A high degree of persuasive skill and effective use of selling methods are necessary for success in this work. Sales representatives are often paid a salary plus a commission determined by their sales performance.

SELLING MERCHANDISE AND SERVICES

All retail store employees have a responsibility to sell the products and services of their employers. The amount of time and effort devoted to selling varies according to job requirements. Merchandise stockers, for example, are not directly responsible for selling merchandise. However, they should be prepared to answer customer questions about merchandise that are similar to those directed to a salesperson. A selling process that can be used effectively in most retail stores includes the following steps:

1. Preapproach
2. Approach
3. Determining customer wants and needs
4. Presenting or demonstrating merchandise
5. Answering questions and objections
6. Closing the sale
7. Suggestion selling
8. Customer departure and follow-up

Preapproach

Preapproach is the getting ready stage of the selling process. It involves studying the various features and benefits of products and services sold. Preapproach activities also include preparing and displaying merchandise.

Approach

When customers enter a store or a particular department, the salesperson should recognize and approach them. Most selling approaches fall into one of four categories: (1) the service approach, (2) the formal approach, (3) the informal approach, and (4) the merchandise approach. An example of a service approach that sales personnel might use is "May I help you?" A salesperson using a formal approach might say, "Good afternoon." A typical informal approach would consist of addressing the customer by name. In a merchandise approach, a salesperson could say, "That table has a scratch-proof top."

Determining Customer Wants and Needs

The goal of this step is to assist customers in identifying a product or service that meets their wants or needs. Some customers know exactly what they want. Others have a general idea but need help narrowing their choices to a single item. Sales personnel who have good listening and observation skills are usually successful in completing this step of the selling process.

Presenting or Demonstrating Merchandise

A most effective way to assist customers with buying decisions is to present or demonstrate the use of merchandise the customer is considering. This step makes it possible to appeal to a customer's senses of sight, touch, hearing, taste, and smell.

Answering Questions and Objections

Customers may raise questions about a product or object to some aspect of an item being presented. Questions or objections indicate the customer's interest in the merchandise. Most customer questions and objections relate to the price or quality of merchandise, store policies, or a reluctance to make an immediate decision. Well-trained sales personnel are prepared in advance to respond to such customer concerns. When their concerns are handled effectively by sales personnel, customers are apt to feel more confident about their selections.

Closing the Sale

Closing the sale is the purpose of the entire selling process. Unfortunately, many beginners in retail selling avoid asking, or apologize for asking, customers to buy. The closing step is a very natural part of the sales process. If the product has been well presented and the customer's questions properly answered, the decision to buy logically follows. Some customers will decide on their own to buy. Others may need some assistance in reaching a decision. Salespeo-

Illus. 6–1 Retailing offers a variety of opportunities for gaining experience in personal selling.

ple should not expect to close every sale, but there is almost no excuse for not trying to close a sale when a customer is interested in products that can fill his or her wants or needs.

Suggestion Selling

Suggestion selling is a service to customers. This step simply involves recom-mending that the customer purchase additional merchandise to complement the original purchase. For example, a salesperson may suggest the purchase of a blouse and scarf that match the purchased suit or, perhaps, a paint roller and tray for use with the paint that has been selected. Sale items or newly arrived merchandise can also be suggested. Suggestion selling should never mean pressuring customers into buying items they cannot use.

Illus. 6–2   *Effective salespeople study their products so that they can provide service to customers.*

Customer Departure and Follow-up

The final step in the selling process gives the salesperson an opportunity to reassure the customer that her or his decision to buy is correct. As the customer departs, the salesperson might say, "Thank you. I know you will enjoy your new coat." This reassurance is a way to build customer confidence and retain goodwill. Even when a sale is not closed, a salesperson should express a willingness to assist customers the next time they visit the store. Depending upon the product sold, a salesperson may perform a variety of follow-up functions. These might include determining customer satisfaction, checking proper installation, instructing on correct use, and determining the need for a product maintenance contract to assure dependability.

SPECIAL SELLING SKILLS

Mastery of the steps in the selling process is important. Additional specialized skills are often needed to provide good customer service. For example, the ability to remember names and faces can build customer confidence in what the salesperson has to say. Skill in selling by telephone also is fast becoming an important job asset. At times, customers may have complaints about the products or services they have purchased. Sales personnel who listen attentively, know store policy, and have a proper attitude toward customer complaints can build goodwill for themselves and their employer. Maintaining customer interest while serving two or more individuals at the same time is yet another skill that competent salespeople can perform.

After a sale has been closed, the salesperson's next responsibility is to assist the customer in completing the actual sales transaction. Generally, a sales transaction involves recording the purchase on a sales register. The salesperson may then give change, provide a receipt, and wrap or bag the merchandise. Although many sales transactions involve cash, the salesperson also must know how to handle personal checks and charge-card purchases. Each procedure must be conducted with speed, accuracy, and friendliness.

SALES SUPPORTING SKILLS

Most retailers agree that selling merchandise is the primary responsibility of a salesperson. However, to be really effective in sales work, the salesperson must perform a variety of duties other than selling. The following examples are typical nonselling duties that retailers assign to their employees.

Stockkeeping

Well-maintained merchandise shelves and racks create a favorable impression of a store. Products properly displayed and in sufficient quantities and variety increase the chances of closing a sale. Salespeople may be responsible for stockkeeping when they are not helping customers.

Housekeeping

Customers like to shop in stores that are neat, easy to walk through, and have a friendly atmosphere. Basic housekeeping duties of sales personnel include cleaning displays, work areas, and walkways. Empty boxes and litter should be removed from the sales area and damaged or shopworn merchandise replaced with fresh products. Every salesperson should assume responsibility for housekeeping duties even if the duties are not assigned.

Preventing Waste and Loss

Careful use of store supplies and materials, such as bags and sales slips, can help reduce the costs of operating a store. Salespeople can prevent losses by being alert to potential shoplifters and vandals and following proper procedures when dealing with them.

Directing Customers

New customers may seek assistance in locating a certain department or product in the store. Salespeople need to be well informed about all areas of the store so that, when customers ask them for help, they can respond courteously, with accurate information.

Store Policy

Most retailers have policies and procedures for dealing with customers. "The customer is always right" is the general policy of most retail stores. "Refunds on returned merchandise are allowed if accompanied by a receipt" is another policy that retailers generally follow. Sales personnel must be thoroughly familiar with those policies since they are usually responsible for explaining them to customers.

Receiving, Checking, and Marking

Sales personnel may be called upon to assist in bringing newly arrived merchandise into the stockroom and checking to make sure that all items ordered have been received. Some merchandise may be brought unmarked to the sales floor where it is priced and placed in appropriate locations by salespeople.

Merchandise Information

When they are not working with customers, salespeople should make every effort to learn the specific features and benefits of the items they sell. A simple review of product labels, directions for use, and manufacturer product data sheets can greatly enhance the salesperson's ability to present merchandise and to answer the customer's questions.

Unit 6 provides additional information about these and other related sales topics—all of which are important to those interested in a career in retail selling.

Summary

Salespeople are the main contributors to a store's success. Retail salespeople must have good work habits and also speak, write, and listen effectively. They need to make calculations, remember customers, and know about the products offered by the store. Retail sales jobs include salesclerks (a typical entry-level job), sales demonstrators, salespeople, and sales representatives. The selling process usually includes at least the following steps: preapproach, approach, determining customer wants and needs, presenting or demonstrating the merchandise, answering questions or objections, closing the sale, suggestion selling, and customer departure and follow-up. In addition to these basic skills, retail salespeople also need to know how to handle special selling situations and perform a variety of sales supporting activities, such as stockkeeping, directing customers, and marking merchandise.

Review

1. Define *personal selling*.
2. List five personal traits that retailers expect sales personnel to possess.
3. State the main differences between a salesclerk and a salesperson.
4. Identify a sales demonstrator's most important task.
5. List the steps of a selling process that can be used in most retail stores.
6. Identify four customer approaches that sales personnel can use.

7.   Define *suggestion selling*.
8.   List the procedures that are involved in most sales transactions.
9.   Identify three sales supporting skills used in retailing.
10. Name two sources of information sales personnel can use to learn more about the products they sell.

Terms

The following terms were introduced in this chapter. Write a separate sentence correctly using each new term.

salesclerk   salesperson
sales demonstrator   sales representative

Discuss

1.   Why are speaking, writing, listening, and computing skills important for success in retail selling?
2.   Why are retail sales representatives paid differently than salesclerks?
3.   If given the responsibility of identifying six special selling skills to include in a store's training program, what would you suggest?
4.   How can merchandise information help salespeople provide service to customers?
5.   Of what value is selling in the retailing industry?

Problem Solving

1.   A customer is looking closely at a pullover sweater on a large display table in your department. What do you believe would be the most effective customer approach in this situation? Give examples of your opening comments to the customer.
2.   Inez has been hired as a salesperson in the sportswear department of Gold's Department Store. After a short time, she appears bored with her job because she feels there is little to do when customers are not in the area. As her supervisor, recommend activities for Inez in her free time.
3.   Juan's employer has indicated that she will offer a bonus to all employees who sell ten or more portable television sets during the week. To earn this bonus, Juan believes he must improve his product demonstration skills. Suggest some ways that Juan could demonstrate the portable television sets to appeal to the customer's various senses.

CHAPTER 7
Operations and Control

CHAPTER OUTCOMES

When you have mastered the information provided in this chapter, you should be able to:

1. List six duties of the operations division of a store

2. Explain the importance of a good control system

3. Define *control system*

4. List the desired characteristics of a control system

5. List the five essential records needed by a business

6. Describe the information contained in an income statement and a balance sheet

7. Describe the control process that leads to effective store management

Operations and control are two of the four functions essential in every retail store. The purpose of both operations and control is to support the buying and selling activities. The employees responsible for the operation function make sure that the store has competent workers and a well-maintained building. Those who carry out the control function keep records and prepare statements necessary for guiding or directing the business.

OPERATIONS

Operations activities usually are the behind-the-scenes work of a retail store. Most customers are unaware of the many activities necessary to provide a clean and attractive store that is well stocked with merchandise. The major duties of the operations division of a store include the following:

1. Recruiting, selecting, and training of store personnel and providing employee benefits and services
2. Arranging and maintaining the store building as well as other store property, such as warehouses and parking lots
3. Extending credit and establishing and following collection procedures
4. Handling store merchandise from receiving to delivery and installation, if necessary
5. Checking, marking, and stocking merchandise
6. Managing store merchandise and security of stock, personnel, and store property

Of the departments within the operations division, customers most often deal with the credit department. The personnel component of store operations is presented in Unit 3. The other activities included in store operations are presented in Unit 7.

CONTROL

Merchants must be alert to new opportunities as well as potential pitfalls when they operate their businesses. Incomplete notes and memory do not provide a reliable picture of what happened last year, last month, or even last week. The daily operation of a modern retail enterprise has too many details for the casual approach to be successful. A retailer must have an adequate system of records to have readily available the data needed for planning profitable growth. In other words, the control function is vital to a successful retail operation.

Some retailers are always aware of the work activity in their companies and, specifically, in each department or merchandise line. They make decisions correctly and quickly and respond to requests for information without delay. Other retailers are unaware of their company's activity, so when decisions must be made, they often guess rather than respond confidently. The probable difference between the two types of retailers is that one has a record system that provides up-to-date facts for making effective decisions, and the other does not.

A good record system is necessary to keep pace with a fast-moving merchandise operation. These records are also needed to determine federal, state, and local taxes; to support requests for loans; and to establish a credit rating. Successful store operators consider record systems so important for planning and control that they invest considerable money in personnel and electronic data-processing equipment.

WHAT IS A CONTROL SYSTEM?

A **system** is a set of procedures or techniques carried out by people and/or equipment to accomplish a given purpose. A **control system** is a set of procedures or techniques used to obtain information for operating a business successfully.

The purpose of a control system is to help a retailer answer questions and make decisions about the business operation. Most merchants believe that a good control system should have at least the following five characteristics.

1. The system should provide quantitative information about the financial condition of the business. This information includes the amounts of cash sales, credit sales, money received on account, money paid out, goods ordered and on hand, and money owed to others.

Illus. 7–1   The merchant regularly checks control information about merchandise sales, expenses, and other data important for effective decision making.

2. The system should protect the merchant against losses due to human errors, such as carelessness, forgetfulness, and theft. The system should report promptly the condition of the company's operation.
3. The system should permit efficient service to customers and suppliers. Customer sales should be recorded accurately and quickly. Payments to suppliers and others should be made promptly. The system should prevent oversight or duplication of billing or payment.
4. The system should be convenient, workable, and practical. The time required to maintain the system should be minimal and should not detract from the selling function of the store.
5. The system should be economical; in other words, it should operate at a reasonable cost. The cost of supplies, equipment, and staff time should be as low as possible without sacrificing the effectiveness of the system.

To plan and control, retailers need specific data about a particular store, department, or even product line. If a merchant has four stores, data on each store are needed—one set of records is not sufficient. Likewise, the merchant needs information for each department or merchandise line within a particular store. The mechanics of control systems will vary. For small stores, a manual system (one kept by hand) may be all that is needed. For most stores, an electronic system (one kept by computer) may be required. Merchants in any size store recognize the value of having fast, accurate, and comprehensive analyses of records.

ESSENTIAL RECORDS

"How much do I have invested in merchandise?"

"How much was earned last month?"

"Which credit accounts are past due?"

"For which merchandise lines are sales increasing? decreasing?"

"What were my total expenses for the last quarter of operation?"

These questions are typical of those retailers ask about their businesses. By looking at the basic retail functions, retailers can identify the records that they must maintain.

A **purchase record** shows what goods have been ordered and from which suppliers and at what cost they have been ordered. Two types of purchase records are purchase orders and invoices. A *purchase order* is a request for merchandise from a supplier. Retailers file purchase orders by date to know when the ordered merchandise will arrive. When the shipment is prepared by the supplier, another form called an *invoice* is sent to the retailer. The retailer uses the invoice to check the shipments. The retailer makes sure that the merchandise ordered was received and the quantities and costs on the invoice are the same as on the purchase order. After checking the shipment, the retailer pays for the merchandise the amount on the invoice.

An **inventory record** shows what merchandise a retailer has in stock. The two main types of inventory records are physical inventory records and book or perpetual inventory records. *Physical inventory records* are prepared by counting the goods on hand. *Book* or *perpetual inventory records* are prepared by subtracting the number of merchandise items sold to customers or returned to suppliers from the number of items received from suppliers. This difference is the number of items that should be on hand. Purchase and inventory records are explained in more detail in Chapter 47.

A **sales record** shows the total dollar amount of sales and the specific items that were sold. Sales records may show that a clothing store sold $1874 worth of goods. More helpful to a merchant is a record of the particular items, sizes, fabrics, and colors that were sold. The amount of cash sales versus credit sales is also important information that sales records reveal to retailers. Sales records are discussed in Chapter 48.

An **expense record** shows the amount of money the retailer has spent for goods, salaries, advertising, taxes, and all other costs of doing business. By regularly examining expense records, a merchant can identify where money is being spent and where costs may be reduced. Various ways of classifying expenses are shown in Chapter 48.

A **financial statement** shows the status and progress of a business in dollars and cents. The main financial records are the income statement and the balance sheet. The **income statement** shows the profit or loss for a given period of operation. The **balance sheet** shows what the business owns and what it owes to others; the difference is the value of the owner's interest in the business. Instructions for preparing income statements and balance sheets are given in Chapter 49.

With these five essential records, the retailer will have the data necessary to answer questions about the business and to make decisions about future actions.

THE CONTROL PROCESS

A record system that provides needed information does not, by itself, ensure good control of the business. Successful retailers recognize that the control process has three other components: (1) standards of performance, (2) measures of current performance, and (3) corrective action.

Standards of Performance

Most retailers set standards of performance in the form of budget goals. The standards may be in terms of expected sales, expected profit, markdowns, or other budget goals. For example, a menswear department may be expected to increase sales by $35,000 in six months as a result of adding a new line of goods. An auto parts store may be expected to increase profit by 1 percent in a year by increasing the amount of advertising. A grocery store may be expected to sell as many turkeys this year as during last Thanksgiving's 15-percent-off sale.

Whether performance standards are set for an entire store or an individual department, product line, or employee, the standard should support the main purpose of the business. Also, to be of value, performance standards must be realistic. Meeting the standards must seem likely.

Measures of Current Performance

To determine whether standards of performance are being achieved, retailers must measure current activity. In retailing,

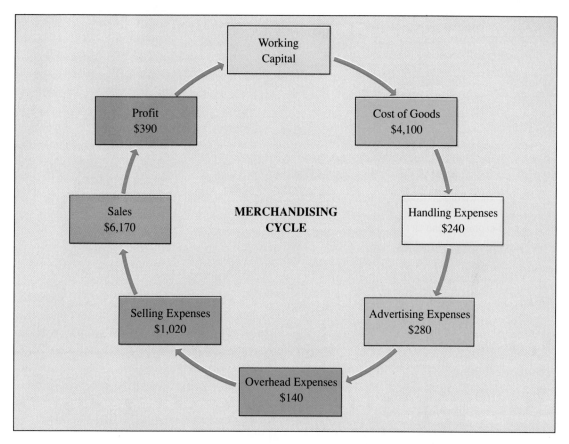

Illus. 7–2 This merchandising cycle, basic to every retail operation, indicates the types of records a retailer must keep.

performance is usually measured in terms of dollars or units of merchandise. The measure of current performance is compared to the preset standard. The difference between standards and performance is noted. Then the retailer looks for one or more reasons to explain the difference. The retailer must consider whether the conditions anticipated when the standard was set actually exist when the current measures of performance are taken. For example, a retailer may note a 10 percent increase in sales in November of this year as compared to last November.

The increase may be due to improved performance by the store staff (see Illustration 7–3). However, the increase could be due to changes in the local economy, the closing of a competitor's store, or the opening of a new highway into the community.

Corrective Action

If current performance does not meet the standards set, corrective action is needed; the retailer must change perfor-

PERFORMANCE APPRAISAL

Employee Appraised

NAME _____ TITLE _____

Manager Preparing Appraisal

NAME _____ TITLE _____

I-far below	II-below	III-average	IV-above	V-far above

These are the symbols to be used in rating employee's performance on position requirements. Discuss with the employee the following performance criteria in relation to her or his duties:

1. Performance of specific duties as stated in description of employee's position
2. Basic knowledge and awareness of current developments in field and ability to keep informed in own field
3. Ability to identify and solve problems
4. Clear expression and tact in both oral and written communication
5. Efficient use of time and scheduling
6. Ability to assist customers and other employees
7. Attitude toward new duties
8. Reliability and common sense
9. Specific goals and plans for future growth and development of employee, related to major job duties
10. Action recommended if performance is unsatisfactory

Employee's signature _____ Date _____

Manager's signature _____ Date _____

Illus. 7–3 Performance standards for an employee, similar to those for an entire store, must support the main purpose of the business.

mance so that standards are achieved or more nearly met in the future. For example, the budget goal for furniture sales for January, February, and March is $96,350; actual sales are $61,500. The sizeable difference indicates a serious problem. When planning corrective action, the retailer should do the following:

1. Gather all the possible facts about the problem: weekly sales, advertising, new competition, lines not selling
2. Identify the most likely causes of the low level of sales
3. Identify possible solutions to these probable causes

4. Make changes or adjustments
5. Follow up to see whether the corrective action is working
6. Repeat the steps if the first corrective action is not working

Too often, retailers are reluctant to take necessary corrective action when performance standards are not met. They seem to forget this vital component of the control process. Correction is as important to a control system as keeping and analyzing records, setting performance standards, and measuring current performance. In short, without corrective action there is no control.

Summary

The store operations function ensures that a store is stocked with merchandise and is ready for customers. *Operations* includes stock handling, customer services, employee services, and security. To control a retail business successfully, the retailer needs to have records and procedures that indicate the health of the business. The control function must provide timely information, be easy to use, and be easy and economical to maintain. An effective control system is made up of inventory records, sales records, expense records, and financial statements. From these records and statements, a merchant can evaluate performance and then make any necessary and appropriate adjustments in the business operation.

Review

1. What six duties are performed by the operations division of a retail store?
2. Why is it important for a retailer to have a good control system?
3. What is a control system?
4. What quantitative information should be provided by a good control system?
5. What information is on a purchase order?
6. What are the two main financial statements needed by a business?
7. Describe the three components of the control process.
8. What six steps are needed to take corrective action?

Terms

The following terms were introduced in this chapter. Write a separate sentence correctly using each new term.

balance sheet   inventory record
control system   purchase record
expense record   sales record
financial statement   system
income statement

Discuss

1. What aspects of store operations directly affect the store's customers?
2. What problems will a new business encounter if a poor control system is used?

3. If you were an owner-manager of a small variety store, what information about your store would you like to have daily? weekly? monthly?
4. Why should a control system be economical?
5. Why would a purchase record file be important to a retailer with limited storage space?

*Problem
Solving*

1. Assume that you are going to open a leather craft shop. You will purchase leather items from a variety of craftspeople. You anticipate sales of about $230,000 for the first year. Which records should you have for your store? Which would be most important in your day-to-day operation?
2. Locate three current newspaper or magazine articles about store control or record systems. Summarize these articles and identify two key points or trends in control and record systems.
3. Evaluate the control system for a women's sportswear store located in a shopping mall. What features would you look for?

CHAPTER 8

Future of Retailing

CHAPTER OUTCOMES

When you have mastered the information provided in this chapter, you should be able to:

1. Identify forces that are affecting consumer life-styles

2. List three technological changes that will have impact on the future of retailing

3. Identify typical retailing problems that retailing research can help solve

4. List some general procedures that can be followed in retailing research

5. Explain the importance of self-assessment and job-seeking skills in starting a retailing career

6. State the importance of career planning and education in preparing for a future career in retailing

President Abraham Lincoln is reported to have said, "We must plan for the future, because people who stay in the present will remain in the past." Today's fast-paced life-style suggests that the future is rapidly becoming the present. Retailers know that success depends on their ability to anticipate change in the way they do business. Just as important is the need to plan for these changes.

To plan effectively, retailers must predict their future markets. Who will be their customers? How many customers will there be? Where will these potential customers be found? What will customers buy? How and when will they make their purchases? To answer these important questions, retailers need to study carefully consumer buying habits, population trends, and changing business practices. Ultimately, continued success of the retailing industry will depend on quality products, competitive prices, and highly skilled retail personnel. This chapter deals with some key factors that may influence retailing practices in the future.

FUTURE CONSUMERS

The key to what the future holds for retailers is the change taking place in consumer life-styles. These new life-styles are influenced by such forces as population trends, mobility, income, personal values, and consumerism.

Population and Income Trends

The U.S. Bureau of the Census reported that this country will increase in population to 268 million by the year 2000. At the same time, the size of various age groups will change dramatically. Middle age and older citizens will become an increasingly larger portion of the retailer's market. Of equal importance will be the single population, which now accounts for approximately 40 percent of all households. Shifts in population represent changes in consumer needs and wants. Progressive retailers recognize that these trends affect the types of goods and services they sell. For example, prepackaged goods may have to be available in a greater variety of sizes because of increased variations in household sizes. Demands for services, such as dry cleaning, home maintenance, recreational facilities, and dining, will continue to expand as people spend less time in the traditional home environment.

Despite the unpredictability of the economy, current signs indicate that Americans generally will experience an increase in spendable income. Retailers think this trend means a greater demand for goods and services. In addition, consumers will expect higher quality goods, greater variety, and increased customer services.

Mobility

Americans are on the move! This has been true since our country was founded. The U.S. Bureau of the Census figures indicate that approximately 10 percent of the population moves each year. Over half of these moves are to other communities. To deal with a constantly changing clientele, many merchants sell easily recognized and highly advertised merchandise. Others locate in shopping centers for convenient ac-

Illus. 8–1   Successful retailers continually change their methods of doing business to provide quality service.

cess. Still others provide rental services, such as moving vans, lawnmowers, trailers, furniture, and similar household goods, to customers who do not want to buy them. Major chain and department stores offer credit cards that are accepted in most parts of the country.

Personal Values

Traditional values are being challenged in today's society. A wide range of life-styles is accepted, and the quality of life, rather than ownership of material things, is becoming important. The role of women has shifted dramatically. More and more women are joining the work force seeking fulfilling careers and economic independence. They will account for 47 percent of the labor force by the late 1990s. Interest in physical fitness and mental health is high, and the desire for personal fulfillment has never been greater.

Retailers interpret these trends to mean increased consumer self-confidence and self-reliance. Customers will be less likely to follow the crowd. Shoppers will be open to new ideas but will demand detailed information and proof before purchasing goods and services.

Consumerism

Undoubtedly, modern consumers are better educated and more sophisticated than consumers of the past, and they expect much more from business. When today's customers suspect unfair treatment, they let someone know. In recent years, that someone often has been a government or private agency established to protect consumer rights. Any activity by a government, business, or private agency designed to protect customer rights is called **consumerism.** Truth-in-lending and packaging laws are typical of the kinds of legislation passed to protect consumers.

In response to growing criticism, many retailers have voluntarily developed programs to protect the interests of their customers. Product-testing services, store advisory committees, and policies designed

Illus. 8—2   Customer buying habits reflect changes in life-styles and personal values.

to resolve complaints quickly are set up to build the confidence and goodwill of retail customers. Efforts are also under way to review advertising, product labeling, and servicing procedures and to regulate practices in these areas. As retailers become more active in policing themselves, government regulation is likely to decline. Consumers, however, will continue to demand fair treatment from the retailing industry.

FUTURE TECHNOLOGY

Technological changes will have a major impact on the future of both large and small retail operations. A key influence on

these changes will be the increasing use of computers. Methods of store operation have changed due to consumer video-ordering systems, electronic banking and payment systems, and check-out and point-of-sale systems.

Consumer Video-ordering Systems

Cable television systems allow consumers to shop at home. Consumers key in requests for product information on a computer keyboard. The information, including a picture of the product, is displayed on consumers' home computer screens. Items selected for purchase may be ordered by computer or by phone. Consumers have the option of picking up the merchandise or arranging for home delivery. Purchases are charged to customers' accounts and bills are issued automatically by retailers' computers.

Electronic-banking and Payment Systems

Electronic fund transfer systems eventually may eliminate the need to handle cash or checks. Electronic banking systems enable customers to deposit money to and withdraw money from bank accounts and to transfer funds from one account to another without going to a bank. Also, some of these computerized systems allow customers to transfer funds automatically from their bank accounts to selected merchant accounts. Some electronic banking systems require use of an automatic teller machine; others permit customers to key payment information on a telephone keypad. It is expected that the innovative use of electronic banking and payment systems will continue to increase.

Checkout and Point-of-sale Systems

Optical character scanners reduce the need for cashiers to key sales transactions on the sales register keyboard. Instead, cashiers simply pass items over an electronic eye. A computer instantly records and displays all pertinent information. Retailers obtain inventory and ordering information and customers receive detailed receipts of purchases. Advanced point-of-sale systems also verify checks and credit ratings and tabulate and analyze sales data. Advanced systems are used to communicate with other stores and report products' profitability.

RETAILING RESEARCH

Predicting the future can be risky for business people. Therefore, most retailers are unwilling to rely on instincts or to guess

Illus. 8–3 Technology will make it possible to shop and carry out bank transactions without leaving home.

what direction their businesses should take. Increasing costs have convinced merchants that they must plan and carefully test new methods before putting them into operation. These planning and testing efforts are called **retailing research.**

Retailers use research methods to solve common retailing problems such as (1) selecting store locations, (2) determining customer buying habits, (3) predicting product demand, (4) choosing effective advertising media, and (5) identifying efficient store operating procedures. Generally, there are no easy or quick ways to resolve problems such as those mentioned. Rather, hard work and good organizational skills are necessary. The nature of these problems suggests the ultimate purpose of retailing research: to improve customer service and increase profits.

Although there is no single right way to organize and conduct retailing research, the following five-step procedure is used by a variety of business establishments:

1. Clearly identify the problem to be solved
2. Carefully study current information and develop new information where needed
3. Analyze collected data and put it in an easy-to-understand form
4. Decide on a plan of action and put the plan into effect
5. Determine later if the plan solved the original problem

Sometimes, plans must be altered to meet changing conditions. Perhaps a plan may fail because of insufficient data or improper organization. The more that consumers and technology change, the more important retailing research becomes. Undoubtedly, retailers in the future will need to apply retailing research procedures. Retailing research and success go hand-in-hand.

STARTING A RETAILING CAREER

There is little doubt that the future of retailing depends on the type of employees and managers it attracts. These personnel will have to be people pleasers, risk takers, and problem solvers. In addition, they will need the following qualities: (1) initiative, (2) willingness to work hard, (3) cooperative team-player attitude, (4) loyalty, and (5) ability to adjust rapidly to change.

Clearly, a decision to follow a career in retailing cannot be made lightly. Employers seek the most qualified personnel they can find. Therefore, a potential employee will want to obtain the best possible educational and work experience. So, where should the search for a retailing career begin?

Self-assessment

Self-assessment is a good place to start. Self-assessment is careful study of your potential for a career in retailing. The self-assessment process requires precise answers to specific questions about your skills and abilities. What follows are examples of the kinds of questions you will want to ask yourself:

1. What are my short-term career goals (one year from now)?
2. What are my long-term career goals (five years from now)?

3. What are my major strengths and weaknesses? For example, do I like dealing with the public or would I rather seek employment where public contact is not necessary?
4. What kinds of job tasks do I do best? Is it displaying merchandise, assisting customers, or operating a sales register?
5. What kind of life-style do I prefer—routine tasks, flexible hours, or constant change?

The more questions you ask, and the more specific the questions are, the more valuable your self-assessment will be. To assess your potential for a retailing career, you need information about retailing jobs. People employed in jobs for which you have some interest can be valuable sources of information. School career planning and placement offices are particularly helpful to students. Help-wanted advertisements and employment agencies are also good resources.

Seeking Employment

The process of preparing, applying, and interviewing for a retailing job is described in Chapter 17. The importance of having a well-prepared personal résumé, a neat and effective application letter, and a good preparation for an employment interview is emphasized in that chapter. Such tasks are necessary for each job application; so it is advantageous to be prepared at all times.

A personal résumé should always be current. A résumé lists educational background and work experience. While it may not be necessary to retype a résumé until it is time to use it for a job change or promotion, the résumé regularly should be brought up to date. Some people wait until they are ready to apply for a new job when they have forgotten that they handled a big inventory project or helped reorganize a department. Include on the résumé any workshops, training seminars, or classes you attended (retain copies of the contents of each presentation). Many people redo their résumés every year; then, if one is needed at a moment's notice, the information is current. A résumé that lists your job-related and educational experiences can be a well-organized presentation of your job qualifications.

A periodic brush-up on your job interviewing skills is a good idea, regardless of whether you are already employed. Employees can practice listening, questioning, and persuading skills during meetings with their supervisors. If it has been some time since a job change, a session with an employment counselor could help you recall the questions most often raised by interviewers. Current work experience will also suggest questions that you want answered before interviewing for or accepting another job.

PLANNING A FUTURE RETAILING CAREER

The person who wants to stand out in the retailing field must plan for success. Once the first retail job is obtained, stepping-stones for moving ahead should be identified. The individual should carefully plan for the next year or two. The plan should include a list of the skills and abilities that advancement will require and a list of ways to acquire them. The plan should also include indications of time. For example, an individual who plans to enroll in a course to learn more about selling should not only decide what course to take but when to apply and actually take the course. Such a plan not only helps the person achieve long-term success but also makes a present job seem more interesting and challenging.

The predicted rate of change in society and business over the next 40 years makes continuing education essential. It is a mistake to assume that major retail career opportunities await high-school graduates who do not continue their education through full-time or part-time study. Some high-school graduates do succeed in retailing without higher education; however, they are few. Most individuals who lack advanced education do not progress beyond minor executive positions. It is true that some older, experienced executives are not college trained, but this is not true of younger executives in large retail organizations. Today, a higher percentage than ever before are college-prepared people seeking retailing careers. Chain stores, department stores, and franchised businesses are competing for the best personnel that colleges and universities can produce.

Thus, a personal career search must go well beyond acquiring a job. You should plan to keep up with developments in the retailing field. Publications such as the *Journal of Retailing, Stores,* or the *Journal of Marketing* along with periodic courses in buying, management, salesmanship, marketing, merchandise information, store control, and computer operation (available at

Illus. 8–4 Having a career plan and following through on that plan are ways to succeed in retailing.

many colleges and universities) will help you to remain aware of new developments. A detailed study of the newest methods of various retailing operations—along with imaginative and creative thinking—can make the difference between just getting along and becoming a future leader in retailing. The purpose of this text is to present those retailing methods in sufficient detail in order to provide the reader with a solid foundation of knowledge about the retailing industry.

Summary

The growth, mobility, and diversity of consumers, in addition to changes in life-style and values, all contribute to an exciting and challenging future in retailing. New technology, and especially new ways to use computers, will bring about new means of communicating with and responding to consumers. As consumers become better educated and better informed about merchandise, they expect more from retailers. Retailers can obtain important information about consumers and their preferences through well-planned retail research. Those who plan to pursue retailing as a career should assess their interests and acquire the skills necessary to get and keep a job. Success in most fields rarely just happens; rather, success must be planned.

*R*eview

1. Name five forces that influence consumer life-styles.
2. State how consumer video-ordering systems, electronic-banking and payment systems, and checkout and point-of-sale systems are used in retail businesses.
3. Identify four typical retailing problems that retailing research can help solve.
4. List five steps to take when conducting retailing research.
5. Identify four questions that will need to be answered in the self-assessment process.
6. List courses that could prove helpful to young retailers who are organizing their future educational plans.
7. State two ways retailers deal with customer mobility.
8. Name ways that a personal résumé can be kept current.

*T*erms

The following terms were introduced in this chapter. Write a separate sentence correctly using each new term.

consumerism   retailing research

*D*iscuss

1. Should retailers anticipate changes in the way they do business?
2. How could population changes affect the goods and services retailers sell to their customers?
3. How does the growth of consumerism affect business practices?
4. Why are many retailers no longer willing to rely on instincts when predicting future business practices?
5. Why are job information sources important in self-assessment?
6. How does educational planning affect future careers in retailing?

*P*roblem
Solving

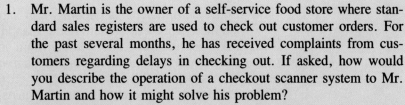

1. Mr. Martin is the owner of a self-service food store where standard sales registers are used to check out customer orders. For the past several months, he has received complaints from customers regarding delays in checking out. If asked, how would you describe the operation of a checkout scanner system to Mr. Martin and how it might solve his problem?
2. You are the assistant manager of a sporting goods department in a locally owned discount store. Sales and profits in this department have almost doubled over the past three years. Your department manager has been authorized to hire three additional full-time employees, two of whom will be in sales positions. What specific recommendations would you make regarding the qualifications of the people to be hired?

UNIT 1 ACTIVITIES

CHECKING KEY POINTS

This exercise is designed to check your understanding of material presented in Unit 1. On a separate sheet of paper, list the numbers 1 to 32. Indicate your response, *T* for true or *F* for false, for each of the following statements.

1. The main purpose of retail marketing is to provide the goods and services desired by consumers.
2. The ultimate consumer is the person who finally uses a product or service for personal benefit or satisfaction.
3. Most retailing is done through in-store retailing.
4. Nearly all retailing jobs require persons with strong selling skills.
5. The informal organization of a business is shown on an organization chart.
6. Store policies set forth procedures for all workers.
7. Large stores are those with annual sales of more than $1 million and/or 15 or more full-time employees.
8. Store operations include the accounting, budgeting, and financial functions of a store.
9. Personal selling involves direct contact between customer and salesperson.
10. Retail wages are about the same in all kinds of retail stores.
11. Long periods of education or training are needed for most retail jobs.
12. Retailing is a highly competitive field.
13. Staple goods are those that customers buy frequently, perhaps daily.
14. Small store merchants generally can improve success by offering merchandise in breadth rather than in depth.
15. Price policies can be used to convey a certain store image.
16. A merchandising plan reflects various merchandising policies set for a store.
17. Promotional stores stress sales, bargains, and price reductions.
18. Comfort, love, and curiosity are social motives for buying.
19. Publicity is nonpaid promotion of a business, product, or service.
20. *Promotional mix* refers to the combination of media used by a retailer to communicate with prospective customers.
21. New retail workers are often employed as salesclerks.
22. The first step of the selling process is determining customer wants and needs.

23. Suggestion selling is a means of getting customers to buy items they really don't need.
24. Salespersons perform a variety of duties other than selling.
25. A control system should help retailers in their planning efforts.
26. Purchase records show what merchandise a retailer has in stock.
27. The main financial records for a business are the income statement and the balance sheet.
28. Good store records ensure good control.
29. Approximately 8 percent of the United States population changes residence each year.
30. Consumerism is any activity that protects business from unscrupulous customers.
31. Improvements in electronic banking will increase use of retail credit cards and store charge accounts.
32. Self-assessment involves a careful study of your own potential.

BUILDING BASIC SKILLS

Calculations

The following calculations were used in Unit 1 to demonstrate certain facts about retailing. Make the calculations necessary to answer each of the questions that follows the chart.

RETAIL STORES AND WORKERS IN WESTWOOD MALL

Store	Sales Last Year	Full-time Workers	Part-time Workers
Pandas	$108,000	2	2
PopStop	482,000	4	3
Deli V	278,000	5	4
Buks4U	190,000	3	9
Score!	541,000	7	4
Prints	170,000	2	5
Mr. D's	210,000	3	4

1. How many retail businesses are located in the Westwood Mall?
2. What were the total dollar sales of the stores last year?
3. How many full-time employees are employed by these stores?
4. How many part-time employees are employed by these stores?
5. What are the average sales for the stores?

6. What is the amount of sales per worker (total of full- and part-time workers)?
7. What is the average number of full-time workers in these stores?

Working with People

Retail workers must work with other employees, supervisors, and customers. Sometimes, misunderstandings, poor communications, and other factors interfere with good working relationships and proper customer service. Many successful workers solve people problems with the four-step *DICE* approach. Each letter of *DICE* refers to a specific action in a four-step problem-solving procedure.

1. *D*—Define the problem
2. *I*—Identify possible solutions
3. *C*—Choose one of the solutions
4. *E*—Evaluate the consequences of the solution selected

Read each of the following problem situations. Then, use the *DICE* approach to find a solution for each. Remember, you must first define the problem before you identify or choose solutions. Describe the consequences of your solutions.

1. You are working as a stockperson in a large discount store. Your job is to move reserve stock to the selling floor, re-mark and rearrange stock on the selling floor, and conduct periodic inventories of stock. Your supervisor speaks softly. Often you misunderstand what she wants done. The result is that you have often moved the wrong stock or repriced the wrong merchandise. You realize these errors make you look incompetent.
2. You are one of two workers in a candy and nut shop in a shopping mall. The other worker regularly excuses himself at noon and makes phone calls to friends. These calls often go on for over an hour. The noon period is often busy and you have to handle all customers who come in.
3. You are a salesperson in a housewares department of a large store. You approach a customer who is looking at glass cookware. After your greeting, the customer says the brand she is looking at is not very good and asks for a brand that you do not have.

Writing Skills

You are asked to be a reporter for the *Retail Times* newspaper. Select one of the feature topics listed below. Your article should be between 400 and 500 words unless your instructor assigns otherwise.

When preparing your article, be sure to credit your resources for any ideas, views, explanations, or quotations that you use.

1. Retailing delivers the goods
2. Selling procedures help customers more than you realize
3. Changes expected in retailing
4. Styles of merchandise are important to some consumers and not to others
5. Retailers report store records resemble a family checkbook
6. Beginning jobs in retailing are many and varied this year
7. Retail advertising improves retailer-consumer communications
8. Organization is essential in retailing

APPLYING YOUR KNOWLEDGE

Can You Do the Following?

1. Name and compare two types of pricing policies that are used in most retail stores.
2. Name four benefits to consumers of an efficient retail-marketing system.
3. List four questions you should ask yourself when performing a self-assessment.
4. List the steps of the selling process.
5. Explain why the study of ultimate consumers is important to retailers.
6. Describe the two major financial statements necessary for a retail-store operation and explain why they are essential.
7. List the three major forms of business ownership.
8. Explain the differences between merchandise breadth and merchandise depth.
9. Identify three differences between the organization of small stores and large stores.
10. Calculate the average of the following numbers: 345, 672, 119, 238, 560, and 491.
11. Develop an organizational chart for a store.
12. Describe the kinds of jobs available in retailing.

Retail Decisions

1. Can the buying and selling functions be separated in small stores? Explain.
2. If you were the manager of a women's sportswear store, what information about consumers in your trade area would be of most interest to you?

3. What are major differences between the activities performed by a salesclerk and a salesperson?
4. What career opportunities in retailing are of most interest to you?
5. What are four changes occurring in the nature and composition of U.S. consumers?
6. What four steps would you take to create an efficient and well-coordinated retail business organization?
7. What technological developments are likely to bring significant changes to retail marketing?
8. What steps could you take to improve your qualifications for employment in retail management?
9. A good store control system provides a variety of information. What information would be of most interest to a department manager of a large store?
10. If you were asked to suggest appropriate merchandise mixes for a family shoe store and for a women's high-fashion specialty store, what would you recommend?

DEVELOPING CRITICAL-THINKING SKILLS

Retail Projects

1. Obtain from your instructor, school library, or other source the annual reports of at least three business corporations. Examine the financial statements of these companies. What information is reported by all firms? What information is unique to certain firms?
2. Keep a record of every purchase you make over a two-week period. Record the name of the item, amount paid, and store or business from which you purchased the item. Classify your purchases into the four categories of goods: staple, fashion, seasonal, and convenience. In which category did you make the most purchases? In which category did you spend the most money? Which purchases were made from stores or businesses nearest your home? If you could have made only half the purchases you did, which items would you still choose to purchase? Explain why.
3. Draw a map of the area around your home or school including the retail businesses that you and your family use. Enter on the map all the retail establishments in the area. Attach to the map a legend that assigns a different number to each type of business and then number each firm on the map appropriately. Are there too many of some types of business? What businesses should be added?
4. Find five quotations about the free-enterprise system and its impact on our economy. Identify the person who made each state-

ment and the title, date, and page of the newspaper, book, magazine, or other source where you found the quotation. Based on these quotations, explain how retailing contributes to the free-enterprise system.

5. Examine the help-wanted advertisements for retail workers in your local newspaper or in the newspapers for large communities nearby. What percentage of the positions appears to be for beginning workers? What percentage is for management positions? For those positions requiring experience, what qualifications are most frequently mentioned?

6. With the development of new electronic technology, many changes are likely to occur in the operation of retail businesses. Locate at least four magazine articles that discuss emerging applications of technology to retailing. What seem to be the major concerns of retailers? What major changes in present practices are apt to be made?

Field Projects

1. Select two items of merchandise that are sold in at least three stores in your community. Visit each store and note the price charged for each item selected. In a written report, state the reasons that you believe justify any difference in the prices on these two items. If the prices are identical or nearly the same, explain why.

2. Visit several retail stores and observe the price endings used. Try to determine if the stores have a certain pattern to their price endings, such as $0.99 or $0.95, rather than even amounts, such as $1.00 or $3.50. If there is a pattern, try to find the reasons for it.

3. Talk to three people who are presently employed in retailing. Find out what they like best about their job and what they don't like. Determine how they obtained their present jobs. Ask all three persons what advice they would have for someone who is considering going into retailing as a career. Prepare a written report of your findings.

CONTINUING PROJECTS

Developing a Career Plan

The opportunities in retail marketing and retail-related businesses are tremendous. It is estimated that, just within the retail marketing sector of business, there are over 29 million jobs, ranging from beginning jobs for the inexperienced persons to top level senior-executive positions. What field of work would be best for you? What type of work best matches your interest and career aspirations? Where should you start your career? What type of work do you expect to be engaged in five years from now? For this continuing project, you are asked to prepare a notebook that will record your occupational interests, your assessment of your personal strengths, and a collection of possible areas of work within retail marketing that best match your interests. As you add material to your notebook at the end of each unit of this text, you will also prepare samples of résumés, application letters, and other documentation that will result in a comprehensive career plan.

For Unit 1, you are asked to develop three lists. The first list should contain those tasks that you like to perform, even though they may not seem to be related to an area of work. On a second list, write down those tasks that you think you would enjoy but have not yet had a chance to try. On a third list, write down those tasks that you are definitely not interested in. Since each list will probably not be completed on your first effort, plan to add items to each list as you proceed through this text. You may even find that some items that are on one list need to be moved to another after you have more information or experience.

Developing a Business Plan

The opportunity to own and operate an independent business is still a realistic goal for many persons interested in retailing. However, no person should try to start a business without carefully planning each aspect of the business operation. As a continuing project, prepare a notebook that can serve as a record of your business plan. Add material to your notebook at the end of each unit of this text. At the end of your studies, you will have a manual that covers all the important elements of planning and operating your own retail store. From the facts you have learned in this unit and the study of other resources, start your manual by completing each of the following assignments.

1. Using library references and local resources such as the Chamber of Commerce or city offices, determine the following facts about your community:
    a.   Total population
    b.   Number of men and women
    c.   Number of persons below age 18
    d.   Number of persons who are age 65 or older
    e.   Number of families
    f.   Number of homeowners
    g.   Average income for workers

    h. Number of persons who move into and out of the community each year

    i. Major types of employers

    j. Number and types of retail stores

    Based on this information, what kinds of retail stores do you think would be successful in your community? Explain your answer.

2. Identify the type of retail store you would like to own and operate. Explain why you selected this type of retail store and how it might contribute to your community.

3. Describe the basic organizational structure of your store. Draw an organization chart for your store.

UNIT 2
Retailing Businesses

In a free enterprise system, the production of consumer goods and services is prompted by the needs and desires of consumers. Through an economic system that allows property ownership, competition, profit, and freedom of choice, consumers influence what goods and services are made available.

A key element in the production, distribution, and consumption sequence is the retail function–the businesses that sell goods and services to the consumer. Retail businesses vary in size and in type of goods carried. They also have different forms of ownership–proprietorship, partnership, and corporation.

Determining the best location for a retail business requires a careful analysis of a community and various shopping districts. The selection of an actual building or business space involves making a decision to buy, rent, or lease the space needed for a business.

Retailing is becoming more and more diverse; many businesses today are managed by people who have a special license (franchise) from the retailer. The number and types of service businesses are growing. Retailing is no longer confined to stores, as the amount of in-home and other nonstore selling increases.

After studying this unit and completing the activities, you should be able to:

1. Identify three means of production
2. Explain four channels of distribution
3. Identify the elements of free enterprise
4. Describe the common measures of an economy
5. Compare the features of various retail businesses
6. Describe what is necessary to start a business with each major form of ownership
7. Identify the major factors that must be considered in selecting a business location
8. Identify and describe each of the four ways to secure business space
9. Identify three main types of special retail businesses and give examples of each

CHAPTER 9

Sources and Distribution of Merchandise

CHAPTER OUTCOMES

When you have mastered the information provided in this chapter, you should be able to:

1. Describe how the four merchandise utilities are created

2. Define the terms *extraction*, *manufacturing*, and *construction*

3. Identify and give examples of four different channels of distribution

4. List the advantages a retailer may gain by purchasing from a wholesaler

5. Describe the two types of agent middlemen or intermediaries

6. Distinguish between physical distribution and channels of distribution

In today's market, there are thousands of different consumer goods. Some goods have been available to several generations of consumers (blue jeans), and some goods are being introduced to the market for the first time (videodisc players). Have you ever wondered where all the goods come from that you see in a department store or a supermarket? Have you thought about how all those goods get to a local retail store? Have you thought about what must occur in order for the stores in your town to have designer dresses, the latest CDs, and fresh fruit whenever you are ready to buy?

Most consumer goods begin as natural resources in mines, fields, forests, or oceans. Every retail worker should understand the way in which these natural resources are changed into consumer goods and then made available to people all over the country, if not the world. As a knowledgeable person, you should know how various businesses work together in the creation and distribution of consumer goods.

MERCHANDISE UTILITIES

Utility is the economic value of goods that makes them useful to consumers. There are four types of utility in goods: form, time, place, and possession.

Form utility is added to natural resources as people or machines change them into useable products such as furniture, clothing, appliances, cars, and foods. For example, grain, such as wheat, corn, or rice, is given form utility when a manufacturer converts the raw grain to a breakfast cereal.

Place utility is added to goods when they are shipped from where they are produced to where they can be sold. For example, the cereal has place utility when it is shipped from the manufacturing plant to supermarkets.

Time utility is added to goods when they are made available at the time customers want to buy. Breakfast cereal, for example, has time utility if quantities of each type of cereal are on the shelves when customers come into the store.

Possession utility is added to goods when a retailer transfers ownership of them to a customer. A package of breakfast cereal has possession utility when a retailer sells it to a consumer.

Thus, the cereal in this example was given form, place, time, and possession utility by a variety of businesspeople, beginning with the farmer who produced the grain and ending with the retailer who sold the cereal to the consumer. Each type of business added something of value to the cereal product.

Firms involved in the mining, growing, manufacturing, or construction of goods are called *producers* and usually create form utility. Firms involved in the distribution of goods add time, place, and possession utilities to those goods.

PRODUCTION

With modern technology, consumer goods can be produced from varied and unexpected sources. Curtains in your home may come from a chemical combination of alcohol and acids. A wood grain appearance on furniture may be created by photography and lamination. A microwave dinner may contain chicken from Ohio, rolls from North Dakota wheat, Idaho potatoes, and a berry tart from California. These products begin as nature's resources and are converted to consumer goods through one or more of the following production processes: extraction, manufacturing, and construction.

Extraction

Those individuals or businesses that remove minerals from the earth, withdraw products from water, or grow crops or raise animals are called *extractors*. The availability of nature's resources is often greatly affected by weather and climate. For example, while a fishing crew might work very hard, it can do little to affect the supply of seafood in the ocean. The farmer or rancher has some control over the production of fruits, vegetables, grains, and animals but has limited or no control over weather conditions and insects. Forest products provided by the lumber industry are dependent on good forest practices, but nature sometimes provides for the destruction of trees. Copper, iron, coal, oil, natural gas, and other minerals are extracted by miners or drillers. The supply of these raw materials is fixed by nature. The fishing crew, farmer, rancher, forester, and miner are all extractors. They supply raw materials to industries for use in the production of consumer goods.

Manufacturing

Changing extracted raw materials into useful products is the major activity of man-ufacturers. Each worker along a production line or in a production group performs certain tasks to add form utility to the goods being made. Products are made up of various components manufactured by many different companies. For example, the various parts of an automobile, such as engines, bumpers, tires, seats, and glass, are brought together at a factory where they are assembled with the features and options requested by consumers.

Many consumer items, such as electronic appliances, are produced in mass quantities by carefully designed machines. Generally, machine production is less costly than handcrafting. Therefore, machine-produced goods can be sold to consumers at lower prices. The use of machinery in the

Illus. 9–1   What is necessary to make this a quality product ready for consumer use?

manufacture of great numbers of identical articles is called *mass* or *large-scale production*. A large-scale producer has costly machinery, buys large quantities of raw materials or component parts from other manufacturers, and produces large quantities of finished products. Manufacturers are constantly seeking ways to improve production processes and products.

Construction

Construction or building is also a means of creating form utility. Lumber, bricks, mortar, and electrical wire have lit-

Illus. 9–2 What advantages do customers receive from the large-scale production of this product?

tle form utility until builders put these items together as a house or cottage. Some builders construct highways, pipelines, power plants, dams, and commercial buildings. Such construction requires many products from a number of manufacturers.

Modern Production Technology

Modern production processes are the result of discoveries in science and technology. Silicon chips, laser beams, robots, and many other developments have resulted in faster and higher quality production processes. Computer-controlled design and production equipment, robot welders, and electronic scanners are examples of technology used in the production of consumer goods. Applying technology to the mass production of goods allows producers to deliver to consumers a continuous supply of new and improved merchandise.

DISTRIBUTION

The path that an item takes from producer to consumer is called its **channel of distribution.** At one end of this path or channel are producers and at the other end are consumers. The process of getting a particular product from a producer to a consumer market is called *distribution*. Actually moving goods from a producer's plant to consumers' homes is called *physical distribution*. Along the path there may be stops, detours, and bottlenecks, which make distribution of goods a long and costly process. Businesspeople are always looking for better and less costly ways of getting goods from the producer to the consumer.

Producer Directly to Consumer

The simplest channel moves goods directly from the producer to the consumer. Direct distribution is ideal for some perishable or easily spoiled goods or for goods manufactured to the specifications of an individual customer. A simple example is a consumer's purchase of farm produce directly from a farmer. Some manufacturers, such as Fuller Brush Company and Avon Products, Inc., have been successful with direct-to-consumer distribution. The direct-to-consumer channel would seem to be the most efficient, least costly means of distribution. In fact, the direct channel is not often used. For most merchandise, the producer-direct-to-consumer channel is more costly and less efficient than moving goods through other channels (see Illustration 9–3).

Channels with One Intermediary

When producers cannot reach the desired number of consumers directly, they might choose to distribute their goods through a retail store. A retail store can make the goods of several producers available to a large number of consumers in a community. The retailer then becomes an intermediary (or middleman) in the distribution channel. An **intermediary** is a dealer who is responsible for the distribution of goods from producer to ultimate consumer. The terms *intermediary* or *middleman* are descriptive marketing terms that cover all businesses, agents, and activities that assist in the distribution of goods from the producers to the users of those goods.

The local retail store, as an intermediary, provides the goods from many producers to a large number of customers. Distribution through retail stores gives consumers a larger selection of products than might be available from one manufacturer. Obtaining merchandise from a manufacturer is called *buying direct*.

The retailer who buys direct gains several advantages. First, the retailer can buy the latest merchandise at low prices. Second, advertising and display materials are often supplied by the producer for use by the retailer. Third, because large retail firms buy huge quantities of merchandise at a time, buying direct from producers saves costs. On the other hand, retailers who buy direct may have to order larger quantities of merchandise than desired, get slow delivery, and make their own credit arrangements.

Channels with Two Intermediaries

If a store does not need to buy goods in large quantities, the retailer may find it easier to buy from a wholesale intermediary than to buy direct from a manufacturer. The goods then pass through two intermediaries on the way from producer to consumer. The first stop in the distribution channel is the wholesaler's warehouse and the second stop is the retailer's store.

A **wholesaler** is an intermediary who buys directly from many producers or manufacturers and then sells to retailers or commercial users. A motel that buys towels from a wholesaler, for example, would be considered a commercial user. Wholesalers buy goods outright and usually store the goods until they are resold through sales representatives to retailers. Wholesalers usually grant credit and make deliveries to their retail customers.

A small retailer, especially, may find it best to purchase from a wholesaler for one or more of the following reasons:

1. Wholesalers sell in smaller quantities than manufacturers.
2. Wholesalers provide faster delivery than producers.
3. Wholesalers usually offer credit and other services.
4. It is easier to deal with one wholesaler for a line of merchandise than with many different manufacturers.
5. In-store inventory can be kept small since orders can be placed frequently.

6. There may be no savings in buying direct from manufacturers.

Many retail chain stores set up their own wholesale warehouses to service their own stores. Thus, the retail chain organization itself becomes the first intermediary in the channel of distribution.

Channels with Three Intermediaries

Some goods, such as imported specialty goods (leather purses, china, silk flowers), pass through three intermediaries—agent middlemen, then wholesalers, and finally retailers—before reaching the ultimate consumer. An **agent middleman** assists in the sale of goods, but, unlike a

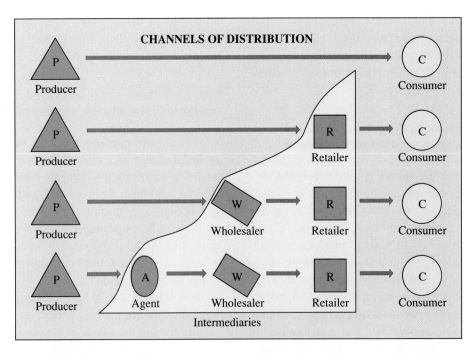

Illus. 9–3 A channel of distribution with no intermediaries is commonly used for door-to-door selling. Clothing may be distributed through one intermediary, while products such as medicines may travel through two intermediaries. Some food lines are distributed through at least three intermediaries.

wholesaler, does not *own* the goods. There are two types of agents: commission merchants and brokers. A **commission merchant** handles the actual goods in which he or she deals. A **broker** does not handle the goods; he or she simply helps sellers find buyers or buyers find sellers.

From the viewpoint of a retailer, a commission merchant is very similar to a wholesaler. However, since commission merchants do not own the goods, they may not be free to set the price or terms of the sale. If commission merchants do have this authority, they are called *sales agents*.

Commission merchants often have exclusive distribution of certain manufacturers' products in a specific geographic area. These merchants are called *manufacturers' agents*. They sell to wholesalers, large department stores, and chains. A retailer who buys from such commission merchants is really buying direct from producers.

Brokers may serve either the producer or the retailer. A producer may ask a broker to sell a quantity of goods. A retailer may ask a broker to find certain types of goods that the retailer would like to buy. The broker's role is to find buyers or sellers and negotiate for exchange of title for which the broker then receives a fee. For example, a large supermarket or a supermarket-chain buyer may ask a broker to find 30,000 pounds of Idaho potatoes at a certain price.

Choice of Channels

Most retailers get the goods their customers want through several different distribution channels. For instance, a drugstore may buy items such as soap, toothpaste, and beauty products, which are sold in large quantities, direct from the manufacturer. The drugstore may obtain combs, stationery, sunglasses, and other items less frequently sold from a drug and sundry wholesaler. Hosiery and greeting cards might be obtained from a commission merchant. Each intermediary adds to the cost of the goods; but the service performed in buying, selling, and storing the goods usually justifies the added cost. Producers and retailers have tried at times to bypass wholesale intermediaries. However, thus far, distribution channels with one or more intermediaries still seem more effective than buying direct for distribution of goods to consumers located in many states or countries.

PHYSICAL DISTRIBUTION

Physical distribution involves those activities associated with the actual handling, movement, and storage of goods. The task of finding a market for goods may involve several intermediaries, but only a few may physically handle the goods; sometimes goods are handled only on paper. For example, a manufacturer may store finished goods in a public warehouse in St. Louis and arrange with a commission agent in New York to sell the goods to a wholesaler or other intermediary. A wholesaler in Knoxville may agree to buy the goods but continue to store them in the warehouse. The wholesaler may provide samples for retailers to show their customers. When a sale is made, the retailer may order the wholesaler to ship the goods directly from the warehouse to the customer. Thus, the physical distribution may be limited to moving the goods from the factory to the public warehouse and from the warehouse to the customer.

The marketing channel thus consists of the producer, the commission agent, the wholesaler, the retailer, and the ultimate consumer. Only the producer, shipping firm, and customer have actually handled the goods. All the intermediaries have assumed ownership or selling responsibility or both. The cost of distributing goods is shared by the producer and the intermediary involved. For many consumer goods, the costs of distribution often exceed the costs of production. In fact, typical consumer goods manufacturers spend nearly half their sales income on distribution and marketing activities. However, without these activities, goods and services would not be readily available to the buying public.

Summary

Consumer goods are produced through extraction, manufacturing, or construction. The distribution of goods to consumers is an important part of retail merchandising. As shown in this chapter, as goods are produced and moved along a channel of distribution, they acquire certain economic values called *utilities* that make them more useful to consumers. The selection of intermediaries involved in the distribution of goods is usually determined by the nature and the quantity of goods to be handled. The intermediaries in a channel of distribution are concerned with transfer of the title of the goods and may not be involved with the physical distribution of the goods.

Review

1. Describe how form utility is created.
2. How does production by extraction differ from production by construction?
3. Name the simplest channel of distribution.
4. What services are provided by wholesale intermediaries or middlemen?
5. Describe the differences between brokers and commission merchants.
6. Why do most retailers use several different channels to obtain goods?
7. What is the difference between physical distribution and channels of distribution?

Terms

The following terms were introduced in this chapter. Write a separate sentence correctly using each new term.

agent middleman   broker

channel of distribution   place utility
commission merchant   possession utility
form utility   time utility
intermediary or middleman   utility
physical distribution   wholesaler

*D*iscuss

1. For which goods is time utility of major importance?
2. How is place utility created for a product such as a newspaper?
3. For what products is producer-to-consumer the best channel? Why?
4. What changes have occurred recently in your community's production businesses? Have any firms adopted new technology in their production processes?
5. Does increasing the number of intermediaries in a channel extend the time it takes to move goods physically from producer to consumer? Explain.

*P*roblem
Solving

1. Describe the distribution channel most often used for small kitchen appliances.
2. Describe the distribution channel most often used for popular paperback books.
3. If you were a manufacturer of a new style hair dryer, how would you decide which channel of distribution to use?
4. What types of products would most likely be sent through a channel with three intermediaries?

CHAPTER 10

Free Enterprise

CHAPTER OUTCOMES

When you have mastered the information provided in this chapter, you should be able to:

1. Define *economic system*

2. State the main difference between a directed economy and a free economy

3. Identify and describe the major elements necessary for a free-enterprise system

4. Explain how competition serves as an invisible control of business

5. Explain the relationships among gross national product, net national product, and national income

6. Describe three kinds of consumer income and spending information that are helpful to retailers

Every society produces goods and services, and every society has certain practices, procedures, and regulations that determine how goods and services are exchanged. All effects of production, distribution, and consumption together make up an economy. An **economy** is a system for producing, distributing, and consuming goods and services. The main purpose of an economic system or economy is to supply the goods and services wanted and needed by the society.

ELEMENTS OF AN ECONOMIC SYSTEM

Every economy is made up of five basic elements: (1) natural resources, (2) a labor force, (3) capital (money and equipment), (4) management, and (5) government.

Natural resources include land, minerals, water, and plant life. The **labor force** includes those persons who are able to work and who are either seeking work or actually working. **Capital** is defined as the machinery, tools, buildings, and money used in the production and distribution of goods and services. **Management** includes the people who decide how natural resources, capital, and labor will be used to make the greatest contribution to business and society. **Government** encompasses all the laws, regulations, taxes, and social services that influence the activities of producing, distributing, and consuming goods and services.

Some economies are directed. In a **directed economic system,** a person or group of persons in authority decides what and how much to produce, when and where to produce it, and for whom and for what purpose to produce it. In a **free economic system,** the consumers of goods and services, by their decision to buy or not to buy, determine what and how much will be produced and when and where the products will be used.

The economic system of the United States is a free economic system, limited by certain laws and regulations. Consumers look for the best buys of goods and services that producers make available to the market. Producers and intermediaries try to sell at the most profitable prices. What is there about a free economy system that makes it succeed at providing people with more and better goods and services? How is the activity of such an economy measured?

ELEMENTS OF FREE ENTERPRISE

The economic system in the United States is based on free or modified free enterprise. Whenever you have some government control, you have modified free enterprise. The theory behind the system is that businesses that serve customers well and efficiently will succeed, and ineffective, inefficient businesses will fail. The free-enterprise system rests on the freedom of people to engage in business and either succeed or fail, depending upon their ability. At the same time, consumers have the freedom to choose what they will eat, wear, and use as well as where they will buy what they want. The freedom of consumers to choose means that all business, but particularly retail business, must be directed toward consumers. As shown in Illustration 10–1, the elements of the free-enterprise system interact to produce and deliver the goods and services that consumers are most interested in having.

The basic elements of a free-enterprise system are property ownership, competition, profit motivation, matching supply and demand, and freedom of choice.

Property Ownership

People in our society may own property both for their personal use and for purposes of production and trade. Anything of value that people use, buy, or sell is called **personal property.** The right to buy and sell tangible personal property and intangible property, such as securities and copyrights, means that people can gain profit from their business transactions. The right to own and accumulate property (including money) is a significant factor in the development of retail businesses. If a person could not accumulate property, there would be no resources to build stores, shopping malls, or large warehouses.

Competition

Since retailers and consumers both have freedom of choice, **competition,** the

Illus. 10–1 The interaction of the elements of a free-enterprise system produce and deliver goods and services to consumers in our society.

FREE-ENTERPRISE SYSTEM

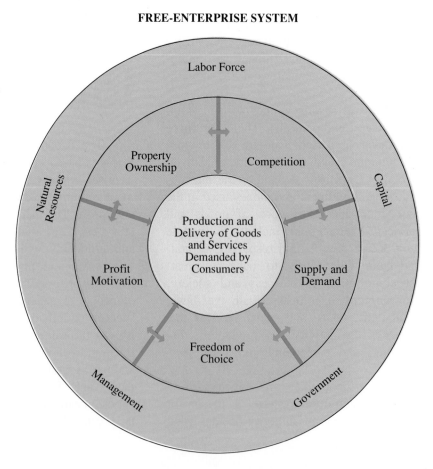

rivalry among businesses for customers, is an important factor in a free-enterprise system. Competition causes business to change and grow, thus improving living conditions for everyone. As long as there is competition, one person or business will attempt to do better than the next. Competition "brings out the best" in everyone. It is this effort that results in economic progress.

Suppose a retailer opens a clothing store in a community, and many people come to purchase clothes. Another person, seeing the success of the first retailer, also decides to open a clothing store. The second person has the freedom to do that. Now the demand for clothing in the community is divided between two stores. In a little while, a third clothing store may open. There may not be enough business for the three stores to operate successfully. The store that succeeds usually will be the one that offers the higher quality merchandise, the lower prices, or the better selection of goods and services.

Competition forces firms to find and develop better products, to offer better services, to keep buildings up-to-date, and to keep operating costs low. The struggle among stores for customers motivates some retailers to offer goods at lower prices than others. This struggle is called **price competition.** Other retailers may choose to offer higher quality merchandise, provide wider merchandise selections, or give better service. These strategies are called **nonprice competition.**

Profit Motivation

Why do people engage in the production and distribution of goods and services?

Illus. 10–2 Competition among different businesses causes each to attempt to do a better job of providing goods and services to consumers.

The two chief motives of all businesspeople are (1) the satisfaction of performing a useful service for others and increasing the well-being of society and (2) the monetary reward received for the efforts expended, skills employed, and risks assumed. The excess of sales income (above the costs and expenses of providing goods and services) is called **profit.** The profit motive is a driving force of a free-enterprise system.

The chance to earn a profit causes a businessperson to produce goods and services for public consumption in competition with other businesspeople. To be in a position to earn a profit, a person must first invest in a business enterprise. A retailer, for example, may invest $350,000 to set up a store. The retailer might use $90,000 of her or his own money and borrow the rest from others or from a bank for a promise to pay it back later. The investment can produce profit only when it is used for buying store buildings, equipment, supplies, and merchandise; paying workers; and making the store known and attractive to customers.

Besides a start-up investment, some of the profits of a business must also be turned into capital. Profits must be reinvested in a retail business to keep it growing and changing to meet customers' needs. Thus, capital makes capital, endlessly. Our private enterprise system is made up of many people investing and reinvesting capital in businesses; therefore, the free-enterprise system is also called **capitalism.** Government regulations and social forces limit competition to some extent—a businessperson cannot do absolutely anything he or she chooses. For that reason, the United States economy is modified capitalism or a **modified free-enterprise system.**

Many people are critical of the profit motive and capitalism. Some argue that businesses influence consumers to buy gadgets and services that they really don't need. They think that, by allowing businesses to make a profit, there is unfair distribution of wealth and, thus, the social needs of the community are not met. To answer those criticisms, defenders of the free-enterprise system argue that the public, not central planners, should decide the priorities for spending. Many countries in Eastern Europe are shifting to consumer choice instead of government central planning. This transition from a directed economy to an economy based on free enterprise is very painful for the consumers as well as for the economies of the countries. It is true that some businesspeople strive to achieve quick financial gain regardless of social consequences. However, most businesses operate to satisfy consumers and social needs as well as to generate a profit. By doing both well, they stay in business.

Matching Supply and Demand

Attempts to balance the supply of merchandise with the demand for goods and services is another driving force of a free-enterprise system. The price of merchandise is important in keeping supply and demand in balance. When supply and demand are out of balance, producers and retailers may have to change prices. If a manufacturer produces more athletic shoes than consumers want at a particular price, prices may have to come down to encourage demand. If consumers want more athletic shoes than manufacturers have provided, consumers will be willing to pay more and prices might increase. High prices tend to reduce consumer demand; low prices tend to increase demand.

Prices alone do not maintain a balance between supply and demand. Producers often can increase the supply of merchandise without increasing the price because the cost of producing an item is not directly related to the number of units produced. Likewise, producers can make and sell fewer products at the old price instead of trying to increase demand by cutting prices. Changing the price has little effect on the amounts of some basic products such as food and gasoline demanded by consumers. It is important for retailers to understand generally the effects of their pricing policies on supply and demand and the nation's economy.

Freedom of Choice

In a free-enterprise system, individuals have a number of important freedoms. Three of the freedoms were already mentioned: the freedom to own property, the freedom to compete, and the freedom to make a profit. Other individual freedoms include the freedom to choose a job, the freedom to bargain collectively with employers, and the freedom to influence government by voting or by lobbying for a change in regulations. These freedoms are essential to a free-market system.

MEASURES OF AN ECONOMY

If retailers are going to be successful and improve an economy, they should understand how the conditions of the economy are measured. The United States economy can be measured (1) as a whole and (2) in terms of consumer income and expenditures.

The U.S. Economy as a Whole

Three key concepts helpful to understanding the United States economy are the gross national product, the net national product, and the national income.

The **gross national product** (GNP) is the market value of this country's total output of goods and services for one year. GNP usually is expressed in dollars. The dollar value of the GNP is made up of four components: (1) the money spent by individuals (consumer expenditures), (2) the money invested by individuals and businesses, (3) the value of exports minus imports, and (4) the goods and services purchased by the government. Changes in the gross national product are watched closely by businesspeople and government officials. Increased spending and investing by consumers, industries, and government are signals to retailers that sales opportunities may be expanding.

It should be noted that the GNP includes the output of United States businesses in other countries. Thus, the GNP inflates the domestic economy. Another measure of the economy, **gross domestic product** (GDP), excludes the output that does not originate in the United States. Therefore, for most retailers, GDP is a more useful measure of the output of goods and services in this country.

Each year, equipment and buildings are used up in the production of goods. They depreciate (wear down) or become obsolete (out-of-date). The value lost because of depreciation and obsolescence is subtracted from the GNP to give a more accurate measure of our economy's production. The figure that results is known as the **net national product.**

FORMULA 10–1

GNP = Individual   + Investments   + Value of   + Goods and Services
           Expenditures   of Individuals   Exports   Purchased by the
                                    and Businesses   Minus   Government
                                                                 Imports

Another measure of the economy that is of interest to retailers is national income. **National income** is the total earnings of workers and business owners resulting from the production of goods and services. The amount of national income is figured by subtracting from the net national product certain indirect business taxes such as sales and excise taxes.

The national income figure is the total of the following categories: (1) compensation for all employees, (2) proprietor's (owner's) income, (3) rental income, (4) corporate profits, and (5) net interest. Employees receive over 67 percent of the national income and proprietors receive about 10 percent. Less than 20 percent goes to the owners of real property and capital. By observing the amount and distribution of national income in these five categories, the retailer can make predictions about consumer purchasing.

Consumer Income and Spending

By buying or not buying products or services, consumers influence what is produced, how much is produced, and for whom it is produced. When consumers buy goods and services, they stimulate production and retailing. When consumers save or do not have funds to spend, there is no demand on retailers or producers. Consumers thus influence the economy in a very direct way.

Information about consumers serves as a measure of the economy. The three kinds of consumer information that retailers watch with great interest are personal income, disposable personal income, and consumer expenditures.

Personal income is the total income of all persons from all sources. The personal income for all persons in the country may be figured by subtracting from the national income all taxable corporate income or other payments not made to individuals for current work or investments. Total personal income for 1988 was estimated at $4,064 billion.

Illus. 10–3 *The income and spending patterns of consumers are of great interest to retailers. Increased discretionary income means consumers are more likely to buy goods other than basic food, clothing, and shelter.*

Retailers are most interested in the amount of money consumers can spend, which is called **disposable personal income.** It is calculated by subtracting from the personal income figure all local, state, and federal taxes that consumers must pay. The first demand on disposable personal income is whatever is needed for the person or family to maintain a minimum standard of living. The difference between a person's total disposable income and the cost of a minimum standard of living is known as **discretionary income.** Discretionary income is what is left after the essentials of food, clothing, shelter, and transportation have been provided. It is income that may be spent on any good or service that appeals to the individual.

Another measure of income that interests retailers is the discretionary fund. The **discretionary fund** is the amount of discre-

tionary income plus the dollar amount of goods and services purchased on installment credit. Many people use installment buying as a means of increasing their discretionary income. Installment buying increases discretionary income by about one third or more.

Personal consumption spending accounts for about 65 percent of the GNP. As shown in Illustration 10–4, consumers spend their money on three types of merchandise: (1) durable goods such as cars and furniture; (2) nondurable goods such as food, clothing, and gasoline; and (3) services such as rent, medical care, recreation, child care, and education.

It is interesting to note that consumers are spending more on services than they are spending on nondurable goods. Retailers are aware of this trend and many now offer a variety of services such as insurance,

PERSONAL CONSUMER EXPENDITURES
(Billions of Dollars)

Category	1965 Amount	%	1975 Amount	%	1985 Amount	%	1988 Amount	%
Durable Goods	63.0	14.7	132.2	13.5	355.1	15.1	455.2	14.1
Nondurable Goods	188.6	43.8	407.3	41.7	847.4	36.0	1,052.3	32.5
Services	178.7	41.5	437.0	44.8	1,152.3	48.9	1,727.6	53.4
Total	430.3	100.0	976.5	100.0	2,354.8	100.0	3,235.1	100.0

Source: U.S. Bureau of the Census, *Statistical Abstract of the United States*, 110th ed. (Washington, D.C., 1990).

Illus. 10–4   *The proportion of consumer spending among the three main categories—durable goods, nondurable goods, and services—has changed over the past 30 years. The percent spent on durable goods and on services has increased, and the percent spent on nondurable goods has decreased.*

banking, home maintenance, and travel planning in addition to traditional merchandise.

The retailer should not think that consumer expenditures will vary directly with changes in personal income or discretionary income. Discretionary spending depends both on ability and willingness to spend. Willingness depends not only on consumers' current income and savings but also on their outlook for the future. If consumers are concerned about the future, their tendency is to save rather than to spend.

*S*ummary

In the United States, the five basic elements of an economy (resources, labor, capital, management, and government) are integrated in a free-enterprise system. The free-enterprise system involves property ownership, competition, profit motivation, matching supply and demand, and individual freedom of choice. Three key measures of an economy are also important to understanding the United States economy: gross national product, net national product, and national income. Consumer income and spending, measured by personal income, disposable personal income, and discretionary income, are vital to understanding the role of retailing in private enterprise.

*R*eview

1. Define *economic system*.
2. Name the elements of an economy.
3. Name the features of a directed economy.
4. List the major elements of a free-enterprise system.
5. Explain how competition influences businesses in a free-enterprise economy.
6. Define *gross national product*.
7. Define *national income* and explain how it is related to gross national product.
8. Name three major categories of personal consumer expenditures.
9. Define *disposable personal income* and explain why it is important to retailers.

*T*erms

The following terms were introduced in this chapter. Write a separate sentence correctly using each new term.

capital	directed economic system
capitalism	discretionary fund
competition	discretionary income

disposable personal income

national income

economy

natural resource

free economic system

net national product

government

nonprice competition

gross domestic product

personal income

gross national product

personal property

labor force

price competition

management

profit

modified free-enterprise system

Discuss

1. What are the advantages and disadvantages of a free-enterprise system to a person operating a retail business?
2. What factors might affect the supply and demand for CDs? for jogging shoes? for sailboards?
3. What changes are likely to occur in personal spending as an individual's or family's personal income increases?
4. Are current economic conditions encouraging consumers to spend or save?
5. What might be the impact on Eastern European consumers as their countries permit businesses to move toward the free-enterprise system?

Problem Solving

1. Identify three countries in the world that have a controlled economy and three countries that have a free economy.
2. What effect would the absence of a natural resource have on a society?
3. What influence would a sharp rise in employment have on the gross national product?
4. What changes have occurred in consumer spending for nondurable goods over the past five to ten years?

CHAPTER 11

Types of Retailing Businesses

Retailing businesses have a tremendous range of sizes, assortments of merchandise, and methods of operation. Stores may be very small or very large. They may carry one type of merchandise or many types. Some are owned by individuals and some are owned by international corporations.

There are several ways these retail stores may be classified. You have already found that stores can be grouped according to their method of retailing: in-store, mail-order, direct, and automatic. Retail businesses can also be grouped by size, type of merchandise carried, type of ownership, and method of operation. Each classification may be useful for a certain purpose. Regardless of the classification, however, stores within a given category vary in personnel requirements, style of goods carried, services provided, and prices.

SMALL-STORE RETAILING

Over 80 percent of all retail firms are classified as small businesses. They each employ fewer than 20 persons and do less than $500,000 in business yearly. When people think of going into retailing, they usually have in mind a small-scale business in which the owner-manager performs duties such as buying, stocking, advertising, selling, and accounting. The chief types of small retail businesses are convenience stores, specialty stores, and service businesses.

Convenience Stores

Items that customers buy frequently and for which they do not wish to make special shopping trips are called **convenience goods.** Examples are basic groceries such as milk and bread, magazines or newspapers, nonprescription medicine such as cold tablets or aspirin, and certain ready-to-eat foods. The best-known convenience store is the general store. Although now limited in number, these stores have served the U.S. public for well more than 200 years. A **general store** carries groceries, staple clothing items, house furnishings, nonprescription medicine, and numerous other articles for local customers. Goods not on hand may be ordered specially for customers. The general store is still found in small communities and in resort areas. It often serves as an informal meeting place for people of the community. Despite the continuing decline in their number, the general store represents a type of retailing important in many small communities.

Because of the increased size and frequent checkout delays in regular supermarkets, customers who want just a few basic food items are turning to quick-service food stores. These stores are small convenience stores carrying limited stocks of the most popular grocery, beverage, bakery, and dairy items. These quick-service convenience stores are open extended hours, often 24 hours per day. They need parking for only a few cars since customer turnover is rapid. The average purchase at quick-service stores is under 10 dollars and the time a customer spends in the store is usually less than three minutes.

Contemporary convenience stores are found in many locations. Some are located in business districts; these cater to people who regularly work in the area. Some are located along main traffic routes between employment centers and residential areas. Some are located in residential neighborhoods to meet the needs of persons living nearby. Some convenience stores are even portable; the flower stall or cookie stand located on a street corner or in a mall is designed to roll away at the end of a business day. The main purpose of the convenience store is to meet the life-style needs of the modern customer who desires quick service, convenient location, and extended hours.

Specialty Stores

Many small retail stores sell just one line of merchandise or a group of closely related items. These stores, often called single-line stores, began as an outgrowth of customer demand for a wider choice of goods than that available in a general merchandise store. Women's clothing, hardware, and shoe stores were some of the early spin-offs of the typical general store. A smaller store that carries a fairly broad selection of a single line of merchandise or a group of closely related goods is called a **specialty store.** A specialty store might carry jewelry, furniture, computers, china and glassware, or high-fashion clothing, for example.

Specialty stores are often found in central business districts or in shopping malls, as malls permit customers to visit several stores in the course of a single shopping trip in order to compare merchandise, prices, and services. Specialty stores are usually among the first to introduce new merchandise. They attempt to offer a complete assortment of colors, styles, and sizes in the line of goods handled. Competition among similar specialty stores is usually keen. Specialty-store merchants strive to know their customers well and select goods that will appeal to an individual customer's tastes.

Illus. 11–1
Convenience stores carry a limited stock of popular items, provide quick service to customers, and are often open 24 hours a day.

Service Businesses

Most service businesses are small, but they provide necessary services, such as dry cleaning, rug cleaning, appliance repair, and interior decorating. Businesses such as pet boarding, car rental, and travel service have become increasingly numerous and popular among working people.

As discretionary income increases, consumers tend to spend more for services. Many people who are interested in going into business for themselves have found that service businesses have great potential. Owners of established retail firms have also become aware of the trend toward service businesses. As a result, department-store owners have introduced departments that sell services, such as insurance, sports lessons, and appliance repair.

LARGE-STORE RETAILING

Successful small-store retailers often expand their businesses into larger operations. A paint and wallpaper store owner may decide to add other lines, such as floor coverings and lighting fixtures. A clothing-store owner might decide to open additional stores in other communities. The roadside fruit and vegetable market owner might add groceries, build a larger building, operate the year round, and begin a mail-order business in specialties such as honey and maple syrup. Most of today's large retail firms started as small retail operations.

The principal types of **large-scale retailing** are the department store, variety store, supermarket, mail-order firm, and low-margin or discount store. Some large retail firms operate their businesses in only one location. Others have hundreds of stores, not only in the United States but in other countries as well.

Department Stores

If several small shops handling a variety of merchandise lines were put under one roof and directed by a central management, they would become a **department store.** A department store offers the people of a community an opportunity to shop in one place for a wide range of general merchandise. Some department stores also include restaurants, automotive services, major appliance showrooms, floral shops, and bookstores. Most department stores permit customers to charge their purchases and most will deliver large items to customers' homes. Other services, such as ordering by mail and telephone, are also provided. Department stores often have several hundred employees at one location.

Department-store owners and managers have won the distinction of being the best-known large-scale retailers because they have successfully pioneered many retail operations. They have been continually alert to current developments in retailing and have adopted practices that maintain their image as the major providers of general merchandise.

Variety Stores

Similar to the department store, the variety store handles a large assortment of general merchandise. Compared with a department store, a **variety store** features lower-priced goods and gives less attention to fashion, furniture, major appliances, and specialized goods. Variety store merchandise includes ready-to-wear clothing, toys, costume jewelry, tableware, light hardware, cosmetics, and candy.

Most variety stores expect customers to serve themselves and bring selected merchandise to a checkout station. Independent variety stores may operate on a cash basis, but most chain variety stores accept credit cards, and some even have their own credit service. The larger variety stores include chains such as McCrory, Woolworth, Murphy, and Newberry. These larger stores approach department-store status in terms of the assortment of merchandise they carry.

Supermarkets

A **supermarket** is a large, departmentalized food store carrying a wide variety of fresh, frozen, and packaged foods as well as many home-related items. Many large supermarkets have bakery, delicatessen, and meat departments. Supermarket cus-

Illus. 11–2   Large supermarkets are arranged into departments such as fresh produce, bakery, canned goods, and delicatessen.

tomers use carts to collect the merchandise they want and take it to a checkout counter where they pay for the goods and have them bagged. The supermarket has experienced amazing growth since it began as a cost-reduction idea in the 1930s. Over the years, competition has led supermarkets to adopt many cost-saving methods of buying, stocking, and handling consumer goods. Many supermarkets are fully carpeted and have piped-in music and the latest fixtures and equipment for maintaining quality foods.

Discount Stores

Many retailers have been able to build successful businesses by selecting low-cost locations; offering few, if any, services; operating on a cash-and-carry basis; and keeping overhead expenses to a minimum. This approach to retailing, known as **discount retailing,** allows retailers to offer customers considerable reduction in prices on many well-known goods.

Discount retailing occurs in nearly all consumer goods areas. In women's clothing, some enterprising merchants buy overruns (production in excess of orders) from top manufacturers with cash. The garments are sold without the designers' labels for about 50 percent less than the price offered by the exclusive specialty stores for the same garments. Some of these merchants have expanded to several stores located all across the country. Other merchants have found appliances, television and stereo equipment, and toys to be excellent merchandise for discount retailing. By placing large orders for a specific item or model, they are able to get an excellent price from the manufacturer. The customer is interested in owning many of these goods as quickly and inexpensively as possible. Price is the major appeal of the discount-retail business.

There are four common types of large discount businesses. An *open-door discount store* sells to anyone and depends on self-service and low overhead to keep prices down. Service Merchandise operates in this fashion. A *closed-door discount store* sells only to members of the store. These stores serve special groups of customers, such as members of the armed services, government workers, teachers, and small-business owners. Sam's Warehouse Club is an example of a closed-door discount store.

The third type of discount operation is the *factory direct store* or *factory outlet*. These stores are either factory owned or have a buying arrangement to sell the manufacturer's line of goods for less than do other types of retail stores. Factory outlets carry only one type of merchandise; examples include shoes, clothing, leather goods, towels and bedding, candy, and frozen foods. Factory direct stores often join together in factory direct shopping malls.

The fourth type of discount operation is the *discount unit* of conventional retail stores. Many well-established, full-service stores have faced the challenge of discount-store operation by starting their own branches or units to operate on a discount basis. These units carry a mixture of specially purchased goods and goods provided by the parent store.

Mail-order Firms

Many people like to shop at home from a catalog or advertisement instead of in a crowded store. The salesperson for the

Illus. 11–3 Factory direct or factory outlet stores attract customers who are primarily interested in quality goods at low prices.

mail-order firm is a well-illustrated catalog or sales brochure that is usually sent free to those who regularly order merchandise. More and more customers are telephoning their orders to local offices of mail-order firms rather than mailing orders. Some firms, such as L. L. Bean and Neiman-Marcus, have a national toll-free telephone number that may be used 24 hours a day, seven days a week for placing orders. Most mail-order firms accept credit cards and have a generous return policy.

General merchandise mail-order firms and specialty mail-order firms are the chief kinds of retail firms doing business by catalog. *General merchandise mail-order firms* carry much of the same merchandise as department stores. Major general merchandise mail-order firms include Sears, Roebuck and Company; J. C. Penney; and Spiegel. Specialty mail-order firms, such as Sheplers, Auto World, Gurney, and Guilford Forge, deal in limited merchandise lines. Over 75 percent of the retail mail-order business is conducted by general merchandise mail-order firms.

To help customers inspect samples and place orders, a number of the general merchandise mail-order firms have set up order offices in small cities and in their regular retail stores. Retail workers help the customers place orders and see that their merchandise is delivered from the nearest warehouse or shipped to the order office for customer pick-up. Similar to department stores, large mail-order firms employ specialists for buying, advertising, and control. They also maintain testing laboratories, which assure high standards of quality at low prices.

ADVANTAGES OF SIZE

It is often predicted that small-store retailers will be eliminated by the success of larger retailers. Actually, retail businesses, small or large, maintain their success by doing what each does best. Small-store retailers have the advantage of being able to quickly adapt their merchandising policies to consumers' needs. Small-scale retailers also have the ability to enter into a market quickly and to move out quickly. In addition, small retailers can use personal ser-

Illus. 11–4 More and more customers are telephoning orders for merchandise selected from well-illustrated catalogs they can examine at their convenience in their homes.

vice, special merchandise lines, and convenience of location to attract and maintain customers.

A large retailer has the advantage of being able to offer great breadth and depth of merchandise; low, competitive prices; trained managers and employees; and a variety of customer services. The large retailer has access to research findings that can guide important business decisions. Also, he or she has the ability to buy in large quantities, to specify certain merchandise features, and to use one advertisement for several products or stores.

For both small and large retailers, success depends on the ability to organize, supervise, and delegate work to other people. Also, success depends on matching the business, merchandise, and service to the needs of consumers in a community.

Summary

Retail stores come in all sizes. The smaller stores, which employ fewer than 20 persons and have sales of less than $500,000 per year, tend to deal in convenience goods, specialty goods, or services. The larger stores—department stores, variety stores, supermarkets, discount stores, and mail-order firms—tend to handle a broad range of shopping goods as well as convenience and specialty merchandise. Because of their large size, they are able to purchase large quantities of goods at favorable prices. An advantage of small stores is their ability to adapt quickly to changes in the market.

Review

1. What percent of all retail firms are classified as small businesses?
2. List three characteristics of a small retail store.
3. Describe convenience goods and list four examples.
4. Explain how shopping goods differ from convenience goods.
5. List five types of large retail firms.
6. Describe the features of department stores.
7. Explain how a discount store differs from a department store.
8. Describe factory outlet stores.
9. What advantages in size do small-scale retailers have?

Terms

The following terms were introduced in this chapter. Write a separate sentence correctly using each new term.

convenience goods
department store
discount retailing
general store
large-scale retailing

mail-order firm
specialty store
supermarket
variety store

Discuss

1. What are the differences between a department store and a variety store?
2. What advantages does a supermarket have over a quick-service convenience store?
3. What advantages do discount stores have over department stores?
4. What are the advantages and disadvantages for consumers of buying from mail-order firms?

Problem Solving

1. Identify four small-retail firms and four large-retail firms that do business in your community.
2. Determine which service businesses have opened in your community in the past three years.
3. What advantages might a mail-order firm have over a specialty store handling the same line of apparel?
4. What store in your community is most like a general store?

CHAPTER 12

Types of Business Ownership

CHAPTER OUTCOMES

When you have mastered the information provided in this chapter, you should be able to:

1. List the three forms of business ownership

2. Discuss the advantages and disadvantages of each of the three major forms of business ownership

3. Explain what is necessary to create a corporation

4. Define the term *par value*

5. Define the term *franchise*

6. Describe the services that a franchisee may expect from a franchisor

When one person is the owner of a retail business, the form of ownership is known as a **sole proprietorship.** When two or more persons join together to own a business, the form of ownership is called a **partnership.** When several people want to own a business, they can choose either the partnership form or the corporation form. In the **corporation** form, they obtain ownership by purchasing shares of stock. Since each of these forms of ownership has its advantages and disadvantages, the type of ownership must be selected carefully. Such factors as capital needed, experience of each prospective owner, type of retail business, goods to be handled, tax laws, and the financial risk that each person is willing to take should be considered. Of course, a business may be started as a sole proprietorship and later changed to a partnership or corporation. It may also be started as a partnership or a corporation.

Approximately 60 percent of all retail stores are owned by sole proprietors. About 15 percent of the retail stores are partnerships and the remaining 25 percent are corporations. The stores that are proprietorships or partnerships are mostly small stores with sales of $250,000 or less per year. The number of retailers using the corporation form is increasing because it seems best suited for large-scale operations.

SOLE PROPRIETORSHIP

For seven years after graduating from high school, Rebecca Statman had worked in a sportswear store. During that time, she had performed just about every job involved in the operation of the store, including the job of acting manager. She eventually decided to go into the sportswear business. She saved some money and borrowed the remainder from friends in order to finance her initial investments. She met several sportswear suppliers and wholesalers who would supply her merchandise. She found a suitable location, obtained from the city and state agencies the licenses to operate the store, and bought her merchandise. Going into business involves much more, but for our purposes these tasks will suffice.

Rebecca Statman became the proprietor of a business. She alone made the decisions regarding buying, pricing, selling, and store policy. She had the freedom to operate the business any way she wished within the restrictions of the law. If the business prospered, Rebecca was entitled to keep any profits; she also was responsible for all losses.

The sportswear store soon became successful. However, the new business demands soon proved to be too much for Rebecca, and her capital (money) was not enough for needed growth. She considered the possibility of adding a partner who could invest additional money and assist in

Illus. 12–1   About 60 percent of retail businesses are owned by sole proprietors.

ADVANTAGES AND DISADVANTAGES OF SOLE PROPRIETORSHIPS

Advantages
+ Easy to start
+ Complete control by one individual
+ Taxation and supervision relatively light

Disadvantages
− Difficult to obtain capital for expansion purposes
− Lack of permanence
− Heavy inheritance taxes
− Lack of exchange of opinion before decisions are made, leading at times to poor management

Illus. 12–2 A retailer must decide whether the advantages of a sole proprietorship will outweigh the disadvantages.

the work. Statman could handle best the buying, inventory control, and promotional activities. The partner needed to be someone who could keep accounting records and handle the selling part of the business.

Statman also knew that the sole proprietorship had disadvantages. The lack of certain abilities, the lack of funds for expansion, the assumption of all losses should they occur, and the closing of the business in case of the owner's death are some of the disadvantages of any sole proprietorship.

PARTNERSHIP

The more Rebecca Statman thought about a partnership, the better the idea seemed. She made inquiries among business associates and friends and placed an advertisement in a sportswear wholesalers' trade paper. Doug Wright, who had worked as a sportswear department manager for a department store and had taken accounting courses at a community college, contacted Statman. Statman decided that Wright should supply as much capital as she had invested in the business and become the operations manager and accountant. In other words, Wright would come in as an equal partner in the established business. With the extra money, the partners decided to modernize and expand the sportswear store.

They put the principal points of their agreement into writing and, with the aid of a lawyer, drew up the **articles of copartnership.** This contract stated the important points of the partnership agreement between Statman and Wright and provided for the dissolution of the partnership in the event of the death of either partner. Other key points included in the articles of copartnership were the rights of each partner, the division of the firm's profits, and procedures to be followed if one of the partners wished to withdraw.

The partnership of Rebecca Statman and Doug Wright had a number of advantages. First, their combined skills resulted in a more efficient retail operation. Second, the increased capital enabled them to stock more merchandise, to use better equipment, to improve their credit position in the market, and to expand the services of their store. Third, each person assumed the financial responsibility of the partnership, dividing the losses, if any.

Statman and Wright found that the partnership also had some disadvantages. The law covering partnerships makes each partner responsible for not only her or his share of the debts of the business but also for the share of any partner who cannot pay. To pay the partnership liabilities (debts), each partner may have to contribute the amount of the business he or she owns, plus personal property such as a house and car. This feature of partnerships is called unlimited liability of partners. **Unlimited liability** means there is no distinction made between the individual owner and the business entity. Any assets, business or personal, may be seized by creditors to satisfy the debts of the business. Furthermore, each partner is bound by the contracts of the other partners. For example, if Statman bought merchandise that Wright did not want, the business still had to pay for it. Such contract binding can be a cause of friction and disagreement between or among partners. Another difficulty is that one partner may think he or she is not getting a satisfactory share of the profits according to the amount of time and effort put into the business. A person may have difficulty withdrawing from the partnership if dissatisfaction occurs. Furthermore, the life of a partnership is always uncertain. Death of a partner ends a partnership, even if the partnership agreement runs for a certain length of time.

While partnerships usually involve only two persons, they may involve more than two. It is possible to organize a limited partnership in which some of the partners have no voice in the management of the business. Limited partners are liable only for the amount of their investment, though they may share equally with other partners in the profits of the business. In a limited partnership, the business is directed by one or more of the general partners.

ADVANTAGES AND DISADVANTAGES OF PARTNERSHIPS

Advantages
+ Skills of two or more persons often better than one
+ More capital obtainable (compared with sole proprietorships)
+ Partners have direct voice in management (compared with corporation)
+ Less regulation and taxation than is true of a corporation

Disadvantages
- Disagreement among partners
- Each partner liable for acts of others
- Liability not limited to investment
- Lack of permanence, since death of partner or addition of new partner dissolves old partnership
- Difficulty of withdrawal from partnership

Illus. 12–3 The partnership form of ownership is efficient and effective for small but growing retail businesses.

CORPORATION

The sportswear store of Statman and Wright prospered under their hard work and direction. Soon, the partners considered opening a much larger store in a new shopping mall about to open nearby. They consulted a lawyer and found that the best way they could raise more capital was to form a corporation. The ownership of the new store would be held by a group of individuals who would each buy shares of stock in the corporation. Each share of stock was to have a **par value** (stated value at time of issuance) of $1. Shares were to be sold in 100-share lots. Statman and Wright talked to their friends and customers and found that several were willing to invest in a shopping-mall store. The partners told their lawyer to apply to the state government for permission in the form of a charter to incorporate their sportswear business. When the charter was granted, the corporation—a person or legal entity in the eyes of the law—was created. The corporation could make contracts, own property, borrow money, and perform other activities necessary to operate a retail business.

The new corporation was to have a beginning capitalization (authorized value of stock to be issued) of $500,000. Statman and Wright bought 85,000 shares each with the money they received by selling their sportswear store to the corporation. They then sold 130,000 additional shares to other persons who were willing to invest in the new corporation. One person bought 20,000 shares, four persons each bought 10,000 shares, eight persons each bought 5,000 shares, and 30 persons each bought 1,000 shares. The remaining 200,000 shares remained unissued but could be sold if the sportswear store later needed money for expansion. The 45 stockholders held a meeting and elected directors. Mostly these directors were the principal stockholders themselves. The directors had the responsibility of outlining the general plans and policies for the sportswear store and of appointing officers to manage the business.

The corporation is the most common form of ownership for large stores. In case of financial difficulties, each stockholder is responsible for losses only to the extent of the stock he or she owns. If a stockholder dies, the corporation need not be ended or closed; it can continue indefinitely. It is easy for stockholders to withdraw ownership by selling their shares of stock to someone else or back to the corporation. If it is needed, more capital for the corporation can be raised through the sale of authorized shares, thus making a large-scale operation possible.

The corporate form of ownership, however, has some disadvantages. Corporations are subject to more laws, regulations, and taxes than other kinds of businesses. It is much more difficult to form a corporation than a sole proprietorship or a partnership. Also, since ownership and management are separated in a corporation, both owners and

ADVANTAGES AND DISADVANTAGES OF CORPORATIONS

Advantages
+ Limited liability—each stockholder liable only for the amount of his or her investment
+ Long life—does not dissolve with the death of owners
+ Much capital can be raised, making large-scale operation possible
+ Easy for a shareholder to withdraw by selling stock

Disadvantages
− Ownership and management separated—danger of irregularities and fraud because of impersonal management
− Subject to many laws, regulations, and taxes
− More difficult to form

Illus. 12−4   Small businesses that grow into large-scale operations often adopt the corporate form of store ownership.

managers may take their roles less seriously than owner-managers of other businesses.

FRANCHISED BUSINESSES

Some people who desire business ownership may find that a franchised business is an attractive option. A **franchise** is granted when the owner of a business or product gives to others the right to conduct a similar business or to sell the product under the owner's name. A franchise is *not* another form of store ownership but a variation in the way a proprietorship, partnership, or corporation may be organized. The **franchisor** (the person or firm that owns an idea or product) gives the **franchisee** (the retailer) the right to use the franchisor's idea or product, name, advertising, and other services.

The most visible franchised businesses are auto service centers, instant copy firms, restaurants, and motels. They are designed to provide a consistent quality of product and service, regardless of location. Many other small retail businesses also operate as franchises.

The owner of a franchised business must give up some freedom of action in business decisions that would be open to the owner of a nonfranchised business. Business operating procedures, advertising, personnel policies, and merchandise are often set by the franchisor. However, franchisees do gain certain business advantages. Among the services franchisors may provide are the following:

1. Location analysis and site counseling
2. Store development assistance, including lease negotiation
3. Building design and equipment purchasing
4. Initial employee and management training
5. Advertising and merchandising planning and assistance
6. Standardized and tested operating procedures
7. Centralized purchasing
8. Financial assistance in the establishment of a business

A good franchise arrangement gives a person without business experience and adequate capital a chance to own and operate

Illus. 12–5 Franchised businesses provide the same products and services and follow the same operating procedures wherever they are located.

her or his own business. The use of a proven product or service and marketing methods lowers a retailer's risk and increases the chance of success.

The cost of a franchise varies considerably by company and by location. For a specialty clothing store, the range is typically $25,000 to $120,000, with additional costs for set-up, fixtures, and initial inventory. Building costs are usually additional and will vary depending on rental, lease, and ownership. Costs for major food franchises are considerably higher, in some cases over $1 million.

*S*ummary

Retail businesses have three forms of ownership. The sole proprietorship is the form of ownership most common for smaller stores. The partnership is used when two or more persons wish to own a business jointly. The corporation involves incorporating according to state law. Ownership is held in the form of stock. Managers of corporation stores may or may not be the business owners. A variation of proprietorship or partnership can occur through franchise-business ownership.

*R*eview

1. Define *sole proprietorship, partnership,* and *corporation.*
2. Name advantages of each of the three major types of business ownership.
3. Explain the purpose of articles of copartnership.
4. Define *limited partnership.*
5. Define the term *par value.*
6. Define *capital* and explain how new corporations are capitalized.
7. Define the terms *franchisor* and *franchisee* and explain how they are related.
8. List the services often provided by franchisors.

*T*erms

The following terms were introduced in this chapter. Write a separate sentence correctly using each new term.

articles of copartnership	partnership
corporation	par value
franchise	sole proprietorship
franchisee	unlimited liability
franchisor	

*D*iscuss

1. Is the unlimited liability of sole proprietors and partners fair to those who want to run their own businesses?

2. Since Statman's store was prosperous at the time of partnership with Wright, do you think it was fair for Wright to become an equal partner by investing only an amount of money equal to Statman's initial investment?

3. If you were to enter into a partnership, how specific would you want the articles of copartnership to be? Name three points you would expect the agreement to include.

4. If you had adequate capital to start a small business, would you consider a franchised business? Explain.

Problem Solving

1. Determine the requirements for a business to incorporate in your state. Are there any additional city or county regulations that must be met?

2. Identify two businesses in your community that are organized as sole proprietorships, two as partnerships, and two as corporations. What difficulty did you have in identifying a firm's type of ownership?

3. Refer to the stock market pages of a major newspaper and determine the current price per share of common stock for three retail corporations.

4. What franchised businesses are located in your community? How many of these businesses were operating in their present location five years ago?

CHAPTER 13

Business Locations

CHAPTER OUTCOMES

When you have mastered the information provided in this chapter, you should be able to:

1. Identify three steps that must be taken in selecting an effective store location

2. Explain why a retailer selecting a location would want information on population, economy, competition, and local laws of a community

3. List several sources for obtaining information about a certain community or trading area

4. Identify six types of shopping districts and describe what types of goods each would carry

5. Describe three types of planned shopping centers

6. Explain how the type of customer traffic should affect store site selection

Selecting a location is among the more important decisions facing a potential retail-store owner. When asked "What are the three factors most likely to ensure retail success?" a well-known store consultant replied, "One, location; two, location; and three, location." In other words, the impact of site selection on the success of a retail operation can't be overemphasized. A retailer may understand consumer needs, economic conditions, and competition; have adequate capital; and manage well but still fail because of location. Far too many retailers select a store site with little consideration as to what it might mean to future success. For some, the search is limited to looking for vacancy signs or an advertisement in a newspaper.

Carol Dride has been employed for several years as a salesperson and manager in the men's clothing department of a locally owned department store. Although successful as a department manager, Carol has few opportunities for advancement at this store. For more than a year, Carol and her husband Chuck have worked on a plan to organize, own, and operate their own clothing store. Their research indicates the community has a need for a medium-scale to up-scale women's clothing store. With the help of two or three part-time employees, the Drides believe they can develop a successful business.

Carol and Chuck have saved their money and decided that now is the time to take action. They realize that selecting a location for their business involves three very important steps. The first is determining the community or general trading area for the store; the second is identifying the specific district within the community or area; and the third is selecting an actual site.

CHOOSING A COMMUNITY

What features make a certain community or trading area most suitable for a particular store? Will the chosen community be really important to the retailer's future success? Selection can be a difficult task since there is no single set of guidelines that can be followed when answering these questions. The aspiring retailer will need to know (1) whether a particular community can support another store of the type planned and (2) whether it will continue to do so in future years. Both concerns require positive answers. To make these judgments properly, the retailer carefully must study information about the community and its residents.

Community Population Trends

The Drides believe that they need a community population study in order to decide on the location of their planned women's clothing store. They need to know the size of the present population and its potential for growth. If the targeted consumer population in the community or trading area is growing, then the need for additional retailers is apparent. If, however, the targeted population is declining, a reduction in demand for such goods could occur. To locate in such a community, unless special conditions justify doing so, would be a mistake. For example, new highway construction or anticipated closing of some existing businesses might result in an enlarged market, making a new store in the area feasible.

Information about local buying patterns is also important. The Drides must de-

UNITED STATES POPULATION

Year	Population
1960	183,285,009
1970	208,066,557
1980	231,106,727
1985	239,279,000
1990 (est.)	251,265,000
1995 (est.)	259,559,000
2000 (est.)	267,955,000

Source: U.S. Bureau of the Census, *Statistical Abstract of the United States, 1990*, 110th ed. (Washington, D.C., 1990), 8.

Illus. 13–1 The U.S. population, including all people abroad and living in U.S. territories, will continue to increase but at a slower rate in the last decade of the twentieth century.

termine if there is a demand for the type and quality of clothing they plan to carry. For instance, how will the incomes and life-styles of the community residents affect the success of the women's clothing store they are planning? In order to answer this and re-lated questions, the Drides obtain U.S. Bu-reau of the Census data from references in the local library, county data from the County Clerk's office, and community pop-ulation projections from the local Chamber of Commerce.

Community Economy

Just as important as knowing some-thing about the number and characteristics of the people in a community is knowing something about their accumulated wealth and incomes. Since income affects cus-tomer buying power, a retailer needs to know per capita (per person) income and

about the ways local residents earn their liv-ings. Answers to the following questions help to provide this kind of information:

1. What is the average family income?
2. How many families are in each income bracket?
3. What is the usual unemployment rate?
4. How many families own their homes?
5. Are the employed heads of households unskilled, skilled, or professional workers?
6. How many and what kinds of industries are in the locality?

One of the best-known guides for de-termining community potential is the *Sales Management Buying Power Index* released annually by the publisher of *Sales Management* magazine. The guide shows for each county of the United States a weighted in-dex based on income, retail sales, and pop-ulation as a percentage of the national total.

INCOME BY U.S. HOUSEHOLDS—1990

Household Income	Percent of Households
Under $5,000	6.2
5,000–9,999	10.8
10,000–14,999	10.3
15,000–24,999	18.6
25,000–34,999	16.0
35,000–49,999	17.3
50,000 and over	20.8

Source: U.S. Bureau of the Census, *Statistical Abstract of the United States, 1990*, 110th ed. (Washington, D.C., 1990), 444.

Illus. 13–2 The second largest percentage of U.S. households have an income between $15,000 and $25,000.

Using data they collect about community population trends and economic conditions, the Drides begin to build a profile of the community where they want to start a business. The community is expected to continue to increase in population; it has a slightly above-average family income, below-average unemployment rate, and a growing and diverse industrial base.

Not surprisingly, retailers do better in communities that have high employment and good family incomes. When buying power is lacking, the demand for retail goods is reduced. In general, retailers conclude that communities with several different forms of industry or employment hold greater promise for retail stores than communities having only one or two major employers. The Drides are encouraged by what they have found thus far.

Retail Competition

Competition is the name of the game in retailing. Selecting a location for a new store requires that all competition be carefully reviewed. The Drides must determine if the community can support another clothing store.

Even if competition studies are positive, they may not reveal a specific need for an additional clothing store. Therefore, the Drides have to include in their store-location study consideration of the following questions:

1. What kinds of stores are already located in this trade area?
2. Are these stores locally owned or part of a regional or national chain-store system?
3. How new are the competitive stores and what is the condition of their buildings and equipment?
4. Are there any major regional or community shopping centers in the area?
5. What is the attitude of the community toward new businesses—supportive or critical?

Before finishing their study, the Drides actually count all clothing stores in the community. For each store, they determine type of ownership, age and condition of store, merchandise lines carried, prices, and quality of the store's management. They also question a number of friends and other persons in the community about the desirability of a new business coming into the community. The Drides conclude that there would be little competition for the type of clothing store they are planning and that the community would welcome such a store.

Community Services and Laws

It is important for new retailers to investigate what regulations and services will allow them to operate efficiently and profitably. Restrictions on where businesses may locate, on when they may operate, and on where and how they may advertise will affect chances of success. Community tax laws and the size and skill of the labor force also can affect how well a business will do in an area. Carol and Chuck Dride realize that community regulations and taxes apply equally to all businesses.

Among the services the Drides should consider in their assessment of the community are accounting, banking, legal, advertising, and credit information offices. Also, transportation and storage services should be available to help provide rapid delivery of merchandise to the store and to the customers. A check on tax rates, property values, and labor conditions also will be necessary.

By walking through or driving around a community, the Drides can observe traffic patterns, parking facilities, building conditions, and public services. Also, trade associations, chambers of commerce, banks, and local retail merchants offer specific information about the particular community. Business and research departments in local colleges and universities are additional valuable sources of location information. However, because few ideal trading areas exist, each trading area must be judged on its own merits. The Drides may have to compromise before selecting a store location.

CHOOSING THE SHOPPING DISTRICT

Several business locations can be found in most communities or trading areas. Many of these locations make excellent store sites if they are matched to a particular type of store and meet the retailer's needs. A fast-food store, for example, needs heavy traffic, while shopping-goods store owners prefer less traffic and more parking space. The Dride's clothing store may need both heavy traffic and a large parking area. In most communities, retailers have six basic types of business locations from which to choose: (1) central shopping district, (2) fringes of the central shopping district,

(3) a secondary shopping district, (4) string-street locations, (5) a neighborhood district, and (6) a planned shopping center.

Central Shopping District

A central shopping district is usually the downtown area of a community. People who live anywhere in the trading area go to the central shopping district to shop, especially when they want to choose from wide assortments of merchandise.

Department stores usually are located in central shopping districts, and specialty shops are located nearby. One of the chief problems in such districts is that it is difficult for customers to find parking space there, even though parking lots and ramps are provided for store customers. For that reason, many customers must use public transportation to reach the shopping districts. Central shopping districts present other problems, too. Rent in a downtown location is high, and in some communities the number of shoppers coming to the central district is decreasing. The result is that this type of location may not be as desirable as it once was—at least not for a new store.

Fringes of the Central Shopping District

Limited-line stores and specialty shops that do not depend on heavy pedestrian traffic often prefer side streets and similar locations near the central district. In such fringe areas, rents are lower and more space is available for goods that require large display areas. Examples of stores that locate on the fringes of the central shopping district are appliance and furniture stores, men's clothing stores, and discount stores.

Secondary Shopping District

In all cities and in most large towns, there are clusters of businesses that include several retail stores. These collections of stores make up a secondary shopping district. The people of the area go to this secondary shopping district because they find it more convenient than going to the central district. Secondary shopping districts vary in size, but they may include restaurants, specialty stores (men and women's clothing, art galleries, religious books, and computers), drugstores, hardware stores, and grocery stores.

In the community that Chuck and Carol Dride are considering, the central and fringe shopping districts have limited potential and are not very attractive. They find several secondary shopping districts, but those having a good mix of businesses are not well located for the potential customers that the Drides plan to serve.

String-street Location

Stores are often located along the main traffic routes leading to the central shopping district or shopping centers. Service stations, fast-food businesses, garden supply stores, and home-furnishings stores are found along these routes known as string streets. Since some suburban shopping centers are becoming crowded, string-street locations may be ideal for some businesses, especially if there are good parking facilities nearby.

Neighborhood Shopping District

Stores may also be located on residential streets and frequently at intersections. These locations are well-suited to businesses that deal principally with people who live in the immediate neighborhood. Drugstores, small grocery stores, beverage stores, and service businesses such as shoe-repair shops are often found in these locations.

Planned Shopping Center

A **planned shopping center** is a facility designed to accommodate many retail and service businesses. Such centers, usually with carefully landscaped pedestrian walks and rest areas, are developed for a predetermined number and type of stores. Most of these centers have been developed in suburban areas where few businesses previously existed. Studies have identified three basic types of planned shopping centers: the neighborhood center, the community center, and the regional center.

Neighborhood Center. A neighborhood center generally serves up to about 20,000 people living within a six- to ten-minute drive from the center. The major store in this center is usually a supermarket. The other stores in the neighborhood center often include a drugstore, a hardware store, a bakery, a variety store, a few specialty stores, and some service businesses such as videotape-rental stores. Most of the stores feature convenience goods or services.

Community Center. A community center can serve up to about 100,000

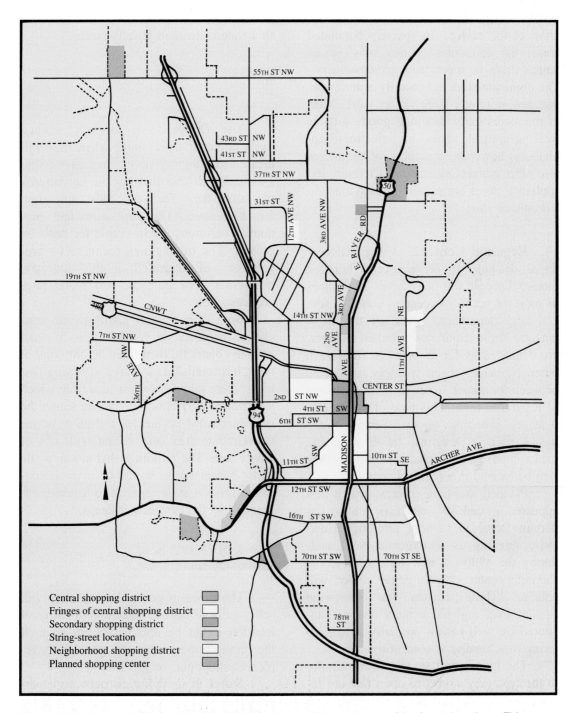

Illus. 13–3 *In most large towns and cities, there are six basic types of business locations. This drawing of a typical city shows the location of each type.*

people living within a 10- to 20-minute drive of the center. (In sparsely populated areas, the community center may be an hour's drive or more from its customers.) The dominant store is generally a junior department store or a large variety store. Most of the stores carry shopping goods such as wearing apparel, shoes, and electronic appliances; however, a number of the stores also offer convenience items. Clothing and appliance stores are usually located close to a dominant store.

Regional Center.   A regional center is designed to serve several hundred thousand people who may travel 20 minutes or more to get to the center. Usually, several large department stores are the major tenants. These major stores, called *anchors,* are distanced as far as possible from each other. Numerous specialty stores are located between the major stores to take advantage of the traffic flow. This type of center emphasizes shopping goods. Service businesses such as theatres, travel agencies, banks, and various medical centers may also be located in a regional center.

Planned shopping centers, which first appeared around 40 years ago, are an important factor in modern retailing. However, retailing is a dynamic field and, during the 1990s, a new form of regional shopping center, called a *power center,* will emerge. These centers are somewhat smaller than regional centers and are anchored by well-known specialty stores offering merchandise at competitive prices.

The Drides find several stores similar to the type they expect to open that are located in the planned shopping centers in their community. The planned shopping centers have stores that will complement their women's clothing store, such as women's shoe stores and jewelry stores.

CHOOSING A SITE

The Drides have carefully studied many factors in determining where they will locate their clothing store. They have found a shopping district that has the characteristics that they feel are most important for their store. The population and economic conditions are favorable for business growth. The trading area seems to be progressive and interested in attracting new businesses. The purchase and rental rates are reasonable.

Next, Chuck and Carol Dride must choose the exact site for the store. In small business districts, there may be only one or two sites available. In large shopping districts, there may be several sites from which a merchant may choose. The site should be near successful businesses and on an active street rather than near vacant buildings or empty lots. The buildings that adjoin a site under consideration should be in good condition since a store, similar to a person, is judged by "the company it keeps."

Types of Goods Sold

The types of goods that the store will sell greatly affect site selection. A different location might be appropriate for each of the three major types of goods: convenience, shopping, or specialty.

Stores in shopping districts are generally grouped so that those with compatible merchandise are close together. Merchants carrying specialty goods that are comple-

STORE SITES WITHIN A COMMUNITY

Downtown or Central Shopping District	Department stores Women's specialty stores Variety stores Women's shoe stores Drugstores (with large novelty and luncheonette sections)
Fringes of Central Shopping District	Specialty groceries Men's specialty stores Home-furnishings stores Automobile agencies Auto-accessory stores Appliance stores Discount houses
Secondary Shopping District	Same as downtown shopping district, but department stores may be absent and specialty stores may be smaller
String Street	Supermarkets Fruit and vegetable stores Garden supplies Furniture and shoe stores Service stations Lunchrooms Discount houses
Neighborhood Shopping District	Unit stores such as grocery stores, drugstores, stationery stores, shoe repair shops, hardware stores, and bakeries
Planned Shopping Center	Commonly built around the branches of large department stores with branches of specialty stores, units of chain stores, discount houses, and some independents

Illus. 13–4   Different stores are located in different shopping districts for particular reasons. Consumers become familiar with their community's shopping districts and know which district to go to for particular kinds of merchandise.

mentary to certain other kinds of shopping goods may desire to locate close to those stores. Buyers of shopping goods like to compare the items in several stores without traveling a great distance. Therefore, an excellent site for stores handling shopping goods is beside or between two large department stores so that walking traffic flows by them. Another good site for a shopping-goods store is between a major parking area and a major department store.

The best location for a specialty-food store is near a supermarket. A supermarket in a planned shopping center is usually best located at one end. An end site in a shopping center is also a desirable place for a drugstore. Because drugstores maintain longer hours than most other stores, they should be easily accessible and not surrounded by stores with shorter hours. Service businesses, such as dry cleaners or banks that depend on a rapid turnover of traffic, should be located where there is always available parking.

Some specialty goods, such as stereos, televisions, sporting goods, and lighting fixtures, are frequently sought by consumers who are already well-informed on the product, brand, or both. Stores catering to this type of consumer may use locations outside a shopping district because they generate their own consumer traffic.

The Drides believe that, to be most successful, their women's clothing store should be located near other women's specialty stores and in traffic generated by major shopping-goods stores.

Customer Traffic

One of the most important factors in determining a location, even in a shopping mall, is the number of people who pass by. The best approach to assessing traffic flow is to do a traffic count, recording each person who passes by the selected location. In an accurate count, the shoppers coming from both directions must be counted during the business day.

The mere fact that a large number of people pass the proposed site does not mean

that a store located there will be successful. A retailer must determine why these people are passing this place. Large crowds may pass a store site on their way to or from work, the theatre, the post office, or the bank. Such traffic, called **structured traffic,** involves persons other than shoppers. The people involved in structured traffic are almost always in a hurry and would not be customers for stores carrying goods that require careful shopping.

Stores selling specialty goods for which a great deal of thought or a large outlay of money are required need not locate where shoppers pass. Customers will seek them out. However, stores selling convenience goods or shopping goods can benefit from being located in the path of shopping traffic. Traffic made up of people looking to buy is called **shopping traffic.** The Dride's selection of a site in Bandana Mall, near three other stores appealing to women and on a shopping traffic path between J. C. Penney and Marshall Field's, best meets the location criteria they established as a result of their business-location study.

Illus. 13–5   The number of pedestrians passing a business location is not necessarily a good indication of the number of potential shoppers.

*S*ummary
Selecting a business location involves several important steps. The retailer must first determine if a community has a need for the type of store planned. Within the community, a certain shopping district must be identified. The next step is to choose a site within a shopping district. Decisions about each of these steps depend on the type of store planned, kinds of goods to be carried, competition, community population and economy, local services and laws, and, above all, the needs and wants of consumers.

*R*eview
1. Identify three steps in selecting a store location.
2. List four questions that should be asked about a community's economy before deciding on the location of a retail business.
3. List three sources of information about the population and economy of a community.
4. List three questions that should be asked about the retail competition in an area during decision-making about the location of a retail business.
5. Identify two local regulations and two services that should be considered in the selection of a retail-store location.
6. Name six types of shopping districts and give examples of the kind of goods each would carry.
7. Describe the differences among the three types of planned shopping centers.
8. Explain how structured traffic differs from shopping traffic and what each means to a retailer.

*T*erms
The following terms were introduced in this chapter. Write a separate sentence correctly using each new term.

planned shopping center   structured traffic
shopping traffic

*D*iscuss
1. Why is location such an important factor in the success of a retail store?
2. Why do planned shopping centers attract such a large percentage of today's retail sales?
3. Why should a new retail store be located near already successful stores?
4. Of what value to the prospective owner is knowing that large numbers of people regularly pass by a potential store location?

Problem
Solving

1. Visit a shopping district or a shopping mall and determine what stores are closest to the primary or anchor stores. Where are the women's clothing stores in relation to other stores? Where are the convenience-goods stores located?

2. What suggestions would you make to Carol and Chuck Dride if, after their study of locations, they had not found an appropriate place for a women's clothing store?

3. Select a shopping-district location and perform a 15-minute traffic count of people passing a specific site. How would you determine which people are potential shoppers?

CHAPTER 14

Business Facilities

CHAPTER OUTCOMES

When you have mastered the information provided in this chapter, you should be able to:

1. Identify key items a retailer should consider when buying an existing business

2. Describe the advantages and disadvantages of store-building ownership

3. Develop a checklist for evaluating a building for possible use as a retail store

4. Compare the relative merits of renting and leasing a store building

5. Describe each of the three basic forms of leases

6. State the major precautions that should be taken by a retailer signing a building lease

"Your market study and consumer analysis on the need for a lamp and lighting fixture store is well done and very interesting." Those are encouraging words to Joe Calderone and Karen Yang, whose banker has just reviewed their request for a loan. The best news is that their request for a business loan will be approved if they can find an appropriate location. As a result of their store location study, Karen and Joe found several good locations for their store. Now, they must choose one of several potential sites. In choosing the exact site, they will have to decide whether to invest in an existing business or start a new store. They must also consider possibilities for buying, building, renting, or leasing a building or shopping-center space. Joe's and Karen's choice is complicated even more by a developer's plan for a new shopping mall in the area they are considering. Should their store become part of this new complex?

No matter how favorable a site may be, it is not acceptable for merchandising purposes unless it can be occupied on favorable terms. These terms—**terms of occupancy**—have to do with the cost of purchasing or leasing a particular building or space. Very often, the terms of occupancy are the determining factor in deciding whether a site should be occupied. Each of the choices faced by Yang and Calderone has advantages and limitations. The following information should prove helpful in making the final decision.

business that can be purchased. The following major questions should be answered before making a decision to buy an established business:

1. Why does the present owner want to sell?
2. How successful has the business been in the past?
3. What are the strengths and weaknesses of the business?
4. Is it necessary to take over the existing inventory and fixtures?
5. Are the business records complete and accurate?
6. Does an audit of the records reveal potential for the desired level of sales?
7. If accounts receivable (amounts due the retailer on credit sales) are to be included in the purchase, do they represent a good investment?
8. How much repair and improvement will be necessary to modernize the store?
9. Does the asking price cover only the physical assets involved? Or does the price include an estimate of the potential earning power of the business?
10. What recommendations are made by a lawyer and an accountant after they examine the business?

As new retailers, Yang and Calderone should enter the purchase of any existing business with extreme care. Caution will help prevent them from taking over another retailer's problems and mistakes.

BUYING AN EXISTING BUSINESS

In some cases, the search for a site and a building results in finding an existing

BUYING A BUILDING

Whether a merchant buys an existing building or builds a new one, ownership assures continued occupancy. The store owner who owns the store building need not worry about being asked to leave the building once her or his store is opened. The decision to stay in business or get out is entirely up to the retailer-owner. Likewise, improvements, renovations, and repairs that meet local building codes can be accomplished without landlord approval. Any increases in property value belong to the building owner. The key advantage of building ownership is, in summary, that a retailer is free to make her or his own business decisions without consulting the owner of the building.

There are, of course, some disadvantages to store-building ownership. These disadvantages should be weighed against the advantages before a building decision is made. For example, when a building is purchased, the initial cost of starting that business increases. More capital is required to cover the added cost of a down payment and monthly expenses involved in maintaining a building. If the building is in need of

Illus. 14–1   The building and location are just a few of the concerns a buyer should consider when buying an existing business.

repairs or remodeling, additional funds are needed to complete that work. Unless the merchant has a great deal of money, building ownership drains away funds needed to start and operate a business. Furthermore, flexibility is lost if moving the business becomes necessary. Because of their limited resources, Calderone and Yang decide that the purchase of a building is not their first choice for obtaining business space.

EVALUATING A BUILDING

Many different types of buildings, including factories and railroad depots, have been converted to successful retail stores. However, it is generally best to operate a store in a building that has been designed for retailing. Modern retailing requires building features that may not be found in buildings planned for other purposes. The dynamic nature of retailing requires that buildings be flexible to change as merchandise and merchandising change.

To evaluate the suitability of a building for a particular business, the prospective retailer should develop a checklist of important features. Such a list permits the retailer to compare the features of one building with those of another. Yang and Calderone decide to write a question about each important feature they need in a lamp and light fixture store and then ask the same questions about each building being considered. The following list contains basic questions that should be asked about the features of any building for retail purposes:

1.   Is the building large enough to accommodate the amount of business the re-

tailer expects to be doing in three to five years?

2. Does the construction meet building codes? Is it soundproof and fireproof? Can additional floors or rooms be added if needed?

3. Does the building have a good heating and cooling system and sufficient insulation?

4. Are the windows suitable for displaying the type of merchandise for sale?

5. Do permanent interior walls or posts reduce the flexibility of floor space?

6. Are there facilities for receiving incoming merchandise that do not block the selling and nonselling work areas?

7. Do the plumbing facilities meet building codes? Are they adequate? What is the condition of the roof?

8. Are the floor surfaces in good condition, or can they be replaced easily?

9. Are there enough exits in the proper places?

10. Does the electrical wiring meet code? Is it modern?

11. Is the zoning, parking, and surrounding area appropriate for the business being planned?

Most of these questions can be answered by careful observation. The technical questions about electrical-wiring, heating, and cooling systems are best answered by a qualified building inspector. The fee for an inspection service is often a small price to pay for an expert analysis of a building's condition.

BUSINESS SPACE EVALUATION

Feature	Building 1	Building 2	Building 3
Size of Space	8	7	9
Quality of Construction	4	5	7
Heating and Cooling	5	6	8
Electrical Wiring and Service	7	5	7
Interior Layout	8	7	9
Windows for Display	9	8	8
Receiving and Storage Area	5	4	6
Restrooms and Plumbing	8	6	8
Roof	4	5	7
Floor Surfaces	6	7	9
Exits and Accessibility	9	7	9
Zoning and Parking	5	6	8
Overall Rating	78	73	95

Illus. 14–2   By rating each business space feature from 1 (low or poor) to 10 (high or very good), the overall rating of the three buildings under consideration can be compared.

The questions should be listed in order of importance. Assuming all necessary questions are evaluated, the building with the highest score is the most desirable. A sample calculation by Calderone and Yang is shown in Illustration 14–2. For them, Building 3 is the most suitable choice.

RENTING A BUILDING

Many store buildings are rented on a monthly basis; the building owner and store operator simply agree on an amount to be paid each month for the use of the building or store space. For example, a $350-a-month rental fee costs a retailer $4,200 a year. Rental terms of occupancy, however, are common only among the smallest of retail stores. Very often, such stores occupy sites of questionable or declining value. In such instances, a retailer and building owner have little or no reason to make a long-term commitment to each other. Actually, few good retail store locations are available on anything other than a lease basis. From a retailer's standpoint, occupying a building on a month-to-month basis is very risky; without some assurance of long-term occupancy, it may be difficult to build a regular customer following. For this reason, most store buildings are rented on the basis of a lease agreement.

LEASING A BUILDING

An agreement for the use of property is called a **lease.** Leasing is a widely used alternative to renting month-by-month or owning a space or building. A lease is made for a certain time period—often three to ten years—and usually contains an option to renew at the end of that period. Why do some retailers choose to lease rather than build or buy their own store buildings? A major reason is that a store operator may lack the capital needed to own land and a building. When funds are in short supply, most retailers prefer to invest this money in inventory and store operating expenses. Some large retail firms can afford to buy their own buildings, but they lease instead because a greater return is earned on money invested in merchandise than on money invested in real estate (land and buildings).

Some merchants have no choice but to lease the land and building they need. This is often the case when a location is ideal and the owner of that space has no desire to sell it. Some retailers simply do not want to be involved in the real-estate business. They prefer to concentrate their efforts on the problems of running a profitable retail operation. Yang and Calderone feel their money should be invested in merchandise and store fixtures rather than in a building. Leasing space for their store seems to be a wise decision, so they will find out more about leasing.

Lease Agreements

There are three basic forms of leases: (1) a flat-amount lease, (2) a straight-percentage lease, and (3) a percentage lease with a guaranteed minimum. One or all may be available for a single property. Each type of lease should be studied before a formal agreement is signed.

Flat-amount Lease.   A flat-amount lease involves a certain dollar amount that must be paid monthly or annually. If a retailer agrees to pay $500 a month for a vacant building or store space, that amount is fixed by a lease contract and cannot be changed. Signing a flat-amount lease can work to a retailer's advantage when business is good. However, if the flat amount is too high, a retailer may suffer financially if business takes a downward turn.

Straight-percentage   Lease.   A straight-percentage lease allows the actual amount paid by a retailer to vary with either the sales volume or profits of the store. One or the other is agreed upon as part of the lease agreement. Thus, when a store's sales or profits go up, the retailer must pay a higher rental rate. When either sales or profits go down, the retailer will pay a lower rental rate. The amount paid is a straight percentage, say 6 percent, of either sales or profits or, sometimes, both. Profit can be calculated several different ways, so a retailer and building owner may disagree on the amount of profit. For this reason, the dollar amount of sales is the better basis for a straight-percentage lease.

Percentage Lease with Guaranteed Minimum.   An arrangement of this kind operates similarly to the straight percentage lease except that the building owner is assured of receiving a minimum payment each month. For example, a percentage

lease with a guaranteed minimum might offer these terms: $400 a month or 3 percent of the sales volume, whichever is higher. If 3 percent of the sales volume in a given month amounts to $430, that is the payment the building owner should receive. If 3 percent of sales equals $390, the retailer must pay the $400 minimum.

Shopping Center Leases

Most shopping-center leases are negotiated. This means that the terms of the lease are arrived at through bargaining between the retailer and the shopping center owner. Rental expense may be a minimum guarantee plus a percentage of sales. Typically, rates are between 4 and 7 percent of sales, but the percentage varies by type of business and other factors. In addition to the guaranteed minimum, fees usually have to be paid to the center's merchant association. Also, retailers may be required to help pay for the maintenance of common areas in a shopping mall.

Generally, a shopping center owner provides bare space. The retailer handles the *finishing-out* at her or his own expense. To finish out a store for specific needs, light fixtures, counters, shelves, paint, and floor coverings are required. In addition, it may be necessary to install heating and cooling units in each store. It is important that the duration of the lease be long enough to enable the retailer to pay off these finishing-out expenses.

Some shopping center developers help tenants plan storefronts, exterior signs, and interior color schemes. This service is provided to make certain that each new store adds to a center's image rather than detracts from it. Thus, shopping-center leases may involve more rules and regulations than just the monthly rental terms.

Precautions in Leasing

Calderone and Yang have decided to locate their business in a small shopping district just off a main thoroughfare. The shopping district has several related businesses (bathroom fixtures, kitchen cabinets, and interior decorating). The stores in the shopping district have joined in developing a large off-street parking area for customers. A suitable building can be leased for two years with a renewal option and at a rate considerably better than any of the shopping center spaces they examined. When they discuss the preparation of a lease with their attorney, she points out some precautions they should take.

Disagreements can develop when lease agreements are not detailed enough. Differences regarding the responsibilities of the retailer (renter) and the building owner (landlord) can occur. For example, Yang and Calderone will need additional electrical circuits to allow them to display a large number of lamps and lighting fixtures. Who will pay for the additional circuits? If Yang and Calderone pay for them, must they be removed if they leave at the end of a lease period? Care in preparing a lease agreement is necessary to avoid misunderstandings and hard feelings. Illustration 14–3 is an example of a lease document.

Since a lease is a legal document, certain precautions should be taken before signing it. Calderone and Yang are advised to do the following before entering a lease agreement:

1. Examine the *property* thoroughly to make sure that it meets the purposes for which it is to be used.
2. Examine the lease *document* thoroughly to make sure that it contains:
   a. no narrow restrictions on merchandise that may be sold or on services that may be provided
   b. statements of the duration of the lease, the amount of rent, the dates on which rent is to be paid, and the conditions in case of nonpayment
   c. arrangements for **subleasing** (leasing property to another person for a shorter term and keeping rights under the first lease) or **subletting** (renting leased property to another person)
   d. provisions in case of fire, flood, or other hazards that prevent the use of the property as intended
   e. mutual obligations concerning major and minor repairs
   f. options and renewal arrangements
3. Make sure that *signatures* on the lease document are properly witnessed.

Karen Yang and Joe Calderone explain to the building owner what they want included in their lease. A copy of the lease is reviewed by their attorney who finds it satisfactory, so they are ready to sign. Deciding whether to buy an existing business or building, rent on a monthly basis, or enter into a lease agreement requires any retailer to go through a process of information gathering and careful thinking before arriving at a decision.

This Lease Witnesseth:

This indenture, made this __third__ day of March 1992 between __George Johnson__ , hereinafter called Lessor, and _Randall and Barbara Miller_, hereinafter called Lessee, witnesseth.

LESSOR HAS AGREED to let and hereby does let and demise to Lessee and Lessee has agreed to take and hereby does take from Lessor the following described real property _one-story yellow brick building with large display window to be used as retail jewelry store facing 232 Collins Avenue, County of Dade, City of Miami, State of Florida_

for a term of _10_ years, commencing _June 1, 1992_, subject to the terms and conditions more particularly set forth in a lease agreement between Lessor and Lessee, consisting of three attached pages bearing even date herewith.

The term of this lease shall be for _10 years_ and shall commence on the _first_ day of June 1992_, and end on the _twenty-eighth_ day of _June 2002_, inclusive. Rent in the total amount of _$9,600.00_ shall be paid to Lessor, without deduction or offset, at such place or places as may be designated from time to time by Lessor, in equal monthly installments of _$800.00_ in advance, on the _twenty-eighth_ day of each and every month during the term of the lease, commencing on the _twenty-eighth_ day of _May 1992_, until the entire amount shall have been paid.

Lessor acknowledges receipt of _$400.00_ deposited by Lessee as security for the performance of his obligations hereunder. Lessor may, but shall not be obligated to, apply said sum or a portion thereof in payment of any obligation of Lessee or as reimbursement for any damage suffered on account of any breach by Lessee. Any balance remaining upon termination of the lease which is in excess of any claim by Lessor shall be paid over to Lessee.

In the event there is any increase during any year of the term of this lease in the City, County, or State real estate taxes over and above the amount of such taxes assessed for the year _1991–1992_, whether because of increased rate or valuation, Lessee shall pay to Lessor monthly during the lease term an amount equal to _½%_ the increase in taxes upon the land and building in which the leased premises are situated. In the event that such taxes are assessed for a tax year extending beyond the term of the lease, the obligation of Lessee shall be proportionate to the portion of the lease term included in such year.

IN WITNESS WHEREOF, the parties hereto have executed this instrument the day and year first hereinabove written.

Randall Miller
Lessee

Barbara Miller
Lessee

George Johnson
Lessor

Howard Levy
Witnesses

Virginia Michaelz

Isabel Garcia

Illus. 14–3   A lease document and the conditions of the lease agreement should be studied carefully before signing the lease. Signatures should be witnessed.

Illus. 14–4 A merchant who obtains space in a planned shopping center is usually required to negotiate and sign a long-term lease.

Summary

Retail space may be obtained in four ways: buying an existing business, buying or constructing a building, renting a building, or leasing a building. Before buying a building, a retailer should develop a checklist for evaluating the structure. Most beginning retailers either rent or lease, though sometimes purchasing is the only way to get a desired location. A retailer should thoroughly review any agreement to buy, rent, or lease before signing. The retailer should understand all terms of a lease agreement—especially the payment arrangement (flat amount, straight percentage, or percentage with guaranteed minimum)—before agreeing to carry them out.

Review

1. List five questions that should be answered by a retailer considering buying an existing business.
2. Identify two advantages for retailers in owning their store buildings.

3. List five questions that should be answered when evaluating a building for use as a retail store.
4. Define *terms of occupancy*.
5. Explain the main difference between renting and leasing a building. Identify one advantage and one disadvantage of each arrangement.
6. Define *flat-amount lease*.
7. Describe a percentage-lease arrangement with a guaranteed minimum.
8. List four precautions that a retailer should take before signing a lease.

Terms

The following terms were introduced in this chapter. Write a separate sentence correctly using each new term.

lease   subletting
subleasing   terms of occupancy

Discuss

1. Under what conditions might a person buy an existing business that is in a poor building and not particularly successful?
2. Why would large-scale retailers choose to build and own their buildings rather than lease them?
3. What kinds of building expenses might a retailer who decides to occupy space in a shopping center have?
4. Why should lease agreements be carefully written?

Problem Solving

1. Identify two new businesses in your community. Try to determine if the retailers own, rent, or lease their buildings. Also try to determine both retailers' reasons for the terms of occupancy they have.
2. Identify two retail business sites that are currently available in your community. Analyze each in terms of how well it might meet the needs of Yang and Calderone. Use the basic questions in this chapter and add three questions about lamp and lighting fixture store features that you believe are important.
3. If Yang and Calderone had chosen to locate in a shopping center, which lease arrangement would you recommend for their lamp and lighting fixture store? Explain your choice.

CHAPTER 15
Special Retailing Businesses

CHAPTER OUTCOMES

When you have mastered the information provided in this chapter, you should be able to:

1. Name services provided by a franchisor

2. Name and describe the items included in a well-drawn franchise contract

3. Define *primary-service retailing*

4. List three reasons for the growth in service businesses

5. List the features of primary-service businesses

6. Describe two main types of nonstore retailing

UNIT 2 *Retailing Businesses*

Sound business organization and careful policy development are necessary for all retail firms. Decisions must be made about organization, merchandise, credit, services, personnel, and training. Three types of businesses merit additional discussion because of their special operating procedures. These special retail businesses are franchised businesses, primary service retail businesses, and nonstore businesses.

FRANCHISED BUSINESSES

Franchised businesses are explained in Chapter 12. A person (franchisor) who owns an idea or product can sell or license to another person (franchisee) the right to conduct a similar business selling the same idea or product. This licensing is called *franchising*. In this form of business operation, the name, procedure, products, and store design of the franchisor are sold to others. Franchised businesses have become commonplace in the United States. A typical business or family trip may find the traveler(s) using several franchised products or services—a car from Budget Rent-a-Car, breakfast at Country Kitchen, lunch at Hardees or McDonald's, and an overnight stay in a Holiday Inn or Howard Johnson motel.

The person who buys a franchised business is able to share immediately in the franchise identity and have access to proven products, services, and operating procedures.

Illus. 15-1 Customers expect similar products, service, quality and price from businesses that operate as franchises.

Structure of a Franchised Business

Franchisors vary widely in what they require of franchisees and in the services they provide them. Some franchisors regularly inspect each franchised business. Others provide help to the franchisee only when requested. Among the services some franchisors provide for franchisees are help in (1) selecting a business location, (2) evaluating a site or building, (3) negotiating terms of occupancy, (4) designing and equipping a store, (5) locating, selecting, and training employees and managers, (6) merchandising and advertising, (7) setting operating procedures, (8) purchasing and storing merchandise and supplies for franchisees, and (9) capitalizing and setting up a business. Illustration 15–2 highlights the wide range of conditions available to franchisees.

Typically, a franchisor provides these nine services in a franchise package. A package may include the actual selection of a business location, construction of a building, staff training, and set-up of the business operation for the opening day. For the franchise and a package of services, a franchisee pays an initial fee ranging from $10,000 to over $500,000. The franchisee also pays a royalty, usually 3 to 6 percent of the monthly sales. In addition, the franchisee often is expected to buy or rent certain equipment, supplies, merchandise, and materials from the franchisor.

The franchisee benefits from the experience of the franchisor and from operating with established policies, procedures, and continuing management supervision from the franchisor's staff. Any person thinking about investing in a franchised business should investigate the franchisor and the franchise system. This study should also include an evaluation of the individual's attitude toward the type of business being considered, particularly the long-term consequences of the franchise and its implications for the individual's future business opportunities.

Franchise Contracts

A franchise agreement is set forth in a contract that delineates the rights and obligations of both the franchisor and the franchisee. The contract includes the terms of the agreement, the length of the agreement, and the method for terminating the contract. The contract typically places most of the obligations on the franchisee. The reasons for this are that the franchisor desires to maintain strict control over the franchise since customers expect similar quality, price, and service from all the businesses within a franchise. To meet this expectation, the franchisor must make sure that a franchisee does not vary too much from established standards and procedures.

Clearly, no person should enter a franchise contract without understanding the terms of the agreement and both parties' obligations. Similar to all other contracts, for the protection of the franchisee, franchise agreements should be reviewed by an attorney.

The structure of a franchised business resembles an independent business in some ways and a chain store organization in other ways. Actually, a franchise is a semi-independent business operating under prescribed structures and procedures. Franchise business opportunities undoubtedly will continue to be attractive to retailers who need

TWO FRANCHISES

Retail Ice-Cream Store

A franchisor selects the site for a store. Upon obtaining a satisfactory lease, the store is completely equipped, stocked with merchandise, and brought to a point where it is ready to open. The complete store is then sold to a qualified individual under a franchise agreement.

Equity capital needed is about $30,000 to $50,000 plus about $15,000 working capital.

On-the-job training in an operating store under the guidance of experienced supervisors is provided. Continuous merchandising programs, accounting procedures, business counsel, and an insurance program are also provided.

Retail Women's Apparel Store

A franchisor provides a line of women's wear, including blouses, pants, suits, dresses, sweaters, shorts, skirts, and hosiery. The franchisees lease their own locations (about 1000 square feet) and install their own fixtures.

The equity capital needed is about $10,000 plus fixtures. Financial assistance is available on fixtures ($7,500) and on start-up inventory of about $10,000, both payable to the franchisor.

Training is informal with some management advice on merchandising, display, advertising, and inventory control. Management counsel is in the form of continuous personal and telephone contact.

Illus. 15–2   Franchisors vary widely in what they require of franchisees and in the services they provide them.

the help and guidance of experienced people in getting their own businesses started.

SERVICE BUSINESSES

Sales of services continue to increase as consumers' discretionary income grows and their life-styles (ways they use and value time) continue to change. **Primary services** include sporting events, theatre entertainment, car washes, dry cleaning, and campgrounds. **Customer services,** such as gift wrapping and store credit, are offered in relation to sales of tangible goods. These are not primary services because they do not have their own value.

Because services are intangible, those who sell the services are not always regarded as retailers. However, primary services satisfy consumer wants. The people who sell the services must adjust the nature and quality of their offerings to meet changing consumer demands. Similar to other retailers, they have pricing policies and contend with competition. Sellers of primary services must have customer policies—ways to handle complaints, for example. Furthermore, most primary services are sold in stores (although some, such as interior decorating, are sold in customers' homes). Therefore, the act of selling these intangible products is deservedly called *primary-services retailing*.

Features of Primary-service Businesses

The main characteristic of a service business is that it deals in intangible merchandise. What a customer buys from a primary-service business is not an item that can be stored or resold. A service affects only the ultimate consumer and often is of value for only a limited time. Also, services are usually paid for with a customer's discretionary income, which means that the purchase of the service can be postponed easily or substituted. Because the purchase of many services can be postponed and many of the services can be performed by customers themselves, a service provider must make it extremely easy for customers to buy. Location, hours, and terms of purchase must be carefully matched to consumer needs.

Primary service retailers often develop close relationships with their customers. For example, an interior decorator must learn in detail the personal preferences of those who live in the house to be decorated. Preferences for art, color, style, type of guests, form of entertaining, and eating habits usually are not shared with retailers of tangible products.

Service businesses are characterized also by their size. Most service retailing businesses are relatively small. They are likely to be owner operated, have a small staff, and have limited sales volume. Primary-service retailers tend to be people oriented rather than product oriented. For this reason, personnel is the major cost for most service businesses. Even in a car wash business, where there is often a large investment in washing equipment, the human labor required for operating the vacuum cleaners, cleaning the insides of windows, and drying the cars represents the major cost of daily operation.

Many service businesses are franchised businesses. Income-tax services, real-estate sales, motels, parking lots, and car rentals are examples of primary-service businesses that are franchised.

Growth of Services

For many years, consumers have tended to spend more and more of their dollars on services instead of goods. Today, consumers spend an estimated 50 cents of every dollar on services. A combination of several factors has caused this increase.

First, life-styles have changed; acquiring goods is less important to many people than in previous years. Consumers' appetites for travel and leisure-time activities have supported and encouraged large transportation, entertainment, and hospitality industries. These wants, along with increases in disposable personal income, have made primary-service selling an attractive business field. Recreation, physical fitness, and sports activities are also some areas that have benefited from consumer demand for services.

Second, there has been a significant growth in the number of women working outside the home and the number of households that have no one at home taking care of homemaking tasks full-time. This trend has caused an increased demand for laundry, dry-cleaning, child-care, interior-decorating, home-cleaning, and home-repair services.

Third, a number of new services have developed in the past years. Theme parks, recreational vehicle campgrounds, and clothing consulting for adults who are too busy to select and manage their own wardrobes are examples. Unless there is a serious economic setback or a major change in life-styles, customers will continue to expect an expansion of primary services to make their lives easier and more pleasant.

Organization and Policies

In the organization of a service business, just as in other retail businesses, there must be a clear understanding of what the business goals are, how the service is to be provided, who is to do what in the business, and exactly how the service is to be sold. The four organization steps described in Chapter 2 are important for a service busi-

ness: (1) group activities into related and manageable units, (2) select employees, (3) specify and assign duties, and (4) provide direction and evaluation of employees' work. Also, the four retail functions—buying, selling, operations, and control—are equally important for service-oriented as for merchandise-oriented businesses. The buying function involves selecting and offering the most appropriate type of services. The implementation of the other functions is similar to merchandise retailing.

Specific policies for retail-service businesses are harder to set forth than policies for product-oriented businesses. Each service customer presents a unique set of needs, and the service may have to be modified or adjusted to meet those needs. A product retailer's money-back guarantee, promise to meet the lowest price in town, and generous merchandise-return policy may not be appropriate or possible for a service retailer. For example, an adjustment may not be possible for a customer who decides after a few days that a hair style, decorating color, or theatre performance isn't

REASONS FOR GROWTH OF CONSUMER SERVICES

1. Consumer life-styles favor more services.
2. Families of two wage earners are becoming the norm.
3. Number of single-parent families is increasing.
4. Women's economic, social, and political roles are changing.
5. Subcultures are increasing in number and importance.
6. Number of retirees desiring "mature" services is increasing.
7. Number of people over age 40 who can afford a variety of services is increasing.
8. Services allowing consumers more time for leisure are increasing.
9. Leisure services desired by all age groups are increasing.
10. New product technologies often require expert service.

Illus. 15–3   Demographic and life-style changes affect what consumers need and want. New life-styles require new products and services.

what he or she wanted. Therefore, customer policies for a service firm may have to be general rather than specific and may have to be interpreted differently for different customer situations. However, service policies should be written as specifically and as clearly as possible.

NONSTORE RETAILING

There are two main types of nonstore retailing. One type involves personal encounters between retailers and customers by telephone or in customers' homes. The second type of nonstore selling substitutes catalogs, advertising, direct mail, or vending machines for personal retailer-customer encounters.

Growth in nonstore retailing has occurred, in part, for the same reasons as growth in service businesses. Customers often turn to a form of nonstore retailing for selecting and purchasing merchandise because they are too busy to shop at retail stores. By ordering merchandise by mail, by telephone, or from in-home salespeople, consumers can save shopping time and the costs, energy, and time spent in traveling to shopping centers.

In-home Selling

Itinerant (traveling) merchants have been a part of our consumer goods delivery system for centuries. Even today, there are certain businesses that sell primarily by calling directly at customers' homes. These businesses include various route-selling businesses (dairy products, household supplies, and bakery goods); individual and party sales (cosmetics, jewelry, and cookware); home-repair services; lawn care; and appliances. In spite of its convenience, in-home selling is not as common as it once was because now fewer people are home during the day. Also, some unethical salespeople have given in-home selling a bad reputation. Legitimate in-home retailers must work extra hard to be sure that their business operations and practices are not criticized.

Telephone Selling

Telephone selling is common to almost all retail stores. Customers call to get product information, to inquire about prices, and, frequently, to place orders. Some nonstore retailers depend primarily on telephone orders for their sales. By advertising in newspapers or directories or on radio or television, retailers invite potential customers to call and place orders for merchandise. Some firms call former customers to solicit new orders.

Telephone selling works best for standard merchandise or goods that can be described easily since customers must make decisions without visually examining the product. A firewood dealer might place a classified advertisement in a newspaper and then receive phone calls from interested persons. The dealer can easily describe the type, size, amount, and price of the wood over the phone. When the firewood is delivered, the customer pays for the order.

For telephone selling to be effective, the retailer must answer the telephone promptly during designated hours and use good telephone techniques. Similar to other

Illus. 15–4   Catalog retailing allows customers to review goods and place orders by telephone. Telephone-order service is often available 24 hours per day.

retail operations, the firm that depends on telephone selling must have definite policies on orders, credit, delivery, adjustments, and returns.

Catalog Retailing

For some retailers, catalog retailing supplements in-store sales and thereby expands business and maintains customer patronage. National chain department stores such as J. C. Penney make a large part of their annual sales through catalog retailing. Stores that are not national chains can reach customers beyond the store's region through catalog sales. L. L. Bean, Shepler's, and Lands' End have built national followings through distribution of their catalogs. The unique merchandise offerings in seasonal catalogs from stores such as Neiman-Marcus and Bloomingdale's are eagerly anticipated by customers.

Many catalog businesses have no retail-store base; that is, all of their business is conducted through catalog sales. In catalogs, merchandise must be presented as effectively as it is in in-store displays, and the catalog design must replace the personal attention of a salesperson. In addition, effective selling requires that an accurate catalog mailing list be maintained. Well-prepared catalogs are expensive, and a catalog retailer must continually verify mailing lists so that catalogs are sent only to those persons who are most likely to order the merchandise. Careful selection of merchandise, an inventory control system, efficient order handling, generous credit, prompt adjustments, and an appropriate return policy are necessary to maintain successful catalog retailing.

Mail-order Selling

Many firms have found that, by placing an advertisement in a newspaper or magazine or by mailing advertisements directly to consumers, they can generate a sizeable business. In fact, it is estimated that about 12 percent of general consumer merchandise is now sold through mail orders. This approach to nonstore retailing is generally most successful for specialty items or products not carried in local retail stores. A mail-order product should be fairly simple and easily described in an advertisement. Mail-order products also must be easy to deliver by mail or parcel service. To succeed, a mail-order firm must fill all orders promptly and accurately.

Some consumer goods companies depend almost entirely on direct-mail advertising to sell their products. Again, just as in catalog retailing, the direct-mail retailer must maintain an up-to-date mailing list of selected customers. Carefully prepared direct-mail advertisements should be sent only to persons who are likely to need or want the featured products.

Vending Machines

Vending machines are used to dispense a wide variety of convenience goods, such as newspapers, candy, and food. Using mechanical and/or electronic technology, vending machines deliver goods in a variety of shapes, sizes, and temperatures.

Some machines accept paper currency, make change, and thank customers for their purchase by means of a synthesized voice. Vending machine merchants have an advantage over in-store and other forms of nonstore retailers because their machines can be located to take maximum advantage of customer traffic 24 hours a day.

Video and TV Retailing

Various forms of nonstore retailing utilizing video or television are certain to increase in the years to come. Advances in home computers, videocassette recorders (VCRs), and video catalogs open new opportunities for sales outside of stores. Video shopping for real estate, automobiles, appliances, and even farm equipment is becoming commonplace. Electronic shop-at-home systems are in regular use nationwide on cable television. Consumers seem to appreciate the opportunity to view possible purchases on their own schedules and in the privacy of their homes. Experimental efforts to use television as a shopping media for groceries, housewares, and other frequently purchased general merchandise continue.

Summary   For all three special types of businesses—franchised, primary-service, and nonstore retailing—the future depends on how well the businesses are organized and operated and how well the market is assessed. The services provided to a franchisee by a franchisor vary, but, in any case, franchising allows many persons, who otherwise could not, to become business owners. Primary-service businesses provide customers with intangible products. The growing number of such businesses is due to economic and social conditions; people now have the interest, time, and money to consume services. The nature of services requires service businesses to be organized and operated differently, in some ways, from stores that sell goods. Nonstore retailing continues to grow, too, as more and more people decide to spend less and less time on in-store shopping. Nonstore retailing includes in-home selling, telephone selling, catalog retailing, mail-order selling, and vending machines.

Review

1. List two advantages a franchisee gains from being part of a franchise system.
2. List three considerations that should be included in a franchise contract.
3. List three examples of primary services and name businesses that offer them.
4. Identify three factors that have contributed to the growth in service businesses.
5. Identify and explain two differences between a primary-service retailer and a product retailer.
6. Name two types of nonstore retailing and give two examples of each type.
7. Describe merchandise that is best suited for telephone selling and list three specific examples.

Terms

The following terms were introduced in this chapter. Write a sentence correctly using each new term.

customer service   primary service

Discuss

1. If a franchisee improves a franchised product or service, who should receive the benefit—the franchisee or the franchisor?
2. What changes in life-style have you observed in your community within the past three to five years?
3. What primary services are frequently used by people in your community? What primary services are not available that people in your community might use?
4. How should consumers deal with unethical nonstore retailers?

Problem Solving

1. Develop a list of six franchised companies that operate in your community. Develop a second list of six nonfranchised stores that also operate in your community. Show your list of twelve businesses to five people and ask each person how these twelve

firms are alike and how they are different. Were the responses concerning similarities and differences related to whether or not the firms were franchised? What conclusions can you draw about the ways these people view franchised businesses?

2. Identify three products that you believe could be sold through a nonstore form of retailing. Name the form of nonstore retailing you would choose for each.

3. Identify four in-home selling businesses that operate in your community. What products are sold by each? How are products sold—through sales calls? party demonstrations? route sales? Are the businesses franchised or independently owned?

UNIT 2 ACTIVITIES

CHECKING KEY POINTS

This exercise is designed to check your understanding of material presented in Unit 2. On a separate sheet of paper, list the numbers 1 to 28. Indicate your response, *T* for true or *F* for false, for each of the following 28 statements.

1. Having goods ready when customers want to buy is an example of form utility.
2. Manufacturers convert or change materials into products that are useful to consumers.
3. Intermediaries assist in the distribution of goods from producers to ultimate consumers.
4. Commission merchants do not physically handle the goods that they sell.
5. In a directed economic system, consumers' decisions to buy determine what will be produced.
6. High prices on goods tend to increase consumer demand.
7. Gross national product (GNP) is the market value of all goods and services produced for a year.
8. Discretionary income is what a person has left after buying essentials, such as food, clothing, shelter, and transportation.
9. A small retail store employs fewer than 20 persons and has annual sales of less than $500,000.
10. Shopping goods stores carry merchandise that customers buy frequently, such as basic groceries.
11. The department store is a well-known type of large-scale retailing.
12. Nearly all types of consumer goods are sold in discount stores.
13. About 20 percent (one out of five) of all retail stores are owned by individual proprietors.
14. Completing a document called *articles of copartnership* allows partners to sell stock in their business.
15. In a partnership, each partner is responsible for the business debts of the other partner(s).
16. Partnerships are limited to two persons.
17. When selecting a location for a business, a retailer should check community population, economy, competition, and services.
18. Traditionally, the downtown area of a city has been the central shopping district.
19. Neighborhood shopping centers serve about 100,000 people within a 30-minute drive from the center.

20. A location with a large number of people passing by ensures a store's success.
21. To be acceptable, a retail site must have favorable terms of occupancy.
22. Buying a building for a retail store usually reduces the cost of starting a business.
23. An agreement for the use of property is called a *lease.*
24. In a straight percentage lease, a retailer pays the same amount of rent each month.
25. A franchisee sells a product and uses the procedures developed by the franchisor.
26. Primary-service businesses deal with tangible consumer goods.
27. Telephone selling works best for unique goods requiring careful descriptions.
28. Catalog retailing is used to supplement in-store retailing or to operate independently of a retail-store base.

BUILDING BASIC SKILLS

Calculations

Various calculations were used in Unit 2 to demonstrate certain facts about retailing, the economy, and consumers. Make the calculations required in the following items.

1. Given the following one-year data for the country of Salisue, calculate (a) gross national product, (b) net national product, and (c) national income.
   Money spent by individuals—$4,875,000
   Money invested by individuals and businesses—$645,000
   Net value of exports minus imports—$400,800
   Goods and services purchased by the government of Salisue—$940,000
   Depreciation and obsolescence of equipment and buildings—$517,000
   Earnings of labor and business owners—$4,515,000
2. Given the following data on Micki Maxwell's personal finances, calculate (a) disposable personal income and (b) discretionary income.
   Personal income—$21,700
   Local, state, and national taxes—$6,940
   Cost of food—$4,300; clothing, laundry, and cleaning—$1,835; shelter—$3,600; and transportation—$2,200
3. A store has a choice of the following lease arrangements:
   Lease A—$400 plus 3 percent of all sales over $6,000

Lease B—5 percent of sales up to $10,000 and 2 percent on sales over $10,000

Lease C—Flat amount equal to $9,600 a year

a. Calculate the monthly rental expense for monthly sales of $18,500 for each lease arrangement.

b. Would you choose lease A, B, or C if you expected sales to increase to $25,000 per month? Why?

c. If you expected sales to remain between $18,000 and $20,000 per month, would you choose lease A, B, or C? Why?

Working with People

Retail workers must work with other employees, supervisors, and customers. Sometimes, misunderstandings occur. Misunderstandings often cause bad feelings among employees and their supervisors and result in poor customer service. Many successful workers solve people problems with the four-step *DICE* approach. Each letter of *DICE* refers to a specific action in a four-step problem-solving procedure. This procedure is described in Unit 1.

Read each of the following problem situations. Then, use the *DICE* approach to find a solution for each. Remember, you must first define the problem before you identify or choose solutions. Describe the consequences of your solutions.

1. You are a checker-cashier in a supermarket. You are assigned to the express checkout register. According to a large sign over the lane, the express lane is for customers who have eight or fewer items and who pay in cash. During every shift you work, several customers come to the express lane with more than eight items (frequently with 15 or 20 items) and want to pay by check instead of cash. Your supervisor wants you to enforce the eight-item, cash-only policy. What could you say to customers who come through with more than eight items? What could you say to customers who check out and then claim they must write a check? What actions might be taken by the store management?

2. You and a friend are partners in a waterbed store. Your partner is supposed to buy most of the waterbeds, and you are responsible for most of the accessories, such as blankets, pillows, sheets, lamps, and mirrors. On numerous shopping trips, however, your partner buys not only bed units but also deals on accessories. These deals are often poor buys of marginal-quality merchandise. You have tried to point out the faults and problems of such buys, but your partner continues to make such buys and has just returned with another big shipment of accessory merchandise that

probably will not sell. What should you say or do to deal with this situation?

3. You supervise a staff of four persons who take telephone orders for department-store merchandise advertised by your employer. One of the order takers often fails to get complete information about the goods being ordered (size, color, model, style) and the correct name, address, and phone number of the customer. What should you do?

Writing Skills

You are asked by the local Chamber of Commerce to prepare a short paper (one or two typed double-spaced pages) on one of the following topics. Reports will appear in the Chamber's publication, *Community on the Grow.* This booklet is distributed to local citizens and businesspeople to make them aware of changes in local business practices.

1. The production and distribution of a locally produced product from manufacturer or producer to consumer
2. The role of the profit motive in the local economy
3. Primary-service businesses respond to local consumer demands
4. Responsibilities of retail business proprietors to themselves and to the community
5. The best site in the community for a women's clothing store
6. What shoe retailers look for in a store building
7. Perfect vending machine goods and locations in the local high school
8. How to pick a business partner

APPLYING YOUR KNOWLEDGE

Can You Do the Following?

1. Describe the benefits or advantages of a small retail business.
2. Describe the benefits or advantages of a large retail business.
3. Explain how each of the four merchandise utilities is created.
4. List the names of two discount stores in your community.
5. Identify five consumer goods that would most likely have a channel of distribution with only a retail store as an intermediary.
6. Name and describe five elements of an economic system.
7. List the names of three businesses in your community that fit the definition of small-scale retailer.

8. List five measures of money that make up a national income figure.
9. List six types of information that would help a retailer understand a community's economy.
10. Explain why a sole proprietor might want to adopt a partnership form of business ownership.
11. List six basic types of store locations from which retailers usually choose.
12. Compare the advantages of buying, renting, and leasing a business building.
13. Identify the features that should be evaluated before a retailer decides to occupy a building.
14. Identify three basic forms of leases and indicate the major differences among the three forms.
15. List eight services a franchisor may provide a franchisee.

Retail Decisions

1. List the steps you would take to select a new supermarket location.
2. What building features would be important for a store featuring discount stereo equipment, CDs, and other entertainment merchandise?
3. How could you roughly estimate the disposable income of families in your community?
4. If you had a successful retail store, why might you also try to sell goods through mail order?
5. What personal qualities would you seek in a business partner if you had an auto-parts store?
6. What local laws and regulations on businesses would be most important to you when starting a physical-fitness center?
7. If you anticipate your retail business in a shopping center is going to grow rapidly over a five-year lease period, what type of lease arrangement would you prefer—a flat amount or a straight percentage?
8. What could happen to retail businesses if government controls restricted each store to the sale of one type of personal property (food, clothing, furniture, appliances, real estate, automobiles)?
9. What building requirements or characteristics would you specify for a store selling new and used bicycles, accessories, and bicycle-repair services?
10. Refer to Illustration 15–2. What additional information about the franchisor services would you want to have before making a decision to become a franchisee of this ice-cream store?

DEVELOPING CRITICAL-THINKING SKILLS

Retail Projects

1. What changes have occurred in the U.S. gross national product, national income, and personal income from 1985 to the present?
2. You are interested in buying a retail sportswear business. The owner wants to sell the business and rent the building to you. The sale would include the inventory, fixtures, and accounts receivable (money due the business from customers). What questions or concerns should you raise before deciding to buy?
3. You are planning to start a variety store. You have two choices for terms of occupancy: (1) leasing a building for $9,000 per year for five years, with a five-year renewal option or (2) buying a building for $85,000, with $10,000 down and the balance due over 15 years at 10.5 percent interest on the unpaid balance. What are the advantages of each arrangement? Which would you choose? Why?
4. Two of your friends would like to start a yard-care business. What factors would suggest that such a business would be successful? What policies should your friends consider for their business?
5. Mr. Ewan is considering two sites for a men's clothing store. The first is a corner location in a particular business district. The corner location has a 40-foot frontage on the main street and extends 90 feet along a side street. The second possible site is on the same street but in the middle of the block. It has a 50-foot frontage and is also 90 feet long. The corner location rents for 25 percent more than the midblock location. What factors should Mr. Ewan consider in choosing one of these locations? Which would you recommend? Why?

Field Projects

1. If you were interested in starting an auto-parts and accessories store in your hometown, what store(s) would be the main competitors?
2. Identify and list the names of six primary-service businesses presently operating in your market area. What additional service businesses might be successful in your home area?
3. Arrange an interview with a small retail business owner and a large retail business owner. Before the interviews, prepare a set of questions about the difference between small-scale retailing and large-scale retailing. Prepare a report on the retailer's responses to your questions.
4. Choose three separate locations in a local shopping center (main

corridor, near one of the anchor stores, a side entrance, for example) and count for 15 minutes the pedestrian traffic that passes each site. Attempt to identify what part of the traffic represents shopping traffic. Compare the traffic counts at the three locations and suggest reasons for the difference in the number of customers counted at each location.

5. Identify and contact three local business persons who have recently purchased existing businesses. Ask them what major questions they considered as they looked for a business to buy. Compare their lists with the ten questions in Chapter 14.

6. Identify the major string-street business locations in your community. What types of retail businesses are located on these streets? Which of these string-street business districts have existed the longest and which are the newest? Which types of businesses seem to be most successful in these locations?

CONTINUING PROJECTS

Developing a Career Plan

In many ways planning a career is similar to planning a business. You need to collect and analyze a great deal of information before making a decision about what action to take. In Unit II, you were introduced to the types of businesses and activities involved in the production and distribution of consumer goods and services. Gather the career information resource books in your school library, help-wanted ads in local newspapers, job-placement information services, and other job sources. Try to obtain a description of at least one job for each type of business along the channel of distribution and one job description for each type of retail business described in Chapter 11. Record each description on a separate sheet of paper. Include job title, description, wages, hours of work, qualifications expected, and the name of the firm(s) offering the job. Include each sheet in your career planning notebook.

When you have completed the collection of job descriptions, develop a tentative career-objective statement. The typical career-objective statement covers five areas: area of interest (sales, research, merchandising); type of organization (wholesaling, retailing, advertising); level of position (usually beginning for new graduates); eventual goals (what you would like to be doing five years from now); and size and nature of the organization (small, large, local, regional, national, international). An example of a career objective statement that you can use as a guide is "Retail Buyer—interested in buying children's clothing for a large regional department store starting as an assistant buyer and moving to merchandise-management responsibilities." Remember, this is just a tentative career-objective statement—you can modify or change it at any time and most people do several times as they plan their careers. Put the current date on this statement and include it in your notebook.

Developing a Business Plan

For your notebook on planning, organizing, and operating an independent business, prepare the following, using the information you have learned in this unit.

1. Write a description of the store you plan to operate. Indicate the type of store, explain why such a store is needed in your community, and list the characteristics you would like your store to have.
2. Develop a list of features you would need in a building for your store.
3. Identify at least three potential locations in your community for your store. Select the one location you believe would be most appropriate and explain why you think it would be the best.
4. Develop a list of questions that you will have answered before you buy, rent, or lease the building for your store.
5. If you choose to operate a franchised business, state in writing why that type of business ownership is most appropriate for you. If you do not choose to be a franchisee, state why.

UNIT 3
Managing Human Resources

The success of any retail business depends on the performance of its employees. Performance, in turn, is affected greatly by the human-resource policies of the store. Therefore, store managers must give much attention to compensation, employee benefits, employee evaluation, scheduling, relocation, labor relations, and communication.

Management also must devote attention to identifying potential employees, selecting new workers, and introducing them to their new employment. The types of training provided affect how well new and experienced employees perform. Thus, successful retail managers are familiar with various methods of initial and continuous training. Many stores have in-store management development programs to prepare employees for management-level positions; some organizations also encourage employees to enroll in marketing education programs.

Supervisors are retail employees who oversee the work of other workers. They must be adept communicators who can help others improve their skills. Effective supervisors have certain characteristics, such as strong interests in human relations, people, and people's abilities. These characteristics

are important because the management of human resources can be exciting, rewarding, and, at times, frustrating. To some extent, all supervisors must plan, direct, motivate, train, control, and solve problems. The chapters of this unit deal with selected human-resource issues that affect everyone in retailing, from newly hired people to those in top management.

UNIT OUTCOMES

After studying this unit and completing the activities, you should be able to:

1. Identify compensation plans and major benefits available to retail employees
2. Describe the procedure most retail businesses follow when selecting job applicants for employment
3. List the training methods used by retailers to train new, experienced, and management personnel
4. Explain why good human-relations and communication skills are important to retail employees
5. Identify and describe the key functions performed by retail store supervisors

CHAPTER 16
Human-Resource Policies

CHAPTER OUTCOMES

When you have mastered the information provided in this chapter, you should be able to:

1. Identify the compensation plans that are used in retailing

2. Name five fringe benefits available to retail employees

3. Describe two procedures used to conduct employee evaluations

4. State the value of a flexible work schedule

5. Explain the difference between job promotions and transfers

6. State the effect of the National Labor Relations Act on certain employer activities

7. Identify three ways to maintain effective communication between employees and management

Retailing is a people-oriented business. That means the success of a retail firm depends to a great extent on how its employees deal with customers. Retailers have learned that satisfied employees are more likely to give their best efforts to the store's operation and the needs of customers. Dissatisfied workers can reduce sales volume, increase expenses, and create a poor store image.

Effective human-resource policies help to develop employee loyalty and productivity. These policies can also ensure that qualified employees will be available in the right place and at the right time. In a small store, human-resource policies usually are developed by the owner-manager. In a large retail firm, human-resource policies are likely to be developed and carried out by a separate department called the *personnel* or *human-resources department*. This department is headed by a human-resource manager who directs and enforces specific policies. Some of the more important human-resource policies concern employee compensation, benefits and services, evaluations, work schedules, employee relocation, labor relations, and communication.

COMPENSATION POLICY AND PLANS

If a store is to attract competent people, it must have a clear policy of offering wages and salaries that are competitive with similar types of jobs in nonretailing fields. A **wage** is typically earned on an hourly basis, while a **salary** is paid by the week or month. Compensation plans must be fair because the result of a poorly administered and unfair compensation policy can be a major source of employee dissatisfaction.

Several types of wage and salary plans are used to compensate retailing personnel for their efforts. It is not unusual for one store to use all these plans, one for each kind of employee. The most common plans are straight salary, salary and commission, quota, straight commission, and special incentive.

Straight-salary Plan

Many stores pay both selling and nonselling employees a definite amount of money per week or month. A flat amount is paid to the employee for the time worked and no direct attempt is made to measure an individual's productivity. This is the **straight-salary plan.** Management personnel almost always are paid a straight-salary plan with the possibility of a year-end bonus if the store's sales or profits are higher than the year before.

Salary and Commission Plan

Another widely used means of compensating salespeople is the **salary and commission plan.** Under this plan, the salesperson receives a straight salary plus an additional amount depending on the individual's sales. This additional amount, called a **commission,** is usually a percentage of the individual's sales for a certain period. Thus, a person whose sales for one week amount to $2,000 and who is paid a commission of 1 percent for all individual sales will receive a $20 commission. If the straight salary is $190, the salesperson's total pay for the week will be $210.

Quota Plan

The **quota plan** is a variation of the salary and commission plan. Under this plan, the store manager sets a definite dollar amount that a salesperson is expected to sell in a given time period. This amount is called a **quota.** If the salesperson sells more than the quota amount, the individual will receive a commission on the amount of sales above quota, plus a straight salary. A person whose quota is $7,000 and whose sales for the month are $5,500 receives no commission, only salary. If next month's sales amount to $8,000, the salesperson will receive a commission on $1,000 in addition to salary.

Straight-commission Plan

The **straight-commission plan** is preferred by capable salespeople who want to earn according to their superior abilities. Under the plan, a commission rate, such as 6 percent of sales, is set. The salesperson then receives a $6 commission for every $100 of individual sales, but no salary. The total amount earned is determined by the amount the salesperson is able to sell. To ensure that the salesperson earns enough even during slow-selling periods, a store often establishes a **drawing account.** Salespeople are paid from their individual drawing accounts at regular intervals, and the payments are charged against commissions they earn later.

Special-incentive Plans

Stores often establish special-incentive plans that supplement the plans previously mentioned. Generally, these special plans are designed to encourage employees to work harder. One special-incentive plan is the **PM (premium money).** It is a reward for selling specific items of merchandise. For example, a $1 PM may be given on each pair of a certain style of slacks to motivate salespeople to move the slacks out of stock.

Profit sharing is another type of special-incentive plan. This plan makes it possible for employees to receive a portion of store profits. Higher store profits mean an increase in the worker's income.

Some firms provide **employee stock-ownership plans.** Under these plans, each employee is given a certain number of shares of stock in the company. If the company is successful, the stocks increase in value. In some retail operations, profit-sharing and stock-ownership plans represent a sizeable portion of each employee's earnings.

Employee-benefits Policy

Employee benefits, sometimes called *fringe benefits,* are the extra rewards that retail personnel receive in addition to their regular wages or salaries. Some employee benefits, such as unemployment compensation and social security, are required by federal law. Others, such as retirement programs, may be the result of a combined effort between the store and employees, with contributions coming from both. Employers voluntarily provide many benefits to keep their present employees content and to attract new employees. Those benefits often make up nearly 32 percent of an employee's income. For years, retailers have been among the leaders in providing benefits and services for their employees. One of the most important benefits today is health insurance. A store usually pays some percentage of the premiums for hospital, medical, and dental care. Dealing with soaring medical insurance premiums has become one of the largest challenges human-resource personnel face. Life insurance is often included in fringe benefits. Group rates are usually less than individual rates even if employees must pay part of the life insurance cost.

Most retailers also give employee discounts of 10 to 33 percent on store merchandise. This practice builds goodwill. Additionally, in a clothing or department store it gives employees an opportunity to buy quality clothing that will improve their appearance.

Many large retailers provide benefits in the form of services, which include facilities and equipment for employees' social, educational, and recreational activities. These activities can range from softball and bowling teams to formal classes and group tours. Often, such activities are planned and organized by the employees themselves. Retail-store owners are usually very willing to support activities that will promote employee morale and loyalty to the store.

Some large stores maintain food-service facilities for employees where well-balanced meals are sold at lower than restaurant prices. Certain retailers may provide child care; medical, dental, and drug-abuse counseling services; and legal-aid assistance at a small cost. An increasing number of stores offer savings and annuity plans.

EMPLOYEE-EVALUATION POLICY

Most employees want their employers to let them know what is expected of them and how well they are doing their jobs. To provide such information, an employer must follow an employee-evaluation or performance-appraisal process. This process involves setting performance standards against which each employee's work may be judged. Retail managers may conduct formal or informal evaluations of employees' work performance.

Formal employee evaluations follow a definite procedure and are often conducted in large retail organizations. The formal procedure calls for regularly scheduled employee evaluations and use of standard performance-appraisal forms similar to the one shown in Illustration 16–1. Typically, appraisal forms are completed by the retail employee's immediate supervisor and a department manager or other store executive. The two ratings are compared and then discussed with the individual being evaluated. Job progress, attendance, willingness to work, attitude, suggestions for improvement, and decisions on promotions and raises are topics often discussed in evaluation sessions.

Small retail operators are more likely to use informal employee ratings and evaluations. The supervisor may offer immediate praise for good job performance and provide suggestions to improve performance. The informal procedure is an ongoing process since the employee's immediate supervisor is always in contact with that individual. Thus, a formal discussion or appraisal interview often is unnecessary. Per-

PERFORMANCE APPRAISAL

Employee's Name_____Title_____

Supervisor_____Title_____

Use the following definitions to rate the factors listed below.

1. **Unsatisfactory**—Deficient; release from job unless improved in 90 days
2. **Fair**—Below requirements for job; less than satisfactory
3. **Satisfactory**—Good; meets all job requirements as in job description; this is the BASIC STANDARD
          for rating any factor below
4. **Very good**—Superior; beyond requirements for satisfactory performance
5. **Exceptional**—Outstanding; approaching the best possible for the job

Rate the employee on each factor by writing the number (1–5) in the blank.

Factors	Descriptions	Rating (1–5)
Ability to work with others	Extent to which employee cooperates and communicates effectively with other employees and customers	_____
Use of time and scheduling	Employee's speed and effectiveness in doing what is assigned	_____
Job knowledge	Extent of employee's job information and understanding and awareness of new developments in field	_____
Judgment	Extent to which employee's decisions and actions are based on common sense and weighing of outcomes	_____
Initiative	Extent to which employee is a "self-starter" in carrying out job duties	_____
Attitude	Amount of interest, enthusiasm, and willingness to accept new duties shown in employee's work	_____
Problem solving	Extent to which employee identifies and solves problems in order to fulfill responsibilities	_____
Overall rating		_____

Use next item for employees still learning the job.

Progress	Speed with which employee is progressing	_____

Rated by_____Date_____
RATER: initial and date this form when you have discussed rating with employee:

Employee's signature_____Date_____
Signature indicates appraisal was discussed with me; it does not indicate approval or disapproval of the ratings.

Illus. 16–1 Performance appraisal forms help an employer inform employees about the quality of their work.

formance appraisal forms, if used at all, are shorter and simpler than those used in large stores.

Employee-evaluation policies are related to compensation policies. If an employee evaluation shows someone doing good work, most stores reward the individual with a raise in wages or salary. Many retailing firms give employees raises once or twice a year if performance is satisfactory. When high salary levels are reached, increases may be given less often.

WORK-SCHEDULE POLICY

What am I expected to do? How well am I doing? What will I be paid? These are important questions for retail employees. Equally important is this question: When do I work? In most cases, retail stores are open more hours than any one employee can work. For example, discount department stores, chain stores, fast-food establishments, and service stations may be open 70 to 168 hours a week. Any one employee, however, typically will work only a fraction of that time—maybe 40 or 45 hours. In fact, the work week for many retail personnel is shortening. In many stores, full-time employees are required to work only seven hours a day, five days a week.

Enough personnel must be available to provide adequate customer service during extended store hours. Doing so often requires a rather complicated employee work schedule and the employment of part-time and seasonal help. The flexible scheduling of part-time employees makes it possible to accommodate many more customers during peak periods and odd hours. Retailers are generally able to attract good part-time help, such as high school and college students, who are willing to adapt to a flexible work schedule.

RELOCATION POLICY

Few employees who remain with a retail establishment for more than several months stay in the same job or department. New jobs may be created as the company grows. Other jobs may become available due to promotions or terminations. Some employees may relocate within a store or move to different stores within a chain or branch store system. Policies governing all types of promotions and transfers must be established.

A **promotion** moves an employee into a new job with more responsibility and authority. An employee's ability and seniority are the two most important factors in determining whether that individual should receive a promotion. Most retailers prefer to fill new or vacant jobs by promoting current employees rather than hiring new ones. Promoting from within reduces the costs of hiring and training new workers. Also, a promotion policy of this kind usually increases goodwill on the part of employees. If employees know their store has a fair promotion policy and good opportunities for advancement, they are more likely to be loyal and enthusiastic workers.

A **transfer** involves the relocation of an employee to another job at about the same level of responsibility. Sometimes an employee is placed initially in a job for which she or he is not suited. A supervisor may realize that the employee would be more productive if transferred to another job. In some cases, an employee is transferred to reduce friction among employees who do not get along with each other. Managerial personnel are commonly transferred from department to department as part of training programs so that they can learn all aspects of a store's operation.

LABOR-RELATIONS POLICY

In the retailing industry, as in other businesses, certain differences of interest between management and workers are unavoidable. Store owners have the right within legislative limits to operate as they see fit. To do so, they depend on their employees to get things done. Workers know that managers depend on them. To do a good job, workers may want some control over their working conditions and compensation. Management may not agree. To deal with potential labor-management conflicts, some workers form labor unions to advance their interests.

The National Labor Relations Act—passed in 1935—prohibits employers from interfering with unions, from discriminating against union members, and from refusing to bargain with union representatives. A retailer's labor-relations policy must be based on this act. Unions negotiate most often for direct pay increases; but they also negotiate for holiday pay, vacation length and pay, insurance and health programs, provision of educational incentives, and seniority rules. The policies of both sides—retail management and labor—should seek to avoid complete work stoppage (strike or lockout) because of differences in employer and employee interests. If a store loses customers

because of labor problems, both store management and employees will suffer.

Retailing has not been a fertile field for unions because differences in management-labor interests have not been as great in retailing as in other fields. Most retail establishments are small, with high labor turnover and many workers who strive for management-level jobs. In the larger stores, where unions do exist, enlightened union leaders now recognize that a store must be profitable to offer secure jobs and adequate employee benefits. Retailers realize that bargaining with a union may reveal a valid need to change one or more employee policies.

COMMUNICATION POLICY

A major area of concern in large stores is communication among employees and between employees and management. The owner of a small store usually has fewer communication problems than an owner of a larger store. A small store retailer knows the employees by name, and employees can easily talk with the employer if they have complaints or suggestions for improving the store's operation. The large discount or department store has hundreds of employees, so it is necessary to set up definite lines of communication.

Illustration 16−2 shows that communication between employees and management can take many forms. Employees discuss their work-related problems with the supervisor, and the supervisor relays the information to management. When any action on a problem is taken, the information is given first to the supervisor who then relays it to the affected employee(s). Communica-

Illus. 16-2   Information is communicated in many different ways between employees and management in large retail stores.

tion among managers usually is conducted through reports and memorandums or committee meetings and conferences.

If a store is unionized, employees can report work-related problems to a union representative. In a unionized store, executives should avoid taking action on a worker's complaint until the employee's supervisor also has an opportunity to present her or his view of the problem.

Illus. 16-3   Direct communication between supervisors and employees is often used to relay store policies and procedures.

Employee manuals are a helpful means of presenting company policies and procedures to all employees. Bulletin boards placed in obvious spots, such as near the time clock or in the employees' lounges, are also useful tools for passing along information. Some large department stores print a weekly newspaper or monthly magazine that contains articles about employees and other topics of general interest.

Summary

Retailers depend on store personnel to help assure the success of the business. Therefore, human-resource policies that develop employee loyalty and productivity are important. One such policy involves the compensation plans offered to workers. Typical plans include straight salary, salary and commission, quota, straight commission, and special incentive. An employee-benefits policy also provides employees with rewards, such as retirement programs, health and life insurance, merchandise discounts, food services, as well as social, educational, and recreational activities. Many retailers have personnel policies that deal with employee evaluations and relocation decisions. A policy related to management-worker relationships often involves a labor union. Such a policy usually includes statements about the importance of open communication between management and employees and suggests ways in which this can be accomplished.

Review

1. State the compensation plans that are used in retailing.
2. Identify five fringe benefits available to retail employees.
3. Name and describe two procedures used to conduct employee evaluations.
4. Explain the value of a flexible work schedule.
5. State the difference between job promotions and transfers.
6. Describe the effect of the National Labor Relations Act on certain employer activities.
7. List three ways to maintain effective communication between employees and management.

Terms

The following terms were introduced in this chapter. Write a separate sentence correctly using each new term.

commission   PM (premium money)
drawing account   profit sharing
employee benefits   promotion
employee stock-ownership plan   quota

quota plan   straight-salary plan
salary   transfer
salary and commission plan   wage
straight-commission plan

Discuss

1. Why should the development of effective human-resource policies be a priority for retail store managers?
2. Why are there several forms of retail compensation plans rather than one plan for all retail stores?
3. Why do retail employers offer benefits to their employees?
4. Of what value are employee evaluations to the employer? to the employee?
5. Why do certain differences of interest exist between management and workers?

Problem Solving

1. For several years, Carlos Alvarez has been responsible for all employee hiring at a local discount department store. The owners of this rapidly expanding business now believe it is time to establish specific human-resource policies. Carlos has been given this responsibility and is seeking your help in identifying areas that should be considered. What policy areas do you suggest that are not included in this chapter?
2. Tatsu Umeki has been employed on a part-time basis in a local department store while attending college. She will be graduating soon and has two retail job offers to consider. Both positions offer similar opportunities and benefits. However, one offer is on a straight-salary plan while the other is on a straight-commission plan. What factors would you recommend Tatsu review before making her decision?
3. You are employed as a personnel assistant in a large discount department store. Ellie Smythe, human-resource manager, has assigned you the responsibility of designing an appraisal form for use in evaluating new salespersons after they have been employed for three months. Identify aspects of the job you would evaluate and give reasons for your choices.

CHAPTER 17

Locating and Selecting Employees

CHAPTER OUTCOMES

When you have mastered the information provided in this chapter, you should be able to:

1. Describe two laws that affect the hiring of retail employees

2. Identify sources that retailers use to find potential employees

3. Explain the difference between a job analysis and a job description

4. State why most employers require potential employees to complete an application form

5. Describe information that should be contained in a résumé

6. State the importance of a letter of application and how it should be written

7. State the purpose of an employment interview and describe how to prepare for, conduct, and close an interview

8. State two benefits of formally introducing newly hired employees to their jobs

Jobs in retailing can be found almost anywhere at any time. This does not mean that employers will hire anyone who asks for work. On the contrary, most retailers prefer to employ workers who (1) have initiative, (2) are willing to work for their pay, (3) are team players and will be loyal to the store, and (4) like working with people in a variety of business situations. Decisions about how many and which individuals should be employed and when they should work usually result from a review of store needs. This review examines store policies and goals and the resources needed to reach those goals. Long store hours, employee turnover, and rapid growth have forced many retailers to continually seek new, well-trained employees. Thus, finding qualified employees is a key responsibility of most retail-store operators.

When making decisions about whom to hire, employers must consider many laws. For instance, the Civil Rights Act of 1964 prohibits discrimination in hiring on the basis of race, national origin, sex, and religion. The Age Discrimination Act of 1967 prohibits discrimination in hiring on the basis of age. Federal laws also prohibit discrimination against the physically disabled.

LOCATING POTENTIAL EMPLOYEES

Retail employers who are successful in locating qualified employees use many strategies to find the personnel they need. Typical among these strategies are (1) placing help-wanted signs in store windows or other heavy-traffic areas in the store;

(2) placing advertisements in local and regional news media (newspapers and television); (3) obtaining referrals from current employees who know of and can recommend interested applicants; (4) offering promotions and transfers; (5) consulting with state and private employment agencies that provide up-to-date listings of persons seeking work in retailing; (6) speaking with high-school and college career-planning and placement offices that make it possible for employers to have direct contact with students seeking full- and part-time employment; (7) contacting marketing education programs that provide in-school and on-the-job training for enrolled students and are excellent sources for employers seeking qualified and well-trained employees; and (8) participating in job fairs.

Regardless of the kinds of employment strategies a retail employer might choose, the store's image in the community is probably the best means of attracting new personnel. Retailers who have a reputation for treating their employees fairly, providing satisfactory employee services, and offering chances for advancement will easily attract new employees. Employers who project a negative image will not.

SELECTING JOB APPLICANTS

Retailers generally follow a fairly simple set of employee-selection procedures. These procedures make up a selection process designed to help a store owner pick the best-qualified person for a particular job. Job analysis, application forms, résumés, letters of application, and personal interviews are some of the tools that employers use in the selection process.

Job Analysis

Sometimes in the selection process employers make decisions too quickly. As a result, mistakes occur and the wrong individual is hired. One way for a retailer to avoid making such a mistake is to develop a list of key requirements for each job opening. For example, a group of retail department-store managers were asked to determine key requirements for the job of department-manager trainee. They agreed on the following: (1) neat personal appearance, (2) willingness to relocate, (3) capability of learning many details, (4) above-average communication skills, (5) dependability, (6) interest in the job, (7) physical fitness, (8) effective management of personal affairs, (9) desire to succeed, and (10) record of honesty.

While general information of this kind is helpful, some employers prefer to develop their own lists of specific job requirements. Specific requirements are best developed through a job analysis. A **job analysis** is a detailed study of a particular job that includes (1) job title; (2) location of the store where the job is performed; (3) job duties and responsibilities; (4) experience and education required; and (5) pay, hours of work, and promotion possibilities. After a job analysis is completed, a summary called a **job description** is written. A job description gives an employer a clear notion of the type of employee needed. A job de-

Illus. 17–1 Retailers often place advertisements in the help-wanted section of newspapers in an effort to attract qualified job applicants.

scription also helps the applicant understand what the job entails. An example of a job description for an advertising manager follows: Responsible for staffing, developing, and supervising full copywriting and layout operations. Interacts daily with senior merchandising managers. Requires extensive (minimum three years) apparel experience and knowledge of direct-mail and newspaper-insert techniques.

Application Form

Most retailers require all job applicants to fill out an application form such as the one shown in Illustration 17–2. From an application an employer gets vital information such as the applicant's name, address, phone number, type of employment desired, educational background, work experience, and personal references' names and addresses. Receipt of a completed application form is often the first step in the employment process. It can also be the last step since some employers use the completed application form as a final check to match the applicant's qualifications with those contained in a job description. Some employers interview all who apply. Others select for interviews only those individuals whose application form shows the qualifications that meet the store's immediate needs. Even when no openings currently exist, a retailer may decide to interview good prospects for possible future employment.

In some stores, no employment is final until the applicant has passed a written test and/or a physical examination. Stores try to avoid hiring people who may not have the basic skills needed to handle a certain job or who are unable to work long hours, for example. Pre-employment tests can help pro-

tect both the store and the prospective employee from mistakes in hiring.

Résumé

In addition to the completed application form, many employers appreciate receiving a summary of the job applicant's background. This summary is prepared by the applicant. It is called a **résumé** or *personal data sheet* and contains personal, educational, and occupational facts. The résumé is an important and useful document for both the employer and the prospective retail worker. The applicant either mails the résumé to potential employers along with a letter of application or hand delivers it at the employment interview. Whether or not a person is hired for a certain job, the résumé usually becomes a part of the applicant's file. Then, when the next job vacancy occurs, the retailer can check such files for possible candidates.

Information for the Résumé.
Employers expect the information in a résumé to be relevant to a particular job and to be fairly detailed. For instance, employers like to know the kind of job an applicant is seeking as well as the applicant's long-range career plans. Recognizing one's immediate readiness for a job and having a career goal are signs of maturity that are most appreciated by employers.

In giving information about education, employers generally prefer that the applicant start with the most recent schooling and go back in time. It is usually unnecessary to go back further than high school. Any diplomas or degrees earned should be mentioned. Applicants may wish to list specific courses they have taken, especially if

Employment Application

NAME	LAST	FIRST	MIDDLE	SOCIAL SECURITY NUMBER
PRESENT ADDRESS	STREET			HOME PHONE NUMBER
CITY	STATE	ZIP CODE		BUSINESS PHONE NUMBER
PERMANENT ADDRESS (if different from above)	STREET			
CITY	STATE	ZIP CODE		

EDUCATION

Type of School	Name and Address of School	Last Year Completed	Did you Graduate?	Major Course of Study and Degree Granted
High School		1 2 3 4	☐ Yes ☐ No	
College		1 2 3 4	☐ Yes ☐ No	
Other (specify)		1 2 3 4	☐ Yes ☐ No	

EMPLOYMENT HISTORY

Have you ever worked for us before? ☐ Yes ☐ No   If yes, from _____ to_____

May we contact your present employer? ☐ Yes ☐ No   May we contact <u>you</u> at your present employer's? ☐ Yes ☐ No

Please list employment history in chronological order with most recent position first.

Present or Last Employer_____ Name & Title of Supervisor_____

Address_____ Phone No. _____

Dates: From _____ to _____ Salary $ _____ $ _____
              (month and year)   (month and year)   (beginning)   (end)

Starting Position _____ Ending Position _____

Reason for Leaving_____

Previous Employer_____ Name & Title of Supervisor_____

Address_____ Phone No. _____

Dates: From _____ to _____ Salary $ _____ · $ _____
              (month and year)   (month and year)   (beginning)   (end)

Starting Position _____ Ending Position _____

Reason for Leaving_____

REFERENCES

Please list persons whom we may contact who know your qualifications.

Name	Address	Phone No.	Occupation

Illus. 17–2   An application form is a good way for an employer to get information about an applicant's job qualifications.

these courses are related to the job in question. The applicant who earned high grades should also mention that fact. Most employers are also interested in any extracurricular activities in which the applicant has participated, particularly if they involved leadership.

When giving information about previous work experience, employers also expect the applicant to start with the most recent job and go back in time. Descriptions of work experiences should be brief and clear. They must give the potential employer a picture of the applicant's past responsibilities and job activities.

Businesspeople prefer that an applicant list a variety of types of references. However, four or five personal references are sufficient. For example, one reference should provide information about the applicant's work in school, another about work on a job, and another about character. No person's name should be used as a reference without his or her permission. Complete titles, addresses, and telephone numbers of references should be given so that the employer can contact them easily.

If a résumé is to be sent to a large number of potential employers, it is better to indicate "References provided upon request" than to list the references.

Appearance of the Résumé. There is no standard form that employers require for setting up a résumé. The example shown in Illustration 17–3 is just one of many possible formats. Résumés should always be typewritten. Similar to effective advertisements, the résumé should be well-balanced and neat. A one-page résumé is easier for the employer to handle than one that is two or three pages long. It is preferable, though, to use two or three pages than

to crowd information onto one page and leave out important data.

There should be margins of at least one inch of white space at the top, bottom, and sides of each page of the résumé. The first page should have the title *Résumé* or *Personal Data Sheet* centered at the top. Beneath the title, the applicant's name, address, and telephone number should appear; these, too, may be centered. The topics of *education, experience, extracurricular activities,* and *references* should appear as headings on the résumé. The headings may be underlined or written in all capital letters to set them apart from other material. Most persons prefer to use short statements rather than complete sentences in their résumés. Complete sentences may be used if space permits, but one should be consistent, using either complete sentences or brief statements.

Application Letter

Normally a letter of application accompanies a résumé. An application letter is one of the most important letters a person writes. It presents the individual to a prospective employer. The objective of an application letter is to sell the applicant's services. Thus, it must first attract favorable attention through its physical appearance. The contents of the letter should be planned not only to gain favorable attention but also to develop interest in the applicant and to create a desire for her or his services. Finally, the letter should induce action on the part of the employer.

Whether an applicant gets a job may depend upon how well the application letter is written. If a potential employer receives a poorly written, unattractive letter, he or she

RESUME

Lawrence C. Graves
3973 Piccadilly Square
Noblesville, IN 46060-3125
(317/639-7435)

OBJECTIVES

Part-time salesperson leading to full-time selling after business college. Career in retail sales management (menswear and general merchandise).

EDUCATION

Graduate, 19--, Willow Grove High School, Noblesville, IN 46060-3347
Marketing Education Program
Related subjects studied in high school:

Merchandising—2 years	Business Law—1 semester
Selling —1 year	Keyboarding—1 year
Accounting—1 year	Economics—1 year
Business English—1 year	Advertising—1 semester

STUDENT ACTIVITIES

Treasurer, Junior Class
Advertising Editor, High School Yearbook
Member, DECA

WORK EXPERIENCE

Stockkeeper, Elder's Discount House, 15 hours a week for 3 months. Duties included bringing goods from stockroom to sales floor, ticketing items, and housekeeping.
Salesperson, Hogan's Hardware, summer 19-- and Saturdays from 19-- to 19--. Duties included selling, stocking, and display.

REFERENCES

Mr. Robert Goodall	Dr. B. R. Albin
General Manager	Vocational Counselor
Elder's Discount House	Willow Grove High School
3242 Booker Road	Noblesville, IN 46060-3347
Noblesville, IN 46060-3236	(317/638-8424)
(317/638-8535)	
Ms. Ellen Schroeder	Mr. George Hogan
Marketing Education Program Coordinator	Manager
Willow Grove High School	Hogan's Hardware
Noblesville, IN 46060-3347	1147 Mission Road
(317/638-8535)	Noblesville, IN 46060-3347
	(317/638-3809)

Illus. 17–3   A résumé should contain specific information that supports the applicant's qualifications for the job.

will probably not consider the applicant for employment. Thus, the letter must be carefully planned, written, and arranged on a page. A correct letter style should be used, and all the rules of English grammar and punctuation should be applied. Each letter should be a high-quality original—never a photocopy.

Application letters, such as the one shown in Illustration 17–4, typically contain three or four paragraphs. The first paragraph should be designed to attract the employer's attention. It should indicate the job in question, the candidate's educational and occupational experience, and what the applicant can do for the potential employer. Other paragraphs can expand on the opening statements and stress job qualifications. Also, if a résumé is enclosed, attention should be drawn to it. The last paragraph of the application letter should be a direct request for an interview at the employer's convenience. If an interview has already been scheduled, the closing paragraph should thank the employer for that appointment.

Some job applicants think they must make their letters unique, so they try to be clever. They may use anecdotes, questions, or breezy language in an effort to attract interest. Letters using such unnatural approaches are seldom successful; few businesspeople finish reading them. Most employers are impressed by a natural-sounding, straightforward letter that gives useful information about the job applicant.

Employment Interview

Employers generally require a personal interview with prospective employees. From the employer's point of view, the purpose of an interview is to learn or confirm valuable information about an applicant. For an applicant, an interview is a chance to sell oneself and to learn more about the job and the employer. During a job interview, an employer evaluates personal appearance, posture, grammar, voice, and job knowledge. An applicant should prepare for a personal interview as carefully as a salesperson prepares to meet a customer.

Before an Interview. An applicant should be careful about personal appearance. Lack of personal grooming or carelessness in dress will greatly reduce chances for employment. One also should find out as much as possible about the prospective employer and the business in advance of the interview. An applicant should be prepared to tell how he or she can fit into the prospective employer's business. Also, an applicant should decide what information he or she wants to obtain in the interview and prepare appropriate questions.

During an Interview. Sometimes an interview is simply a casual conversation, but it is a conversation with a purpose. It must give the interviewer and interviewee needed information. The following are typical questions that an interviewer may ask an applicant. The applicant should give a short, clear answer to each question.

1. What work have you done?
2. Did you use any special tools or equipment?
3. How would you handle a difficult customer?
4. Have you done any volunteer work?
5. Do you have any hobbies or special interests?

3973 Piccadilly Square
Noblesville, IN   46060-3125
April 24, 19--

Mr. Willard J. Robinson
Personnel Manager
Closson's
401 Race Street
Indianapolis, IN   46230-4236

Dear Mr. Robinson:

My retailing instructor, Ms. Schroeder, suggested I write you concerning
a sales trainee position in your Men's Department. I will be a senior next
year and have had prior retail experience. With this background, I
believe I have those qualities you are seeking in a new employee.

Currently, I am enrolled in the Marketing Education Program at Willow
Grove High School. My classes have included basic retailing principles
and skills, and I have consistently earned A's and B's in these classes.
The program has also included a model store, where I took rotations in
the stockroom, on the sales register, and on the floor meeting with
customers (other students and teachers). I am presently finishing a three-
month intern experience at Elder's Discount House.

More information about my qualifications is on my résumé, which is
enclosed. I will be available for full-time employment starting June 11,
following graduation from Willow Grove.

At your convenience, I would like to talk with you about my
qualifications. May I have an interview? You may call Ms. Schroeder's
ME office (555-8535) to leave a message for me. Also, you can reach
me at home (555-7435) in the evenings.

Sincerely yours,

Lawrence C. Graves

Lawrence C. Graves

Enclosure

Illus. 17-4   The letter of application should attract attention, develop interest, create desire, and induce action.

6.   What education have you had?
7.   What is your goal for the future?
8.   Why do you want to work for us?
9.   What kind of work do you want?
10. How much in salary or wages do you expect to earn?

In answering such questions or in giving a personal history, an interviewee should speak clearly and briefly. He or she should avoid elaborate details but respond beyond giving a simple "Yes" or "No". The interviewee should take care not to air personal problems. More important than the answers themselves is the impression that the applicant creates. Keep in mind that an interview is not just a one-way flow of information. The applicant should also feel free to ask questions of the employer about the job, training, hours, and business policies and procedures.

After an Interview. A personal interview may end with an applicant getting a job. In that case, the newly hired employee should ask where and when to report for work and then thank the interviewer in a businesslike manner and leave immediately.

The interviewer may close the conversation with a promise to contact the applicant later. If this occurs, the applicant should thank the interviewer for her or his time and leave promptly. It is appropriate to ask when such a call can be expected. However, it is often a good idea not to wait for the employer to call. An applicant who is persistent, courteous, and tactful can make a good impression. A letter, telephone call, or return visit to offer thanks for the interview stresses the applicant's interest in the job and keeps his or her name in the mind of an employer. When an appropriate job is open later, the unhired applicant who has shown interest and demonstrated courtesy will be remembered.

Introducing New Employees

Formally introducing new workers to the job is an important step once they have been located and selected. Meeting other workers and seeing the work area gives a new employee a sense of belonging. An individual who is helped to fit in can be more relaxed and confident during the first day at the store. Such a person usually finds long-term satisfaction in a job.

Summary   Retailers prefer to hire workers who (1) have initiative, (2) are willing to work for their pay, (3) are team players and will be loyal to the store, and (4) like working with people in a variety of situations. Locating potential employees who meet these qualifications is a key responsibility of most retail-store operators. To be successful in their search, retail employers follow a fairly simple set of new-employee selection procedures. These procedures start with the writing of a job description based on a thorough job analysis. Applications are then sought from job seekers who may submit letters of application and résumés or personal data sheets. Qualified applicants are interviewed and the final selection is made. Job candidates who know how to prepare for an interview and what to do during and after an interview have the best chance of being offered employment.

Review

1. Identify two federal laws that can affect the hiring of retail employees.
2. List four strategies that retailers can use to locate potential employees.
3. State the main difference between a job analysis and a job description.
4. Explain why most employers require potential employees to complete an application form.
5. List two types of information that should be included in a résumé or personal data sheet.
6. Explain the importance of a letter of application in obtaining employment.
7. State two purposes of an employment interview and what the candidate should do to prepare for that interview.
8. State three benefits of formally introducing newly hired employees to their jobs.

Terms

The following terms were introduced in this chapter. Write a separate sentence correctly using each new term.

job analysis   résumé (personal data sheet)
job description

Discuss

1. Why is locating qualified employees a key responsibility of retail-store operators?
2. Of what value is a properly prepared résumé in the search for retail employment?
3. Why should application letters be composed to gain favorable attention?
4. What kinds of questions is a retailer likely to ask the job applicant?
5. What should an applicant do to prepare for an interview?
6. What are some questions an applicant may want to ask during a job interview?

Problem
Solving

1. Lydia Nestor is interviewing for a salesperson position in the children's wear department of a locally owned specialty store. She is anxious to obtain this position so she asks you for suggestions on how to prepare for the interview. How would you assist her?

2. You are a trainee in the personnel department of a nationally known discount furniture store. The store manager plans to hire eight full- and part-time employees, and the personnel manager has given you the responsibility of locating qualified candidates. How would you accomplish this task?

3. A classmate has asked you to help him or her write a letter of application for a customer-services position. This position is available in a food store in a large shopping center. Referring to other texts dealing with job application material, develop an outline of specific information to include in the application letter.

CHAPTER 18

Training Employees

CHAPTER OUTCOMES

When you have mastered the information provided in this chapter, you should be able to:

1. Explain the benefits of training to employers, customers, and employees

2. Identify the major groups of employees who receive retail training

3. List the types of subjects that are presented in general and specific store training sessions

4. Describe some of the methods used in initial retail training sessions

5. Explain why continuous retail training is necessary and identify some topics frequently covered in such programs

6. Name some of the methods used in continuous training sessions

7. Identify job competencies that must be learned in retail-management training programs

8. Define the term *Marketing Education* and describe the role of DECA in it

189

Everyone gains when retail employees are properly trained—the customer, the employer, and the employees. Training can help employees become more effective by increasing their job skills and keeping their morale at a high level. Well-trained personnel also can increase an employer's chance to realize a profit by reducing supervisory costs and keeping worker turnover at a minimum. Also, properly trained employees bring about improved service, increased customer satisfaction, and more store loyalty.

In a small store, the manager or owner is usually responsible for training employees. Often this instruction is informal—new workers are expected to learn by observing other employees. Large retail firms are more likely to have centralized training departments that are responsible for all employee-education programs. Closed circuit television, videotapes, individualized instruction, and full-time instructor-trainers are typically used to train large numbers of retail employees.

Retailers who support costly training programs do so because they recognize the value of well-trained personnel. To develop effective training practices and procedures, a retailer must identify persons to be trained, the instruction needed, and the most effective method or methods of providing the necessary training.

RETAIL EMPLOYEES TO BE TRAINED

Retail training is offered to three major groups of full-time store employees: (1) **inexperienced personnel**—new employees who have not had prior experience in retailing, (2) **new, experienced personnel**—employees who have had prior retailing experience with another employer, and (3) **experienced personnel**—long-term employees who require regular retraining. In addition, special types of training programs are available for new and experienced part-time employees. Retailers also provide highly organized programs called *development programs* for their management personnel.

Some retailers conduct training programs for new and experienced nonselling personnel. These personnel might include stock clerks, office workers, security officers, and other employees whose duties are important to a store's overall operation. Normally, there are not enough nonselling employees hired at any one time to justify formal training classes for them. Most employers, however, recognize the importance of some form of training for their support personnel. They know that customer dissatisfaction can result from errors made by any untrained employee.

Needless to say, the training needs of each group of employees are different. Therefore, various types of training are used.

INITIAL TRAINING FOR NEW PERSONNEL

The amount of time devoted to the training of new employees varies from store to store. Even in those stores where little attention is given to formal training needs, a commitment to teaching new employees is evident. Progressive retailers, however, approach the formal training of new employees in two phases. Phase 1 usually involves the presentation of information about the store's general operation and basic job skills; phase 2 deals with specific job preparation.

The following topics are often handled in phase 1 training sessions:

1. Personnel policies regarding dress, employee discounts, pay and work schedules, and absences from work
2. Operation of sales registers, handling of various sales forms, and basic selling techniques
3. Basic business organization; policies and procedures for seeking help with job tasks and job-related problems
4. Review of the store's merchandise lines, including the various kinds of products sold and their locations in the store
5. Error prevention and where to seek assistance when it is needed
6. Customer relations policies, including customer service, merchandise returns, and customer complaints

When new employees have unique job responsibilities, specific training information related to their job needs should be presented. Phase 2 training sessions for sales personnel typically involve the following:

1. A detailed explanation of the duties and responsibilities of the job
2. Information about stock arrangements and merchandise-display techniques in a particular department
3. Specific product information, including major selling points and methods of answering customer questions and overcoming objections

Illus. 18–1   The thorough preparation of personnel can result in customer satisfaction and increased store profits.

4. Techniques for closing a sale and providing follow-up services

The main objective of an initial training program is assuring that new employees get a proper start. Many retail organizations believe that the proper training of new personnel is key for future business success. Care must be taken when selecting training methods for new retail employees. The choice of a method or methods depends on the individuals to be trained, the instructional materials to be presented, and whether the training is to be informal or formal. Several of the most commonly used methods for initial retail training are summarized here.

Lecture-Discussion Method

The lecture-discussion method allows a trainer to cover a large amount of information in a relatively short time. Store policies, rules, and procedures are presented with this formal method. Very often, new employees are given printed materials to follow during the presentation. Normally, time is allowed for trainees to ask questions before and after the discussion. The lecturer then leads a group discussion.

Demonstration-Practice Method

Training sessions involving the use of the formal demonstration-practice method are particularly helpful when trainees are learning to perform specific tasks, such as displaying merchandise, wrapping packages, recording credit charges, and fitting clothes. First, the trainer demonstrates the correct way to perform the task. Then, each new employee is required to practice the task until the trainer is satisfied with the worker's performance. When several tasks have been learned, trainees may be required to perform the tasks separately or in a particular order.

Computer-assisted Instruction (CAI)

Computer-assisted instruction relies on the use of specially designed software packages and a computer to provide step-by-step instruction in various retailing tasks. CAI, which is a formal training method, is particularly valuable for teaching such skills as processing charge transactions and refunds and following check-cashing procedures. CAI allows an employee to tackle new tasks as rapidly or as slowly as the individual wishes.

Illus. 18–2   Sponsor-led demonstration-practice training sessions help trainees learn to perform specific tasks.

Sponsor Method

Some retailers rely entirely on the sponsor method for training new employees. In this informal approach, it is the responsibility of the sponsor (experienced worker) to see to it that the trainee (inexperienced worker) receives instruction and practice in all phases of the job for which he or she has been hired. The success of the sponsor method depends almost entirely on the effectiveness of the person selected as the sponsor. Besides job skills, a sponsor must have good teaching skills and treat the new employees with tact, patience, and understanding. New employees must learn facts and procedures from their sponsors.

Sink-or-Swim Approach

The sink-or-swim approach is not really a training method; instead, it is the lack of a method. Some retailers place new, inexperienced workers in situations where they must learn on their own; in other words, they must sink or swim. Each new worker is expected to develop job skills by watching and listening to other employees while trying to perform the job. Everyone loses when the too-informal sink-or-swim approach is used. The employee loses the satisfaction that comes from doing a job well. The customer loses the services that knowledgeable employees provide them. The employer loses profits as dissatisfied customers avoid the store. The sink-or-swim "method" is best forgotten.

CONTINUOUS TRAINING FOR EXPERIENCED PERSONNEL

At times, the educational needs of experienced workers are overlooked while the retailer focuses on new-employee training programs. This situation can cause experienced workers to become careless in their jobs. Morale also becomes a problem as poor attitudes toward the employer, the job, and the store's customers develop rapidly. To maintain a staff of quality personnel, continuous training is needed for everyone on the staff. Among the most frequent topics covered in continuous retail training programs are the following:

1. Features and customer benefits of major items of merchandise
2. Advanced selling and merchandising techniques
3. Prevention of common errors in handling various sales transactions
4. Changes in store policies, rules, and regulations

The training methods described for preparing new workers can be effective for experienced personnel as well. Leading retail-store operators suggest that individual supervision plus departmental and storewide meetings can provide opportunities to use several other proven training methods. A brief description of some of these methods follows.

Case Study

The case-study method is one way to assist experienced employees in developing their ability to deal with problem situations. A difficult imaginary problem is presented to the training group. The members of the group are then asked to discuss the problem. The discussion centers on naming the facts of the problem, identifying likely causes, and presenting possible solutions. Solutions may be identified by the group through discussions of personal experience or brainstorming, for example. Consequences of each solution are considered. Then, the trainees together choose the best solution to the case.

Role-playing

Role-playing is an effective strategy for dealing with problem-solving situations. A store may, for example, be losing sales because salespeople are overlooking opportunities to suggest additional merchandise to customers. To help solve this problem, role playing may be used in a mock selling situation. One employee acts as a customer and another as the salesperson who portrays suggestion-selling techniques. Following the role-playing, the training group reviews the actions of the participants and discusses ways of improving the portrayed sales techniques.

Brainstorming

Brainstorming is a challenging and somewhat different approach to the training of experienced retail employees. A group of salespersons may, for example, be asked, "What do you think is the most effective way to demonstrate this new product?" Each participant is encouraged to use her or his imagination and to suggest any ideas that come to mind. No limitations are set and all suggestions are recorded without being judged good or right or possible. A shorter list of suggested solutions is presented to the store's management for possible action. Brainstorming, as a training method, allows employees to learn from each other.

MANAGEMENT-DEVELOPMENT PROGRAMS

For many years, family ownership and management dominated the field of retailing. Family-owned businesses typically had little interest in formally hiring and training management personnel. Most large department stores and chain stores now see the competitive advantage of having well-trained department managers, store managers, and top executives. Most retail leaders think that management-development programs are needed to attract high-quality managers of retail operations.

The content of management-development programs varies depending on needs within each store. However, basic management principles and required job competencies are the same everywhere. To begin, management trainees need to be fully exposed to all aspects of the selling function. Practical sales experience together with sales-register operation skills and knowledge of selling techniques are absolute necessities for anyone wanting to be a retail manager.

An orientation to other store functions, such as store operations, personnel, and control, makes up a major part of many management-development programs. Instruction in these areas is usually accomplished through lectures, demonstrations, group tours, and videotapes. Job rotation is a common way of organizing management training. A trainee works in one retail job for a few weeks or months and then rotates to another job in the store. Job rotation continues until the trainee has experienced all of the functional areas of retailing.

As the management trainee progresses through a development program, in-depth

Illus. 18–3 Many retailers hire students enrolled in Marketing Education programs. ME students make excellent employees.

instruction in such subjects as merchandising, sales promotion, display, and customer services takes on greater meaning. To become successful managers, trainees must also develop supervisory, leadership, communication, and motivational skills. Following management training, one normally can expect to become an assistant buyer or department manager. Many stores provide additional training and development to help these individuals become store managers or executives.

MARKETING EDUCATION (ME) PROGRAMS

Marketing Education (ME) represents a cooperative effort between local businesses and educational institutions. The purpose of ME is to provide quality retail training for high-school and post-secondary students. In most cases, ME students are also part-time retail employees. Their training involves formal in-school instruction directly related to on-the-job experiences at a store that participates in the program. ME

has proved to be an excellent source of well-qualified workers for the retailers that participate. Many businesses that could not otherwise provide training opportunities for their employees have taken advantage of the opportunity that local Marketing Education programs offer.

One important aspect of the Marketing Education program is the National Association of **DECA.** This student organization provides opportunities for its members to participate in a variety of job enrichment activities. DECA activities supplement and support business training that local schools and businesses offer. Examples of the learning experiences DECA members receive are the competitive events conducted annually on local, state, and national levels. Competition allows club members to demonstrate their knowledge, attitudes, and skills in various competencies. Career areas such as general-merchandise, apparel and accessories, hospitality and tourism, vehicle and petroleum, finance and credit, and restaurant services are covered in these competitive events. DECA also provides extensive leadership-development activities. The main goal of Marketing Education programs is to educate and train qualified workers for successful marketing careers.

Summary

Everyone—the customer, the employer, and the employee—benefits when retail employees are well trained. Retail training is usually provided for three major groups of employees: (1) inexperienced personnel, (2) new, experienced personnel, and (3) experienced personnel. In addition, training programs called *management-development programs* are available to supervisory and management personnel. Training for all new personnel includes the lecture-discussion method, the demonstration-practice method, computer-assisted

instruction (CAI), the sponsor method, and the sink or swim approach. Case study, role-playing, and brainstorming methods are
used to train experienced employees. An excellent source of quality
candidates for full- and part-time retailing positions are Marketing
Education programs operated by various educational institutions.

*R*eview

1. Name some advantages to an employer of having well-trained retail employees.
2. List three groups of employees who receive retail training.
3. Identify five subjects that are often presented in general (phase 1)
   store training sessions.
4. Name three topics that are typically covered in specialized (phase
   2) store training sessions for sales personnel.
5. List and describe four methods commonly used in conducting
   initial retail training programs.
6. Explain why continuous retail training is important.
7. List four topics often covered in continuous training programs
   and identify three methods used to present these topics.
8. Name four job competencies that must be covered in retail man-
   agement-training programs.
9. Define *Marketing Education* and describe the role of DECA in
   this program.

*T*erms

The following terms were introduced in this chapter. Write a
separate sentence correctly using each new term.

DECA	Marketing Education (ME)
experienced personnel	new, experienced personnel
inexperienced personnel	

*D*iscuss

1. Why do differences exist in the kinds of retail-store training programs offered to employees?
2. What methods seem to be most effective in conducting initial retail training programs. Why?
3. Why do some retailers consider management-development programs a necessity?
4. Why is a Marketing Education program an excellent source of
   well-trained retail personnel?

Problem
Solving

1. You have been employed as a training assistant by a discount chain store soon to open in a new shopping center. Your immediate task is to organize a one-day training session for 50 part-time salespeople. What topics would you recommend be covered? What would be the most effective methods of presenting the material?

2. LeeAnn Richards has been thinking about enrolling in the Marketing Education program offered in the high school she attends. She is interested in a career in retailing, but she is not sure the program will help her attain that goal. Identify some ways the ME program may help LeeAnn.

3. Oscar Diaz has been appointed manager of the sporting-goods department in a fashionable department store. Most department employees are experienced workers. Oscar notices a morale problem seemingly caused by personality conflicts among workers. Management has given him approval to do what is needed to improve the situation. Since there is no formal training program available, Oscar decides that he will start one. As a member of the department, you are asked to suggest topics to be covered and means of presenting each topic. What suggestions will you make? Give reasons for each of your recommendations.

CHAPTER 19

Working with Others

CHAPTER OUTCOMES

When you have mastered the information provided in this chapter, you should be able to:

1. Explain why working effectively with others is an essential skill in retailing

2. Define the term *human relations*

3. Define the term *personality*

4. List four positive attitudes

5. Identify five ways an individual can contribute to teamwork

6. Explain the difference between passive and active listening

7. Name five guidelines for developing active listening

8. List three guidelines for both spoken and written messages

Sue Lowery, a salesperson for Hampton Department Store located in Southgate Mall, has over 300 job-related contacts in a typical working day. Each of these contacts represents an interaction between Sue and another person. In each contact, there is some form of communication. While most contacts are person to person, some are by telephone, some by computer mail, some by FAX (facsimile machine), and others in written form. About a third of Sue's contacts are with customers, another third are with other employees of Hampton Department Store, and the remaining third are with persons such as suppliers and employees from other businesses. A contact with fellow employees may consist of a simple "Good morning" to the security guard when she enters the building or a 30-minute discussion with the sportswear buyer who is presenting new merchandise to the department staff.

Retailing is a people-oriented business. Some retail workers—managers, buyers, and salespeople such as Sue—are in high-contact positions. Other retail workers, such as stockkeepers, may have fewer daily contacts, but their interactions are equally important. The ability of all retail employees to work effectively with others is essential for a productive retail business. Harmonious relationships among people do not occur automatically. Each worker, such as Sue, must learn and use the skills that make contacts not only pleasant but also effective.

Skills in listening, speaking, and writing are primary. The basis for developing these skills is sensitivity to the viewpoints and feelings of others. The purpose of this chapter is to explore the skills that are needed for working well with others in a retail setting.

HUMAN RELATIONS

Human relations is the study of behavior of individuals in personal contacts. If people were all alike, behaving in the same way, human-relations skills would be simple to acquire. But people are not alike. Each person is unique.

Basic Needs

All of us have basic physical and emotional needs that are inborn or derived from our experiences. Throughout our lives, we attempt to meet or satisfy these physical and emotional needs.

Physical needs are made up of survival needs and safety needs. Survival needs include food, clothing, shelter, rest, and activity. Thus, workers must earn enough money to buy adequate food, clothes, and housing; have breaks and time off for relaxation; and have tasks that require movement and mental alertness. Safety needs include the needs to feel safe and secure. Thus, people require a workplace where they will not be injured or become ill.

Emotional needs include the need to be accepted by others (to belong), the need to be recognized for accomplishments, the need to achieve personal goals, and the need to feel good about oneself. Sue Lowery is a good example of an employee whose emotional needs are met through her job at the department store. Sue is pleasant with her coworkers so that they accept her into their group. She performs especially well those parts of her job that her coworkers compliment her on and notice. Sue continually tries to meet the goals she has set for herself. Through her work, she has found self-respect and a feeling that she is always doing her best.

As we go about meeting our basic needs, we are influenced constantly by experiences in our families, schools, society, and workplaces. Differences in needs and experiences give rise to the unique thoughts, feelings, and actions of each individual.

Personality

The total of a person's thoughts, feelings, and actions is her or his **personality.** In human-relations terms, your personality is mostly how you are seen by others as they observe you talking, working, and interacting. However, psychologists point out that each individual has three personalities: (1) the person as seen by herself or himself, (2) the person as seen by others, and (3) the person he or she wishes to be.

Attitude is a mental position with regard to a particular fact, person, or situation. Attitudes form automatically as we experience life. Each new attitude that a person forms changes her or his personality in some way. However, attitudes do not change easily. To adopt a new attitude, a person must work at it. Employees who want to change their attitudes about work must first attempt to see themselves as coworkers see them. Then, they need to identify their actions that others may not like. Finally, they should begin the process of replacing these attitudes with attitudes that will let them be the people they wish to be.

The changed attitudes will produce different behavior. By practicing this new behavior, the employee strengthens her or

his new attitude. The result: better human relations on the job.

All employees should attempt to develop the following attitudes toward work and fellow workers:

1. *Enthusiasm.* This is a go get 'em position. To have enthusiasm about work, one must be physically and mentally healthy and be able to solve most everyday problems on the job and at home.

2. *Openness.* To be open, an individual must realize that he or she has much to learn from everyday experiences. Learning must be viewed as a lifelong process. Open people also realize that others need to hear them share what they know.

3. *Tolerance.* Tolerance is an attitude based on an inescapable fact: People are different. Some coworkers will be more like you—therefore, more liked by you—than others. But every employee contributes something to every other employee's job. Finding qualities to like or admire in another person is usually the first step in releasing that worthwhile contribution.

4. *Purposefulness.* This is an attitude that gives direction to work. Purpose is set by young people who plan their careers as though they were looking backward from their retirement years. People who work with purpose think about what they can do today that will bring them satisfaction many years later.

Teamwork

The quality of human relations in a work group directly affects the group's productivity. Worker relationships help to meet the emotional needs of each worker. As members of a team, employees gain recognition and a sense of belonging and share mutual achievements. Because team relationships are built on the motivations and personalities of the individual members, teamwork begins with individual efforts. It is each employee's responsibility to do the following—not just for her or his own success and satisfaction on the job but also for building a team of productive workers:

1. Respect coworkers at all levels; be friendly and honest with them.
2. Be positive about your life and work, doing all you can to turn negative situations into positive ones.
3. Be proud of your work; stop now and then to think about not only what you have done but how you have done it and how other people have been helped by it.
4. Cooperate in group tasks; give your coworkers a helping hand.
5. Be patient; try to understand the needs of others on your work team.

Illus. 19–1 Retailing is a people-oriented business. Employees should try to develop enthusiastic, open, tolerant, and purposeful attitudes toward work and fellow workers.

6. Maintain self-control; when you are criticized, look for an element of truth in the criticism—and forget the rest.
7. Keep the objectives of the business firmly in mind; pay attention to supervisors.
8. Learn from all associates; stay busy and show them that you care about the team.

VERBAL COMMUNICATION

Sue Lowery interacts with more than 300 people daily as a salesperson at the Hampton Department Store. Most of these contacts, as noted at the beginning of this chapter, involve verbal communication. The main verbal communication skills involved are listening, speaking, and writing. These vital skills are the tools of human relations. Teamwork is possible only when team members communicate with each other. Communication is more than hearing, saying, or writing words; communication is the understanding that results.

Listening

There are two kinds of listeners: passive and active. Passive listeners hear the words that are in a message, but, because they do not concentrate on what the message means, they often do not completely understand the message. With incomplete information, the passive listeners then proceed to make mistakes in the performance of their work. The habit of passive listening builds negative relationships among coworkers.

Illus. 19–2   Active listening is a skill that is essential for retail workers and requires concentration on what the speaker is saying.

4. Identify the speaker's purpose as soon as you can to aid your understanding.
5. Listen for the general idea of the message as well as for specific facts.
6. Avoid trying to guess what the speaker will say next.
7. Think about the meaning of the message; push other thoughts and problems to the back of your mind.
8. Summarize key points for the speaker and ask her or him to clarify any part of the message that is not clear.
9. Add relevant information to show the speaker that you have listened to and understood the message.
10. Make sure you have all the information you need before you act.

Speaking

The speaker also is responsible for assuring that communication (understanding) takes place. When speaking, the retail worker should strive for accuracy, clarity, and economy (ACE). **Accuracy** means conveying only information that you know is reliable. **Clarity** means using words and gestures that will make the message clear. **Economy** means using only the words that are necessary. Extra words only confuse the listener by covering up the intended message.

The following set of guidelines will help retail employees become ACE communicators:

1. Plan each message; organize the ideas and information so that the hearer or receiver gets the sense of it.
2. Get to the point immediately; if background information or explanation is needed, add it after the main point of the message.

In contrast to the passive listener, the active listener hears and concentrates on the meaning of messages. Active listeners ask questions to increase their understanding. Active listeners also pick up additional clues from the speaker's facial expression and tone of voice. For example, a supervisor may say, "Please pick up the special-order merchandise from the marking room." The tone of the supervisor's voice may convey this added message: "Right now!"

Successful retail employees work at developing active listening skills. An employee would do well to follow the following guidelines when receiving a message from another worker, supervisor, manager, or from an employee from another business:

1. Look directly at the speaker.
2. Check posture and facial expression: Do you appear interested?
3. Check attitude: Are you allowing the speaker's delivery or appearance to turn you off to the message?

3. Keep the message concise; practice using words as though they were $1,000 bills and you a miser.

4. Choose short, simple words that say what you intend; for example, say "use" instead of "utilize," "next" rather than "ensuing," and "try" for "endeavor."

5. Make specific, detailed statements instead of hinting at your meaning; include names, dates, and times.

6. Expand your vocabulary; the more you know about words and their meanings, the easier it is to choose the words that say precisely what you mean.

7. Pronounce words carefully; practice pronouncing words that you find difficult or that are new to you.

8. Ask a question of the listener to be sure he or she understands the message.

Writing

Many firms ask that messages involving requests or directions be written to avoid the misunderstandings that often result from poor speaking or listening skills. Written communications, similar to spoken messages, should be accurate, clear, and economical. Most of the guidelines on pages 202–203 also apply to written communications. In addition, written messages should include the names of the receiver and sender and the date. Many retail firms use message/reply forms for written communications within the company. (See Illustration 19–3). The sender writes a message in the left-hand section of the form, keeping the second copy and sending a copy and the original. Then the receiver replies in the

Hamilton Department Store	
MESSAGE	REPLY
TO:	DATE:
DATE:	
SUBJECT:	
SIGNED:	SIGNED:

Illus. 19–3   *A message/reply form is used by many retail firms for written communications within the store.*

right-hand section of the form, returns the original to the sender and keeps the copy.

If messages are handwritten, the writing must be legible. Correct spelling of all words is essential to prevent misunderstanding on the part of the reader. Every message should end with an indication of what the reader should do next. Stating if and when a reply is expected is particularly important. Every written message should be checked before it is sent. Messages that do not meet the ACE standards should be revised or rewritten.

*S*ummary

Retailing is a people-oriented business. The ability of retail workers to get along with each other is crucial. How a person gets along with others—human relations—is the result of her or his physical and emotional needs and experiences. No two people have identical needs or experiences; therefore, no two have exactly the same thoughts, feelings, and actions. In other words, everyone's personality is unique. The key to a change in personality is a change in attitudes. Four attitudes that promote good human relations are enthusiasm, openness, tolerance, and purposefulness. Good human relations within a group of workers causes members of the team to work more productively than people who do not get along.

Through their listening, speaking, and writing, employees affect human relations on the job. Communication takes place between a speaker and listener or writer and reader when understanding results. Active listeners focus on the speaker and the meaning of what they hear, while passive listeners merely hear the words. Speakers and writers improve communication if they strive for accuracy, clarity, and economy in their messages.

*R*eview

1. Name the main reason that working effectively with others is important in a retail job.
2. Define the term *human relations*.
3. Define the term *personality*.
4. List four positive attitudes for all workers.
5. Name five ways that a person can contribute to good human relations.
6. Explain the difference between passive and active listening.
7. List five guidelines for developing active listening.
8. List three guidelines for speaking or writing on the job.
9. List five guidelines for spoken messages.

Terms

The following terms were introduced in this chapter. Write a separate sentence correctly using each new term.

accuracy	emotional needs
attitude	human relations
clarity	personality
economy	physical needs

Discuss

1. How can one determine that good human relations are present in a work group?
2. How may active listening affect a retail worker's future career?
3. How do verbal communication skills help to build teamwork?

Problem Solving

1. Read the following memo sent by Mark Wills to Kreb Knotts. Then rewrite it using the guidelines suggested in this chapter. Note: The junk boxes are used boxes to be folded and put in the trash. The nuts are mixed nuts that are to be weighed and put into plastic bags, one pound per bag.

   "K—had to leave early to gas the car and get redy for the jr. aud show. How about moving the junk boxes and bagging the nuts for me. MW"

2. Refer to the guidelines for active listening on page 202 and complete the following.
   a. Describe two listening situations in which you did not follow one or more of these guidelines.
   b. Explain why you did not follow the guidelines.
   c. Who lost as a result of your failure to follow the guidelines? the speaker? the listener (you)? both?
   d. Add three more guidelines on the basis of your listening experiences.

3. Norma appeared to have excellent potential as a salesperson in your department. Lately, however, fellow workers have complained to you about Norma. They say that she doesn't help with some tasks, doesn't talk with them, and complains to customers about working conditions in the department. As department head, you decide it is time to discuss this situation with Norma. What will you suggest to her?

CHAPTER 20

Effective Supervision

CHAPTER OUTCOMES

When you have mastered the information in this chapter, you should be able to:

1. Name eight characteristics of successful retail-store supervisors

2. Name six functions performed by supervisors

3. Define the term *planning*

4. Explain why supervisors must be objective rather than emotional when giving direction

5. Name three motivation tools

6. Identify four steps that supervisors should follow when training employees

7. Explain the importance of controlling to good supervision

8. List five steps of problem solving

The person who oversees the work of others is called a **supervisor.** Supervisors in retail stores may be department heads, buyers, division managers, or assistants who are responsible for the work of a group of employees. Being a successful supervisor requires the ability to get work done by delegating tasks to others. Retail supervisors must understand the goals of the business, the needs of employees, and ways of helping employees achieve their full potential. Successful supervision in retailing often requires more skill than similar positions in other industries. Retailing employs a large number of young, part-time, and temporary workers, and a rapidly changing mix of merchandise. Therefore, retail store supervisors must spend more time working with their personnel in order to build and maintain effective performance.

CHARACTERISTICS OF EFFECTIVE SUPERVISORS

Retail supervisors usually are individuals who have been employed in retailing for several years. They have shown a dedication to retailing, probably have had various jobs within one or more stores, and have an education that qualifies them for work beyond initial employment. Among other common characteristics of effective retail supervisors are the following:

1. They enjoy working with people and get along well with coworkers, supervisors, and customers.
2. They understand and perform their work well.
3. They continually look for better ways of doing things.

4. They take initiative and are capable of making decisions quickly.
5. They assume responsibility easily and accept criticism gracefully.
6. They like helping other people improve and change.
7. They are positive thinkers and thrive on handling a variety of duties and problems.
8. They have good health and a high energy level.

Effective supervisors understand that their own attitudes and needs are a part of the human-relations picture within their work group and their organization. They also know that attention to the above characteristics is essential to their success.

SUPERVISORY FUNCTIONS

There are certain functions performed by nearly all retail store supervisors. These functions include (1) planning, (2) directing, (3) motivating, (4) training, (5) controlling, and (6) problem solving.

Planning

Planning means deciding in advance what needs to be done, who will do it, and when it will be accomplished. Without planning, there can be no short- or long-range objectives for the store or employees. Retailers who recognize the need to keep their personnel productive carefully plan work schedules and employee assignments.

Customer traffic, for example, may vary considerably during the day. The supervisor must have enough sales personnel to handle those periods when many customers need assistance. When customer traffic is slow, the supervisor must make sure that enough work is available to keep personnel busy. This means assigning salespeople to maintain stock, price merchandise, build displays, or perform other activities. Such planning requires that store management spell out its goals and that supervisors understand them. Goals may include increased sales volume, increased customer service, improvement of store image, and reduction of merchandise losses. Such goals should be the basis of any planning by supervisors.

A good plan is one that is well organized, realistic, comprehensive, and easy to understand. Also, a good plan is one that can be carried out efficiently. In other words, the time, money, and effort required to carry out the plan should be reasonable in relation to the outcomes. Supervisors are constantly seeking new ideas and new ways to carry out their plans.

Directing

Retail supervisors play a key role in directing the efforts of the workers for whom they are responsible. **Directing** is helping employees complete their work. Directing involves informing workers of the organization's goals and influencing them toward meeting those goals. Therefore, supervisors must communicate their ideas clearly and concisely. To promote good human relations, supervisors must direct their employees by following the listening, speaking, and writing guidelines presented in Chapter 19. In addition, supervisors must be especially alert to possible gaps or breakdowns in the communication process as they direct others.

Essential to directing employees is knowing how tasks are to be done. For example, a retail supervisor who directs workers to rearrange displays in a department must know how to physically move the displays and how they should look when they are rearranged. Otherwise, the results may be frustrating for both the supervisor and the employees he or she directs.

Supervisors should treat subordinates (those they direct) with the same respect that is shown to other supervisors and their superiors. Therefore, they must be able to control emotions when giving direction. Signs of unexplained anger or frustration on the part of the supervisor tend to raise the emotional level of the workers and undermine their confidence. By the tone of voice used, a supervisor may send the message, "I'm angry"—but nothing more. In this case, the supervisor has not communicated because he or she has not brought about understanding of a situation on the part of the employee.

Directions to workers should be given under suitable conditions. It makes little sense, for example, to explain procedures for repricing merchandise to a salesperson who is busy writing a refund for a customer. The supervisor should make sure that he or she has the undivided attention of a worker when speaking with her or him. Good supervisors move from behind a desk or counter when talking with an employee. Getting rid of a physical barrier tends to remove relationship barriers as well. Eye contact with the employee should be maintained while talking or listening. A steady gaze may make the employee uneasy, but shifty eyes may be even more discomforting. Whether the message is positive or negative, serious or light, the supervisor should maintain eye contact with the employee.

Effective supervisors practice active listening. They listen carefully to questions, comments, and suggestions offered by employees. The supervisor need not agree with the employee, but it is vital for the supervisor to convey that he or she understands and appreciates what is being said. When talking with employees, the effective supervisor listens for hidden messages. If an employee makes many speech errors when talking to a supervisor, the hidden message may be "I'm afraid of you," "I don't like you," or

"I'm not sure about what I'm saying." A good supervisor will ask questions to draw out the employee to get at the real message.

Organizing messages is another important aspect of directing. Even when ideas are clearly stated and presented in an orderly fashion, some employees may need to have the message repeated. Stating information unclearly or out of order is, therefore, a serious error in supervision.

Direction accompanied by explanation is an effective way to communicate. Instead of saying to Joan, "Move this merchandise to the front of the department," her supervisor may say, "Joan, will you please move these items to the big display table in the front of the department. There is going to

THE MANY ROLES OF A RETAIL SUPERVISOR

A retail supervisor is a PLANNER, who sets goals and makes plans to meet the goals.
A retail supervisor is an ORGANIZER, who arranges jobs, equipment, and people to most effectively complete the work.
A retail supervisor is a COMMUNICATOR, who sends oral and written messages that are accurate, clear, and economical.
A retail supervisor is a MOTIVATOR, who stimulates people to want to do what is needed for a successful business.
A retail supervisor is a STAFFER, who selects and hires the right number of qualified people.
A retail supervisor is a TRAINER, who instructs new and experienced employees in job procedures.
A retail supervisor is a CONTROLLER, who makes sure that work is done correctly and on time.
A retail supervisor is a PROBLEM SOLVER, who efficiently deals with operational and human-relations problems.
A retail supervisor is a TEAM BUILDER, who makes the results of a work group more than the sum of the individuals' work.
A retail supervisor is a DIRECTOR, who coordinates the efforts of people, getting them to carry out the policies and plans set by management.

Illus. 20–1 Effective leadership is required to perform the many roles of a retail supervisor. The successful supervisor is a leader of her or his work group and the retail business.

be a special sale on this merchandise tomorrow." The specific direction, plus the explanation, helps build Joan's morale by telling her that she is an important part of the store and that she is contributing to the store's success.

Motivating

Motivating employees to do a good job with a minimum of direction is an important supervisory function. To **motivate** means to provide with a cause, need, or desire to act. As has often been said, "Motivating is not making a person work; motivating is making a person want to work." Motivating employees is not a single task. Directly or indirectly, almost everything a supervisor does either positively or negatively motivates workers.

Motivating individual workers involves (1) identifying their basic needs and (2) providing ways for each employee to meet those needs through work. Since every person has different needs, supervisors must have a variety of motivational tools from which to choose. Recognition of jobs well done; assignment to new, more responsible tasks; awards and contest prizes; and bonuses are examples of motivational tools. Many supervisors find that competition in any form is excellent motivation. Most people have a strong need to win (achievement) or to be first (recognition). For those with such needs, the chance to be the first to make a sales quota, win more awards than coworkers, or receive a certificate from the management is a source of job satisfaction. On the other hand, some employees are not motivated by needs of recognition or achievement. They may have unmet physi-

cal needs that keep them from seeking recognition or achievement. These individuals may be motivated by the opportunity to earn more money. Still others may be highly self-motivated, so they do good work without encouragement from the supervisor.

Training

Retail management expects supervisors to be able to train employees. In fact, employee training is a major function of a supervisor. Retail employees learn their jobs in various ways—trial and error, explanation, and demonstration-imitation. Each method has merit, but each also has serious limitations when used alone. Effective employee training involves four steps: (1) preparing the employee, (2) presenting the material, (3) monitoring practice, and (4) checking performance. Following these

Illus. 20–2   Recognition of a job well done is an excellent way to increase employee motivation and to maintain a high level of morale among all workers.

four steps will help supervisors provide clear, well-organized instruction and opportunities for practice of each job task.

Prepare the Employee. Supervisors must make the employee feel comfortable in the workplace with her or his coworkers. They should explain the whole job and relate it to what the employee already knows about the job or parts of the job. Supervisors set learning goals for the employee and discuss with the individual which job skills should be mastered in the first week, the second week, the third week, and so on. They also let the employee know how long it should take to master each goal as well as the whole job.

Present the Material to Be Learned. Supervisors organize instruction for an orderly presentation and decide how much material can be presented at one time so that the employee will not be overwhelmed with new tasks. A good supervisor will choose the best training method for the content and the learner. For a job made up of many dissimilar tasks, employees will learn more quickly if the supervisor presents the easiest tasks first (psychological order). For jobs consisting of few or similar tasks, the supervisor should present the tasks in the order in which they are done by experienced workers (logical order). The supervisor first should present a section of the material and then summarize the key points and ask questions to determine if the employee has understood the instruction.

Monitor Practice. As soon as the employee shows understanding of what was presented, he or she should perform the task in the supervisor's presence; the employee may role-play some tasks, such as greeting a customer. If the employee makes serious mistakes, the supervisor should re-explain or redemonstrate the appropriate parts of the task. Little mistakes can be ignored because minor errors usually disappear as the employee gains experience in the task. To find out if the employee knows what is to be done, how the task is to be done, and why it is to be done a particular way, the supervisor should ask specific questions about the task. The employee should practice the task in the supervisor's absence and should know what to do or who to see if things go wrong.

Check Performance. Initially, a supervisor must check on the employee often. If the trainee is performing well, checking can be done less frequently. It is important for the supervisor to keep asking questions to check the employee's understanding of the work and its relationship to the business goals. If mistakes persist, the supervisor should explain and redemonstrate the correct procedure. Employees need praise for a good performance and

Illus. 20–3 Retail supervisors are expected to be able to train new employees to do their jobs well.

gradually increased responsibility and independence. When the trainee can handle all tasks without assistance, the supervisor can shift to regular supervision.

Properly applied, these four steps are an effective structure for training. The steps also help supervisors assume their leadership role. Training employees to do their work well and to like their jobs is a vital part of a supervisor's job.

Controlling

Directing or training on an as-needed basis is not enough to assure that the necessary work will be done. The supervisor must check to see that her or his directions and instructions have been carried out. **Controlling** means making sure that all assignments have been carried out according to a set schedule. The amount of time a supervisor devotes to controlling activities is not the same for experienced and for new employees. For instance, the head of receiving and marking may simply ask an experienced employee, "Is everything going OK?" and find that question to be all of the follow-up needed. But a new employee in the same situation may need time to ask questions, review the work he or she has completed, or to see another demonstration of the procedure.

A wise retail supervisor checks regularly to be sure that information, equipment, and supplies required to do a job are available. By controlling, supervisors assure that information is timely and that equipment is in good repair. Routinely checking the workplace for cleanliness, lighting, safety, and ventilation is also a supervisor's responsibility.

Controlling can be overdone. Supervisors should avoid placing themselves in the position of being "backseat drivers," "nit-pickers," or "nosey" or of "lacking confidence." Generally, though, a store's goals are better met by a supervisor who overcontrols than by one who controls too little or not at all. For example, when a retail supervisor is coordinating storewide sales campaign to sell merchandise purchased in large quantities, the need for controlling is great. The store cannot afford to be left with unsold inventory just because unmarked sale merchandise remained in the backroom while shelves on the selling floor stood empty. Simply put, supervisors who ignore controlling ask for trouble.

Problem Solving

A significant function of many supervisors is to solve operating or human-relations problems. Operating problems usually involve store policy or procedures. Human-relations problems usually involve employee performance, relationships with customers, and working arrangements with other store units or outside businesses. Supervisors can solve most difficulties with employees through evaluation, correction, or discipline.

If an employee complains about the work schedule, the supervisor may snap, "Do you think the work schedule is made for your personal benefit?" This question is apt to make the employee defensive; her or his response likely will be emotional—moving away from, rather than toward, a solution to the problem. A better question for the supervisor to ask is, "How would you arrange the schedule if it were up to you?" This question has the opposite effect of the first question. It gives the employee a chance to contribute useful suggestions and to feel important in doing so; also, the question helps the supervisor discover the real problem—which may not be the work schedule. Upon hearing the question, the employee may decide that her or his complaint was groundless. It is better for the employee to conclude that, than to be told "this is how it's going to be."

When an employee must be disciplined, the disciplining should be done in private. The supervisor's comments to the employee should be specific. As a result of the discussion, the supervisor and employee should understand the situation better than before the disciplining session. "I have noticed that usually you do not return tools to the display work room" should be followed with "Why not?" This statement and question tend to get at the reason for the unreturned tools. The employee's answer should

suggest action that the supervisor can take to prevent future problems.

When proper supervision techniques are used, the need for problem solving and disciplining is reduced. To eliminate the need for all problem solving, though, is nearly impossible. Therefore, effective supervisors follow these five problem-solving steps:

1. Identify the problem to be solved.
2. Gather the facts related to the problem.
3. Decide on possible courses of action.
4. Take the selected action to resolve the problem.
5. Check results to be sure the problem has been solved satisfactorily.

Steps 1 and 2 are most critical in most situations. If the problem is accurately identified and all the facts are known, action in steps 3 and 4 may be obvious. Step 5 can be part of regular controlling activities.

Summary

Retail supervisors must understand the goals of the business, the needs of employees, and the policies and procedures for tasks. Good supervisors share certain characteristics; mainly, they like working with people and helping them to improve and change. Nearly all supervisors perform these six functions: planning, directing, motivating, training, controlling, and problem solving.

In planning, a supervisor decides in advance the what, who, and when of the work to be done. In directing, the supervisor clarifies the organization's goals and helps employees meet the goals. Motivating involves giving employees a reason to want to perform well. Training is a teaching function; in training, supervisors prepare a new employee, present the job tasks, monitor the trainee's practice, and check up often on the new employee's progress. Controlling is a follow-up function. Effective supervisors do not assume that work will be done exactly right and on time by everyone; instead they check to be sure the right work is being done by the right person at the right time. In problem solving, supervisors deal with the operating and human-relations problems that arise in spite of good planning and directing. To solve any problem, the supervisor must first identify it and gather facts related to it. Then, he or she decides on the possible solution and acts on it. Finally, the supervisor makes sure that the problem is indeed solved.

*R*eview

1. Identify eight characteristics of successful retail-store supervisors.
2. List six functions performed by supervisors.
3. Define the term *planning*.
4. Describe what is likely to happen if a supervisor directs an employee when the supervisor is very angry.
5. Describe three ways supervisors can motivate employees.
6. List the four steps to follow when training employees.
7. Describe the controlling function.
8. List the five steps to be followed in solving problems.

*T*erms

The following terms were introduced in this chapter. Write a separate sentence correctly using each new term.

controlling   planning
directing   supervisor
motivate

*D*iscuss

1. Which of the characteristics of successful retail-store supervisors would be most important to supervisors in a small store?
2. What is the relationship of the planning function to the other supervisory functions?
3. If you and your classmates were retail salespersons, what motivational tools would motivate you?
4. Why do some supervisors tend to give too little attention to the controlling function?

*P*roblem
Solving

1. It is the practice of management in your store to ask supervisors to give presentations at weekly meetings. You have been asked

to discuss the importance of communication skills in directing workers. Outline the points you would cover in your presentation.

2. One of your employees is consistently late for work. You have spoken to the employee about the situation, but the problem continues. How would you go about correcting this problem?

3. Recently your store was expanded and remodeled. Six additional part-time employees will be needed in your department to handle the expected increase in business. What steps will you take to train these people in the shortest time possible?

UNIT 3 ACTIVITIES

CHECKING KEY POINTS

This exercise is designed to check your understanding of material presented in Unit 3. On a separate sheet of paper, list the numbers 1 to 25. Indicate your response, *T* for true or *F* for false, for each of the following 25 statements.

1. Wages are typically earned on an hourly basis.
2. Marketing Education programs are an excellent source of new retail employees.
3. Properly trained employees mean improved customer service.
4. People have few basic needs in common.
5. Successful retail supervisors usually accept responsibility easily.
6. Controlling requires making sure that all assignments have been carried out.
7. An attitude is how others feel toward an individual.
8. In general, experienced retail personnel do not require regular job training.
9. The work week for many retail employees is shortening.
10. A letter of application seldom accompanies a résumé.
11. Recognition is an effective means of motivating employees.
12. Sales experience is not important for one who aspires to be a retail executive.
13. Communication skills play a minor role in directing the efforts of others.
14. Promoting from within avoids the costs of hiring and training new workers.
15. Personal appearance is of little importance in seeking employment.
16. With serious effort, an individual's personality can be modified and improved.
17. Planning is not a key function of the retail-store supervisor.
18. Lecture-discussion is an effective method of covering a few topics in a short time.
19. Retailers have been leaders in providing benefits and services to their employees.
20. A job analysis is a brief written description of a job.
21. The same guidelines apply to both written and spoken communication.
22. The Civil Rights Act of 1964 prohibits discrimination in hiring practices only on the basis of race.

23. Continuous training is needed to maintain a quality staff of retail personnel.
24. Few communication problems occur between management and employees in large retail stores.
25. Good human relations is the ability to get along with others.

BUILDING BASIC SKILLS

Calculations

1. The following facts describe some aspects of the operation of Steven's Leather-Fashions Store:
   a. Steven's store is open Monday through Saturday from 9 A.M. to 9 P.M.
   b. Full-time employees work eight hours per day and have one day off per workweek.
   c. Steven's employs 12 full-time workers.
   d. Full-time workers are paid a weekly salary of $200.00.
   e. Part-time employees are paid $4.25 per hour.
2. Consider the information provided above when making the calculations necessary to answer the following:
   a. How many hours each day is Steven's open?
   b. What is the total number of hours the store is open each week?
   c. Two full-time employees are absent on a given day because of illness. How many *hours* of part-time help must be assigned to cover the two full-time employee positions?
   d. What will be the total amount of part-time wages paid to cover the two positions?
   e. What is the total amount of the store's weekly payroll for all full-time employees?
3. Complete the following calculations. Then answer the questions that follow.
   a. *Wages*
      Hours: 40 per week
      Wage: $5.10 per hour
      Expected sales: $2,500 per week
      Total wages = _____
   b. *Salary Plus Commission*
      Base salary: $170.00
      Commission on sales: 2.5 percent
      Expected sales: $2,500 per week
      Salary plus commission = _____

   c. *Straight Commission*
       Commission on sales: 8.5 percent
       Expected sales: $2,500 per week
       Total commission =_____
   d. In this case, which payment plan offers the highest weekly income?
   e. Identify an advantage and disadvantage of each method of payment.
   f. Which plan would you select? Give specific reasons for your choice.

Working with People

   Successful retail-store supervisors get work done through the people they supervise by planning, directing, motivating, training, controlling, and problem solving. Recently you were promoted to the position of department head in the sporting-goods department of a locally owned department store. Among your immediate duties are handling the following situations.

1. John Lopez has been hired to work at the customer service counter in the sporting-goods department. His major duties will include handling returns and providing general customer assistance. Because an all-store sales promotion is scheduled within the week, John must be trained quickly. Identify the four basic instructional steps that many successful supervisors use to train employees. Include with each step some general topics you think would be helpful to John in preparing for his new job.

2. Management has proposed that all sales personnel in the sporting-goods department be paid a salary plus commission rather than an hourly wage. Initial salaries would be slightly less than employees' current hourly wages. During a coffee break, you overhear a long-time employee telling others that the proposed payment plan is a poor idea. "Management is just looking for a way to pay us less money," the employee says. You decide to address this issue at your next department meeting. What will you say?

3. Two of your most productive salespeople constantly argue with each other and are beginning to cause friction among other employees. A possible solution is to change work schedules so that the employees will work at different times. However, neither salesperson wants the current schedule changed. As department head, what other solutions can you identify? Give reasons for your suggestions.

Writing Skills

Select one of the situations described below as the subject for a written communication. Investigate the topic presented using interviews, written materials, or other references as sources of information. When preparing the written assignment, be sure to credit your resources for ideas, views, explanations, or quotations you use. The assignment should be no longer than two double-spaced typewritten pages.

1. Your store publishes a monthly newspaper containing articles written by employees and management. You are asked to write an article entitled "Current Trends in Retail Employee Benefits and Services."
2. Recently you were introduced to the owner of a very successful business in your community. During your discussion, you expressed an interest in working for that firm. Write a letter of application to the employer confirming your interest.
3. Your employer is thinking about beginning a training program for all new sales personnel. You are asked to identify topics that should be included in the training sessions and explain why you believe these topics are important. Write a paper to help your employer decide.
4. You have been assigned the topic "The Importance of Writing and Speaking Skills in Retailing" as a final project for your speech communications class. You must provide a written copy of your project.
5. You are the assistant personnel manager for a local chain of food stores. Recently you received a letter from a student seeking information about the characteristics and skills needed by retail-store supervisors. Write a response to the student.

APPLYING YOUR KNOWLEDGE

Can You Do the Following?

1. List the types of personnel who are usually included in retail training programs.
2. Define the term *Marketing Education.*
3. Explain how controlling can be overdone.
4. Explain the ACE qualities of written and spoken communications.
5. Name the functions performed by retail-store supervisors.
6. List five questions an interviewer is likely to ask a job applicant.
7. Contrast active and passive listening.

8. Compare employee evaluation procedures used by large and small retail-store operators.
9. Identify four employee characteristics that employers look for when hiring workers.
10. Explain the purpose of the National Labor Relations Act of 1935.

Retail Decisions

1. As a retail-store supervisor, what are some questions you would ask about any planning that you do?
2. What would you tell a new employee who asked how to develop good human relations on the job?
3. What personal characteristics do you believe are most important for success in a retailing career?
4. What topics would you include in a general information session for new retail employees?
5. If you were the owner of a small retail outlet, how would you evaluate your employees' performance?
6. How would you select employees for your business?
7. How would you follow up on an interview two weeks later? (The interviewer has not called you.)
8. What would you suggest when asked to recommend an effective method of solving store personnel problems?
9. How would you use the sponsor, role playing, and brainstorming methods to train employees?

DEVELOPING CRITICAL-THINKING SKILLS

Retail Projects

1. Identify five specific retailing skills that you believe are important for success in business. How would you teach these skills to new employees?
2. Study each of the various compensation plans discussed in Chapter 16. List each plan in order of your personal preference and give reasons for your choices.
3. Obtain copies of application forms used by four businesses from your instructor or the career-planning and placement office in your school. Study each form and make a list of questions that are identical or similar on all the forms. Make a separate list of questions that appear on only one form. In a third list, compile questions from the forms that you cannot answer. Discuss with your

instructor the importance of finding answers to these questions and where they can be found.

4. Make a list of five occupations in which you are currently interested. Write the list a second time, placing each occupation in order of importance to you right now. Finally, identify three actions you could take (plan) to improve your qualifications for the first, second, or third choice on your list. You may wish to obtain help from your teacher, school counselor, or other sources in developing your plan.

Field Projects

1. Opinions vary regarding the contents and layout of an effective résumé or personal data sheet. Select a minimum of five sources that you feel could provide useful information about résumé writing. Consider employers, employees, teachers, placement counselors, various publications, and, of course, your own opinions. On the basis of the information you collect, prepare a résumé that best reflects your current qualifications for a job in retailing.

2. Identify three occupations that currently interest you and for which you would like more background information. Make a list of the types of career information you would want, such as educational requirements, previous occupational experience, opportunities for advancement, wages, and hours. Select and contact three sources that could provide answers about the occupations you have chosen (school career-planning and placement offices, employment services, and persons currently employed in the occupation). Compose and list any differences found among the job requirements of the occupations you have selected.

3. Identify three new state or national laws that affect relationships between management and employees. Possible sources for this information include local labor-union officers, chambers of commerce, libraries, or local government officials. Explain ways in which the laws you have identified could affect your job-seeking activities.

4. To prepare for the kinds of training you may receive when you accept full-time employment, do the following:

   a. Identify five employers who offer the kinds of job opportunities that you are seeking.

   b. On lined paper, draw six vertical lines about one-half inch apart, beginning about three inches from the left edge of the paper.

   c. In the spaces to the left of the lines, list seven or eight training techniques. At the top of each column created by the lines, write the name of one of the employers identified in *a*.

    d. Arrange an interview with the supervisor in each firm who is responsible for training new employees.

    e. Ask each trainer to identify the training techniques he or she found to be most effective in preparing new employees. Check the appropriate box on the chart as each training technique is mentioned.

    f. Analyze the responses you obtained to determine the most frequently used training methods. Give reasons that these methods are used to train new employees.

5. Identify three retail salespeople and three store supervisors who you feel are effective workers. After receiving their permission, observe each salesperson and supervisor on the job at least three times over the next two months. Pay particular attention to the way in which each demonstrates her or his personality, attitude, and job motivation. What conclusions can you draw from your observations?

CONTINUING PROJECTS

Developing a Career Plan

A key activity in developing career plans and finding employment involves the preparation of a personal "employment package." This package often consists of a letter of application, résumé, and follow-up letter. Unfortunately, the development of an individual employment package is often postponed until the last minute. The quality of this package can be increased if the job seeker 1) prepares the needed information well in advance and 2) continually updates that information as qualifications and career goals change.

The purpose of this project is to help you prepare an employment package that accurately describes your current qualifications. You may wish to refer to one of the occupations you selected in the second Field Project. Also review the résumé and letter of application shown in Chapter 17. Additional help is available from your teacher, employer, library, and career-planning and placement office. Remember, this is your own personal employment package. Therefore, it will contain information different from that of other students. Include the completed package in your career-planning notebook. Be sure to update its contents as the year progresses.

Developing a Business Plan

From the facts you have learned in this unit and the study and research of other resources, add to your manual by completing each of the following assignments:

1. Locating and employing competent workers is a key management responsibility. Devise a plan that will help you find the kinds of employees you seek by:
    a. Preparing job descriptions for at least three different positions in your store
    b. Listing specific questions to be included in your store's application form
    c. Identifying key items of information you expect applicants to provide in their letters of application or résumés
    d. Stating the questions you will ask applicants during job interviews
2. Competent workers are more likely to be retained if fair and equitable compensation policies are established. Review (a) the payment plans used for management, supervisory, and sales personnel in stores similar to yours; (b) the kinds of benefits provided by these employers, and (c) the methods used to evaluate worker performance. Outline the compensation policy and employee-evaluation policy for your store.

UNIT 4
Merchandising

The planning activities associated with having the right goods in the right quantities at the right prices at the right places at the right times is called *merchandising*. A merchandise plan is based on the objectives of the business. Essential to a good merchandise plan is a merchandise budget that details the retailer's expectations for profit, sales, purchases, prices, and expenses over a planning period.

Selection of a product line is another merchandising activity. Retailers use various methods of finding out what customers need and want as a basis for selecting store merchandise. After a product line is selected, the quantity and variety of goods within that line must be chosen.

Information about specific merchandise and where to buy it is available from several sources. Having collected market information, a retailer then purchases the planned merchandise.

An important part of buying merchandise is negotiating with the suppliers. Buyers work with the supplier to get discounts, set up favorable terms of sale, and arrange for special services.

Pricing is a vital part of merchandising, too. Retailers give much thought to setting retail prices and are concerned with the markup on goods. Reductions in prices are necessary for various reasons and are controlled by a markdown policy.

A store's prices are regulated by a sales policy or set of pricing guidelines. Once prices are set, tracking price adjustments, or markdowns, is important to continue an effective merchandising effort.

After studying this unit and completing the activities, you should be able to:

1. Describe the four steps of merchandise planning
2. Describe key items in a merchandise budget
3. Name the tools retailers use to plan merchandise assortment
4. Describe major sources of market information
5. Name and explain five types of discounts on merchandise
6. Calculate markup, retail price, and cost, given any two of these figures
7. Describe four in-the-market buying methods
8. Explain the relationship between prices, costs, and expenses
9. Name and describe three types of operating expenses that affect prices

CHAPTER 21
Planning and Budgeting

CHAPTER OUTCOMES

When you have mastered the information provided in this chapter, you should be able to:

1. Describe the four steps in the merchandise planning process

2. Identify the four levels of merchandise planning

3. Distinguish between top-down and bottom-up planning

4. Describe each of the five main planning figures in a six-month merchandise budget

5. Calculate stock turnover on a retail, cost, or unit basis

6. Calculate planned purchases and open-to-buy

7. Calculate planned markup to achieve a given profit goal

Planning means deciding what is to be done and how it is to be done. It involves setting policies, assigning responsibilities, and developing procedures. The retailer also looks at the results of past plans as a guide for future plans. **Budgeting** is an essential part of a store's merchandising plan. A budget spells out the merchandising plan in terms of money. In addition to being an important planning tool, the budget is a control tool. As explained here and in Unit 8, deviations from a budget are often the first signs that a merchandise plan is not being carried out as intended.

MERCHANDISING ORGANIZATION

Merchandise planning and budgeting activities may be carried out in different ways depending on store size and form of organization. In small stores, the owner or manager plans the merchandise to be carried and establishes the merchandise budget. The owner or manager also selects and buys the goods from suppliers and sets and controls the prices. Salespersons assist in these activities by reporting slow- and fast-selling goods, keeping prices up to date, and noting customer preferences.

In larger stores, the responsibility for merchandising is held by a merchandise manager. Under the merchandise manager, there may be divisional **merchandise managers** for each major type of goods. For example, there may be a divisional merchandise manager for appliances, another for men's clothing, another for housewares, and so on for each major merchandise classification carried by the store.

Within each of these divisions, there also may be buyers for certain lines of goods, such as large kitchen appliances (stoves, dishwashers, refrigerators), laundry appliances (washers, dryers), and small appliances (toasters, food processors, coffeemakers). In some large stores, the buyers also manage the departments that sell the goods they buy. Generally in large stores, the departments have sales managers and the buyers work full time on selecting and buying merchandise.

If the store is part of a chain, the store manager reports sales and expenses to a district or regional manager at the chain-store headquarters. The district or regional manager has responsibility for all the company stores in a certain geographic area. Merchandise planning and budgeting are performed by the merchandising management and staff at headquarters. The actual merchandise selection and buying are conducted by specialists at the chain headquarters, as shown in Illustration 21–1.

MERCHANDISE PLANNING

Careful merchandise planning leads to a healthy and profitable business. Good planning starts with a specific statement of purpose of the particular business. A statement of purpose includes the type of merchandise to be carried, the types of customers to be served, and the business image to be projected. Having a workable merchandise policy usually involves emphasizing one or two—but not all—of the following: fashion leadership, exclusive lines,

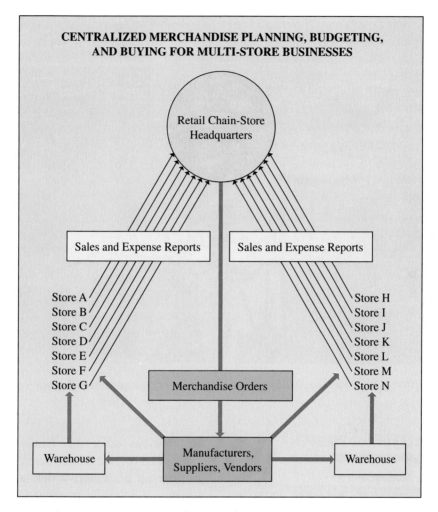

Illus. 21–1 In multi-store organizations, merchandise planning, budgeting, and buying are often centralized in the firm's headquarters. Each store manager provides sales and expense reports to headquarters or district managers. The headquarters staff decide what merchandise is to be purchased and from which manufacturers, suppliers, or vendors. Then, goods are sent either directly to the stores or to a warehouse for distribution to the stores as needed.

high quality, large assortments, low prices, personal service, and customer convenience. Once a merchandise policy has been set for a business, it is time to plan all of the activities that will make the policy effective.

A good **merchandise plan** contains definite goals for each merchandise area of the store. These goals are usually expressed in dollar amounts in a merchandise budget. When developing a merchandise budget, it is important that profit be planned first. Only then can realistic goals be set for other activities such as sales, purchases, stocks, expenses, reductions, and markups. Meeting each of these dollar goals results in profit, which is the long-term goal of every business.

Illus. 21–2   Having the right merchandise for customers is a major objective of every store.

Levels and Types of Planning

In a large store and even in some small stores, the merchandise plan is developed at several specific levels. These levels usually are (1) the entire store, (2) major store divisions, (3) departments within each division, and (4) merchandise classifications within each department. The merchandise plan can be developed from the entire store down to the specific merchandise categories or from the various merchandise categories to an overall plan for a store.

In **top-down planning,** the overall goals for stock, sales, expenses, and other figures are established at the store level and then subdivided into divisions, departments,

and various other merchandise classifications. The reverse of this sequence is called **bottom-up planning,** which starts with estimates of sales by merchandise classifications. Data are accumulated upward through each department and division to the overall store level. This approach may result in goals that differ from those of the top-down approach. The salespeople who sell certain kinds of goods may see merchandise trends not known to management. Some department managers may be more or less optimistic than those in higher levels of management.

Neither top-down nor bottom-up planning is best. By blending both systems, the store and department managers determine the information necessary for an effective merchandise plan. However, even with accurate information, a merchandise plan serves only as a road map; management can make merchandise decisions that may be contrary to the plan.

Within a department, goals usually are set for each class of merchandise. Merchandise may be classified by kind, material, price, color, size, brand, or supplier. Each specific classification is called a **stockkeeping unit** and is referred to by retailers as an **SKU.** This kind of planning is justified where knowledge of each SKU is essential to the success of the store's merchandise plan. A major appliances department would need such information, for example. With computerized inventory and sales records, more merchants than ever before are building merchandise plans on specific SKUs.

MERCHANDISE BUDGET

The retailer can set up a merchandise budget for any period—a month, a season, or a year. Most retailers find that it works well to set up a general budget for one to three years and then to develop specific budgets for six months in advance. The six-month period is long enough to make specific planning useful. A six-month plan serves as a guide to definite action. The merchandise budget, and the plan it controls for the upcoming six months, can be adjusted to meet expected market changes and the sales performance of the current six-month period.

A *six-month budget* includes estimates of sales, inventory, purchases, expenses, and profit. For larger stores the six-month budget also contains estimates of markup and gross margin, stock turns, average inventory, and stock reductions, including markdowns, employee discounts, and stock shortages.

Planning Profit

As already pointed out, profit is the long-term goal of every business. To plan sales, reductions, stocks, purchases, expenses, and especially markup, it is necessary to set a profit goal or an estimate of profit either as a percentage of sales or as a dollar figure. This profit goal is based on a variety of considerations: the profit earned during the past few years or seasons, the potential for increases or decreases in both sales and expenses during the upcoming period, changes in business policies or managerial personnel, and competitive conditions.

Planning Sales

Once a profit goal has been set, the next budget figure to be set is sales. Planned sales are based on past sales, changes in business policy, management, and the general business conditions, all of which may make customers more willing or less willing to buy. Illustration 21–3 shows the distribution of planned season sales among seven classifications of pajamas (Column 1) and the relationships among planned sales, planned stock, and planned season purchases. Note that planned season sales minus opening stock plus planned closing stock equals planned purchases for the season. Since sales are heavily influenced by outside conditions, it is better to estimate them and then to adjust the stocks, markups, and expenses to meet the sales possibilities. It is difficult to plan these factors first and then try to reach a sales goal consistent with them. Inflation is one outside condition that must be considered. If a department manager plans total sales of $90,000 for a six-month period, and inflation is expected to be 5 percent per year (2.5 percent for six months), then total sales may have to be increased to $92,250 to compensate for expected inflation.

Six-month sales plan	×	Inflation for six months	=	Increase due to inflation
$90,000	×	.025	=	$2,250

Six-month sales plan	+	Increase due to inflation	=	Six-month sales plan with inflation
$90,000	+	$2,250	=	$92,250

Planning Reductions

Markdowns (reductions from original retail price), **merchandise shortages** (goods lost because of damage or theft), and **employee discounts** (price reductions given to employees who buy goods) are all called **reductions.** They represent the inability to sell goods at original retail prices. Reductions are commonly planned for a six-month period and sometimes for each month. In the six-month merchandise plan for the children's department, shown in Illustration 21–4, reductions are planned at $6,000 for the six-month season. As shown later, this $6,000 expected reduction is a factor considered in planning the initial markup for the department.

CLASSIFICATION CONTROL PLAN—CHILDREN'S PAJAMAS

Class of Pajamas	Planned Season Sales	−	Opening Stock	+	Planned Closing Stock	=	Planned Season Purchases
A-11	$ 1,620		$ 540		$ 480		$ 1,560
A-16	1,940		610		560		1,890
B-14	2,630		480		640		2,790
B-15	2,200		440		540		2,300
C-32	1,450		360		340		1,430
C-44	1,800		660		480		1,620
D-17	3,400		710		640		3,330
Total	$15,040		$3,800		$3,680		$14,920

Illus. 21–3 Planning purchases by classification is more precise than planning by department. Here the various classifications of pajamas (knit, flannel, cotton, and nylon in various styles) are listed with planned sales, stocks, and puchases for each. In many cases, these season figures are further broken down by the amounts for each month of the season.

SIX-MONTH MERCHANDISE PLAN FOR THE CHILDREN'S DEPARTMENT

Season's Profit Goal . . . .$8,000   Last Year. $7,000
Season's Reduction Goal . . . . . .$6,000   Last Year. $5,500

	Feb.	Mar.	Apr.	May	June	July	Aug.	Total
Sales Last Year	$11,800	$15,100	$17,400	$13,700	$11,650	$ 9,600		$ 79,250
Planned Sales	13,100	16,600	19,500	17,200	12,300	10,550		89,250
Actual Sales								
Stocks Last Year (First of Month)	$23,500	$26,500	$28,000	$29,500	$24,500	$21,000	$19,500	$ 24,643 (average)
Planned Stocks (First of Month)	22,000	25,000	26,000	26,000	24,000	21,000	20,000	23,429 (average)
Actual Stocks								
Purchases Last Year	$14,000	$16,600	$18,900	$ 8,700	$ 9,150	$ 8,100		$ 75,450
Planned Purchases	16,100	17,600	19,500	15,200	9,300	9,550		87,250
Actual Purchases								
Selling Salaries Last Year	$ 1,600	$ 1,850	$ 2,000	$ 1,750	$ 1,500	$ 1,450		$ 10,150
Planned Salaries	1,750	1,900	2,000	1,900	1,850	1,750		11,150
Actual Salaries								
Advertising Last Year	$ 350	$ 500	$ 550	$ 400	$ 350	$ 300		$ 2,450
Planned Advertising	400	600	650	450	400	350		2,850

Illus. 21–4   This six-month merchandise plan and budget is discussed in this chapter. It is important to record actual results and compare them with the plan to determine if the goals are being met. Refer to this illustration frequently to better understand the relationships among the factors discussed.

SIX-MONTH MERCHANDISE PLAN FOR THE CHILDREN'S DEPARTMENT (cont.)

Season's Profit Goal . . . .$8,000   Last Year $7,000
Season's Reduction Goal . . . .$6,000   Last Year $5,500

	Feb.	Mar.	Apr.	May	June	July	Aug.	Total
Actual Advertising								
Other Expenses Last Year	$800	$ 900	$1,050	$ 950	$ 950	$900		$5,550
Planned Other Expenses	850	1,000	1,100	1,100	1,000	950		6,000
Actual Other								
Markup Last Year								36.2%
Planned Markup								35.7%
Actual Markup								

Planning Stocks

After sales are planned for each month, the next step is to plan the amount of stock to have on hand at the beginning of each month. For staple merchandise, retailers develop a **basic stock list.** This is a list of goods that should be in stock at all times. For fashion and shopping goods, retailers develop a **model stock plan** that divides the stock according to size, color, or any other notable characteristic used by a retailer when ordering stock. Using these guides, the merchant may plan increases or decreases of the amount and assortment of stock according to anticipated monthly variations in sales.

Finding Average Stock or Inventory. An essential figure in making stock calculations is **average stock.** The average stock figure for a year may be determined by adding the stock in inventory on the first of every month to the year-end stock and dividing this sum by 13 (the number of times stock inventory is counted during the year). Average stock may be calculated on the basis of retail prices or cost prices or by the number of units, as shown in Illustration 21–5.

Inventory Date	Retail	Cost	Units
Jan. 1	$ 31,000	$ 18,600	413
Feb. 1	35,100	21,060	468
March 1	36,000	21,600	480
April 1	37,410	22,400	498
May 1	34,700	20,800	462
June 1	31,200	18,700	416
July 1	30,000	18,000	400
Aug. 1	33,750	20,250	450
Sept. 1	34,000	20,400	453
Oct. 1	36,650	21,990	488
Nov. 1	36,400	21,840	485
Dec. 1	32,840	19,700	438
Dec. 31	30,000	18,000	400
Total	$439,050	$263,340	5,851
Divided by 13	$ 33,773	$ 20,257	450

Illus. 21–5   Average stock or inventory can be calculated in three ways—by retail, by cost, or by stockkeeping units.

Computing Stock Turn.

Stock turn or the stock turnover rate is the number of times the average stock is sold during the year. Every retailer should understand stock turn to make the best use of investment capital, to control inventories, and to realize maximum profits. If a retailer buys $200 of goods and then prices them to sell for $300, there will be a $100 margin when the goods are sold. At this price ($300), it may take a whole year for the goods to be sold. If, however, the $200 worth of goods are priced at $275 and sold in six months, then two lots of goods may be sold during the year. The retailer will then have attained a $150 margin on a $200 investment.

Stock turn may be computed on three different bases: retail, cost, and unit. The equation for each is as follows:

1. Retail basis: stock turn = net sales ÷ average stock at retail price
2. Cost basis: stock turn = cost of stock sold ÷ average cost of stock
3. Unit basis: stock turn = number of units sold ÷ average number of units in stock

The retail basis for computing stock turn is preferred when stores keep records of the retail value of their stock. When information about stock is available only in terms of cost, however, the cost basis of computing stock turn is satisfactory. The unit basis is useful for studying the number of items carried in relation to the number sold. For example, a store stocks 60 jackets in a certain style in order to provide a sufficient assortment of sizes. The stock is replenished as sales are made; by the end of the year, 300 jackets are sold. So, the stock turn for the year is five (*300 ÷ 60 = 5*).

Suppose a retailer stocks an average inventory worth $5,000 at retail price. From that $5,000 worth of stock, there are annual sales of $30,000, six times the average inventory amount. Thus, the rate of stock turn is six. It is possible to achieve a sales total of $30,000 with an average inventory of $5,000 because, as the goods are sold, the merchant orders more goods, so that the stock level is always kept at about $5,000.

Stock turn may be computed for any convenient period, though typically it is figured for a year. When stock turn is computed for a shorter period, the yearly rate may be found by multiplying the stock turn rate by the number of such periods in a year. For example, if the stock turn for three months (one-fourth of a year) is two, the yearly stock turn rate is eight (*4 × 2*).

Varying Stock Turn. Different lines of merchandise have different rates of stock turn. For instance, the rate for food stores is greater than the rate for furniture stores. Many food items must be sold quickly or they will spoil. Food is also purchased frequently by customers. Consequently, despite the large assortment of stock in grocery stores, their average number of stock turns per year typically ranges between 18 and 24. Furniture stores also have a large assortment of merchandise, but, because their customers shop and buy so infrequently, the stock turn for many furniture stores is less than two. The furniture retailer must have an assortment of stock large enough to meet customer demands but small enough to reduce the risk of goods going out of style or of tying up funds unnecessarily.

Planning Purchases

Once sales and stocks have been planned, it is fairly easy to determine the amount of **planned purchases,** or stock to be purchased, for each month. The planned purchases may be calculated by using Formula 21–1:

FORMULA 21–1

Planned Purchases = Planned Sales + Increase (or − Decrease) in Inventory

In the merchandise plan for the children's department in Illustration 21–4, the planned sales for February are $13,100. The planned retail stock on February 1 is $22,000, and the planned retail stock on March 1 is $25,000. Therefore, the desired increase in inventory is $3,000 (*$25,000 − $22,000*). By inserting these figures into Formula 21–1, we find that planned purchases for February are $16,100 (*$13,100 + $3,000*).

Actual purchases are kept in line with planned purchases by putting a limit on merchandise orders. The limit on orders is called an *open-to-buy*. **Open-to-buy** is the difference between planned purchases for a period and the merchandise orders already placed for delivery in that period. The open-to-buy may be calculated by using Formula 21–2:

FORMULA 21–2

Open-to-Buy = Planned Purchases − Orders

From Illustration 21–4, we know that the planned purchases for the children's department for February amount to $16,100. Assume that orders for $8,700 of merchandise for delivery in February have already been placed. By using Formula 21–2, we find that the open-to-buy for February is $7,400 at retail value (*$16,100 − $8,700*). Therefore, additional orders for merchandise to arrive in February should not exceed $7,400.

Planning Expenses

Expenses are the cost of items and services needed to operate a business and make a profit. Heat, lights, salaries and wages, advertising, and taxes are a few of the expenses necessary for operating a business. Based on experience and comparisons with other businesses, a percentage allowance for each category of expense can be included in a six-month budget. Salaries and wages for store employees are often the largest expense of a retail store, ranging from 5 percent to 20 percent of sales, depending upon the type of store. Generally, the ratio of salaries and wages to sales is lowest in self-service stores and highest in full-service stores. In the merchandise plan shown in Illustration 21–4, the planned selling salaries for the season ($11,150) are about 12.5 percent of the season's planned sales ($89,250).

In the preparation of a complete budget, a list is made of all expenses. An estimate is made of the minimum outlay necessary to meet each expense. For example, in the merchandise plan shown in Illustration 21–4, planned advertising ($2,850) is estimated at about 3.2 percent of planned sales ($89,250). The various categories of expenses are explained more fully in Chapter 48.

Planning Markup

Establishing an appropriate retail price on merchandise is necessary if the retailer is to cover expenses and earn a profit. The retail price also must be attractive to customers. The amount that a merchant adds to the cost of merchandise to arrive at the retail selling price is called **markup.** Suppose a retailer buys a belt at a cost of $6 and sells it for $9. The $3 that the retailer adds to the

cost is the markup on the belt. In this case, the markup ($3) is 33.3 percent of the retail price ($9).

The planned markup is the amount needed to achieve the planned profit goal and to cover expenses and reductions. It is based on the amount of sales planned and is expressed as a percentage of those sales. While there may be variations in actual markups from one month to the next, the important figure to plan is the markup for the entire season or period. Markup, therefore, is usually set for an entire season or six-month period rather than for each month. The planned markup for the children's department (Illustration 21–4) is calculated in Formula 21–3.

FORMULA 21–3

Planned Markup = planned profit + planned expenses + planned reductions ÷ the sum of the planned sales + planned reductions

$8,000 (profit) + $20,000 (salaries + advertising + other expenses) + $6,000 (reductions) ÷ $89,250 (sales) + $6,000 (reductions) = $34,000 ÷ $95,250 = 35.69 percent (35.7%).

Since, in the children's department, the planned markup of 35.7 percent is close to last year's actual markup of 36.2 percent, the figure probably needs no modification. If there is a big difference between the estimated markup and the past year's actual markup amount, all budget items should be reviewed carefully and the merchandise plan revised to reflect a more realistic plan.

Summary   Merchandise planning requires that the retailer set a profit goal. Once a profit goal has been set, estimates can be made for sales, reductions, and expenses. From these figures, inventory, purchases, and markup can be planned. These goals are meaningful only if (1) store personnel understand them and (2) they can be attained. Therefore, attainable goals should be communicated to the business staff. From time to time, actual sales, purchases, prices, stocks, and expenses should be compared with budget estimates. Differences between actual and budgeted amounts should be carefully noted.

Review
1. List the four steps in the merchandise planning process.
2. List the four levels of merchandise planning.
3. Explain the advantages of top-down planning and of bottom-up planning.
4. Explain why most retailers use six-month periods for merchandise planning.
5. List the five main planning figures in a six-month merchandise budget.
6. Define the term *stock turn*.
7. If net sales are $20,000 and average stock retail is $5,000, what is the stock turn?
8. How is it possible to have sales greatly in excess of average inventory?
9. Define the term *open-to-buy*.
10. If planned purchases are $12,000 and orders for the period are $8,500, what is the open-to-buy?

Terms   The following terms were introduced in this chapter. Write a separate sentence correctly using each new term.

average stock	merchandise shortage
basic stock list	model stock plan
bottom-up planning	open-to-buy
budgeting	planned purchase
employee discount	reduction
markdown	stockkeeping unit (SKU)
markup	stock turn
merchandise manager	top-down planning
merchandise plan	

Discuss
1. Is merchandise planning equally important to both the small store and the large store? Explain.
2. For which types of stores would analyses of past records be most helpful in deciding which merchandise to carry?

3. Why do past figures have less meaning to the store if there is to be a change in policies and procedures in that store?
4. Why do different lines of merchandise have different rates of stock turn?
5. If a merchant finds that sales are exceeding those planned for a six-month period, what adjustments in the budget will be necessary?
6. If a merchant finds that actual selling salaries and advertising costs are above planned levels, what adjustments can be made?

Problem Solving

1. Select one of the following categories and develop as many classifications of it as you can: sweaters, crackers, auto tires, gloves, and shoes. At what point do the classifications no longer have value to merchandise planning?
2. Jake Smith has operated a small general store in the resort village of Splitwood for over 20 years. The store is packed with all sorts of merchandise; in fact, there is so much that Jake doesn't know where to put new merchandise. What reasons would you give Jake for introducing a system of merchandise planning? How would you go about setting up a merchandise plan for this general store?
3. The Willow Tree clothing store had the following dollar value of stock at the beginning of each month: January, $11,900; February, $12,100; March, $9,800; April, $10,300; May, $10,800; June, $11,200; July, $10,600; August, $10,400; September, $11,700; October, $12,300; November, $13,400; and December, $12,600. The store had a December ending inventory of $10,800. What is the average stock figure for the year? What is the average stock figure for the six-month period between January and June? What is the average stock figure for the six-month period between July and December?
4. The manager of the Willow Tree (see Problem 3) has planned sales of $9,100 for the month of March. What are the planned purchases for March?
5. On March 15 the manager of the Willow Tree (see Problem 3) found that orders amounting to $6,700 had been placed for delivery in March. What is the open-to-buy figure?
6. If the Willow Tree clothing store (see Problem 3) management plans $7,500 in profit, $38,000 in expenses, $4,100 in reductions, and $117,100 in sales, what is the store's planned markup percentage? If expenses could be reduced to $32,500, what would the store's planned markup percentage be?

CHAPTER 22

Product Lines and Assortments

CHAPTER OUTCOMES

When you have mastered the information provided in this chapter, you should be able to:

1. Identify techniques a retailer can use to determine what items customers are likely to buy

2. Explain the difference between national and private brands and the advantages of each for retailers

3. Define the term *shopping goods* and explain the difference between standardized and nonstandardized goods

4. Make a distinction between style, fashion, and fad and explain why retailers must clearly understand each

5. List the steps in a fashion cycle

6. Identify important merchandise assortment considerations that every retailer should understand

7. Identify the assortment planning tools that are commonly used in retailing

As noted in Chapter 21, good retail merchandising is having the right goods in the right quantities at the right prices in the right places at the right times. When the merchandise plan and budget have been established, the next major decisions to make are what specific goods potential customers will buy; what brands customers want; what styles, sizes, and colors should be carried; and what prices should be listed. Since no store can carry all possible goods, careful selection of product lines is essential for attaining the goal of good retail merchandising.

ANALYZING CUSTOMER NEEDS

Successful retailers must know their potential customers' wants and needs in order to plan proper merchandise lines and assortments. If customers do not want an item, the merchant should not buy it, no matter how good a bargain or how eye catching it may be. It is so important to know customers' needs that merchants have developed various methods of finding out what customers want and when and why they want it.

Some merchants invite typical customers to sit in with their stores' staffs to discuss buying, advertising, and services. Such groups are called *customer panels*. These customers can provide helpful opinions on merchandise and store procedures and services. Some stores select groups of high-school or college students, called *teen boards,* to advise them on youth activities and fashion trends. Other merchants send their customers letters asking for comments on the goods and services offered by the store. Many stores test customers' preferences for styles, colors, sizes, and price ranges; small initial orders are placed for a large variety of merchandise and then customer reactions to each item are carefully observed. Preferred products are reordered in larger quantities than other products.

A study of customer characteristics, including level of education, financial status, and buying habits, is also a basis for selecting merchandise lines. The retailer who takes time and trouble to study customers—to listen to them and to analyze what they have bought in the past—has taken the first step toward offering merchandise that will sell.

Analyzing Past Records

A careful analysis of past sales records tells much about what customers want and are likely to buy again. Sales records provide information about the kinds, quantities, colors, sizes, and prices of merchandise that have been sold. By reviewing the past sales records, a variety-store owner knows that each week a certain amount of candy, envelopes, yarn, zippers, and picture frames is sold. Past sales records give a fairly reliable indication of recurring customer demand.

Want Slips

Another way to find out what customers want is to talk to them and require salespeople to report on merchandise requested but not in stock. Since it is easy to forget details regarding such merchandise, salespeople are supplied with forms called *want slips* on which they jot down those items asked for but not available. When a salesperson succeeds in selling an article other than that asked for, the substitution is also reported on the want slip (see Illustration 22–1). By studying these reports every day, a store buyer may find that there is a definite demand for certain articles not normally carried. For example, a men's store that does not sell hats may have so many requests for hats that management may decide to open a hat section. The report of substitution sales on want slips indicates which goods in stock can be substituted readily for articles asked for but not carried. This knowledge may prevent the retailer from stocking merchandise in which customers show only a passing interest.

Comparison Shopping

An indirect way of determining customer demand is to study the activities of competitors. Merchants watch the advertisements and the store displays of competitors.

Local merchants sometimes find it desirable to watch the advertisements of stores in nearby towns and metropolitan centers as well. By watching the offerings in these places, merchants may find out what goods will eventually become popular locally.

Occasionally, merchants have their staffs visit competing stores to note the lines of goods that are available and to record prices, styles, colors, and so on, as though they were customers. Such comparison shopping may indicate to a merchant that a competitor is successful at selling a classification of merchandise that the merchant does not have in stock. Comparison shopping supplements the want slip system and provides the merchant with many good ideas for new merchandise lines.

STAPLE GOODS

In Chapter 4, you were introduced to the four kinds of consumer goods—staple or regular goods, fashion goods, seasonal

Illus. 22–1
Merchandise requested but not carried should be reported by salespeople on want slips.

ITEMS CALLED FOR	WANTED				WHAT WAS SUBSTITUTED	BUYER'S DISPOSITION
	Style	Color	Size	Price		
Blouse	shirt-waist	white	10	$28.00	—	On order
Sweater	turtle-neck	Grey	36	$34.50	V-neck	On order
flannel pajamas	coat style	Blue	10	$16.95	Lounger	Discontinued
Coat	coat-coat	Red	14	$115.00	—	In reserve
Gloves	leather	white	6	$19.95	—	On order

Date March 11, 19-- — WANT SLIP — Dept. No. 42 — Employee No. 14

Whenever an item is called for that is not in stock, whether the item is carried regularly or not, record that fact at once. Make certain that you record every call.

goods, and convenience goods. In this chapter, you will examine in more detail the nature of staple goods and fashion goods.

From the retailer's viewpoint, *staple goods* consist of merchandise for which there is a continuing and repetitive customer demand. Some examples of staple goods are work gloves, floor polish, bed sheets, and athletic shoes. In general, the buying of staple goods for resale is a relatively simple procedure. Since staples typically enjoy long periods of customer demand, retailers can easily review records of previous purchases and maintain lists of such goods. Staple goods, however, should never be regarded as unchanging. By observing customer wants and developments in the wholesale markets, a merchant can discover new items that should be added to the list of staple items. Many items that were originally novelties may become staples with continued customer acceptance. Frozen food is a typical example of a specialty good that has now moved to the staple category.

Brand-name Staples

Most staple goods that have widespread consumer appeal are readily identified by their advertised brand names. Levi's, Nike's, and Pepsi are examples of brand-name merchandise items that have become staples for many consumers. A brand—or the legal term **trademark**—is used by manufacturers and others to identify a product. It may be a word, mark, symbol, device, or a combination of these. A brand may appear on the product or the container, or a brand may be attached to the product on a tag or label. The use of a reg-

istered trademark or brand name is limited to the firm that owns it.

A brand name may be used for only one specific product, or it may be a blanket name used for a family of related products. For example, Escort is an individual brand because it applies to only one type of automobile. Zenith is a blanket brand because it is used for various products such as radios, stereos, and television sets.

National Brands. A brand used by a major manufacturer or producer of products is frequently called a **national brand** because such products are distributed all over the country. The producer of a national brand may invest a great deal in building customer acceptance and preference for that brand. If the producer can show that the features and qualities of a product are different from and better than the features of other similar products, more customers probably will buy his or her brand. Furthermore, when customers shop, they tend to buy brand-name products in which they have confidence as opposed to unknown products that may prove disappointing.

Wise retailers carefully choose national brands to be used as staple merchandise lines. By carrying a line of national-brand merchandise, the retailer will enjoy specific benefits. First, the goods he or she carries will have been developed carefully and will be of consistent quality. Second, those goods already will have been promoted heavily through national media. Many customers will recognize the brands and know special features of the merchandise. Third, national brands often carry a suggested standard price that customers can expect regardless of where they buy.

Private Brands.   When a product is brand named by an intermediary such as a wholesaler or retailer, it is referred to as a **private brand.** When a middleman has a producer make and identify a product with the middleman's trademark, the product becomes a private brand. In some instances, middlemen produce or pack private brands themselves.

Well-known private brands are usually sponsored by chain stores that insist on quality standards and excellent packaging. These products are often made by the producers of national brands and vary little, if any, from the national-brand specifications. The private brand price is often 20 to 30 percent less than the price of national-brand merchandise, largely because the producer does not have to include heavy advertising expenses in the cost. By developing private brands, the merchant is not at the mercy of changes that the national-brand producer

may make in price and markup; nor does he or she have to abide by a minimum resale price.

As noted in Illustration 22–2, private brands give a store certain advantages, such as freeing it from direct competition and allowing it to buy for less; but there are disadvantages. New, private brands are more expensive for a store to promote and to sell than well-known national brands. There also may be considerable customer reluctance to buy new private brands, and a store may lose sales if nationally advertised brands are not available.

Department stores, supermarkets, and drugstore chains often carry their own private brands and also several leading national brands. The advantages of both national and private brands are thus realized. In general, small retailers—unless they are affiliated with a buying group—have difficulty developing a high level of

ADVANTAGES AND DISADVANTAGES OF PRIVATE BRANDS

Advantages	+ Generally cost the retailer less
	+ May be sold for less than competing national brands
	+ May allow higher markups to be realized, even with lower retail prices
	+ May build repeat sales
	+ Avoid direct price competition with other stores
	+ Allow goods to be made to specifications of the retailer
	+ Permit store to carry exclusive merchandise
Disadvantages	− Bring about higher selling and advertising costs
	− Encounter customer resistance, which may lead to markdowns and ill will for the store
	− Involve packaging, labeling, and making commitments for large amounts of merchandise

Illus. 22–2   Before stocking private brands, a retailer should consider their advantages and disadvantages carefully.

customer acceptance for their private brands. As a result, many retailers believe that it is better for them to feature well-known national brands and to depend on personal service to attract repeat customers.

Generic Brands

Goods with no brand name are labeled with the generic name or description of the merchandise. These generic labeled items are typically staple goods and are generally packaged by an outside distributor for chain stores. For example, paper towels or canned pineapple are simply labeled "paper towels" or "pineapple." Labels on generic products carry only the names and basic information required by law, such as a list of the ingredients. The packaging is simple and the contents are satisfactory, but the quality of no-brand or no-name goods may not be uniform. Peas, for example, may be of mixed sizes rather than all small or all large. The price of generic brands is considerably less than the price of national or private brands. In a sense, no-name brands are a variation of the private brand. Generic products are sold at a low price, and usually without advertising or special promotion.

Illus. 22–3 Consumers tend to buy products in which they have confidence. Retailers are wise to carry those brands that give satisfaction to the majority of customers.

SHOPPING GOODS

A **shopping good** is one that the customer believes requires careful selection and comparison. Although some staple goods of low unit cost are "shopped," most shopping goods are big ticket or infrequently purchased items such as automobiles, appliances, and major home furnishings.

Shopping goods can be viewed as two types of merchandise: products that appear to be standardized but differ in special features and price and products that apparently are not standardized in quality or price. In the first instance, the customer may shop primarily for price. Most home appliances fall in this category. Examples of nonstandardized shopping goods are furniture, draperies, and decorative art. The price of these goods is often secondary to their style, quality, and brand. Customers are more willing to spend the additional time required to find exactly what they want when shopping for nonstandardized goods, especially decorative art.

FASHION GOODS

Fashion goods present the retailer not only with profitable sales opportunities but also with costly pitfalls. When fashions change, prices must be reduced sharply or the declining fashion items will not sell. Resulting losses may eat away profits. Merchants are able to reduce losses that arise in fashion merchandising only by keeping stocks low in relation to sales and by making prompt adjustments to changing conditions.

Since fashion is such an important buying motive for many consumers, retailers of high-fashion merchandise must consider the effects of fashion trends when selecting goods for resale. In addition to studying customer buying habits and store sales results, fashion-goods merchants also must know fashion trends and the fashion cycle.

Studying Fashion

The desire to be different, the desire for something new, and the desire to identify with prevailing cultural or social ideas are the forces that create fashion. **Fashion** may be defined as the style of merchandise, art, or activity that appeals to a large number of people at a given time. Fashion is most often thought of in connection with women's and men's apparel. Also, the youth market has unique fashion demands.

While fashion is important in the apparel industry, fashion can be found in nearly all other areas of consumer goods as well. There are fashions in home furnishings, automobiles, sports equipment, art, and books, for example. In fact, there is fashion in almost everything we buy. Besides fashion, people today want comfort, convenience, health, beauty, and an escape from a humdrum existence. If a new style contributes to one or more of these wants, it has a good chance of becoming the latest fashion.

Language of Fashion

To understand fashion goods and trends, it is necessary to know the exact meaning of three common terms: *style, fashion,* and *fad.*

Everything has style. By **style** we mean the lines and characteristics of an article or activity that make it different from other articles or activities of the same kind. One refrigerator may have square corners, a door, and a vertical handle. Another may have rounded edges, two doors, and horizontal handles. Each has its own style, and the style of one may have more appeal to certain customers than the style of the other.

When a particular style appeals to a large number of people who then want that style, the style is said to be **in fashion.** A style that is in fashion today, however, may not be in fashion six months or a year from now because people's tastes change. That item is then labeled as having an old-fashioned style. When something new appeals to a large number of people, the new article, in turn, becomes fashionable. This ever-changing element that people want in merchandise is good for business. When a new style becomes fashionable, the wheels of industry and business turn, and thousands of people are employed to produce and sell the new fashion.

When a style catches the fancy of a sizable group of people, has brief popularity, and dies out quickly, it is called a **fad.** Generally, fads are confined to minor apparel accessories, but sometimes fads may be found in other types of goods. Some dolls and other children's toys are extremely popular for just one selling season. Fads are probably more common among young people than among any other consumer group.

The Fashion Cycle

A style that becomes a fashion passes through rather definite steps in its rise and fall from popularity. These steps—origination, rise, acceptance, mass production, decline, and abandonment of a style—make up the **fashion cycle.** This sequence of steps is shown in Illustration 22-4.

The speed with which styles pass through the fashion cycle vary greatly. Some styles are abandoned shortly after creation or adaptation without ever becoming popular or being sold in large quantities. Normally, styles in staple goods (basic food and clothing items and some shopping

goods, such as home furnishings and automobiles) have a cycle of several years. Styles in accessories, such as jewelry and handbags, have a very short fashion cycle—often only a few months or a season. The length of a cycle also varies with different features of a style. For example, the basic lines of some garments have a much longer fashion cycle than the color or fabric. Thus, to stock a store, the wise buyer always looks for garments that have classic lines but details that are on the rise in the fashion cycle.

ASSORTMENT CONSIDERATIONS

In addition to understanding customer needs and the nature of various categories of merchandise, successful merchants must also maintain well-balanced stocks of merchandise. A **balanced stock** is an assort-

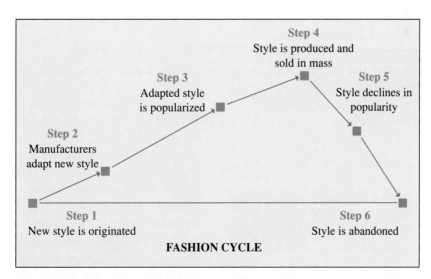

Illus. 22-4 Buyers of fashion goods must know the fashion cycle for their line of goods in order to know when to stock a new style.

ment of goods that will appeal to most customers. To achieve appropriate balance, a retailer must consider both merchandise depth and breadth. Merchandise depth refers to the quantity of items stocked in any given brand, size, color, style, or price of a particular kind of merchandise. A store such as County Seat, which specializes in the sale of jeans, likely has more merchandise depth in jeans than the clothing section of a large department store. On the other hand, the department store probably offers a greater breadth of men's and women's clothing to its customers. Merchandise breadth refers to the variety of selections, sizes, colors, styles, prices, and materials in a given product line.

Merchandise assortment considerations may include decisions about special kinds of merchandise. Some retailers sell nothing but special assortment merchandise such as discontinued lines, manufacturer overruns, bankruptcy merchandise, and damaged goods. Other merchants place limitations on the prices at which they will offer merchandise for sale. For example, a merchant may decide that blouses will be priced at three levels—$10.99, $16.99, and $22.99—and only the brands that can be offered at those prices will be carried. Other retailers may limit assortments to certain sizes, colors, or styles.

ASSORTMENT PLANNING TOOLS

Most merchants keep detailed lists of the merchandise they need to buy in order to have an appropriate assortment of staple, shopping, or fashion goods. Three types of assortment planning lists are common: (1) the basic stock list, (2) the model stock plan, and (3) the never-out list.

Basic Stock List

The **basic stock list** contains those items that are staples for the store; that is, those items for which customers maintain a continuous demand. Basic-stock lists are often very specific and show brand names, sizes, colors, and other pertinent product features. Since staple goods tend to sell steadily, these products quickly go out of stock. To avoid the out-of-stock problem, the merchant maintains a complete list of basic stock and checks the list frequently. As a result, complete assortments of steady-demand goods are likely to be in stock at all times.

Model Stock Plan

The **model stock plan,** similar to the basic stock list, can be used for a wide variety of products. It is particularly useful when planning fashion and shopping assortments, such as clothing and shoes, where a proper distribution of sizes and colors is important. Because of the speed with which customer demand may change, it is more difficult to maintain specific lists for fashion-oriented merchandise. Nevertheless, many merchants rely on model stock plans to guide them in determining which price lines, sizes, colors, and current styles to carry in their main fashion lines. Each time merchandise is ordered, the distribution of colors, sizes, styles, and prices is checked against the model stock plan. The growing use of the computer in developing stock lists has greatly assisted retailers in planning fashion and shopping-goods assortments. Illustration 22–5 shows a model stock plan for men's pajamas.

Never-out List

A never-out list is used for all types of merchandise including staple, fashion, and shopping goods. As the name implies, the never-out list identifies products that the merchant has classified as key items or high-demand merchandise. Great care is taken to ensure that ample supplies of never-out items are always stocked.

MODEL STOCK PLAN: MEN'S PAJAMAS, FALL	Dollars	Units
Total planned stock	$9000	
Reserve for specials and clearance	−1328	
Available for model stock	$7672	476
Price lines: $14	$2128	152
$16	3744	234
$20	1800	90

DISTRIBUTION TO CLASS, MATERIAL, COLOR, AND SIZE

Class	Material	Price	Units	Navy & Blue				Brown & Gold				Green & Olive				Prints			
				S	M	L	XL	S	M	L	XL	S	M	L	XL	S	M	L	XL
Button-down	Cotton broadcloth	$14	36	2	2	2	2	2	2	2	2	1	1	1	1	4	5	4	3
		$16	58	2	4	3	3	3	4	3	2	1	2	2	1	6	8	8	6
		$20	25	1	2	1	1	1	1	1	1	1	2	2	1	2	3	3	2
	Dacron polyester	$14	43	1	2	2	1	1	2	1	1	1	2	1	2	6	8	8	4
		$16	60	1	2	2	1	1	3	2	2	2	3	3	2	9	11	10	6
		$20	35	1	1	1	1	1	3	1	1	1	2	2	1	4	5	5	5
	Cotton flannel	$14	22		1	1	1	1	1	1	1	1	1	1		2	4	4	2
		$16	32	1	2	2	2	2	3	3	2	1	2	2	1	2	3	3	1
		$20	30	1	2	2	2	1	2	2	1	1	3	3	1	2	3	2	2
Pullover	Cotton broadcloth	$14	12	1	1	1	1					1	1	1	1	1	1	1	1
		$16	20	1	1	1	1	1	1	1	1	1	1	1	1	2	3	2	1
	Dacron polyester	$14	12		1	1		1	1	1	1	1	1			1	1	1	1
		$16	26	1	2	2	1	1	2	2	1	1	2	2	1	2	3	2	1
	Cotton flannel	$14	27	1	2	1	2	2	3	3	1	1	1	2	1	1	3	2	1
		$16	38	2	3	3	2	2	3	3	1	2	3	3	2	2	3	2	2
TOTAL			476	16	28	25	21	20	31	26	18	17	27	26	16	46	64	57	38

S = Small   M = Medium   L = Large   XL = Extra Large

Illus. 22–5 Many merchants rely on model stock plans to guide them in determining which prices, sizes, colors, and styles to carry in their main lines of merchandise.

Summary

To plan what merchandise to stock, retailers must know customers' needs. These needs can be learned from customer panels, teen boards, opinion surveys, observations, and customer characteristics. What people will buy also can be predicted from sales records, want slips, and comparison shopping.

Different kinds of goods involve different considerations. National, private, and generic brands are an issue for staple goods. Whether shopping goods are standardized or nonstandardized requires consideration. For fashion goods, not only styles but also fads and the place of fashionable products in their fashion cycles must be considered. Retailers use basic stock lists, model stock plans, and never-out lists to plan balanced stock—an assortment that is both broad and deep enough to appeal to many customers.

Review

1. List four techniques retailers use to determine what customers are likely to buy.
2. What is the difference between national brands, private brands, and generic or no-name brands? Name one advantage to retailers of stocking each type.
3. Describe the two groups of shopping merchandise.
4. Define *standardized shopping goods* and give two examples.
5. Explain the difference between a fashion, a style, and a fad.
6. List the six steps in a fashion cycle.
7. Explain the difference between balanced stock, merchandise depth, and merchandise breadth.
8. Name and describe three assortment planning tools used in retailing.

Terms

The following terms were introduced in this chapter. Write a separate sentence correctly using each new term.

balanced stock	model stock plan
basic stock list	national brand
fad	private brand
fashion	shopping good
fashion cycle	style
in fashion	trademark

Discuss

1. What is the purpose of analyzing customer needs when determining merchandise assortments?
2. How can customer panels and teen boards be of value in analyzing customer needs and wants?

3. Why should a retail store operator understand the classifications of consumer goods?
4. How can a retailer of fashion goods reduce the risks involved in selling fashion merchandise?
5. How can retailers use assortment planning tools to identify items that should be offered for sale?

Problem Solving

1. If you were managing a shoe store in your community, how would you determine your customers' needs and preferences?
2. Select a grocery store item such as coffee, cereal, soup, or jam. Examine the item in a local grocery store. How many different brands of the item does the store carry? How many are national brands? private brands? generic brands? How many different sizes or flavors does the store carry in each brand? What changes would you suggest the store make in the depth or breadth of assortment of this item?
3. Identify a fashion item that is currently popular among students in your school. At what step in the fashion cycle is the item? How long will it be before it moves to the next step of the cycle? Why do you think so?
4. Select an item of clothing that is purchased by students in your school. Assume that you are a retailer and could have 36 of this item in stock. Develop two assortments: one that is an assortment with depth and another that has breadth. Which assortment would be better for your store in your community? Why?

CHAPTER 23

Selecting and Buying Merchandise

CHAPTER OUTCOMES

When you have mastered the information provided in this chapter, you should be able to:

1. Describe five sources of market information

2. List five merchandise-selection factors in a buying plan

3. Describe two means of buying goods in store

4. Explain how cooperative buying arrangements serve stores

5. Describe four means of buying goods in the market

6. List factors important in selecting merchandise resources

7. Explain how to set up a resource file

Determining the type and assortment of goods is only one phase in obtaining the right merchandise. Information about specific merchandise and their sources is equally important. A store handling convenience goods may buy from regional wholesalers or join other stores in a cooperative buying arrangement. A store handling fashion goods would more likely make direct contact with manufacturers rather than buying through intermediaries. Regardless of business size or product lines, retailers should go to suppliers rather than waiting for suppliers to call on them.

OBTAINING MARKET INFORMATION

Manufacturers and wholesalers are continuously making new merchandise available. To know what items are available or soon to be introduced, the merchant must obtain up-to-date product information. Most merchants use a variety of methods to find out what new items or models are coming into the market.

Supplier Representatives

Representatives of manufacturers and wholesalers are often excellent sources of new product information. They can show the retailer samples and indicate which items are expected to sell best to customers in that area. Some representatives may not have or present the most up-to-date merchandise or offer the best prices. Therefore, a merchant should not depend entirely on supplier representatives to learn about new products.

Nevertheless, personal acquaintanceship with product and supplier representatives can prove helpful in many ways. Information about products being developed and the retailer's needs can be exchanged. If the retailer wants to clarify an order or to get special assistance, knowing someone in the supplying firm is helpful.

Market Centers

Retailers must keep in touch with the entire wholesaling and manufacturing market. Ideally, the merchant makes periodic trips to the major market centers, such as New York City, Chicago, San Francisco, St. Louis, Philadelphia, Dallas, and Los Angeles. In these and other market centers, the retailer can inspect merchandise that otherwise would not be seen and can become acquainted with supplier representatives who may not make store visits.

Trade Shows

Often, exhibits or products from many suppliers are organized by manufacturers' associations, wholesalers, or groups of retail stores. These exhibits are known as *trade shows*. They may feature specific product lines or consist of several types of related merchandise areas. Trade shows are held regionally, serving retail stores in one geographic area, or nationally, serving retailers from all over the country.

The scope of a national trade show is illustrated by the National Housewares show. Under one roof are nearly 2,000 manufacturer exhibitors. This annual show represents the ultimate opportunity for the retailer looking for new and improved merchandise in the housewares area. Similar shows are held for almost all other consumer merchandise lines. In some cases, these shows become permanent displays and are maintained as showrooms year round. Typical examples include the Chicago American Furniture Mart, the Merchandise Mart of Chicago, and the Merchandise Center in Dallas.

Trade Papers

If merchants cannot afford to make trips to market centers or trade shows, they can get product information from trade publications. Almost every line of staple or fashion merchandise has a trade publication available on a subscription basis. A trade paper or trade journal is a publication containing information about products, merchandising, and other information of value and interest to people in a particular field or line of goods. For instance, *Women's Wear Daily* presents information about women's apparel; *Modern Retailer* provides valuable information for discount-store operators; and *Daily Men's Record* is of interest to retailers who sell menswear.

Trade Services

Many merchants subscribe to specialized trade services that provide specific market and product information. For example, the Retail News Bureau, a well-known trade service, employs shoppers to report their responses to the advertisements of

leading stores in New York, Chicago, and Los Angeles. Detailed reports, sometimes called *action item reports,* of each promotion are prepared and distributed to the Bureau's clients. Thus, a retailer, knowing the degree of success of a specific item in a certain store, can come to an intelligent decision as to whether to buy and promote that item. Trade services also are able to locate the wholesale source of an advertised item that is reportedly doing well. Also, some trade services conduct customer research and make projections of likely best-sellers in future seasons.

While each of these five methods of obtaining market information can be helpful, most retailers, like customers, prefer to see and touch the merchandise in which they are interested. Personal examination of an item can give a far better understanding

Illus. 23–1 Trade papers and magazines are an important resource for retailers. Almost every line of goods and type of store has a trade publication with information on merchandise and vendors.

of its qualities and features than a picture or written description. Thus, for new merchandise, retailers make a special effort to go to market centers or trade shows.

BUYING PLAN

The first step in choosing specific merchandise is to make a buying plan. A **buying plan** shows the classifications, price lines, and other important characteristics of the merchandise that is expected to meet customer demand. The total merchandise investment for any given period is set by the planned purchases and controlled by the open-to-buy figure (explained in Chapter 21).

The amount of open-to-buy for a merchandise classification must be further broken down in the buying plan by selection factors: color, size, style, material, and price. The breakdown of how much money will be invested in specific items can be quite detailed for staple and convenience goods. In the buying plan for fashion goods, the breakdown of an open-to-buy figure usually is less detailed because the buyer will want to see what is available before making specific plans.

Buying plans are more often set in merchandise units than in dollars. If the open-to-buy for children's playsuits is $800, the buyer may plan for 20 units at $8, 40 units at $12, and 10 units at $16. By noting the planned size and color breakdown, the buyer then divides the open-to-buy for each price line into sizes and colors. Thus, the 20 units for the $8 price line may be composed of six in size 4, eight in size 6, and six in size 6x. About half of each

size may be in blue and the rest equally divided between red and yellow. Similar plans are needed for each of the other price lines.

Styles are selected based on market information and expected customer preferences. The most difficult part of buying fashion goods is the need to anticipate customer demand long before merchandise is available. The manufacturers of clothing items begin production of a style and a material only after substantial orders have been received. Retailers must place orders many months in advance of the time they wish to have the goods in the store for sale to customers. It is often not possible to reorder best-selling styles and receive them within the selling season.

IN-THE-STORE BUYING METHODS

For stores handling primarily convenience goods, it may not be necessary for buyers to go into market centers to buy. Needed merchandise may be obtained from sales representatives who call at the store or ordered from wholesalers or other suppliers under cooperative buying arrangements.

Buying from Sales Representatives

Wholesalers and manufacturers whose lines contain a wide variety of items can afford to send sales representatives to call on stores. Depending on the merchandise lines, sales representatives, often called *sales reps,* may visit stores on a weekly, monthly, or even semiannual basis. Sales reps for greeting cards or hosiery may call on their accounts (retailers) every week or so. Sales reps for clothing lines or housewares may visit stores only once a year. Some suppliers supplement sales representatives' contacts with catalogs from which the retailer may place direct orders.

Sales representatives who call on retailers are of two types. One type provides product information and advice on merchandising strategy. The second type provides more comprehensive merchandising service, which may include inventory, display, and rotation of stock.

Sales representatives who provide merchandising services may ask the retailer for a certain amount of shelf or display space for their products. The representative may even assume responsibility for the display, inventory, and reordering of the merchandise. These persons may be called *rack jobbers* if they agree to maintain a rack or counter with their line of merchandise. Examples include cosmetics, ladies' hose, and bakery goods. The rack jobber regularly visits the store, replenishes items on the rack or counter, removes old or slow-selling items, and makes sure that the display is in good condition.

A wise merchant sets aside regular days and hours to see sales representatives. Otherwise, he or she is constantly interrupted in the performance of other duties. Exceptions may be made for those representatives who make advance appointments. A schedule for a hardware store is shown in Illustration 23–2.

By planning for each visit by a sales representative, the retailer can get the most from the contact. In addition to product information, ideas about promotion, product features that are moving well in other communities, and effective selling techniques may be obtained.

Cooperative Buying Arrangements

For many convenience goods stores, the most practical method of making market contacts is a cooperative buying arrangement. In such an arrangement, several retailers agree to buy a large part of their stock from a wholesaler or manufacturer who agrees to provide needed goods. Probably the most widely used cooperative buying arrangement is the voluntary chain. In this arrangement, a wholesaler contracts to

	Monday	Tuesday	Wednesday	Thursday	Friday	Saturday
A.M.	Inventory	Sales representatives	Weekly advertisements	Receiving new merchandise	–	–
P.M.	Account billing	New displays	Special deliveries	Stocking	–	–

Illus. 23–2   In this schedule of visits and other store activities, Friday and Saturday are left open because of heavy store traffic those days. Tuesday morning, when traffic is lighter, the staff can concentrate on visiting with sales representatives.

act as the buying and servicing agent for a group of stores. By serving a number of stores at one time, the wholesaler can reduce selling expenses. The wholesaler knows the specific needs of member stores and is able to buy large quantities of goods for which there is an assured market. The wholesaler can provide goods at a low price and provide merchandising and promotional assistance.

IN-THE-MARKET BUYING METHODS

Illus. 23–3   Retailers who attend central markets and trade shows can compare many different lines of goods and meet large numbers of vendors in a short period.

Large retail stores and those dealing with shopping goods tend to make their contacts with the market directly rather than through intermediaries. They, of course, may buy some merchandise through sales representatives, but larger stores concentrate on other means of making market contacts. These means include (1) market trips, (2) resident buying offices, (3) group buying, and (4) central buying.

Market Trips

Certain cities are well-known centers for the marketing of certain consumer goods. For instance, New York City, Los Angeles, Dallas, and San Francisco are known for women's wear and fashion goods. Boston, St. Louis, and Chicago are considered central markets for shoes. Central markets for furniture are High Point, N.C.; Chicago; Dallas; and Los Angeles.

Buyers who visit these central markets go to the individual showrooms of the vendors whose lines are of interest. These showrooms usually are located together or in a central facility, so that buyers may visit several vendors in a short time. One advantage of going to the central market is that the buyer can see the offerings of several manufacturers before placing an order.

How often a buyer visits the central market depends on the type of merchandise in question, the size of his or her retail store, and the distance of the store from the central market. Buyers of fashion goods may find it necessary to visit the central market frequently to keep up to date on style trends and new merchandise. Buyers of housewares may go to market only once a year to examine new products. Some small store houseware buyers may buy entirely from sales reps who call on their stores.

Resident Buying Offices

For merchants who are some distance from the central market and who make few market trips, the use of a resident buying office is essential. There are two distinct kinds of resident buying offices.

An independent office contracts with stores to provide them market services. Most independent buying offices charge a fee to the stores they represent. Others, however, collect a commission from the manufacturers on orders they obtain and make no charge to their store customers.

A store-owned office is owned by one or more stores. Buying offices owned by chain stores are known as *syndicate buying offices*. When a buying office is jointly owned by a group of independent stores, it is called an *associated buying office*. Some independent stores have their own private offices in central markets. Whatever the name, store-owned offices provide only buying services to their own stores. The services of a resident buying office are listed in Illustration 23–4.

Group Buying

Resident buying offices sometimes arrange group buying for their member stores. Under this plan, the buyers from a group of stores meet and select styles that all stores can sell. The usual procedure is for the resident buyer to assemble newly designed styles by different manufacturers. These styles are inspected at a meeting where each store's buyer votes on her or his preference. Usually, every buyer agrees to take at least a minimum number of all styles approved by the majority.

SERVICES OF A RESIDENT BUYING OFFICE

1. Gives advice as to the best sources for goods of every classification, price, and style. These sources are obtained from its up-to-date file of all manufacturers.
2. Keeps the store in touch with all developments in the wholesale market, including new styles, price changes, and bargains.
3. Buys goods for the store whenever the store buyer is unable to go to the market in person. The buying is based on a description of what is needed by the store.
4. Follows up on store orders to see that goods are shipped on time.
5. Handles adjustments involving returns or cancellations of orders.
6. May consolidate purchases made from different manufacturers into one large shipment, thus saving transportation charges.
7. Provides a store buyer with office space, a secretary, and personal service, and it notifies manufacturers when the store buyer will be in town.
8. Provides one of its own buyers to help the store buyer make selections.
9. Is occasionally able to get price concessions and exclusive styles for the store because of its association with other stores that buy the same styles.
10. May arrange for group and central buying, as explained in this chapter.

Illus. 23–4   Resident buying offices provide these and other services to stores and buyers.

CENTRAL BUYING

In a chain operation, central buyers specialize in the selection of merchandise, and store managers specialize in selling. Groups of independent stores also join to use central buying. There are three main kinds of central buying: (1) central merchandising, (2) listing system, and (3) central warehousing and requisitioning.

Central Merchandising

The central merchandising method is used extensively in fashion merchandising. The store sales supervisor sends to the central office a regular report of (1) styles received in stock and (2) styles sold. Once a week, the sales supervisor reports local trends and customer interest and sends in an inventory report listing goods in stock. On the basis of reports from all stores, the central office decides which merchandise to buy for the group, what to send to each store, and even when goods in the various stores should be marked down. The widespread use of electronic point of sales registers networked with computers has aided retailers in maintaining increasingly complex data on both sales and inventory.

Listing System

Under the listing system, central buyers choose the items that stores may carry. The central office sets specifications, selects styles, determines prices, and makes shipping arrangements. Individual store management decides when and how much to buy and then orders from the listed sources. The listing system is often used for buying shopping goods that do not change rapidly.

Central Warehousing or Requisitioning

Using the central warehousing or requisitioning method, a central buyer purchases and warehouses the goods. The stores order what they need by means of a requisition to the warehouse. Thus, the central buyers actually buy—they do not just make buying arrangements. The local store management decides when and how much to requisition from the warehouse.

SELECTING RESOURCES

There are many factors that a buyer must consider before deciding from whom to buy. Buyers are constantly urged by sales representatives, manufacturers, wholesalers, and other vendors to place orders with them. Unless the buyer is aware of some of the important factors in selecting a resource, he or she will probably make costly mistakes. Specifically, the following factors must be considered:

1. Suitability of supplier's goods to store customers. Are goods similar to what customers have been buying and of a consistent quality?
2. Completeness of line. Does the vendor have a broad assortment of goods and in sufficient quantities to meet the store's needs?

3. Ability to supply or manufacture to a store's specifications. Can the supplier meet the needs of buyers who have specific requirements in terms of materials, workmanship, and design?
4. How much a vendor can and will ship. Will the vendor supply small lots as well as large shipments depending on store need?
5. Favorable prices. Are the prices competitive for the quality offered? If the prices are not competitive, are they justified by other reasons?
6. Up-to-date lines. This applies particularly to fashion goods. Does the vendor carry goods that are in the upswing of the fashion cycle?
7. Creativity. Does the vendor show a flair for developing new ideas in merchandise?
8. Speed of delivery. Can the vendor deliver goods promptly according to an agreed-upon schedule?
9. Credit terms. Is credit available? How much time does the vendor allow for paying bills?
10. Dealer aids. Does the vendor supply displays, advertising materials, or other sales aids?
11. Pricing and brand policy. Does the vendor insist on a standard retail price? Are both national and private brands available?
12. Fairness in handling complaints. Are the vendor's guarantee and adjustment policies favorable? Is the vendor reliable?
13. Facilities for repairing or servicing products. Are factory-authorized repair centers set up throughout the country? Will customers find it convenient to return merchandise for repair?
14. Length of time in business. Has the vendor been in business long enough to have proven ability to serve customers? (Incompetent vendors cannot stay in business long.)

PREPARING A RESOURCE FILE

Buyers should develop a resource record for each vendor contacted. The record should show the name and address of the vendor, the kinds of goods carried, the price ranges in which the vendor specializes, the terms allowed, the names of the sales representatives, and general impressions of the firm. If a purchase is made, notations should be made as to promptness of delivery, correctness of the order received, and marketability of the goods. The resource record should be filed by merchandise classification(s) and price line(s). If this is done, the buyer has a convenient up-to-date resource file to refer to when in need of new stock.

Retailers find it advantageous to concentrate their business with vendors that have been found to be most satisfactory. Such a vendor, called a **key resource,** often supplies goods for which the retailer enjoys large sales volume and substantial markup.

There are other special resources that retailers may need to use for special buying situations. For example, auction houses often are good sources for items such as Oriental rugs and antiques. Import houses or foreign exporters may be the best and often the only sources for certain foreign-produced goods. Retailers need to be particularly careful in the selection of sources of imported goods. Federal laws on such merchandise, especially on fabrics, toys, and foods, must be observed.

EVALUATING MERCHANDISE OFFERINGS

Regardless of the resource or buying method used, merchandise should be evaluated carefully before it is purchased. A buying checklist is helpful in evaluating merchandise offerings. A checklist may be written, or it simply may be carried in the buyer's head. What follows are some of the questions that may be asked:

1. Is the item suitable for my department or store?
2. Does the item have appeal for a specific customer group?
3. Will it stand up well in use?
4. Is the item clearly not a duplication of goods already in stock or on order?
5. Will my customers be able and willing to buy it at the retail price that I will have to set?
6. Is it a good value at its price?
7. Will it provide a satisfactory profit margin in view of volume opportunities?
8. Is the item properly packaged?
9. Are special services available from the resource and are they desirable?

If the buyer can answer *yes* to most of these questions, the merchandise item is likely to be a good choice. In evaluating merchandise, the buyer should consider how the item will be sold. Can the item be promoted enthusiastically? Will salespeople willingly bring it to the attention of customers? A buyer must keep in mind that an item not worth promoting is not worth buying.

Summary

The procedures used in selecting and buying merchandise vary depending on the type of merchandise being handled and the size and organization of the retail store. Information about new merchandise can be obtained from suppliers' representatives, by going to market centers and trade shows, by reading trade papers, and by subscribing to services that provide trade information. After preparing a buying plan, the retailer must decide whether to use in-the-store or in-the-market buying methods. In either case, numerous factors must be considered in deciding which vendor will be used. A resource file may be developed to provide a record of the important features of each vendor's service. A buying checklist is a valuable tool in evaluating merchandise offerings regardless of the buying method used.

Review

1. Describe five means of obtaining market information.
2. What are the five selection factors in a buying plan for a typical merchandise classification?
3. What are the two in-store methods of buying goods?
4. What role do wholesalers play in cooperative buying?
5. List four means of buying goods in the market.
6. Name two kinds of resident buying offices.
7. How does a central merchandising plan work?
8. What is the purpose of a resource file?
9. What questions should be asked when evaluating merchandise?

Terms

The following terms were introduced in this chapter. Write a separate sentence correctly using each new term.

buying plan   key resource

Discuss

1. Of what value is an action item report?
2. What information about customer demand should a merchant have before talking to a sales representative?
3. Why would a retailer want a sales representative to perform merchandising services, such as arranging stock, in addition to selling?
4. Which services of a resident buying office would be most helpful to a large department store in setting up a new line of merchandise?
5. If a central buyer selects the new clothing styles and then has the merchandise shipped to member stores, how can the support and cooperation of the store department managers be assured?
6. Which questions asked in evaluating merchandise would be most important for a retailer handling convenience goods?

Problem Solving

1. Illustrate how an open-to-buy of $880 could be arranged into a buying plan calling for 48 units at three prices—$15, $18, $22—with an equal number of units at each price in two colors.
2. What are the major merchandise markets in your state or region? Which major trade shows are attended by one of the merchants in your community?
3. Assume that you are the owner of a small variety store. Sales representatives from both manufacturers and wholesalers frequently call at your store. What policies or procedures would

you establish to make these calls as productive for you as possible?

4. Assume you are the buyer for men's and women's dress gloves for a department store. A vendor offers you a line of leather gloves with cotton lining in black or brown. The wholesale price is $64 per dozen in assorted sizes of your choice. What questions would you need answered before deciding whether or not to buy?

CHAPTER 24

Negotiations with Suppliers

CHAPTER OUTCOMES

When you have mastered the information provided in this chapter, you should be able to:

1. List three ways to estimate prices of merchandise

2. Identify five forms of discounts that may be allowed by vendors

3. Explain the purpose of each of the five forms of discounts

4. List and define common billing and shipping terms

5. Describe special services that may be available from vendors

6. Name the conditions that make a merchandise order a binding contract

The buyer who has identified good resources that offer appropriate merchandise is ready to actually buy. Buyers must obtain goods that can be sold at favorable prices to customers and provide a profit to the retail store. Buying the right goods is much more important than saving a few cents on the purchase price. Buyers make no effort to bargain when the seller's price and terms are right. However, successful buyers do not hesitate to press for concessions if they think circumstances may warrant a lower price.

The relationship between buyer and seller should be characterized by honesty and a spirit of fair play. Experienced buyers and sellers know that it is to their advantage to work together to provide goods that consumers want and need. To build a good relationship, both the buyer and the seller should adhere to principles of good business conduct and established trade practices. There must be a common understanding of prices, the buying process, discounts, billings, shipping terms, special terms, and the importance of each order.

ESTIMATING PRICES OF GOODS

A capable buyer can estimate, from a close inspection of the merchandise, the approximate cost price and probable retail price. This valuable skill is developed through study and experience. Buyers will take every opportunity to estimate prices on merchandise. Prices may be estimated in three ways.

The first is to estimate the retail price and then determine what an appropriate cost price would be. If the buyer's cost price is typically two-thirds of the retail price, then an item estimated to sell at retail for $17.95 should cost about $12.

A second means of estimating prices is to memorize them. The buyer may collect and memorize all price information for items that he or she may buy. Some buyers amaze people with their vast knowledge of prices and the ability to quote the retail or cost prices of hundreds of items in a store. Such a storehouse of price information is gathered by repetition, concentration on price information, and close attention to price and product changes.

The third means of estimating prices is to build up prices. This method is used when the buyer has a good knowledge of the cost of materials and labor necessary to produce the product. For example, upon being shown a selection of decorative drapery rods, a buyer might build up the price of each rod by adding the cost of the materials and labor to make one rod, the expenses involved in selling a rod, and a profit amount for the manufacturer. An example follows:

- Basic manufactured materials—rod, rings, and brackets—for 90-inch rod: $9.50.
- Labor for partial assembly: $2.75
- Labor for packaging: $.75
- Overhead, transportation, and manufacturer's profit margin: $4.25.

The total of these three figures ($17.25) represents the estimated cost price per rod to the buyer. If the retailer normally takes a 50 percent markup on cost, the approximate retail price to customers would then be $25.95.

With this estimate, the buyer is in an excellent position to judge the reasonableness of the supplier's price. If the vendor offers the rod at a price much more than $17.25, the buyer must assume there is some value in the rod that was not noticed. If the rod is quoted at considerably less than $17.25, the buyer must suspect poor materials, poor workmanship, or a poor seller that the manufacturer is eager to move.

DISCOUNTS

In retail merchandising, a **discount** is a reduction from the **list price,** the price set by the manufacturer or vendor. A discount is stated as a percentage of the list price. Some store managers insist on a certain percentage discount when purchasing from vendors. The merchandise manager may even refuse to confirm buyers' orders that do not carry expected discounts. Store management may actually set a specific discount rate that buyers are to obtain. If the buyers fail to obtain that rate from vendors, the difference is charged against the budgets of the buyers' departments. The most commonly offered discounts are the quantity discount, seasonal discount, trade discount, cash discount, and anticipation discount.

Quantity Discount

A buyer may qualify for a **quantity discount** by buying unusually large quantities. For example, an order for 1000 items at $5 each, instead of a usual order of 100 items, may qualify a buyer for a 5 percent quantity discount. Thus, the price for the 1000 items would be $4,750 rather than $5,000. Quantity discounts are regulated by

law to prevent unfair discrimination. (The Robinson-Patman Act governs the question of price discrimination among business customers.) Quantity discounts are permitted as long as the discount is limited to the amount the seller saves by selling an unusually large quantity. A quantity discount is unlawful if it exceeds the savings gained by the seller in selling the larger quantity. Also, a quantity discount must be made available to all buyers who buy a particular quantity.

Seasonal Discounts

Vendors sometimes grant buyers a seasonal discount if purchases are made in the manufacturer's off-season. In many product lines, consumer purchasing is highly seasonal and store buyers tend to concentrate their buying within a few months. As a result, the vendors are swamped with orders at one time, while, at other times, the production plants are nearly idle. To keep plants and skilled workers producing evenly, the manufacturer or vendor finds it worthwhile to offer concessions to the buyer who will place an early order. Thus, the buyer who will order Halloween costumes in January or February may pay a lower price than one who orders in July or August.

Trade Discount

A **trade discount** is usually not a true price reduction. It is a deduction from the *list price that has been set to include a retail profit margin.* In the hardware trade, for example, retailers are granted a trade discount of perhaps 40 percent off list prices.

Wholesalers and other buyers may receive an additional percentage trade discount. The percentage is set high enough to cover the average dealer's necessary markup for expenses and profit.

A trade discount is sometimes called a **functional discount** since the discount is given because the buyers perform certain functions for the seller. Differences in the functions performed account for the differences in the amount of the trade (functional) discount. Wholesalers usually buy in larger quantities than do retailers, and they sell to markets beyond those that the manufacturer ordinarily serves. Therefore, wholesalers generally are granted larger trade discounts than are retailers. Occasionally, a group of retailers will qualify for a wholesaler's functional discount by organizing buying offices and by setting up a warehouse operation. Thus, a 40 percent discount for the retail function and a 10 percent functional discount to the wholesaler may be quoted as "less 40, less 10." Thus, if the list price is $10, the cost is computed as follows:

List price	$ 10.00
Less 40%	− 4.00
	6.00
Less 10%	− .60
Cost	$5.40

It should be noted that where there is a series or chain of discounts, each discount is a percentage of the previous balance, not of the original list price. In the preceding example, the 10 percent discount is a percentage of $6, not of $10. If a manufacturer sells an article to be used by another manufacturer, an additional small discount may be granted. Thus, if an additional 5 percent discount usually is given manufacturers, the trade discount will be shown as "less 40, less 10, less 5 percent" or simply "40/10/5."

Cash Discount

A **cash discount,** a percentage reduction of the list price, is given if a buyer pays within a specified number of days after the invoice (billing) date. Most sellers offer a cash discount to induce buyers to pay for merchandise before the due date of the billing. Sellers offer cash discounts to obtain prompt payment, to avoid having to borrow operating cash, and to avoid the costs of collecting late payments. Late payments and bad debts often result when no special inducement for prompt payment is offered retail buyers.

To obtain a cash discount, it is seldom necessary for a retailer to pay as soon as goods are shipped or even as soon as they are received. The common practice is to allow a discount if goods are paid for within ten days from the billing date, which usually is the same as the shipment date. A ten-day period generally provides ample time for the goods to arrive at the retail store and for the retail buyer to inspect the goods, check them against the invoice (list of goods and charges), and process the invoice for payment. Thus, if goods are shipped on July 5 with terms of 6 percent discount if paid within ten days and net (full, no discount) payment due in 30 days (6/10, net 30), the invoice must be paid by July 15 to earn a discount of 6 percent. The full amount for the merchandise is due August 4 (see Illustration 24–1).

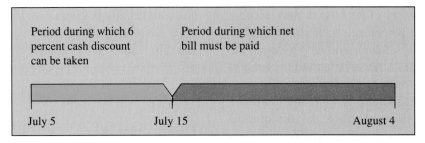

| Period during which 6 percent cash discount can be taken | Period during which net bill must be paid | |
| July 5 | July 15 | August 4 |

Illus. 24–1   This scale compares the time during which a cash discount is available with the time allowed for paying the net invoice amount.

Every retailer should take advantage of cash discounts when they are available. These discounts lower the cost of goods to the store. Also, by paying within the discount period, a retailer builds a good credit rating in the market.

Anticipation Discount

Buyers with plenty of ready cash sometimes pay a bill even before the cash discount date. From the discounted price, they deduct the interest, at the going market rate or in the amount allowed by the vendor, for the number of days of prepayment. The amount deducted is called an **anticipation discount.** For example, suppose that goods are billed on March 10 at $100, 4/30, net 60. The buyer may decide to pay the bill immediately on March 10, 30 days before the discounted amount is due. At an annual interest rate of 8 percent, the rate for one month (30 days) is two thirds of 1 percent (0.667%). For paying ahead of time, the buyer may deduct, in addition to the 4 percent cash discount ($4.00), an extra 0.667 percent from the cost of the goods. Thus, the buyer in this example deducts 4.67 percent from the billed amount and pays $95.33 instead of $100.

TERMS OF SALE

The indication of a cash discount, such as 4/30, net 60, is called the *billing term*. Arrangements for shipping goods from the seller also are indicated on the invoice in abbreviated forms. These arrangements are called the *shipping terms*. Together, the billing and shipping terms make up the *terms of sale*.

Billing

The billing terms of a sale indicate how much time the seller gives the buyer to pay for the goods (another word for the billing terms is *dating*). Billing terms include the following frequently used terms:

- *Cash on delivery* (**COD**) means that the goods must be paid for upon delivery at the retail store.
- *End of month* (**EOM**) means that the payment date is figured from the end of the month. Thus, an April 5 shipment of clothing dated 8/10 EOM, net 30 means that the terms begin after April 30.
- *Receipt of goods* (**ROG**) means that the date of payment may be computed from the date goods are received by the store

rather than from the date of the invoice (shipment). Thus, the terms 8/10 ROG, net 30 on a shipment made April 5 and received April 17 means that the net does not have to be paid until May 16. Retailers who are some distance from the market may be granted ROG terms.

- **Extra dating** means that the buyer is given a specific number of extra days in which to pay. Thus, in the terms 8/10, net 30 X60, the buyer has 60 extra days for payment or a total of 90 days from the invoice date.
- **Postdating** or **advance dating** means that the invoices are dated after the date of shipment, giving buyers extra time for payment. For example, the invoice for a shipment on April 5 might be dated May 5. This postdating would give the buyer an extra 30 days to pay the bill.

A less frequently used billing term, *cash in advance* (**CIA**) may be required of new merchants or of those who have poor credit ratings.

Shipping

The shipping terms on the invoice indicate the shipping arrangements for merchandise and whether the seller or the buyer is to pay for the shipment. There are four common FOB shipping terms. *FOB* means *free on board*.

- **FOB factory** means that the buyer is to pay all transportation costs and is to own the goods from the moment they are shipped.
- **FOB destination** means that the seller is to pay all transportation costs and is to own the goods until they arrive at the store.

- **FOB shipping point** means that the seller pays any cartage necessary to the place where the goods are turned over to a transportation company.
- **FOB destination, charges reversed** means that the seller owns the goods until they get to the store, though the buyer agrees to pay the transportation charges.
- **FOB factory, freight prepaid** means that the goods are owned by the buyer as soon as they are shipped, but the seller pays the freight charges.

When negotiating the method of shipment, the buyer has two major factors to consider: time and cost. When merchandise needs can be estimated well in advance, the slower but less expensive means of shipment should be chosen. Such means might be railroad freight, railway express, motor freight, or fourth-class mail. If merchandise is needed quickly, then faster means such as air express, first-class postal service, or private parcel delivery would be preferred.

SPECIAL SERVICES

When all other factors are equal, any special services that might be negotiated with a manufacturer or supplier may influence the buyer's decision to purchase. These services may involve promotional aids, an allowance by the seller for advertising, packaging or ticketing services performed by the buyer, or the provision of additional merchandise by the seller. Such special services are lawful if they are available on proportionally equal terms to all buyers.

Illus. 24–2 Retailers must be sure that promotional materials provided by suppliers or manufacturers are appropriate for their stores.

Promotional Aids

Certain promotional aids may be an important service to the buyer. Cooperative advertising is an arrangement in which the manufacturer agrees to pay part of the retailer's costs for advertising the manufacturer's product. The manufacturer may agree to pay a flat sum or a certain percentage of the retailer's advertising expenses. If a flat sum is set, it may be deducted from the cost of the merchandise. If a percentage of the advertising cost is paid by the manufacturer, the retailer usually must show detailed records of advertising and request a credit or payment for the amount allowed.

If the buyer agrees to provide choice display space, the seller may be willing to give the buyer an allowance from the regular price. Sellers may provide the buyer with material for window, interior, or point-of-purchase displays. Care must be taken that materials provided by sellers are appropriate for the buyer's store and promotional efforts. Sellers may also agree to provide

specially trained product demonstrators for a certain number of days in the buyer's store.

Packaging and Ticketing

Buyers who can negotiate special packaging or ticketing with suppliers can eliminate some store expenses and, at the same time, improve sales. The seller, for example, may be willing to pack merchandise in convenient or eye-catching packages—all ready for store shelves. In some cases, the supplier will preticket merchandise before it is shipped to the retailer. **Preticketing** simply means that the retail price of the item is attached, often on tickets supplied by the retailer or on the item itself as marked by the supplier. Preticketing is a savings to the retail store and allows goods to be placed on the selling floor more quickly.

Merchandise Deals

The retail buyer is often offered a merchandise deal in which a certain amount of goods is given free by the seller if the buyer orders in quantity or performs a promotional service. For instance, a grocer may be offered a dozen free boxes of Brand A tea if ten dozen boxes of the tea are ordered. This reduces the cost of Brand A tea to a more attractive price. According to the Robinson-Patman Act, the same offer must be made to all other buyers. The buyer should thus realize that all grocers in the area will sell Brand A tea at low prices because the cost price of the tea was the same for all. Merchandise deals are common in

Illus. 24–3   Manufacturers or suppliers often agree to develop special packaging for buyers who purchase in large quantities.

the grocery, housewares, and drug sundries trades, where they are frequently used to introduce new items.

ORDERING

A buyer's merchandise order must be prepared carefully. An order properly filled out, signed, and accepted by the vendor is a legal contract. This means that the order is an agreement containing a promise enforceable by law. The order has a lawful purpose (sale of goods); is made by competent parties (people over age 21, or 18 in some states, who are sane and are not alien enemies of the United States); contains an offer and acceptance (buyer offers a price for goods and offer is accepted by vendor); shows consideration (buyer promises to give up money, seller is to give up goods); and involves a meeting of the minds (both buyer and seller understand and agree on every condition in the order). Many stores today have a computerized purchasing system. Data is entered by the buyer and a standard order form is generated on the printer, with the specific order information completed. Often, stores insist that their buyers use their order forms and not those provided by suppliers. This policy cuts down on inaccurate or incomplete orders.

Preparing the Order

Common errors in completing order forms include omitting credit terms and discounts, omitting transportation instructions, and using incorrect shipping dates. Checklists, such as the one in Illustration 24–4, help eliminate errors in orders. On a store order form, the buyer should know where each of the negotiated selling terms is to be entered. Also, the forms should be numbered and an accurate record maintained of each order.

Buyers should write their own orders, even though suppliers or manufacturers' sales representatives may be glad to do it for them. Every order should be made out in multiple copies. The original copy is for the seller and duplicates are for the buyer. In large stores, four or more copies may be required. The copies go to the accounting offices, the receiving departments, the merchandise managers, and the department heads.

Confirming the Order

Before shipping goods, a careful vendor makes sure that the order is confirmed by an authorized person connected with the store. Some stores may require that the merchandise manager sign all orders to vendors. The purpose of the order confirmation is to exercise a check on the buyer. Requiring order confirmation prevents the purchase of any goods that the merchandise manager believes is unwise or orders that exceed the buyer's open-to-buy. Some stores require the merchandise manager's signature only on orders over a certain dollar amount.

INFORMATION CONTAINED IN AN ORDER

- Names and addresses of both buyer and seller
- Department for which goods are being purchased
- Date of order
- Quantity
- Description of the goods
- Unit cost
- Extension
- Total cost of order
- Credit terms
- Discounts
- Transportation instructions
- Delivery date
- Terms and agreements that cover all orders placed
- Signatures

Illus. 24–4   *Buyers should make sure that the correct information is included in their order forms because, once an order is accepted by the seller, it is a legal document.*

Summary   The retail-store buyer goes into the buying process with a good understanding of prices for the goods he or she plans to buy. Through experience and training, the buyer is able to estimate the price of goods offered by a manufacturer or vendor. Once locating desired merchandise, the buyer negotiates discounts, sales terms, and special services with the seller. Merchandise managers often expect that buyers will negotiate discounts on all orders placed with suppliers. Discounts commonly offered are quantity, seasonal, and trade discounts, as well as cash and anticipation discounts. Also, the buyer must obtain favorable billing and shipping terms as well as any special services that might assist in the sale of the goods purchased. Because of the detail on a merchandise order, buyers are often required to use order forms prepared by their stores. Vendors should confirm orders with a store's merchandise manager before shipping goods to the store.

*R*eview

1. List three ways a buyer can estimate prices of merchandise.
2. List the five kinds of discounts usually available to the retail buyer.
3. Explain the primary purpose of a cash discount to the seller.
4. Explain the primary purpose of a trade discount.
5. List and define five frequently used billing terms.
6. List and define four frequently used shipping terms.
7. List three types of special services a vendor may provide a buyer for a retail store.
8. What conditions must an order meet to be considered a legal contract?

*T*erms

The following terms were introduced in this chapter. Write a separate sentence correctly using each new term.

anticipation discount	FOB factory, freight prepaid
cash discount	FOB shipping point
CIA	functional discount
COD	list price
discount	postdating or advance dating
EOM	preticketing
extra dating	quantity discount
FOB destination	ROG
FOB destination, charges reversed	trade discount
FOB factory	

*D*iscuss

1. Are quantity discounts a fair practice from the small-store owner's point of view? Why or why not?
2. Under what conditions would a retail buyer particularly want to have billing terms of extra dating?
3. If you were a small retailer some distance from the market, would you prefer an EOM or an ROG dating on your purchases? Why?

4. A vendor offers a long-time, loyal buyer an inexpensive personal gift. Should the buyer accept? Why or why not?

*Problem
Solving*

1. What is the net amount of an invoice for $2,500 if the trade discount terms are minus 20 percent, minus 10 percent?

2. On a $500 invoice dated November 1 with billing terms of 8/10, net 30, what is the amount due if it is paid on November 10? on November 27?

3. A buyer has found two suppliers with comparable products; both suppliers quote a price of $8 per unit. Company A provides the following: 2 percent cash discount, net 60 days, a 5 percent quantity discount for over 115 units, shipment FOB destination, $50 cooperative advertising allowance for 100 or more units, and free display materials valued at $35. Company B provides the following: 2 percent cash discount, net 30 days, a 6 percent quantity discount for an order of 100 units or more, shipment FOB factory, 1 percent advertising allowance, and display materials valued at $10. The buyer knows that freight costs are about $65. If the buyer wants 100 units, based on just these facts, which company is it best to choose? If the buyer wants 125 units, from which company is it best to buy?

4. A chair is listed at $95 with a trade discount of 30 percent, 10 percent. If the terms of the sale to the retailer are 2/10, net 30, and the invoice is paid within the discount period, what is the net cost of the chair?

CHAPTER 25

Markups and Markdowns

CHAPTER OUTCOMES

When you have mastered the information provided in this chapter, you should be able to:

1. Identify the major elements in the markup equation

2. Calculate markup, retail, and cost when any two of these figures are given

3. Explain the difference between initial-markup percentage and maintained-markup percentage

4. Identify the figures necessary to plan desired markup

5. Calculate markdown percentage when dollar markdown and total sales are given

6. Explain the two major purposes of markdowns

7. Identify the five main reasons markdowns are necessary

8. Describe two general plans that stores may follow in their timing of markdowns

The setting of an appropriate retail price on merchandise is important to the retailer in two ways. First, the price must be one that is attractive to customers. Second, the price must be sufficient to cover the cost of the goods plus the retailer's expenses and to provide a profit margin. As mentioned in Chapter 21, the amount that a merchant adds to the cost price of merchandise in arriving at the retail price is called **markup.** For example, a retailer buys a pair of shoes for $45 and sells them for $60. The $15 that the retailer added to the cost price is the markup on the shoes. When an item that has been priced by the retailer at $18 is reduced in price to $12 in order to sell, that reduction is called a **markdown.** As will be explained in this chapter, there are several reasons retailers take markdowns.

THE MARKUP EQUATION

The basic markup equation is as follows: *cost (C) + markup (M) = retail (R)* or *C + M = R*. Using the same elements, the equation can be expressed as retail − markup = cost and retail − cost = markup. Thus, for the shoes in this example, the cost is $20, the markup is $10, and the retail price is $30.

Most merchants think of markup as a percentage rather than a dollar-and-cents figure. With percentage, it is easy to compare markups, even though the prices differ. Once the dollar amount of markup is known, it is simple to convert this figure into a percentage. Markup may be expressed either as a percentage of retail price or as a percentage of cost price. *Most merchants prefer to treat markups as a percent-*

age of retail and, in this book, markup percentages are expressed on the retail basis unless noted otherwise. If markup is to be expressed as a percentage of retail, it may be calculated by using Formula 25−1:

FORMULA 25−1

Markup Percentage of Retail = Markup in Dollars ÷ Retail Price

Suppose that a merchant buys women's blouses for $18 each and plans to sell them for $30 each. The markup for each blouse is $12, or 40 percent (M$/R$ = M% of R; 12/30 = 0.4 = 40%).

If markup is to be expressed as a percentage of cost, it may be calculated by using Formula 25−2:

FORMULA 25−2

Markup Percentage of Cost = Markup in Dollars ÷ Cost Price

In the preceding example, the markup on each blouse, expressed as a percentage of cost, is 66.67 percent (M$/C$ = M% of C; 12/18 = .6667 = 66.67%). Note that, although the percentage based on retail and on cost differ, the amount of markup in dollars is the same.

INITIAL AND MAINTAINED MARKUPS

Two kinds of markups are commonly used in retailing: the initial markup and the maintained markup. Suppose that a towel costs a retailer $7 and is priced to sell at

$10. The $10 price is called the **original retail selling price.** Later, the towel may be reduced to $8.95 and finally sold at that price. The $8.95 price is the **final selling price.** The difference between the cost price and the original retail selling price is the **initial markup** (also called *markon*).

The difference between the cost price and the final sales price is the **maintained markup.** Some stores use the terms *maintained markup* and **gross margin** interchangeably. In the preceding example, if the towel had been sold at the original price of $10, the initial markup and the maintained markup would have been the same. The *maintained markup* should be enough above the cost to pay expenses and provide a profit. The initial markup must be even higher to provide for possible price reductions. The relationship of initial markup and maintained markup to sales price is shown in Illustration 25–1.

Determining Initial Markup

To plan initial markups, the retailer must estimate the following figures:

1. Total sales for the coming year or season
2. Expenses for that period
3. Price reductions (markdowns, shortages, discounts)
4. Profits planned for that period

The initial-markup percentage can be calculated by inserting the estimated figure, as shown in Formula 25–3:

FORMULA 25–3

Initial-Markup
Percentage = (Expenses + Profits + Price Reductions) ÷ (Sales + Price Reductions)

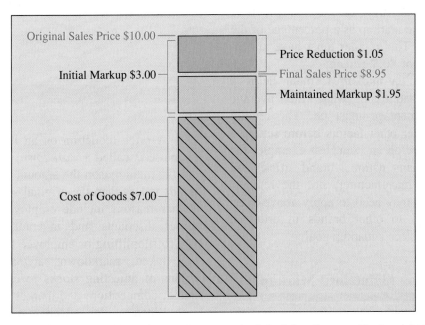

Illus. 25–1 The concept of initial markup is shown on the left of the diagram. On the right is the concept of maintained markup.

Suppose that a retailer estimates the annual sales in a department to be $100,000, expenses to be $30,000, and price reductions to be $10,000 and has set a profit goal of $5,000. The result is as follows:

Initial-Markup
Percentage = ($30,000 + $5,000
+ $10,000) ÷ ($100,000 + $10,000)
= $45,000 ÷ $110,000 = 0.4090 × 100
= 40.9%.

The dollar markup the retailer must have is the sum of the expenses, profits, and reductions ($45,000). The estimated sales of $100,000 is the expected result after reductions have been made. Thus, the estimated reductions of $10,000 must be added to the sales of $100,000 to find the total retail at which the goods must first be priced and put into stock ($110,000). Finally, $45,000 is divided by $110,000 to determine the markup as a percentage of the retail price. This retailer must have an initial markup of 40.9 percent.

The initial-markup formula helps a merchant determine what the average markup percentage must be. The retailer must consider other factors before setting a specific price on an item. For example, the prices of many national brand articles are set by the manufacturer, not the retailer. The retailer may need to apply above-average markup to other brands in order to achieve the store's markup goal.

Determining Maintained Markup

Maintained markup is determined after goods have been sold. For example, a re-

tailer buys ten ladders at a cost of $23.70 each. A maintained markup goal of 35 percent is desired. The ladders are marked up by 40 percent and offered at a retail price of $39.50. Three are sold at this price. During a special sale, the ladders are offered at $34.50. Four ladders are sold at this price. Following the sale, the remaining ladders are again offered and sold at $39.50. When the ten ladders have been sold, the retailer's records show that six were sold at $39.50 and four were sold at $34.50. Thus, the ten ladders sold for $375, cost $237, and produced a margin of $138. The maintained markup on the ten ladders is 36.8 percent; that is, the total markup ($138) is 36.8 percent of total sales ($375). Had seven ladders been sold in the special sale, the maintained markup on the ladders would have been 34.2 percent, or less than desired. If this had happened, the merchant might set the initial markup on the next shipment of ladders at 42 percent.

MARKDOWNS

A price reduction on an item of merchandise is called a *markdown*. Markdowns are the main reason the amount received for goods is less than the original selling price. (Other reasons include employee and customer discounts and inventory shortages due to shoplifting or employee theft.) Properly taken, markdowns are an effective means of adjusting stocks to customer demand, competition, and market conditions.

When retailers advertise markdowns to customers, the reductions are stated most often as a percentage off the original retail price. "Half-price sale," "20 percent off," and "clearance sale" are advertising phrases indicating markdowns. For their own use, however, merchants express markdowns as a percentage of the final sale price of all goods sold during a period—a month, a season, six months, or a year. If the markdown percentage for a period is larger than expected, the merchant is alerted to examine the type or quality of merchandise as well as advertising and sales efforts.

The markdown percentage is calculated by using Formula 25–4:

FORMULA 25–4

Markdown Percentage = Dollar Markdown ÷ Total Sales

While markdown percentages may be calculated for individual units of merchandise, the dollar markdown and total sales figures are usually on a class of goods or an entire department. For example, if ten items originally priced at $10 apiece are reduced to $8.95 each, the total markdown is $10.50; that is, *10 × ($10.00 − $8.95) = 10 × $1.05 = $10.50*. If the total sales during the period, including the sales of the marked down goods, are $400, the markdown is 2.625 percent of the total sales *(MD% = M ÷ TS; $10.50 ÷ $400 = .02625 = 2.625%)*.

REASONS FOR MARKDOWNS

There are two major purposes of markdowns: (1) to reduce prices on merchandise that customers are not buying in the expected quantities or at the planned rate and (2) to stimulate the sale of the reduced item or to increase the sale of regularly priced goods during the period of a special sale. Most markdowns are caused by errors made in merchandise selection (buying), in initial pricing, or in selling techniques. Also, many markdowns are also taken because of poor inventory control or because of merchandise policy.

Buying Errors

If a merchant buys at the wrong time, buys too much, or fails to spot the best-sellers in a merchandise line, markdowns probably will be necessary. Therefore, to prevent markdowns, a buyer should plan purchases by class or price line and, if possible, experiment with the sale of small quantities before placing large orders. Often, goods are not examined carefully, and, as a result, merchandise that is faulty in workmanship, color, or style is put into stock and later must be marked down. Goods that are styled right, bought right, and priced right usually sell without a markdown. That is why the buying function is so important to a retailer.

Pricing Errors

A buyer may misjudge what customers will pay and price goods too high. For example, one buyer purchased several dozen summer slacks at a cost of $22 each and priced them at $42.95. The slacks did not sell well; when they were marked down to $34.95 each, they sold in large quantities. If the slacks had been priced originally at $34.95, no markdown would have been necessary.

REASONS FOR TAKING MARKDOWNS

Buying errors—wrong styles, sizes, colors, patterns, prices, quantities

Selling errors—careless and high-pressure selling; neglect of old stock

Pricing errors—marking goods too high at first

Poor control—failure to spot slow sellers promptly

Policy reasons—store policy that calls for markdowns in given merchandise

Illus. 25–2   Retailers may be forced to take markdowns to ensure even a small profit on merchandise, and they also may take markdowns voluntarily for policy reasons. Listed here are five reasons for taking markdowns.

Selling Errors

The training and attitude of salespeople are important influences on markdowns. Salespeople may encourage customers to take merchandise that is wrong in color, style, fit, or quantity, hoping that they will not return it. Generally, goods returned by customers must be marked down before they are sold again. Sometimes, salespeople show only the styles of merchandise they personally like. As a result, some merchandise stays in the store for a long time because of a salesperson's failure to show it to customers. Other salespeople tend to show only what is new and neglect to show basic stock. Markdowns can be prevented by training salespeople to avoid these common mistakes.

Poor Inventory Control

When accurate inventory records are not kept and checked, some classifications of stock can accumulate. So markdowns are necessary to reduce stock to an acceptable level. An organized follow-up system on every piece or class of merchandise is essential to ensure that goods do not remain in stock too long and ultimately require a drastic price cut. Stores having an effective stock-management system usually spot slow-selling merchandise promptly and avoid a stock buildup in such goods.

Policy Reasons

Stores that try to maintain full assortments until late in a buying season may need to take large markdowns to sell or close out stock at season's end. Some stores purposely take a high initial markup and then quickly follow with a large markdown to appeal to bargain seekers. Other stores set policies that prompt a particular pattern of markdowns. For example, a store may regularly take markdowns to meet competition. A retailer may stock expensive goods for prestige purposes but have to sell most of them at reduced prices. However, not all markdowns are due to errors or miscalculations. Merchants may have a policy about running frequent special sales to attract customers to the store. If sale markdowns are truly reductions from regular prices, they will stimulate customer traffic and increase purchasing interest.

MARKDOWN POLICIES

In addition to the reasons for markdowns just discussed, stores may take markdowns as a matter of merchandising policy. Decisions about when to take markdowns and the amount of markdowns to take depend on the merchandise being sold and the particular selling situation.

Timing of Markdowns

Stores follow two general plans in timing their markdowns. Markdowns may be taken several times within a selling season, either as soon as an item's rate of sale begins to drop or after the item has remained in stock for a fixed length of time. Stores that prefer not to have frequent sales may take markdowns late in a selling season in the form of a clearance sale.

With fashion merchandise, it is generally best to mark down items as soon as customer demand begins to drop. Daily sales records indicate the stage of customer demand. With staple merchandise, the markdown should be taken as soon as there is a danger of the goods becoming shopworn. Some stores set a limit on the amount of time merchandise can remain in stock at the original price. When that time limit has been reached, the goods are marked down. A four-, six-, or eight-week limit is common for fashion merchandise. Staple goods may not be marked down as long as stock turnover is rapid enough to maintain fresh stock.

Clearance sales held late in a season are favored by many stores. Such clearance sales do not interfere with the sale of regularly priced merchandise as do markdowns that are offered several times within a selling season. A late markdown means that the goods are given every chance to be sold at the original price. Also, the quantity of stock accumulated during a season will determine whether the clearance sale can be an important selling event. End-of-season markdowns can be widely advertised. For example, bargain hunters look forward to holiday sales and end-of-summer sales every year.

Amount of Markdown

No definite rules specify the amount of markdown to be taken. The merchant must determine the markdown for each item or class of goods in each selling situation but always keep in mind the need to cover expenses and make a profit. Some stores, however, do mark down their goods a fixed percentage, such as 10 percent, after the goods are in stock for a certain period of

Illus. 25–3 When goods must be marked down to sell, it is usually due to an error in buying, wrong selling price, poor selling techniques, or store policy.

time. This practice is called an *automatic markdown*.

Seldom does a retailer come out ahead by making a series of small markdowns instead of one large markdown. The first markdown that is taken should be large enough to sell most of the items that are be-ing reduced in price. It is also important that the markdown be large enough to make the goods seem a bargain to the customer and to make customers want to buy. The longer merchandise remains in stock, the more shopworn it becomes, decreasing its chances of being sold.

MATHEMATICS OF PRICING

Given	Calculation Goal	Formula
Cost price, retail price	Markup in dollars	Subtract cost from retail
Markup in dollars, retail price	Cost price	Subtract markup from retail
Markup in dollars, cost price	Retail price	Add cost to markup
Retail price, markup in dollars	Markup percentage (retail)	Divide markup by retail
Cost price, markup in dollars	Markup percentage (cost)	Divide markup by cost
Cost price, original retail selling price	Initial markup	Subtract cost price from original retail selling price
Cost price, final sales price	Maintained markup	Subtract cost price from final sales price
Retail price, markup percentage	Cost price	Multiply retail price by $(100\% - M\%)$
Cost price, markup percentage	Retail price	Divide cost by $(100\% - M\%)$
Estimated expenses, profits, price reductions, sales	Initial markup	Add expenses, profits, price reductions; divide this figure by (Sales + Reductions)
Original retail selling price, final sales price	Markdown	Subtract final sales price from original retail price
Dollar markdown, total sales	Markdown percentage	Divide dollar markdown by total sales

Illus. 25–4   Every retailer should memorize these formulas used in setting prices.

Summary

The amount added to the cost of goods in arriving at a retail price is called *markup*. The markup equation is cost + markup = retail. The first markup must be enough to cover estimated sales, expenses, price reductions, and profits for the period. The maintained markup, however, may be less than the initial markup.

Any reduction in retail price to a new selling price is called *markdown*. The markdown equation is retail − markdown = new retail. Markdowns are taken to stimulate the sale of goods. Markdowns are necessary if errors are made in selecting or pricing merchandise, if poor selling techniques are used, or if poor inventory control allows a buildup of goods. Markdowns also may be taken as a matter of a store's merchandising policy.

Review

1. What is the basic equation for markup?
2. What is markup if retail is $14 and cost is $10? What is cost if retail is $24 and markup is $7?
3. What is the difference between initial markup and maintained markup?
4. What figures are necessary in order to plan desired markup?
5. What is the markdown percentage if total sales are $4500 and markdowns are $90?
6. What are the two main purposes for markdowns?
7. List the five main reasons markdowns are needed to move goods.
8. Describe the two plans stores may follow in timing their markdowns.

Terms

The following terms were introduced in this chapter. Write a separate sentence correctly using each new term.

final selling price   markdown
gross margin   markup
initial markup   original retail selling price
maintained markup

Discuss

1. If two merchants located in the same shopping mall were selling identical articles, would it be reasonable to assume that they also were using the same percentage markup? Why or why not?
2. Why is it important for a merchant to know whether markdowns are due primarily to buying errors, selling errors, or pricing errors?

3. Should a store have a policy of taking a fixed markdown percentage on all merchandise after a certain time in stock? Why or why not?
4. What options does a retailer have if competition prevents pricing goods at a desired markup?
5. Is it fair to customers that some goods are initially overpriced and then marked down to give the appearance of a savings?

*Problem
Solving*

1. For each of the following three items, calculate the percentage markup on retail and the percentage markup on cost:
    Item A—Markup = $2.00, Retail = $7.00
    Item B—Cost = $7.50, Markup = $3.50
    Item C—Cost = $22.00, Retail = $34.00
2. If an article costs $10 and you desire a retail markup of 38 percent, what would be the minimum retail price?
3. If an article cost $8, the original retail was $12, and the sale price is $10.50, what are the (a) initial-markup percentage, (b) maintained-markup percentage, and (c) markdown percentage (assume no other sales)?
4. A retailer bought 25 lawn chairs for $11 apiece. The initial retail price was $18.50 apiece. Total sales on 25 chairs was $432. What were (a) the initial-markup percentage and (b) the maintained-markup percentage?

CHAPTER 26

Pricing and Adjustments

CHAPTER OUTCOMES

When you have mastered the information provided in this chapter, you should be able to:

1. Explain the relationship of cost and expenses to pricing

2. Name the three categories of expenses to be considered in pricing merchandise and give examples of each

3. Identify two demand factors in pricing

4. Explain why there might be a variation in markup on items carried in the same department of a store

5. Recommend when a lower- or higher-than-average markup may be justified

6. Explain the relationship of a store's sales policy to the way it prices merchandise

7. Explain why price adjustments should be recorded

A retailer computes the retail prices necessary to realize a desired markup. The discussion of markups and markdowns in Chapter 25 suggests that, in actual practice, merchants tend to vary considerably in pricing of individual merchandise items. Overall, however, they attempt to achieve a maintained markup that will cover expenses and provide a profit. Several important factors enter into the decision about exactly what price should be set on a given item or service. These factors involve the relationships among cost of merchandise and expense of operation, customer demand for goods, need for variation in markup, and store policy on sales and pricing.

COST AND EXPENSE FACTORS IN PRICING

The largest single factor in establishing a retail price is the cost of the merchandise to be sold. An additional factor is the expense of handling the merchandise to get it ready for sale. There are also expenses associated with selling the goods and keeping the store open for business. The terms **cost** and **expense** are frequently used interchangeably. There is, however, a technical difference. The term *cost* identifies the expenditures required to purchase the goods, to transport them to the store, and to alter or prepare them, if necessary, for sale. The term *expense* identifies all the expenditures required to operate the store; maintain the building; buy, sell, and handle the merchandise; and administer or manage the business. Money paid for buildings and equipment, except for repairs, is not included in expenses, but the annual depreciation (loss of value) on these assets is an expense.

In determining the original retail selling price of goods, three kinds of expenses must be considered: flat, variable, and overhead expenses.

A **flat expense** is an expenditure that is about the same for every article of merchandise, regardless of its cost or retail price. Classified as flat expenses are expenditures for handling goods, such as in receiving, marking, storing, wrapping, and delivering merchandise.

A **variable expense** is an expenditure that is different for each type of good. Some goods require more space to be stored, more time to be sold, greater advertising effort, or more capital to be carried in stock. Variable expenses include salespersons' salaries, advertising, insurance, and interest on the investment in goods.

The third kind of expense is called **overhead**—expenditures required for operating the store or department. Overhead expenses do not vary with the number or value of the specific items being sold. Overhead includes rent and store maintenance, record keeping and accounting supplies, and salaries of department and store managers.

To illustrate how the knowledge of costs and expenses can influence the setting of a retail price, examine the case of Big Lake TV Store. The store manager has purchased a new television model that costs $140. Flat expenses run about $22 a set, and variable expenses have been found to be about 10 percent of the total price of the television. The manager is considering three possible prices: $180, $190, and $200. Which should be the selling price? To decide, the retailer must first estimate how many sets will be sold at each price. This manager estimates ten sets per week at

$180; eight sets at $190; and six at $200. If the price is $180, then:

Retail Price	$180
Estimated Sales/Week	× 10
Total Sales/Week	$1,800
Cost ($140 × 10)	$1,400
Flat Expenses ($22 × 10)	220
Variable Expenses ($18×10)	+ 180
Total Cost and Expenses	$1,800

At a price of $180, an estimated ten TV sets could be sold per week. The total sales and total cost and expenses are equal and there would be no contribution to overhead or profit regardless of the number sold.

If the price is $190, then:

Retail Price	$190
Estimated Sales/Week	× 8
Total Sales/Week	$1,520
Cost ($140 × 8)	$1,120
Flat Expenses ($22 × 8)	176
Variable Expenses ($19 × 8)	+ 152
Total Cost and Expenses	$1,448

At a price of $190, an estimated eight TV sets in this model could be sold. The total sales would exceed total cost and expenses by $72.

If the price is $200, then:

Retail price	$200
Estimated Sales/Week	× 6
Total Sales/Week	$1,200
Cost ($140 × 6)	$840
Flat Expenses ($22 × 6)	132
Variable Expenses ($20 × 6)	+120
Total Cost and Expenses	$1,092

At a price of $200, an estimated six TV sets in this model could be sold. The total sales would exceed total cost and expenses by $108.

Of the three possible prices, the $200 price would contribute the most to overhead and profits. Thus $200 is the best of these three prices, at least over the short run. Knowing this information, the manager can make an informed decision on which price to set on the new line of TV sets.

An example of how price is affected by differences in expenses is the **multiple price** (the price for several units of the same item). An item may be retailed at $0.35 a unit or at $1 for three. Since the expenses of handling three items may be no more than handling one, variable expenses may not be increased by the larger transaction. Thus, the profit margin at the multiple price may be even larger than that on three separate sales at the unit price of $0.35. For example, canned whole-kernel corn may cost the grocer $0.39 per can, flat expenses of $0.06 per can, and variable expenses for one or three cans of corn of $0.05. If the grocer sells one can of corn at $0.53, the difference between the retail price and cost plus expenses is $0.03 [0.53 − (0.39 + 0.06 + 0.05)]. If three cans are sold for $1.54, the difference is $0.14 [1.54 − (1.17 + 0.18 + 0.05)].

DEMAND FACTORS IN PRICING

The initial price of merchandise must be set at a point at which the goods will readily sell. Thus, the nature of a store's customers and competitors has an important influence on markup.

Knowing the Customer

If customers expect stores to have numerous services, a high markup on certain goods may be acceptable. A high markup does not ensure a large profit for the retailer, however, since customer services increase a store's expenses and its losses from reductions. On the other hand, if customers tend to be price conscious, low markups may be appropriate. Low markups may be possible with low expenses, small markdowns, fast-selling items, and minimum service.

By talking with customers and observing their buying patterns, a retailer may find that customers prefer to buy when there are distinct differences in merchandise prices. For example, a shoe retailer found that customers bought more readily when shoes were in three price lines: $35, $55, and $75. Shoes were purchased at many different cost prices from suppliers but are offered at retail in one of these three price lines. The differences among these three prices shows a clear distinction in quality and style.

Another shoe retailer may be in a market where customers prefer to buy from among many price lines. Shoes may be priced anywhere from $34.50 to $95.50, with prices only a few dollars apart, such as $34.50, $39.50, $44.50, $47.50, and so on to the top price. The merchant uses whatever prices will move a style quickly.

Illus. 26–1   Most customers compare prices and base their selections on quality and appropriateness to their needs.

Knowing customer price and shopping preferences helps the retailer select the best price pattern for merchandise.

Studying the Competition

One of the major considerations in setting the price of individual items is the price that competitors are receiving for the same items. A supermarket, for example, sets most of its individual prices so they are the same as its competitor's prices. It will then try to set lower prices than its competition on certain featured items. Knowledge of competitors' prices is obtained by checking their advertising, visiting their stores, or talking with customers. Although most stores try to meet competition in prices, many compete in the offering of service. Thus, it is possible for a store to succeed and yet not meet competitors' prices. For example, a convenience food store open 24 hours per day may carry higher prices on all goods, except perhaps milk and bread, than a supermarket. The convenience of location and extended hours attract customers who will buy at higher prices. Stores may also attract customers by offering credit or other services, such as check cashing or home delivery.

VARIATIONS IN MARKUPS

In the same store and even in the same department, the markups on items may vary greatly. This variance is due partly to differences in variable and overhead expenses on items. In a furniture store, for example, a large table requires a great deal of storage and display space and surely will have to be delivered to the customer. Thus, it normally will require a higher markup than a lamp sold in the same department. The lamp occupies little space, and the customer will probably take the lamp at the time of the sale.

Another reason for differences in markup is the likelihood of a later markdown and the risk of stock shortage. For instance, clothing in basic styles and high-fashion styles is commonly carried in the same department. The likelihood of having to mark down a classic-style dress is much less than on a garment with new style. Thus, the classic dress warrants a lower markup than the high-fashion dress. Similarly, the markup on basic shoe styles is generally less than on the latest fads in footwear. Goods that are prepackaged in protective covers are more likely to remain fresh and salable. Goods carried in open displays are more likely to be shoplifted than goods in closed displays.

Higher-than-average Markup

A higher-than-average markup is generally justified when one or more of the following conditions is present:

1. When the risk of later price reduction is great, such as on a high-fashi   fad, or seasonal item
2. When the expense of han   to be abnormally high
3. When the goods a   art, handcrafts,   when the retai'   ership and *   competit'

4. When customers expect a great deal of service either at the time of the sale or because of installation and maintenance

Lower-than-average Markup

A lower-than-average markup is generally justified when one or more of the following conditions is present:

1. When staple merchandise, which is carried by most similar retailers, is stocked
2. When no packaging, delivery, or other special services are provided
3. When customers expect little personal service or can select desired items by themselves
4. When the stock turn is high, resulting in low space cost and few shopworn goods
5. When the volume opportunities at a lower-than-average markup will yield a larger dollar profit than could be obtained with an average markup

In any situation where lower-than-average markup seems justified, the merchant must be sure that the margin is still sufficient to cover expenses and provide a profit.

SALES POLICY AND PRICING

A store's special sales policy has a good deal to do with pricing. Some stores attempt to make use of the same merchandise to cater to three groups of customers: (1) those searching for new merchandise, (2) those who buy when they feel the need, (3) those looking for bargains. New styles are put into stock early in the season at markups sufficiently high to cover later markdowns. Later in the season, they are marked down sharply to appeal to price-conscious customers. The merchant's goal is to achieve the desired markup on the entire operation over the season.

Sales of Regular Goods

Some stores hold frequent special sales of regular goods. It is assumed that the extra volume realized during the sale, even at lower prices, will yield a profit since overhead expenses will not be increased as a result of the sale. After the sale, the goods are restored to their regular prices.

Special-purchase Goods

Often the special sale consists of goods purchased just for the sale and not carried regularly. The merchant attempts to find goods on which the store can take a substantial markup and still offer a bargain price. But the management knows that there will be remainders of unsold sizes and colors that will have to be closed out at sharp markdowns.

Some retailers arrange to buy extra quantities of regular goods to feature at special prices. With specially priced regular goods, the merchant is not faced with sharp markdowns for closeout—goods can be incorporated into regular stock. However, when these special price events become a regular part of the promotional effort of the store, customers may defer buying until those goods are at special prices.

Illus. 26–2 Prices set by retailers must cover the cost of the goods, expenses, and profit, but customer needs and competition must also be considered.

Leader Merchandising

Items are sometimes priced below their most profitable point or below the average markup simply to attract customers to the store. Whenever a store sells an article at a reduced price for the purpose of increasing customer traffic, the item is being used as a **leader.** For example, an article costing $1.20 customarily may retail at $2.00. A store may cut the price to $1.59, not in the hope of making money from increased volume on the item but to attract customers who will then buy other goods. The leader is thus used as an advertising device.

When a store sells an article at less than cost, the item becomes a **loss leader.** If the item in the preceding example were sold for $1.19, the merchant would be losing at least $0.01 on every sale, without considering flat expenses, variable expenses, or overhead.

Some retailers misuse leaders. Once the customer is in the store, purchase of the leader is sometimes discouraged and attempts are made to sell other higher-priced goods. This tactic is called *bait and switch* and it is illegal.

Premium Merchandising

A *premium* is something of value given free or at a low price in order to induce a customer to purchase merchandise. Many times, premium offers are established by manufacturers. The manufacturer's objective is to grant an indirect price cut that will introduce a new product or make the merchandise the leading product in its field. This may be done by the use of coupons, gifts, or trading stamps.

Coupons may be carried in advertisements, sent by direct mail, or printed on the package of the product. At the time of purchase of the item at the retail store, the customer presents the coupon which allows a reduction in the price of the item purchased. To obtain a gift offered by a manufacturer, the customer usually must return a proof-of-purchase insert from a box or label with a small sum of money. In return, the customer may receive a household gadget, T-shirt, poster, book, or other item of interest. Often inexpensive premiums are enclosed in the package containing the product. Cereal packages, for example, often contain puzzles, character cards, or toys.

A form of premium merchandising that used to be widespread is the trading stamp. With each purchase of merchandise, the customer is given trading stamps that, when accumulated, can be redeemed for merchandise at a redemption center. The use of trading stamps has decreased substantially. A current variation is the frequent-flier offer of some airlines, rental car agencies, and hotels. When the customer has accumulated sufficient points, he or she receives free airline tickets or upgrades in seating.

Similar to leader merchandising, the various premium devices can be successful in attracting customers. Many merchants, however, question the continued or expanded use of premiums. They believe that a product should be sold primarily on the basis of its merits, not because of gifts or extras.

TRACKING PRICE ADJUSTMENTS

Good retail practice requires that all merchandise markdowns be accurately recorded. Both the dollar amount of the markdown and the reason for the markdown should be recorded.

As described in Chapter 25, the dollar amount of the markdowns on a category of goods must be recorded so that the retailer will know what the final or maintained markup is on those goods. In addition, as

Illus. 26–3 Retailers must keep accurate records of all merchandise price adjustments so that the final or maintained markup is known on all goods.

each markdown is made on merchandise, the reason for the price adjustment should be recorded. Typical reasons for markdowns are features of products that customers find unappealing:

1. Color
2. Size
3. Style
4. Fabric or pattern
5. Quality of workmanship

Other reasons for markdowns include the following:

1. Overstock of specific styles
2. Special-purchase stock remaining after promotion
3. Broken assortments, remnants, and dated or shopworn goods
4. Special sales from regular stock
5. Price adjustment to meet competition
6. Customer returns or adjustments
7. Timing of purchases, delivery delays, or weather conditions

Many stores have price-change forms that are filed for each price adjustment. By analyzing the reasons for the price changes, the buyer or merchandise manager can determine what steps need to be taken to reduce future markdowns.

Summary

The largest component of retail price is the cost of the merchandise. In addition there are variable, flat, and overhead expenses and, of course, provision for profit. In deciding the initial retail price, the merchant must consider the customers' buying preferences and the competitors' prices. Variations in markup are due to differences in variable and overhead expenses. Higher-than-average markup is justified if there is likelihood of markdowns, stock shortages, high handling costs, and extra customer services or if goods are unique or exclusive. Lower-than-average markup is justified for staple goods when no special services are required and when stock turn and sales volume are high. A store's sales policy and use of specially purchased goods, leaders, and premiums also will affect pricing. In addition to keeping a dollar record of price changes, the merchant should keep a record of the reasons for markdowns.

Review

1. Define *cost* and *expense;* distinguish between the two terms; explain the relationship of both to pricing.
2. Name a flat expense, a variable expense, and an overhead expense.
3. List two demand factors that will affect pricing.
4. Explain why the markup on two items in the same department might be different.
5. List five reasons for a lower-than-average markup.

6. Explain the relationship between a store's sales policy and pricing.
7. What is the difference between a leader and a loss leader?
8. Give two reasons retailers need to keep a record of price adjustments.

Terms

The following terms were introduced in this chapter. Write a separate sentence correctly using each new term.

cost   loss leader
expense   multiple price
flat expense   overhead
leader   variable expense

Discuss

1. What would a retailer consider when deciding whether an expense should be classified as flat or variable?
2. What justification is there for a retailer to offer an item for $0.69 each or three items for $1.99?
3. Is it good business practice to put high markups on infrequently purchased goods with the idea that the customer will buy such items if they really need them?
4. What merchandise is most frequently used as a leader in the supermarkets in your community?

Problem Solving

1. If an item costs $6, retails for $9, and includes a flat expense of $2 and a variable expense of 10 percent of sales, what is the overhead and profit contribution from sales of 15 items? of 30 items? of 60 items?
2. In Number 1, 40 items can be sold each week at $9. At a price of $11, though, 20 items per week could be sold. Which retail price, $9 or $11, will contribute the most to overhead and profit?
3. If 20 items cost $5 each and 14 are sold for $9, four are sold for $8, and two are sold for $6, what is the maintained markup?
4. Obtain five different examples of coupons on consumer goods offering an incentive for customers to buy. Describe how each coupon was provided to the customer (newspaper, direct mail, package) and how effective you believe the coupon offer to be in generating sales.
5. Visit two retail stores featuring a special sale. Examine four sales items in each store. Determine the original retail price of each item and the apparent reason the goods are on sale. Write a description of each store's sales policy, according to what you observe.

UNIT 4 ACTIVITIES

CHECKING KEY POINTS

This exercise is designed to check your understanding of material presented in Unit 4. On a separate sheet of paper, list the numbers 1 through 28. Indicate your response, *T* for true and *F* for false, for each of the following 28 statements.

1. In top-down planning, overall stock, sales, and expense figures are first established for each classification of goods.
2. A basic-stock list is a list of goods that should be in stock at all times.
3. If average stock is $10,000 and net sales are $40,000, then stock turn is three.
4. If you plan to buy $1,700 of goods for a period, and $600 worth of goods are already on order for delivery in that period, the open-to-buy is $2,300.
5. Customer panels provide helpful opinions on merchandise, store procedures, and services.
6. Want slips are filled out by customers who cannot find the goods they want.
7. A brand may be a word, mark, symbol, or device or any combination of these used to identify a product or service.
8. Although styles change, fashions remain, even though they may not be popular.
9. Merchandise depth refers to the quantity of items stocked in a particular brand, size, color, style, or price of one kind of merchandise.
10. Trade shows may feature specific product lines or exhibit several related merchandise areas.
11. Action-item reports are used by buyers to report dollar amounts of markdowns.
12. The first step in choosing specific merchandise is to make a buying plan.
13. Stores may obtain market services by contracting with independent resident buying offices.
14. A buyer's resource file contains the names and addresses of vendors and details on each vendor's goods and prices.
15. Estimating prices is a valuable skill for a buyer.
16. If an invoice of $2,000 carries a functional discount of less 40, less 10, the amount to be paid is $1,000.
17. *FOB factory* means that the seller pays transportation charges.

18. *FOB destination* means that ownership of the goods remains with the seller until the goods are received by the buyer.
19. Buyers should write their own orders on their own company's order forms.
20. Most retailers prefer to treat markups as a percentage of cost.
21. If retail is $18 and markup is $11, then cost is $29.
22. If markup is $4 and retail is $10, then markup percentage on retail is 66.67 percent.
23. If total sales are $12,000 and markdowns are $900, then the markdown percentage is 13.3 percent.
24. *Automatic markdown* means that stores regularly mark down goods after they have been in stock for a certain number of weeks.
25. The term *cost* identifies expenditures for the goods offered for sale.
26. Overhead expenses vary with the number and value of items being sold.
27. Lower-than-average markups are justified when goods are unique.
28. Higher-than-average markups are justified when stock turn is high.

BUILDING BASIC SKILLS

Calculations

The following calculations were used in Unit 4 to demonstrate certain facts about retail merchandising. Make the calculations necessary to answer each of the questions that follow.

1. Over the past 12 months, the average stock at retail for the Red Hot Boutique has been $12,500. The net sales for the 12 months amount to $71,000. The cost of the merchandise sold in these 12 months was $21,300. The average cost of stock was $3,750.
    a. What is the stock turn on the retail basis?
    b. What is the stock turn on the cost basis?
2. At the end of January, the Red Hot Boutique has stock on hand of $12,400 at retail. If stock at the end of February should be $13,500 and February sales are $6,000, what should be the planned purchases figure for February? If the planned stock at the end of February were to be $11,700, what would be the planned purchases for February?
3. For the next year, the Red Hot Boutique plans sales of $84,000. Total cost and expenses are estimated at $41,000. Markdowns

are expected to be $2,700, and the profit goal is $9,000. What should be the initial-markup percentage? If the profit goal were set at $5,000, what initial-markup percentage would be needed?

4. A buyer for the Red Hot Boutique estimates that an article retailed at $15 (a markup of 40 percent) will sell at the rate of 20 a week; if the price is set at $17.50, 12 per week could be sold; if the price were at $12, 30 a week could be sold. Flat expenses for each item are $3, and variable expenses are 10 percent of the retail price. At which price will the item make the largest contribution to overhead and profit? Explain the possible objections to pricing the item at this so-called best price.

5. Calculate the net cost of each of the following items:
   a. Sportcoat—list price $85; trade discount 40 percent; terms of sale 8/10, n/30; invoice paid within discount period.
   b. Computer monitor—list price $185; trade discount 30 percent, 10 percent; terms of sale 8/10, n/30; invoice paid within discount period.
   c. Moped—list price $550; trade discount 35 percent; terms of sale 8/30, n/60; anticipation 5 percent; invoice paid 45 days before net is due.

6. Twenty-four dresses, costing $18 each, were offered at $39. During a special sale, eight were sold for $28, and, later, two were sold for $16 each. The rest of the dresses were sold at the $39 price. What was the maintained markup on the 24 dresses?

Working with People

Retail workers must work with other employees, supervisors, and customers. Sometimes, misunderstandings occur. Misunderstandings often cause bad feelings among employees and their supervisors and poor service to customers. Many successful workers solve people problems with the four-step DICE approach. Each letter of DICE refers to a specific problem-solving action and was described in Unit 1 (see page 78).

Read each problem situation below. Then, use the DICE approach to find a solution for each. Remember, you must first define a problem before you identify or choose solutions. Describe what you think the consequences of your chosen solution would be.

1. You are a salesperson in a women's clothing store. Most of the store's customers are young women who work in banks, insurance firms, law and government offices, and business-service firms. The store manager buys all merchandise. The customers frequently want merchandise in other colors, styles, or newer fashions. You have made these requests known to the store manager, but he continues to buy large amounts of goods that must

be marked down drastically to sell. What is the problem? What steps will you take?

2. A customer is interested in buying a four-slice toaster. The price is $39.95, but the customer knows that it was on sale last week for $31.95. She insists, even though the sale is over, that she be able to buy the toaster for the lower price. What is the problem? What action will you take with this customer? At what price would you sell the toaster? Why?

3. You are the merchandise manager for a large variety store. One of your buyers has made errors recently on several large orders of merchandise. Some prices have been wrong; the terms of sale were inconsistent with store policy; and the shipping dates have been incorrect. How would you deal with this situation? Be specific.

4. You are manager of the children's clothing department in a chain store. You have noticed that your returns and markdowns have increased over the past six months. Most of these seem to be traceable to two of your salespeople. Both are aggressive and try to make a sale to every customer who comes to the department. What action should you take?

Writing Skills

Communication skills, oral or written, are essential for nearly all retail jobs. They are especially important in those areas of retailing where orders for merchandise are placed with vendors. The omission of a term or the wrong use of a word could cause the vendor to send the wrong goods or the wrong quantity or ship at the wrong time. Prepare a letter to the vendor in each of the three cases that follow.

1. Your order, RZ-709 (dated 9/30), to the Cripple Creek Glove Company asked for 120 pairs of lined deerskin gloves with 36 pairs in medium, 60 pairs in large, and 24 pairs in extra large. Cripple Creek shipped, and you received on 10/20, 120 pairs of medium. You want approval to return 84 pairs in exchange for the correct sizes. If the correct sizes cannot be shipped by 11/10, you want a credit memo (refund) for the 84 pairs of medium. Have you included all the facts?

2. An invoice from the Tiger Square Rug Company bills you $3,168 for 24 rugs with the terms 6/10, net 30. On your order placed with their salesperson, the terms were to be 6/10, net 30, 60 extra. If you cannot get the original billing terms, you wish to return the entire shipment.

3. The Turtle Top Manufacturing Company makes a line of women's and men's tank tops that sell very well in your store. Next year will be your store's tenth anniversary, and you are planning a month-

long sale featuring all your regular lines. You want to find out if Turtle Top can provide 60 dozen of a special style, costing no more than $96 per dozen and delivered at least 30 days before your sale. You want billing terms allowing net payment 30 days after your month-long sale ends.

APPLYING YOUR KNOWLEDGE

Can You Do the Following?

1. Describe the merchandise planning process that should be used by a retailer.
2. Calculate the stock turn when average retail stock is $15,000 and net sales amount to $90,000.
3. List the advantages and disadvantages of carrying private brand merchandise.
4. Explain the four steps of the fashion cycle.
5. Explain the uses of a basic stock list, model stock list, and never-out list.
6. List the elements necessary to calculate an open-to-buy figure.
7. Explain the services of an independent resident buying office.
8. Calculate the net amount of an invoice for $5,000 if there are discounts of 15 percent and 6 percent.
9. Find the retail price and markup percentage on retail when cost is $10 and markup is $6.
10. Calculate the markdown percentage when markdown is $216 and sales are $1,800.
11. Calculate contribution to profit and overhead when the selling price on an item is $389, flat expenses are 10 percent of cost, variable expenses are $59, and the merchandise cost is $260.
12. Calculate the maintained markup percentage on the sale of 20 items costing $8 each, ten of which sold for $17 and ten of which sold at $11.

Retail Decisions

1. The Pier Ten Clothing Store has been operating in a major shopping mall for ten years. The manager is concerned that past merchandising policies and procedures may not be meeting the needs of today's customers. What could the manager do to determine if current merchandise and store policies and procedures are meeting the needs of current customers?
2. You are a buyer for the Pier Ten store. How would you prepare for a buying trip to purchase staple merchandise?
3. Who should set the retail prices on the merchandise you buy for

Pier Ten: you, the buyer, or the department sales manager? Why?

4. Why would it be important for you as the buyer to specify the shipping terms and type of transportation on goods that you purchase?

5. If Pier Ten is 500 miles from the market (seller), would you prefer an EOM or an ROG dating on your purchase? Why?

6. You submitted a handwritten purchase order to a vendor. Because of your poor handwriting, the vendor misread the quantity of goods to be shipped. Whose fault is the error? Why?

7. Is it ethical for you as a buyer to try to get a lower price on goods than that quoted by a supplier?

8. You ordered merchandise for a special sale, and the vendor shipped the items late. The goods did not arrive until after the sale. What immediate action should you take? What can you do to prevent this in the future?

9. A competitor offers two best-selling items at cost price to attract customers to his store. What will you do to meet the competition?

DEVELOPING CRITICAL-THINKING SKILLS

Retail Projects

1. In your store, 100-watt light bulbs sell at the rate of 25 per week and require one week to be delivered by the supplier. You have set 40 as the normal reorder number for the bulbs to provide a reserve in case sales increase. Stock is checked and items are reordered every two weeks. What should be your maximum stock? If you have 30 items on hand, how many should you reorder?

2. While a buyer was looking over a manufacturer's line of jackets ranging in price from $18 to $24, the representative showed the buyer a group of 30 jackets that would sell for the flat sum of $450. About eight jackets were in the $24 price line, and the rest of the jackets came from the $18 price line. Three of the jackets were in a style that likely would not sell at all. Five jackets would have to be offered for sale at $12. The buyer thought the rest of the jackets could be sold at the regular store price of $30. Should the buyer purchase this group of jackets? Why or why not?

3. A merchant estimates that an article retailed at $25 (a markup of 40 percent) will sell at the rate of 20 a week. If the price were set at $35, sales probably would be 12 per week. If flat expenses for each item are $5 and variable expenses are 10 percent of the retail price, at which price will the merchant make the larger contribution to overhead and profit?

4. It costs a manufacturer $810 to make and sell a dining-room table and six chairs. The manufacturer wants to make a profit of $100 on each set of furniture. If trade discounts of 10 percent and 5 per-

cent plus a cash discount of 3 percent are offered, what should be the manufacturer's list price for the dining-room set?

5. Calculate the net cost of each of the following items:
   a. Topcoat—list price $95; trade discount 40 percent; terms of sale 8/10, n/30; invoice paid within discount period.
   b. Chair—list price $235; trade discount 30 percent and 10 percent; terms of sale 6/10, n/30; invoice is paid within the discount period.
   c. Ten-speed bicycle—list price $450; trade discount 35 percent; terms of sale 6/30, n/60; manufacturer allows anticipation of 4 percent; invoice is paid 45 days after the invoice date.

6. Your employer has allocated $1,500 for the purchase of goods in your department. Show how you would distribute these dollars over the purchase of five different items each selling for $12 and costing $7.50. Products sell at the following rates: A at 15 per period; B at 60 per period; C at 30 per period; D at 40 per period; and E at 55 per period.

7. Calculate the planned purchases and open-to-buy figures for the following:

   Planned stock on September 1 . . . .$26,400
   Planned stock on October 1 . . . .$25,200
   Planned sales for September $11,800
   Orders already placed for September $5,300

Field Projects

1. Visit a housewares or small-appliance store or the housewares or small-appliance department of a chain store in your community. Observe the different lines of merchandise carried (cookware, toasters, utensils, and similar lines). Develop a list of all the goods included within two such lines. Prepare a list of questions that you would want to ask before reordering or repurchasing new merchandise in these two lines.

2. Select one line of consumer merchandise, such as women's sportswear, men's shoes, or fresh produce. Determine where in your community such lines might be purchased by a retail-store buyer. List up to five resources that might be used.

3. Interview a local retail businessperson and report on the following:
   a. The extent of buying by sales representatives who call at the store
   b. The extent to which trade journals and market publications are used as aids in buying merchandise
   c. The kinds of information and services provided the store by vendors and manufacturers and the degree to which these services are used

d.   The extent of buying done by means of market trips
4.   Most large supermarkets use optical scanning equipment to read and record merchandise prices at the time of customer checkout. Interview a supermarket manager to determine how the frequent price changes made in supermarket merchandise are recorded and how maintained markups are determined.
5.   Determine what the legal requirements are for a person in your state to be considered a competent party to a contract such as an order for merchandise. You may wish to consult state statutes in your library, the business-law teacher in your school, a local businessperson, or other person suggested by your instructor.
6.   Contact your local chamber of commerce, better business bureau, or your state consumer affairs office to determine if in your community or state there are any regulations regarding minimum markup on consumer goods or the advertising or conduct of consumer-goods sales.

CONTINUING PROJECTS

Developing a Career Plan

As you have already discovered, there are many different occupations in the field of retail merchandising. One of the keys to making a good career decision is having current and accurate information about the jobs within the occupation you are considering. The difference between an occupation and a job is that an occupation is a broad category, such as merchandise manager, buyer, or salesperson, while a job is more specific, such as men's clothing merchandise manager for Aldo's Department Store, toy buyer for Games Galore, or paint salesperson for Redi-Color. Within each of these jobs, the person performs a number of tasks, such as taking inventory, analyzing sales records, greeting customers, and using an electronic sales register.

Identify what might be the beginning job for the occupation you selected for your tentative career. By observing people in that job, by talking with persons in that job or persons who know about that job, or by reading career materials, develop a list of tasks (specific things that are done) in that job. Try to list at least ten different tasks that would need to be performed in that job. For each task, determine what knowledge or skill you would need. Place a check next to each task you feel you have the knowledge and skill to perform. Include this analysis in your career-plan notebook. As you become interested in other jobs, complete similar analyses and include them in your notebook.

Developing a Business Plan

From the facts you have learned in this unit and from your own research, record the following in your planning notebook:

1. Select a group of products or a line of merchandise you plan to carry in your retail store.
2. Identify the primary central market in which vendors for your merchandise would be located.
3. Start a resource file including at least four potential suppliers.
4. Design an order form that you could use for your store's purchases and make four copies.
5. Write a sample order to each of the four suppliers in your resource file using the four copies of the order form you made.
6. Estimate the number of buying trips you would need to make to the market each year.
7. For each trip, estimate the number of days you would need to spend in the market to make purchases for one selling season. Then, estimate the total expenses for the buying trip. Include travel, meals, hotel, and all other expenses that you are likely to incur from the time you leave your city until you return.
8. Compare your markets, resources, and buying trip plans with those of other students who are planning similar retail businesses.

UNIT 5
*P*romotion

Successful retail promotions depend upon the careful coordination of the five methods of promotion: advertising, visual merchandising, sales promotion, public relations, and personal selling. Advertising is covered in Chapters 27, 28, 29, and 30. Sales promotion and public relations are presented in Chapter 28. A detailed discussion of visual merchandising is presented in Chapters 31, 32, and 33. Unit VI, Selling, discusses personal selling.

The first step is to determine objectives of a coordinated promotion; then the goods or services to be promoted must be carefully selected. Another vital aspect of successful promotion is planning an advertising budget.

Advertisements make up a large proportion of most promotional campaigns. Choosing from among a variety of media is important to successful promotion.

Visual merchandising—particularly the use of exterior and interior displays—permits an up-close inspection of goods. To design displays that sell, a retailer must know the six elements and five principles of display design. Besides careful planning, skillful installation helps make displays effective.

Sales promotions offer special inducements to customers to purchase goods and services. Sales promotion techniques include (1) product sampling, (2) premiums, (3) coupons, (4) rebates, and (5) contests and games.

Good public relations and favorable publicity also contribute to the overall effectiveness of promotional plans.

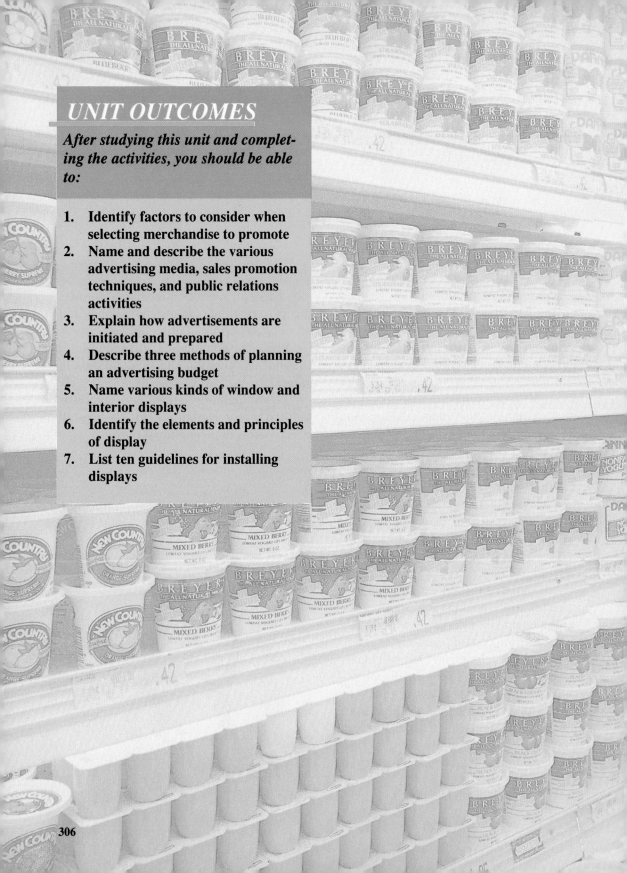

UNIT OUTCOMES

After studying this unit and completing the activities, you should be able to:

1. Identify factors to consider when selecting merchandise to promote
2. Name and describe the various advertising media, sales promotion techniques, and public relations activities
3. Explain how advertisements are initiated and prepared
4. Describe three methods of planning an advertising budget
5. Name various kinds of window and interior displays
6. Identify the elements and principles of display
7. List ten guidelines for installing displays

CHAPTER 27
Selecting Goods to Be Advertised

CHAPTER OUTCOMES

When you have mastered the information provided in this chapter, you should be able to:

1. Define the terms *promotional advertising* and *institutional advertising*

2. Identify the objectives of retail advertising

3. List the key considerations of retail promotion

4. Name seven factors affecting merchandise selected for advertising

5. Describe the types of merchandise that should not be advertised

The selection of the right goods to advertise is considered by many as a very important factor in retail promotion. Experienced advertisers know that even good advertising will not sell unwanted merchandise. Thousands of dollars have been lost in advertising goods for which there was no demand. No amount of advertising will sell obsolete goods or goods that people consider unattractive. On the other hand, wanted merchandise can be, and often is, sold by poor advertising. A combination of good merchandise and good advertising will give the best results.

OBJECTIVES OF ADVERTISING

Advertising by a retailer can be classified as either promotional or institutional. **Promotional advertising** focuses on attracting immediate customer traffic and creating sales. **Institutional advertising** focuses on building store prestige and store acceptance over a long period of time. Thus, the usual pattern is that merchants who have decided to operate a promotional store stress promotional advertising. Merchants who have decided to operate a nonpromotional store tend to stress institutional advertising. Some stores follow a **semipromotional policy** by combining promotional and institutional advertising techniques.

There are several goals that retailers hope to achieve by using either promotional or institutional advertising or both:

1. To bring customers into the store to inspect the goods offered and to use store services
2. To introduce new goods, styles, and services

3. To stimulate demand for a product
4. To teach customers new uses of a product
5. To prepare the way for sales presentations
6. To keep the business name or slogan before the public
7. To keep the customer satisfied with previous purchases
8. To create goodwill, leading to customer selection of the store for future purchases

SELECTING MERCHANDISE TO BE ADVERTISED

The right merchandise, timing, and appropriate advertising media are key considerations in any retail promotion effort. Of particular importance is the selection of the merchandise to be advertised. Stores cannot advertise all the merchandise they have in stock. Doing so would ensure high advertising expenses but would not ensure high sales volume. Thus, retailers must choose representative items that will attract the largest number of possible buyers and build the most goodwill. Which goods in the store will win the approval of the largest number of people? Which goods will bring customers to the store? To answer these questions, a retailer must understand the factors that affect customers' points of view.

Customers are attracted by merchandise that is distinctive and currently popular. Customers are attracted to a store that offers reduced prices and specials, particularly if a number of bargains are available at

The young must try their wings.

Painted faces. Drum beats. Figures in a heap. Then, out of chaos comes form. The painted faces begin to be mime actors. Drum beats, a dance.

Eager youngsters leap up to twirl into ballet. And one more time the Oklahoma Summer Arts Institute has worked its magic. Here at Quartz Mountain, teenage winners of a state-wide competition bring their talents to be polished by encouraging instructors. Dance. Acting. Music. Writing. Visual Arts. It's work and it's fun. And Phillips Petroleum gladly gives to its support. Not for money. Just for a song.

Oh, baby.

Small wonders from Tiffany & Co. Sterling silver baby cup, $135. Spoon, $75. Rattle, $115. Baby sets of plate, porringer and cup; "Seashore," $85. "Tiffany Tiny," $90. Available at Tiffany & Co. in New York, Beverly Hills, San Francisco, South Coast Plaza, Dallas, Houston, Washington, D.C., Chicago, Atlanta, Boston, Philadelphia. Also available at selected fine stores. To inquire: 800-526-0649.

TIFFANY & CO.

Illus. 27–1   Promotional advertising, as in the ad on the left, attracts immediate customer interest and generates sales. Institutional advertising builds store prestige over a long period of time.

one time. Customers loyal to a store's own brand of products look to advertisements to guide their selections of private-brand items.

Current Demand

The advertising of fast-selling, popular items will bring customers into a store and will increase sales. Stores that sell moderately priced merchandise generally feature articles that are in current demand: fans in hot weather, hit musical recordings, or clothing in season. Advertising these goods shows customers that the store is up-to-date

and that it will sell goods they want at prices they are willing to pay. A fast-selling item has won the approval of many customers. It is merchandise for which there is steady demand.

Fashion

The store with a policy of fashion leadership does not advertise the accepted best-seller; instead, it advertises new styles that the retailer believes will become the fashion. Customers will watch the store's advertisements for new and unusual merchandise, not established items. Customers who know the policy of this type of store and are interested in wearing the latest styles are sure that they are getting up-to-the-minute merchandise when they buy the store's advertised goods.

In most stores, however, new styles should be put before the public cautiously. Many stores test the sales possibilities of new goods by a small advertisement or a small display to get customers' reactions. Should demand suddenly become brisk, the

SPECIAL PROMOTIONAL EVENTS

Store opening	Manager's day
Store anniversary	Sports event
Back to school	School and college
Supplier's special	event
Wholesaler's	Civic function
promotion	Holiday
Remodeling	Season
Expansion	Outdoor activity
Founder's sale	Home and garden
	improvement

Illus. 27–2   Advertising merchandise for special events is usually successful.

goods may be stocked in large quantities and advertised heavily.

Exclusiveness

Many people not only desire new things but also want exclusive merchandise; that is, merchandise produced in very small quantities and not easily found. Custom-made clothing, furniture, and luxury cars, such as the Rolls Royce, are examples of exclusive merchandise. Advertising can be an effective means of bringing attention to unique products, provided the advertising media are carefully selected and the advertisements are targeted to the potential market.

Special Events

Merchandise associated with a special occasion is also a good choice for advertising. Toys and gifts have high promotional value at Christmastime, spring clothes at Easter, flags before the Fourth of July, and children's clothing prior to the opening day of school. With just a little imagination, retailers can turn almost any day of the year into a special event. Illustration 27–2 lists special occasions for which particular types of merchandise might be promoted.

Price

Retail stores generally advertise merchandise that has a distinct price appeal because many people must economize, and almost everyone is looking for a bargain.

Discount houses, for instance, use the drawing power of reduced prices and feature merchandise that has already won customer favor. They attract even wealthy customers, who buy most of their clothing and furnishings in high-class department stores and specialty shops, by carrying such standard merchandise as stockings, shoes, towels, and linens.

Single and Multiple Promotions

A discount house seldom devotes an advertisement to a single item. Rather, it uses an **omnibus** (relating to many things at once) **advertisement** that features 15 or more bargains of various sorts on the same page. The price endings of advertised merchandise are usually in odd cents—for example, $1.31, $3.93, and $6.57—which are not the customary price endings for most stores.

Large promotional stores, however, may advertise single items that are of interest to a great many people. Examples of such items are television sets, women's hosiery, and men's shirts. The store must be reasonably sure that the sales of that one item will make buying the advertising space worthwhile. For example, a blouse with an advertised price of $13.89 may cost the store $11.30, thus providing a profit margin of $2.59 on each blouse. If the advertisement costs the store $320, it would be necessary to sell 124 (320 ÷ $2.59) blouses simply to cover the cost of the advertisement, without any allowance for other expenses. Many more than 124 blouses would have to be sold to make the advertising profitable. Occasionally, a high-class store will promote a very expensive item, such as a $6,000 diamond necklace, that few people

in the community could afford. This is a form of institutional advertising instead of a promotional offering. It is a dramatic attempt to impress the public and make known the fact that the store carries the best products that money can buy.

Food and household goods that are bought regularly should be advertised regularly to ensure steady repeat sales. Supermarkets advertise weekly, but they carefully select different products to advertise each week. Advertisements are most effective if customers see an interesting variety of promoted products.

Private Brands

When a retailer is building a market for private brands (store brands), the merits of these products should be advertised often. One large department store ran a series of advertisements comparing national brands with the store's private brands, pointing out the difference in prices for similar items. This advertising approach gave the private-brand items an identity and the products almost sold themselves. People could easily see why it was advantageous for them to buy the store's private brands. Private-brand advertising became a theme of that store's success story.

MERCHANDISE THAT SHOULD NOT BE ADVERTISED

Many advertisers make the mistake of regularly featuring leftover merchandise, slow-selling goods, and old stock. They do this in the hope of making up for mistakes in purchasing. However, such goods will fail to attract customers unless the price is greatly reduced. Salespeople do not like to sell old or overstocked merchandise—another reason why advertising such merchandise is not effective.

One retailer advertised a good quality woolen blanket for sale at $29.95. The advertisement brought many buyers to the store. The retailer failed, however, to state in the advertisement that only a limited quantity was available. The sale blanket was soon sold out; when customers asked for the blanket, salespeople tried to sell a substitute. Many people felt the advertisement had tricked them and they left the store without making a purchase. Merchants can lose many customers through the blunder of advertising goods available in very limited quantity (see Illustration 27–3). When the quantity of an item is not enough to fill the demand created by the advertisement, the item is better promoted through an in-store display than through a newspaper or radio advertisement. Also, merchandise that cannot be reordered quickly is not an ideal choice for advertising purposes. The advertising may create a demand that the store is not able to meet, and the result would be a lowering of the store's prestige.

The temptation is often great to advertise goods before they arrive at the store. A delay in shipping may, however, result in the advertised goods not being on hand when customers call for them. This practice could result in loss of customer goodwill and, over time, loss in sales. Thus, it is sometimes necessary for a store to pass up advertising opportunities to keep goodwill. In chain stores, advertisements almost always are released before the goods are in the stores and marked with the advertised

GOODS THAT SHOULD NOT BE ADVERTISED

- Leftover merchandise offered at regular prices or available in a quantity insufficient to justify the advertising expense
- Quantities of desirable merchandise that may prove too small to fill the demand created by the advertising or quantities of merchandise for which prompt refills by the manufacturer are not possible
- Goods that may not be in the store, properly priced, on the day the advertising appears
- Goods that have not been moved by previous advertising and that do not give any indication of becoming more salable
- Goods that salespeople are not aware of

Illus. 27–3   *To keep customer goodwill, retailers should never promote the kinds of merchandise listed here.*

price. Thus, the advanced advertising problem is particularly difficult for chain-store retailers.

Goods that have not been sold as a result of previous advertising should not be advertised again unless there is a change in the situation that makes them more salable; otherwise, the expense of a second advertisement will be wasted.

Finally, no goods should be advertised without salespeople being informed. Few situations are more annoying to a customer than to have salespeople show ignorance about goods that were advertised.

Summary

    Selecting the right goods to promote is key in helping to assure the success of a retail-advertising effort. Retailers use promotional advertising when the objective is to build customer traffic and sales. Emphasis is placed on institutional advertising when the purpose is to build store prestige and customer acceptance. In either case, choosing the right goods to advertise is important. To make proper choices, retailers need to consider current product demand, fashion trends, merchandise exclusiveness, special events, pricing, single- or multiple-product promotions, and the merits of advertising private brands. Leftover, slow-selling, or old stock items should not be advertised. Merchandise available in limited quantities, out-of-stock goods, and items that salespeople know little about should not be included in promotions.

Review

1. State the difference between promotional advertising and institutional advertising.
2. List five specific objectives of retail advertising.
3. Identify three considerations in developing a retail promotion effort.
4. Name seven factors that affect the kinds of merchandise selected for promotion.
5. List five kinds of merchandise that should not be advertised.

Terms

    The following terms were introduced in this chapter. Write a separate sentence correctly using each new term.

institutional advertising   promotional advertising
omnibus advertisement   semipromotional policy

Discuss

1. Why is proper goods selection an important factor in the success of a retail promotion?
2. Upon what bases would a retail merchant choose a promotional advertising or institutional advertising policy?
3. How do single-item advertisements differ from omnibus advertisements?
4. Is the statement "Good advertising will not sell unwanted merchandise" true or false? Why?
5. How can the promotion of merchandise in short supply create problems for the retailer?

Problem
Solving

1. You are finalizing plans to open a jewelry store in a large metropolitan shopping center. Your business will be located next to a
   department store that features distinctive merchandise. You will
   carry national-brand goods. Make up an advertising policy for
   the store. The policy should include promotional and institutional
   advertising. The policy must include a description of the types of
   merchandise that will be promoted and of how often and when
   you will promote them. Also include a list of jewelry-store items
   that never will be advertised.

2. You have just completed arrangements for a back-to-school advertisement featuring specially priced school supplies. One of the
   featured items will be a three-ring binder selling for $1.98. The
   usual retail price is $2.59. You have ordered 50 cases of this
   merchandise in anticipation of a large customer demand. A
   phone call from your supplier indicates that two shipments of
   notebooks will be sent rather than one. The first shipment will
   consist of ten cases, and the second will consist of 40 cases. Outline a plan of action for promoting the binders.

3. Wilkens Clothiers carries a complete line of men's and women's
   clothing. The store is experiencing rapid growth and has gained a
   reputation for selling quality merchandise at reasonable prices.
   Ben Wilkens has decided to add a line of goods carrying the
   "Wilkens Clothiers" label. Outline the steps that Ben should follow to attract customer attention to this merchandise. Try to find
   newspaper or magazine advertisements similar to the ones you
   recommend for Ben Wilkens.

CHAPTER 28

Advertising Media

CHAPTER OUTCOMES

When you have mastered the information provided in this chapter, you should be able to:

1. Define the terms *target market* and *medium*

2. Define the terms *advertising media, coding,* and *market segmentation*

3. Identify and describe the various kinds of printed media

4. Compute the milline rate in a given situation

5. Identify the major types of electronic media

6. Compare the relative advantages and disadvantages of radio and television advertising

7. List six types of supplementary media

8. Distinguish between sales promotion and public relations

There are many ways that retailers can communicate information about their stores and merchandise to potential customers. For example, a merchant or store employee can talk with individuals in or out of the store, or satisfied customers can tell their friends about the store and its merchandise. This person-to-person communication is often called *word-of-mouth advertising*. However, to have control over what is said and to be sure many people receive the message, a retailer also must use other forms of communication. Retail advertising can be placed in newspapers and magazines, sent through the mail, broadcast on radio or television, or carried through other media. Selecting the right media is not an easy task. Advertising that has the best chance of reaching potential customers in a given market must be selected. Potential customers are often referred to as the **target market.** The means by which advertising can be presented is known as a **medium.** Together, these retail channels of communication are called **advertising media.**

COMMUNICATING THROUGH ADVERTISING MEDIA

Obviously, not all people listen to the same radio station or read the same newspaper. A retailer must determine which channel or medium will reach the greatest number of potential customers. Once a communication channel is identified as likely to reach a certain type of consumer, the next step is making sure that the advertising is properly coded. **Coding** an advertisement involves choosing words and pictures to send the right message. Coding includes the voice and music used for radio or television advertisements.

It is important for retail advertisers to get feedback from receivers of advertising messages in order to evaluate the effectiveness of the communication channel. For example, if a hardware store is promoting a new line of lawnmowers, it may present its advertising through a particular radio station to reach the intended audience. That store may, on another occasion, advertise those same lawnmowers through another medium, perhaps a newspaper. By comparing the number of lawnmowers sold as a result of the radio and newspaper advertising, the retailer will know which medium is more effective for carrying a message to the right people. The relationship of media to sales revenue is shown in Illustration 28–1.

Effective advertising is more than sending a message. Good advertising carries a message to the specific people who are likely to want the advertised product or service. Getting the message to the right consumers requires planning. Retailers classify all consumers in categories or segments on the basis of characteristics—such as income and age—that they have in common. Then, a retailer decides which advertising media are likely to appeal to each kind of people. This process is called **market segmentation.** Market segmentation is necessary for two reasons: (1) few merchandise offerings appeal to everybody and (2) it is wasteful to try to communicate a message to everybody if only a few persons will be interested.

PRINTED MEDIA

Printed media include all written communications that can be delivered or carried into consumers' homes. Typical printed me-

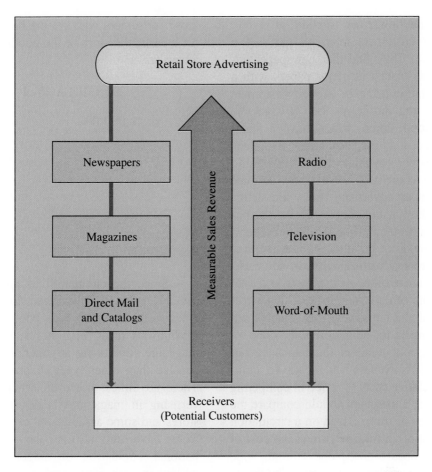

Illus. 28–1   The means by which advertising can be presented is known as a medium. These retail channels of communication are called advertising media.

dia are newspapers, magazines, direct mail, and catalogs.

Newspapers

Although there is a high level of competition in a newspaper for each reader's attention, newspapers remain the chief advertising medium for most retail stores. Eighty-nine percent of all adults look at a newspaper at least once a day. Stores will, however, make a careful study of the character and the circulation of a particular paper before they place their advertisements. They want to know how many and what type of people read that newspaper. They want information as to which parts of the city the newspaper serves most, which parts it serves least, and why.

The best newspaper for any retailer is the one that is read by the market segment to whom the store sells. Stores that are located in the downtown section of a city draw their customers from all parts of a trading area. They find that newspaper advertisements placed in major papers with a high circulation bring in enough customers for sales and profit to be satisfactory. Neighborhood stores, which have a small trading area, may use local rather than general newspaper coverage. Local advertising is the best choice for these stores because (1) newspaper advertising rates are determined by how many people receive the paper and (2) people outside the neighborhood usually would not be attracted into the area by newspaper advertisements. In some cities, there are weekly newspapers and special editions of daily newspapers that cover just part of the city; these are valuable advertising media for neighborhood stores.

Successful retailers must balance advertising effectiveness and cost. To compare the relative costs of space in competing newspapers, a merchant should compare the milline rates of each. Based on a circulation of one million, a **milline rate** is the cost of one agate line (a space one column wide and 1 $\frac{1}{14}$ inches deep) adjusted to the actual number of copies circulated. See Formula 28–1 for figuring milline rate. For example, if a newspaper charges $0.25 an agate line and has an actual circulation of 100,000, its milline rate is $2.50, as computed in Formula 28–2. The newspaper with the lowest milline rate is not necessarily the best, however, for it may not reach

FORMULA 28–1

Milline Rate =

Agate Line Rate $\times \dfrac{1,000,000}{\text{Actual Circulation}}$

those consumers who are the best prospects for a particular store or the goods it plans to advertise.

FORMULA 28–2

$$0.25 \times \frac{1,000,000}{100,000} = 0.25 \times 10 =$$
$2.50

Magazines

Since the circulation of magazines is usually national rather than local, magazines would seem to be a poor advertising medium for most retail stores. In addition, magazine advertising is generally more expensive than other types of printed media. There are times, however, when retail advertising in magazines is desirable. Chain stores and some associations of independent stores have units all over the country. The national circulation of magazines is not wasted in such cases because almost every reader of the magazine lives or works near one of the chain's or the association's outlets.

In recent years, many national magazines have developed regional advertising programs that permit retailers to buy space in just those issues of the magazine that are circulated in their area. This practice is often referred to as offering a **split run.** For example, a large men's store in Chicago may advertise in the issues of *Time* or *TV Guide* that are circulated in the Midwest. Some magazine advertisements are concerned with only a single city and its environs—for example, *New York* magazine in New York City.

Direct Mail

Direct-mail advertising includes letters, enclosures in bills, postcards, and other mailable items that are sent directly to prospective customers. Although direct-mail advertising is often thrown away without being read and costs more and more to send, it is favored by many merchants. For one thing, direct-mail advertising offers merchandise to the public without informing competitors about it. Some stores like direct-mail advertising because target marketing can be accomplished in a personal manner. Results of direct-mail advertising can be easily determined, and expenditures for this medium can be controlled accordingly. Some stores make direct mail their major advertising medium. For example, closed-door discounters who sell only to a select clientele rely almost entirely on direct mailings to their members.

Catalogs and Directories

While catalogs mailed to customers may be thought of as direct mail, they deserve special mention as an advertising medium. Many large general merchandise catalogs, such as J.C. Penney's, must be purchased. In addition to one or two annual catalogs, many retail stores find it worthwhile to prepare special catalogs, particularly for holidays. Items advertised in catalogs vary from novelty items for about $1 to expensive gifts. While catalogs may sell considerable merchandise directly, some merchants have found that catalogs also stimulate many people to come into the store to examine the featured merchandise.

Local and regional directories usually contain a yellow-pages section. This advertising media is helpful to both merchants and customers because it lists businesses alphabetically by the products and services they sell.

ELECTRONIC MEDIA

Radio and television are electronic media. Most individuals spend several hours every day listening to radio or watching television. Both radio and TV are cumulative media; that is, repeated advertising is necessary to reach an audience and to stimulate listeners to take action. Many retailers, in both large and small firms, are finding that electronic advertising, if carefully done, is an effective means of communicating with customers.

Radio

Radio continues to be a popular medium for retail stores. In addition to 24-hour programming, radio appeals to specialized markets and is not limited by listeners' locations. Some merchants sponsor particular programs, but most use **spot announcements**—advertising messages lasting 30 to 60 seconds. Most radio advertisements of specific products have musical backgrounds or sound logos to draw attention in addition to the words and illustrations. Illustrations take the form of word pictures, created by the expressive voice of an announcer.

The time of a broadcast is important. Some stores like to advertise before, during, and after a program that is popular with their target audience. Other stores are less concerned with the program but wish to broadcast their advertisements when potential customers are most likely to be listening, such as in the early morning or during rush hour.

Small retail stores frequently think radio advertising is too expensive. Some, however, select a local station, either AM or FM, and use short spot advertisements that can be given between programs. These spot announcements contain a message about goods or services and emphasize the store and its location. Several retail stores in a business area or shopping center may arrange to share the cost of a program with each store broadcasting a message.

Television

In spite of its cost, television is becoming an increasingly important medium for many retailers. Cable television has segmented the target markets and reduced the cost of advertising. Television advertising makes it possible for potential customers to see the product being used. Many stores advertise over local stations; however, some large chains use the national networks.

Television is an excellent advertising medium that reaches almost all U.S. homes. Its high cost, however, may limit use by some advertisers. Generally, the cost of a promotional piece broadcast on television is determined by the size of the audience at a particular time. Daytime and late-night advertising rates tend to be less expensive than those charged for promotions run during prime-time evening hours. Almost all the ads are 30-second spot announcements; ten-second spots follow the half-minute spots in popularity   A few

stores use television for institutional advertising, but most concentrate on specific merchandise or a related assortment.

SUPPLEMENTARY MEDIA AND PROMOTION METHODS

Too often, retailers consider the typical printed or electronic media but overlook other useful advertising media. However, these supplementary media have been proven so successful that some retailers have invested most of their advertising budgets in them.

Outdoor Advertising

Billboards, posters, painted signs, electrical displays, and merchandise are used by retailers primarily for gaining recognition, rather than for advertising specific merchandise. Promotional stores and discount houses often use banners, floats, and placards on motor vehicles as part of their outdoor advertising.

Transit Advertising

Small posters in public transportation vehicles are read daily by all types of people. Transit advertising may be used by stores wishing to advertise a prestige image or to advertise a particular line of goods or a special sale. Generally, transits are best suited for the promotion of national-brand convenience goods and widely used services.

Illus. 28–2   Most people spend several hours every day listening to radio or watching television. Thus, these electronic media are good ways to send retailing messages to customers.

Handbills

Single sheets of advertisements distributed to people's homes or handed out in stores are good for highlighting a small number of products. To get the best results from handbills, a retailer should advertise only one or two leaders, urging customers to buy regular merchandise of good value. Care must be taken not to create ill will by littering doorways and lawns with this type of advertising. Handbills distributed in stores call attention to specials not advertised by other media.

Shopping News

Papers containing nothing but advertisements and distributed by mail are used by major retailers to supplement advertising in the printed and electronic media. Advertisements in a shopping news are less likely to be seen than are those appearing in newspapers.

Inside Posters

Attractive signs placed near entrances, in elevators, near escalators, and at other key points in large stores draw attention to special offerings in various departments and to special services.

Specialty Advertising

Printed messages on often-used items such as calendars, pencils, and notepads have the advantage of keeping a store's name, address, telephone number, and logo before customers' eyes almost constantly. Gifts with a store's imprinted message are also often used for specialty advertising. Examples are paint stirrers from a hardware store, shopping bags from a department store, and windshield scrapers from an auto-parts store.

Illus. 28–3   Some specialty advertising is used to gain recognition rather than to advertise specific merchandise.

SALES PROMOTION

Sales promotion is often described as all marketing activities, other than advertising, visual merchandising, public relations, and personal selling, that promote the sale of goods and services. Retailers use a variety of sales-promotion techniques to attract new customers, meet competition, introduce new goods and services, and offset seasonal sales declines.

Product Sampling

Sampling makes it possible for customers to try a product before making a purchase. Because sampling is generally not difficult to arrange, manufacturers and retailers find it to be an effective and inexpensive way to promote goods to the public. Merchandise selected for a sampling promotion is usually low in price and has repeat sales potential. Toothpaste, shampoo, pizza, cheese, and pastries are typical examples of products used in a sampling promotion.

Premiums

A premium is an item of merchandise presented to a consumer as an inducement to purchase another product or service. Banks may give dishware for opening a savings account. Cosmetic and fragrance sales might include the offering of designer tote bags, sunglasses, and similar merchandise at half price. Manufacturers may provide additional products, such as soap or cereal, in an attached package or the origi-

nal package at the regular or reduced price. The success of this kind of promotion depends on the appeal of the premium.

Coupons

Coupon promotions are among the most widely used of all sales-promotion techniques. Manufacturers and retailers who issue coupons give consumers a price reduction in order to encourage the use of new products and to build brand loyalty. Direct mail, newspapers, and in-store displays are the primary means used to circulate coupons to potential customers.

Rebates

Rebates make it possible for consumers to receive a partial refund on the purchase price of a product simply by completing a rebate form and returning it to the manufacturer. Rebate forms can be found on or near displays of products being promoted. Some retailers provide rebate display racks that contain forms for all items in the store that qualify.

Contests and Games

Contests and games (sometimes referred to as *sweepstakes*) make it possible for customers to win money, merchandise, and even vacations. Purchases are not required to enter. All that is necessary is the completion of a game card or entry blank. Contests and games are an effective means of building repeat traffic because there is usually no limit on the number of times a customer may participate. In all cases, such promotions must follow the legal regulations that apply.

PUBLIC RELATIONS

Public relations includes all those activities designed to build a positive attitude toward a particular business. Participants in this process can include employers, employees, and suppliers, as well as financial and governmental institutions. Successful public-relations programs usually reflect involvement in local affairs, active membership in civic organizations, and concerted efforts to meet special community needs. A good public-relations program also considers the store's internal environment. When employer-employee relationships are positive, customers are better served and the community in general benefits.

Publicity plays an important role in any public-relations promotion. **Publicity** occurs when any advertising medium mentions a retail business or product at no cost. When an event appears to be newsworthy, media will often carry information about the event as a news story. The retail business(es) or products named in the story are thus brought to the public's attention free of charge. Obviously, publicity cannot be planned and managed as carefully as other promotion efforts. However, many merchants have found that special store events or introduction of special products can be made newsworthy. Many stores organize their annual promotion plans to include events that will likely be of interest to the media—for example, fashion shows that introduce new lines of clothing. The potential for publicity should not be overlooked by retailers.

Summary   Merchants use a variety of communication techniques to reach customers. Salesperson-to-customer and customer-to-customer, or word-of-mouth, advertising are common communication methods. However, retailers rely heavily on planned retail advertising methods to make sure potential customers receive the messages. These methods involve the use of channels of communication called *advertising media*. Major forms of advertising media include printed media, electronic media, and supplementary media. Newspapers, magazines, direct mail, and catalogs are forms of *printed media*. Radio and television are referred to as *electronic media*. Supplementary media include outdoor advertisements, car cards, handbills, shopping news, posters, and specialty advertising. Some stores receive indirect benefits by paying for advertisements that promote community educational, artistic, and civic programs. Retailers also seek to promote their businesses through publicity, a form of free advertising of goods and services as well as of the business.

Review

1. Define *target market, medium, advertising media, coding,* and *market segmentation*.
2. List four major printed media used by retailers.
3. Calculate the milline rate for a newspaper that charges $0.35 an agate line and has a circulation of 200,000.
4. Name two major electronic media and identify one advantage and one disadvantage of each.
5. Identify six types of supplementary media.
6. Explain the difference between sales promotion and public relations.

Terms

The following terms were introduced in this chapter. Write a separate sentence correctly using each new term.

advertising media	publicity
coding	public relations
direct-mail advertising	sales promotion
market segmentation	split run
medium	spot announcement
milline rate	target market

Discuss

1. What are the relative merits of newspapers, magazines, and direct mail for promoting retail goods?
2. Defend the following statement: "Television is more effective than radio for advertising."
3. Why is market segmentation important to selecting an advertising medium?
4. Why is publicity more difficult to manage than other types of promotion?

Problem Solving

1. Pizza Classics is a reputable restaurant and take-out business that relies heavily on radio, television, and direct-mail coupon promotions to draw customers. This promotion plan has changed little over the past five years. The combination of increased competition and declining sales has caused management to consider using some form of sales promotion to increase sales. Which sales promotion techniques do you suggest? Give reasons for your suggestions.
2. Carmen Ramos has been employed to manage a new health-foods store in a small neighborhood shopping center. The center is located in a community of 48,000 people. The owners have

given Carmen full responsibility for all merchandising, promotion, and operations activities. Considering the type and size of the shopping area, location of the store, and product line, recommend answers to Carmen's questions:

a. What market segment—what type of customers—should I try to reach?

b. What advertising medium should I use to get the most coverage for my advertising dollar?

c. Should I use more than one medium?

d. If so, which should I use most and which least?

e. How often should I advertise?

3. You are employed by a small retail mail-order outlet. This business specializes in unique household goods including dishes, kitchen utensils, small rugs, planters, pictures, and knickknacks. Until recently, the owners depended on catalogs as the major means of promoting their goods. With the purchase of a computer and word-processing equipment, the decision has been made to drop catalogs in favor of direct mail. For the first mailing, the customer mailing list will be divided into three lists. Each of the three customer groups will receive a slightly different sales letter. The first letter will emphasize service while the second will bring attention to price. The third will concentrate on merchandise quality. Suggest ways to measure the effectiveness of each letter.

CHAPTER 29

Preparing Advertisements

When you have mastered the information provided in this chapter, you should be able to:

1. Name four sources that small and large stores might use to initiate advertisements

2. Explain the three psychological levels of an individual's action

3. List the four psychological steps brought on by good advertisements

4. Identify the major elements of a printed or electronic advertisement

5. Define the terms *signature plate* (logotype), *layout,* and *dummy layout*

6. Create and evaluate an advertising layout

7. Identify three sources of help for advertisers

Retailers generally have four basic sources of help in developing needed advertisements. These include the production departments of various media, store-operated advertising departments, manufacturers or suppliers of products, and advertising agencies. To prepare an effective advertisement, a retailer must have clearly defined objectives in mind. In small stores, the owner or manager may make rough notes of what is wanted and call for outside assistance to complete the advertisement. In most large stores, the buyer or head of the department indicates to the store's advertising department—consisting of artists and copywriters—just what is wanted in the advertisement. Completed advertisements are then distributed to the appropriate media.

REQUIREMENTS OF SUCCESSFUL ADVERTISEMENTS

Psychological studies show that people act on three levels: (1) the **conscious level** when they deliberately take actions; (2) the **subconscious level** when they act on the basis of emotional urges but do not admit the real reason for their actions; and (3) the **unconscious level** when they act in certain ways but do not know the reasons for their actions. Advertisers attempt to design advertisements that encourage specific customer action on one or more of these levels.

To help assure the success of a proposed advertisement, a retailer must carefully consider the merchandise to be offered and the nature of consumers in the intended market. The retailer will then select an appeal to match one of the three levels of action. A rational appeal encourages conscious buying. An emotional appeal stimulates subconscious decisions to buy. Appeals to momentary impulses encourage unconscious decisions to buy.

A successful advertisement takes the reader, viewer, or listener through the psychological steps of a sale. Good ads (1) attract attention, (2) develop interest, (3) create desire, and (4) induce favorable action. The favorable action induced by an advertisement is a phone call or a visit to the store to purchase the advertised merchandise.

Attracting Attention

To be effective, an advertisement first must be seen or heard or both. Consequently, the problems of attracting the eye and the ear should receive serious thought in the preparation of an advertisement. Psychologists tell us that attention must be caught and held before a message can be impressed upon the mind. Often, this attention grabbing can be accomplished by means of contrast. If, for example, a speaker finds that an audience is not listening, the speaker may suddenly stop. Attention is then immediately focused upon her or him. An advertisement cannot perform its function unless it attracts the attention of customers, so an ad attracts attention by being different.

Various methods are used to catch and hold the potential customer's attention. Illustrations; vivid colors; strong headlines; movement; sound; contrasting situations; and short, forcible sentences are some of the devices used to attract attention.

Developing Interest

Attention is momentary. When it is held for any length of time, it is called *interest*. The initial attention to the advertisement must, therefore, be prolonged in order to develop interest. People are always interested in matters that relate to themselves, therefore, they will be interested in merchandise and services that satisfy their needs and desires. To be most effective, descriptions of merchandise and customer benefits should be presented in a manner that everyone understands. Long explanations and technical descriptions should be avoided.

Creating Desire

Successful advertisers, like successful salespeople, are students of human nature. They try to create a desire for their merchandise by appealing to their customers' emotions as well as to their reason. Among the buying motives that advertisers appeal to are hunger; curiosity; imitation; companionship; sex appeal; pride; ambition; a desire for good health; a desire for comfort; and a desire for pleasure, fun, and even excitement.

Just which buying motive or motives should be appealed to depends on the kinds of goods advertised and the kinds of customers to be reached. If an appeal is to create a desire for goods, it must have the *you* approach; that is, it must answer the questions that are always in the customer's mind: What will the goods do for me? Why should I buy them? How shall I benefit from them?

Inducing Favorable Action

If all the preparatory steps of an advertisement have been carefully planned, the desired action (customer purchase) should result. The action suggested should be easy to perform. In other words, the advertiser should make it easy for the customer to buy. Buying may involve making a trip to the store, filling out a simple order form, or placing a telephone call. In many instances, advertisers induce action by calling attention to the fact that there is a limited supply of an article or that the goods must be ordered at once in order for them to arrive in time for a holiday or special occasion. Gift certificates, coupons, special sales, and closeout promotions are also effective means of stimulating prompt action. Institutional advertising is less intense than promotional advertising in its appeal for immediate action. Nevertheless, the institutional advertisement should induce the customer to visit the store for whatever kinds of goods or services the store sells.

ELEMENTS OF A PRINTED ADVERTISEMENT

Every advertisement is made of four basic elements: headline, illustration, copy, and signature plate or business identification. Sometimes, there is a fifth element included: price. Advertisers use these elements to accomplish the objectives of printed advertising.

Headline

The first line of an advertisement, called a headline, is the most important element in the opinions of some advertisers. A headline must accomplish three functions:

1. It must attract the attention of potential customers.
2. It must arouse readers' interest.
3. It must lead readers into the copy that follows.

Large type is often used in headlines to attract the reader's attention. Using small type in the rest of the copy also helps call attention to the headline. Several headlines of different sizes, all larger than the ad copy itself, are often used to get attention. Furthermore, any message printed in different sizes of type is easier to read than one printed in all the same type size. Additional guidelines for writing headlines and copy are listed in Illustration 29–1.

A good headline not only gets attention; it keeps it and leads readers into the ad copy. An advertisement must not only be seen; it must be read and understood. To arouse a reader's interest, a headline must relate to her or his needs or wants. Therefore, it is a good idea to put *you* in the headline along with words that name a product's strong features. Consider the following two headlines:

(1) ELI BRAND JEANS!
(2) ELI: THE JEANS THAT FIT
at savings that fit your budget

The second headline is stronger than the first. Even a two- or three-word headline has the big job of sifting customers interested in the advertised product from those not interested. The content of the headline does the sifting. For instance, few men will notice either of these headlines:

BEAUTY AIDS
BEAUTY AIDS SALE

However, the second headline will get the attention of most budget-conscious women.

BASIC GUIDELINES FOR WRITING HEADLINES AND COPY

- Write from customers' points of view.
- Write as though talking to a customer.
- Put the *you* approach and product information into the headline.
- Focus on one main idea in the headline, copy, and illustration.
- Tell about merchandise in new, exciting ways—but accurately.
- Keep words, sentences, and paragraphs of copy short, simple, and easy to understand.
- Urge customers to act now and make it easy for them to do so.

Illus. 29–1   Following the "basics" when preparing headlines and copy can improve the effectiveness of an advertisement.

The best headlines, then, are short and speak directly to customers about the uses and benefits of a product or service.

Illustration

It is a well-established fact that more inquiries and more sales result from an advertisement that contains a picture than from one that is a block of copy only. Many people are eye minded; that is, they are most readily impressed by what they see. Pictures can make a definite appeal to people's intellect and emotions.

A picture that is related to the product advertised and is tied in with the copy will attract attention to the whole advertisement as well as develop an interest and a desire for the product. The illustration, like the headline, must connect the reader's experiences to the product advertised. The illustration should usually appeal to human interest. For example, a picture of a smiling, apparently happy man wearing an advertised shirt is more effective than a picture of the shirt alone.

Illustrations—photos and drawings—are often used by advertisers to direct readers' eyes to the copy or to the name of the product or service advertised. Illustrations show the selling points of merchandise while words can only describe them. In printed advertisements, a picture truly is worth a thousand words!

Copy

Advertising *talks* to people. The talking part of printed advertising is the *copy*. Copy gives readers information about the goods. It creates desire to own the goods and leads to action.

A successful copywriter said, "I write as though one customer were standing in front of me and I am talking directly to that individual, trying to convince the person why he or she should have the merchandise. I write from the customer's viewpoint— how the individual looks at the goods, what the goods will do for that person."

The reader whose interest is aroused by the headline(s) is almost always interested in details about the goods. Therefore, complete and specific merchandise facts should be included in advertising copy. Advertisements should talk naturally to readers—like a salesperson talking with a customer. The copy should contain short, simple sentences made up of specific, commonly used words.

Signature Plate or Logo

Clear identification of the store in all ads makes it easy for customers to act favorably. Another term for store identification is **signature plate** or **logotype.** A logotype, or logo, usually contains a distinctive typeface, trademark, emblem, or symbol that may help readers identify a particular store. The logo is placed near the top or bottom of the advertisement. Close to the store name is the address of the store and sometimes the store's slogan.

Other items of information commonly considered part of the signature plate are lists of the main store's hours, information about whether mail or telephone orders will be accepted for the advertised product, and the names of branches where the same product is available.

Price

There is no agreement among advertisers regarding the inclusion of price as a key element in an advertisement. Clearly, the decision to include price depends on the advertiser's purpose. If the advertisement is to build goodwill and a favorable store image, price will likely not be used. If the purpose is to motivate customers to buy, then price may be a key element in getting customers to act. Typical advertising copy seeking action might read, "Special Sale," "While the Supply Lasts," or "Year End Clearance." In each example, price could play a prominent role in catching customer attention.

Illus. 29–2   The person who plans a layout imagines how the ad should look in order to motivate customers to buy.

COMBINING THE ELEMENTS

The arrangement of the headline, illustration, copy, signature plate, and price is called the **layout.** As shown in Illustration 29–3, an effective layout has a definite starting point; there is one spot in the headline or illustration that attracts attention. From that point, the layout should lead the eye through the remainder of the advertisement. This sequential movement should take the reader through the psychological steps of arousing interest, creating desire, and inducing action.

To get these results, an advertiser who is planning a layout has several important details to consider. The exact size and arrangement of the headline, the selection of the illustration and its position, the copy arrangement, and the location of the signature plate must be determined. In addition, the backgrounds and borders of the advertisement as well as the type sizes and typefaces to be used must be selected.

The person who prepares an advertisement imagines how it should look in order to motivate customers to buy. A rough sketch of this idea is made which reveals the general layout and may even include a specific headline. In a large store, this sketch may be prepared by the advertising manager and turned over to an artist, a copywriter, and a layout person who work out the ideas for the advertisement. This sample, called a **dummy layout,** is a model of the proposed advertisement, showing size and arrangement of the elements. When approved by the advertising manager or store manager, the dummy layout is worked out in detail and submitted to a newspaper or magazine for reproduction and printing. For a small store, the layout

Flair for Elegance?

Imported Designer Fabrics by Mario

$15.95 a yard

No need to look all over town. No one can match our selection of fine fabrics.

Mendez Designs, Inc.

DALLAS
300 North Park Center / 363–2280

1. Headline is meaningful, attractive

2. Subhead is pertinent, supporting

3. Price is prominent, not screaming

4. Illustration is dominant, arresting; adequately portrays merchandise

5. Copy is appealing; creates desire; details provide an overview

6. Place of purchase is clearly identified; individuality is obvious in logotype

Illus. 29–3 Notice how the eye is drawn naturally from the headline through the illustration, copy, price, and signature plate in this well-designed advertisement.

may be prepared by a staff member of a local newspaper.

ELEMENTS OF ELECTRONIC ADVERTISEMENTS

Advertisements presented over radio or television contain the same five elements as printed advertisements. The functions of each element are also the same, although, because of the medium, they may be presented in different ways. For example, on television or radio, a headline and signature plate may be accompanied by a musical theme that is used with every one of a store's ads. Soon, listeners or viewers associate that music with the store. The illustration on a radio advertisement may be sound effects; on television it may be an actual display or demonstration of the product. The copy is in the form of a script.

SCRIPT FOR TELEVISION ADVERTISEMENT
(30 seconds — The Kitchen)

Video (suggested technique: tape)	Audio
Modern kitchen with full range appliances. Countertops should display a variety of holiday food. Containers and utensils should be appropriately placed so that the focal point is on a large ham ready to go into the oven. Two children and an adult are seated at the breakfast bar with a dining table and chairs directly behind. The table is set for a holiday meal. Camera should pan left to right sweeping from oven and appliances to people to table and back to main course and open oven door. Fade away on oven appliances.	[Holiday] time means company and company means special food and lots of it. That's why it's important to own a kitchen range you can depend on. [Product] means quality and dependability, and meals prepared on time just the way you like them. Here are just a few of the [product] outstanding features: heat elements that carry a 15-year unconditional replacement guarantee, an all-porcelain finish available in three colors to match most decors and, best of all, a self-cleaning oven that can reduce post-holiday clean-up time. So, why not visit your [product] dealer today? You'll be glad you did and so will the whole family.

Illus. 29–4 Television spots are prepared from a script listing the scenes and action at the left and the words to be spoken at the right. A script is the copy element of electronic advertising.

In electronic media advertisements, it is generally a good idea to have the advertiser's signature plate appear more than once. Customers should be made aware of the source of the message before and after the other elements of the advertisement are given. An advertising message should close with the signature plate and/or slogan because people tend to remember the end longer than any other part of a message.

HELP FOR ADVERTISERS

A beginner in advertising may want to seek the help of local media experts. Print and electronic media people will, in most instances, be glad to make suggestions. They will help store advertisers with illustrations, copy, scripts, and layouts. Other sources, such as the Retail Advertising Bureau of the American Newspaper Publishers Association, provide an excellent monthly service for retailers. Such groups provide advertising help through the space sales staff of local newspapers. In addition, the manufacturers and wholesale suppliers of products often provide, as a part of their customer services, newspaper, radio, and television ads.

Some large retail advertisers utilize the services of advertising agencies to carry out their promotion activities. Frequently, these agencies will develop a total advertising plan or campaign which involves the use of several media to promote the clients' products or services. Generally, however, retail advertisers do not use advertising agencies in the same way that most national (manufacturer-wholesale) advertisers do. This is true for two reasons: (1) retail advertisements must be planned and executed quickly at short notice and (2) most media charge local stores a rate that is considerably below the national rate. Stores that depend largely on institutional advertising, which can be prepared long before actual use, make effective use of advertising agencies.

*S*ummary

Effective advertisements attract attention, develop interest, create desire, and induce favorable action. Most advertisements are made up of four major elements: headline, illustration, copy, and signature plate or business identification. Sometimes, there is a fifth element included: price. All elements of a printed or electronic advertisement need to be arranged so that the layout leads the reader through the psychological steps of arousing interest, creating desire, and inducing action. To attain the desired advertising results, retailers can rely on a number of sources of help. These sources of help include local advertising media personnel, advertising associations, and advertising agencies.

*R*eview

1. Explain how advertisements are initiated by large and small stores.
2. Describe the three psychological levels of an individual's action.
3. Name the four psychological steps caused by a successful advertisement.
4. Point out the major elements of a printed or electronic advertisement.
5. Define *signature plate, layout,* and *dummy layout.*
6. Describe an effective advertising layout.
7. List three sources of help for advertisers.

Terms

The following terms were introduced in this chapter. Write a separate sentence correctly using each new term.

conscious level   signature plate or logotype
dummy layout   subconscious level
layout   unconscious level

Discuss

1. Why is incorporation of the psychological steps of a sale an effective way to develop a successful advertisement?
2. Why do copywriters say, "Write from the customer's point of view"?
3. Why do some stores use a musical theme to accompany their signature plate when advertising on radio or television?
4. What are the unique functions of each of the elements of printed or electronic advertisements?
5. Why do only some retailers use advertising agencies?

Problem Solving

1. Joy Lu has experienced a successful first year in the operation of her business. This year, she has increased her advertising budget and is thinking about placing advertisements in the local electronic media for the first time. She asks you how radio and television advertising will differ from the newspaper promotions she has used. List as many differences as you can; then identify the three most important differences.
2. You are the manager of a card shop located in the downtown mall of a medium-sized metro area. The empty store next to your business is now being remodeled, and the new operator Joy Lu intends to open a fabric shop within the month. During lunch one day, Joy indicates that she is meeting with the local newspaper-advertising salesperson to plan an ad for the opening of her store. Since her experience in developing ads is limited, she asks your advice regarding what she should try to accomplish in this first promotion. What suggestions would you provide?
3. Your neighbor Kunio Akita owns and operates a neighborhood convenience store. His primary advertising media are window signs and word of mouth. Occasionally, he circulates handbills in the surrounding area to promote a specially priced item or new merchandise. He would like to make greater use of handbills but has not had a good response to this medium. Because he knows

you have some knowledge of advertising, he seeks your help in designing an effective handbill that will successfully promote a new type of frozen pizza. Prepare a dummy layout of a one-page handbill promoting the sale of the pizza. Assume any product information you think would be appropriate in promoting this merchandise.

CHAPTER 30

Advertising Strategies

CHAPTER OUTCOMES

When you have mastered the information provided in this chapter, you should be able to:

1. Identify eight factors that influence how much a retailer might spend on advertising

2. Describe three methods of planning an advertising budget

3. Define the term *cooperative advertising*

4. Identify three possible problems of cooperative advertising

5. Explain how advertising results may be measured

6. State how governmental agencies affect advertising

7. Explain the importance of advertising and how it serves consumers

8. Define the term *bait and switch*

Good advertising doesn't just happen. Careful planning is very important. A retailer must decide when and what to advertise and what combination of media will be most effective. A retailer also must decide how much to invest in advertising, evaluate the results, and meet social and legal advertising standards.

Business conditions are constantly changing, and demand for both new and traditional products tends to vary. Thus, time spent in developing an advertising plan is key to business success.

PLANNING AN ADVERTISING BUDGET

Retailers invest large amounts of money in advertising. The usual measure of advertising expenditures is a percentage of sales. On average, retail firms spend about 3 percent of sales on advertising. As can be seen in Illustration 30–1, there are wide variations in amounts spent to advertise different types of goods. Some firms, such as furniture stores, spend as much as 5 or 6 percent of sales to advertise. Other businesses, such as food stores, spend as little as 1.4 percent of sales.

Factors to Be Considered

A number of factors influence how much money should be invested in advertising: the age and size of the business, competition and competitors' advertising, type of merchandise offered, store location, size and nature of market area, available media, and business philosophy.

Age. During the first few months and often for the first few years, a business needs to advertise heavily in order to become established in a community. A common rule for businesses that are just starting is to spend about twice as much as established competitors.

Size. Small neighborhood stores spend very little on advertising—occasionally, they'll place a small advertisement in a neighborhood shopping paper or a weekly newspaper. On the other hand, a large department store, located among competing department stores and specialty stores, needs to invest much more in advertising. A large store must advertise often in a variety of media to reach a broad market of potential customers.

Selected Types of Retailers	Ad Dollars as Percentage of Sales (%)
Apparel and accessory stores	2.4
Catalog showrooms	3.5
Convenience stores	0.4
Department stores	3.1
Jewelry stores	5.1
Shoe stores	1.8
Variety stores	2.3

Source: "Ad-Sales Ratios by Industry Compiled." Reprinted with permission from the October 12, 1987, issue of *Advertising Age*, p. 50. Copyright © by Crain Communications, Inc.

Illus. 30–1   The choice of a percentage-of-sales figure can be based on what similar businesses are setting aside for advertising purposes.

Competition.   Retailers who compete with big-budget advertisers will need to spend more for advertising than retailers who have little competition. Established retailers should be alert to new competition and should be ready to adjust their advertising plans accordingly. Hard-hitting advertising by a new retailer should not be ignored, even by successful and well-established businesses.

Merchandise.   Retailers of convenience goods aim advertising at the general public. Stores that feature fashion merchandise or unique goods need to reach a very specific group of customers. These customers must be informed of the latest fashions and reminded that the store has fashion goods that cannot be obtained elsewhere. Appealing to a particular audience usually requires more varied advertising—and more advertising dollars—than appealing to a general audience.

Location.   It may seem strange, but, usually, the better a store location, the more the owner invests in advertising. For a store in a heavy traffic location, additional advertising attracts more people who are already coming to that area. A large advertising budget for a store in an inconvenient location may not increase store traffic because of customer difficulty in getting to the store.

Market.   Retail firms with large-market areas generally need to invest additional dollars in varied media. Stores in regional shopping centers, for example, need to send their advertising messages over large areas in order to reach all potential customers. Stores in neighborhood shopping centers, though, reach most customers with media that cover one or two miles around the store.

Media.   Retailers in communities having one newspaper and one radio station often will not spend as much on advertising as retailers in communities with more media. Small-community retailers know that a sizable number of potential customers will be reading that single newspaper or listening to the local radio station. Large communities usually have several newspapers, several radio stations, and one or more television stations as well as opportunities to use direct-mail, transit, and billboard advertising. Because so many advertising media are available, advertising rates in large communities are usually higher than the rates in small communities.

Philosophy.   The merchant who decides to operate a store with a strong promotional philosophy will likely spend more on advertising than a similar store with a nonpromotional philosophy. If the typical store invests about 3 percent of sales in advertising, the strong promotional store may go above the average by 1 or 2 percent because of the increased amount of advertising required to continually promote products and services.

Methods of Planning

For most retailers, advertising is the second or third largest expense—less than payroll but often equal to rent. Accordingly, advertising expenditures must be planned carefully. To get the most value from advertising dollars, retailers budget advertising expenses. Most advertising budgets are one-year plans that are based on

Illus. 30–2   Careful planning is important to good advertising. The retailer must consider a number of factors when deciding how much to spend on advertising activities.

one of the following: last year's sales, anticipated sales, and the store's merchandising objectives.

Last Year's Sales.   A retailer may plan to spend a certain percentage of last year's sales for the current year's advertising. Thus, if last year's sales in March amounted to $80,000 and the retailer wants to spend 3 percent on advertising, then $2,400 will be budgeted for advertising in the month of March this year. This plan usually works, but it is not very progressive. By using a fixed percentage of last year's sales, a retailer bases future action on past results, which does not allow for changing conditions or new store objectives.

Anticipated Sales.   An advertising budget may be based on estimated sales for the coming year. This is a good method because a retailer plans on the basis of future goals rather than on past performance. However, problems arise when merchants rigidly follow the plan once the amounts have been set, even in the face of changing conditions. For example, a merchant might estimate sales for October at $56,000 and plan to spend 3 percent or $1,680 on advertising that month. However, when a new product is introduced, more than $1,680 would be needed for advertising in October. A similar situation can develop if actual sales are much lower than estimated. A retailer may have to go over the budget in such situations. Rather than go over budget often, though, retailers should select another basis for the advertising budget.

Merchandising Objectives.   Another budgeting method involves setting a year's sales goal. With this method, a sales objective is set for the coming year and then two six-month objectives are set. Within each six-month period, regular and special shopping events for each month are identified. The total dollars needed to promote each event properly are estimated. Also, the dollar amounts for each event are budgeted among the various merchandise lines. At the end of each week or month, the advertising budget is reviewed and adjusted according to how well the merchandising objectives were met. If sales were below expectations, an increase in advertising may be needed. If sales exceeded plans, maybe the advertising budget should be decreased. Major advantages of this planning method are its flexibility and ability to deal immediately with specific advertising events and merchandise lines. Because of these advantages, it might be expected that all retailers would use this budgeting method. Actually, many do not use merchandising objectives because the method involves careful figuring, constant watching during the year, and a willingness to change the advertising budget as conditions indicate.

Cooperative Advertising

Many manufacturers and suppliers are willing to share the cost of advertising their products in retailers' local media. This shared approach is called **cooperative advertising.** If a retailer agrees to advertise selected products, the manufacturer or supplier may share the costs of those advertisements, usually on a 50–50 basis. Cooperative advertising has an advantage for manufacturers and suppliers and for retailers. Manufacturers get more benefits for their advertising dollar by paying the retailers' local advertising rates than by paying the higher national rates. Retailers reduce

advertising expenses greatly, especially if they can promote products for which there is cooperative advertising support. Cooperative advertising arrangements are particularly effective when the manufacturer or supplier also has an aggressive national advertising campaign under way that can be tied in with a local promotion. With the extra help on advertisements, local retailers can often use media that would be too expensive if they had to pay the entire cost themselves.

Retailers should not use cooperative advertising, however, just because it is available. First, cooperative advertising should fit the retailer's advertising budget. Second, the cooperative advertisements must be consistent with the usual style and purpose of the retailer's ads, even if prepared by the manufacturer or supplier. Third, the additional record-keeping time and demands made by the manufacturer or supplier on the retailer must not amount to more than the advertising savings.

EVALUATING RESULTS OF ADVERTISING

Judging the results of advertising is easy if clear and measurable goals have been set in the beginning. (If you know where you are going, it is easy to know when you get there!) One way to evaluate advertising is to monitor the sale of advertised items. An advertisement tends to attract the most customer traffic within three days of the time it first appears. A sales record of items or services to be advertised is kept for a week before the advertisement is released. Then, a record of sales is kept for the week following the release of the advertisement. A comparison of pre-advertising sales with post-advertising sales provides clear dollar-and-cents information about the effectiveness of the advertisement.

There are other ways to find out if advertisements are reaching their target. Some retailers hide or bury a special offer, such as a 10-percent reduction in price or free installation, in advertisements. Since the offer appears nowhere else, customers who accept the offer give a clue to the effectiveness of that advertisement.

Coupons are also effective means of determining ad readership. By asking customers to present a coupon to take advantage of an offer—and it should be really worthwhile—a merchant can get an idea of both readership and market coverage of the advertising medium.

Generally, if an advertisement pulls in sales amounting to ten times its cost, it is doing very well. Considering unadvertised merchandise purchased by customers who responded to the advertisement, the advertising cost is probably 2 to 3 percent of total sales. If an advertisement does well, a merchant should use it again. A good seasonal advertisement can be used year after year with only minor changes.

MEETING ADVERTISING STANDARDS

The multibillion dollar advertising business has been subjected to much criticism. One of the more common misuses of advertising is promotion of false leaders. To advertise an item that has been marked down from a fictitious regular price is clearly an attempt to deceive the public. Another unethical practice is to advertise an item at a remarkably low price and then try to sell a high-priced substitute to the customers attracted by the advertisement. This abuse of advertising is called **bait and switch.**

Trade associations, both national and local, and the Better Business Bureau have contributed much to improving ethics in advertising. Through their efforts and those of concerned businesspersons, legislation preventing fraudulent and dishonest advertising has been passed. Most states now have statutes that make deceptive advertising, such as bait and switch, illegal. Legal or not, deceptions, such as advertising false leaders, are not ethical and are not practiced by legitimate businesses.

In recent years, many governmental agencies have increased their activities to assure the protection of consumers from harmful and hazardous merchandise. Also, legislation provides that consumers be informed through labeling, packaging, and advertising about the products they buy.

The federal government, through the Federal Trade Commission (FTC), has handed down trade practice rules for advertising and selling the products of many industries. These rules have the force of law. For example, the Textile Fiber Products Identification Act requires that the fiber content of most textile products be shown to the potential buyer on labels and in advertising. Similar federal laws govern the labeling of wood products, furs, foods, and drugs.

It is natural to expect advertisers to stress the good points of their products or services. Suppose that an individual wanted to sell a used car. If the car had an AM/FM radio and new tires, the seller would want

344 UNIT 5 Promotion

ADVERTISING OF FIBER PRODUCTS	
CORRECT	**INCORRECT**
$165 CLASSIC YEAR-ROUND NAVY BLAZERS in a fine Dacron/worsted wool. Our price: $95	$165 CLASSIC YEAR-ROUND NAVY BLAZERS in Worsted Wool w/Dacron. Our price: $95
Fibers listed on order of content by weight.	Fibers not listed in proper order.
$300 LIGHTWEIGHT CASHMERE-AND-WOOL SPORT COATS imported from Italy — sensuously soft and rich! Our price: $145	$300 LIGHTWEIGHT CASHMERE SPORTS COATS FROM ITALY. Blended with wool—sensuously soft and rich! Our price: $145
Fibers identified in same size type.	Fibers disclosed in different size type.
THE "SHEEPDOG" OF SWEATERS: Big, bulky, lovable, cotton Shaker-knit crewnecks in bold, bright colors. Our price: $30	THE "SHEEPDOG" OF SWEATERS: Big, bulky, cozy-knit crewnecks in bold, bright colors. Our price: $30
Fiber content given.	Fiber content not disclosed; "sheepdog" may suggest "wool."

Source: With permission of Better Business Bureau, Metropolitan New York.

Illus. 30–3 Under the Textile Fiber Products Identification Act, the fiber content of textile products must be shown in advertisements. The statements in the ad on the left do not conform to the act. The statements in the ad on the right are acceptable.

to mention that. He or she would not advertise that the car needed painting or that the carpeting was worn. The advertisement is most effective when it lists the best features of the car. So it is with store advertisements. The retailer advertises the qualities that make a particular item a good value for the price. In general, *truth in advertising* means that an advertisement does not make claims that are untrue or misleading. If readers understand this limitation, they will

soon realize that most advertising is accurate.

Some people do not understand that advertising serves to educate and inform consumers about the great variety of merchandise and services available. They fail to see that, by increasing demand for specific items, advertising reduces retail prices because production costs usually go down as more of a certain item is manufactured. Such people also miss a point that has been proven time and time again: Advertising cannot sell poor goods or items that people do not want to buy. Undoubtedly, advertising has been a contributing factor in the improvement of living standards and the quality of life in this country. Yet, every year, cases of poor and misleading advertising create doubt and dismay in the buying public. To earn and keep the confidence of consumers, advertisers must maintain certain standards of ethical and legal behavior.

Summary

Planning is an important aspect of any effective advertising strategy. Part of this planning requires the development of an advertising budget. Factors that influence how much money should be invested in advertising include the age and size of a business, competition, merchandise offered, store location, nature of the market, available media, and the advertiser's philosophy. The retailer must also select a method for budgeting advertising dollars. The most common methods are based on the previous year's sales, anticipated sales, or the store's merchandising objectives. The results of a particular advertising effort must be evaluated in terms of clear and measurable goals. Finally, every advertising effort should meet legal and ethical standards.

Review

1. List eight factors that influence how much a retailer should invest in advertising.
2. State three methods that can be used to plan an advertising budget.
3. Describe cooperative advertising.
4. Name three possible problems of cooperative advertising.
5. List ways in which advertising results can be measured.
6. Explain how governmental agencies affect advertising.
7. State how advertising serves consumers and explain the importance of truthfulness in advertising.
8. Define *bait and switch*.

Terms

The following terms were introduced in this chapter. Write a separate sentence correctly using each new term.

bait and switch   cooperative advertising

Discuss

1. How can careful planning help to ensure the success of a retail-store advertisement?
2. How do competition and store location influence the amount of money that a retailer will invest in advertising?
3. What are the relative advantages and disadvantages of the methods of planning advertising expenditures involving last year's sales, anticipated sales, and merchandising objectives?
4. Under what conditions might cooperative advertising not be a wise choice?
5. What are some ways in which the quality of today's advertising could be improved?

Problem Solving

1. Richard Johnson is the owner of a convenience food store located near a heavily traveled freeway and a large shopping center. His advertising effort to date has been limited to a sign placed in front of the store. Three months ago a new off-ramp was completed. It has diverted 30 percent of the usual traffic flow away from Richard's store. Richard has decided that he must increase his advertising efforts but is not sure how much. What factors should he consider in making his decision? How could each of these factors influence his final plan?
2. After careful consideration, Richard has decided how much he will budget for advertising. He has also decided to rely on a local newspaper as the major means of promoting the store. Because you are an advertising salesperson for that newspaper, Richard asks your help in determining an effective way to measure the success of his advertisements. Outline a plan for Richard to use.
3. You are employed as a copywriter in the advertising department of a locally owned discount department store. On occasion, you visit with your neighbor to talk about the weather and sports. In a discussion, your neighbor says, "I see your store is having a big sale this weekend. Looks like some good buys although you can't believe what is in the ads most of the time." What exactly would you say to help clarify your neighbor's opinion?

CHAPTER 31
Visual Merchandising-Display

When you have mastered the information provided in this chapter, you should be able to:

1. Explain the purpose for which window displays are designed

2. Name the three kinds of window display units

3. Identify five ways in which window display units can be used

4. State at least five purposes of interior displays

5. Identify the two major types of interior displays

6. List the six basic kinds of interior displays

7. Name the five basic types of display arrangements

8. State what is required for a display to be judged a success

Advertising, sales promotion, public relations, visual merchandising, and personal selling all promote customer interest in a particular business and the goods and services it offers for sale. Visual merchandising, however, is most effective in making it possible for customers to view merchandise firsthand. **Visual merchandising** includes displays, descriptive signs, merchandise presentations, descriptive labels, and the overall image created by the decor of a business.

There are two common types of retail store displays: window displays and interior displays. Both types of displays and their uses are discussed here.

WINDOW DISPLAYS .

Window displays provide the first impression many customers get of the character of a store and its merchandise. Signs, banners, building materials, and window displays are designed to be viewed by customers from outside the store. Most often, window displays are located near the main entrances, but they also may be found in other areas where traffic outside the store is heavy. In open-front mall businesses, the entire view of the firm is an exterior display.

People who are passing by often react favorably to well-designed window displays. They may even decide to enter the store to make purchases based on their reactions to the window displays. The ability to plan and build effective window displays is an important skill that every retailer should possess. One way to develop this ability is

to understand how window display units are designed and used.

Window Display Unit Designs

There are three kinds of window display units. One is a **closed window design** which uses a full background panel. This kind of display completely separates the store's interior from the window display. A second is the **semiclosed window design** which uses a half-panel background to separate the store interior from the display. This style allows potential customers to see over the displayed merchandise into the store itself. Drugstores, jewelry stores, and hardware stores often use this kind of window display. A third design, the **open window display** makes it possible for customers to look directly into the store. Since this kind of window has no back panel, it is possible to see merchandise that is located on nearby counters, tables, and racks from outside the store. In effect, the store interior becomes the merchandise display.

Window Display Uses

Window display units are used for various purposes: special events and sales, related merchandise, line-of-goods, and mass-merchandise displays.

Special Events. Special-event window displays are created to feature merchandise that is related to the event: Christmas, Easter, the Fourth of July, or Labor Day. Business and community promotions, such as store anniversaries, annual local events, and back-to-school days, are also occasions for special displays.

Illus. 31–1   Retail stores often make use of three kinds of window display units. These include the closed window, the semiclosed window, and the open window displays.

Sale Merchandise. Sale display windows are easy to spot because they usually contain both sale merchandise and large colorful sale signs. Sale displays are effective attention getters that appeal to customers seeking bargains.

Related Merchandise. One of the more popular uses for window display units is to present related merchandise. A typical example of a related-merchandise display is a man's sport coat shown with matching slacks, shirt, and shoes, all attractively arranged. Another is a woman's suit with such items as a fall coat, gloves, and scarf placed in an eye-catching arrangement.

Line of Goods.

A line-of-goods window display centers on the promotion of a complete assortment of one kind of merchandise such as jeans, leather goods, and household items. Sometimes a line-of-goods window display presents the products of a single manufacturer. For example, you have probably seen windows containing one brand of VCRs, television sets, camcorders, and stereo sets with the name of the product's manufacturer prominently displayed.

Mass Merchandise.

Mass-merchandise displays are windows filled with a broad assortment of related and unrelated merchandise. Little attention is paid by most retailers to any specific plan of merchandise arrangement in these displays. Mass-merchandise displays hold a particular appeal for persons who are looking for bargains. As a result, merchants who use price to promote their goods make extensive use of mass-merchandise displays to attract customers. Variety stores, drug stores, and discount stores are among the major users of mass-merchandise display windows.

INTERIOR DISPLAYS

Displays located on the sales floor in retail stores are called *interior displays.* These displays, like window displays, allow customers to see the merchandise. More importantly, interior displays permit customers to inspect the merchandise firsthand. To be successful, interior displays should contain some of the merchandise that customers have seen in the store windows. Interior displays usually are found in high-traffic areas of the store. They also can be effective in attracting customers to areas where traffic is light.

With the rapid growth of self-service retailing, there has been a dramatic increase in the use of interior displays as a major means of selling merchandise. Perhaps as important has been the development of new and attractive ways of packaging merchandise. Prepackaged foods, clothing, tools, hardware, and small appliances are among the many products shown in interior display units.

Interior Display Unit Designs

Retailers generally agree that there are two major designs of interior display units: open interior and closed interior. An **open interior display** makes it possible for customers to inspect and handle merchandise without the help of a salesperson. **A closed interior display** is used when it is necessary to protect the merchandise on display from damage or theft. These displays require that customers seek a salesperson's assistance. Jewelry, fine silver, fashion clothing, and most unpackaged food items are examples of goods that must be kept in closed display units.

Both types of interior display unit designs have proved effective in selling packaged and nonpackaged merchandise. Marketing studies show that increased sales result when merchandise is (1) highly visible, (2) easily accessible to customers, and (3) attractively displayed. Interior displays are designed to accomplish all three objectives.

Kinds of Interior Displays

Most display people agree that there are six basic kinds of interior displays: (1) island, (2) end, (3) platform, (4) shadow box, (5) background, and (6) point of purchase.

Island.   Island displays usually are large, open tables stacked high with one or several types of merchandise and separated from surrounding displays. Such displays are most effective when placed in heavy customer traffic areas. They are often used to display sale merchandise.

End.   End displays present merchandise in closed cases, in open bins, or on racks, depending on the type of merchandise to be promoted. In any case, such displays are located at the end of store merchandise aisles. Their main use is for displaying timely and specially priced merchandise. Supermarkets and discount department stores are the most common users of end display units.

Platform.   Platforms are open interior displays that are used on the sales floor. Merchandise that is displayed on platforms (stands) is raised above surrounding products. The added height of the platforms increases the visibility of the displayed merchandise to passing customers. Clothing, furniture, and appliances are often displayed on platforms.

Shadow Box.   Shadow boxes are small closed interior displays built into walls or placed on counters or ledges. Their main purpose is to highlight items available for sale in the various departments of the store. Gloves, purses, jewelry, shirts, ties, and shoes are excellent choices for display in shadow-box units.

Background.   Background displays as their name implies, make use of store space that might otherwise be left empty. Typical of such space are the tops of department backgrounds, escalator ledges, and partitions. Seasonal items and store decorations are frequently displayed in this manner. Although background displays are usually open, customers generally do not have access to displayed goods because of their location.

Point of Purchase

A **point-of-purchase (POP) display** is an open display that is usually tied in with a manufacturer's advertising program or promotional effort. These displays are most often located near checkout counters where purchases are made. Department stores, discount stores, supermarkets, and most other self-service operations rely heavily on point-of-purchase displays. The displays are normally provided by manufacturers and are easy for retailers to set up and maintain. In recent years, point-of-purchase displays have become a popular means of promoting fast-selling merchandise in all types of retail stores.

Interior Display Uses

Without a doubt, the most important reason retailers use interior displays is to

Illus. 31–2   Interior displays allow customers to inspect merchandise firsthand.

sell merchandise. Interior displays also accomplish other important store purposes:

1. Routing customer traffic through the entire store
2. Directing customer attention to new and specially priced merchandise
3. Carrying out themes of the store's window displays
4. Creating a pleasant store atmosphere
5. Helping customers quickly identify various departments in a store
6. Suggesting other products related to the customer's major purchases

However, no display is effective unless it is properly located and attractively arranged.

BASIC DISPLAY ARRANGEMENTS

There are five types of display arrangements that most retailers rely on when developing window and interior display ideas: (1) repetition, (2) step, (3) zigzag, (4) pyramid, and (5) radiation. Each can be used alone or in combination with any of the other arrangements to build a single display. Knowledge of each arrangement can save the retailer time and effort when designing and building displays that will sell merchandise.

Repetition

In display work, repetition-type arrangements can be quickly built simply by stacking rows of one kind of merchandise on top of each other, until a desired display size is reached. Retailers who use self-service and large displays to sell merchandise find such arrangements well-suited to their volume operations. Repetition-type displays are most effective when placed in heavy customer traffic areas, for example, near checkout counters and at the end of merchandise aisles.

Step

Similar to steps in a staircase, this type of arrangement involves placing merchandise in straight lines at different heights or levels in a display unit. Very often, differences in the height of the steps are equalized, so that the display design resembles stairs. Shoes are often displayed in this manner. Props, such as platforms, stands, shelves, bricks, boxes, and even different sizes of merchandise, can be used to create the appearance of steps.

Zigzag

A zigzag arrangement is similar to a step design. As the name implies, merchandise is placed in a zigzag pattern. Unlike a step arrangement, a zigzag display does not require exact differences in height and distance between each level of merchandise. However, like a step arrangement, the zigzag usually consists of three or more levels, with the highest level placed at the rear of the display.

A zigzag arrangement often is used to display exclusive or high-fashion merchandise. Merchandise that is available in a variety of sizes, shapes, colors, and textures is particularly appealing when placed in a zigzag arrangement.

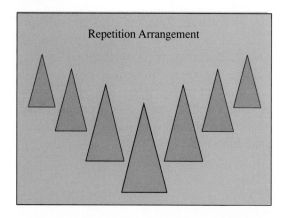

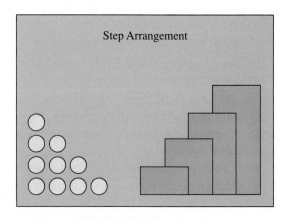

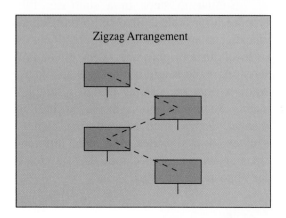

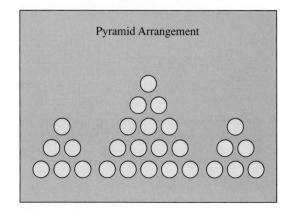

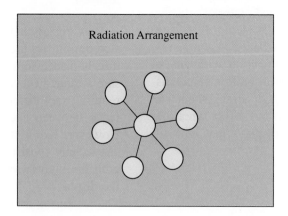

Illus. 31–3 Repetition, step, zigzag, pyramid, and radiation display arrangements are used in window and interior displays.

Pyramid

The pyramid arrangement is simply a display built in the form of a triangle standing on its base. It consists of straight or curved rows of merchandise stacked and rising to a peak. The pyramid arrangement is easy to construct and is most effective for displaying canned goods or hard-covered packages.

Radiation

Radiation-type arrangements are used by retailers to direct customer attention to a major merchandise item in the center of a display. This is done by surrounding the main item with related items of less importance. An example of this arrangement might be a lawnmower displayed with such related merchandise as a garden hose, rakes, and bags of grass seed, all radiating from the lawnmower. Another example is a fall jacket surrounded by shirts or blouses, sweaters, and caps. If the retailer's purpose is to quickly draw customers' attention to a certain product, the radiation arrangement is an excellent choice.

REQUIREMENTS FOR SUCCESSFUL DISPLAYS

Successful displays please the eye, tell a story, and induce customers to buy merchandise. To be successful, a display, like a good advertisement, must attract people's attention. Second, it must develop interest with its timeliness and appeal to each customer's wants and needs. Third, the display must build customers' desire to own the displayed merchandise. Finally, a successful display convinces customers to take action.

In the case of a window display, customer action means entering the store to examine the goods more closely. With interior displays, customer action means asking a salesperson for assistance. In a self-service operation, action takes the form of customers bringing the displayed merchandise to a checkout counter for purchase. In any of these situations, a display is successful when the merchandise is sold.

Most successful displays are the result of careful planning by a retailer. Chapters 32 and 33 offer helpful suggestions for designing and creating effective displays.

Summary   Although customers may be influenced by what they see in advertisements, many prefer to view products firsthand before deciding to buy. To accommodate customers, retailers use visual merchandising; that is, merchandise displays. These displays give customers a chance to inspect goods.

There are two common types of store displays: window displays and interior displays. Window displays are designed so that customers can view merchandise from outside the store. Typical window-display designs include the closed, semiclosed, and open window units. These units are especially effective when used to promote special events, sale and related merchandise, a line of goods, or mass merchandise.

Interior displays, as the name implies, are located inside the store and are used to present all merchandise available for sale. Basic kinds of interior-display designs include island, end, platform, shadow box, background, and point of purchase.

Merchandise is placed in window and interior displays in repetition, step, zigzag, pyramid, and radiation-type display arrangements. Successful displays are those that please the eye, tell a story, and sell merchandise.

Review

1. State the purpose for which window displays are designed.
2. Identify the three kinds of window-display units.
3. List five ways in which window displays can be used.
4. Explain five related purposes of interior displays.
5. Name the two major types of interior displays.
6. Identify the six basic kinds of interior displays.
7. List the five basic types of display arrangements.
8. Explain what is required for a successful display.

Terms

The following terms were introduced in this chapter. Write a separate sentence correctly using each new term.

closed interior display
closed window design
open interior display
open window display

point-of-purchase (POP)
 display
semiclosed window design
visual merchandising

Discuss

1. What kind of interior display would be best suited for the following items: (a) earrings; (b) jogging clothes; (c) paint.
2. What type of window and display arrangement is appropriate for promoting low-priced, fast-moving merchandise?
3. How do window displays and interior displays differ in their approach to convincing customers to take action?

Problem
Solving

1. You are the manager of a card and gift shop in a large shopping mall. Williams Outdoors, which specializes in men's and women's sportswear, is located next to your store. Recently Williams was sold. The new owners intend to remodel the store and place

greater emphasis on promotion. During a conversation with you, the new owners express concern about the kind of window design that would be most effective for their business and they ask you to help. First, list all the factors you can think of that should be considered. Then, select the three or four most important factors for the new owners to consider. Finally, describe the window-display design you would recommend for Williams Outdoors and explain why you chose it.

2. Victor Medina is the owner-manager of Stanfield Jewelry store. To increase sales volume, Victor has decided to add several new lines of medium- and low-priced watches and costume jewelry. Because he has almost no closed counter space, he needs to find other ways in which to display the new merchandise. Considering the type of merchandise, what other kinds of interior display units do you recommend for Victor's use?

3. In the past, Victor has relied on the repetition arrangement for displaying most merchandise in his store. Now that he has decided to try several new interior display units, he believes new arrangements would be helpful. Because you are a display consultant, he asks your assistance in identifying new ways to display his merchandise. What types of display arrangements might Victor use? What requirements must Victor's displays meet in order to be successful? Which of the arrangements you identified would be best to use first?

CHAPTER 32

Designing Displays

CHAPTER OUTCOMES

When you have mastered the information provided in this chapter, you should be able to:

1. Identify and describe the elements of display design

2. Explain the effect of color on customer buying decisions

3. Describe the difference between complementary colors and adjacent colors

4. Name and describe the principles of display design

5. List four sources of display ideas

6. Contrast small- and large- store procedures in selecting merchandise for display

7. Name three appeals that should be considered when selecting merchandise for display

When retailers design displays, they usually have very specific goals in mind. The most important goal is to create displays that sell merchandise. Another is to present a favorable store image to customers. To achieve these goals, an understanding of the basic elements and principles of display design is necessary.

The *elements of display* include line, shape, size, texture, weight, and color. Each can be used to describe the appearance of the components of a merchandise display: display unit, props, lighting, and merchandise. The *principles of display design* determine the proper placement of the elements in the display unit. Knowing how to use basic design techniques is necessary for the beginning display designer.

Illus. 32–1   *Lines can create certain moods. For example, curved lines appear free flowing while vertical lines seem stiff and formal.*

ELEMENTS OF DISPLAY DESIGN

The elements of design are important because they influence the way customers react to a display. Positive reactions induce customers to buy. The following are examples of how each element should be used by retailers to build good displays.

Line

When straight and curved lines are joined in various combinations, such as those shown in Illustration 32–1, they form the physical outline of the merchandise and the display unit. These lines can create certain moods or impressions. For example, vertical lines appear stiff and formal to many people. Curved lines give a sense of free-flowing movement. Diagonal lines, on the other hand, communicate a sense of action. Horizontal lines give a feeling of restfulness or sleep.

Shape

Shapes, such as squares, circles, and triangles, convey the physical appearance of merchandise; cubes, rectangles, and ovals are typical display-unit shapes. Similar shapes placed together create an impression of harmony. Opposite shapes in the same display attract attention. For instance, an oval-shaped display unit containing oval-shaped picture frames may not sell as many frames as a rectangular display unit containing oval picture frames. Since the main purpose of a display is to attract customer attention, shape is an important factor in display design.

Illus. 32–2   The use of shape, size, and texture in a display usually attracts attention.

Size

Merchandise that is small may not sell if it is placed in a large display area. Jewelry items in a full-size window display may attract little notice from passersby because of their small size. On the other hand, large size merchandise in a small display area can result in low sales because, although potential buyers pay attention, they react negatively to the cramped or out-of-place appearance of the display.

Texture

In display design, the term **texture** refers to the surface of a product or display unit. *Shiny, dull, smooth,* and *rough* describe texture. Display designers use texture to create contrast in displays because contrast draws attention to key merchandise. For example, smooth, shiny dishes are most noticeable when displayed on a dull, rough tablecloth. Likewise, rough-textured wool sweaters get attention if displayed before a smooth, shiny background such as silk.

Color

Of the six display elements, color is probably the most important. Too much or too little color confuses and even irritates some customers. Often, the best advice is to use as few colors as possible and to choose colors that provide a pleasing contrast. To do so, of course, requires a basic understanding of (1) what color is, (2) how it affects customer buying decisions, and (3) what constitutes the best combination of colors for a particular display.

Effects of Color.   The influence of color on customer buying decisions is important knowledge that every display person should possess. Each of the primary and secondary colors creates an impression and causes a similar reaction in most people. The impressions typically conveyed by colors are shown in Illustration 32–3.

For example, red suggests power and strength, while blue and green (a combination of yellow and blue) cause a cool or calm reaction. Yellow and orange (a combi-

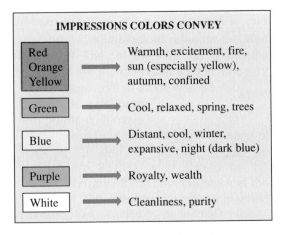

Illus. 32–3   The impressions that colors convey influence customer buying decisions.

nation of yellow and red) suggest warmth and sunshine, and purple (a combination of red and blue) reflects quality and wealth. Air conditioners, for instance, may best be displayed against a blue or green background to create a cool feeling on a hot day. Electric blankets or winter coats in a red or orange display create an impression of warmth, even when it's freezing outside.

Selecting Colors.   To help solve the problem of selecting attractive color combinations, many retailers use a color wheel (see Illustration 32–4). **Complementary colors** are found on opposite sides of the color wheel (blue/orange; yellow/purple; red/green). The colors that complement each other are most effective in creating color contrasts. **Adjacent colors** are found next to each other (red—red-orange, red-purple; yellow—yellow-orange, yellow-green; blue—blue-green, blue-purple) and create the least contrast when used together in a merchandise display. Color selection should include consideration of the display unit, props, and lighting as well as the merchandise. All display components must blend together for a design to be effective.

Weight

The weight of an item of merchandise can be real or imagined. Size and color together give an impression of weight. Generally, the larger and darker a product is, the

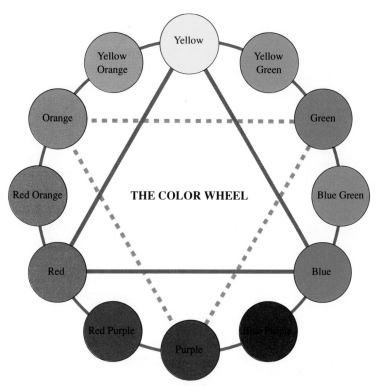

Illus. 32–4   The colors connected by the solid-line triangle are the primary colors; colors connected by the dotted-line triangle are secondary colors. Knowledge of the color wheel is essential to display planning.

heavier it appears and the more noticeable it is. Like shape and texture, weights are contrasted in a display to draw the customer's attention from one item to another.

PRINCIPLES OF DISPLAY DESIGN

The elements of display design deal with the appearance of the individual items contained in a display. Retailers also should know how to apply the principles of display which determine where the items should be *placed* in relation to each other. Principles of display design include harmony, contrast, emphasis, balance, and proportion.

Harmony

Harmony in display simply means that all the displayed items look good together. Everything flows together well. The sizes, shapes, lines, textures, and colors, when placed in the same unit, create a display that is pleasing to the eye. A display of matching shoes, purses, and gloves would have harmony; but a display of summer shoes, umbrellas, and winter coats would lack harmony. Merchandise items that would be used together in everyday life are more likely to create a harmonious blend.

Contrast

Contrast is used to draw attention to differences in the merchandise on display. Display elements such as color, shape, and size provide an excellent way to show contrast in whatever is presented. A display of red coats against a white background provides color contrast. A display of cordless portable phones and table-model phones with built-in answering machines contrasts sizes and shapes.

Contrast is a powerful display design principle so care should be exercised in how it is used. Too much contrast can produce a negative customer reaction. Although surf boards and ice skates in the same display create contrast, customers may not respond because of the lack of connection between the two products. Strong contrast in products and their uses can be too much to overcome when convincing prospective customers to buy. When contrast is used, it should suggest something about the displayed merchandise.

Emphasis

Emphasis is a very effective way to attract attention to key merchandise. Every display should have one or two highlighted items, although several pieces of merchandise are in the display. One simple technique for emphasizing a display item is a sign directing the customer's attention to the key merchandise. Another method is to use the design elements to emphasize one or two items. Keep in mind that each of the display elements can provide an excellent means for developing emphasis. Merchandise items with different lines, sizes, shapes, textures, and colors are natural attention getters. Cleverly used, emphasis can be the strongest visual attraction in a display.

Balance

Balance is a key principle in display. Skill in planning balanced displays should be a priority for display designers. Two types of balance are used in display arrangements: formal and informal. **Formal balance** is achieved when an imaginary line can be drawn through the display, resulting in two identical halves. **Informal balance** results when the halves are not equal. For example, an informal-balance display may have three items in one half of the display and one item in the other. Because of the contrasting halves, informal balance is generally more interesting than formal balance and more likely to attract attention.

Proportion

People are attracted to merchandise displays that are pleasing to the eye. Designing an attractive display requires careful selection of merchandise, props, and signs having shapes and sizes in proportion to the display area. **Proportion** is defined as the correct relationship between object and space. For example, a large window display containing popcorn poppers, an electric stove, and a small electric mixer is out of proportion because of the size differences of the merchandise relative to the display unit. On the other hand, cookware, dishes, and utensils would fit well because of the similarity in their shapes and sizes.

SOURCES OF DISPLAY IDEAS

New and interesting displays are not always easy to develop. Even the most experienced display designer must rely on outside sources for new ideas. Numerous sources of display ideas are available to retailers who are willing to take time to look for them. Easy-to-find sources include the merchandise itself, trade publications, other

merchants' displays, and customer feedback. A retailer should keep a record of all displays used and the origins of the designs. Later, designs can be pulled from the retailer's own idea file.

Merchandise

Items that have been selected for display can provide valuable clues as to how they might best be presented. Such features as the product's construction or its use are proven sources of ideas for the display planner. Consider, for example, a display of color television sets with each set turned on to show picture and sound quality; or, perhaps, a set of unbreakable tableware surrounded by fragments of dishes that break when they are dropped. The potential displays suggested by the merchandise itself are innumerable.

Printed Materials

The main offices of most retail chains regularly supply illustrations of completed displays for use by their local stores. Manufacturers often provide a similar type of service to their dealers. Other excellent sources of display design ideas are the various trade publications such as *Visual Merchandising and Store Design* and *Signs of the Times* which contain many creative ideas. Even some newspaper advertisements and television commercials can spark ideas for eye-catching display designs.

Other Merchant Displays

Some surprisingly good sources of design ideas are the displays of other merchants. It would be a mistake, however, to look only at displays of merchandise similar to that for which a display is being designed. In fact, some of the best ideas come from displays containing completely different merchandise. It is entirely possible that a well-designed jewelry display can provide a design idea for athletic gear.

Customers

To some extent, it is possible to measure a display's effectiveness by the number of customers who stop, look, and buy. Customers who respond to a display can be asked to explain why they were attracted to it. The display designer's responsibility is then to translate these customer responses into new, action-producing displays.

SELECTING MERCHANDISE FOR DISPLAY

The selection of specific merchandise items for display must be made with an understanding and awareness of the overall objectives of display design. In most small retail stores and specialty shops, the selection procedure is simple; the number of items that can be displayed is usually very limited. The season of the year, displays recently used, and special advertising plans reduce the selection to a few items. Inquiries by customers or comments by friends may prompt the small-store owner to prepare a display of a certain kind of merchandise. The store manager can also draw on a multitude of local events—even a change in weather—to make a decision on a merchandise display. In a small store, the time between selection of merchandise and building of a display usually is very short.

Large stores must follow different procedures in merchandise selection. The amount of merchandise from which they can select is extensive, and there are many display areas to be used and coordinated. Because displays are usually elaborate, additional time is needed between merchandise selection and the actual creation of the display. In a large store, buyers, department heads, the merchandise manager, the display manager, and the display staff are all involved in each display. Communication among these people must be carefully organized.

Whether the selection of merchandise is made by the owner-manager in a small store or by the department head or display director in a large store, that decision should not be made carelessly. Whoever makes the decision can be sure that it is correct if each display item has (1) sales appeal, (2) eye appeal, and (3) time appeal.

Merchandise with Sales Appeal

Some merchants make the mistake of using displays to promote merchandise that customers are not interested in buying. Customers are sure to lose interest in such a store. Naturally, customers would think the displays contain merchandise that represents the whole store. Therefore, only those items that have a proven sales appeal for the largest number of customers should be selected for display.

Merchandise with Eye Appeal

Items placed in a store display should be pleasing to the eye because of their attractive appearance and special customer interest. Damaged merchandise or merchandise that is ill fitted or incorrectly placed in the display will detract from the display's appeal. Of all the potential good sellers, some items are sure to have more eye appeal than others. These should be selected for display use.

Merchandise with Time Appeal

Timely merchandise is often tied in with important national or local events, changing weather conditions, holidays, and fashions. An important local football game in November presents a good opportunity to display heavy sweaters, coats, gloves, scarves, caps, and blankets.

Constant attention to world events and their effect on customer taste and demand is necessary if displays are to have time appeal. For example, developments in the 1991 Persian Gulf War stimulated interest in patriotic music, flags, and military-style clothing. Retailers pulled out all the stops in their efforts to promote their support for the U.S. troops with attention-getting, action-inducing merchandise displays.

Summary

Retailers want to create displays that will sell merchandise and maintain a favorable store image. To accomplish these goals, they apply the basic elements and principles of display design when constructing displays. Elements of display design deal with the appearance of displayed items: lines, shapes, sizes, textures, colors, and weights. Principles of display design refer to the proper placement of the elements in a display. Proper arrangement involves harmony, contrast, emphasis, balance, and proportion.

Successful display designers constantly seek new and interesting display ideas. Innovative ideas can often be obtained from the merchandise itself, from printed materials, from other merchant displays, and from customers. However, consideration of display elements and principles along with creative thinking do not guarantee an effective display. Merchandise for display must also be carefully selected. Items that have sales, eye, and time appeal are the goods that belong in displays.

Review

1. Name and describe the elements of display design.
2. Explain how color affects customer buying decisions.
3. Explain the difference between complementary colors and adjacent colors.
4. Tell how the principles of display design are different from the elements of display design.

5. Identify four sources of display ideas.
6. Compare small- and large-store procedures of selecting merchandise for display.
7. List three appeals that should be considered when selecting merchandise for display.

Terms

The following terms were introduced in this chapter. Write a separate sentence correctly using each new term.

adjacent colors   informal balance
complementary colors   proportion
formal balance   texture

Discuss

1. Why is an understanding of the basic design techniques necessary for the beginning display designer?
2. How do balance and proportion attract customer attention?
3. Why do experienced display designers use a variety of sources for display ideas?
4. Why do large and small stores differ in the procedures they follow when selecting merchandise for display?

Problem Solving

1. The Chamber of Commerce in your community is sponsoring a seminar for small retail businesses. The seminar is entitled "Creative Promotion Techniques." Several local retailers have been asked to give presentations on selected topics. Because you are a successful display designer, you have been asked to discuss new sources of display ideas. What will you suggest to the other merchants?
2. After the seminar is ended, several merchants tell you that they are confused about the differences between display elements and principles. What could you do to clear up their confusion?
3. You are employed in the display department of a clothing store. This store is owned and operated by a large national chain. Your major responsibility has been to install displays designed by specialists in the chain's national headquarters. Recently, the store display-department manager was informed that display policies had been changed to allow each store to design and build its own displays. You are asked to help design several displays that could be used in the upcoming fall promotion. What procedure will you suggest for developing display designs?

CHAPTER 33

Installing Displays

CHAPTER OUTCOMES

When you have mastered the information provided in this chapter, you should be able to:

1. Identify the six most important objectives of display

2. Name five merchandise aids that affect the visual impression given by a store

3. List five steps involved in planning and setting up a display

4. Define the terms *display requisition, display planning calendar, display planning budget, functional prop*, and *decorative prop*

5. Identify ten guidelines for installing a display

6. List five factors that should be considered when evaluating a completed display

7. Explain the difference between promotional displays and institutional displays

Katie Lin and Jerry Perez are seniors at Apollo High School. Both are enrolled in the school's Marketing Education program, and both are employed part-time at a local department store. Mr. Jon Harris, the store's display director, is aware of Katie's and Jerry's interest in developing basic display-building skills. Because both students have proven themselves good workers, Mr. Harris has arranged for their temporary transfer to the display department as display assistants. In preparation for their transfer, Katie and Jerry have been provided with reading materials explaining the basic elements and principles of display design. They have been informed that the most important objectives of display are the following:

1. To sell goods
2. To show new uses for merchandise
3. To introduce new goods
4. To build prestige and goodwill
5. To show proper care of merchandise
6. To suggest merchandise combinations

After a tour of the store's display areas and workroom, Mr. Harris has invited the two new assistants into his office to explain to them the procedures followed in planning and building effective displays.

DISPLAY REQUIREMENTS

Effective merchandise displays are the result of careful planning and skill in installing displays. This kind of work involves more than the occasional creation of a visual presentation. It requires a level of excellence that must be constantly maintained week after week. Careful attention must also be given to meeting specific deadlines for completion of store presentations. Quality displays are no accident. Rather, they are the result of careful design planning and rapid completion. Every retailer wants visual presentations that will attract customers, increase sales, and, in general, please more people. An important fact to remember is that visual merchandising includes not only displays but other features of the store. In addition to merchandise, features such as the color of the walls, carpeting, lighting, and even the appearance of salespeople influence the customer's impression of a store. The following is a list of visual merchandising considerations that affect the customer's impression of a store:

- department layout
- selling fixtures
- display fixtures
- wall colors
- lighting
- signs
- floor coverings
- arrangement of aisles
- furniture
- fitting rooms
- wrappings (bags and boxes)
- color and arrangement of background stock
- grooming and dress code of store staff
- color of telephones

Certain procedures in the planning and installing of effective displays are common to all stores, regardless of their size. These procedures generally include requesting a display, planning the display, preparing the display area, installing the actual display, and evaluating the display. An understanding of these basic procedures will permit the potential display worker to advance quickly to more involved display-building assignments and to learn faster under the guidance of an experienced display specialist.

REQUESTING DISPLAYS

The process of planning and installing a display begins with the selection of the merchandise to be presented. For example, in a large department store, a buyer of children's clothing may advise the department head that a new line of children's play clothes and accessories has been ordered and will arrive in ten days. The department head believes that the price and quality of this new merchandise are excellent and that window and interior displays of the merchandise will stimulate additional sales for the department. The department head also wants to feature this merchandise in newspaper and television advertisements.

To reserve the display space needed, the department head must complete a **display requisition,** similar to the example in Illustration 33–1, which is then sent to the display department. The display director checks the completed requisition to determine whether (1) the merchandise recommended for display will blend with other displays planned for that period of time, (2) the display department can complete the displays by the time requested, and (3) the necessary props and other display materials needed will be available. If all of these requirements can be met, the display director and the department head will meet to discuss the appropriate window and interior display designs and their locations.

The display director usually makes the final decision as to the actual colors and sizes of the merchandise selected for display. This is particularly true if the display department is planning a central theme for a storewide sales promotion. Often, the display director will ask each merchandise-department head to submit a list of items that will contribute to the success of the promotion. Finally, the display director will select those products that can be developed into a series of attractive window and interior displays.

The process of selecting merchandise for display in a small retail store is not unlike that just described. The major difference, of course, is that most of the responsibility for getting these jobs done belongs to the store owner or manager.

PLANNING DISPLAYS

A retail-store display department receives many requests to plan and install window and interior displays. Display people must decide which are the most important items to present to the public. The total store promotional effort and the space available for display purposes are major considerations.

Once a specific display area has been determined, the location of each item to be included in that area must be decided. Next, a theme or selling story is developed that will appeal to the largest number of shoppers. A sketch is made of the display and a list of needed props and display materials is prepared. The sketch provides a general layout of the display and the position in which merchandise is to be arranged. Any special effects such as lighting, color, or

ENGLEWOOD'S

DISPLAY RECORD

DEPARTMENT Children's Wear DATE OF DISPLAY 11/9-18 COST $75

WINDOW 1 INTERIOR 2 INSTALLED BY William Ruitt

LOCATION Window 3; platform near center escalator; Children's Wear Dept.

SALES $2,800 (nine selling days)

MERCHANDISE Children's playsuits with related accessories (mittens, caps, and boots). Window display showed five different colors in various sizes—2 to 6x. Platform display featured two suits with show-card message "Weather or Not" and departmental location. Architectural display showed same colors and sizes and accessories as in window.

SETTING Window—background of playground scene done in watercolors; foreground covered with grass turf and scattered colored leaves; merchandise and accessories on child mannequins placed randomly as if children at play. Platform—floor covering of gold burlap; two suits French wired with large card message. Architectural—four sided, merchandise and accessories on child mannequins playing on jungle gym. See attached photos of displays.

SIGN COPY See attached sign requisitions and photos.

REMARKS Customer response highest to architectural display. Few stopped at platform display. Window drew some response, especially first three days. Reaction to merchandise very favorable, although some customers questioned the wearing quality of material in suits.

Illus. 33–1   Here is a display requisition that might be used in a department store. Study the form and note the kinds of information required before display materials can be obtained and the display installed.

showcards that may be needed are also noted on the sketch.

Routine displays may take only a few days to prepare. On the other hand, major store themes and special promotions may take many months to plan and complete. Since most retailers display merchandise throughout the entire year, planning becomes a year-round job. Two important techniques can make display planning and

installing easy and effective, reducing the amount of time and money spent on display work. A *display planning calendar* is a list of all the displays to be built during the coming weeks and months. A *display planning budget* is a record of the expected costs of building each display. Both, of course, are subject to change should the need arise. To reduce planning and scheduling time, retailers may use window and in-

Illus. 33–2   Display people use a sketch (left) to determine the general layout and appearance of the finished display area (right).

terior displays prepared by product manufacturers. Of course, there is always the danger that such displays will not reflect the store image or that too much emphasis will be placed on a single brand of merchandise.

PREPARING THE DISPLAY AREA

In the normal cycle of display work, one display must be taken down before another can be installed. New display installation should be done as quickly as possible.

Valuable promotion time is lost every minute that any display space stands empty. To reduce lost time, displays are often installed during the early-morning or late-store hours or whenever customer traffic is light.

Care should be taken to see that display area preparation is done with as little interference as possible with other work areas. Inconvenience to customers in the store's sales areas should be avoided. A curtain is usually drawn across the window display space to prevent customers from viewing the dismantling of the present display.

The first step in arranging a new display is to remove the accessories from the present display. These items are placed in plastic bags, wrappers, or other appropriate containers. The display merchandise is then removed from the props, neatly folded or placed on hangers, and returned with the accessories to the respective departments to be placed in stock and sold. The props are removed and loaded on a stock truck for return to the display-department workroom. If a mannequin has been used, special care must be taken to protect it from damage while it is being moved. The next steps are to clean the glass, floor, ceiling, sides, and background of the display unit. Lights should be replaced if necessary and any other display materials removed.

Every display person should be aware of the potential hazards that exist when arranging a window or interior display. Sharp bumps to window-display glass can produce disastrous results. Protruding staples and nails can cause serious injury. Overloaded electrical outlets can cause serious fires and burns. Careless handling of props, merchandise, and equipment can result in serious accidents. All these mishaps can be avoided if reasonable care is taken and established display-removal procedures are followed.

SETTING UP DISPLAYS

The actual steps followed in installing a display vary from store to store. Such factors as store size, merchandise to be displayed, and available display space must be considered. Most displays start with an idea presented in a sketch (see Illustration 33–2 on page 371). As soon as the details of the display have been approved, the actual display-building process moves ahead.

The display person begins by selecting the needed functional and decorative props. If necessary, special props are constructed especially for the display. Functional props are basic items, such as mannequins, shirt forms, and shoe stands, that hold or support the merchandise on display. Decorative props are important frills, such as artificial flowers, leaves, and background scenery, that are used to indicate the season or setting and to attract the eyes of customers. The display background and large, bulky props are arranged according to the display sketch. Merchandise is then placed on the props. If clothing is to be displayed on mannequins, the fitting and arranging of garments should be completed before the forms are placed in the display area.

After all featured merchandise has been arranged and necessary accessories added, the remaining decorative props should be properly placed and the display sign set in position. Lighting effects should be checked and shadows eliminated or

Illus. 33–3   As soon as the details of a display have been approved, the next step is to select the needed functional and decorative props.

added, as needed. A final inspection should be made; details should be checked and the display viewed from all angles to make certain it is attractive to passing shoppers.

Regardless of the steps followed when installing displays, every display person adheres to certain guidelines to accomplish her or his objectives. The following are typical of the installation guidelines used by many successful display designers:

1. Suggest how displayed merchandise can be used.
2. Mark prices plainly (unless the store has a policy not to show prices in order to emphasize quality and leadership).
3. Display related articles together.
4. Group merchandise; do not scatter it.
5. Do not crowd the display.
6. Make displays simple.
7. Gather together everything needed before starting to work on the display.
8. Change displays frequently (once a week if possible—never use a display over a month).
9. Keep window and interior display units spotlessly clean.
10. Make certain that each display sells merchandise.

EVALUATING DISPLAYS

After Mr. Harris, Katie, and Jerry finished discussing display-building procedures, Mr. Harris pointed out the importance of knowing how to evaluate each completed display. From a technical point of view, such factors as (1) attracting attention, (2) merchandise and prop arrangement, (3) timeliness, (4) lighting, and (5) construction are major considerations. The real test of a successful display, however, is the number of customers it brings into the store and the amount of display merchandise it sells.

Some retailers keep a record of traffic, inquiries, and sales in each department with a display (see Illustration 33–5). Recording

Illus. 33–4   All displays should receive a final inspection. Customer reactions to displays should be observed, too.

ENGLEWOOD'S

DISPLAY REQUISITION

DEPARTMENT _Children's Wear_   DATE REQUESTED _10/12_   DATE OF DISPLAY _11/9-18_

NUMBER OF DISPLAYS NEEDED _3_   WINDOW(S) _1_   INTERIOR(S) _2_

MERCHANDISE

TO BE FEATURED _Children's playsuits with mittens, caps, and boots as accessories. Playsuits are of new style in five colors for either boys or girls, sizes 2 to 6x. Fabric is polyester, ankle and wrist cuffs of cotton rib-knit, elasticized back for better fit, ankle zippers, front zipper with large ring, and two snap-close side pockets._

DEPTH OF STOCK _More than adequate for anticipated customer response. Item will be carried as regular stock for remainder of season. Additional shipments of goods already ordered._

LOCATION DESIRED _Prefer Window 3 be used and that one of each color be shown (red, blue, yellow, rust, and lime). Small platform display with three items near center escalator. Large architectural display in center of children's wear department._

RELATED PROMOTION _Newspaper advertising on 11/8 (Sunday) 1/2 page and on 11/12 (Thursday) 1/4 page; 30-second spots on "Noontime" TV show._

REQUESTED BY _Peg Baruoarskee_   APPROVED _Toni Shaw_

Illus. 33–5   A display record should include the dates the display was used and a description of the background, merchandise, and design (including sketch or photo) of the display. The form also should show the cost of the display, sales of the merchandise during the display period, and other remarks. Display records are good sources of ideas for future displays.

the average daily sales of merchandise prior to the construction of the display and during the time the display is visible can give an indication of the effectiveness of the display. If various advertising media are used to promote the display merchandise, the ef-fect of each on sales must be considered separately.

A display featuring merchandise for sale—**a promotional display**—can usually be evaluated through measurable sales re-sults. More difficult to evaluate, however, is the display designed to create goodwill—the **institutional display.** Displays of this kind often promote community activities in which the store is involved. Fund-raisers, fashion shows, and school and organization activities are typical subjects for institutional displays. The effects of these displays are most often determined through customers' expressions of appreciation or through the general public's approval of the store's efforts.

Professional display people constantly seek ways to evaluate and improve their display results. Some display people often pose as passersby and observe customer reactions to the display being evaluated. Sometimes customers are approached directly and asked for their opinion of a display. Personnel in the department containing the display are excellent sources of evaluation, since they see and hear customers' reactions.

ORGANIZING DISPLAY ACTIVITIES

Jon Harris suggested that, time permitting, Katie and Jerry become acquainted with the various ways in which stores in the shopping center organize their display activities. Following is a summary of their observations.

In a very small store or service establishment, the owner or a salesperson does the display work. The slightly larger specialty shop probably requires the services of a part-time display designer. This individual is usually a regular store employee or a freelance display specialist who plans and builds major displays for a fee. Since the display budget is usually small, care must be taken to assure that the greatest benefit (dollarwise) is obtained from each completed display.

In a medium-size store, the display staff may consist of a lead display specialist with one or two part-time assistants. Often, there are limited workroom facilities where window and interior displays are prepared and where display equipment is stored.

In most large-volume retail operations, display is an important store function. Here, a display director operates at the executive level—often directly under the sales-promotion manager or publicity director. A staff of 10 to 30 or more people may work on display activities. The display director serves as coordinator among general managers, buyers, and department heads to plan store promotions, to schedule displays, and to assign appropriate display areas. Display staffs often specialize in one type of display in order to design and install displays efficiently. Assistant display directors may be designated for window display, interior display, or special store promotions. Display assistants, who specialize in the design and construction of specific kinds of merchandise displays, may be assigned to such areas as ready-to-wear, home furnishings, appliances, hardware, and high-fashion merchandise.

Regardless of the size of the store, the people responsible for the display function should have two objectives clearly in mind. One is to sell merchandise; the other is to create a favorable image of the store to the buying public.

Summary

Displays that sell merchandise are usually the results of careful planning and skilled installation. Regardless of store size, there are certain procedures to be followed in planning and organizing displays. After merchandise has been selected, appropriate display space should be identified. Then, a display theme and the placement of merchandise should be decided and outlined on paper. A list of props and materials needed to build the display must also be completed. After the plan for the display has been finalized, the previous display must be removed and the area made ready for the new display. The actual display-building process may vary depending on the type of store and the designer's preference. Generally, props are selected, the background is prepared, and the merchandise is placed in the display. Necessary lighting and signs are then added. Effectiveness of the display should be evaluated. Factors such as (1) attracting attention, (2) merchandise and prop arrangement, (3) timeliness, (4) lighting, and (5) construction should be considered. The before and after sales of displayed merchandise should be measured. Store size often determines how display activities are organized. In a small store, the owner or a salesperson may do the display work. Large stores may employ a display director and a large staff of display specialists.

Review

1. List the six most important objectives of display.
2. Identify five merchandise aids that affect a customer's visual impression of a store.
3. List the steps that should be followed in planning and setting up a display.
4. Define *display requisition, display planning calendar, display planning budget, functional prop,* and *decorative prop.*
5. State ten guidelines for installing a display.
6. List five elements of a completed display that should be evaluated.
7. State the difference between promotional and institutional displays.
8. Explain how the organization of the display activities differs among small, medium, and large stores.

Terms

The following terms were introduced in this chapter. Write a separate sentence correctly using each new term.

display requisition   promotional display
institutional display

Discuss

1. What is meant by the statement "Quality displays are no accident"?
2. What are some steps that should be considered when preparing a display area for a new presentation?
3. Why do retailers always look for ways to evaluate and improve their displays?
4. Why do small, medium, and large retail stores differ in how they organize their display function?

Problem Solving

1. Assume that you are a display assistant in a department store. You have been asked to suggest ways in which the visual impression of the store could be improved. Visit three stores of your choice and make a list of the visual merchandising aids you think are particularly effective. Be ready to explain why these aids made you feel good about the stores.
2. As the display manager for a new department store, your first task is to organize all display activities. Set up some new general guidelines for installing displays.
3. Talk with a display person in each of three different stores. Ask each individual to describe the methods he or she uses to evaluate the effectiveness of the store's displays. Compare your findings. Identify common methods. Try to explain differences in methods.

CHECKING KEY POINTS

This exercise is designed to check your understanding of material presented in Unit 5. On a separate sheet of paper, list the numbers 1 to 28. Indicate your response, *T* for true or *F* for false, for each of the following statements.

1. Good advertising sells unwanted merchandise.
2. A successful advertisement takes the reader, viewer, or listener through these steps: attention, interest, desire, and action.
3. The better the store location, the less a store owner needs to invest in advertising.
4. Few states have statutes that make deceptive advertising illegal.
5. Window displays are designed to be viewed outside the store.
6. Placement of merchandise is the most important principle of display design.
7. A display sketch provides a detailed description of the display to be installed.
8. No goods should be advertised without salespeople being informed of the ad.
9. Because of its relatively low cost, television is fast becoming the main advertising medium for many retailers.
10. Sales promotion includes advertising, visual merchandising, public relations, and personal selling.
11. Informal balance is more interesting and less likely to attract attention than formal balance.
12. A display planning budget is a list of the displays to be built during the coming weeks and months.
13. The signature plate describes the advertised product.
14. A fast-selling item is one that has won the approval of many customers.
15. Platform displays are an example of closed displays.
16. Personnel in the department containing a display are among the best people to evaluate the display.
17. Direct mail remains the chief advertising medium for most retail stores.
18. Of all the display elements, color is probably the least important.
19. The process of planning and installing a display begins with the selection of the merchandise to be presented.
20. Most discount houses devote an advertisement to a single item.

21. Publicity is free advertising of a business or product.
22. Coupons are an effective measure of advertising readership.
23. Complementary colors are found on the same side of the color wheel.
24. A successful display is one that sells merchandise.
25. Any means by which advertising can be presented is known as a *medium.*
26. Contrast is not an effective means of attracting attention.
27. An effective headline is short, clear, and relates to a particular product.
28. Interior displays are not effective for attracting customers to light traffic areas.

BUILDING BASIC SKILLS

Calculations

1. Study the following data and then answer the questions:

Item A		Item B	
Retail price	$ 5.80	Retail price	$ 2.98
Store cost	3.40	Store cost	1.75
Advertising cost	420.00	Advertising cost	194.00

   a. What is the gross profit (Retail price − Store cost) for Item A?
   b. What is the gross profit (Retail price − Store cost) for Item B?
   c. How many units of Item A would have to be sold to generate enough gross profit to pay the cost of advertising that item?
   d. How many units of Item B would have to be sold to generate enough gross profit to pay the cost of advertising that item?
   e. If 260 units of Item A were sold, how much gross profit would remain after the advertising costs are paid?
   f. If 370 units of Item B were sold, how much gross profit would remain after the advertising costs are paid?
   g. Which item would you advertise (Item A or Item B)? Why?

2. You have decided to spend 4.0 percent of last year's monthly sales in each of the corresponding months of the new year. Study the information below and complete the necessary calculations.

	Previous Year Monthly Sales	Current Year Monthly Advertising Budget
January	$13,500	_____
February	13,900	_____
March	14,750	_____
April	15,100	_____
May	16,250	_____
June	17,150	_____
July	18,200	_____
August	15,300	_____
September	16,800	_____
October	17,100	_____
November	17,600	_____
December	19,700	_____

Total Previous   Total Current Year
Year's Sales   Advertising
                        $ _____   Budget $ _____

Working with People

Retail personnel in charge of the promotional activities of their stores have an important responsibility. To do their job well, they need to know how to (1) select attractive merchandise, (2) choose the right advertising media, and (3) devise creative merchandise displays. To accomplish these tasks, they also must have the ability to work with a wide range of store employees. As a retail person in charge of promotion at Phillips Department Store, how would you handle the following situations? Be specific.

1. Tony has above-average skill in planning and designing visual presentations. His main responsibility, however, is to install displays. You observe that he is slow, occasionally damages display merchandise and props, and is careless in making a final inspection of his work. As Tony's supervisor you believe he has potential and you want to keep him in your department. He is a hard worker but needs some assistance.

2. As the person responsible for coordinating store promotion, one of your responsibilities is to assist department managers in choosing merchandise to be promoted. The new manager of the appliance department has given you a list of eight items to be featured in the next storewide promotion. You note that four of the items have been slow sellers and stocks are limited.

3. For a number of years, Phillips Department Store did not budget money for promotion purposes. Instead, management approved spending for advertisements and displays as the need arose. Although not convinced that it is necessary, the store's new owners have asked you to recommend plans that could be followed to organize or coordinate advertising and display activities.

Writing Skills

Select one of the situations described below as the subject for a written communication. Investigate the topic presented using interviews, written materials, or other references as sources of information. When preparing the written assignment, be sure to give credit to your resources for the ideas, views, explanations, or quotations you use. The assignment should be no more than two double-spaced typewritten pages.

1. You have applied for a position in the advertising department of the Trane Discount Department Store. You are asked to submit an example of the copy you would write for a product of your choice and of the arrangement of that copy in an advertisement.
2. Currently, your class is studying sales promotion techniques. Your assignment is to identify a specific retailer's sales-promotion efforts and report these findings in writing to your instructor.
3. Currently your store has no formal means of evaluating window and interior displays. Your job is to develop a rating sheet that would help measure the quality and appearance of a display.
4. There are three new part-time employees in the display department of your store. To speed up their training, you prepare a handout containing sketches of the basic display arrangements. Provide a brief written description with each sketch.
5. The business department in your school regularly provides articles for publication in the school paper. You have been asked to write an article entitled "Ethics in Advertising."

APPLYING YOUR KNOWLEDGE

Can You Do the Following?

1. Explain the difference between a display-planning calendar and a display-planning budget.
2. Explain why advertising merchandise that is limited in supply is a mistake.
3. List three ways in which a retailer can communicate information about the store or its merchandise to potential customers.

4. Name five kinds of special promotional events.
5. Name three functions of the headline in a printed advertisement.
6. Describe an open window display design.
7. Define *texture* and describe its importance to a display design.
8. List six basic kinds of interior displays.
9. Name the three primary colors.
10. Explain the meaning of the *you* approach when creating desire in an advertisement.
11. Explain the purpose of the Federal Trade Commission.
12. Describe how promotional and institutional displays can be evaluated.
13. Identify four kinds of printed media used by the typical retailer.
14. Describe the anticipated-sales method of budgeting for advertising.

Retail Decisions

1. What is required to create and install effective displays?
2. How could display merchandise and props be the right color, size, shape, texture, line, and weight and still produce an ineffective display?
3. If you were asked to explain how color affects your buying decisions, what would be your response?
4. What are three ways to measure the results of a radio advertisement?
5. What medium would you use to promote a new style or fashion for the first time?
6. What are four sources you could use for help with your advertising program?
7. How would you use a dummy layout to create an advertisement?
8. What are four ways in which you could use window units for display purposes?
9. What methods could you use in an advertisement to catch and hold a potential customer's attention? Name as many as you can. Which are the best?
10. Why would the age of your business affect the amount you would budget for advertising?

DEVELOPING CRITICAL-THINKING SKILLS

Retail Projects

1. Select a product of your choice and identify two different media you would use to advertise that product. Compare the advantages

and disadvantages of each medium. Decide which would be most effective in promoting your product.

2. You have been given the assignment of designing and installing a window display. What steps will you follow in preparing the display area and setting up the display?

3. Review each of the methods of planning advertising budgets discussed in Chapter 30. Choose the method you believe would be most effective and give reasons for your choice.

4. Obtain two newspaper advertisements promoting similar kinds of merchandise. Identify and compare the elements contained in each ad. Then, evaluate the advertisements on how well they attract attention, develop interest, create desire, and induce action.

5. Name the basic kinds of interior displays found in most retail stores. Select a product that you would present in each kind of display. Give reasons for your choices.

Field Projects

1. Too often, supplementary media are overlooked in favor of the typical printed or electronic media. To determine the effectiveness of outdoor advertising, car-card advertising, and specialty advertising, obtain the following information:
   a.   the availability of these media in your community
   b.   the size and kinds of markets they reach
   c.   costs of promoting a product through each medium
   d.   means of measuring the effectiveness of each medium.
   Based on the results of your study, which medium would you choose?

2. Beginners in advertising can often enlist the assistance of local media experts when writing copy for advertisements. Contact three local advertising media of your choice and ask their assistance in identifying some basic rules to follow when writing advertising copy. Summarize their recommendations in a written report.

3. Make a list of five popular consumer goods that can be found in a variety of retail stores. Locate these products in at least six different stores. Record the kind of display unit, arrangement, and location of each display. Summarize your observations in writing by indicating for each product what appears to be the most-used means of display. Indicate why you think each product-method combination is effective.

4. Observe the merchandise displays in four stores of your choice. Select one display that you believe could be made more effective. Make a sketch of the display that includes those changes you would recommend. Keep in mind the elements and principles of display design.

CONTINUING PROJECTS

Developing a Career Plan

An understanding of the advantages, disadvantages, and future prospects of a variety of jobs is essential to career planning. Although most persons have a very good knowledge of 3 or 4 occupations, this is generally not enough to make wise career choices. Reading about potential jobs is time well spent. But career information obtained directly from those who are currently employed is just as valuable.

This activity is designed to help you expand your knowledge of career opportunities available in the retail-promotion field. First, identify those advertising and visual-merchandising jobs that may be of some current personal interest. Then, ask your teacher or the career planning and placement office in your school to help you identify businesses where these jobs can be found. Prepare a list of job-related questions, arrange interviews with the appropriate firms, and record the answers to your questions. Review the information you have gathered and place it in your career-planning notebook. You may wish to repeat this process as you learn about other careers in the business field.

Developing a Business Plan

From the facts you have learned in this unit and the study and research of other resources, add to your manual by completing each of the following assignments:

1. Determine the kinds of advertising media and public-relations activities that are most likely to be effective for the type of business you have chosen. To accomplish this task, you may want to contact representatives of the local media, interview operators of similar businesses, or visit with a local Chamber of Commerce or trade association. Among the questions you will want to ask are the following:
    a. What goals should I set in planning my advertising program?
    b. Which media will be most effective in accomplishing my advertising goals?
    c. How much should I budget for my advertising effort?
    d. What kinds of merchandise should I advertise?
    e. How often should I advertise?
    f. How can I determine the effectiveness of my advertising program?
2. Prepare a rough sketch of the floorplan for the business you intend to operate. Possible sources of information for store design

and layout might include trade associations, store display and fixture outlets, merchandise wholesalers, and architects and general
contractors. Include in your plan the following:

a.   overall dimensions of the store
b.   customer entrances
c.   stockroom space and service entrances
d.   customer-service counter locations
e.   window-display locations (indicate types of window displays)
f.   interior display-unit locations (indicate types of display units)

3.   Check the floorplan you have completed with one of the resources
     mentioned in question two. Does the plan make it possible for
     customers to move freely throughout the store? Will the plan en-
     courage customer traffic into those areas where slower-moving
     merchandise is on display? Does your floorplan create the impres-
     sion you want customers to have of your business?

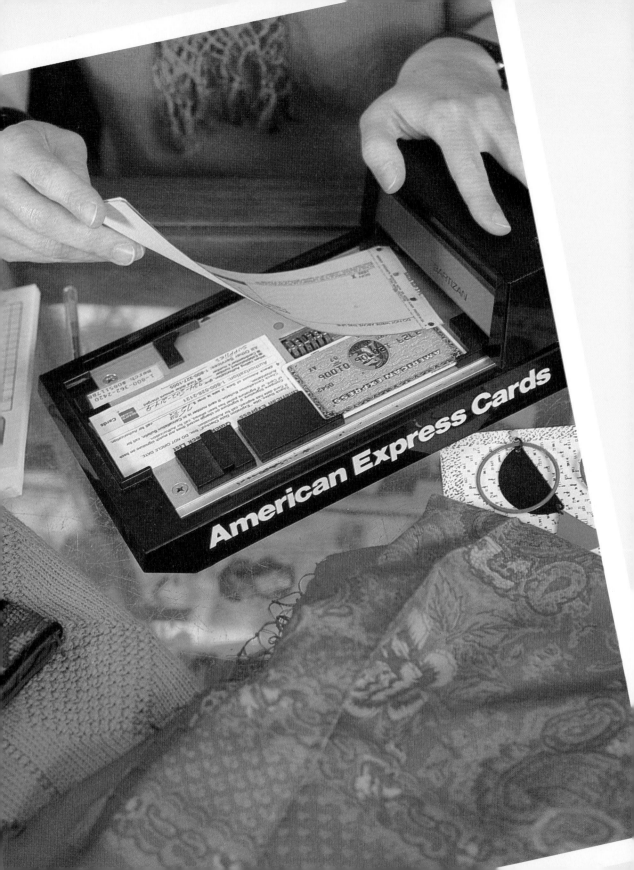

UNIT 6
*S*elling

  The activities involved in personal selling are an important part of promotion. Most retail-store employees are involved in the sale of merchandise to customers. In addition to this responsibility, they are expected to perform a variety of nonselling duties. These duties might include stockkeeping, housekeeping, preventing waste and loss, directing customers, and handling complaints. To perform the selling duties satisfactorily, salespeople need to understand why, what, and when customers will buy. In addition, they must know the essentials of a good sales presentation and how to apply the steps of the selling process. Completion of a sale may also require special skills such as remembering names, using the telephone, selling services, serving several customers at a time, and meeting the needs of customers out of the store.

After studying this unit and completing the activities, you should be able to:

1. Identify the various nonselling duties performed by retail salespeople
2. State what retail salespeople must know in order to understand customer buying behavior
3. List the essentials of a good sales presentation
4. Name and explain the steps of a sale
5. Describe the tasks a salesperson should be able to perform when completing a sales transaction
6. List six special skills that a salesperson may use in conducting a sales presentation

CHAPTER 34

Duties and Characteristics of Retail-Sales Personnel

CHAPTER OUTCOMES

When you have mastered the information provided in this chapter, you should be able to:

1. Identify a major responsibility of most store employees

2. State the importance of stockkeeping in making a favorable first impression on customers

3. List three housekeeping tasks that are usually performed in a retail store

4. Name ten ways to prevent waste and loss

5. Explain the importance of being courteous and accurate when giving customers directions or handling complaints

6. Define the term *store policies* and explain the importance of these policies to the customers, employees, and store managers

7. List four key salesperson characteristics

8. Explain the importance of a proper selling attitude and how it can be developed

Retailers depend entirely on satisfied customers for their existence. When customers enter a store, they expect friendly and competent service from all personnel. Retail employees have varying duties and responsibilities, depending on the types of stores in which they are employed. A major responsibility of most store employees is to sell merchandise by meeting the wants and needs of customers. This usually happens through direct contact with customers, by means of direct personal-selling techniques.

Selling directly to a customer requires that a salesperson be able to (1) greet a customer and quickly determine his or her needs, (2) provide sufficient information to the customer, (3) present merchandise in an interesting manner, (4) answer customer questions, (5) close the sale, (6) handle the transaction accurately, and (7) package merchandise properly. (The direct-selling process is discussed in detail in the chapters of Unit 6.) Selling also takes place through indirect-promotion means such as creating effective advertisements or eye-catching merchandise displays that influence customers to buy.

shelves contain a good selection and are well-filled, customers usually react favorably. It is understandable, then, why most retailers consider stockkeeping an important duty of salespersons.

Daily, before customers enter the store, salespeople must replenish stock. Care is taken to make sure that ample amounts of merchandise in the correct brands, models, sizes, styles, and colors are kept available for purchase. On busy days, stock may have to be brought from the stockroom several times. When shelves are stocked, fresh merchandise is normally placed behind or beneath the stock already on hand. This procedure ensures that older goods are sold before new goods. Efficient stockkeeping helps sales personnel do a better job and results in increased sales for the retailer.

Housekeeping

In almost all retail stores, salespeople are required to perform a variety of housekeeping duties. These usually include such

NONSELLING DUTIES

To be an effective retail salesperson, an individual must perform a variety of nonselling duties. The most important nonselling duties are presented in this chapter.

Stockkeeping

First impressions are often the most lasting ones. When merchandise racks and

Illus. 34–1 The visual impression of a store is enhanced when displays are well-stocked and sales areas are kept clean.

tasks as (1) regular cleaning and straightening of display cases, counter tops, and sales register areas; (2) the removal of cover cloths placed over merchandise at night to protect against dust; and (3) the removal of trash, boxes, and other unusable materials from the sales floor. The majority of housekeeping duties should be completed in the morning or near closing time, when customer traffic is lightest. Untidy sales areas destroy the effectiveness of merchandise displays and generally downgrade the image of the store.

Preventing Waste and Loss

An important duty that is in the interest of both the store and the customer is the prevention of waste and loss of merchandise. What follows are suggested ways to accomplish this duty:

1. Handle goods carefully.
2. Keep all merchandise in its proper location.
3. Maintain merchandise in good condition.
4. Avoid wasting store supplies.
5. Be careful not to damage equipment and fixtures.
6. Avoid sales pressure which leads to customer complaints and returns.
7. Perform all sales transactions accurately.
8. Measure and weigh products accurately.
9. Arrive on time and make effective use of time on the job.
10. Promote honesty among co-workers and customers.

How valuable each salesperson is to a store may be judged not only by the sales that are made but also by the salesperson's ability to keep store operating expenses at a minimum. The physical presence of alert salespeople in a department can prevent shoplifting and vandalism. This kind of protection reduces the retail losses and could, as a result, produce savings for the store's customers. Specific techniques that can be used by employees to help prevent theft are presented in Chapter 45.

Directing Customers

Customers frequently enter a store not knowing where to find the items they wish to buy. In a small store, directing customers is relatively simple, since each salesperson should be familiar with the entire stock and its location. In a large store where there are many departments, customer assistance may be more difficult to provide. Salespeople are frequently asked where a product is located, and the customer's goodwill depends on a prompt and accurate answer. Nothing is more annoying to a customer than to be directed first to one department, then to another, and then perhaps to a third, in a vain attempt to find something that the store probably stocks but that poorly informed salespeople know nothing about.

Directions to customers should always be given courteously and accurately. A customer should never be directed unless the salesperson is sure the information provided is correct. If the salesperson is unsure about the location, she or he should seek the assistance of a coworker who can provide the necessary information. Directions should also be given clearly and in a helpful tone so that the customer will understand every word.

Handling Complaints

There is a growing trend to centralize the handling of customer complaints. However, many stores still expect their sales personnel to handle routine complaints and to make adjustments. This responsibility requires patience, understanding, and a desire to work with the public. Handling complaints successfully requires a salesperson to be thoroughly familiar with the store's merchandise and customer policies. Very often, a kind word can disarm an angry customer; a courteous salesperson may not only adjust a problem but increase the goodwill of a customer. Particular complaints that may arise during the course of a sale are discussed in Chapter 39.

Carrying Out Store Policies

Most retailers have established rules or guidelines that they expect employees to follow in the daily operation of the business.

Illus. 34–2 Salespeople should know the location of all merchandise in their store so they can help customers find the products they wish to purchase.

These rules are known as **store policies.** Store policies, ranging from not permitting gum chewing on the sales floor to procedures for granting credit to new customers, can affect a range of employee activities. Well-designed and fairly administered store policies build goodwill for the store in its dealings with customers, suppliers, and the business community. For store policies to be effective, every salesperson must understand them and follow the procedures required to carry them out.

Working in a store is easier when everyone understands the rules and how to apply them. When sales personnel accept enforcement of store policies as part of their job duties, several benefits result: There is less confusion and disagreement among store employees, and there is loyalty to the employer and increased job satisfaction for the employee. Most important, however, customers receive fair and equal treatment and store sales and profits increase.

SALESPERSON CHARACTERISTICS

Training, experience, and a clear understanding of one's job duties can help assure a happy and satisfying career in retailing. To reach this goal, a salesperson must possess certain characteristics. Katie Lin and Jerry Perez, you may recall, quickly learned their job duties as display assistants. Jon Harris, the display director, proved to be an excellent teacher. Whenever necessary, he took time from his many other duties to explain and demonstrate job skills needed by the new display assistants.

After their display training, Katie and Jerry were transferred back to their respective departments to gain additional experience as retail salespersons. Before the transfer, Mr. Harris reminded them that they would be expected to assume the following additional responsibilities related to the specific duties of retail salespersons.

Personal Habits

It is each salesperson's responsibility to maintain high standards of personal cleanliness, health, and grooming. This means that regular attention must be paid to proper rest and diet. The development of speaking, listening, and writing skills is also important to project a favorable image to the buying public and other store employees. Enthusiasm makes routine duties interesting and challenging. Often, it is easy to tell when people like their work because their attitude is reflected in a desire to provide good customer service. As a result, a pleasant and agreeable atmosphere can be enjoyed by salespeople and customers alike.

Mental Skills

Retailing is a challenging and fast-moving field, which means that stores need alert salespeople with sharp mental skills. These skills can be developed, but individual desire and responsibility are prerequisite. Some of the more important job-related mental skills are a good memory, creativity, imagination, and a high degree of accuracy.

A good memory is very helpful in remembering names and faces and is a valuable asset in any situation that requires direct contact with the public. Because people generally like to think they are important, remembering and using a customer's name in a selling situation is a compliment to both the customer and the salesperson. A good memory also helps the salesperson remember major merchandise information which is important to good job performance.

Accuracy in such activities as inventory counting and sales-register operation, however, is the name of the game. Without accuracy, most retailers stand to lose more than they can gain. Merchandise and cash are only two of many items that must be accurately accounted for if a business is to show a profit.

Unique, rapid, and efficient ways to accomplish job tasks are objectives of most progressive retail-store owners. Suggestions for new and effective ways of performing job tasks, along with a good memory and a high degree of accuracy, have saved millions of dollars, improved merchandising techniques, and increased sales for countless retail stores.

Business Ethics

Retailers seek employees who demonstrate high ethical standards. Such behavior is an important factor in creating customer goodwill and gaining acceptance from co-workers and employers. **Ethical behavior** can be defined as conduct that reflects honesty, dependability, fairness, and loyalty to oneself, the employer, and the public. Unethical behavior, on the other hand, causes feelings of distrust, anger, and suspicion. Behavior such as giving certain customers preferential treatment, ignoring store policies, and avoiding responsibility, while not illegal, could result in the loss of customer goodwill or even one's job.

Human-relations Skills

Retail salespeople face an interesting challenge in trying to determine how best to please customers and coworkers. Getting along with others is often not easy, but, in retailing, cooperation is vital. A customer's health on a given day, a coworker's previous job experience, and even a personal, unexplainable problem can account for differences in a person's behavior.

A good starting point in working effectively with others is to put yourself in their shoes. In other words, try to look at situations from their viewpoints. Don't you like to receive fast, friendly service in a store? Most customers do. Would you rather have someone work with you or against you? Coworkers usually prefer to cooperate. Letting the other person know that he or she matters can go a long way in maintaining good human relationships.

Proper Selling Attitude

Every salesperson has a responsibility to develop a selling attitude that is service oriented. To do so requires a sincere interest in meeting customer wants and needs and an understanding of the selling process. Not only must salespeople understand their customers and the motives that move them to make purchases, but they also should be able to present the right merchandise in the proper manner to each customer.

Illus. 34–3   Dealing effectively with customers and coworkers is a key responsibility of all retail employees.

Summary   A major responsibility of most retail salespersons is to sell merchandise. In addition, they are expected to perform a variety of nonselling duties. Nonselling responsibilities include stockkeeping, housekeeping, preventing waste and loss, directing customers, handling complaints, and carrying out store policies. Salespeople who are effective in their work usually share common characteristics. Among these are good personal habits, sharp mental skills, high ethical standards, effective human-relations skills, and a proper selling attitude.

Review
1. Name a major responsibility of most store employees.
2. Explain the importance of stockkeeping in making a favorable first impression on customers.
3. Identify three housekeeping tasks that are usually performed in a retail store.
4. List five ways to prevent waste and loss.
5. Explain the importance of being courteous and accurate when giving customers directions or handling complaints.
6. Define *store policies* and explain the importance of these policies to customers, employees, and retailers.
7. Name four characteristics of an effective salesperson.
8. State the importance of a proper selling attitude and explain how it can be developed.

Terms   The following terms were introduced in this chapter. Write a separate sentence correctly using each new term.

ethical behavior   store policies

Discuss
1. Why are housekeeping duties an important part of a salesperson's responsibilities?
2. How can the physical presence of a salesperson help reduce shoplifting and vandalism?
3. How can well-designed and fairly administered store policies build customer goodwill?
4. Why are high ethical standards a must for retail employees?

Problem Solving
1. You are one of six individuals who has just been hired as a salesperson in the local outlet of a national chain-store operation. Each of you has been given a store-policies booklet to study

prior to beginning work. Two of the new employees have told you it's not worth the time to learn the store's policies. How will you respond?

2. You are an area manager in a locally owned department store. One of your employees who, until recently, showed great potential now complains about the workload, is often late, and treats customers with a general lack of respect. What might you do to get this employee "back on track"?

3. Within the past week, you have heard five customers complain about inaccurate directions given by the salespeople in your department. Two customers looking for gift wrapping were directed to the credit desk rather than customer service. One who asked to see curtain rods ended up in hardware instead of the drapery department. Two who wanted children's jeans were directed to the teen shop and then to menswear before finding their way to the correct department. As the department manager, what suggestions would you make to the personnel?

CHAPTER 35

Customer Buying Behavior

CHAPTER OUTCOMES

When you have mastered the information provided in this chapter, you should be able to:

1. State two general reasons customers buy

2. Identify *basic needs* and explain how needs motivate

3. Identify *secondary wants* and explain how wants motivate

4. Name five rational buying motives

5. List five emotional buying motives

6. State the difference between convenience, shopping, and specialty goods

7. Describe how timing can affect a customer's decision to buy

8. Define the term *store personality*

9. Identify six customer personality types and explain how each should be handled

"I just don't understand it, Joan. Last year we sold twice as many of this model video equipment. Now we can't give them away." "I know what you mean, Wes. It seems as though customers are always changing their minds about what they want to buy. Have you noticed lately that more and more of our regular customers are going out to the new mall to do their shopping? I wonder why."

The job of trying to predict changing customer needs, wants, and buying habits is always filled with uncertainty. Retailers, however, cannot afford to ignore the behavior patterns of their customers. To do so could mean a loss of business. Some factors that may affect the customer's behavior and buying decisions during the selling process are reviewed in this chapter.

WHY PEOPLE BUY

Since no two customers are alike, their reasons for buying certain merchandise may differ. Generally, customers buy to satisfy their needs and wants. As you may recall, in Chapter 5, *needs* are defined as conditions basic to an individual's existence, work, and welfare. *Wants* are the conditions or items that a person desires, though they are not essential to life.

For example, Allan Wilson shops for a microcomputer and letter-quality printer for use in his home. He tells the salesperson he needs the microcomputer because it is fast, easy to operate, and dependable.

Sue Randall, the office manager of a large law firm, has a typewriter in her office. Since her workload increased, she has been looking for a high-speed microcom-puter and printer that can handle large legal forms, produce large mailings, and simplify other word processing tasks.

It is the salesperson's job to identify as many of a customer's reasons for buying as possible so that the reasons for buying can be matched with the right merchandise. The salesperson's experience, product knowledge, and skill in observing and listening to customers are useful tools in identifying reasons customers may buy. These skills are particularly important when two customers such as Allan and Sue buy the same item for entirely different reasons. Determining a customer's exact motives for buying can be difficult.

Some customers may not be able to state clearly their reasons for buying; others know their reasons but prefer not to reveal them. Sometimes, buying motives are so complex that they cannot be identified by either the salesperson or the customer. In any case, a basic understanding of how buying motives work can prove valuable to a salesperson who is trying to help customers make wise buying decisions.

BUYING MOTIVES

Experts have struggled for years to answer this question: What motivates people to buy? Much remains to be learned about consumer motivation, but there is some general agreement on two key points. First, buying decisions are determined by the customer's basic needs and secondary wants. Second, the strength of each basic need and secondary want varies depending on whether the customer is thinking rationally or emotionally at the time of the sale.

Basic-need Motives

Basic needs are not learned; they represent conditions that are essential to human nature and survival. Everyone has basic needs and satisfies them in a variety of ways. Food, water, rest, freedom from fear and danger, security, self-esteem, and sociability, including the need for love and affection, are examples of strong human needs that motivate. Remember Allan Wilson? His real reason for buying a home computer and printer may have been self-esteem or social approval—to be the first person in the neighborhood to own such equipment. Obviously, salespeople who can detect the customer's real motives for buying can build those reasons into the sales presentation. When this is done effectively, increased sales and satisfied customers are the result.

Secondary-want Motives

Unlike basic needs, **secondary wants** are learned. The customer's background, experience, and education determine which secondary wants are most influential during purchases. Secondary or learned wants are generated by a desire for bargains, convenience, efficiency, dependability, style, or cleanliness. Sue Randall's motive for buying computer equipment probably was a desire to be an efficient worker. Secondary wants usually are easy to determine, since most customers willingly discuss such reasons for buying. For example, a customer might say, "Do you have something a little less expensive?" when economy, or a desire for a bargain, is the motive. They might say, "How well does this material wear?"

when quality or dependability is the secondary want.

Secondary wants may be of a rational or emotional nature. Rational motives are those based on sound thinking. They include desires for economy, durability, reliability, and usefulness. Emotional buying motives, on the other hand, are those based on feelings. These include desires for status, pride, romance, adventure, and positive self-image. For example, Rick shopped at Sports Arena because he knew the store offered long-wearing sportswear at low prices. He reasoned that he could save money on clothing to have more to spend on his car. His was a rational motive for shopping at a particular store. Marsha, however, shopped at LaRacquette, a high-fashion boutique offering designer-label sportswear. She felt that, by wearing such clothing, she would convey the same elegant image and status as LaRacquette itself. Her motive was emotional.

Consider the kinds of images that each store conveys in Illustration 35–1. Rational buying motives, centered on economy, may lead a customer to shop in Store 2; but emotional buying motives, centered on self-image, may draw a customer to Store 1. Clearly, however, buying motives cannot be placed in neat little packages and labeled. A customer may have both rational and emotional motives that affect one buying decision.

WHAT PEOPLE BUY

As mentioned in Chapter 11, retailers traditionally have classified consumer merchandise into convenience, shopping, and

RETAIL-STORE IMAGE COMPARISON

Store 1	Store 2

Located in a new shopping center	Located away from main shopping areas; no parking or public transportation available
Elegant decor and attractive displays	Eighty-year-old building in need of repair
Name-brand and high-fashion merchandise; high prices	Some nationally known brands; mostly off brands and low prices
Charge accounts and delivery service	Cash and carry

Illus. 35–1   Rational buying motives will influence the customer to shop in Store 2, while the customer influenced by emotional buying motives will tend to shop in Store 1.

specialty goods. Examples of convenience goods are bread, milk, soft drinks, and canned goods. Because the customer's motives for buying these items are likely to have been influenced earlier by various promotional techniques, little time is usually required to identify customer needs in a direct-selling situation. Unlike the decision to buy convenience goods, the decision to buy shopping goods (automobiles, large appliances, and furniture) or specialty goods (gourmet foods, expensive clothing, and specially designed items) is extremely important to the customer. As a result, the customer may spend considerable time and effort reaching a decision to buy. Salespeople who can combine product knowledge with the ability to identify the customer's real motivation for making a shopping or specialty-goods purchase can provide a valuable sales service to patrons.

WHEN PEOPLE BUY

A major consideration in the customer's decision to buy is the timing of the purchase. Buying motives can be seriously altered if neither cash nor credit is available to make the purchase. When delays occur, regardless of the reasons, the customer may lose interest in buying. Also, delays in buying sometimes lead to less-expensive substitutions for the original item—a CD player instead of a full stereo system, paint rather than wallpaper, resoled shoes instead of new ones, and so on.

Timing of purchases can also be affected by other factors: the availability of certain brands, store hours, holidays, special sales, economic conditions, and the customer's health and mental attitudes. Some purchases cannot be made unless several members of a family are present. This is particularly true when the purchase is expensive and affects a number of family members. Because timing is so important in successfully completing a sale, retailers must be alert to those factors that influence the timing of the selling process and the customer's decision.

CUSTOMER STORE PERSONALITIES

No study of customer buying behavior is complete without mentioning the effect that each customer's store personality can have on the selling process. *Store personality* is defined as a customer's behavior while making a purchase. Every customer is different. No two customers will react exactly the same to the salesperson or to the merchandise. It is possible, however, to describe in general terms some typical customer behavior patterns. Retail salespeople agree that there are several identifiable customer personality types. How to be helpful to each is reviewed in the following paragraphs.

Undecided Customers

Undecided customers are ones who cannot make buying decisions. Often a fear of making a wrong choice causes a prolonged delay in buying. Customers of this kind should not be shown too much merchandise. It is best to narrow each customer's choice by removing those items that the customer does not seem to like. The article that the customer keeps returning to should be highlighted by the salesperson. Usually, a few words of encouragement are sufficient to help undecided customers decide to buy.

Just-looking Customers

Customers who are just looking usually are not interested in making immediate purchases. On the other hand, some customers may say they are just looking, but in reality they want to make their own buying decisions. Prolonged inspection of certain merchandise or occasional questions are strong indicators of the customer's real interest in buying. If the salesperson is alert and prepared to talk about the purchase, a sale is likely in that case. A salesperson must be careful not to high-pressure a customer who is truly just looking.

Silent Customers

Because silent customers are difficult to draw into conversation, the salesperson may have difficulty determining their exact needs and wants. Close attention must be paid to silent customers' actions and reactions during the sales presentation. A technique that often works is to ask questions

Illus. 35–2 What, when, and why customers buy is directly influenced by their store personalities.

that require more than a *yes* or *no* response. For example, the salesperson might say, "Mrs. Walters, how would you compare these two microwave ovens?"

Know-it-all Customers

These individuals know what they want, and are not particularly interested in product information or the opinions of others. If the customer's product information is correct, sales should not be too difficult. If the customer does not know all the facts, the salesperson can often provide correct information with little resistance from customers. For example, the salesperson might say, "Mr. Smith, you're right; this camcorder does have automatic focus and a

zoom lens. I think you also mentioned that it has a one-year warranty." Salespeople must always remember that their job is to sell merchandise, not to win arguments. In selling, an argument means that everyone loses.

Deliberate Customers

Customers who decide to buy only after careful consideration are deliberate shoppers. Their buying behavior should not be confused with that of the undecided customer. Deliberate customers make decisions but only after weighing all the facts. It is best not to hurry this type of customer but, rather, to slow the pace of the sale and provide as much merchandise information as needed. Thorough preparation by the salesperson is necessary for helping deliberate customers.

Friendly Customers

Friendly customers are a pleasure to serve, but they can take up valuable selling time if permitted to do so. It is easy to become lax and careless when assisting this type of individual. It is important to focus the customer's attention on the merchandise and to complete the selling process as rapidly as possible. Properly treated, friendly buyers can easily become regular customers.

Summary

Determining customer buying behavior is filled with uncertainty. Since no two customers are alike, their reasons for buying differ. In any case, customer buying decisions are influenced by basic needs and secondary wants. Basic needs are inborn conditions essential to human nature and survival. Secondary wants are learned from experience. Salespeople who can identify a customer's real motives for buying can use this information to advantage by building it into the sales presentation. Products that consumers purchase are classified in three ways: as convenience, shopping, or specialty goods. Little direct selling is required to sell convenience goods. Because major decisions may be necessary to buy shopping and specialty goods, salespeople need to be alert to the motivations that would cause customers to consider such goods. In addition, timing of purchases affects the customer's decision to take action. Availability of merchandise, current prices, and a holiday mood are a few examples of circumstances that could encourage or postpone a decision to buy. The customer's personality could also influence a decision to act. Customers who are undecided, just looking, silent, know-it-all, deliberate, or friendly must be motivated to act based on sales appeals that match their particular needs or wants and personalities.

Review

1. Identify two general reasons customers buy.
2. Define and give examples of *basic needs*.
3. Define and give examples of *secondary wants*.
4. Identify five rational buying motives.
5. Name five emotional buying motives.
6. Explain the differences among convenience, shopping, and specialty goods.
7. State how timing affects customers' decisions to buy.

8. Define *store personality*.
9. List six identifiable customer personality types and describe how each should be handled.

Terms

The following terms were introduced in this chapter. Write a separate sentence correctly using each new term.

basic needs   secondary wants

Discuss

1. Of what value to the retail salesperson is an understanding of why people buy?
2. How does store image influence a customer's rational and emotional buying motives?
3. State reasons customers delay making purchases. How can salespeople overcome reluctance to buy in each case?
4. How does a customer's store personality affect the selling process?

Problem Solving

1. Ron Valdez is employed by a large discount appliance store. A certain customer has been in the store on three occasions in the last week to look at a washer and dryer. Each time Ron approaches the customer, she either does not respond or says, "I'm just looking." What would you suggest Ron do to help the customer make a decision to buy?
2. At lunch one day, Joan and Wes express their concerns to you about the way customers seem to always be changing their minds about what they buy. How would you respond?
3. You have decided to open a high-fashion store specializing in exclusive men's and women's sportswear. What type of store image would you create and to what buying motives would you appeal?

CHAPTER 36

The Sales Presentation

CHAPTER OUTCOMES

When you have mastered the information provided in this chapter, you should be able to:

1. State the importance of personal selling and services as retail functions

2. Explain the difference between nonpersonal selling and personal selling

3. Define the term *sales presentation* and list its essential components

4. Identify the eight steps of the selling process

5. Explain the purpose of the preapproach

6. List and explain the four approach categories

7. Explain how listening, questioning, and observation skills can help the salesperson determine customer wants and needs

8. List four demonstration techniques

9. State the purpose of the presentation

"I don't shop there anymore." "I can never find anything in this store." "Can't anyone answer my questions about this jacket?" "Isn't there someone who knows the difference between these two exercise bicycles?" Sound familiar? Unfortunately, when customers react negatively to some retail stores, it could be because certain salespeople did not make use of good personal selling techniques. There are some retailers, however, who say that personal selling and service are no longer important as retail functions. They maintain that self-service has replaced the need to provide direct personal customer service. But most people, whether shopping in a self-service store or a conventional retail store, expect some amount of personal attention. Even the space-age technology that makes it possible for machines to show merchandise, give change, and dispense products cannot respond to individual customer questions. These machines can't listen with attention and interest to each person's expressed needs and wants. For most customers, salespeople are their key personal contact with a store. This reality can be positive or negative, depending on the salesperson's personal selling skills and job interest.

WHAT IS PERSONAL SELLING?

"Me sell? No way! I couldn't sell a life jacket to a drowning sailor." Some retail employees shy away from sales duties because they lack understanding of what personal selling is all about. There are two kinds of selling activities in retailing: nonpersonal selling and personal selling. **Nonpersonal selling** uses advertising, visual merchandis-ing, and other promotion to inform customers about merchandise and to encourage them to come in the store and buy. **Personal selling,** on the other hand, requires direct contact between the customer and the salesperson. It also means providing customers with the products and services they need and want. In personal selling, a salesperson must use a variety of basic selling techniques when helping the customer make buying decisions. These techniques do not include high-pressure, fast-talking, hard-sell tactics. Such methods have no place in any retail store committed to serving its customers.

But you may ask, "Why should I study personal selling techniques? I'm never going to use those skills." Actually there are few, if any, existing jobs that do not require the use of some basic selling skills. In fact, most successful job applicants are employed because they were able to convince (sell the idea to) the employer that they had the qualifications necessary to do the job.

Illus. 36–1 Customers very often need assistance in deciding which products or services to buy.

An old saying in retailing is that nothing happens until something is sold. In other words, selling is of central importance in any retail business operation. Thus, it is vital for every salesperson to master personal selling techniques.

ESSENTIALS OF A GOOD SALES PRESENTATION

Each year, product manufacturers and retailers spend millions of dollars advertising and promoting their goods to the buying public. Customers may, however, require additional product information before reaching a decision to buy. Salespeople who know how to use correct selling techniques can be of great service to customers trying to make proper choices.

Some customers will need assistance in identifying their specific needs and wants. Once this assistance has been provided, the salesperson can suggest certain products or services that will satisfy those needs and wants. Information about price, model, size, style, and color can help the customer decide to buy the merchandise. If the store's price is right and the timing of the purchase is correct, the customer, with the salesperson's assistance, will make an appropriate purchase.

Salespeople are most helpful to customers when the information they provide is accurate and well-organized. Providing such information is called a **sales presentation.** Beginning salespersons can test the effectiveness of their presentations by asking themselves the following questions: (1) Is my presentation complete? (2) Is it clear? (3) Does it build customers' confidence in me?

A Complete Presentation

To be complete, a sales presentation must contain enough merchandise information to answer the questions that customers often ask. A presentation should also build up a customer's initial interest in the merchandise. When this is done well, the customer's desire to own the product may increase to the point where he or she will decide to make a purchase.

A Clear Presentation

There is no room for misunderstanding in any sales presentation. When a misunderstanding occurs, the most likely result is a dissatisfied customer and an unhappy salesperson. Every effort should be made to make sure that the salesperson and customer understand each other and that no hazy areas exist.

A Confidence-building Presentation

No matter how clear or complete a sales presentation may be, little chance exists that customers will buy if they doubt the truth of what they have been told. Customer confidence in the salesperson is critical to most sales situations. In fact, sales are often made on that basis alone.

A LOGICAL PRESENTATION

Sales presentations that are complete and clear and that build confidence are usually organized around a flexible, logical selling sequence. What follows is one such selling sequence that is effective in most retail settings:

1. Preapproach
2. Approach
3. Determining customer needs and wants
4. Demonstrating and presenting merchandise
5. Answering objections
6. Closing the sale
7. Suggestion selling
8. Customer departure and follow-up

This chapter contains a discussion of steps 1 through 4; Chapter 37 is devoted to steps 5, 6, 7; and Chapter 38 covers step 8.

ASSISTING CUSTOMERS

Customers often need assistance in deciding which products or services to buy. To help customers make appropriate decisions, a salesperson makes use of several steps in the selling process. These steps include the preapproach, the approach, determining needs and wants, and demonstrating and presenting merchandise.

The Preapproach

The preapproach is the getting-ready stage of the selling process. This step requires salespersons to prepare themselves, the merchandise, and the department for customers who are about to enter the store. The store building, equipment, lighting, and displays should be carefully checked to see that everything is clean and neatly arranged. The first impression a customer receives of the salesperson and the store will have an important bearing on the rest of the sales presentation.

The most important aspect of the preapproach is the salesperson's product knowledge. Salespeople who know the features and qualities of their merchandise give better service and have greater confidence in their sales ability. Every salesperson should know the merchandise that is in the store and where it is located.

Many successful salespeople know that customers really buy products because of what those products do for them (benefits) rather than because of specific physical product features. For example, one feature of a certain lawnmower is its light weight. This feature is a benefit to the customer because the lawnmower is easy to push. Also, because the lawnmower is lightweight, less time is needed to cut the lawn. When prospective customers learn the benefits of the products they are interested in, increased sales result, and the salesperson gains a satisfied customer for the store.

Salespeople have many excellent sources of information about various product features and benefits: (1) merchandise tags and labels, (2) product manufacturers, (3) advertisements, (4) previous customers, (5) other salespeople, and (6) store sales-training sessions. Some retailers provide product information sheets that list product features on one half of the page and corresponding benefits on the other. When these are not available, individual records of product features and benefits should be prepared and kept on file by the salesperson. Regardless of how it is done, thorough preparation in the preapproach sets the stage for the steps that follow.

The Approach

Just when to approach (actually meet) a customer who enters the store depends upon the type of store and the customer's store personality. The approach should always indicate that the customer is welcome and is not intruding or interrupting the salesperson's duties. The salesperson's approach should give the assurance that he or she is ready to help satisfy the customer's shopping needs.

In small stores and service stores that handle convenience goods, customers generally want fast service. In large stores, especially those that sell shopping goods such as clothing, furniture, appliances, and household items, customers may want to look around before being approached. In specialty-goods stores, customers expect a prompt and personalized approach. In self-service stores, however, there may be no approach at all.

In a busy store, people are usually willing to wait a reasonable length of time for service. However, shoppers resent having to wait while store employees arrange stock, visit with friends, engage in long telephone conversations, or gossip with other employees. Almost as offensive as keeping a customer waiting is approaching a customer the instant he or she walks into the department. Careful observation of every customer who enters a store or department, supported by product knowledge, will aid the salesperson in approaching customers at the right time.

It's safe to say that no two salespeople approach customers in exactly the same way, even in the same type of store. However, most sales approaches are similar enough to be grouped into one of four categories: (1) the service approach, (2) the formal approach, (3) the informal approach, and (4) the merchandise approach.

Service Approach. "May I serve you?" "May I assist you?" "What can I do for you?" and "May I help you?" These questions are typical of the service approach. They indicate a salesperson's willingness to serve a customer. But the service approach can be overused. For example, the question "May I help you?" does not show that the salesperson expects the customer to buy something. "No, I'm just looking" is often the customer response to this particular service approach.

Formal Approach. An approach that receives more general approval of retailers and shoppers than any other is the formal approach. Examples are simple, courteous, and cordial greetings such as "Good morning," "Good afternoon," and "Hello." The advantage of a formal approach over a service approach is that it is likely to draw a positive response from the customer. A "Hello" will usually bring a similar greeting rather than a "No, I'm just looking" response.

Informal Approach. The informal approach requires that the salesperson be acquainted with the customer. Examples of the informal approach are "How are you today, Mr. Percy?" and "Wasn't that your daughter who won the award, Mrs. Johnson?" Of course, the salesperson's remark should not be too personal or reflect unfavorably on the customer. Needless to say, the informal approach would not be a good choice if the customer could possibly be offended by it.

Merchandise Approach. When a customer has indicated interest in particular merchandise by examining it closely, the merchandise approach may be best. This approach involves an immediate reference to that merchandise: "That watch is waterproof" or "This chain is 14K gold." As these examples suggest, the merchandise approach requires the salesperson to have thorough product knowledge. This kind of approach cannot be used by salespersons who do not know the features and benefits of their departments' merchandise.

Studies show that customers think the approach is the most important part of the selling-buying process. What is said and done during the first few seconds after the salesperson and customer meet often determines the rest of the presentation.

Determining Customer Needs and Wants

Customers have all kinds of motives for buying. When a salesperson detects the customer's buying motives, a sale is much easier to complete. Some of these motives are easier to determine than others. As was mentioned in Chapter 35, purchases are in some way tied to basic human needs and secondary wants. Comfort, welfare of loved ones, bargains, safety, status, and convenience are just a few of the many buying motives.

In determining customer needs and wants, it is important to recognize that the customer may be in one of several buying moods:

1. The customer may already *know* which item is needed. If so, the customer will probably ask for the merchandise without delay.

2. The customer may be *undecided,* knowing her or his need for an article of a general type but not the specific details, such as price, material, and color.

3. The customer may be *just looking,* having no immediate need to buy but showing an interest that may be converted into a sale with the salesperson's help.

Discussions with successful retail salespeople indicate the importance of good listening, questioning, and observation skills in a sales presentation. This is particularly true when the salesperson is determining customer needs and wants.

Listening Skills. Customers often reveal their wants and needs by what they say or don't say. When a customer says, "I need two pounds of turkey salad," the wants or needs are clear. But what happens if the customer says, "I'm not sure what to buy; I am looking for a gift for my 12-year-old nephew who is visiting from out of town"? If the salesperson has been listening, three obvious clues to the customer's wants and needs have been given: (1) the purchase is for a 12-year-old boy, (2) it is intended as a gift, and (3) the nephew will be traveling to return home. The salesperson could reason that a 12-year-old may be interested in such items as books, video games, watches, and sunglasses, and so on—items that a child could easily use while traveling. Suggesting any of these items as a possible gift could bring a favorable response from the customer. If not, additional information may be necessary.

Questioning Skills. Questioning is an excellent means of obtaining important information that can help customers make correct buying decisions. Sometimes a few questions well-chosen by the salesperson may be all that is necessary to complete a sale. "I need a new suit," says the customer. "Something for a special occasion?" asks the salesperson. Having received an answer to this question, the salesperson may also ask, "Do you have a particular color in mind?" "A price range?" The conversation continues in this way until the customer's needs have been determined and met.

There is always a danger that the salesperson may ask too many questions. Customers should never be made to feel that they are being given the third degree. Therefore, salespeople should learn to ask three or four questions to learn most of what they need to know to complete a sale.

Observation Skills. There are many ways in which customers will react to the salesperson's attempts to help them. Facial expressions, tone of voice, the direction eyes travel, and even the way merchandise is handled are signs of a customer's reaction. Salespeople must be quick to observe these signs when asking questions and listening to customer responses.

Salespeople who become skilled in determining customer wants and needs through observation will find that (1) the selling process takes less effort, (2) the customer will have confidence in the salesperson's suggestions, and (3) the number of satisfied customers will increase.

DEMONSTRATING AND PRESENTING MERCHANDISE

Salespeople should appeal to a customer's senses—sight, touch, hearing, taste, and smell—when demonstrating and presenting merchandise. Customers should also be encouraged to take an active part in this demonstration step of the sale so that they can ask questions and try out the merchandise.

Demonstration Techniques

Illus. 36–2 Successful salespeople possess good listening, questioning, and observation skills.

There are a number of ways in which merchandise can be creatively demonstrated:

1. Show the product in use.
2. Ask customers to operate or try on the merchandise.
3. Demonstrate the major features of one product over another.
4. Show and explain an unusual product feature or benefit.

The salesperson's attitude during a product demonstration can influence the final outcome of the sales presentation. For instance, salespeople who handle merchandise carelessly may create the impression that they have little respect for what is being sold. If so, why should the customer buy it? In addition, customers can become confused when too many items are shown. Some professional salespeople recommend that no more than three items be demonstrated and that the customer's choice be narrowed from that number. Whenever possible, customers should be encouraged to take part in sales demonstrations. When this is done, the chances of making a sale are greatly enhanced.

Presentation Techniques

During the demonstration, the salesperson calls attention to the features and benefits of the merchandise. This is the main part of the presentation and includes verbal appeals to the customer's emotions and reasoning. Facts and figures about the product and the satisfaction the customer likely would gain from owning it are pointed out. Customers are more likely to purchase if they have an opportunity to say something rather than just listen to the salesperson; so, encouraging the customer to talk is an important presentation technique.

Illus. 36–3   Generally, a customer should be shown no more than three items from which to choose.

Special needs of customers often can be readily identified from discussion. Also, discussion can bring out objections the customer may have to the merchandise. Even customers who raise strong objections should be allowed to complete their statements. It is a psychological fact that if customers have a chance to express their opinions fully, they will be more likely to pay attention to another point of view. Successful salespeople are good communicators. During a sales presentation, they speak and listen well.

Summary

Some retailers contend that personal selling has been replaced by a variety of self-service functions. Most customers, however, prefer some amount of personal attention, depending, of course, on the merchandise being considered for purchase. There are two kinds of selling activities in retailing. Nonpersonal selling uses advertising, visual merchandising, and other promotion to reach customers. Personal selling requires direct contact between the customer and salesperson. To give an effective sales presentation, a salesperson must provide customers with accurate and well-organized information. The sales presentation should also capture attention and interest. One selling process that is effective in serving customers involves eight steps: (1) preapproach, (2) approach, (3) determining needs and wants, (4) demonstrating and presenting merchandise, (5) answering objections, (6) closing the sale, (7) suggestion selling, and (8) customer departure. The preapproach step requires that salespersons prepare themselves, the merchandise, and the department for potential customers. Approaching the customer is accomplished by using the service approach, formal approach, informal approach, or merchandise approach. Success in determining the customer's needs and wants depends on the salesperson's skill in listening to, questioning, and observing customers. Salespeople who make an effort to appeal to the customer's senses—sight, touch, hearing, taste, and smell— are effective in demonstrating and presenting merchandise. The remaining steps in the selling process are discussed in Chapters 37 and 38.

Review

1. Explain the importance of personal selling skills in retailing.
2. Explain the differences and similarities between nonpersonal selling and personal selling.
3. Identify and explain the essential qualities of a sales presentation.

4. List the eight steps of the selling process.
5. State the purpose of the preapproach.
6. Identify and explain four types of approach.
7. Describe how listening, questioning, and observation skills can help the salesperson determine customer wants and needs.
8. Identify four demonstration techniques.
9. Explain the purpose of the presentation step of selling.

*T*erms

The following terms were introduced in this chapter. Write a separate sentence correctly using each new term.

nonpersonal selling   sales presentation
personal selling

*D*iscuss

1. Why might some retailers believe that personal selling is no longer an important retail function?
2. What are the means by which a salesperson can test the effectiveness of her or his sales presentation?
3. What cautions should a salesperson observe when applying questioning skills in a selling situation?
4. How can a product demonstration affect a customer's attitude?
5. Is this statement ultimately true or false: "Nothing happens until something is sold"?

*P*roblem *S*olving

1. Robert approaches customers well and is effective in determining their wants and needs. He also possesses a great deal of product knowledge. Lately Robert has noticed that customers appear puzzled and somewhat confused following his presentations. Suggest some features of his sales presentations that Robert should check.
2. You have just been employed as a part-time salesperson in the greeting-card and stationery department of a local department store. The department manager has provided you with materials designed to help you understand the various selling techniques used in that department. Another new employee tells you that it's not worth the effort to study the information because selling skills are not very important. Do you agree or disagree with this co-worker? If you agree, prepare to tell your department manager why you will not be studying the materials. If you disagree, prepare to tell the other new salesperson why you believe you

both should master the selling skills. Write notes so that you include all the important points of either case.

3. Carla is a pleasant and enthusiastic salesperson who works part-time in the jewelry department of a large discount department store. She is effective in approaching customers but often fails to complete a sale when asked questions about more expensive items such as watches and gold chains. As Carla's supervisor, recommend ways for Carla to follow through after the approach. Be very specific since Carla is a new, part-time employee.

CHAPTER 37

Closing the Sale

CHAPTER OUTCOMES

When you have mastered the information provided in this chapter, you should be able to:

1. Identify the four basic kinds of objections and explain why customers raise them

2. Explain how objections can be forestalled

3. List and explain five techniques that can be used to answer objections

4. Identify three ways salespersons can prepare to answer objections

5. Identify the natural process involved in closing a sale

6. Define the term *trial close*

7. Name and explain four closing techniques

8. Identify the ABCs of selling

9. Explain suggestion selling

Every new salesperson needs to remember that no two sales presentations are exactly alike. Even when identical products are presented, differences in customer personalities and buying moods require that the salesperson use a variety of sales techniques. To close a sale, the salesperson must be prepared to answer customer questions or objections in an attempt to get the customer to buy. In addition, the effective salesperson suggests additional items that the customer may consider buying. In this chapter, steps 5, 6, and 7 of the selling process will be discussed.

ANSWERING OBJECTIONS

As a salesperson presents merchandise, the customer may state objections. These objections should be welcomed since they indicate the nature of the customer's interest. Generally, there are four basic kinds of legitimate customer objections encountered in a selling situation. These include objection to price, objection to quality of merchandise, objection to store policies, and objection to buying immediately. In no case should salespeople allow themselves to become annoyed, regardless of the objections offered by customers. Nor should a salesperson be drawn into an argument to prove a point. The saying "The customer is always right" applies—at least in the store.

When customers raise objections during the sales presentation, they often do so in hopes of obtaining additional product information. For instance, a customer may say, "I like this product, but it costs too much." This question indicates interest in the product. What the customer may mean

is, "Tell me why this item is worth the price you are asking." It may be true that the customer cannot afford to buy at the asking price, but a good salesperson welcomes customer objections as opportunities to further explain a product's features and benefits.

One way to handle objections is to *forestall* them; that is, to answer them before they are raised by the customer. For example, a sporting-goods salesperson may say, "This jogging suit is washable and will not fade," anticipating a common customer objection to buying clothes that require special cleaning. Illustration 37–1 lists typical kinds of customer objections. It is not always possible to anticipate and forestall every objection a customer raises. However, several techniques may be effectively used in actually answering objections: (1) the direct-denial method, (2) the yes, but method, (3) the reverse-English method, (4) the superior-point method, and (5) the questioning method.

Direct Denial

The direct-denial technique can be used when a customer's objection is incorrect. For example, if a customer says, "I think these jeans will shrink too much," the salesperson could promptly reply, "No, they definitely will not. Tests have proven that they will not shrink, and our store guarantees it!" Since this method tends to put customers on the defensive, proof must be given in a friendly and helpful way. In no instance should a customer's ego be threatened or damaged. The intent of the direct-denial method is to provide accurate information, not to point out the customer's ignorance.

KINDS OF OBJECTIONS

Objections to Price:	"That's more than I want to pay." "The price is too high." "I can get it for less somewhere else."

An objection to price means that the customer is not convinced that the value of the merchandise justifies the price asked. The salesperson should *build up the value of the merchandise.*

Objections to Merchandise:	"This is poor-quality material." "It looks too light." "I'm afraid it won't hold up."

An objection to merchandise means that the customer is not sure about the point raised about the merchandise. The salesperson should *give the facts or show other goods.*

Objections to Store Policy:	"Why don't you deliver?" "Why won't you accept this credit card?" "I want my money back—not credit toward another purchase." "I've never heard of this brand."

An objection to store policy means that the customer is not sure about the point raised about the store. The salesperson should *state the appropriate store policy and suggest alternatives.*

Objections to Buying Immediately:	"I'll look around first." "I didn't bring enough money." "I'll have to talk it over with my wife (husband)."

An objection to buying immediately means that the customer cannot decide whether or not to buy the merchandise. The salesperson should *suggest the advantages of buying right away.* Of course, this objection may be an excuse to leave without revealing the true objection.

Illus. 37–1   Customers often make comments similar to these when expressing objections to making a purchase. Here are some of the statements and actions a salesperson might use to answer each objection.

Yes, But

The yes, but method of meeting customer objections is one of the most effective methods. It fits many selling situations and can be used with more customers than any other method. Simply put, the yes, but method disagrees with the customer in an agreeable way. It avoids telling the customer directly that he or she is wrong. For instance, a salesperson may say, "Yes, your point is well taken, but don't you think that . . . ?" Or, the salesperson may say, "I understand how you feel. I felt the same way until I found out that this product could

. . . ." Yes, but responses, like the direct-denial method, are actual denials of what a customer believes to be true. Therefore, yes, but should be handled diplomatically. It's a good idea not to use the method too often with a particular customer. Instead, use other methods along with yes, but in countering the customer's objections.

Reverse English

In the reverse-English technique, the customer's objection becomes the major reason for buying the product. "But this luggage seems so lightweight, I doubt that it will last very long." "Actually, this luggage is designed for lightness and strength. The manufacturer provides a three-year guarantee against breakage under normal use and care." The manner of the salesperson is important in the use of the reverse-English method of overcoming objections. A friendly and sincere desire to provide information is much more effective than an attempt to outsmart the customer.

Illus. 37–2   Several methods of overcoming objections may be necessary during a sales presentation. For example, the salesperson may start with the yes, but technique, but follow it by the reverse-English and superior-point techniques.

Superior Point

A fourth way of meeting objections is the superior-point method. In this approach, the salesperson agrees with the customer's objection to a particular product feature. However, offsetting advantages are also pointed out. For example, the customer may say, "This car battery has only a 24-month warranty." The salesperson responds, "That's true, but this battery costs $16 less than the others." While selling, one should remember that no product is perfect for every customer. Each has its advantages and limitations. The superior-point method gives the salesperson an opportunity to admit to product disadvantages in good faith, while pointing out offsetting reasons for buying.

Questioning

The questioning technique allows customers to answer their own objections by letting them explain why they think as they do. Notice the pattern of conversation in the following example:

Customer: This brand can't be good.
Salesperson: Tell me why you think so.
Customer: The price is so low, there must be something wrong with it.
Salesperson: But doesn't our product have the same features as Brand X?
Customer: Yes, I guess it does, but what about a guarantee?
Salesperson: Our guarantee is for six months rather than three months.
Customer: Is that right? Well, maybe I'll try one.

Through a series of questions, a salesperson can often determine the customer's real objections to a product. In the previous example, price and brand probably were smoke screens for the real objection, which was product guarantee. By careful probing, the salesperson can sometimes bring the real objection to the surface in order to answer it. However, it is better to accept the excuse than to offend by being overly insistent. Whether making a sale or not, it is important to maintain the customer's goodwill.

Sometimes it is a good idea to combine the questioning method with the other methods of answering objections. The salesperson should first ask questions to clarify the customer's thoughts and to determine the nature of the objection. Then, the salesperson should proceed to other appropriate methods of answering the objections if they still exist.

Preparing to Overcome Objections

Most retailers agree that objections should be answered as soon as they are raised. The best way to do this is to be prepared. To have success in overcoming sales resistance, salespersons need to (1) know their merchandise, (2) apply correct selling procedures, and (3) understand customer buying behavior.

No matter which method or methods are used to meet objections, the salesperson should (1) listen carefully before answering, (2) be interested in the customer's point of view, and (3) not hurry a response—be sure of the answer. A successful salesperson is familiar with often-heard objections to the product and is prepared to answer

each one. The effective salesperson also thinks ahead and includes answers to common objections raised in the sales presentation. Care should be taken, though, not to make the presentation so complete that the customer goes away feeling totally overwhelmed—and without the product. Keep in mind that the customer should be allowed to participate in the selling process. Allowing customers to ask a few questions or to raise valid objections is an effective way to involve them in the selling process.

A salesperson should not attempt to close a sale until all of the customer's objections seem to have been answered. To press for a close when objections remain may be interpreted by the customer as high-pressure selling. Such a tactic seldom results in a satisfactory sale.

CLOSING TECHNIQUES

Many beginning salespeople are afraid to close a sale; instead, they avoid a direct closing or apologize for it. One reason for this is an inner fear that the customer may say, "No, I don't want that." Actually, everything a salesperson does during the selling process is for one purpose: to close a sale. Except in some self-service situations, decisions to buy usually require the help and encouragement of a salesperson. Salespeople cannot expect to close every sale. But there is no excuse for not trying when the customer has an obvious need.

Closing a sale should be a very natural process. This process involves (1) obtaining small favorable decisions during the presentation, (2) making each new decision more forceful, (3) seeking agreement of the customer as the sale comes to an end, and (4) narrowing the customer's choice to a certain item that is at a price the customer is willing to pay. When a buying signal is received from the customer, the salesperson should make a comment or ask a question that will lead the customer to a decision to buy. Such a comment or question is called a **trial close:** "How many would you like?" "Will that be cash or charge?" "Do you prefer the aqua or maroon one?" "We can deliver your computer this afternoon if that is convenient." These are examples of trial closes that can lead to a sale.

Occasionally, a customer may have difficulty deciding. If this happens, the selling process goes on after the trial close. The salesperson, acting as an adviser, may give more help to the customer by using a specialized closing technique. Popular specialized closing techniques include the (1) which close, (2) related-merchandise close, (3) service close, and (4) asking-for-the-sale.

Which Close

The which close is an attempt to narrow a customer's choices and put an end to indecision. Using the which close, a salesperson pointedly requests a buying decision. The objective of the which-close method is to give the customer a choice between something and something rather than something and nothing. To say or to imply "Do you want these shoes or don't you?" would almost certainly result in no sale. Consider, for example, the salesperson who has shown a customer three or four different styles of basketball shoes. The salesperson helps the customer make a decision by re-

Illus. 37–3 The which close helps the customer make a decision to buy by narrowing the choice of goods to two items.

moving from view those shoes in which the customer shows the least interest. With two styles remaining, the salesperson says, "Which pair do you prefer—the white and red one with double laces or the high tops?" The customer usually makes a choice and the sale is closed. However, the customer may say, "I can't decide" or "Neither one, really." In such a situation, the salesperson may make a decision for the customer: "I would take the high tops." An alternative is to start the sales presentation again.

Related-merchandise Close

Many sales are closed because of the customer's interest in merchandise that is related to the principal item. This is especially true of merchandise that can help care for or enhance the value and appearance of the principal article. A salesperson may say, "These shoes will go well with the suit." If the customer responds, "Yes I'll take them," this is a signal that the customer has already decided to buy the suit.

Helping a customer decide first on buying smaller, related merchandise opens the opportunity to close the sale of the principal item.

Service Close

The service close, similar to the which close, asks the customer to make a decision. The decision is to accept or reject store services connected with the assumed purchase. "Is your car near the pickup area?" "Would you prefer to take advantage of our layaway plan?" "Would you like this gift wrapped?" All are examples of typical store services that may help the salesperson close a sale. All that is needed is a positive response from the customer.

Asking for the Sale

One experienced salesperson has wisely advised, "If all else fails, ask the customer to buy!" The point, of course, is that many salespeople don't even ask for the sale. This omission may be due to a fear of failure or simply to forgetfulness. When a sales presentation has been conducted in a friendly, matter-of-fact manner, it is only natural for the salesperson to ask the customer to buy. However, the question should not be a do-you-or-don't-you-want-it inquiry. Comments such as "I know you will enjoy your purchase," "We will have it taken to your car," or "That should take care of it" can close the sale. If a customer indicates readiness to buy, the salesperson should never let the opportunity to close slip by even if the sales presentation is just getting under way.

Timing the Close

When is the ideal time to close a sale? Normally, of course, closing occurs toward the end of a sales presentation. Often, this occurs after the salesperson has responded to the customer's questions or objections. Most professional salespeople point out, however, that anytime is the best time to close: Always Be Closing—better known as the ABCs of selling—is a good principle to follow. For example, if the customer says early in the sale, "I really like this framed poster," the salesperson might respond, "An excellent choice; this poster is very popular. Do you prefer to pay by cash, check, or charge?" The professional salesperson is constantly on the alert for signals that the customer is ready to buy. These signals can be comments, facial expressions, or actions such as picking up the merchandise for closer inspection.

SUGGESTION SELLING

After all major buying decisions have been made and before the sales transaction is completed, an important customer service should be performed. This service is called *suggestion selling.* For example, a home owner decides to paint a lawn chair but does not have the right kind of paint to do the job. A visit to a paint store or hardware and paint department of a large retail store appears to be necessary. The paint is selected and the sales transaction completed. The salesperson in this case does not include suggestion techniques in the selling process. At home, the customer discovers that the old can of paint remover has dried up. To make matters worse, there is no sandpaper to smooth the wood surface of the chair and the paint brush has been thrown away! A happy customer? Probably not. If only the salesperson had suggested paint remover, sandpaper, and paint brushes, the customer's memory might have been jogged, time would have been saved, and perhaps more items could have been sold.

There is virtually no limit to the kinds of merchandise that can be suggested to customers. Related items, more of the same item, higher-quality merchandise, sale items, and newly arrived merchandise are just a few. Suggestion selling should not be confused with loading down customers with unwanted merchandise. *Remember that selling means providing customers with goods and services that they need and want.* If the following rules are observed, a valuable service can be performed for the customer in addition to increasing the amount of the sale:

1. Make suggestions precise. Instead of saying, "Anything else?" say, "Do you need polish for those shoes?"
2. Show the item as you suggest it; do not just talk about it.
3. Give a reason for making the suggestion. Point out how well the plant will grow with the correct fertilizer.
4. Do not overdo suggestion selling. Considerable ill will can be caused if the salesperson attempts to sell the customer every item in the store.

Illus. 37–4   *Suggestion selling is a valuable service to customers and it enhances a store's ability to increase profits.*

Up to the close of the sale, many salespeople do exactly the right things to build goodwill. Then, in handling the cash or charge card or handing the purchase to the customer, they do or say something foolish or tactless. As a result, the customer may say, "Never mind!" or complete the purchase but leave the store irritated. Slow and inefficient sales recording, change making, and packaging are common customer irritants. Advertising, word-of-mouth recommendations, attractive store appearance, good merchandise, and a sincere interest in creating goodwill all attract customers. However, these will not make goodwill last unless they are supported by salespeople who are courteous and helpful at the beginning *and* end of a sale.

Summary

To bring a sale to a successful conclusion, the salesperson must be able to answer the customer's objections, close the sale, and use proper suggestion-selling techniques. Some customer objections can be forestalled by answering them before they are raised. Other objections require the salesperson to employ such techniques as the (1) direct-denial method, (2) yes, but method, (3) reverse-English method, (4) superior-point method, and (5) questioning method. The salesperson must always be prepared to close the sale. Lack of confidence and fear of failure cause some beginning salespeople to avoid the use of effective closing techniques. These techniques include (1) the which close, (2) the related-merchandise close, (3) the service close, and (4) asking for the order. Suggestion selling allows the salesperson to provide a valuable service to the customer. It is accomplished when related items, more of the same item, higher-quality merchandise, sale items, and new merchandise are brought to the customer's attention. Selling means providing customers with the goods and services they need and want.

Review

1. List four basic kinds of objections and explain why customers raise them.
2. State how objections are forestalled.
3. Identify and explain five techniques that can be used to answer objections.
4. State three ways salespersons can prepare to answer objections.
5. Explain the natural process of closing a sale.
6. Define *trial close*.
7. List and describe four closing techniques.
8. Explain the ABCs of selling.
9. Explain suggestion selling.

Terms   The following term was introduced in this chapter. Write a sentence correctly using it.

trial close

Discuss

1. Have you ever raised objections during a sales presentation? Why?
2. Why is it sometimes a good idea to combine the questioning method with other methods of answering objections?
3. What reasons can you give for failing to close a sale? Why should closing be considered a natural part of the sales presentation?
4. What customer signals would you look for when deciding to close a sale?
5. Is suggestion selling a valuable customer service? Explain

Problem Solving

1. The customer says "I like all three coats, but I have nothing to wear with any of them." Which closing methods would you use? Provide examples of what you would say for each method.
2. During one of the monthly store sales meetings, your manager asks each salesperson to write on a slip of paper two frequently heard customer objections. The manager collects the slips and redistributes them with instructions to prepare a response to each objection. The first objection on your slip says, "I can purchase that same item at X Store for $8.00 less." The second objection reads, "My neighbor told me these cups stain easily." Which method would you use to answer each of these objections? Exactly what would you say to the customers?
3. You have just received a large shipment of folding lawn chairs. These chairs will be featured in a special spring promotion. Make a list of items that salespeople could suggest to customers who buy the chairs.

CHAPTER 38

Completing the Sales Transaction

CHAPTER OUTCOMES

When you have mastered the information provided in this chapter, you should be able to:

1. List the activities that make up a sales transaction

2. Identify three sales transaction functions performed on sales registers

3. Name two sales register functions

4. List seven of the most common errors made in the operation of a register

5. Describe the procedures of making change for a cash sale

6. Identify means of authorizing a customer's use of credit when the floor limit has been exceeded

7. Explain the procedure that retail stores typically follow when completing a credit-card purchase

8. Explain the salesperson's responsibility when bagging merchandise for the customer or preparing it to be delivered or mailed

9. State why a customer's departure is considered part of the sales transaction

10. Explain why a follow-up to certain sales may be necessary.

After the majority of steps in the selling process have been completed, the sale must be recorded properly and the customer provided with a proof of payment or charge. In addition, the purchased merchandise usually must be wrapped or bagged to be taken from the store. These activities make up a **sales transaction** and must be conducted with speed, accuracy, and friendliness. A sales transaction is a store owner's only record of sales. It may also be the last opportunity a salesperson has to create a favorable impression and to encourage the customer to return to the store. The successful sales transaction, along with customer departure, usually mark the completion of the sales process described in Chapter 36.

SALES REGISTERS

The most commonly used device for recording retail sales and providing customer receipts is the sales register. Sales registers help perform three very important sales-transaction functions. First, they serve as information-collection centers. The department merchandise classification, salesperson identification, amount of the sale, kind of transaction, and change due the customer can be recorded easily. Second, sales registers provide a place to keep cash, checks, charge slips, layaway slips, refund slips, and coupons after a transaction has been completed. Third, registers can be used to print the necessary information on a receipt. Of course, sales registers are only as reliable as the information that is fed into them by salespeople.

Computer-assisted Sales Registers

Most sales registers are designed to perform complex operations. Much depends on the merchant's individual needs. Complex registers are linked with a computer. Sales information is entered directly into a main computer that summarizes it for sales reports, budget analysis, inventory records, and purchasing. For example, a product marked with a bar code (called the Universal Product Code or UPC) might be passed over an electronic scanner which is installed in the checkout counter or hand held by the salesperson. The scanner reads the code and records the coded information electronically in a computer system. At the same time, the correct selling price is reported back to the sales register on a digital readout and/or paper tape.

In some retail outlets, a portion of the price ticket is inserted in the register which reads the magnetic-ink characters on the tag and records all pertinent information about the merchandise. This kind of system also can be designed to verify credit, calculate returns, and compute any applicable discounts. The sales register then shows the amounts being recorded and prints a customer receipt or sales check and an audit tape. Computerized sales registers are sometimes the basis of the retailer's inventory system. Each time a transaction is entered in the register, the item of merchandise is subtracted from inventory. When the inventory reaches a set minimum, the computer automatically reorders from the supplier.

Illus. 38–1   In many retail stores, products containing Universal Product Codes are passed over an electronic scanner at the sales register.

Sales Register Operators

The operator of any sales register usually is the salesperson, but the operator may be a cashier or checkout clerk whose main job is sales-register operation. Cashiers are essential in self-service stores. Even in stores where there are salespeople, cashiers stationed at customer-service counters are sometimes provided to relieve salespeople of this aspect of selling.

Sales registers provide fast and efficient recording of sales only if the operator is properly trained. A checkout operation involves more than scanning, bagging, making change accurately, and giving courteous service. Sales register operation means working under pressure, especially when long lines of customers are waiting for service. It requires knowledge of the store's register system and procedures for handling various sales transactions.

Some of the most common errors made by sales register operators are (1) recording prices incorrectly, (2) pressing the wrong department keys, (3) failing to record all of a customer's purchases, (4) leaving cash drawers unattended, (5) running out of change, (6) forgetting to give the customer a receipt, and (7) improperly handling money and giving incorrect change. It is extremely important that salespeople know what their register is designed to do and how to operate it quickly and accurately.

CASH TRANSACTIONS

A cash sale occurs when a customer pays for purchases with money or a check. Customers often pay cash to speed up a sales transaction. It is especially important, therefore, that cash sales be completed rapidly but without error. A salesperson's money-handling skills must include knowing and following the store's check-cashing policy.

Cash-sale Procedures

For cash sales, the amount of the sale plus any applicable tax is totaled by the sales register and stored in the computer (where available). If a customer is paying by check, store policy may require check writer identification. To simplify this process, an increasing number of stores are using on-line check acceptance services. This service reduces loss and speeds up the handling of checks. A limit may also be set on the amount of a check that can be cashed. Each purchased item probably has a depart-

ment code to enter. For some items, particularly wearing apparel, a portion of the price tag may be removed to serve as the store's record of the sale.

Making Change

Although most automated registers have eliminated the change-making step in the sales transaction, many salespersons and cashiers still are required to make change. Considerable practice in the procedures for making change is often necessary. The total amount of the sale should be announced to the customer. When the customer offers payment, the amount of the bill or check should also be announced. When currency is received from a customer, it should be placed on the shelf above the cash drawer. This eliminates the possibility of a dispute as to how much money the customer gave the salesperson.

Change should be made with as *few* coins as possible—for example, a dime should be given rather than two nickels. The change should also be counted following a definite procedure; that is, the salesperson should count the change silently as it

Illus. 38-2 Making correct change is an important responsibility of salespeople and cashiers.

is removed from the sales register. The usual procedure is to count *up* from the purchase price, selecting the smallest denominations of currency or coins first. The same procedure is used when counting change out loud to the customer. Thus, if a sale amounts to $3.15 and the customer gives a $10 bill, the salesperson should count back out loud as follows: $3.15 out of $10, $3.25 (giving the customer a dime), $4 (giving three quarters), $5 (giving a $1 bill), and $10 (giving a $5 bill). When more than one bill is given in change, each should be counted separately and placed one by one in the customer's hand.

If a customer is shortchanged, efforts to rebuild goodwill usually fail. Some customers who are shortchanged never return to a store. On the other hand, giving too much change causes a direct loss to the store.

CHARGE TRANSACTIONS

Increasing numbers of retail-store customers rely on credit cards to make purchases. Some large department stores maintain their own credit accounts and provide charge cards to creditworthy customers; that is, customers whose credit standing has been checked and approved. When a customer charges a purchase in these stores, a charge slip indicating the merchandise, the amount of the sale, the department, the date of the sale, and the salesperson is given to the customer.

Some sales may exceed a certain dollar amount called the *floor limit*. A store's **floor limit** is the maximum amount a customer can charge without management ap-

proval. Once the floor limit has been exceeded, the salesperson may have to request authorization by the store's credit manager or by a central credit office at another location.

More and more stores are now using electronic credit authorizers. Credit authorization is obtained by inserting the customer's credit card in a telephonelike device usually located near the sales register; the salesperson is given an audio, light, or printed response indicating that credit is authorized or that the credit department should be asked to check the customer's credit standing.

Electronic authorizers are part of most computer-assisted, point-of-sale systems so that data from the price ticket, the customer's credit card number, and the salesperson's identification number are all recorded at once. Not only is the credit standing checked, but, if credit is approved, the customer's account is charged or billed auto-

Illus. 38–3 Charge transactions are often made with a credit card.

matically. Also, the salesperson and the department are credited automatically for the sale, and the stock or inventory records adjusted to reflect the sale.

Most retailers accept credit cards issued by banks such as MasterCard or Visa. Each card contains the name, signature, and account number of the card owner; the name of the bank; and the expiration date of the card. At the time of a charge purchase, the card is given to the salesperson or cashier. The card number is checked for credit approval against a list of delinquent accounts (customers who are behind in payment of their bills). This checking is usually done automatically by the register or a separate computer system. If credit is approved, the customer signs the charge slip and is then given a copy of it for her or his records.

Illus. 38–4 Most customers expect their purchases to be packaged correctly.

BAGGING MERCHANDISE

Most customers expect their purchases to be bagged or wrapped. Although some customers may say, "That's OK; I'll take it the way it is," the offer always should be made.

Merchandise should be bagged so that it can be carried easily. It also should be covered enough to protect it from damage between the store and the customer's destination. Proper bagging also protects the customer from suspicion that may fall on a person who leaves the store carrying unwrapped merchandise. The sales receipt assures that the customer has proof of purchase and it should always be included with the bag.

Concern for the environment has prompted retailers to be more selective when choosing packaging materials. Recyclable paper and environmentally safe containers are increasingly popular. Many food stores now encourage customers to bring their own reusable cloth or nylon shopping bags.

Some discount stores provide facilities for customers to package their own purchases. However, in many supermarkets, a checkout person or a courtesy clerk is responsible for bagging customer's purchases. Care must be taken to put larger and heavier items, such as canned goods and cartons, at the bottom of a correct size bag and light and perishable merchandise on top. Wet or frozen foods should be put in plastic or insulated bags before being placed in the outer bags; otherwise, the moisture may break the outer bag or damage other items.

If a customer is carrying several packages, even though not all of them were bought in the store, the salesperson should offer to place all items in one large bag. Customers usually appreciate this service.

When a customer asks to have a package gift wrapped, the salesperson should be careful not to enclose the sales slip, price ticket, or customer's receipt. Some stores have a centrally located gift-wrapping service that provides tissue-paper linings, colorfully designed wrapping paper, ribbons, and even small gift cards.

PREPARING MERCHANDISE FOR DELIVERY OR MAILING

When merchandise is to be delivered by the store's truck or by common carrier, it is often necessary to prepare the goods to withstand rough handling. With a little practice, a retail employee can become expert at this skill. It is also necessary to make sure that the customer's name and address are correct and legible and that the store's return address is clearly marked on the package.

In some large stores, goods to be delivered are not wrapped and packed by salespeople but are sent in bags, with directions for mailing or delivery attached, to a central station. Fragile articles are sent to the packing department where experienced workers prepare the merchandise for delivery. Then, the packages are sent to the store's shipping department where they are sorted according to delivery routes.

At one time, it was considered necessary to pack for rough handling all goods that left the store—regardless of expense. In recent years, however, this practice has been changed. If customers plan to take goods directly to their cars, they can take the merchandise unwrapped, with a sales-

register receipt attached. If the goods are to be delivered, they are often best left exposed.

Prepackaging merchandise in advance of sale—in unit prepacks (individual packages) ready for delivery to customers—is a standard practice. This prepackaging is generally done by the manufacturer in consultation with the retailer. In supermarkets, however, the store usually prepacks its own produce and meats. In some chain stores, meats are prepackaged in the warehouse, and each manager orders the particular assortment of cuts required for sale.

Manufacturers are constantly improving the packaging of their products, and recent developments in packaging have been remarkable. However, the impact on the environment of materials used in prepackaging is a major concern. This will influence the way in which products will be made ready for sale.

CUSTOMER DEPARTURE AND FOLLOW-UP

In Chapter 36, you learned that the salesperson's approach to the customer depends on the conditions existing in the store or department. Similarly, after completing a sales transaction, the method of taking leave of the customer will vary with the kind of merchandise sold, the length of time the salesperson has spent with the customer, and the number of customers waiting for service. In some cases, all that the salesperson needs to do is say, "Thank you" as the sales transaction is completed. In other cases, the salesperson may accompany the customer to the store or department exit and

Illus. 38–5   The customer's impression of the salesperson and the store is often influenced by how the departure and follow-up step in the sales process is handled.

state such pleasantries as, "I'm sure you will enjoy your purchase," "We shall be glad to see you again," or "It was a pleasure to serve you; have a nice weekend." The departure can be used to retain customer goodwill. Shoppers who do not buy should be provided the same courteous farewell.

Some sales transactions require some follow-up by salespersons, service personnel, or other store representatives. Delivery of goods, installation where necessary, and simply calling the customer to inquire about product performance helps build goodwill and repeat business.

*S*ummary

After a sale has been closed, the purchase must be recorded, paid for, and bagged. Creating a favorable impression on the customer is also important to the completion of the sale. Sales registers are used to record sales transactions. Salespeople must know how to operate this equipment quickly and accurately. Doing so requires proper handling of various sales transactions, including cash and charge transactions. In addition, customers expect purchases to be properly bagged in preparation for removal from the store, whether by the customer or store delivery person. Finally, when the customer departs, it is the salesperson's responsibility to make sure goodwill is retained and that the customer is encouraged to return to the store.

Review

1. Identify the activities that make up a sales transaction.
2. Name three important sales-transaction functions performed on sales registers.
3. List two functions, other than totaling the sale, that are performed by computer-assisted sales registers.
4. Identify common errors in the operation of a sales register.
5. State the procedures for making change in a cash transaction.
6. Name means of authorizing customer credit when the floor limit has been exceeded.
7. Describe the procedure that retail stores typically follow when completing a credit-card purchase.
8. State the salesperson's responsibility when bagging merchandise.
9. Explain why the customer's departure is viewed as part of a sales transaction.
10. Explain why follow-up may be required after certain sales.

Terms

The following terms were introduced in this chapter. Write a separate sentence correctly using each new term.

floor limit   sales transaction

Discuss

1. What types of skills would a well-trained sales-register operator possess?
2. Why is it important for salespeople and cashiers to possess good change-making skills?
3. What techniques should be employed to make sure that merchandise is packaged properly?

Problem Solving

1. You are a department head in a women's high-fashion clothing store. Recently, you have noticed that one of your salespeople simply hands the package to the customer at the close of the transaction and walks away. What would you suggest this salesperson say and do during the departure stage of the sales process?

2. Susan has been employed at Borden's Gift Shop for approximately six months. During Susan's recent employee review, the store manager indicated overall satisfaction with her work. However, the manager did express concern about her occasional errors when making change. The manager has asked you to review change-making fundamentals with Susan. What will you include in your discussion?

3. Your customer requests that the following items be packaged so that he may carry them easily to his car: a small unassembled TV stand in a box, a package of nails, ten pounds of laundry soap, two quarts of paint, and a paint roller and tray. Describe how you would package or bag these items.

CHAPTER 39

Special Skills in Selling

CHAPTER OUTCOMES

***When you have mastered the information provided
in this chapter, you should be able to:***

1. List five strategies for remembering names

2. Name four ways a salesperson can help a customer visualize a service

3. Explain how to serve more than one customer at a time

4. Describe the attitude a salesperson should demonstrate when handling customer complaints

5. Name three major kinds of customer complaints

6. Identify four factors that influence the adjustment a store will make

7. Identify the best policy for apprehending shoplifters

8. Identify five kinds of information to obtain during a telephone order

9. Describe characteristics of salespersons who are most successful in telephone selling

10. Define *in-home parties* and list factors that should be considered in a home-selling situation

Manufacturers, distributors, and retailers spend millions of dollars a year promoting their products. These efforts usually include national, regional, and local advertising campaigns designed to attract the buying public. In support of such efforts, retail stores create interior and exterior displays containing the advertised merchandise. However, the success of these promotional activities really depends on the selling skills of retail salespeople. Lack of training and little desire to assist the buying public can greatly reduce the effectiveness of any sales campaign.

Customers want and deserve the help of effective salespeople. This service often involves special skills in selling that go beyond the basic techniques described in the preceding three chapters. Some of these special skills are highlighted in this chapter.

REMEMBERING NAMES

The ability to remember names and faces is an important asset to any salesperson. Although judgment must be used in determining the appropriate time to address customers by name, most customers appreciate this kind of personal recognition. Usually, customers are addressed by their last names: "Good afternoon, Mrs. Lopez." "That is a lightweight fabric, Miss Conners." "In the second aisle, Mr. Shen." First names are used only if it is apparent that the customer prefers to be addressed that way.

What follows are some strategies that might be helpful in developing the ability to remember names:

1. *Get the name right;* write it down; learn how the name is spelled.
2. *Repeat* the name often; try to recall the names of customers served at the end of each workday.
3. *Associate* the name with something familiar such as a customer's purchases, address, or appearance—Miss Brown wore a brown coat.
4. *Be interested,* determined to learn customers' names.
5. *Practice* constantly; review names of regular customers with co-workers.

Following these suggestions will build confidence in using names correctly. Practice, of course, is a key element and will help prevent the embarrassment of incorrectly identifying customers.

A true test of skill in remembering names is the ability to recognize and greet customers personally each time they enter the store. Using the customer's name in the sales presentation is one way to demonstrate a sincere desire to be of service. Saying the customer's name occasionally helps build the customer's confidence, but overusing a name distracts the customer from the sales presentation.

SELLING SERVICES

Products that can be seen and touched by customers give salespeople a selling advantage when completing a sale. Increasingly, however, retailers are offering intangible services, such as insurance, stocks, travel, and repair and maintenance contracts, on tangible products.

The sales process followed when presenting services is essentially the same as that used when selling goods. To sell services, a salesperson needs to be able to create a strong image of the service in the customer's mind. In addition, the salesperson must help customers visualize how they would use a particular service. This visualization can be done through such techniques as (1) using visual aids, (2) quoting a previous satisfied customer who used the service, (3) using words that paint a picture, and (4) emphasizing how the customer will benefit if a purchase is made. These techniques only make a sales presentation more effective; they are not substitutes for clear interesting presentations of the service.

SERVING MORE THAN ONE CUSTOMER AT A TIME

One of the most difficult situations faced by most salespeople is serving several customers at once. This problem can occur in a self-service grocery store, a fast-food operation, and a full-service department store. There are, fortunately, some techniques that can help a salesperson provide personal and efficient service under such circumstances.

The most obvious solution is to call for the assistance of other salespeople. If none is available, the salesperson should continue to serve the first customer and, at the same time, recognize other customers who are waiting. Often a simple nod of the head or word of recognition, such as, "Good morning. I'll be with you shortly," is sufficient. Sometimes, directing waiting customers' attention to merchandise can prove effective. For example, the salesperson may suggest that the customer examine some new merchandise, consider some matching accessories, or use the mirror to check for proper fit and appearance. Experience and skill are required in effectively serving customers who must wait. Under no circumstance should customers be ignored; service should be provided as quickly as possible.

Another difficult selling situation is created by two or more persons shopping together. A husband and wife, a mother and daughter, or a peer group can present selling situations where not only the buyer, but also the others, must be sold. In such cases, a salesperson should try to determine and answer the objections of all parties. This requires additional concentration on listening and questioning. It may do little good to sell just the buyer in the group and not answer the objections of others. Such selling usually results in no sale at all or in returned merchandise.

Illus. 39–1 Selling experience and skill are required to serve more than one customer at a time.

HANDLING COMPLAINTS

"Three of the plates were broken when I took them out of the box." "I thought you said there was a one-year warranty." "I wanted a size 15 1/2 collar. This is much larger." "This isn't what I ordered." Complaints such as these are almost certain to be heard by retailers. No matter how carefully a store develops and implements its merchandising policies and procedures, there are always some dissatisfied customers. A variety of circumstances cause customer complaints, and realistic retailers expect them. Usually, a retailer makes an **adjustment** (finds ways to correct the situation) for customers.

In most small stores, listening to the customer and making certain adjustments, such as even exchanges, are the responsibilities of the salesperson. Some large retail outlets provide customer-service counters where returns and exchanges are centralized. Since the adjustment must satisfy both the customer and the store, store personnel must develop special skills in handling customer complaints.

Maintaining the Proper Attitude Toward Complaints

A salesperson with the right attitude toward customer complaints can earn much goodwill for the store, but a salesperson with a poor attitude can cost the store many customers. Some salespeople and department managers become defensive when a customer comes to them with a complaint. They believe that the complaint reflects badly on the store and on them, even though they did not make the original sale to the customer. A few salespeople become angry with the customer and resist making the adjustment, even before they have heard the customer's explanation. Such an attitude will almost certainly lead to loss of the customer's goodwill and future patronage. What is more important, additional customers can be lost. A dissatisfied customer is certain to tell friends and acquaintances who consequently may also stop buying at the store.

The salesperson—or anyone else who handles complaints—should always assume that the customer believes they have good reason to complain. The person handling the complaint should listen with an open mind to the customer's explanation before making a suggestion concerning settlement. The most important thing to remember is that a properly handled complaint is a great opportunity to create customer goodwill. A fair and speedy adjustment can make as favorable and lasting an impression upon a customer as an efficient sale.

Kinds of Complaints

There are three major kinds of complaints: (1) complaints about merchandise, (2) complaints about service, and (3) complaints about billing. A merchandise complaint may be about an article of clothing that does not fit properly or about a defective home appliance. A service complaint may be about late delivery. A billing complaint may concern an incorrect price recorded on a customer's charge account. Complaints may be caused by poor quality merchandise, carelessness in sales transactions, inefficient service, and poor supervision of new salespeople.

Determining the Facts

A salesperson should first try to determine the facts surrounding a complaint. Many customers have justifiable complaints caused by defective merchandise or store errors. However, the salesperson can expect to meet some customers who are sincere in their complaints but whose ignorance of or inexperience with the product or store policies makes the complaints unjustifiable. Unfortunately, the salesperson also will encounter customers who make unreasonable claims in an effort to take advantage of the store's policy of trying to please all customers. Regardless, persons who handle complaints should always assume that the claim is a just one until all the facts have been reviewed.

Customers should be allowed to explain their reasons for making a complaint, and the salesperson should listen attentively. The salesperson should then ask questions to uncover any facts that seem to be missing. If the item in question is defective, the salesperson should examine it in front of the customer. The salesperson should, of course, express regret for the inconvenience caused and reassure the customer that the store wishes to make a fair adjustment. The salesperson should take immediate action to see that the problem is settled.

Making an Adjustment

Most large stores instruct salespeople to listen attentively and sympathetically to a customer's complaint. The salesperson will exchange merchandise or refund the purchase price if nothing more is necessary to retain the customer's goodwill. However, major adjustments usually must be referred to a department manager or a customer-service office.

Whoever makes it, the adjustment will be influenced by several factors: (1) the cost of the item in question, (2) the value of the customer to the store, (3) how often the customer makes complaints, and (4) the validity of the complaint.

How might a salesperson use each of these factors? Suppose a customer complains that a can opener that cost $13.95 broke the second time it was used. The salesperson would examine the can opener quickly to see if it had any signs of unusual abuse and would most likely give the customer a new one. The price of a new can opener, $13.95, is too small to risk losing the customer's goodwill by refusing to make the replacement.

How valuable the customer is to the store is an important factor in making an adjustment. Suppose a customer complains about a hole in the upholstery of a chair that has just been purchased. The salesperson may wonder whether the hole was in the chair before it was delivered or whether the customer accidentally tore the upholstery. However, if the customer has just placed an order with that salesperson for two rooms of new furniture, the store would be wise to replace the chair or offer to repair it rather than risk cancellation of the large order.

How often a customer makes complaints is also important in making an adjustment. There are customers who shop carelessly with the attitude that they can always return merchandise. There are some customers who are chronic complainers. Perhaps a salesperson recognizes a customer who often returns used goods with the complaint that they do not meet advertised claims. Replacing these goods obviously represents a direct loss to the store. If a number of adjustments have already been made and if, upon examination, the goods do not seem to be in a condition that warrants a complaint, the salesperson should refer the customer to the department manager or to the customer-service office where the adjustment may be refused. The store may lose the customer's patronage, but the cost of making the adjustment demanded is probably greater than the loss of business.

REDUCING SHOPLIFTING AND THEFT

State laws and store policies regarding shoplifting problems vary. Some laws and policies dictate that shoplifters should be apprehended outside the store. Apprehension of this kind strengthens the store's case against a shoplifter. Furthermore, scenes or any commotion a shoplifter might make in the store can interfere with store operation. However, many states do not require that apprehension of a suspected shoplifter be initiated outside the store. Seeing a person conceal merchandise is enough to charge the individual with shoplifting in some states. A shoplifter is generally apprehended in the store if the merchandise involved is of substantial value or if it is likely that the shoplifter would get away with the stolen goods when outside the store.

A good approach to stopping a suspect is to identify yourself and say, "I believe you have some merchandise on you or in your bag that you may have forgotten to pay for. Would you mind coming back to the store to straighten out this matter?"

Never touch the suspect. Any physical contact could be interpreted as roughness.

TELEPHONE SELLING AND ORDERS

The use of the telephone in retailing is increasing. Salespeople often are required to sell by telephone. More and more people are finding it convenient to shop by telephone, especially if they are buying food, services, clothing, or items advertised in newspapers or catalogs.

Telephone Selling

Telephone selling is a special skill that can be mastered with practice. Salespeople develop lists of customers whom they know personally. They call these customers when interesting offers are available. Calls that are made tactfully and at reasonable hours can bring in much additional business.

A store that uses telephone selling must arrange for deliveries and customer credit and train personnel to be effective telephone salespeople and order takers. Telephone selling allows for greater use of store facilities. In times of slow in-store traffic, especially, telephone selling means higher profits and lower selling costs.

Selling by telephone presents some problems that differ from those of over-the-counter selling. When customers come to the store, the salesperson can greet them, present the merchandise, and observe their reactions. Since it is not possible to show customers the merchandise, the telephone salesperson must be able to paint a word picture of it. Selling over the telephone requires unusual ability in applying the eight steps of the selling process. For example, telephone salespeople should place calls at times likely to be most convenient for customers and identify the store, the department, and themselves. They should remain courteous throughout the conversation, using the customer's name occasionally and answering the customer's questions or objections. Good telephone salespeople clearly and enthusiastically describe the merchandise to build the customer's desire for the goods. At the end of the call, they close the sale, possibly by suggesting related merchandise, and, of course, they thank the customer.

Telephone Orders

Do not confuse telephone order taking with telephone selling. While the telephone is used for both activities, order taking is a simpler procedure than selling. Customers generally call in orders when they find it difficult to go to the store because of transportation problems or family commitments. Alert retailers who realize the potential of telephone orders advertise this service and provide telephone-order departments with specialists to handle called-in orders. Some stores keep telephone-order departments open 24 hours daily. A store that accepts telephone orders must arrange for deliveries, offer customer credit in most cases, and employ capable people to record orders.

When a customer places an order, the following information must be recorded accurately:

1. Name of the person ordering
2. Name of the person to whom goods will be shipped
3. Address to which goods will be sent

4. Any special delivery instructions
5. Exact descriptions of each article, including price, quantity, brand, color, size, and special preparation

After recording the information, the order specialist should read it back, asking the customer to confirm or correct the information.

Order specialists must know the sizes, colors, prices, and quantities of merchandise on hand to tell the customer whether or when an order can be filled. The specialists must be careful not to leave customers waiting on the phone for more than a few seconds while looking up merchandise information. Telephone customers resent indications that they have been forgotten.

SERVING CUSTOMERS OUT OF THE STORE

Certain types of selling require that the sales presentation take place at the customer's home or place of business. Examples of products for in-home selling include appliances, cookware, and interior decorating products. Landscaping items, such as shrubs and trees, window awnings, and playground equipment, are frequently sold on site. Some firms sell household cleaning products by calling regularly on home customers. Other firms sell household cleaning products through in-home parties to which a customer invites several friends for a display and demonstration of the company's products.

Although the basic principles of good retail selling apply, there are some additional rules to follow when selling in customers' homes. It may be necessary for the salesperson to make specific appointments, present samples rather than actual products, and plan for callbacks to demonstrate additional merchandise or to answer follow-up questions. Salespeople who sell outside the retail store must remember that they are guests and act accordingly. They also must be attentive to certain details. For example, they should make sure that parking in the customer's driveway is not going to cause difficulties and that the customer does not object to having samples or products arranged on a table or carpet. They should refrain from smoking (even though the customer does) and adhere to an agreed-upon time schedule.

Actually, certain goods can be sold more effectively in customers' homes than in the store because the customers' needs and wants are more apparent to the salesperson and the customers themselves. Also, customers can see better just how certain merchandise will fit into their homes or lifestyles. Usually, in-home sales presentations are made with fewer distractions or interruptions than may occur in the retail store.

Summary

Mastery of basic selling techniques is important to a retail salesperson. But it is not sufficient! A salesperson must also possess knowledge of special skills that go beyond basic selling methods. For example, the ability to remember customers' names is an important asset to any salesperson. The ability to sell services, such as stocks and insurance, also requires skills beyond those needed to sell items that can be seen and touched by the customer. Knowing how to deal with more than one customer at the same time and the ability to resolve customer complaints provide opportunities to retain customers and build goodwill. Reducing shoplifting and theft is high on the list of special skills needed by successful salespeople. So are the abilities to conduct the selling process and to record orders by telephone. Increasingly, retail salespeople are being called on to go to customers' homes to present a variety of products, such as drapes, carpeting, interior decorating products, and landscaping articles.

Review

1. Name five strategies for remembering names.
2. List four techniques that the salesperson can use to help a customer visualize a service.
3. Describe how more than one customer can be served at a time.
4. Describe the kind of attitude a salesperson should demonstrate when handling customer complaints.
5. Identify three major kinds of customer complaints.
6. Name four factors that influence the adjustment a store will make.
7. Describe the best way to apprehend shoplifters.

8. Identify characteristics of salespersons who are most successful in telephone selling.
9. Describe in-home parties and identify factors that should be considered in an in-home selling situation.

Terms

The following term was introduced in this chapter. Write a sentence correctly using it.

adjustment

Discuss

1. Why is remembering names an important asset for retail salespeople?
2. Why are more and more people shopping by telephone?
3. Why should customers be given time to explain their reasons for making a complaint?
4. What are some basic rules, other than those in the chapter, that a retail salesperson should follow when selling in a home?

Problem Solving

1. Your store encourages personalized service for its customers. One way this is done is to remember and use customers' names in selling situations. In some instances, however, a few customers have appeared upset when they were addressed by name during the sales presentations. Why would this occur? Write a brief set of rules for using customers' names to prevent anyone's being upset.
2. As a retail store salesperson, you are occasionally asked to call customers to sell specially priced merchandise. Some customers say, "I don't have time to talk now" or "I'm not interested." How should you respond? How could you approach the customer to get positive responses?
3. A week ago, a customer bought a wall clock from you ($59.95). Today, the customer, who is a "regular," returned with the clock. The customer demanded a return of the purchase price because the clock did not run. A casual inspection of the clock showed that it was wound too tightly. How might the problem have been prevented? What steps should be taken now to resolve the problem?
4. You are completing a sales transaction for a customer who is trying to locate a credit card. A second customer in line has a single item to purchase and has the correct amount of the sale in hand. A third customer has a question about the sizes available in a particular line of slacks. What should be done to provide good service to all three customers?

UNIT 6 ACTIVITIES

CHECKING KEY POINTS

This exercise is designed to check your understanding of material presented in Unit 6. On a separate sheet of paper, list the numbers 1 to 24. Indicate your response, *T* for true or *F* for false, for each of the following statements:

1. Retailers depend entirely on satisfied customers for their existence.
2. Buying decisions are not affected by a customer's basic needs and secondary wants.
3. Salespeople are most helpful to customers when the information they provide is accurate and well-organized.
4. In the reverse-English technique, the customer's objection becomes a less important reason for buying the product.
5. The departure has little influence on retaining customer goodwill.
6. A salesperson should first try to determine the facts surrounding a complaint.
7. Salespersons are required to perform few housekeeping duties.
8. Rational buying motives include status, pride, and self-image.
9. Personal selling requires direct contact between the customer and the salesperson.
10. As a salesperson presents merchandise, customer objections may be encountered.
11. Change should be made with as many coins as possible.
12. The ability to remember names and faces is an important asset to any salesperson.
13. Few stores expect personnel to handle routine complaints and make adjustments.
14. Store personality is a customer's behavior while making a purchase.
15. Customers seldom need assistance in deciding which product or service to buy.
16. Closing a sale should be a very natural process.
17. The use of the telephone in retail selling is decreasing.
18. A customer should never be directed unless the salesperson is sure the information provided is correct.
19. Predicting customer needs, wants, and buying habits is always filled with uncertainty.
20. An approach that receives less general approval than any other is the formal approach.

21. Most retailers agree that objections should be answered at the end of a presentation.
22. Sales registers serve as information-collection centers.
23. The cost of an item is not a factor in making an adjustment.
24. A checkout operation involves more than making change accurately and giving courteous service.

BUILDING BASIC SKILLS

Retail Calculations

In each of the following situations, indicate the total amount tendered, total amount of change, and the kind of coins and bills in change.

1. The customer's total purchase is $18.86. The customer gives you (tenders) a $20 bill and 1 penny.
   a. Total amount tendered _____
   b. Total amount of change _____
   c. Coins and bills in change _____
2. The customer's total purchase is $12.81. The customer gives you (tenders) a $20 bill, two $1 bills, and a penny.
   a. Total amount tendered _____
   b. Total amount of change _____
   c. Coins and bills in change _____
3. The customer's total purchase is $6.60. The customer gives you (tenders) a $10 bill, a dime and a $0.50 coupon.
   a. Total amount tendered _____
   b. Total amount of change _____
   c. Coins and bills in change _____
4. The customer's total purchase is $26.90, and the customer is receiving a refund on a returned item for $8.70. The customer gives you (tenders) a $20 bill. In addition, the customer gives you a $10 bill and requests five $1 bills and a $5 bill in exchange.
   a. Total amount tendered _____
   b. Total amount of change _____
   c. Coins and bills in change _____

Working with People

Duties of retail-sales personnel include a wide range of responsibilities. Among these are stockkeeping, housekeeping, preventing waste and loss, and offering personal services to customers. Personal selling skills are of particular importance. An effective salesperson conducts sales presentations in such fashion as to meet the needs and wants of most customers. Doing this requires the ability to deal with a variety of customer personalities and selling and nonselling situations. How would you handle the following? Be specific; indicate precisely what you will do or say *first* and how you will follow through.

1. While closing the sale with one customer, another insists on immediate service.
2. You have presented three different sports coats to a customer. The customer, however, cannot decide what to do.
3. You notice that a particular customer is looking carefully at a brass floor lamp which is on display in your department. You approach the customer and begin describing the various features and qualities of the lamp. The customer remains silent.
4. An obviously upset customer approaches you and says, "Can you tell me where the stainless-steel dinnerware that is on sale is located? I've asked two other salespeople. One was not sure and the other gave me wrong directions."

Writing Skills

Select one of the situations described below as the subject for a written communication. Use interviews, written materials, or other references as sources of information. Then organize your thoughts carefully. (Be sure to credit your resources for ideas, views, explanations, or quotations that you use.) The memo, outline, or list should be no more than two double-spaced typewritten pages.

1. The training director is not convinced that a discussion of customer wants and needs should be included in the sales-training program. As assistant store manager, you decide to send a memo to the director suggesting that this topic be included.
2. Your employer is concerned about reducing waste and loss in the store. She asks for a memo suggesting ideas and offers a bonus to the individual who submits the most useful idea.
3. As part of a term project, your instructor asks you to hand in a list of at least ten effective methods for demonstrating clothing.
4. Develop an outline of what you consider to be the main steps in the selling process. Include any subpoints you feel should be listed under each step. The outline will appear in the updated sales manual and will be followed generally in sales-training seminars.
5. You have just attended a special demonstration session on the use of the steps of the sale in a telephone selling situation. Your assignment is to outline a sales presentation to be used on the telephone.

APPLYING YOUR KNOWLEDGE

Can You Do the Following?

1. Explain how to handle a selling situation in which two or more persons are involved.
2. List three tasks that salespersons typically perform as part of their housekeeping duties.
3. Name five methods of overcoming customers' objections.
4. Describe how an electronic credit authorizer functions.
5. Explain why customer confidence in the salesperson is critical in a selling situation.
6. Name the eight steps of the selling process.
7. Explain how fresh merchandise should be stocked.
8. List four techniques that can be used to sell services.
9. Explain what effect a store's image can have on the kinds of customers it attracts.
10. State rules that should be followed to make suggestion selling a valuable service.
11. Identify seven common errors made in operating a sales register.
12. List four convenience goods.
13. Explain how the related-merchandise close can be used to complete a sale.
14. Explain how timing affects a customer's decision to buy.
15. Name five ways to learn and remember customers' names.
16. List six sources of information about product features and benefits.
17. State how a good memory helps salespeople.
18. Explain how telephone selling differs from order taking by phone.

Retail Decisions

1. You have just received a shipment of a new type of battery-operated can openers. How would you demonstrate this product?
2. How would you apply the preapproach step in the selling process to prepare yourself for a sales position?
3. How would you deal with a customer who regularly returns merchandise?
4. Give three examples of how you might respond to the customer who says, "Isn't this product rather expensive?"
5. How would you apply your understanding of basic needs and secondary wants to help customers make buying decisions?
6. What would you say if asked to demonstrate differences in the skills needed to sell convenience, shopping, and specialty goods?

7. Explain why giving a customer too much change is as serious an error as shortchanging the customer.
8. If you were asked, "Why should I study personal selling techniques?" what would be your response?
9. What would you do to assist an undecided customer?
10. How would you explain the importance of knowing how to apply good human-relations skills to new retail workers?

DEVELOPING CRITICAL-THINKING SKILLS

Retail Projects

1. Identify three customer store personalities in addition to those discussed in the text. How would you handle these customer types?
2. There are many opinions regarding those characteristics needed to be successful as a retail salesperson. Develop a list of salesperson characteristics you consider to be most important. Then, obtain the opinions of your teacher and a counselor in the career planning and placement office. Finalize your list by adding characteristics frequently mentioned and deleting those rarely mentioned.
3. Select a product of your choice and make a list of possible customer objections to that product. Prepare a response to each objection and indicate the technique used to overcome each objection.
4. Since no two customers are alike, their reasons for buying certain merchandise will vary. Select a product that you believe most of your classmates would be interested in owning. Ask each one to list on paper (no names) her or his own reason(s) for needing or wanting the product you are presenting. Collect the results, eliminate duplicate reasons, and make a final list of buying motives.

Field Projects

1. A good sales presentation is complete and clear and builds customer confidence in the salesperson. Select five retail salespeople that you feel are highly qualified. Ask each one to respond to this question: "If you had your choice, what kind of selling sequence would you use in presenting merchandise to your customers?" Study their responses and determine a sequence of selling steps. Then, compare your results with the selling process discussed in this unit. Point to major differences and similarities.
2. Compare the change-making procedures followed by five salespersons who use sales registers with automatic change-making equipment with those of five salespersons who use standard sales

registers. What do they do differently? What do they do the same?
3. Contact a department manager in three different retail stores of your choice. Ask each manager to list the housekeeping duties workers are expected to perform. Combine these duties into a single list.
4. Ask three classmates, three store managers, and three retail salespeople to describe the processes they would follow in conducting a sales presentation. Compare your results with the sales process described in this unit.

CONTINUING PROJECTS

Developing a Career Plan

Retailers know that employees who possess effective selling skills are key to the success of their operations. Therefore, they seek individuals who show an interest in becoming and have potential to become good retail salespersons. In fact, most, if not all, retail managers and executives have extensive retail-sales experience. There is little doubt that a sales background can help provide the basis for advancement in the retailing field.

The purpose of this activity is to help you 1) identify a variety of retail sales positions, 2) determine the qualifications necessary to obtain and hold these positions, and 3) become aware of the potential each kind of position offers for future advancement. To accomplish the above, prepare a concise list of questions you wish to ask store or department managers. Then, arrange to interview at least five different retail operations in your community. Compare the answers you obtain and rank each sales position you have identified using 2 and 3 above as your criteria. Place this information in your career-planning notebook.

Developing a Business Plan

From the facts you have learned in this unit and the study and research of other resources, add the following to your manual:

1. Obtain copies of sales-training outlines used by several retail outlets to prepare new employees for sales. From the information gathered, do the following:
   a. Prepare an outline of the topics you would cover if you were asked to present a sales training program.
   b. For each sales topic you identify, suggest one activity you would use to help new workers better understand the material being presented.

    c. Indicate how you would determine if your new salespersons could do what was taught.

2. Selling is a key responsibility of all employees in your store. Employees are also expected to perform other duties which you plan to describe in a handbook for new employees. Some of those duties will include stockkeeping, housekeeping, preventing waste and loss, directing customers, handling complaints, and operating sales registers.

    a. Write a statement that describes the tasks that must be completed when performing each duty.

    b. Add any other duties you feel are important in the operation of your store and provide a description of each one.

    c. List and describe any special skills you expect your employees to possess.

    d. In your handbook, describe in detail how you expect employees to behave toward the public.

UNIT 7
*O*perations

Retail operations are those activities that support the buying, selling, promotion, and control functions of a retail business. The interior design of a store, the way merchandise is presented, and the way customers are served are important concerns of an operations division. Store maintenance, general housekeeping, security, and provision of supplies and equipment are other concerns.

A store's policies for offering services to customers are vital to its image. Underlying all services is a store's customer relations policy — its attitude toward customers.

Few policies are more important to a store than its credit and collection policy. Every successful retailer has a carefully written collection policy that describes the collection procedures to be followed.

Handling merchandise efficiently when it comes to the store from the supplier is another operations activity. Marking and stocking merchandise, the next operation after receiving, requires a policy for marking methods and a planned arrangement for stocking goods.

Managing stock involves keeping the right balance between the goods on the sales floor (forward stock) and those in the stockroom (reserve stock). Controlling stock requires means for measuring the value of the stock and a system of stock records. People who work in store operations also must know special techniques for moving slow-selling merchandise and for protecting the merchandise against theft and damage.

UNIT OUTCOMES

After studying this unit and completing the activities, you should be able to:

1. List at least eight considerations in planning a store layout
2. Name the main activities of proper store maintenance
3. List the four major categories of store services and give two examples of each
4. Explain the three C's of granting credit and describe a credit scoring procedure
5. Demonstrate four ways to measure the effectiveness of a collection policy
6. Describe five steps in checking merchandise at the receiving point
7. Name and describe five procedures for marking merchandise
8. Give examples of unit pricing, cost codes, and merchandise dating
9. Explain how to use a checklist system of stock control

CHAPTER 40
Store Layout and Maintenance

CHAPTER OUTCOMES

When you have mastered the information provided in this chapter, you should be able to:

1. Identify and describe the retail activities of the operating division of a store

2. Explain how store design relates to store image

3. Explain why different parts of a store have different potentials for sales

4. Develop appropriate layouts for feature, impulse, and staple goods

5. List points that should be considered when planning a store layout

6. Describe five types of store lighting systems

7. Name some activities necessary for good store maintenance

The retail activities included under operations cover a wide range of responsibilities. As described in Chapter 2, store operations include all of the necessary activities other than buying, selling, promotion, and control. For a store to promote and sell merchandise successfully, many supporting activities need to be performed.

In large stores, operations activities are performed by the store's *operating division*. The operating division is usually headed by an executive titled *store manager, store superintendent,* or *store operations manager.* In small stores, the operations activities are performed by the owners or by members of the staffs. Regardless of store size, these store operations activities must be performed smoothly and efficiently if the store is to be successful. Unit 7 describes some of the main operation activities; namely, store layout and maintenance; service policies; credit and collections; and the handling, stocking, and managing of merchandise. The operations area often includes personnel responsibilities, such as employee services, which are described in Chapter 16.

This chapter deals primarily with the functions of design, layout, and maintenance. Stores that have poor designs and inadequate lighting and are not well maintained lose customers and have unnecessarily high costs.

STORE DESIGN

Store design involves all of the physical objects of a store, both inside and outside, and the ways they are combined. The store front, landscaping, parking lot, display windows, and entrances make up the outside design qualities of a store. The walls, floors, ceilings, equipment, lighting, layout of selling and support areas, display fixtures, and decorations make up the inside qualities of a store. The exterior and interior qualities are put together or arranged to convey a particular image to customers.

A careful combination of materials, fixtures, colors, lighting, and layout produces a distinct impression of quality, bargains, excitement, fashion, or any other image desired by the merchant. A men's clothing store may use solid wood fixtures and interior trim, natural colors, indirect lighting, and sports decorations. A store selling at discount prices may create an image of bargains and low prices by designing a bright, carnival atmosphere. Chrome, glass, carpeting, and spot lighting may convey an image of high fashion. Store design is usually created by specialists called *store planners.* Store operations personnel also must be involved in design for they will be responsible for making sure that the planned design is used properly and maintained.

Illus. 40–1   The operations division of a store is responsible for developing and maintaining store design and layout.

STORE LAYOUT

Surveys show that customers tend to stay longer in, buy more in, and return frequently to stores that they find warm, attractive, and comfortable. Store planners strive to provide the modern atmosphere and convenience desired by today's customers. The physical arrangement of a store for receiving, displaying, selling, and delivering goods is called the **store layout.** Many large retail firms have special departments that analyze customer behavior and plan layouts for various departments and stores.

Merchandise Arrangements

Merchandise layouts should be planned with customer as well as merchandising principles in mind. In almost any store, the space nearest the customer entrance has the potential for the greatest

amount of sales. As noted in Illustration 40-2, the farther you move from the store entrance, the less potential space has for generating sales. Merchants recognize this fact and select the location of merchandise accordingly. The back of the store or the upper floors are best used for nonselling activities such as receiving and marking or as stockrooms and store offices.

Decisions about merchandise arrangements usually depend on the potential for sales, space requirements of the merchandise, and customer needs. Department stores place furniture, rugs, and outer clothing above or at the rear of the main floor because of the space needed to show such goods. Retailers assume correctly that most customers will make special trips to see these goods. Department stores generally carry smaller clothing and accessory items, such as hosiery, neckwear, jewelry, handbags, and umbrellas near the front of the main floor. Suits and dresses are often placed so that they are visible from the en-

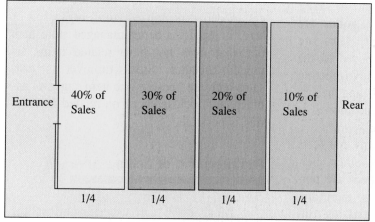
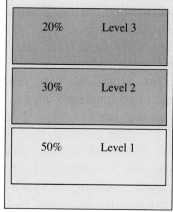

Illus. 40-2 *The selling space nearest the store entrance and on the first level generates the greatest amount of sales. The value of selling space decreases as it is farther from the customer entrance. Retailers make merchandise layout adjustments to counteract the typical results shown.*

trance. A method commonly used to determine the merchandise arrangement is to calculate the amount of sales per square foot of space assigned each type of goods. Goods that provide the highest dollar sales per square foot are likely to be located close to the store entrance or along main traffic flow of customers. Some sophisticated retailers are now assigning locations based on profit per square foot.

Merchandise Attractiveness

Feature goods are usually advertised and often displayed in the outside store windows to attract customers to the inside. Fashion merchandise, seasonal items, and novelties may be featured because they have timely appeal. Other goods may be featured because of low price. Customers will look for these items. Therefore, feature goods need not be located on major traffic aisles but may be in parts of the store that customers usually do not visit.

Impulse goods are usually placed near checkout lanes, at entrances, and in major traffic areas. Because impulse goods are purchased without prior intent, sales are best when these items are exposed to the maximum customer traffic. Candy, greeting cards, magazines, film, health and beauty aids, and sunglasses are often positioned at checkout lanes.

Staple goods are basic items that form the framework around which other merchandise is arranged. These goods are purchased repeatedly by customers; therefore, they need not be located where passing traffic is heavy. Staple goods should be assigned permanent places in the store where customers can expect them to remain.

Related-merchandise Lines

Related articles should be grouped together. If a customer comes into a store for one article, other merchandise closely related to the first should be displayed nearby. Handbags and gloves may be sold close to the neckwear department. In drugstores, shaving creams, after-shave lotion, shaving talc, razors, and blades should be close together.

Placing similar lines of goods together saves the customer both time and energy by calling attention to goods that will be needed later but can be bought now. For example, batteries might be placed near toys, calculators, cameras, flashlights, and smoke alarms. Customers find this arrangement convenient and retailers gain additional sales by using it. The grouping of related merchandise also makes it convenient for the salesperson to serve the customer quickly and offer suggestions.

Merchants who divide their stores into selling departments soon can tell which lines move quickly and which are slow sellers. A departmentalized store, regardless of size, is usually a better managed store than one that does not have related items arranged together. Stock turnover is fast, sales increase because one item suggests another, and a close check on related inventories is possible.

Arrangement of Selling Area

Most stores can use standard selling fixtures to meet the needs of most merchandising areas. Some arrangements do, however, require special fixtures. A **feature**

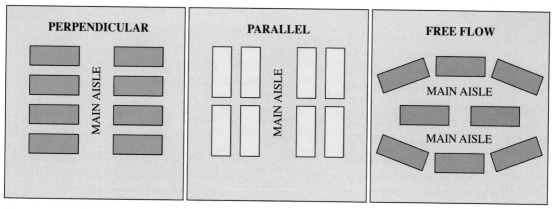

Illus. 40–3   Placing counters and fixtures perpendicular to the main aisle is preferable to placing counters parallel to the aisle. Some stores use layouts with gentle curves, instead of rectangular floor layouts, for better distribution of customer traffic.

unit may be used to call attention to impulse items or marked-down goods that many people would miss if the goods were carried only in the regular department fixtures. An aisle table, portable cart, and on-the-floor stack allow a great deal of merchandise to be placed at a favorable spot, grabbing the attention of many people.

A **merchandise island** is a selling fixture that has an open space in the middle where a salesperson is stationed to serve customers. The island allows for effective display and protection of goods as well as very rapid handling of sales. An **end fixture** features merchandise specials for a few days. These fixtures are placed at the end of a merchandise aisle and display goods regardless of their normal location in the store. Ends are frequently used in supermarkets to attract customers' attention by displaying items in unexpected places.

Self-service fixtures are designed to display all of the stock in a product line and to make these goods accessible for customer self-selection. When the store is arranged as a complete self-service operation, sales register checkout stations must be installed at all store exits. The stations control losses by preventing shoppers from leaving the store without paying for merchandise they selected.

The following points should be considered when planning a store layout.

1. Major aisles should be wide enough for three or more people to walk side-by-side. Minor aisles should be wide enough for two people to walk abreast.

2. Major aisles should run without interruption from entrances to elevators, escalators, and stairways.

3. Fixtures and aisles at store entrances should guide customers away from the entrance area so as not to interfere with incoming traffic.

4. All merchandise should be readily visible to customers and easy for them to examine.

5. Counters should be positioned so that customers examining goods are not jostled by passing traffic.

6. Checkout counters should be positioned so that traffic flow of outgoing customers does not cross or interfere with incoming traffic.

7. Service desks, such as returns and gift certificates, should be well marked and centrally located in the areas they serve.

8. Dressing rooms for trying on clothing should be spacious, well lighted, and located where the store staff can provide maximum service and control.

9. Departments and merchandise should be clearly identified by signs, decorations, and merchandise arrangement.

LIGHTING

Good store lighting is carefully planned and coordinated with the store's interior design. Effective store lighting can add glamour and elegance to the overall store decor (decorations and layout) and increase the appeal of merchandise.

Three categories of lighting must be considered when planning for the lighting needs of a store. First, **general lighting** is almost always installed in the ceiling and provides the light for most store purposes. Second, **wall lighting** provides the light for the walls and other interior surfaces. This lighting is usually individually designed for each store. Wall lighting is used to make a store seem larger and assures that all parts of the store are equally inviting. Third, **display lighting** supplements general and wall lighting and serves to highlight special displays.

Types of Lamps

Fluorescent or incandescent lamps (or both) are used for store lighting. Fluorescent lamps are more widely used, for they give more light per watt and are less expensive to operate. Fluorescent lamps are available for either cool or warm lighting, and certain types (such as quartz or mercury vapor lamps) show colors very close to their appearance in natural light. Incandescent lamps, however, give a broader range of natural-light color.

Types of Lighting Systems

The chief factors to be considered in planning a lighting system are (1) the type of fixtures, (2) the number and types of lamps used, (3) the length and width of the room, (4) the height of the room, (5) the color of the walls and ceiling, (6) the nature of the merchandise, and (7) the energy effectiveness and cost of the system. The appropriate lighting system can be created by using one or a combination of the following types of lighting:

1. *Direct*—virtually all the light comes straight down from the lighting units.

2. *Semidirect*—most of the lighting is direct, but some light is reflected from the ceiling.

3. *Semi-indirect*—some of the light is transmitted directly, but over one half is reflected from the ceiling.

4. *Indirect*—practically all the light is reflected from ceiling or wall areas.

5. *Panel*—light comes as a glow from an electrified glass panel.

Semidirect lighting is usually used for store interiors because it is inexpensive and the lighting fixtures are easy to keep clean. Semidirect lighting fixtures should be at least 12 feet from the floor to prevent glare. Light units of 300 watts, placed 10 to 15 feet apart, are commonly used.

Semi-indirect and indirect lighting fixtures are very popular when an image of quality and elegance is desired. The diffused, soft light enhances the appearance of most merchandise. Semi-indirect and indirect lighting fixtures use more electricity, though, than semidirect lighting.

To get the most out of a good lighting system, light-color walls and ceilings are necessary. Flat paint, as opposed to gloss paint, minimizes reflected glare. Dirty ceilings and walls may reduce the effectiveness

ADVANTAGES OF GOOD LIGHTING

Increases the selling power of
  displays
Makes the store look pleasant and up
  to date
Permits customers to inspect
  merchandise carefully, decreasing
  the likelihood of merchandise being
  returned
Lessens salespeople's fatigue
Allows complete utilization of selling
  area
Creates a good shopping atmosphere

Illus. 40–4   Only a few of the many advantages resulting from good lighting are listed.

of a lighting system by as much as 40 percent, so they should be kept clean.

FLEXIBILITY IN LAYOUT AND LIGHTING

Store flexibility determines how easily a merchant can rearrange the fixtures of a department or a section of the store. Such flexibility is important in modern merchandising. Quick adjustments for seasonal goods, fast-selling items, redirection of customer traffic, or simply a new look require considerable flexibility.

If sales of certain goods have been unsatisfactory in a particular department, the retailer may change the lighting and layout to direct traffic to that department. Often customers' habits, such as going to the right when entering the store, influence the layout and level of lighting. Increasing the level of lighting or changing the width of aisles gets customers to follow a different traffic pattern. To attract fashion-conscious customers also interested in high quality, the store layout and lighting must be elegant and encourage leisurely shopping. Attracting customers interested in bargains and self-selections calls for quite a different layout and lighting design.

STORE MAINTENANCE

Maintenance, repair, periodic remodeling and rearrangement of the store building; upkeep of equipment and fixtures; and general security are major activities of the operating division. Custodial and day-today housekeeping are also necessary to assure that the entire store is clean, appealing, and ready for customer traffic.

Housekeeping

Customers like to shop in stores that are well lighted, comfortably heated or cooled, neatly arranged, and clean. The operating staff of a store makes sure that the overall maintenance and cleaning are done according to store standards. The operations manager, or the owner-manager in smaller stores, assigns persons to keep sidewalks clean, wash windows, collect trash from each department, sanitize restrooms, and maintain floor surfaces. Cleaning and maintenance schedules are established to make sure that the premises are kept as clean as possible during store hours and that equipment is maintained as well as replaced regularly.

Salespeople are responsible for some housekeeping duties, regardless of store size. Salespeople rather than the operations staff arrange stock, dust shelves and counters, and clean selling areas and equipment. Unfortunately, many salespeople believe that these tasks are unimportant or are not part of their jobs. However, an unattended department soon becomes untidy and disorganized, customers disappear, and sales are lost, which ultimately affects the salesperson. Every salesperson should make sure that merchandise stocks are properly arranged by size, color, style, price, or any other classification necessary to enable customers to locate items. Adequacy of selling supplies, such as bags, boxes, and charge slips, also needs to be checked regularly. Some signs of poor housekeeping are shown in Illustration 40-5.

SIGNS OF POOR HOUSEKEEPING

Dirty or stained floors

Dusty, half-filled, or empty bins, shelves, and displays

Soiled or torn price tags and price signs

Wrappings, cartons, and register receipts on sales or checkout counters

Hand trucks, stock carts, and merchandise in aisles

Inventory memos, requisitions, and price lists left where customers can see and read them

Unused display fixtures, sign holders, and point-of-sale material on counters or floor

Illus. 40–5   Salespeople are responsible for preventing these conditions by attending to their housekeeping duties.

Supplies and Equipment

Stores require a large amount of supplies and equipment for housekeeping and maintenance as well as for support of the selling activities. Paper or plastic bags, boxes, cleaning supplies, vacuum cleaners, light bulbs, lamps, and a variety of business forms must be regularly purchased and distributed to staff by the operations division. From time to time, the purchasing manager also must order such items as sales registers, stock carts, counters, and delivery equipment.

The purchase of regular supplies is often just a matter of reordering periodically. However, the operating staff must make sure that the current sources of supplies are indeed the best, both in quality and price.

Also, quantities must be checked and maintained accurately. Too large an inventory of supplies and equipment means poor use of funds and store space. Running out of necessary supplies means emergency purchases from local sources or rush orders which are likely to be more expensive. It is important that salespeople not misuse the supplies and equipment provided. Consistent use of an oversize bag or box, instead of the correct size, can cost the store hundreds of dollars each year. Rough handling of carts or machines can cause breakage or excessive wear that shortens their expected lives.

Store Security

Protecting against shoplifting and employee pilferage, discussed in Chapter 45, is a vital behind-the-scenes activity in any store. Theft, fire, and general protection, along with customer and employee safety, are also the concerns of the operations division.

Those assigned security responsibility should check regularly and often to make sure fire extinguishers are properly located and functioning. Employees should be trained in the use of extinguishers, location of fire alarms, and emergency evacuation procedures. More and more local ordinances forbid smoking in stores. The security staff must enforce this regulation.

Often, local fire departments make routine checks of stores. Many retailers are found to be careless. Exits may be locked during store hours and some exits may be blocked with cartons of merchandise or supplies. Emergency lighting systems may be faulty or inadequate. In some communities, there are heavy fines for such dangerous practices.

The security staff must also watch for conditions that can cause harm to customers or store staff. The 1970 Occupational Safety and Health Act, OSHA, requires employers to furnish employees a workplace that is free from hazards. Torn carpeting, protruding counters or displays, slippery floors, and worn stair treads should be reported promptly and then repaired or corrected. Attention must be given to areas surrounding the store as well as all inside areas. Customer entrances, merchandise receiving areas, and parking areas are sites of potential accidents. Store security staff should report to management any potential dangers to workers or customers in these areas.

While many large business firms employ their own security personnel, owners of small stores and shopping malls often subscribe to independent protection services. Independent protection services may be contracted to regularly check the business premises when the store or mall is closed and may be used during special store events when additional security is needed.

Summary

Customers enjoy shopping in stores that are attractive, comfortable, and clean and that present an image consistent with the type of merchandise offered. Store design and layout vary depending on the merchandise carried, the space requirements of the merchandise, and customer needs. In most cases, retailers can use standard selling fixtures, but some arrangements may require special fixtures.

When planning a store layout, several points should be considered: location and dimensions of aisles, size and location of fixtures, fitting and service areas, checkout counters, and signs. Most stores have a combination of the five main types of lighting: direct, semidirect, semi-indirect, indirect, and panel. Store maintenance is important to keep the store attractive to customers. Salespeople should assist in housekeeping duties such as keeping the stock and the equipment on the selling floor arranged and clean. Other parts of store maintenance are carried out by a custodial staff. The operating division of a store maintains supplies and is responsible for store security.

Review

1. List four activities carried out by the operating division of a retail store.
2. Explain how store design contributes to store image.
3. Define *store layout*.
4. Where should impulse goods be located?
5. Explain the difference between a merchandise island and an end display fixture.
6. Identify nine points that should be considered in store planning.
7. List the five types of store lighting systems.
8. List six signs of poor housekeeping.

Terms

The following terms were introduced in this chapter. Write a separate sentence correctly using each new term.

display lighting	merchandise island
end fixture	store design
feature unit	store layout
general lighting	wall lighting

Discuss

1. Why would store management decide to change a store layout?
2. If you managed a men's clothing store offering both dress clothing and sportswear, what merchandise items would you group together?
3. Which types of goods will a supermarket display on end units?
4. How may a merchant tell if too little or too much merchandise is located in one selling area?
5. Should members of the sales staff be expected to perform housekeeping duties in their selling areas? Why? Give specific reasons for your answer.

6.   A store policy directs salespeople and cashiers/checkers to use as few bags as possible in packaging a customer's purchase. Is this a good policy? Why or why not?

7.   The security officer for a store has asked management to arrange for all employees to attend a fire and crisis training session twice a year. Is this a reasonable request? Why or why not?

Problem Solving

1.   Visit a retail store in your neighborhood and observe the arrangement of the selling area. After leaving the store, develop a diagram of the store layout. List the ways you believe the layout could be improved and develop a revised diagram of the store layout.

2.   Identify a retail store in your neighborhood that you believe has a good lighting system. List the various types of lighting used, the background (walls and ceiling) colors used, and the merchandise featured under any special lighting system. Repeat this study in a store that you believe is poorly lighted.

3.   Visit a supermarket, a hardware or variety store, and a clothing store. Observe the quality of maintenance and housekeeping in each. Rate these qualities on a scale of one (very poor) to five (very good). What problem areas did you find in each? What action would you suggest be taken in each store to correct or improve maintenance and housekeeping?

CHAPTER 41

Service Policies

CHAPTER OUTCOMES

When you have mastered the information provided in this chapter, you should be able to:

1. List the four major categories of store services

2. Identify at least five selling and shopping services

3. Define the term *personal shopping services*

4. List five different delivery policies that a store may adopt

5. Give examples of *convenience services*

6. Name two kinds of profit services

7. Explain the purpose of a store's community service activities

Many customer conveniences are provided through good store location and layout. Other services are provided through credit and merchandising policies. Many stores, however, provide a large number of other customer services. Some of these services are merchandise related (wrapping, delivery, and installation), while some are nonmerchandising services (restaurants, parcel checking, exhibits, and entertainment). In larger stores, these services are under the supervision of a customer-services manager who is in the operating division.

SERVICE POLICIES

The service policies of the retail store, such as those listed in Illustration 41–1, are intended to reinforce a certain image in the minds of customers before, during, and after the sale. All the services that a store provides help to create the personality of the store. There are four different categories of services that a store may provide: selling and shopping services, convenience services, profit services, and community services. Most customers are influenced by the store's **selling and shopping services.** These services, such as delivery, are associated with the selling of the merchandise carried by the store. **Convenience services** are the many nonmerchandise services provided for customers, such as rest rooms. The third category of services in retail stores is **profit services.** These services are available for a charge, and the store expects to make a profit from them. Engraving of jewelry bought in the store is a profit service. **Community services** are activities, such as

sponsorship of art shows, undertaken by the store on behalf of the community. The provision of services in any of these categories depends upon the image that the store is attempting to project.

SELLING AND SHOPPING SERVICES

The services associated with merchandise are the most used customer services. The presence or absence of a selling or shopping service, such as personal assistance, alterations, or delivery, may influence a customer's decision to buy.

Personal Selling and Self-services

Merchants are constantly asked how much personal selling effort is necessary to sell the merchandise carried in the store. In **personal selling,** a store staff person assists the customer in making a merchandise selection. Some customers perceive the salesperson as a source of accurate and detailed product information. Other customers see the salesperson as an obstacle and would rather serve themselves. People are particularly willing to wait on themselves when they think they are getting a low price by doing so. Others prefer personal attention and assistance, especially when buying major clothing items, home furnishings, or appliances.

If a store decides not to depend on personal selling, is it better to adopt self-service or self-selection? Under a **self-service** policy, the customers select items from an open display and take them to the checkout point where they pay for them. Under **self-**

SERVICE POLICIES

1. Selling and Shopping Services	2. Convenience Services	3. Profit Services	4. Community Services
Personal selling	Greeters at door	Installation and	Entertainment
Mail-order selling	Lounges and	repairs	Exhibits
Telephone selling	playrooms	Restaurants	Demonstrations
Personal shopping	Information desk	Snack counters	Lectures
service	Lost-and-found desk	Travel and ticket	Sponsorships
Fashion shows	Parcel checking	bureaus	Contributions
Wrapping and	Parking space	Insurance	
bagging	Telephones	Rentals	
Returns and	First-aid station	Photo finishing	
adjustments	Convenient store		
Delivery	hours		
Alterations			
Credit			
Layaway plans			

Illus. 41–1   The services a store provides help to create the store's personality.

selection, customers examine merchandise samples that are carefully labeled and described. After making a decision, the customer asks a clerk to get the selected article from stock to complete the sale.

Many department stores use a combination of service methods depending on the nature of the goods. For clothing and major home furnishings, personal selling is used. Candy and stationery are sold on a self-service basis. Other merchandise, such as accessories or housewares, is sold from self-selection counters.

Shopping Services

When developing a shopping-services policy, retailers must decide whether to provide mail and telephone orders, personal shopping, and similar services to help customers buy from the store. Mail-order and telephone shopping are becoming increasingly popular, but specialized store personnel are needed to handle these services well. The merchant must decide whether the added sales will be enough to cover the additional expenses of catalogs, large reserve stocks, extra employees, credit, and delivery of ordered goods.

A **personal shopper** provides individual assistance to customers who have little time to shop or need extra help in choosing merchandise. A personal shopper assembles articles in advance of the customers' store visits; accompanies customers to various departments; selects items for gifts; and, when the store has many boutiques, helps customers decide in which to shop. Personal shopping services are usually found in

Illus. 41–2 A careful selection of store services makes shopping easy and convenient for customers. Most services help the retailer indirectly by getting and keeping customers in the store.

prestigious stores, especially during certain holidays.

A **fashion show** is another form of shopping service. Whether conducted in the store or at other locations, fashion shows present a variety of merchandise and information in an interesting and appealing manner. The show permits the customer to see an entire collection of the latest fashions, compare choices, and make tentative selections.

Wrapping or Bagging

Almost all retail stores wrap or bag merchandise purchased by customers, though some retail stores sell merchandise, such as lawn mowers and furniture, that cannot be wrapped. The wrapping and bagging service may range from placing groceries in bags to placing high-fashion clothing in specially designed boxes or shopping bags. Other stores, such as specialty stores, make an effort to provide complete and unique store wrapping for customer purchases.

If store policy dictates that customer purchases shall be wrapped or bagged, the service policy also must indicate where it shall be done and by whom. Should the wrapping be done by the salesperson, by a special employee in the department, or by an employee at a central location in the store? In small stores, the most logical choice is to have the salesperson handle this task. In large stores, however, it is likely that a policy may provide for all three locations, depending upon the nature of the merchandise. The **salesperson wrap** is done at the point of sale by the person who has assisted the customer in the purchase.

Illus. 41–3 For most nonfashion goods, customers prefer self service, but they do want expert help if they have questions.

The **department wrap** is used when the wrapping may be time consuming or take special skills, such as the ability to pack china or crystal. **Central wrap** is used when a customer has made several purchases from various departments in the store and wishes them to be packed in one carton. Also, if merchandise is to be delivered or if there are special packaging requirements, central wrapping is used. Store policy must make it clear how the wrapping is to be done and under what circumstances it should be done in each location.

Returns and Adjustments

Many stores have adopted a liberal return policy. Thus, the customer who wishes to return an item or believes that an adjustment should be made is given prompt and often generous treatment. Many adjustments for returns are made in cash; if the returned item was purchased on credit, an adjustment consists of crediting the account. Merchants know that a cash adjustment is less costly because it eliminates record keeping and the red tape of a rigid return policy. Some stores, however, will not give cash when an item is returned. Instead they mail a check or give a credit slip that can be applied to other purchases, often within a certain time limit. Store policy may require that a return be accompanied by a sales slip and price tag and occur within a definite number of days after purchase.

Many stores have found that having returns, adjustments and complaints handled by the operating division, rather than by the sales staff, results in greater consistency and control. While most returns and exchanges can be handled better by the people who made the sales, serious complaints are handled more objectively by a unit of the operating division.

Delivery Services

The delivery policy of a store depends on the type of store and on its other service policies. For example, supermarkets that make low price a major appeal may offer no delivery service. Department stores, furniture stores, and appliance stores usually make deliveries because it may be inconvenient for their customers to carry their purchases. Such stores usually insist that the value of the purchase be greater than a prescribed amount if the delivery is to be made at no cost to the customer.

A store may adopt one of five delivery policies:

1. It may provide no delivery service.
2. It may refuse to deliver or may charge for the delivery of small packages or those that cost less than a stated amount, such as $50; but it may deliver costly and bulky articles free.
3. It may charge for all deliveries.
4. It may deliver in case of emergency only.
5. It may deliver all purchases at least to the immediate market area, free of extra charge.

Until recently, stores that provided delivery service usually made no charge except for out-of-town deliveries involving mail or express deliveries. The delivery costs were viewed as operating expenses. In effect, then, all customers were sharing the cost of delivery even though many did not use the service. Today many stores, as standard practice, charge for delivery and price the goods at a take-with price.

What follows are the major kinds of delivery service:

1. *Independent delivery service:* the store owns and operates its own service, and delivery people act as store representatives.
2. *Consolidated delivery service:* a private agency, such as United Parcel Service, contracts for the delivery service of a store or group of stores; the agency is paid a fee based on the number and types of parcels.
3. *Cooperative delivery service:* a group of stores in the same community or shopping mall agree to provide joint delivery service.
4. *Express company or messenger company delivery service:* an outside transport company provides delivery service for a store as a sideline.
5. *Parcel-post service:* delivery is made through the U.S. Postal Service. While slow for local delivery, it is commonly used for out-of-town delivery.

Alterations

For many stores, especially those selling clothing or home furnishings, an important service is that of alterations. Workroom operations, such as clothing alterations and drapery finishing, are often essential to selling clothes and home furnishings. Clothing often needs to be shortened, lengthened, or adjusted in some way to get the desired fit. Customers like the convenience of having alterations made by the store where the goods are purchased.

Traditionally, the better clothing stores provided free alterations on regularly priced merchandise. This tradition is changing. Some stores are charging even for minor clothing changes. In most cases, though, the customer is charged the retailer's cost for the alterations—the retailer does not earn profit on the alteration services.

Workroom operations need close supervision. The variability of workloads, for example, may result in excess alterations staff during some periods and overtime rates during other periods.

For these reasons, some stores have stopped making alterations and refer customers to private individuals. When making such referrals, retailers should be sure that the person will do a good job, since the quality of work will reflect on the store.

CONVENIENCE SERVICES

Many retail stores provide services that are designed to make shopping a pleasure. These services need not relate to any products or services the stores may sell. In many cases, stores may cooperate with other stores to provide convenience services. For example, several stores located in a shopping district may share the cost of developing a parking lot for customers.

In-store Services

Stores may have door attendants or greeters and provide lounges for customers. At Wal-Mart, it is standard policy for an employee to greet each customer and offer a cart. Information desks, lost-and-found departments, rest rooms, and first-aid stations are provided by large stores and shopping malls. Some stores provide playrooms where preschool-age children can play under supervision while parents shop. Pay phones and parcel-checking lockers are also conveniences that many shoppers appreciate. Parking near or adjacent to the store is, of course, one of the important convenience services.

Store Hours

In the past, most stores, except neighborhood and convenience-goods stores, had a policy of being open from about 9:00 A.M. to 6:00 P.M. six days a week. Changes in customer life-styles have led to marked changes in store hours. Many stores now stay open seven days and six evenings a week. In many cities, the common opening hour is 10:00 A.M. Some supermarkets stay open 24 hours a day, seven days a week.

In communities where laws do not prevent it, many stores, especially those in shopping malls, are open on Sundays from noon to 6:00 P.M. Store hours depend partly on the policies of competing stores in the shopping area. The added cost of extended hours has to be measured against the added sales. Most merchants have found that the extra business and customer goodwill justify the extra hours.

PROFIT SERVICES

Profit services provided by retail stores are of two kinds. One relates directly to the merchandise carried by the store. For exam-

ple, installation of carpet sold by the store is provided to customers for a charge. The other kind of profit service relates to customer convenience and is illustrated by food service. Customers who can get a meal in a store restaurant or a snack in a coffee shop will also tend to spend more shopping time in the store or mall. The purpose of profit services is to earn enough income to cover all expenses of offering the services and also provide a profit.

The number of profit services being adopted by retail stores is increasing. Some stores provide travel and ticket bureaus where customers can buy tickets for sporting events, theatre events, and travel tours. Examples of other profit services include hair styling, optometry, key cutting, photo finishing, insurance, and car or equipment rentals. Some of these services may not always produce significant revenue, but they do have immense value in getting and keeping customers in the store.

Some profit services are made available through lease agreements. Under a **lease agreement,** or concession, service is provided by nonstore personnel who pay the store a fee, often a percentage of sales. Thus, space for a travel agency or a restaurant may be leased to an independent operator to run according to certain store policies. Because a service is leased does not mean that the store operating division can forget about the service. The fact that such services are provided within the store makes it essential that customers be completely satisfied with them. Customers often judge the entire store by the quality of service they get from an in-store restaurant or insurance office. Because of such customer reaction, stores must consider carefully whether to actually provide such services or to sign a lease agreement.

COMMUNITY SERVICES

Stores are often asked to sponsor softball and bowling teams and beauty contestants and to supply holiday baskets for the needy. To attract community interest, stores may set up exhibits of art, sports cars, or antiques. They may also provide live entertainment or informative lectures by well-known persons. The store manager and other store staff may be members of Lions, Rotary, Kiwanis, or other civic groups engaged in community projects. More and more stores include in their budgets financial contributions for community activities. Some stores make space available for community activities. The use of store meeting rooms, parking lots, and the common areas of malls by various community groups brings additional people into the stores. The purpose of store involvement with community activities is to tie the people of the community more closely to the store as a center for community events.

Development of policy on involvement in community services must be taken seriously by both large and small retail firms. Community requests for money or employees' time can quickly exceed what the store can realistically provide. Store policy must specify what and how much will be provided.

CUSTOMER RELATIONS

Customer relations is not a service in the same sense as the others mentioned in this chapter. Policies on customer relations set forth the attitude that store personnel should have while the other services are being provided. The adage "The customer is always right" is a simple customer-relations policy. Store policies, no matter how generous and accommodating, do not in themselves assure good customer relations. The way in which customer services are provided often makes as much of an impression as the service itself. The store's customer-relations policy should assure that customers are given polite attention and their comments are listened to carefully. When the response is—as it must be at times—a refusal to make an adjustment, store personnel should make every effort to maintain the customer's goodwill.

Summary   Merchants must set four different categories of service policies: selling and shopping services, convenience services, profit services, and community services. The services most commonly used by customers are those associated with merchandise. Selling and shopping services include personal selling, self-service, self-selection, wrapping or bagging, returns and adjustments, delivery, and alterations. Convenience services are nonmerchandise efforts to make shopping more comfortable to customers. Examples of convenience services are information desks, parking, and appropriate store hours. Some stores provide services for the purpose of making a profit. Profit services include restaurants, insurance desks, and equipment rentals. Community services are contributions of money, staff time, or store facilities for the purpose of supporting some activity of interest to the community. These services may include sponsorship of sports teams, contests, or entertainment programs. As important as the service policy is the way in which the service is provided. A store's customer relations policy states how, in general, customers are to be treated to maintain their goodwill.

Review

1. List and describe the four major categories of store services.
2. List five selling and shopping services.
3. What is the difference between self-service and self-selection?
4. List five delivery policies.
5. List the major kinds of delivery services.
6. Give two examples of convenience services.
7. What are the two kinds of profit services?
8. How do customer relations differ from other store services?

Terms

The following terms were introduced in this chapter. Write a separate sentence correctly using each new term.

central wrap
community services
convenience services
department wrap
fashion show
lease agreement
personal selling

personal shopper
profit services
salesperson wrap
self-selection
self-service
selling and shopping services

Discuss

1. What customer services would help give an image of quality merchandise and good value?
2. For what types of goods is personal selling better than either self-service or self-selection?
3. Many discount food and variety stores are asking customers to wrap or bag their own purchases after checkout. Is this a good strategy for these merchants? Why?
4. Some supermarkets and drugstores are offering free delivery within 24 hours on any telephone orders over $25. What benefits do the stores get from this service?

5. Although a cash adjustment on a merchandise return is less costly to a retailer, more and more merchants are making adjustments only by credit slips. Is this a good policy? Why?

*Problem
Solving*

1. The Desert Shop is a small gift and western antique store located in a shopping mall. The shop features a variety of items for home and office. The store, owned by Trish Moore, has three full-time and three part-time employees. Prepare a complete set of suggested service policies for this store.
2. Find two retail stores in your community that deliver purchases. What is the delivery policy of each store?
3. Identify a large store in your community. Develop a list of the community services provided by this store. Beside each service, give what you believe to be the reasons the store provides that service.

CHAPTER 42

Credit and Collection

CHAPTER OUTCOMES

When you have mastered the information provided in this chapter, you should be able to:

1. Describe the three basic types of retail credit plans

2. Explain how retail stores use bank credit-card plans

3. Explain the three C's of credit granting

4. Describe the credit-scoring procedure

5. Describe the features of a good credit collection procedure

6. Explain the legal actions a retailer may take when a customer fails to pay a credit obligation

7. Describe four measures that can be used to determine the effectiveness of a collection policy

In modern American society, there is little reluctance to buy goods on credit or to finance a major purchase such as furniture or an automobile. Low-income customers must be granted credit if they are to buy many of the goods they desire, and nearly all customers expect to be able to buy on credit as a personal convenience. Most retailers who wish to make shopping easy and convenient for their customers are faced, therefore, with providing credit and developing a credit and collection policy.

The retailer who is just getting started in business or who is operating with limited capital is wise to do business on a cash basis so as to conserve capital. Also, where merchandise has low unit value and the typical customer purchase is fairly small, cash-only sales are advisable. For example, most food stores operate well on a cash-only basis. Other stores handling more expensive merchandise, such as clothing or home appliances, must grant credit. The nature of our economic system makes both cash and credit selling necessary.

RETAIL CREDIT PLANS

Once a retailer decides that customers should be allowed to make credit purchases, the next question is whether the store should operate its own credit program. Merchants who establish their own credit programs usually adopt one or more of these basic retail credit plans: (1) open, or regular, credit account; (2) deferred, or revolving, credit account; and (3) installment plan. A modified form of credit is the layaway plan.

Open Account

Under the first and most common credit plan—the **open,** or **regular, account**—a customer is billed each month for purchases made during the previous month. The customer is expected to pay promptly. Limits as to the amount each customer may purchase on credit and owe at one time are set, but the store may allow the customer to exceed these limits. The store does not have the right to repossess (take back) the goods bought on an open account but not paid for, but the store can sue for the amount owed.

Deferred Credit Account

In recent years, retail stores have introduced a modified open account called a **deferred,** or **revolving, account.** For buyers of nondurable goods who want to pay a small sum each month rather than the full amount of their monthly purchases, a **service charge**—generally about 1 to 1¾ percent of the balance due—is added to their monthly account balances. As the customers make their monthly payments, they are allowed to buy more as long as their account balance does not exceed the credit limit established for their accounts.

Installment Plan

For those customers who wish to make a major purchase of an expensive durable good and pay for the item over a long period, the *installment plan* of credit is available. Under the **installment plan,** the buyer is required to sign a contract agreeing to make a series of payments of a stated amount for the merchandise purchased. Usually, a finance charge is added to the purchase price of the item, a downpayment is made, and the balance due is spread over a series of 12, 24, or 36 monthly payments.

Layaway Plan

To help customers who may not qualify for credit, many stores provide a **layaway plan.** If the customer selects an item that costs more than he or she can afford to pay in cash, the store will hold the item in a layaway, or holding, room. The customer agrees to make regular payments until the full purchase price of the item has been paid. The goods are then delivered to the customer or picked up on a scheduled date. Most retailers charge a small fee, sometimes a percentage of the purchase, for use of the layaway plan.

OUTSIDE FINANCING OF RETAIL CREDIT

For many retailers, the cost of operating their own credit systems is more than the cost of using outside systems. They may choose to operate their own systems, however, because of their value in attracting and holding customers. Retailers who prefer using outside credit systems may select from several that are available in our credit-oriented society.

Bank Credit Plan

Under the **bank credit plan,** a bank grants a customer a certain amount of credit and charges a 1 to 1¾ percent monthly service fee on the unpaid balance. For instance, Lee Williams arranges for bank credit of $500. He can write checks for up to $500. As the amount charged is repaid, the money again becomes available to Lee. He pays a service fee only on what he owes. For example, Lee buys two tires for $190 and pays for them with a bank-credit check. Sixty days later, he pays $190 to the bank. The bank charges Lee 1 percent (monthly rate) on the $190 for 60 days *($190 × 0.01% = 1.90 × 2 = $3.80 fee).*

Factoring

Retailers who sell on installment plans often lack the capital to carry a great number of contracts for long periods of time. In such situations, the retailer may resort to factoring. **Factoring** is the practice of selling installment contracts, or accounts receivable, to a finance company at a discount. Thus, a retailer with $4,000 in installment contracts may sell these contracts to a finance company for $3,760. The customer's responsibility for payment is then no longer to the retailer but to the firm that has bought the contract.

Bank Credit Card Plans

A **bank credit card** is issued to an approved applicant who pays an annual fee, usually about $20. The major bank card

Charge Account Agreement

THIS IS A COPY OF YOUR ORIGINAL AGREEMENT WITH WHITES . . . .

PLEASE RETAIN IT FOR YOUR RECORDS.

CHARGE ACCOUNT AGREEMENT: WHITES — Cleveland, Ohio: I agree to the following regarding all merchandise and services purchased on my Whites Charge Account:

1. For all purchases made on my account—I will pay the time sale price consisting of the cash sale price, delivery and handling charges, and taxes, if any, plus any **FINANCE CHARGE** computed at the following monthly periodic rates: **1.75%** (minimum **50¢** on balance under **$28.85**) on the portion of the "Average Daily Balance" of my account of **$350.00** or less, and **1%** on that portion of such balance in excess of **$350.00**. **"ANNUAL PERCENTAGE RATE"** is **21.0% and 12%** respectively. I understand and agree that the **"FINANCE CHARGE"** and other credit terms of this Agreement may be changed by you upon prior notice to me in the manner provided by law and in such event the new terms will be applicable to my previous balance effective on the billing date after such notification and to all subsequent purchases made by me.

2. If I do not pay the entire "New Balance", you may assess a **FINANCE CHARGE** (or 50¢ minimum) computed on the amount appearing as the "Average Daily Balance" on my current statement. The daily balance outstanding in my account is determined by deducting payments and credits from the previous day's ending balance and by adding charges and purchases, if any. The "Average Daily Balance" is the sum of the outstanding daily balances in my account during the monthly billing cycle, divided by the number of days in the monthly billing cycle. The length of monthly billing cycles may vary. Unpaid **FINANCE CHARGES** shall be a part of the daily balances upon which the **FINANCE CHARGE** is computed.

3. When there is an unpaid balance in my account at the close of a billing cycle, I will make a payment on the account within 20 days of the closing date shown on my monthly statement. That payment may be any amount up to and including the "New Balance," but not less than the minimum payment each month (shown below). I have the right at any time to pay in full the amount of the "New Balance" of my monthly statement. If payment of the full amount of the "New Balance" is actually received by you each month by the date shown on the bill (my next closing date), I will avoid payment of a **FINANCE CHARGE** on purchases shown on the statement. If I have a "Previous Balance," I will also avoid payment of an additional **FINANCE CHARGE** on that balance by paying the full amount of the "New Balance" by the date shown. If I choose to make monthly payments, I will pay by the date shown on my current statement, not less than my scheduled minimum monthly payment, which will

remain at the highest amount required by my highest account balance as shown in your current table of credit terms below until my account is paid in full.

*Minimum Monthly Payment	$ 7	8	9	10	11	12	13	14	15	16
Highest Account Balance	$140	160	180	200	240	280	310	340	370	400
*Minimum Monthly Payment	$ 17	18	19	20	21	22	23	24	25	
Highest Account Balance	$430	460	490	520	550	580	610	640	670	

*The monthly payments stated are based on the item price without delivery and handling charges. For account balances over $670, the minimum monthly payment is increased by $1 for each $30 (or any part thereof) additional credit.

Payments made by me shall be applied first to the payment of **FINANCE CHARGES** and then to the payment of the respective amounts financed in the order in which the entries to my account are made.

4. You may add a charge of **$2.00** to my account for any check or other type of remittance tendered as payment on my account which is returned as unpaid or uncollected for any reason. You may investigate my credit record and furnish information on my account to credit reporting agencies or others who may properly receive such information.

5. Upon default by me, unless I cure the default, you may declare the entire balance due and payable without notice and you may take such steps as are provided by law to require payment of the unpaid balance of my account.

6. This Agreement and each purchase made on my account shall be subject to acceptance by you at Cleveland, Ohio. This Agreement shall be deemed a contract made in Ohio and I acknowledge and agree that the laws of the State of Ohio shall govern all credit terms and our respective rights and duties under this Agreement and its enforceability. Should any provision hereof be finally determined inconsistent with or contrary to applicable law, such provision shall be deemed omitted or amended to conform with such law without affecting any other provision or the validity of this Agreement. If I have applied for a joint account, I represent that my spouse has authorized me to do so and that both of us agree to be jointly and severally bound by the terms of this Agreement. You also have the right, from time to time, to determine and modify the amount of credit that will be extended on my account and to terminate my charge privileges without prior notice.

NOTICE TO ACCOUNT HOLDER: DO NOT SIGN THIS AGREEMENT BEFORE YOU READ IT OR IF IT CONTAINS BLANK SPACES. YOU ARE ENTITLED TO A COPY OF THE AGREEMENT YOU SIGN. KEEP YOUR COPY, WHEN RECEIVED, TO PROTECT YOUR LEGAL RIGHTS. YOU MAY AT ANYTIME PAY OFF THE FULL UNPAID BALANCE OF YOUR ACCOUNT.
I authorize you to investigate my credit record.

Sign Here: Account Holder's Signature   Date   Signature of Spouse or Co-account Holder if Joint Account   Date

NOTICE: ANY HOLDER OF THIS CONSUMER CREDIT CONTRACT IS SUBJECT TO ALL CLAIMS AND DEFENSES WHICH THE DEBTOR COULD ASSERT AGAINST THE SELLER OF GOODS OR SERVICES OBTAINED PURSUANT HERETO OR WITH THE PROCEEDS HEREOF. RECOVERY HEREUNDER BY THE DEBTOR SHALL NOT EXCEED AMOUNTS PAID BY THE DEBTOR HEREUNDER.

Illus. 42–1   This credit agreement accommodates state-to-state differences in credit requirements. It is a contract for a revolving credit account that may be treated as an open account. Retailers must be sure that charge account agreements are clearly written and fully explained to credit customers.

systems belong to either the Interbank (MasterCard) or Americard (Visa). The banks and stores agree to accept cards issued by any member bank. Subscribing stores sell on credit to any customer presenting a card, provided that validation verification indicates the card has not been cancelled, the credit limit has not been exceeded, and the customer is who she or he claims to be. Charge slips for each bank card credit purchase are given to the bank that issued the credit. The bank credits the store's account for the amount of the customer's purchase, less an agreed percentage, usually about 1 to 3½ percent. Thus, if a retailer sells a bank credit card customer an item for $100, the bank will pay the retailer from $96.50 to $99.00 depending on their agreement. The bank then, rather than the retailer, bills the customer and accepts the risk of customer default. Customers who do not pay within a given period, usually 30 days, are charged a finance fee that may be from about 11.4 to 19.8 percent annually.

Other Credit Card Plans

Carte Blanche, Diners Club, American Express, and similar organizations specialize in granting credit for customer's use in member restaurants, hotels, airlines, and various retail establishments. These cards are usually referred to as T & E (travel and entertainment) charge cards and are issued for a yearly fee (typically $40 to $100) to persons who are recognized as excellent credit risks. Merchants who accept these cards are reimbursed by the card grantor for the amount of the customer's purchase minus a fee, usually from 3 to 5 percent. The charge card grantor assumes the risks and collection costs.

Abuse of Credit Cards

With the dramatic increase in the use of credit cards, credit abuse has increased. To counteract this, merchants regularly verify credit card purchases to assure the card is not stolen and the credit limit has not been exceeded. The merchant may be required to call a central bureau for clearance of *all* charges above a certain amount. Usually, the credit cardholder is responsible for only $50 worth of charges made by an unauthorized user. The cardholder is responsible for no unauthorized charges if loss of the card is reported immediately.

Illus. 42–2   A customer's credit record usually is checked by the cashier before a credit-card purchase can be completed. Some electronic cash registers have systems built in that verify credit-card purchases.

Illus. 42–3 Important factors about a credit applicant must be determined before a retailer grants credit.

GRANTING CREDIT

When retailers, bankers, or other lenders decide to give credit, they must determine the standards that prospective credit customers must meet. Three important factors must be considered in granting credit to an applicant: (1) character, (2) capacity, and (3) capital. These are called the three C's of credit.

Character

Character, as it relates to granting credit, is the customer's honesty. This honesty may be indicated by the customer's liv-

ing habits and reputation in the community, by the judgment of associates, by the stability of the customer's employment, and by his or her payment habits in the past.

Information about character is obtained largely from a **retail credit bureau** to which a merchant and lender may subscribe. The credit bureau accumulates from each merchant complete information about her or his experience with each credit customer. The local credit bureaus are generally members of a national association, which makes it possible for any member merchant to obtain information about the payment habits of almost any customer in the United States. Customers who think they have been unfairly denied credit have the legal right to examine their files and correct any inaccuracies.

Capacity

Capacity, as a factor in granting credit, is the customer's ability to earn and to pay. The merchant must decide whether the applicant's education, skill, and intelligence are such that the applicant will retain steady employment with enough income to warrant the granting of credit.

The credit grantor must develop the ability to forecast an applicant's probable earnings. When credit is extended to low-income customers, capacity is the chief consideration. The credit manager who is able to forecast earning power accurately will be successful in increasing the store's business without undue loss.

Capital

Capital, as it relates to credit, is the applicant's assets that can be seized in case he or she fails to pay. Owning a home or having a savings account indicates ability to pay that influences merchants in granting credit.

An applicant's capital can be determined from personal references, statements of bank accounts, business ownership, or a credit bureau. In the past, capital was given more weight by the credit evaluator than it is today. Ability and willingness to pay in the future, rather than present assets, are what really count.

CREDIT SCORING

A formal rating plan may be developed to evaluate applications for credit. The characteristics of those customers who regularly pay their bills and those who do not are analyzed. Studies show that a person's marital status, occupation, salary bracket, presence of a home phone, length of time at present address, type of residence (owned or rented), length of time with present employer, and status of other charge accounts are factors clearly related to credit performance.

Point values are applied to each of these factors. For example, three points may be awarded if you rent an apartment, five points if you rent a house, eight points if you own your apartment, and ten points if you own your house. The actual point value for each factor would be based on past repayment success of credit applicants. Applicants who do not exceed a total minimum score will not be extended credit. Customers who score well above the minimum are given a higher credit line than those who score the minimum. The point values and the minimum acceptable scores have to be developed by each store or lender.

COLLECTION PROCEDURES

A credit sale is not complete until the customer has paid the bill. The merchant who does a large volume of business on credit and who does not insist on prompt payment will soon be short of capital with which to purchase additional goods and to pay expenses. The merchant needs sound policies and procedures for collecting late payments to make sure that too much money is not tied up in accounts receivable.

The term *collection* does not refer to the normal receipt of payments at the time agreed upon by merchant and customer. Rather, *collection* refers to getting payments that are past due. Perhaps the most important part of setting up a good collection procedure is to do everything possible to encourage prompt payment. Merchants who have their own credit program have learned that the following steps encourage prompt payment:

1. Choosing carefully the customer to whom credit will be extended
2. Emphasizing to new credit customers that they have an obligation to make their payments promptly
3. Sending out bills at exactly the time agreed upon
4. Following up immediately on any accounts in which there is a delay in payment

With good credit management and effective collection procedures, most stores have been able to keep their losses on uncollectible accounts to a fraction of 1 percent of their total credit sales. An effective credit policy specifies when and how the retailer will follow up to collect from customers whose payments are overdue. In addition, the policy indicates how the effectiveness of collection procedures will be measured.

Follow-up Plans

An orderly follow-up plan for credit accounts must be established. Accounts-receivable records should be reviewed at regular intervals to spot those that are delinquent (past due). Computerized credit records make it possible to determine automatically those credit accounts that are de-

linquent. As charges and payments are made on an account, the transactions are automatically stored. Periodic reports on the status of each or all accounts can be obtained.

In stores without computerized records, a manual system called a **tickler file** is used. A card for each delinquent account is filed under the date when the next collection effort is to be made. Payments received are marked on the cards that are checked each day. If payment on an account has not been received by the date specified for it, a follow-up notice is sent to the person having the delinquent account.

Classifying Delinquent Accounts

The same collection methods are not applied to all delinquent accounts. Stores usually classify customers having past-due accounts as good risks, fair risks, or poor risks.

A **good risk** is a customer who, in the past, has shown character, capacity, and capital but who is temporarily negligent. Such a customer is treated leniently in the retailer's collection policy.

A **fair risk** is a customer who can be relied upon to pay but who tends to put off payments. Most delinquent accounts belong to customers who are fair risks. A fair-risk customer with an open or revolving account should not be pushed too hard for payment. However, quick, positive action is warranted on any customer with a delinquent installment plan.

A **poor risk** is a customer whose credit rating is barely good enough to be granted credit and who has a low credit limit. Some poor-risk customers will prove unwilling to pay unless collection pressure is prompt and stern. A small percentage may have no intention of meeting their obligations.

Communicating with Delinquent Account Customers

An account is not considered delinquent until the customer has failed to respond to the regular statement mailed by the store at the end of the billing period. To give the customer every opportunity to make payment, the store generally allows some time to elapse between the time the statement is sent and the time collection follow-up begins. The collection follow-up usually begins with the mailing of a duplicate of the regular statement. No additional comment or reminder is included in the first step. The second step may be to send a similar statement that contains a notice or a special message, such as "Please note this account is 30 days past due." If the second statement brings no results, a series of letters probably should follow. In an automated credit system, the follow-up statements and letters are issued automatically by computer at specified times. Each letter in the series is more urgent in its demand for payment. Key phrases in a series are: "Your account is overdue; prompt payment of outstanding balance is requested"; "We have had no response to our notice that your account is overdue. If payment cannot be made in 15 days, please call"; "Since no payment has been made on your overdue account, no additional credit can be extended until the account is paid in full."

Some merchants prefer to call the customer on the telephone rather than send a reminder through the mail. A telephone call gives the customer a chance to air complaints about a product, price, or service that may be delaying payment. Telephone communication with a credit customer often leads to a quick settlement of the overdue account.

When a customer fails to pay after receiving several overdue notices, the merchant must decide whether the individual should be continued as a credit customer. Some merchants put a hold on an account after it has been delinquent for a certain period, say 90 days, permitting no more charges to be made. Other merchants do not withdraw credit privileges until legal action is taken to obtain payment. The goal of careful credit collection communication is to keep the individual as a satisfied customer, one who will continue to do business with the store.

Legal Action

If letters and phone calls fail to get the customer to pay, the merchant may have to resort to other actions. For some, this means using an outside agency to collect payment of the delinquent account. Customers should be notified when their accounts are being turned over to an outside **collection agency.** The agency will charge the merchant a certain percentage of the amount collected as a fee for services.

Some merchants choose to bring legal action in court. **Legal action** can be pursued in three ways. When goods are sold on an open or a revolving account, the merchant can recover the amount due only by suing in court for the amount of the debt. If, however, the merchandise is sold on an installment plan, with the seller retaining title, the merchant has the right to repossess the property and resell it. If the amount received on resale is less than the amount owed, the customer can be held responsible for the balance. Another form of legal action that can be brought by a merchant against a debtor is *garnishment.* In **garnishment,** the merchant obtains in court an order to the debtor's employer to pay the merchant a certain percentage of the debtor's wages until the amount of the debt has been paid.

Using a collection agency or taking legal action should be considered carefully. Loss of customers' goodwill as a result of these actions can have a serious impact on a store. Persons who feel that a store deals unfairly with customers are likely to take their business elsewhere. A collection agency may proceed in a manner that could reflect poorly on the store. In the case of legal action, the cost of a lawsuit can sometimes exceed what might be recovered from the debtor.

EFFECTIVENESS OF COLLECTION POLICIES

Merchants mostly rely on four measures to determine whether collection policies are effective: (1) the bad debt loss index, (2) the collection percentage, (3) the accounts receivable turnover rate, and (4) the age analysis of accounts. A particular retailer would likely use two or more of these measures.

A **bad debt** is an account due that the merchant feels will not be collected. It is a

loss for the merchant. The **bad debt loss index** is calculated by dividing the bad debts incurred during a period (usually a month or year) by the total credit sales for that period. For example, Sand Hill Fashion Store had credit sales of $29,300 for the past year. During that period, it was determined that $879 in credit accounts could not be collected. The bad debt loss index is 0.03 *($879 ÷ $29,300).* The bad debt loss index and other debt collection calculations are shown in Illustration 42–4.

Separate indexes can be calculated for open accounts, revolving accounts, and installment sales. A merchant may have a policy that all past-due accounts that are not collected after 18 months are to be considered bad debts. If the bad debt index rises over several months, the merchant knows that the credit granting and collection procedures of the store are not working very well. If, on the other hand, the bad debt index remains at a satisfactory level or falls, then the credit procedures may be working as planned.

To figure out the **collection percentage,** the merchant divides the payments made by credit customers during a certain period by the accounts receivable outstanding at the beginning of that period. If accounts receivable at the beginning of a month amounted to $4,450 and customers made payments of $3,738 on credit accounts during the month, the collection percentage would be 84.0 *($3,738 ÷ $4,450 = 0.84 × 100).*

The **annual accounts receivable turnover rate** is computed by dividing the total yearly credit sales by the average amount owed each month. The Sand Hill Fashion Store had average monthly accounts receivable of $3,755 during the year it had $29,300 in credit sales. The accounts receivable turnover rate is 7.80 *($29,300 ÷ $3,755)*.

A goal for the Sand Hill Fashion Store management might be to get the accounts receivable turnover rate closer to ten. The

PERFORMANCE MEASURES FOR DEBT COLLECTION

Bad Debt Loss Index

Divide bad debts incurred by total credit sales for same period. Example: Credit sales for past year equal $48,000; bad debts equal $960.

$$\$960 ÷ \$48,000 = 0.02$$

This means that for every dollar of goods sold on credit there was a bad debt loss of 2 cents.

Collection Percentage

Divide payments made on credit by the accounts receivable outstanding at the beginning of that period. Example: Customers made credit payments of $3,600 during March. Accounts receivable on March 1 was $7,200.

$$\$3,600 ÷ \$7,200 = 0.50$$

This figure represents a 50 percent collection rate.

Accounts Receivable Turnover Rate

Divide total yearly credit sales by average amount owed each month. Example: Yearly credit sales equal $48,000 and average accounts receivable each month equal $6,000.

$$\$48,000 ÷ \$6,000 = 8$$

Note: To get average monthly accounts receivable you need to know the monthly accounts receivable. Add all months and divide by 12.

Aging of Accounts

Determine length of time accounts are past due. Use a classification system to determine the number or percentage of accounts past due for certain periods of time. Example: Your store has 100 past-due credit accounts: 36 are 30 days past due; 24 are 4 months past due; 21 are 7 months past due; and 19 are more than 1 year past due. Thus, using a four-category classification:

30 to 60 days past due	36	= 36 percent
60 days to 6 months past due	24	= 24 percent
6 months to 1 year past due	21	= 21 percent
1 year or more past due	19	= 19 percent
	100	100 percent

Illus. 42–4   Knowing these calculations helps retailers understand the need for efficient credit collection.

higher the turnover, the more efficient the store's collection procedures are.

Finding out how long a merchant's accounts receivable are past due is called **aging of accounts.** To age accounts, a store may set up four classes of past-due accounts: (1) accounts 30 to 60 days past due; (2) accounts 60 days to six months delinquent; (3) accounts six months to one year past due; and (4) accounts more than one year overdue. Computer analysis of accounts can provide store credit staff the age of all accounts receivable at any time.

Many accounts in classes three and four indicate that the collection procedures are not effective. Merchants have observed that retail credit accounts less than three months overdue are about 90 percent collectible. Accounts that are one year or more past due are likely to be only 30 percent collectible. Only a small percentage of accounts two years overdue are ever collected. These figures emphasize the importance of establishing good credit and collection policies and procedures.

Summary

Customers expect most retail stores to provide credit for the purchases they make. The retailer may make one or more credit plans available: open or regular credit, deferred or revolving credit, and installment credit. Merchants may design and operate their own credit systems or use outside credit systems. Outside systems include bank credit, bank credit cards (Visa and MasterCard) or specialized credit or charge-card plans (Diners Club, Carte Blanche, and American Express). When operating their own credit plans, retailers will consider applicants' character, capacity, and capital. A formal rating plan, called *scoring,* can help determine which applicants should be given credit and how much.

Collection procedures are an important part of extending credit to customers. *Collection* refers to how the merchant intends to collect past-due payments from credit customers. Prompt follow-up on all overdue accounts is vital. Customers may be classified as good risks, fair risks, or poor risks. Collection procedures will be different for each. Direct communication with customers who have overdue accounts is important. When planned follow-up efforts on overdue accounts fail, the retailer may use an outside collection agency, take legal action by suing in court, repossess property sold under an installment contract, or obtain court-ordered garnishment of the debtor's wages. Effectiveness of collection procedures can be measured by calculating a bad debt loss index, collection percentage, and accounts receivable turnover rate or by aging accounts.

Review

1. Name three basic credit plans.
2. Define *layaway plan*.
3. Describe how bank credit-card plans work.
4. Name the three C's of granting credit.
5. What customer characteristics are considered in credit scoring?
6. List four actions that can be taken by merchants to encourage prompt payment of credit obligations.
7. Describe a fair-risk credit customer.
8. What three types of legal action can a merchant take against a customer having a delinquent credit account?
9. List four measures of collection policy effectiveness.

Terms

The following terms were introduced in this chapter. Write a separate sentence correctly using each new term.

aging of accounts	factoring
annual accounts receivable turnover rate	fair risk
	garnishment
bad debt	good risk
bad debt loss index	installment plan
bank credit card	layaway plan
bank credit plan	legal action
capacity	open or regular account
capital	poor risk
character	retail credit bureau
collection agency	service charge
collection percentage	tickler file
deferred or revolving account	

Discuss

1. Which types of stores are least likely to need or use a credit program? Which stores are most likely to need a credit program?
2. What should retailers consider when choosing between bank credit-card plans and their own revolving credit plans?
3. Under what circumstances should a store take away the credit privileges of a customer?
4. At what point in the collection process is a telephone call to the debtor likely to be most effective?

Problem Solving

1. Assume that you are the owner of a sporting goods store and that you operate your own credit program. Would you extend credit to either of the following applicants? Why or why not?

A. Doug R.: age 23, single, currently unemployed. Owns a 2-year-old sports car and has half interest in a water-skiing boat. Attends a community college and lives in the college dorm. Doug R. works on a painting crew in the summer and lives on his savings during the year.

B. Lisa S.: age 27, married, one child, currently employed as a delivery person. Owns a 5-year-old car that is paid for. Rents a small house and is taking evening classes in interior decorating.

2. Assume that you extended credit to both Doug R. and Lisa S. Doug has charged $560 worth of merchandise and made one payment of $60. The balance of $500 is now 120 days overdue. Lisa S. has charged $520 worth of merchandise and has made five monthly payments of $60. The balance of $220 is 120 days overdue. What collection procedure would you use in each case? Describe step-by-step what you would do in each situation.

3. After a year of business, you find that you have incurred $350 of bad debts on credit sales of $33,000. At the end of the next year, you find that you have incurred $575 of bad debts on credit sales of $42,500. What is your bad debt loss index for the first year? the second year? If the average bad debt loss index for stores such as yours is 0.009, how do you assess your performance?

4. If, on annual credit sales of $43,000, you have an average monthly accounts receivable of $3,800, what is your annual accounts receivable turnover rate? If the next year you have annual credit sales of $56,000 and an average monthly accounts receivable of $7,100, what is your annual accounts receivable turnover rate? Would you consider this an improvement in your credit procedures? Explain.

CHAPTER 43

Receiving and Checking Incoming Merchandise

CHAPTER OUTCOMES

When you have mastered the information provided in this chapter, you should be able to:

1. Explain how to achieve efficiency in handling incoming merchandise

2. Describe the activities that take place when merchandise arrives at the receiving point of a retail store

3. Discuss the kinds of receiving records and identification procedures that are followed when processing newly arrived merchandise

4. Describe each of the five basic steps in checking merchandise

5. List and describe methods that are commonly used to check merchandise quantity

6. Identify steps used to check merchandise quality

7. State the steps that should be followed when handling returns and claims against vendors

Shipments of new merchandise are received at Meadowbrook Hardware Store almost every day. Deliveries are made by the United States Postal Service, United Parcel Service, Emery Express, and various wholesale hardware freight trucks. The store manager expects that all new merchandise will be on the selling floor or in reserve stock one day after it is received. Store staff responsible for receiving goods must be constantly on the alert for any problem that will prevent merchandise from moving quickly to the selling floor or to stockrooms.

Merchandise coming into Meadowbrook Hardware Store goes through a series of steps that prepare it for sale: receiving the goods from the shipper, checking the merchandise, marking or tagging the individual items with a price and other identifying information, and placing the goods in stockrooms or moving the goods to an appropriate place on the selling floor. Proprietors of small stores may perform all of these steps themselves and use little special equipment in getting the goods prepared for selling. In large stores, however, elaborate equipment and several people may be employed to handle the movement of incoming merchandise.

EFFICIENCY IN RECEIVING MERCHANDISE

Successful retailers control operating expenses by efficiently handling incoming merchandise. What follows are several ways retailers hold down the costs of handling incoming goods.

The first way to hold down cost is to eliminate unnecessary reserve stockroom space. Reserve stock space is where goods are kept until they can be moved to space near or on the selling floor. Reserve stockroom space may be necessary because of limited forward stock (stock that is in the selling area) or selling space or because the firm buys goods in very large quantities. An alternative to moving stock for resale to the selling floor is to sell from models on the selling floor. Customers receive selected items directly from the stockroom. This procedure works especially well for appliances, power tools, and some furniture. Use of a reserve stock area means, however, that goods must be handled at least one extra time. Reducing or eliminating reserve stock space means that goods are handled less often and, therefore, more efficiently.

The second way is to reduce or eliminate duplication in the handling of goods in the checking and marking processes. Some merchants request that goods be delivered during a period when store traffic is light. Thus, goods can be received directly on the selling floor, checked, and placed into stock by sales staff. This method saves handling of goods and is an efficient use of store staff.

A third method to reduce costs is to place goods on the selling floor immediately after removal from the delivery truck, if possible. Some efficiency-minded retailers ask manufacturers to ship ready-to-wear garments on racks instead of placing them in boxes or cartons. Certain transportation companies will then take charge of the merchandise at the point of origin, premark it, and deliver the goods directly to the retail selling floor on racks. No additional preparation or marking is necessary.

The fourth method is to assign to one responsible employee all activities involved in getting incoming goods ready for resale. When one person is designated to handle receiving activities, that person can concentrate on procedures and practices that will be most effective for the store. He or she becomes an expert and can train others. This employee should have charge of the goods from the time the order is written by the buyer until the goods are placed in stock. In a large store, this employee may be called the **receiving manager** or the **traffic manager** and he or she may have a number of assistants to carry out the various activities of receiving goods.

Young people with limited retailing experience often qualify as receiving clerks, checkers, and markers. These are good beginning retail jobs for young persons because the jobs offer excellent opportunities to learn about merchandise, sources of supply, and pricing policies.

RECEIVING POINT

Receiving—actually taking physical possession of goods in the store—must be carried out quickly and smoothly. Every store should have a definite place where all merchandise is received, unpacked if necessary, checked, marked, and distributed. Most goods are shipped in containers and must be received at a definite location for unpacking and for completion of the other activities involved in getting the goods ready for sale.

The receiving point for many large stores and most shopping centers is a specially constructed dock area with platforms that can be adjusted to match the height of the tailgates of trucks. This arrangement facilitates the use of hand carts, forklifts, and conveyors that can move goods directly to where they will be checked. It avoids repeated handling of goods which often leads to merchandise damage. Receiving platforms are usually situated near the area where the goods are to be checked, marked, and stored.

Many merchandise shortages have been traced to losses occurring at the receiving point. Therefore, careful physical control is necessary. The fewer the number of receiving points, the more control a store has over its incoming merchandise. Sidewalk receiving points should be avoided if possible. Cartons should be moved inside the store quickly so that they will be safe from theft and weather. The back doors of the store that are used as a receiving point should be closed and locked when unattended.

Many stores receive at one or more warehouses or service buildings in addition to the store. Where there are several store units of a chain or branch system in a community, a warehouse may be used as the central receiving point for all units. Merchandise is received, checked, and marked at the warehouse and then distributed to each of the several stores. Use of electronic inventory systems permits every store immediate access to the status of any merchandise item in the warehouse or at any other store. Some merchandise received at a warehouse may be held there until sold and then shipped directly to customers. When customers select a model or style of appliance, furniture, or lawn equipment from a display at the retail store, delivery is often made from stock at the warehouse.

Illus. 43–1   In larger warehouses or stockrooms, cartons marked with bar codes can be electronically scanned and automatically conveyed to an area for checking, stocking, or shipment.

RECEIVING RECORDS AND IDENTIFICATION

When goods arrive at the receiving point, the receiving process begins. First, a receiving clerk carefully examines the unopened boxes, cartons, or containers. Next, the condition and the number of packages are noted on the delivery person's receipt or book. The delivery receipt is signed by a designated store employee, usually the receiving manager. A copy is kept in case a claim for lost or damaged merchandise becomes necessary. If the transportation charges have not been prepaid, the delivery person may be given a voucher at the receiving point. The voucher may be cashed at the store office or submitted later for payment. In addition, the receiving manager, or a subordinate, checks and verifies transportation bills and makes claims against transportation companies for any overcharges.

A record of the number of packages received, the date and time, the vendor's name, the method of shipment, the transportation charges, and other facts about the receipt of the goods are entered in a **receiving book** or **receiving record.** This receiving information may be entered manually or keyed into a computer. This first record of an incoming shipment shows whether goods have been received, thus preventing the payment of invoices for which no merchandise has been received. The receiving record entry should be made by the same individual who signs the delivery person's receipt, so that the goods may be moved immediately to the checking area. Also, prompt computer entry allows buyers and department heads to check on the status of expected merchandise by means of their computer terminals.

An example of a receiving record used in many stores is shown in Illustration 43–2. Sets of forms having three or four copies each are arranged so that only the top line of each set appears on a writing board. When the facts on a shipment have been entered on the top line, all the copies of the set are removed from the board and attached to one of the cartons in the shipment. Beneath these sets of forms is a receiving sheet (see Illustration 43–3 on page 495) which remains on the board until about 25 entries have been made.

As soon as a shipment is entered on the receiving record, the shipment must be assigned a receiving number by the receiving clerk. The number must be noted on the receiving record and on each package of the shipment. The clerk also writes on each carton with a crayon or marking pen the number of the department for which the goods are intended and the number of packages in

Illus. 43–2 Facts about incoming shipments are recorded on a receiving record at the receiving point. Copies of one form are pulled from the receiving record and attached to a carton in the shipment.

the shipment. This numbering procedure helps get the shipment to the correct checking station and ensures that all packages are on hand before checking begins. The set of three (four in larger stores) sheets is attached to one of the packages of the shipment.

The first copy is called the **apron;** the checker may make additional notations on it. The apron is attached to the invoice when it becomes available. The second copy becomes the **marker's record,** and the third becomes the **buyer's record.** When a set has a fourth copy, that copy usually is sent to the merchandise manager. These copies accompany the shipment to

the checking area where the receiving record is verified and completed.

CHECKING MERCHANDISE

The checking activity consists of five steps: (1) comparing the store's purchase order and the vendor's invoice; (2) opening the containers in which the goods have been shipped; (3) removing and sorting the merchandise; (4) checking the quantity of goods received against the amount specified on the invoice; and (5) inspecting the goods for quality. These steps differ slightly from

Each line of this KEY-SHEET speeds and controls one shipment and invoice

Rec By	Shipper or Vendor	Shipped From	Received Via	Carrier's No	Pcs Rec	Weight	Charges ($)		KEY-REC 51026	Date Rec	Check-Out
Bc	FASHIONS	N	X	20017	3	92	1.62	5	26	/18	
Bc	SMITH BROS	N	X	13201	2	60	99	6	27	/18	
Bc	JONES INC	B	PRR	16·04	6	91	1.06	10	28	/18	
Bc	BROADWAY	N	E	36210	18	63	2.20	4	29	/18	
Bc	DOE DRESS	S	LTK	6102	8	161	2.03	5	30	/18	
Bc	SULTAN SHOE	S	MTK	5100	20	393	5.90	33	31	/18	
Bc	WHITE SHIRT	P	BO	51632	1	50	*(1 carton SHORT)*		32	/18	
Bc	NEW BLOUSE	N	NIT	2108	½	90	2.63	1	33	/18	
Bc	DAINTY DR	N	OP	316·26	1	53	1.46	5	34	/18	
Bc	KIDDYWEAR	LA	X	612·330	3	80	4.13	2	35	/18	
Bc	METRO	N	P		1		.62	5	36	/18	
Bc	REED INC	Smithtown	P		1		1.31	1	37	/19	
Bc	A+B	Tol	P		1		*(shipment DAMAGED upon receipt)*		38	/19	
Bc	REEVES	Hammond	P		1		1.21		39	/19	
Bc	VOGEL	N	X	321·140	2	70	2.15	9	40	/19	
Bc	BROWN HDW	CITY			1		DISPLAY		41	/19	
Bc	APEX COAL	CITY					EXP	B	42	/19	
Bc	TALBOT STATY	CITY			1201	5		SUP	5	43	/19	
Bc	TYPE SERV	CITY				1		ADV	5	44	/19	
Bc	NRMA	N	X	162·103	1	10	PD	MR.VIP	45	/19	
Bc	UNITED MUS	SALEM O.	U+T	6101	5	156	PD	17	46	/19	
Bc	BRANCH SALE	SEATTLE	NO	4162	3	1	*(carton SHORT from #51033 received the next day)*		47	/19	
Bc	NEW BLOUSE	N	NIT	F/A2108	½	45	—	1	48	/19	
Bc	ALLIED/EGRY	DAYTON	Co	1250	10	200	3.20	REC	8	49	/19	
Bc	CANNON	KANN	PX	831056	19	800	10.51	21	51050	/19	

Illus. 43–3   This is a completed receiving record of 25 shipments. Each line is identical to the top line of one of the 25 forms pulled from the record (see Illustration 43–2). Diagonal lines through the receiving numbers indicate shipments that are short or damaged. A claim must be filed with the supplier or shipper for such shipments.

store to store, but the aims of the checking activity are the same in all stores. Retailers must make certain that they are getting the goods in the quantity and quality ordered; they must move the goods to the selling floor as quickly as possible; and they must keep the expense of handling goods as low as possible.

LAYOUT OF RECEIVING AREA

The **receiving area** of a store is the place where shipments are opened, checked, and marked. The size and arrangement of a receiving area naturally varies with the type of store, design of building, volume of goods to be handled, and receiving system in use. The receiving area for many older store buildings typically has been a large room with stationary tables on which space has been assigned to different kinds of goods carried. Goods are laid out on the tables, counted, and marked with price tickets or stickers. They are then loaded on trucks or carts and moved to the stockroom or the selling floor.

Today, many large stores and warehouse-type discount stores use two or more rooms, one for the checking and others for the marking of merchandise. Portable double- or triple-decked tables are stationed first in the checking room. Goods are placed on the tables and counted; then the tables are wheeled to the marking room. After the price labels have been attached, the goods are moved either to the stockroom or to the selling floor. Stationary tables require less space, but portable tables offer other advantages. Portable tables eliminate the need to load marked goods on carts or hand trucks to move them to where they are needed. Also, with portable tables, marking is done in a space free from the litter and dust of the checking room.

More and more large retail operations are using merchandise conveyor belts or roller conveyors to speed up the movement of merchandise from the receiving point through the receiving area and into the selling area. A central conveyor moves newly arrived merchandise to side conveyors, where checking and marking are performed. New stores are designed with conveyors to move goods directly to the selling floor to reduce physical handling.

QUANTITY CHECK

Standard merchandise received in cartons containing a half dozen, a dozen, or a gross need not be opened for checking. There is usually enough information on the carton to make counting the number of cartons a sufficient check. If a shortage or a damaged item is found later when a carton is opened for marking, the manufacturer usually can be relied upon to make a satisfactory adjustment. For most merchandise in which there are size, color, and style variations, all containers must be opened and the items counted. Each carton should be opened carefully so that the contents are not damaged. The merchandise should be laid out on the checking table systematically. All merchandise of a particular size, color, or brand should be placed together. This sorting helps in counting the merchandise. Problems a checker may find in a shipment are listed in Illustration 43–4.

Direct-check Method

Neatly arranged stacks of merchandise make it easy for the checker to accurately count the quantities received. The checker may compare the quantities against the invoice that was sent by the vendor of the goods or against a copy of the order. Checking goods against the invoice is more common than checking them against a copy

WHAT A CHECKER MAY FIND WRONG IN A SHIPMENT

Breakage	Fragile merchandise that has been incorrectly wrapped may be found broken when the container is opened.
Damage	Rough handling in transportation may have caused damage to contents.
Shortage	Invoice or packing slip may call for a larger number than that received.
Overage	Invoice or packing slip may call for a smaller number than that received.
Substitution	Invoice or packing slip may list a different style, number, color, material, or size than that received.

Illus. 43–4 Each carton of a shipment must be checked carefully to be sure the quantity and quality of merchandise received are as ordered.

of the order. However, the use of the order allows merchandise to be checked as soon as it is received, even though the invoice has not yet arrived. Checking goods against either the invoice or the order copy is called a **direct check.** For a direct check, the checker counts the quantity and features of each item received and lists the quantity on the apron (the first of the three copies sent with the shipment by the receiving clerk). As indicated in Illustration 43–5, the checker then looks at the quantities on the invoice or order to see if the numbers agree with those on the apron. If the quantities are the same, the checker places a small checkmark beside the item on the invoice or order. This procedure is repeated until all the items in the shipment have been verified. If the quantities, colors, sizes, and other features of the items are correct, the invoice or order is signed by the checker, or the apron may be signed and attached to the invoice. If errors are found, they are noted on the invoice or order. Depending on store policy, the buyer may be called to check and initial an invoice or order on which errors are found.

Blind-check Method

The direct-check method is quick and inexpensive, but it is not always accurate. After direct checking many shipments and finding them to be correct, the checker may come to believe that the goods received will always agree with the vendor's count or the order quantity. The checker may, therefore, check the items without counting them carefully. To avoid this difficulty, a method known as the **blind check** is sometimes used. For a blind check, neither the invoice nor the order is given to the checker. Instead, the checker prepares a list, called a **dummy invoice,** of the actual contents of a shipment. Then, the checker compares the contents listed on the dummy invoice with the original invoice.

In some large stores, the checker is provided a copy of the invoice that is complete except for the quantity column. It is then necessary to record only the quantities as the count is completed. The blind-check method provides an excellent invoice control because the original invoices are not

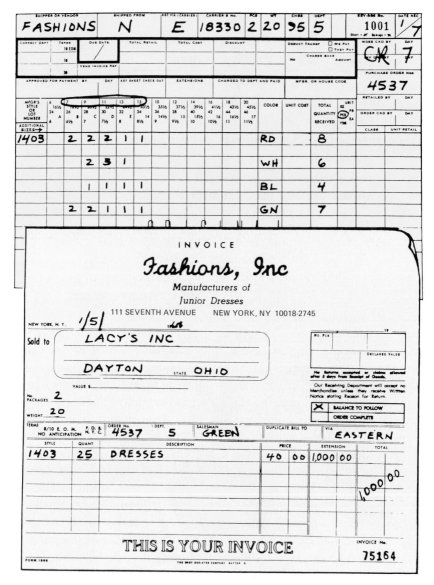

Illus. 43–5 *A checker writes the quantity of merchandise on the apron (top); then the apron and invoice (bottom) are compared.*

scattered about the receiving area but are kept in the office. This method is particularly useful for expensive items for which a small error in checking would involve the loss of a large sum.

Choosing the Checking Method

The checking method that a store chooses usually depends on whether the invoice arrives before the shipment, with the shipment, or after the shipment has arrived. When a store's shipments originate locally, invoices commonly accompany the goods, and the direct-check method can be used. If the invoice arrives before the shipment, the invoice should be held in the receiving area office so that it is available for a direct check when the corresponding shipment arrives.

If the invoice does not arrive with the goods or by mail before the shipment is received, the blind-check method must be used, or the shipment may remain unopened until the invoice arrives. Since the merchandise was ordered because the store needed the goods, sales may be lost if the merchandise is kept in the receiving room until the invoice arrives. Particularly if the merchandise is perishable or seasonal, the store may suffer a loss. Also, the receiving room may become crowded with unopened cartons.

To move goods through the receiving room and onto the sales floor as quickly as possible, some stores use a combination of the direct- and blind-check methods. All shipments are opened immediately after arrival and checked against the invoice if it has arrived. If the invoice has not arrived, the checker prepares a dummy invoice which is held in the receiving office until the vendor's invoice arrives; then, the dummy and regular invoice are compared.

QUALITY CHECK

Many consumer goods must be checked for quality as they come into the store. Usually, the buyer who ordered the goods or a trained assistant should examine the merchandise to see if it is of the quality expected. It is the duty of the quality checker to verify that the styles and materials are those selected, that the workmanship is satisfactory, and that the goods meet all other store standards. Inspection of new styles of shopping goods is particularly important. Some stores have experts in fabrics who inspect all textiles for quality and correctness of description.

Brand-name and packaged merchandise, such as canned goods and toothpaste, usually are not checked for quality. Periodic quality checking of privately branded goods is important, though, because production control for such goods may not be as rigorous as it is for national brands.

RETURNS AND CLAIMS AGAINST VENDORS

It is during the checking process that breakage, damage, shortage, overage, and substitutions are discovered and adjusted. The checker must be alert to discover any irregularities in a shipment. If an irregularity is found, it should be noted on a **discrepancy report.** The discrepancy report may then be used for returning merchandise to the supplier or possibly for filing a claim against the shipper or transportation company.

The person who fills out discrepancy reports and packs and ships returns must be skillful and careful. First, the person must know if a particular vendor accepts returns without written approval. If approval is required, the person handling discrepancy reports must obtain it. Then, that person needs to know the acceptable procedure for returning merchandise to each vendor. A complete, accurate list of the returned merchandise must be enclosed with the returned shipment. A copy of the packing list of re-turned goods and a request for credit should be sent separately by mail. Goods already purchased by customers that must be sent back to the supplier for repair should be handled in much the same way by the person in charge of returns.

Summary

Retailers develop procedures for handling incoming merchandise efficiently. Efficiency can be improved by eliminating unnecessary stockrooms, reducing duplication in handling, moving goods directly to the selling floor, and assigning responsibility for handling incoming goods to one individual. Stores should have one receiving point that is used for all incoming merchandise. The receiving process used by most stores involves checking the condition and quantity of the cartons or containers and entering appropriate information on a receiving record. The checking process involves comparing the purchase order with the shipment invoice; opening the containers; sorting the goods; and checking the quantity, quality, and other features of the goods.

Work can be done more efficiently and accurately if conveyors are used to move goods from the receiving area and if goods are checked in an area separate from the receiving point. Quantity checks of merchandise can be done by either a direct-check or a blind-check method. The blind-check method is particularly useful for expensive items and when the invoice does not arrive with the goods. Quality checks of goods verify that the merchandise is of the type ordered and meets store standards. If breakage, damage, shortage, overage, or other errors are found during checking, a discrepancy report is completed. Special procedures need to be followed in returning goods to suppliers.

Review

1. Identify four ways in which retailers reduce expenses through efficient handling of merchandise.
2. List the steps in the receiving process of a typical retail store.
3. Define *receiving point, receiving area, receiving book,* and *apron.*
4. Describe the five steps of the merchandise checking process.
5. Identify five things that could be wrong with a merchandise shipment.

6. Explain the difference between the direct-check method and the blind-check method for determining the quantity of merchandise received.
7. Describe the use of a discrepancy report.

Terms

The following terms were introduced in this chapter. Write a separate sentence correctly using each new term.

apron
blind check
buyer's record
direct check
discrepancy report
dummy invoice

marker's record
receiving
receiving area
receiving book or receiving
   record
receiving manager or traffic
   manager

Discuss

1. What are some advantages of a centralized receiving warehouse for a multistore operation?
2. Why is it important for a store checker to record where a shipment originated, the name of the carrier, and the number of pieces in the shipment?
3. How is the layout of the receiving area important to the efficiency of the checking process?
4. For what types of goods would quality checks be particularly important? Why?
5. Why would some vendors request that returns of goods have prior approval?

Problem Solving

1. You are the receiving manager for a large variety store. The store receives shipments of 20 to 60 boxes and packages daily. Diagram and describe how you would like to handle incoming merchandise.
2. You are the store operations manager of a full-service family clothing store. Your receiving manager has reported that certain buyers want incoming merchandise set aside for them to check personally. This creates a storage problem in the receiving area because buyers may wait several days before coming in to check. What action(s) should a store operations manager take? What action(s) should the receiving manager take?
3. Determine how the receiving procedures in supermarkets, where there is a rapid turnover of merchandise, differ from receiving procedures in a furniture store, where merchandise turnover is slow.

4. You own and manage a small housewares store. Shipments of goods to your store are usually a mixture of items, some fragile such as cups and glassware. You have just hired a person to work three afternoons each week to help with the receiving and checking of incoming merchandise. Develop a step-by-step procedure that you could use in training this person in receiving and checking (both quantity and condition of) your shipments. Design your step-by-step procedure so that the new worker could use it as he or she receives and checks merchandise for your store.

CHAPTER 44

Marking and Stocking Merchandise

CHAPTER OUTCOMES

When you have mastered the information provided in this chapter, you should be able to:

1. Explain the requirements of a good marking system

2. Name and describe five standard marking procedures

3. Explain the use of a Universal Product Code (UPC) as a marking

4. List at least six items of information that may appear on a price ticket

5. List a variety of price tickets that are used to mark merchandise

6. Give examples of unit pricing, cost codes, and merchandise dating

7. Name and explain the three main objectives of proper stock arrangement

Once merchandise has been received and checked, the goods must be marked before going to the selling floor or reserve stock area. Marking is the process of stamping merchandise with a price or attaching to the merchandise tags or tickets containing price and other important information. A good marking system requires that close attention be paid to neatness and that all information be marked clearly. Marking also must be done in such a way that it will not damage the merchandise or be difficult for customers to find. In addition, the marking system should be designed to prevent customers from altering or changing information or removing tickets.

In some stores, only the price is marked on the merchandise or on the merchandise display. More and more, however, additional information is being marked on goods. For example, marking the merchandise department and product classification numbers allows sales and inventory records to be kept and sales, profits, or losses to be recorded by store department or division. Having vendor numbers marked on goods assists the buyer in reordering and in deciding whether to buy from the same or different suppliers. Style, color, and size marking make unit control possible. Purchase dates help in avoiding an accumulation of old goods. Thus, modern marking practices mean improved merchandise information systems for retailers.

Such practices also benefit customers by giving them information on the tags for making quick buying decisions. When merchandise price is clearly marked, customers are assured that everyone pays the same price for the goods. An effective marking system also improves the service provided by salespeople and is absolutely necessary in a self-service store. In short, proper marking procedures build customer confidence and goodwill as well as contribute to effective merchandising.

MARKING MERCHANDISE

A variety of procedures is used for marking merchandise, as suggested in Illustration 44–1 and in Illustration 44–3. Marking may be done by attaching gummed labels, tickets, tags, or stamps to the merchandise or by writing on the merchandise itself. The use of electronic equipment, such as optical scanners or wands, for recording sales has increased the marking options available to retailers. The choice of a marking procedure depends on the size of the store, the types of merchandise, and the method of operation (self-selection, self-service, full service). Several standard marking procedures are used in the retailing business in preparing merchandise for the selling floor. Descriptions of the five most common procedures follow.

Illus. 44–1   There are a variety of procedures for marking merchandise. Retailers will choose the method of marking that is most appropriate for the size of their stores, type of merchandise, and methods of operation.

Hand Marking

In some small or very exclusive stores, the marking is handwritten. A felt pen or marking crayon is used to mark items carried in the small store. Calligraphy pens may be used to make elegant tickets for fine jewelry, art, and furs carried by some exclusive stores. Of course, the method of marking merchandise by hand is relatively limited.

Preretailing

When a merchandise shipment is inspected for quality, the checker may record on the invoice or attached apron the retail price of the goods and related information. Sometimes, though, the buyer writes the retail price on a duplicate of the purchase order before the goods are received. The goods can then be marked accordingly as soon as they are checked. Such advance marking from the purchase order is called **preretailing.** Preretailing saves time and speeds merchandise through the marking process. Preretailing may be done even before the goods are shipped to the store. A practice that is becoming very popular is for manufacturers to receive tickets or price information from store buyers and then to attach tickets before shipping the goods.

Premarking

Manufacturers who distribute national brands sometimes mark each item with the required information and a price before shipping orders to retail stores. Premarking, as this practice is called, may be included as part of the product package. This practice is done as a service and as a means of reducing the time retailers must spend marking the manufacturer's products. Many large chain stores premark merchandise in a central warehouse before it is sent to the individual outlets, so that merchandise can be moved directly onto the sales floor for immediate sale.

Re-marking

Some goods are not sold at the originally marked price, requiring the merchandise to be marked a second time. For example, a retailer may decide to mark down shopworn or outdated items. Occasionally, goods increase in value while in stock and are marked up. In either case, the original markings must be changed. Re-marking may be done by creating a new ticket or by reprogramming the electronic scanner computer to reflect the new price. To maintain an accurate inventory, careful records of all price changes should be kept. Large stores, especially, have set up elaborate control systems to account for all price changes.

Nonmarking

Certain kinds of goods may not be marked by the retailer at all. Examples include items that can be displayed in bins or on tables with large price signs. When the cost of marking is out of proportion to the value of the product or when the goods, such as fruits and vegetables, can be damaged by marking, nonmarking is a wise choice.

Bar-code Marking

Over the past 15 years, nearly all consumer-goods manufacturers have adopted the **Universal Product Code (UPC)** marking system. First used extensively by supermarkets, the UPC is a machine-readable block of thin and thick vertical lines that indicate brand, item, size, manufacturer, production lot, production date, and other product information. The UPC block, as shown in Illustration 44–2, is most often printed on the product container or package by the manufacturer. However, the UPC block can be on the tag or ticket attached to merchandise. When this block of vertical lines is read by an optical scanner, the scanner automatically inputs this information into the sales register. The sales register is programmed to display and print the price and other data associated with that code. Thus, items that have a UPC do not need to be marked by the retailer. Retailers that do not mark individual products print UPC shelf labels. These labels are placed on the edge of the shelf displaying the products. The customer can read the label to determine product information, size, and price. If the retailer wishes to change the price of a product, the new price can be programmed into the sales register and a new label can be computer-generated for the shelf display.

Illus. 44–2 The various combinations of thin and thick vertical lines on a Universal Product Code enable a manufacturer or merchant to record a vast amount of product data in a minimum amount of space.

PRICE TICKETS

Individual price tickets are placed on most shopping goods because tickets are a direct aid to selling. A ticket acts as a silent salesperson and eliminates the possibility of misquoting prices—intentionally or unintentionally. Price tickets also can be the basis for a store's merchandise-control procedures. The increasing use of computerized control systems encourages the inclusion of a price ticket or UPC on each item.

In large stores, price tickets often are prepared in a central marking room separate from that in which the tickets are attached. The ticket markers are experts in preparing neat, complete tickets in the exact quantities called for on the marker's copy of the receiving form. When the markers apply the tickets, they must be sure that the quantity of tickets matches the quantity of goods. If they have too many tickets, it is clear that part of the shipment has failed to reach them. If there are too few tickets, there is an overage in the shipment or an error in applying tickets. This procedure also verifies the accuracy of the merchandise checkers in the receiving area. Types of information that may be found on a price ticket are listed in Illustration 44–3.

Kinds of Price Tickets

Several kinds of price tickets are used for marking merchandise. These tickets may be prepared by hand or by machine.

INFORMATION THAT MAY BE FOUND ON A PRICE TICKET

Retail price
Unit price and quantity (on packaged goods)
Cost price in code
Identification of season or date when goods were received into stock
Date on which goods, if perishable, are to be removed from sale
Size and color
Kind of material
Style number
Manufacturer or vendor number
Department and classification
Code that identifies the item for stock-control purposes

Illus. 44–3   A price ticket provides a great deal of information, though few tickets contain all of the data listed here.

Gummed labels and pin tickets are the most popular types because they are inexpensive and easy to attach. Gummed labels typically are used for items with a hard surface, such as books and appliances; pin tickets are used on merchandise, such as socks and underwear, that will not be damaged by pinholes. String tags are commonly used for dresses and large articles. Another kind of price ticket is fastened onto items—particularly yard goods—by looping part of the goods into a slot on the ticket. Some tickets are punched with holes that can be read automatically by electronic equipment. For packaged goods, prices are often stamped directly on each package. Types of often-used price tickets are shown in Illustration 44–4.

Unit Pricing

In many localities, packaged goods, such as fresh meat, fruits and vegetables, and groceries, must be marked with the price per pound, ounce, or other unit of measure, as well as with the total selling price of the package. This marking is known as **unit pricing** and is required to make it easy for customers to compare prices of different-sized packages. For example, a package of cheddar cheese may weigh 1.8 pounds and be priced at $2.52. It is important for the customer to know that the price of a pound (unit) is, in this example, $1.40.

Cost Codes

If the store values its stock at cost rather than at retail price on inventory records, the cost of the article must be shown on the price tag. Customers may not consider the heavy expenses of store operation and assume that the difference between the cost and retail price is the retailer's profit. Therefore, the cost price almost always is indicated in code. Some retailers

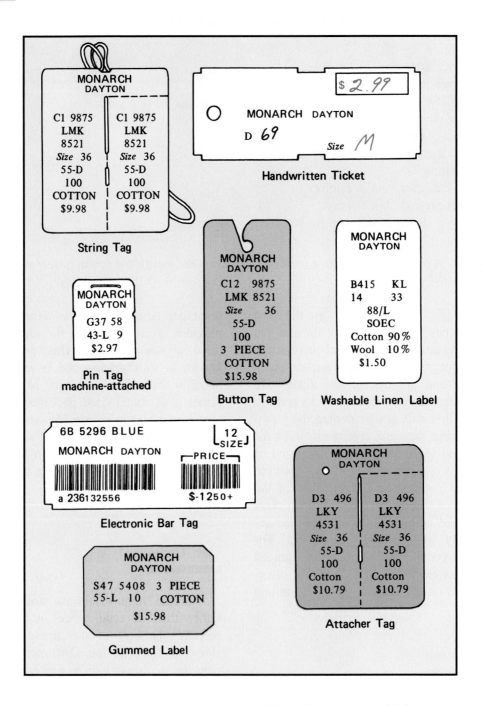

Illus. 44–4 These are the most frequently used price tickets. For each type of ticket, name merchandise items with which you have seen it used.

use a word or phrase of ten letters, with each letter representing a specific digit:

C	A	M	P	S	H	I	R	E	D
1	2	3	4	5	6	7	8	9	0

An article that costs $17.50 would be coded CISD. Other examples of word codes are MAKE PROFIT and MONEY TALKS. Another simple code consists of the cost figure with two digits expressing the year in front and two digits expressing the department number behind it or the year purchased in front and the month received behind it. Omitting the decimal, a cost figure of $13.20 purchased in 1993 and received in June (the sixth month) would be written 93132006.

Merchandise Dating

In addition to cost and retail price, stores often mark the date when merchandise was received into stock or the last date on which it may be sold at the original price. **Code dating** is a system whereby a letter or symbol indicates to store personnel when the goods were received. **Open dating** is a system whereby the actual date is marked and can be read by customers. For nonperishable goods, a common code plan is to designate a six-month season by letter and the month in the season by a number. Thus, A could represent the spring and summer season (February through July) of a specific year, say 1993, and the numeral 3 would represent April. An item marked A3 is one received in April 1993.

For perishable goods, the date, commonly stamped by the supplier, may be the date of production or the last date that the goods should be sold to customers. The freshness period for milk, for example, may be set at seven days. Thus, milk cartons filled on November 2 would be marked NOV 9. This indicates to the retailer and the customer that the product should not be sold after November 9. Open-date marking for fresh meats and dairy products is required by law in many localities.

ARRANGING STOCK

When goods arrive on the selling floor—whether directly from a carrier, from the central marking room, or from a reserve stockroom—they must be arranged on shelves, counters, or racks. In small stores, this work is done along with other duties by salespeople. In large stores, employees called *stockpersons* move merchandise from the marking rooms or stockrooms to the selling floor where they arrange it. Stockpersons also pick up goods from the display and advertising departments, try-on areas, and buyer's and merchandise manager's offices and return the goods to the appropriate selling areas.

Proper arrangement of stock has three objectives: (1) it aids in the sale of goods; (2) it allows the salesperson (and the customer) to learn the location of stock and to obtain the required goods quickly; and (3) it facilitates the control of stock. Merchandise should be arranged with these three goals in mind.

To Aid in Selling

All related items that a customer may want to inspect should be displayed together. These items should be placed where the customer can easily see them and handle them if desired. They should be attractively arranged and well lighted. Fast-selling goods, which are in continuous demand and not bought on impulse, should be placed to draw customers' attention to other merchandise. Impulse goods should be placed along the main lines of traffic. Profitable goods—those on which markup is high—generally should be displayed in a conspicuous place. The stock arrangement of fashion merchandise should be shifted from time to time so that the department may give new interest to regular customers.

Stock should be rotated; that is, it should be arranged to sell the merchandise that arrives first. Stock rotation involves putting new goods behind or beneath old goods on the shelf or counter. If new goods are placed in front or on top of goods already there, the danger of accumulating old, shopworn, spoiled, or otherwise unsalable merchandise is greatly increased. The stock rotation principle is so important—particularly for food, drug, and fashion items—that supervisors of chain stores in these lines almost always check the rotation of stock when visiting their stores.

To Aid New Salespeople

The arrangement of stock should be logical and simple so that new salespeople may learn the stock quickly. In a shoe store, for instance, one wall may be devoted to women's shoes; the opposite wall to men's shoes; and the back wall to children's shoes. Each wall, then, may be divided into three sections: the first for black shoes, the second for brown, and the third for fashion colors. Sizes may be arranged from low to high within each section.

Illus. 44–5   Goods should be arranged in a simple but logical manner, with new goods going behind or below current stock.

This arrangement can be explained easily to a new salesperson. When asked for a man's brown brogue, the new employee can go immediately to the proper section of the store for the suitable style in the correct size. All salespeople, as well as customers, benefit from this simple but logical arrangement, which saves time in serving customers' needs.

To Aid Stock Control

Stock should be arranged so that it can be replenished and counted easily. Visible dividers should be used where possible. Dark bins and corners, where goods may be overlooked, should be avoided. The stock arrangement should be flexible enough to allow for new style numbers. If an item shows an increasing rate of sale, a good arrangement makes it easy to expand the space for it in proportion to its rate of sale.

Every item that the store sells normally should have a place set aside for it in the selling area. Only one of a low-selling item may be displayed, but a sign should state that additional items are available in reserve stock.

Summary

Marking merchandise involves placing the price and other information on the product. In addition to price, retailers may mark goods with information about the supplier, cost, date received, and style or model. Tickets or tags may be handwritten by the retailer, printed by the retailer or supplier, or premarked on goods by the manufacturer; or the goods may carry no marking at all. Merchandise may be marked with a Universal Product Code (UPC), a bar code that can be used by retailers who have electronic scanners and computerized sales registers.

Among the several kinds of price tickets used by retailers are gummed labels, pin tickets, string tags, loop tags, and stamps applied directly to the merchandise. Two forms of merchandise dating— code dating and open dating—are used. Merchandise dating allows a retailer to keep track of how long goods have been in stock. Arranging stock is an important part of making sure goods are available for sale. Good stock arrangement helps new salespeople learn the stock, helps in stock control, and aids in providing prompt service to customers.

Review

1. List the requirements of a good marking system.
2. Define the following terms: *marking, preretailing,* and *unit pricing*.
3. Identify five items of information that may be found on a price ticket.
4. Name the various kinds of price tickets and explain how each is used.
5. Explain how a UPC is used in marking.
6. Define and describe *cost* and *dating codes* and explain how they are used by retailers.
7. List the three goals of proper stock arrangement.

Terms

The following terms were introduced in this chapter. Write a separate sentence correctly using each new term.

code dating	unit pricing
open dating	Universal Product Code (UPC)
preretailing	

Discuss

1. Why is a good marking system important to the retailer? to the customer?

2. For what types of goods is premarking most likely to be done by manufacturers?
3. Of what value is unit pricing to the retailer? to the customer?
4. Under what circumstances would retailers prefer code dating over open dating? For what types of merchandise would code dating be preferred?
5. Many customers know that the most recently received goods will be stocked near the back or the bottom of a display. Should salespeople insist that customers take merchandise only from the front or top of an arrangement? Why or why not?

Problem Solving

1. Visit a department or variety store and observe the types of tickets used. Identify products using each of the following types of tickets: pin tag, string tag, gummed label, and electronic bar tag.
2. You work in a small hardware store, selling and marking goods. The owner wants prices marked directly on goods with a marking pen whenever possible. Some customers have complained that it is difficult to get the price mark off goods that they buy. Some have even refused to purchase an item that has been so marked. What do you suggest to your employer to solve this problem?
3. Make up two cost codes different from those shown in this chapter. Develop one code using letters and one using numbers. Record these cost prices using your codes: $1.23, $23.45, and $345.00.
4. Visit a supermarket and observe which items have code dating and which have open dating. List ten code-dated and ten open-dated items.

CHAPTER 45

Stock Management and Control

An operations division's responsibility does not end when the goods are on the selling floor or in reserve stock. Stock management involves a plan for handling, recording, and reporting types and quantities of merchandise on hand and on order at all times. A good stock-management system makes possible efficient and secure control of merchandise assortments and inventory. Main elements of stock management include stock reserves, stock-control records and reports, and merchandise security.

STOCK RESERVES

Stores vary in what they can and must do with the large quantities of goods prepared for resale. But almost all retailers would have the following to say regarding stock reserves:

1. Goods that cannot be seen cannot be sold.
2. All space in a retail store costs money.

So, whenever possible, merchandise should be on the selling floor (forward stock), and as little space as possible should be given over to stockrooms (reserve stock).

Forward Stock

The **forward stock,** merchandise maintained in the selling area, should be adequate for at least a few days of expected customer demand. Once each day, however, the forward stock should be checked carefully to determine which items need replenishing. A list of needed items may be made by a salesperson and sent to the re-serve area so that the forward stock can be replenished promptly. Such a list of reserve items may be used also for analyzing inventory to determine buying needs. Since goods are ordered from the reserve only because sales have depleted forward stock, the reserve lists approximate actual sales.

Supermarkets and discount stores attempt to reduce their storage space by stocking large amounts of merchandise on the selling floor, on shelving units above the selling floor, and in the drawers of counters and display fixtures. Although this stock is not accessible to customers, it keeps it convenient for replenishment. Certain sections of the selling area may be assigned to cashiers and wrappers or to selling personnel who have the responsibility of keeping their assigned sections fully stocked with merchandise for peak selling periods. Stockkeepers may bring merchandise from stockrooms to the selling floor during the day and before business hours, when salespeople and cashiers may have time to restock, re-mark, and arrange merchandise.

Reserve Stock

The **reserve stock** is the merchandise that is held or stored off the selling floor and is used to replace goods that are sold from the forward stock. The layout of merchandise in reserve stock should be similar to the way the goods are arranged on the selling floor. For example, if forward stock is arranged by size and color in each classification, the reserve stock should be arranged in the same manner. Employees should be able to access the reserve stock area from the receiving area without needing to pass through the selling area.

Illus. 45–1   Large stores that handle bulky merchandise often require separate storage warehouses. Only samples are kept in the store. Customer orders are filled from the warehouse.

Because of the high value of space in selling departments, it may be necessary to have reserves located on upper floors or in basements of the retail building. Telephone or intercom connections between selling floors and remote reserve areas are important so that a salesperson can get in touch with a stockkeeper while a customer is waiting for information. In larger retail facilities, quick access to reserve may be assured by service elevators.

METHODS OF STOCK CONTROL

The two methods for controlling stock are the dollar control method and the unit control method. Using the **dollar control method,** retailers calculate the dollar value of forward and reserve stock at frequent intervals. The dollar value may be figured from the store's receiving and sales records (book inventory) or by actually counting and recording the price of stock (physical inventory). These checks show whether the stock is too high or too low in relation to the planned stock figure. Using the **unit control method,** retailers record the number of units or items in stock rather than the dollar value.

Dollar Control Method

The dollar control method provides the retailer with the dollar value of stock. It does not provide specific information about items that may be out of stock or slow selling. To use the dollar control method, the retail dollar value of the opening inventory (forward and reserve stock at the beginning of a period) is determined. The retail dollar value of purchases during the period is added to the opening inventory value. From this total, markdowns and sales are subtracted. The result is an estimate of the retail value of the current stock. Some retailers prefer to use cost prices rather than retail in dollar control. The procedure using cost values would be to determine the cost value of the opening inventory, add the cost of purchases, and subtract the cost value of merchandise sold during the period. Using the dollar control method, the retailer can determine the stock turn rate (see Chapter 21).

What the retailer cannot determine is whether the right number of each item is stocked, because the method does not involve a record of the number of units of each type of goods in stock. There may be too few best-selling items and too many slow sellers. With too few popular items in stock, a retailer creates ill will by not having the merchandise customers desire and expect.

Unit Control Method

For the unit control method, a complete record of merchandise by classification, style number, size, color, material, or other characteristic is maintained for the entire stock. As discussed in Chapter 21, each item of merchandise so recorded is called an SKU (stockkeeping unit). If 20 pairs of red wool mittens, size seven, are in the opening inventory, 12 pairs are received, and 18 pairs sold during the period, then the current stock of this SKU should be 14. By using unit control of the entire stock, a retailer can tell exactly which items and how many of each are on hand at any time.

When using the unit control method, a merchant can compare the dollar markup on the quantity of each SKU sold with the number of that item in merchandise inventory. Thus, the retailer can concentrate on items that sell well even at a substantial markup.

KINDS OF UNIT STOCK CONTROL SYSTEMS

There are many different stock control systems in operation today. The paragraphs that follow discuss several of the most common systems. These systems may be implemented by either manual (handwritten) or electronic (computer-keyed) recording of inventory data. While a store of almost any size can benefit from a computerized unit control system, such systems are particularly important when a store has sales of over $1 million or has more than one store unit. Each store must determine the best type of system for the size of its operation and the merchandise it handles.

Checklist System

The simplest unit stock control system is the checklist or never-out list system. The checklist contains all of the regular merchandise items. The buyer usually indicates a maximum or model stock level for each item. The quantities appear on the checklist, too. Once a week or at some other regular interval, the list is compared with a count of the stock to see if an adequate quantity of each item is on hand. If there is not, an order is placed. The checklist system or never-out list is particularly satisfactory for convenience goods and shopping goods that are not subject to fashion change.

STOCK CONTROL GOALS

To maintain correct quantities within merchandise assortments

To guide the purchase of new merchandise in each classification

To determine price ranges that will serve the store's clientele

To simplify merchandise ordering

To identify appropriate items for sales promotion

To point out slow-selling merchandise items

To increase the return on the investment realized from each item handled

Illus. 45–2   To meet the many goals of a stock control system, information must be supplied quickly to buyers and store managers.

Unit-sales Analysis

For fashion goods, such as women's dresses or sportswear, a fairly elaborate control is necessary for each style number. Sudden changes in demand for some styles make it necessary for the buyer to know the stock condition every day. For a unit-sales analysis, the first step is to list what is sold at the end of each day. An electronic sales register may provide a printed sales list. Or, these daily lists may be prepared from copies of the sales checks or from stubs of price tickets that are removed from the merchandise when the sale is made. Also, a unit-sales analysis may be prepared from reserve stock requisitions (lists). When forward stock is limited, these requisitions provide a fairly accurate count of what has been sold since the last requisition was made. For large forward stocks, the daily sales list is a better way of obtaining a unit-sales analysis.

Perpetual-inventory System

By using a unit-sales analysis along with records of goods ordered and received, a retailer can maintain a perpetual record of goods in inventory. A perpetual inventory is calculated for each style or SKU. For example, if 12 items of style No. 710 are on hand, 24 more are received, and 16 are sold, the new inventory would be 20. A perpetual-inventory record may be kept on cards (with one card for each item), in an electronic sales register, or in a computer. For fashion goods, the retailer may wish to have a report of inventory status each day. For other items, a weekly or bimonthly report may be adequate.

From time to time, the on-hand figures appearing on inventory reports are checked against the actual stock. If only seven items are found in stock when the perpetual inventory figure indicates eight, the one missing is a shortage. An effort is made to find it, and records are checked to make sure that no error was made in calculation. If the difference cannot be accounted for, the item may have been stolen or mismarked in receiving.

The perpetual inventory type of unit control is usually more expensive to maintain than periodic physical inventories, because it requires that every sale and all SKU data must be recorded. Fortunately, the use of UPC or other coding and electronic sales registers with point-of-sale inventory-control programs makes collecting such data relatively easy. Perpetual inventory control is desirable under the following conditions:

1. When stock shortages must be watched carefully
2. When styles change rapidly
3. When it is difficult to count stock frequently
4. When an electronic sales register or a computer makes it efficient to report sales for each SKU

Warehouse Control System

When the physical stock cannot be readily inspected because it is in a warehouse or in one or more units of a chain, the **warehouse control system** may be used. This system is also used for items of high unit value, such as furs, jewelry, computers, stereo components, and furniture. A control file is prepared for each separate unit of the merchandise. Thus, if 24 units of one item are received, 24 units are entered into the file (or 24 cards are prepared). In each file or on each card, the history of the piece is indicated, including when it was ordered, when it was received, its cost, its original retail price, any markdowns or markups taken, and when each item was sold. As an article is sold, it is deducted from the computer inventory or the card is removed from the file. Thus, the file presents a picture of the stock for each item at all times.

A variation of the warehouse control system involves attaching to the price ticket a number of stickers, one for each item received into the warehouse or reserve stockroom. The price ticket, in turn, is attached to a sample item on the selling floor. As a sale is made, one sticker is removed from the ticket and attached to the sales check. Thus, there is little risk of taking a customer's order for something that is not in stock.

SLOW-SELLING MERCHANDISE

Unit stock control systems are invaluable in pointing out slow-selling merchandise. For a stock assortment to yield a profit, old stock must be moved out quickly to make room for new stock. Slow-selling merchandise is merchandise that has been in stock a longer period than experience indicates is desirable. Department stores set the limit for much of their merchandise at six months. Experience shows that goods that fail to sell within that period likely will not sell at all unless given special attention. The time limit for fashion merchandise is much shorter—in some cases, only four weeks.

Rugs, furniture, and other household furnishings may be allowed a year or more because there will be little depreciation in that time. Forcing the sale of merchandise with markdowns before the time limit leads to unnecessary loss.

On the other hand, slow-selling merchandise is a serious problem to the merchant. Money tied up in slow sellers could be used more profitably if invested in fast-selling goods. Often, the merchant is prevented from buying desirable goods because money invested in the slow sellers cannot be recovered. Even if funds are available to purchase needed merchandise, the slow sellers may be tying up selling and storage space.

When faced with the problem of slow-selling merchandise, a retailer should consider the following six methods of moving the merchandise:

1. *Take Large Markdowns.* One large markdown moves merchandise faster than three or four small markdowns. When a markdown is taken, it should be large enough to make buying worthwhile for the customer.
2. *Offer Incentives to Salespeople.* Extra sales effort may be needed to sell certain goods. Salespeople can be offered special incentives or extra commissions for selling these items.
3. *Give Extra Attention to the Merchandise.* Since odds and ends of merchandise are hard to sell, perhaps the retailer should fill in sizes, round out assortments, or complete missing parts to clear the goods from stock.
4. *Advertise the Slow Sellers.* Special promotional effort can be given to slow sellers if the quantities, styles, and col-

ors are worthy of being advertised. If the merchant believes that he or she has merchandise that is wanted or needed, it might be wise to invest in advertising those items.

5. *Display the Slow Movers.* A feature display might be set up in a noticeable spot to attract attention to and create interest in the product and create a desire to buy.

6. *Offer Special Promotions.* Perhaps a new idea for selling the merchandise could be developed. Tie-in sales, a free-gift offer, special service, and extra time to pay are possible special selling ideas for moving merchandise that has been in stock too long.

STOCK SECURITY

Depending on the type of store, merchants lose the equivalent of 1 percent to 5 percent of stock to shoplifters and employees each year. While shoplifting losses are extensive, a more discouraging fact is that two thirds of the shortages in some stores are due to dishonest employees. Protection of merchandise is a responsibility of the operations staff, but assistance is needed from all store workers.

Protective Measures

Most large stores employ security officers or contract with private agencies for protection services. Security officers are trained to observe any questionable conduct throughout the store. They know how to approach suspicious-looking customers without running the risk of making a false

arrest. Since security personnel cannot be everywhere at once, they often use closed-circuit television screens and cameras. Thus, from a central monitoring station, as shown in Illustration 45–3, a single security person can monitor activities in many parts of the store.

To supplement the work of security persons, many other devices are used. Magnetic tags are attached to selected merchandise, and an alarm sounds if the items are taken from the store before the tags are removed or deactivated by a cashier. Some merchandise is fastened by chain or cable to the rack or counter. To protect against ticket switching, a form of stealing, stores may use hard-to-break plastic string or conceal extra price tickets in unexpected places on the merchandise. Some stores color code the price tickets. If the color of the ticket does not match the type of article, then a switch likely has taken place.

Store layout can encourage or discourage shoplifting. High fixtures and tall displays provide cover for shoplifters. Low fixtures and open views across the selling area allow store staff to observe all customers better. Valuable and easy-to-hide items should be displayed at counters that are attended by salespeople or placed under glass so that customers must ask a salesperson for help.

Employee Theft

Currently, an overwhelming problem for store-operations and security personnel is employee pilferage. Internal theft by employees accounts for a far greater loss than theft by customers. Some employees seem to feel they have a right to take store merchandise or supplies. Theft may be done by

Illus. 45–3   Through closed-circuit television, one security person can observe activities in several areas of a store.

an individual employee or achieved with a partner who poses as a customer. Areas in which employee theft is most common include pricing, refunds, cash handling, exchanges, and employee purchases. Large-scale employee theft is carried on more often through the back door than through the front door. For example, a box from a shipment may be left on the receiving dock; merchandise may go out with the trash; a door may be left ajar; or an extra box may be set out for return to a vendor. In each case, the dishonest employee or her or his partner can carry merchandise away from the store unnoticed by supervisors or managers. Sooner or later, though, such stealing is seen by other employees. Watchfulness on the part of honest employees; willingness to reprove dishonest fellow workers; and, as necessary, reporting them to management are all required safeguards against employee theft. Many large retailers reward employees monetarily for reporting employee theft.

Summary   To sell merchandise, it must be available where customers can see it. Therefore, as much merchandise as possible should be kept in the forward stock area and as little as possible in the reserve stock area. The two methods of keeping track of stock value are dollar control and unit control. The dollar control method provides the dollar value of goods in stock, and the unit control method provides details on each type of merchandise carried. Retailers may choose a checklist system, unit-sales analysis, perpetual-inventory system, or a warehouse control system, depending on their store operation and types of merchandise. Nearly all stores could receive benefits from computerized unit stock control. An effective unit control system aids in identifying slow-selling merchandise. Knowing which goods are not moving well allows a retailer to take appropriate action to sell such goods. An important part of merchandise management is to provide for stock security. Main losses in inventory are due to shoplifting and employee theft. Protective measures such as security personnel, closed-circuit television, special merchandise tags, careful store layout, and employee training can be used to reduce losses.

Review

1. Define *forward stock*.
2. Explain why reserve stock should be kept at a minimum.
3. Explain the difference between the dollar control method and the unit control method of stock control.
4. Describe the operation of a checklist system of stock control.
5. Describe six ways in which slow-selling items may be moved.
6. What measures can be taken by retailers to protect against stock losses?

Terms

The following terms were introduced in this chapter. Write a separate sentence correctly using each new term.

dollar control method	unit control method
forward stock	warehouse control system
reserve stock	

Discuss

1. In which types of stores is reserve stock unnecessary?
2. If a store uses computerized stock control, is it assured that there will be no slow-moving stock or shortages? Why or why not?
3. Is it feasible for a store to use several different stock control systems at the same time? Why would more than one be necessary?
4. Should legal action be taken by the retailer against any customer or employee caught stealing merchandise?

Problem Solving

1. Visit a store or a large selling department and observe the arrangement of merchandise on the selling floor. After leaving the store, draw a diagram of the stock arrangement in the selling

area. Which items will likely have a reserve stock? Describe in detail how you would arrange the reserve stockroom for this merchandise.

2. Assume that you are the manager of a hardware store and are using a perpetual-inventory control system. When physical inventory checks are made, shortages are usually found in the same merchandise areas. What could cause these shortages and what steps could you take to control them?

3. Assume that you are planning to open a bicycle shop and intend to carry a full line of bicycle parts and accessories. Design an inventory and stock control system to be used for this business.

4. You are working in a large variety store. A close friend comes into the store and you observe your friend shoplifting. What action, if any, would you take? State specifically what you would do and what you believe the outcome of your action would be.

UNIT 7 ACTIVITIES

CHECKING KEY POINTS

This exercise is designed to check your understanding of material presented in Unit 7. On a separate sheet of paper, list the numbers 1 through 26. Indicate your response, *T* for true or *F* for false, for each of the following 26 statements.

1. Store design includes the exterior and interior of the store, including lighting and fixtures.
2. Space near the back of the store, away from the constant traffic of the entrance, has the greatest potential for sales.
3. Direct or semidirect lighting usually would be used where an image of quality and elegance is desired.
4. Well-lighted and comfortable stores encourage customer shopping.
5. In self-service stores, the customers examine samples of goods and then ask a clerk to get the desired items from stock.
6. Store staff who try to sell by telephone are called *personal shoppers.*
7. Department wrap is done by the salesperson who assisted the customer in the sale.
8. Profit services may be associated with the merchandise sold or provided just as a customer convenience.
9. A customer with open or regular credit is expected to pay each monthly bill promptly.
10. Customers using deferred or revolving credit are required to sign a contract agreeing to a series of stated payments.
11. In credit granting, *capacity* means the customer's ability to earn and pay.
12. A fair credit risk is one whose credit ratings are barely good enough to be granted credit.
13. An analysis of the length of time credit accounts are past due is called *aging of accounts.*
14. The activity of taking physical possession of incoming goods is called *receiving.*
15. Checking goods involves verifying both the quantity and quality of merchandise.
16. Using the direct-check method, the checker prepares a list called a *dummy invoice.*
17. Boxes of merchandise should not be opened until the vendor's invoice has arrived.

18. A discrepancy report is used as a basis for a merchandise return or claim against the shipper.
19. Individual price tickets are placed on most shopping goods.
20. If the cost code is CODING MARK (C = 1), then *DNK* means *$4.75*.
21. *JULY 25* on a product is an example of code dating.
22. New merchandise should be stocked behind or below old goods.
23. Forward stock is maintained in the selling area.
24. The dollar control method is preferred by most retailers.
25. Unit-sales analysis works best on staple or convenience goods.
26. Slow-selling merchandise is any merchandise that has been in stock longer than desirable.

BUILDING BASIC SKILLS

Calculations

The following calculations were used in Unit 7 to demonstrate certain facts about retail merchandising. Make the calculations necessary to answer the questions that follow.

1. A retailer has the following seven installment contracts from customers: H. Jones, $550; R. Smith, $270; A. Brown, $890; F. Golden, $720; S. Brooks, $190; I. Jensen, $440; and B. Cortz, $630. The retailer can sell installment contracts to a finance company at the following rates of discount: under $300 at 10 percent; $300 to $600 at 9 percent; and over $600 at 8 percent. What is the total value of the seven contracts? How much would the retailer get if all seven contracts were sold to the finance company?
2. The Blue Nugget Shop had $12,300 accounts receivable on January 1; a year later, on December 31, $1,600 of accounts receivable were classified as bad debts; during the year, $34,100 was paid on accounts by credit customers; total credit sales for the year were $36,500. What is the Blue Nugget's bad debt loss index for the year? What is the store's collection percentage for the year?
3. Review the unit receiving and reserve stock requisition record for the SKUs indicated on the chart on page 525. Calculate the amount currently on hand for each SKU.
4. The retail prices of SKUs in problem 3 above are as follows: A31 = $7.95; R61 = $11.50; S28 = $5.50; W11 = $24.95; and X40 = $17.50. Based on the record shown in problem 3, what is the retail

value of goods received in each SKU and in total? Assuming that requisitions from reserve stock represent sales, what is the retail value of goods sold in each SKU? in total?

SKU	Beginning Reserve	Requisitioned from Reserve	Received
A31	36	— 8 18 12 16	12 24 18
R61	42	18 12 — 20 32	24 12 24
S28	61	24 48 18 — 24	36 18 32
W11	16	4 8 2 4 6	6 9 6
X40	22	8 — 10 18 14	14 8 12

Working with People

Retail workers must work with other employees, supervisors, and customers. Sometimes, misunderstandings occur. Misunderstandings cause bad feelings among employees and their supervisors and poor service to customers. Many successful workers solve people problems with the four-step DICE approach. Each letter of DICE refers to a specific problem-solving action described in Unit 1 (see page 78).

Read each problem situation below. Then, use the DICE approach to find a solution for each. Remember, you must first define a problem before you identify or choose solutions. Describe what you think the consequences of your chosen solution would be.

1. You are responsible for reviewing credit applications. Many applicants do not supply all the information requested, such as employment history and current bills. When you request this information, the person often becomes upset and defensive. However, to do an effective review of each application, you must have this information. What is the problem and what action might you take?

2. You are receiving manager of a medium-sized department store in a downtown location. You have three clerks who are responsible for receiving all incoming goods for the store. All three clerks have worked in the receiving area for several years. Every week, there are several errors noted in the receiving record. You have noticed that the errors seem to occur when you are not in the receiving area. What could be causing these errors and what action(s) might you take?

3. The price tickets used in your store show, in code, the date the merchandise was brought into stock. Store policy is that older goods should be sold first. Moving stock from reserve into forward stock is done by both stockkeepers and sales personnel. When

you check stock in any department, you frequently find that newer goods are stacked on top of older goods. When you ask the stock-keepers, they say it is being done by the salespeople; when you talk to department managers or salespeople, they say it is customers who are moving new stock to the top. What is the problem and what action should you take?

4.   You are the operations manager of a large variety store. The responsibility for stock security from the time goods come into the store until they leave the store rests with the operations division. However, salespeople help with security in the selling areas. Your store has a single receiving area, an employee entrance, and one line of checkout stands. A store security person checks employees in and out at the employee entrance. Store security reports few cases of shoplifting, but stock shortages have been substantial over the past six months. What could be causing the stock shortages and what action(s) might you take?

Writing Skills

Communication skills, oral or written, are essential for nearly all retail jobs. Writing skills are important when communicating with customers, employees, suppliers, or the public. The clarity and tone of a letter may either antagonize them or retain their goodwill. Prepare a positive, goodwill-building letter for each of the situations that follow.

1.   A person has just moved to your community. Write a letter inviting her or him to come to your store and open a credit account. Because you cannot be sure that the individual will be qualified for credit, your letter must not imply assurance of a credit account.

2.   A qualified person has applied for a job as a checker and marker in your store. Write a letter informing the individual that he or she may have the job and explain some of the expectations you have for a person working in your store as a checker/marker.

3.   A credit customer is nine months late in paying a $280 bill on a revolving account. You have written the customer before but received no answer. You called the customer on the phone six weeks ago, and the customer promised to pay within three weeks. Write a letter to the customer requesting prompt payment and explain what action will be taken if payment is not received.

4.   A customer recently purchased a pair of lamps and a small table from your furniture store and requested delivery for the following Saturday morning. You provide free delivery on Tuesday and Thursday from 9:00 a.m. to 5:00 p.m. Customers who want delivery on weekday evenings or Saturdays must pay a delivery charge. The customer feels that the policy is unfair. Write a letter to this customer explaining and defending your delivery policy.

APPLYING YOUR KNOWLEDGE

Can You Do the Following?

1. Draw a diagram of a store floor layout and show which part would have the greatest potential for sales and which part would have the least potential for sales.
2. List guidelines for good store maintenance.
3. Describe the five selling and shopping services that a store might provide.
4. List three nonmerchandise for-profit services provided by stores in your community.
5. Describe the three C's of credit and how they are applied in granting retail store credit.
6. List the steps you would take in collecting past-due payments from retail credit customers.
7. List the procedure to be used in a direct quantity check of incoming merchandise.
8. Explain how to use a dummy invoice.
9. Describe five procedures that may be used to mark merchandise.
10. Describe the types of information that are often found on a price ticket.
11. List six methods for moving slow-selling merchandise.
12. Describe four unit control systems and explain under what conditions each may best be used.

Retail Decisions

1. You have been appointed assistant store manager in charge of store operations. Which aspects of store operations do you want to look at most closely during your first two weeks on the job? Why?
2. You have been asked to make suggestions regarding the design and layout of a sportswear store (men's and women's) to be located in a small shopping mall. Compile a list of your recommendations.
3. What convenience services would you recommend the store described in item 2 provide? Give your reasons for offering each service.
4. As owner of a new retail clothing store dealing in high-quality and fashion merchandise, you have decided to handle your own credit program. Of the three widely used plans, which would you choose? Why?
5. What information should a receiving clerk write in the receiving

record? What information should be written on each carton of an incoming shipment?

6. You are the merchandise manager for a variety store. What type of ticket would you ask the receiving/marking manager to put on each of the following types of goods: bath towels, silk scarves, glass-bottled bath oil, purses, and stuffed animals?

7. You are working in a quick-service food store handling many convenience goods such as milk, bread, sandwich meat, cheese, and some prepared delicatessen items. Which type of dating would you recommend be shown on each of these products?

8. Which stock control method—dollar or unit—is more appropriate for a line of fashionable women's business and evening wear? Why? Would you use the same control method on accessories? Why?

9. What steps can a store take to control employee theft?

DEVELOPING CRITICAL-THINKING SKILLS

Retail Projects

1. For several years, Willobee's Department Store has hired the Midnite Moppers janitorial service to clean the store during nonstore hours. The Midnite Moppers do all the general cleaning, floor polishing, and trash removal; they install light bulbs or tubes; and do whatever else must be done. Mr. Willobee, the store owner, has noticed that, as the store has grown in size and as business has increased, additional janitorial service is needed during the day. Some floors require additional cleaning; trash must be taken out during the day, and it is not always convenient to wait until the end of the day to replace burned-out light bulbs. List at least six factors Mr. Willobee should consider before changing the present maintenance and janitorial plan.

2. A variety store has one selling floor. The basement is used for checking, marking, and storage. Receiving is done at a dock at the rear of the building. The store has nine employees—the owner, four cashiers, three stockpeople/salespeople, and an office worker. Incoming goods are received and prepared for selling in a haphazard fashion. The owner does not want to hire more help, but he wants to improve the handling of incoming merchandise. Outline the procedure he should use and the duties he should assign to the different members of the store staff.

3. Nordak's is an independent department store chain that consists of the parent store and three branch stores in the city of Delrio. Two of the branch stores are larger than the parent store and each nearly equals the parent store's sales volume. The receiving

and marking for all stores is done in the basement of the parent store. Goods are then sent to the branches. Buyers operate out of the parent store but have no responsibility for supervision of the selling departments for which they buy. A problem has emerged as the four-store operation has grown. Merchandise that is received takes as long as five or six days to reach the selling area of the parent store, and branch stores may not receive goods for ten days after arrival at the parent store. What additional facts do you need in order to assess the merchandise-flow problem of this department store? Based on the information provided, what suggestions do you have for improving the handling of incoming merchandise?

4. Nordak's offers qualified customers open or regular credit accounts. One of the customers, Alan Clarke, has had a credit account for several years. His credit purchases have been relatively small ($50 to $100), but payment has always been slow, sometimes as long as six months overdue. All credit purchases over $50 have to be cleared by salespeople with the credit office. Alan Clarke wants to charge $500 in purchases. What additional information would you like to have before approving or rejecting the credit request? What action do you recommend?

5. Calculate each of the following items:
   a. What is the bad debt loss index if credit sales have been $27,000 and bad debts amount to $550?
   b. What is the accounts receivable turnover rate if annual credit sales are $56,000 and average monthly accounts receivable amount to $4,200?
   c. What is the collection percentage if the total accounts receivable at the beginning of the period was $5,600 and payments made by customers for the period amounted to $48,300?

6. Prepare a cost code made up of a word or slogan of ten letters. Show how each of the following prices would be written with your cost code: $17.50; $4.80; $0.71; $110.00; $35.00; $6.60; and $5.45.

Field Projects

1. Visit three retail stores selling the same type of goods. For each store, identify the merchandise that is located within 15 feet of the main store entrance. What type of goods were found most often close to the entrances? Where were the checkouts (sales registers) in relation to the store entrances?

2. Obtain the credit application form from a retail store in your community. Based on your examination of the information requested on the form, what criterion seems most important in the decision to extend or reject credit applicants?

3. Many stores have their merchandise ticketed or marked with a universal product code or optical characters. The retailer can quickly program electronic sales registers to adjust prices in the case of sales or price increases. With your instructor's help, set up a visit with a merchant who uses optical scanning (supermarkets are likely choices) and find out how price adjustments are made. Prepare a written report on your findings.

4. Stores use a variety of merchandise security controls. Arrange to visit three major stores in your neighborhood. What merchandise security devices do they use? How effective are these devices? What suggestions do you have for improvement of stock security in these stores? Prepare a written report on your findings and recommendations.

5. The receiving, marking, and stocking arrangements vary for stores largely because of differences in size, type of merchandise, and method of retail merchandising. With your instructor's help, set up a visit to one large store and one small store in your community. Observe how each store handles the receiving, marking, and stocking activities. Prepare a paper describing the procedure used in each store and the strengths of each store's procedure.

CONTINUING PROJECTS

Developing a Career Plan

Retail operations require workers with a broad range of interests and skills. Most persons who advance to management levels in retailing have worked, at least for some period of time, in retail operations. Some retail workers, including management personnel, spend their entire careers in retail operations. Persons who have good skills with people; who can deal effectively with records, financial detail, and merchandising systems; and who enjoy making sure the retail enterprise runs smoothly may find challenging careers in retail operations.

The purpose of this activity is to help you (1) identify a variety of positions in the retail operations area, (2) determine the qualifications necessary to obtain and hold these positions in stores of various sizes, and (3) become aware of the potential that each kind of position offers for future advancement. To accomplish the above, prepare, in advance, a list of questions you wish to ask operations or store managers. Then, arrange to visit at least five different retail businesses in your community. Determine what retail operations positions are in each business, what qualifications are expected for each, and what potential each position has for career employment or advancement. Compare the answers you obtain from different types and sizes of stores. Place this information in your career planning notebook.

Developing a Business Plan

Develop the following for the retail business you plan to organize and operate:

1. A floor plan of your store showing the location of the selling area, reserve stock area, receiving and marking area, and offices and customer-service area
2. A diagram of your selling area showing the location of various merchandise, forward stock, and sales registers
3. A statement on the type of credit you will offer customers and your credit policy
4. A description of your credit application and approval procedure
5. A description of your credit collection procedure
6. The procedure you plan to follow in the receiving, checking, and marking of incoming merchandise
7. A list of information you plan to include on your price tickets
8. A description of the stock control system you plan to use in your store
9. A list of stock security methods you plan to use in your store

UNIT 8
Business Control

Control involves determining whether goals are being met and taking appropriate action if they are not being met. Business control begins with the initial financing of a business and continues throughout the life of the business. For effective business control, a retailer needs detailed information, especially financial data, about the business. Furthermore, the right information must be available in an easy-to-understand form at the time a decision is required.

Unit 8 discusses basic issues of financing a business, major merchandise records, and essential financial statements. You will learn the main sources of capital, how capital needs are determined, how retailers obtain capital funds, and how they distribute capital for different purposes. You will also learn about the major merchandise records – namely, purchase and inventory records – and different ways of valuing merchandise inventory. Also, sales and expense records are studied in the unit; expense and tax records receive special treatment. Two financial statements basic to business control, the income statement and the balance sheet, are also presented in the unit.

Finally, Unit 8 will give you insight into the planning and use of retail information systems, particularly electronic systems, to record transaction data, compile vital retailing reports, and serve other special retailing needs.

After studying this unit and completing the activities, you should be able to:

1. Identify major sources of business capital and explain the difference between fixed and working capital
2. Describe the kinds of information that lending agencies want from loan applicants
3. Describe purchase orders and invoices and explain procedures for handling these forms
4. Explain the difference between physical and book inventory and calculate book inventory
5. Describe the procedure for doing a sales register proof of cash
6. Classify operating expenses in several ways and identify expenses that are frequently mishandled
7. Describe the five most common taxes retailers are required to pay
8. Describe procedures for preparing an income statement and a balance sheet
9. Describe five common reports used for retailing decisions
10. Describe five applications of computer technology to the retailing field

CHAPTER 46

Financing a Business

CHAPTER OUTCOMES

When you have mastered the information provided in this chapter, you should be able to:

1. Explain the difference between fixed and working capital

2. Explain why fixed capital should be kept at a minimum in relation to working capital

3. Describe three ways a person may become an owner of a retail business

4. Describe the three classifications of building equipment

5. Describe the kinds of information lending agencies want when considering granting a loan

6. Identify the major sources of capital that are available to most store owners

To establish and operate a retail business, a merchant must have adequate funds to cover business facilities, merchandise, salaries, and operating expenses. The amount of funds needed depends on how the business facility is obtained, the nature of the merchandise carried, the type of business equipment needed, and the scope of the business operation. If the business is to be successful, it is important that initial financing methods as well as operating records and procedures be used that will effectively control the funds used in the business. Good records are necessary if the owner is to have accurate information about the financial condition of the business. This chapter presents the type of funds needed by a retailer and the sources of business financing. Subsequent chapters in this unit present the various operating records needed for effective control of the business.

Determining Capital Needs

Any potential store owner needs to study carefully location, equipment, layout, merchandise lines, insurance needs, and other operation expenses before making decisions about the amount of money required. Banks and private lenders expect to see a detailed and well-planned financial proposal before giving any thought to approving a loan.

Two kinds of capital investments are required to operate a retail business. One kind, called **fixed capital,** is money invested in such things as land, building, store fixtures, and equipment. The other, referred to as **working capital,** is the money available to buy merchandise for re-

sale and to cover operating expenses. Part of the margin between the cost of goods and the selling price received when the goods are sold becomes working capital.

Important, but often overlooked, is the need to have a cash reserve as part of the working capital of a business. A **cash reserve fund** is money readily available to cover any unexpected expenses. Unfortunately, some new store owners discover too late that certain expenses were overlooked when the capital needs of their businesses were determined. Even if such an error does not occur, many retailers believe that it is better to have a cash reserve and not need it than it is to need it and not have it. New retailers should remember that three to six months pass before most stores begin to bring in enough money to cover expenses. Some new, larger businesses do not reach a break-even point on income and expenses for two or three years after starting. Lacking a cash reserve fund, a new store owner could be under great financial pressure to pay store bills.

Money needs naturally differ from store to store. The type of store, management experience, and length of time the business has existed affect many of the financial decisions that have to be made. It is generally good management policy to keep fixed capital, as a percentage of the total capital needed, as low as possible. Renting instead of buying a building or leasing instead of buying equipment and fixtures on the installment plan are ways to limit the amount of money that is tied up in fixed capital investments. In every instance, though, care should be taken not to short-circuit the store's chances to succeed. A penny saved may be a dollar lost if customers go elsewhere to shop because a store owner chose a poor location, outdated fixtures, or old equipment to keep fixed capital costs down.

SOURCES OF CAPITAL

Store owners have often discovered that money is easier to borrow when it is not really needed than when a real need exists. One reason for this tendency may be that lenders generally view an established business to be a better risk than a newly formed business. Experienced retailers also know not to depend on just one source for all financial assistance. For these reasons, anyone planning for store ownership should be aware of common sources of retail store capital: personal savings, bank loans, part-

nerships, incorporation, and trade credit. The major sources and types of funds needed by a retailer are shown in Illustration 46–1.

Personal Savings

The initial investment required to start a new business usually comes from the retailer's own savings. This investment in the business by the owner is also called **equity capital.** When the equity capital investment is small, the retailer must look to other sources to provide the balance of needed funds. Some beginning business owners seek financial help from friends and relatives. In most cases, however, it is wise to check other capital sources first, since business, family, and social relationships often

SOURCES OF BUSINESS CAPITAL

Types of Funds	Sources
Equity capital • proprietorship; stocks; retained earnings	• owner investment; reinvested profits
Long-term debt • mortgage loans on real estate; equipment • bonds with collateral • term loans	• banks; loan agencies; insurance companies • individuals • trade creditors; suppliers
Short-term debt • open-trade accounts • notes and drafts • pledged accounts receivable	• wholesalers; vendors • banks; finance companies; loan agencies • banks; finance companies

Illus. 46–1   *The type of funds needed by a retailer can be provided from several sources. Equity capital investment and long-term debt are used for fixed capital expenditures. Short-term debt is used for working capital.*

are unstable. The size of the personal financial investment made by the owner is almost always a factor in determining lenders' willingness to provide additional capital.

Banks and Loan Associations

Commercial banks and loan associations are major sources of capital for retail-store operators. Two types of loans are available from these sources. Short-term debts are loans for one year or less and are most often used as working capital. Long-term debts are loans to be repaid after one year or more. Long-term loans may be used to meet the fixed capital needs of a business. Most loans to new businesses are short-term, but some banks will consider providing loans for up to ten years. In either case, the decision to approve or disapprove a loan depends on the retailer's financial condition and ability to repay the loan. Since the policies of lending institutions vary widely, it is wise to shop around before choosing a bank or association with which to do business.

Banks are generally willing to lend money when the retailer has collateral that can be used to back up the requested loan. **Collateral** is anything of value a bank can sell to recover its money if the loan is not repaid. Examples of acceptable collateral include the store owner's merchandise inventory, equipment, store building, life insurance policies, and accounts receivable (money owed to the store by customers).

Retailers can also obtain money from personal loan companies. Similar to banks, these firms are more willing to lend money when acceptable collateral is available. Loan companies may also lend money if the prospective borrower can get another responsible person to sign a note guaranteeing payment if the store owner is unable to pay. Such a loan is called a *cosigner loan*.

Partnership

One of the easiest and often best ways to obtain capital for a retail store is to take a partner. A partner, who will invest funds in return for part ownership, can have either an active or a silent role in the operation of the business. The advantages and disadvantages of business partnerships are described in Chapter 12.

Corporate Financing

Many large, well-established companies raise capital by using corporate financing. Corporate financing is done mainly through the sale of stocks or bonds. As described in Chapter 12, stock represents shares of ownership in the corporation. Owners of stock (stockholders) are entitled to a share of the business profits (dividends) if any are earned and declared. A bond does not represent a share of ownership but is a debt owed by the corporation. Bonds are issued to people called *bondholders* who provide capital for the business. The bond is a written promise by the corporation to repay the bondholder a definite sum of money at a certain time and to pay interest at regular intervals. Bondholders must be paid interest before stockholders can receive any dividends.

Trade Credit

When a new store owner finds it difficult to obtain short-term loans, trade credit can provide much-needed working capital. **Trade credit** is credit granted by wholesalers and other store suppliers for the purpose of buying merchandise for resale. When a retailer orders merchandise, the supplier may agree to postpone payment for 30 or 60 days or longer periods. If payment is made in less time, the supplier may allow the retailer to take a discount on the amount to be paid. As explained in Chapter 24, these terms are negotiated at the time orders for goods are written.

Trade credit is the most widely used source of financing available to retail store owners today. Newcomers to store management should, however, use extreme caution in selecting the kinds and amounts of merchandise they intend to sell when using trade credit. Only merchandise that has the best chance of being sold rapidly should be ordered. When a plan of action for store operation includes trade credit, increased business, satisfied customers, and additional cash reserve can result if that credit is used wisely.

Retailers may get extended trade credit in some situations. If the retailer agrees to carry a particular line of goods, the supplier may agree to provide funds in addition to the delayed billing on merchandise. The advantage to the supplier is the assured access to a market for an extended period and, in all likelihood, a strong voice in how the goods will be promoted and displayed. If the supplier's line of merchandise is what the retailer would like to carry, extended trade credit can be a profitable arrangement for both supplier and retailer.

OBTAINING CAPITAL FUNDS

Knowledge of the financial facts and practices of business life can save a borrower time and embarrassment. The ability to obtain capital when it is needed is as important as knowing how to choose a good store location, proper equipment, capable personnel, and quality merchandise.

Lack of experience with lending practices can lead to frustration and disappointment for retailer borrowers. If the borrower has only a vague notion of how much capital is needed and how the capital will be used, lenders will hesitate. Lenders want to see a carefully laid out plan for the business, including plans for how the capital funds will be distributed between fixed and working capital and estimates of expenses and income. Most lenders will loan more to some businesses than to others, depending upon the characteristics of each business that applies for a loan. Such limitations are for the borrower's as well as the lender's protection. Before a lending agency will

Illus. 46–2 Borrowing capital to start a business can be a difficult hurdle for persons planning to become store owners.

consider lending money to any business, satisfactory answers to questions such as the following need to be provided by the borrower:

1. What evidence of your character and ability to pay can you provide? What sort of person are you—the prospective borrower? What experiences have you had in running a business and managing business funds?

2. What are you going to do with the money? Do you have specific plans for equipment, merchandise, remodeling, or repayment of other loans? The intended use of the loan helps the lender determine the kind of loan needed.

3. When and how do you plan to pay back the money? Do you plan to pay it back in installments? in a lump sum? The lender's judgment as to the borrower's business ability and the type of loan requested provide partial answers to this question.

4. Does the loan provide sufficient funds to accomplish what is intended? Just as you need a cash reserve in planning needed capital, the borrower needs to allow a cushion in the loan for unexpected costs.

5. What alternatives to obtaining this loan have been considered? Some retailers turn to borrowing funds as the first means of resolving a problem. Lenders will want to know if nonfinancial solutions have been considered.

6. What is the outlook for business in general and your proposed store in particular? The lender has to know how many similar businesses exist and how successful they are. Also, the lender requires evidence that the store you are proposing is needed.

Many persons seeking funds for a business operation feel that lenders are prying or are overly critical when they ask questions such as those just listed. However, lenders must have assurance that the borrower is entering into a loan with an understanding of her or his needs and with full awareness of the risks and obligations involved.

DISTRIBUTION OF CAPITAL

Persons who are planning to enter into a retail business are often encouraged to think of the capital they have to invest as being in three piles. In one pile is the fixed capital for long-term investment in building, fixtures, and other equipment. The second pile contains the working capital—the funds for merchandise and for operating expenses. The third pile, also working capital, is the cash reserve needed to cover unexpected expenses. The amount needed in each of these piles varies depending upon how the owner wishes to operate.

Fixed Capital

The fixed capital requirements of a business vary according to how the retailer acquires a business and how the store is equipped.

Buying into a Business. Becoming a partner in an existing business is fairly easy when compared to buying a business or starting a new store. Partnership opportunities can be found by asking manufacturers and wholesalers. Store owners looking for partners may advertise in newspapers and trade journals. The soundness of a business may be determined by having an accountant check the store records and by inspecting the merchandise. Buying into a business often provides a good return on the investment because the new funds increase the fixed and working capital already invested by the original owner. However, buying into a business may limit the changes and procedures that an incoming partner may initiate.

Buying an Existing Business.

The seller of a going business will set an asking price. The buyer must test the fairness of that price by determining the condition of the building, fixtures, equipment, and stock. A good business may be worth ten to twenty times its current yearly profits. Advantages of buying an existing business are that the new business owner can start immediately, the business and the potential of the location are known, and past business records are available to guide future business actions.

The chief disadvantage of buying a going business is that usually more capital is required than would be necessary to establish a new store of a similar kind, since the owner will want to be paid for goodwill as well as for tangible assets. Goodwill, of course, arises from the reputation of the business and its relations with its customers. As an asset, goodwill is that value of a business in excess of the owner's total investment.

Not all stores offered for sale have a customer following that justifies paying for goodwill. Therefore, persons planning to invest in an existing business should view available businesses with caution. Why is the business being sold? Is the business unsuccessful?

However, good reasons for an owner to sell a business include the owner's age or ill health or desire for a change in location or occupation. Sometimes an owner may be unsuited for business ownership and may wish to sell the investment. Nothing may be wrong with the business that careful management cannot correct. Whatever the reason, the capital requirements of buying an existing store should be compared carefully to requirements of other options.

Starting a New Business.

Many persons planning to go into business have the mistaken idea that retailing is an easy road to riches. Such thinking attracts many unqualified people to open stores of their own. The inability of people to judge themselves objectively and to recognize their lack of management skills is a frequent cause of retail failure. On the other hand, a new business, especially in rented space, often may be started with limited funds, limiting fixed capital requirements to fixtures and some equipment.

Building and Store Equipment.

The term *equipment* includes everything, except the building, people, and merchandise, necessary to perform the selling and nonselling functions of a store. Articles of equipment may be classified as (1) building equipment, such as floor coverings, sprinklers, heating and cooling systems, and escalators; (2) selling equipment, such as shelves, counters, display racks, sales registers, and lighting; and (3) nonselling equipment, such as delivery trucks, data processing equipment, ticket-marking machines, and office machines. Equipment necessary for a retail store can require a sizable portion of the fixed capital. Proper equipment reduces operating expenses, minimizes labor costs, speeds and controls the movement of merchandise, and adds to the attractiveness of the store. A retailer with limited fixed capital would probably give priority to building and selling equipment, especially those items that attract customers and help them shop. Nonselling equipment can be upgraded and selling equipment added as the retailer gets more funds.

Working Capital

With careful planning, the amount of capital needed for merchandise and operational expenses can be projected fairly accurately. Many new store owners tend to be overly optimistic about their chances for

success. Thus, it is wise to have sufficient working capital so that income from sales is not the only source of funds for operating expenses over the first several months. Some retail stores will not have enough income from sales to cover operational expenses until after a year or more of operation. Whenever possible, most of the capital available for a business should be earmarked for use as working capital.

Reserve Capital

Reserve capital should be maintained in bank accounts where the funds will earn interest for the retailer. Some of the reserve should be available in 30-day accounts and the rest in 60- or 90-day accounts. A minimum reserve equals all of one month's expenses; a safer reserve equals three months' expenses.

Summary

Two kinds of capital are needed to start or operate a retail business: fixed capital for the building and equipment and working capital for the merchandise and operating expenses. Five sources of capital are the personal savings of the retailer, banks and loan associations, partnerships, corporation financing, and trade credit. To obtain funds, the retailer must have a clear idea of how much money is needed and how it will be used in the business. New retailers must be sure to have adequate working capital to carry them through the first several months of operation. Careful allocation of the capital used in financing a business is an essential first step in the control of the retail business.

Review

1. Explain the difference between fixed capital and working capital.
2. Explain the purpose of a cash reserve.
3. Name three ways in which a person may become an owner of a retail business.

4. Name four ways that additional capital can be obtained for a retail business.
5. Define *collateral* and list five examples.
6. What is a cosigner loan?
7. Name three classifications of equipment in a retail store.

Terms

The following terms were introduced in this chapter. Write a separate sentence correctly using each new term.

cash reserve funds   fixed capital
collateral   trade credit
equity capital   working capital

Discuss

1. What types of retail stores would require large amounts of fixed capital? Which retail stores require a minimum of fixed capital?
2. In what types of retail businesses would cash reserves need to be fairly large? For what businesses could the cash reserves be relatively small?
3. Is it appropriate for a lender to ask borrowers how they handle their personal finances? Why or why not?
4. Should a retailer avoid borrowing capital from relatives or friends? Why or why not?

Problem Solving

1. Ted and Barb, who both have some prior retail experience, plan to start a new sporting-goods store. They are ready to seek financial assistance to buy a store. They have arranged a meeting with a local banker. How should they prepare for this meeting? What information should they have ready to show the banker? What questions should they be ready to answer?
2. Ted and Barb have $14,500 in equity capital. They plan to rent store space (including utilities) at $600 per month and invest $16,000 in merchandise and $4,800 in equipment. They estimate other monthly expenses at $2,400. Based on these figures, what amount of capital will they need? How much will be in fixed capital? in working capital? How much should they have in cash reserve? How much will they have to borrow?
3. Instead of renting, Ted and Barb decided to buy a building at $25,000 down and $400 a month for 15 years. They still plan to invest $16,000 in merchandise and $4,800 in equipment, and they expect other monthly expenses of $2,400. Based on these

figures, what amount of capital will they need? How much will be fixed capital? working capital? How much should they have in cash reserve? How much will they have to borrow?

4. Look in the business opportunity section of the newspaper classified ads. Find six examples of retail businesses for sale. What amounts of capital would be needed to buy these businesses? What financial help, if any, is offered or suggested in these ads?

CHAPTER 47

Merchandise Records

CHAPTER OUTCOMES

When you have mastered the information provided in this chapter, you should be able to:

1. Describe each of the records necessary to maintain control over purchases

2. Describe the purpose of good merchandise-purchase and inventory records

3. Explain what information is contained in a purchase-order file

4. Explain the flow of a vendor's invoice from point of receipt to payment

5. Describe the procedure necessary to take a physical inventory

6. Calculate book or perpetual inventory

7. Calculate the cost of an inventory

In most retail businesses, the greater portion of working capital is invested in merchandise. Through the sale of this merchandise, the business receives income that, in turn, is used to pay for more merchandise and operating expenses and to provide a profit. Thus, it is important to have records that accurately show which merchandise has been ordered, which goods have been received, which goods have been paid for, and the amount of goods presently in inventory. The purpose of good merchandise-purchase and inventory records is to make sure that unneeded goods are not ordered, that needed goods are ordered and received before present stock is depleted, and that merchandise payments are made promptly.

PURCHASE RECORDS

The records of merchandise ordered and received center around two forms. The first is the purchase order (explained in Chapter 24), a form used to order merchandise from suppliers. The second is the invoice (described in Chapter 43), a form from the vendor that charges for the merchandise purchased.

Purchase Order

Merchants usually maintain purchase order files, either manually or in computers, that show what has been ordered and from whom, how the goods are to be shipped, and the date the goods are expected to arrive. Some firms keep this file current by making a copy of each purchase order; others store all purchase orders in a computer file. On the purchase-order copy, retailers may enter the retail price to be marked on the merchandise and may note any changes in the order agreed upon with the vendor. Firms with computerized ordering can key such purchase-order information into a data file.

After the ordered merchandise has been received, it is checked and prepared for the selling floor as described in Chapters 43 and 44. The invoice from the supplier is matched with the corresponding purchase order. Any discrepancies in count, cost, style, color, or size are noted. Special care must be taken when an invoice contains merchandise from more than one purchase order. The cost prices are recorded by the vendors, and the manager or buyer marks the retail prices on each invoice opposite the cost prices. Thus, the record of purchases may be kept at both cost and retail prices. After this verification of invoice against the purchase order, the invoice is filed in the unpaid-invoice file. (Note: Purchase orders for store operation supplies and fixtures are kept separate from merchandise purchases.)

Merchants who want a more complete record of purchases enter the amount of invoices in a purchase book, which is a record of all invoices received. In a department store, the purchases of each department are separated in the purchase book. From this book, accounting clerks transfer the information to a vendor's ledger or accounts payable ledger. In this ledger, each creditor's account is kept on a separate page, and payments made are deducted from each account. Retailers who have computerized invoice records may periodically print out the status of all accounts payable (unpaid invoices) as well as the invoices for each department. A procedure for purchase-order control is shown in Illustration 47–1 and in the description that follows:

1. Purchase order (PO)—showing what is ordered and from whom, how goods are to be shipped, and the date goods are expected to arrive—is sent to vendor

2. Planned retail prices of the merchandise are marked on store copy of the PO by buyer or merchandise manager

3. PO is filed in manual (copy) or computer system

4. Merchandise and invoice arrive from vendor

5. Copy of the PO is pulled from the file system and PO information compared

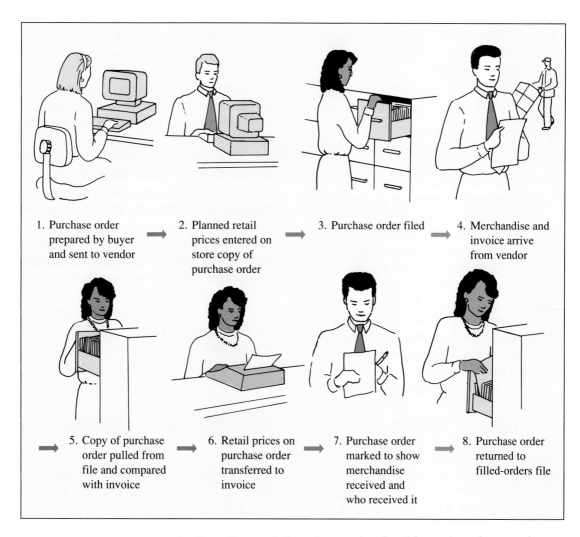

1. Purchase order prepared by buyer and sent to vendor

2. Planned retail prices entered on store copy of purchase order

3. Purchase order filed

4. Merchandise and invoice arrive from vendor

5. Copy of purchase order pulled from file and compared with invoice

6. Retail prices on purchase order transferred to invoice

7. Purchase order marked to show merchandise received and who received it

8. Purchase order returned to filled-orders file

Illus. 47–1 The purchase order lists what goods have been ordered and from whom, how goods are to be shipped, when they should arrive, and what carrier will deliver them. The purchase order begins the process of obtaining merchandise.

with invoice information (quantities, descriptions, unit prices, total prices, and other terms of sale); all discrepancies between the PO and invoice are traced until they are eliminated or reported

6. Retail prices penciled on the PO are transferred to the invoice beside the vendor's cost price, thus keeping purchase records in both cost and retail figures

7. PO is marked to show when and how merchandise was received and who actually received it

8. PO is returned to a filled-orders file

Invoice

Paralleling the flow of merchandise from the receiving point to the selling floor is the flow of the vendor's invoice from the point of receipt to the office for payment. Just as the merchandise must be controlled to avoid loss or delay, so the invoice must be controlled. This control should ensure accuracy and speed so that cash discounts may be obtained and the correct changes made on the purchase records of the various departments. The procedure followed by a store to keep track of the invoice in process is called **invoice control.**

As shown in Illustration 47–2, invoice control begins by checking each invoice against the buyer's purchase order. The invoice is next checked against the appropriate receiving record, and the apron is attached to the invoice. Then, the invoice is checked against the actual goods in the shipment. After these checks have been made and found to be correct, the buyer enters on the invoice the retail price of each item and approves the invoice for payment.

If errors are found, appropriate discrepancy reports must be prepared. As previously pointed out, the buyer may enter the retail price on the store copy of the purchase order; that way price tickets can be made up in advance of the shipment to speed the merchandise through the receiving and marking process. If markers use the invoice to prepare price tickets, they should, when finished, send the invoice to the office for payment.

In the office, checks and payment vouchers are prepared, invoices are charged against the department purchase records, and invoices are filed in a paid vendor file. The actual mailing of the check for payment is normally made in time to deduct any cash discount that may be available. An important part of the invoice control process is that every person who handles the invoice—order clerk, checker, buyer, marker, receiving manager—is required to initial it. Thus, the office knows whether an invoice has passed through every necessary step. When an invoice is paid, it is removed from an unpaid-invoice file and placed in a paid-invoice file. The total remaining in the unpaid-invoice file is the amount due creditors. (Note: Invoices for store operation supplies and fixtures are kept separate from the invoices for merchandise.)

INVENTORY RECORDS

If retailers are to have control over their merchandise, they must know what they have in inventory at all times. An inventory that is overstocked with some goods and understocked with others hinders effective merchandising. The two major

1. Invoice checked against purchase order →
2. Invoice checked against receiving record and apron attached →
3. Invoice checked against goods in shipment →
4. Retail price entered on invoice and approved for payment

→ 5. Invoice used to prepare price tickets →
6. Invoice sent to office for payment →
7. Invoice paid and placed in paid-vendor file

Illus. 47–2   The flow of an invoice from the receiving point to the office is controlled carefully. Persons involved in receiving, checking, and marking should be able to find a particular invoice at any time.

means of maintaining inventory records are (1) an actual physical count of the goods in stock or (2) a running count of goods received and goods sold. The latter is called a *book record* or a *perpetual inventory* of the goods.

Physical Inventory

To determine the financial standing of a business and to determine profit for a certain period, a merchant must know the total value of the stock on hand. This value may be found by taking a physical inventory— actually counting the goods on hand. Most stores take two physical inventories a year—generally, at the end of January and at the end of July. Some stores take only one; and there are still a few small stores that take no complete inventory but merely guess the value of the stock on hand. These merchants lose the opportunity to determine just what is in stock, to analyze it to control buying and promotion, and to familiarize store personnel with the goods on hand.

To minimize the amount of merchandise to be counted, many merchants reduce their stocks on hand to a low point between seasons before taking a physical inventory. This practice accounts for the many preinventory sales in stores. Goods are pulled out of forward stock bins and moved in from reserve stockrooms, reduced in price, and sold before inventory-taking begins.

After stock has been reduced as much as possible through clearance sales, the merchandise is sorted and put back into its proper place. Missing price tickets and labels are replaced. Then, the merchandise is counted—usually at retail value although sometimes at cost. One counting method uses tags numbered in sequence which are attached to each different style or lot number of merchandise. The merchandise is counted, and the count is entered on each tag. A second method uses sheets rather than tags, and many lot numbers are listed on each sheet. A third method usually involves two persons: a counter and a recorder. As the counter calls out the item and number, the recorder enters the data on cards or on electronic counters. In some operations, the counter dictates the data directly into a tape recorder or keys it into a microcomputer. A fourth method utilizes modern scanning equipment. This method, which can update inventory counts already in the computer system, has proved to be very accurate.

In taking physical inventory, it is a good practice to record the age of each item on hand as measured from the date of receipt. Subtotals may then be calculated to show, for example, how much merchandise on hand is new, how much is less than three months old, and how much is three to six months old. If the proportion of old stock is increasing, mark-downs and other promotional steps should be taken to move it.

Book or Perpetual Inventory

The **book inventory** of merchandise shows the amount that should be on hand according to store records. (The **perpetual inventory** is another name for the book inventory.) As explained in Chapter 44, book records may be maintained either in dollar figures for the value of the goods or in numbers of the amount of units or items. With either method, the retailer begins each period with what is called an **opening inventory.** Purchases are added to the opening inventory. Sales are subtracted from the opening figure. The result is the *closing book inventory,* which should be close if not identical to the physical inventory figure.

To have ample stock to meet customer demand and yet keep the investment in merchandise as low as possible, an up-to-date record of stock on hand is needed. With book or perpetual inventory, the value of goods on hand can be determined at any time without the labor of counting the goods. Book inventory is also a great aid in case of loss due to some disaster such as fire. Without such a record, a store has no way of telling the exact value of the goods destroyed. Despite these advantages, some retailers do not use the book method of inventory. In some cases, the amount of inventory is too small or the per-unit value of the merchandise is so low that the cost of recordkeeping is not justified. Other retailers feel that a periodic physical inventory is sufficient.

BOOK INVENTORY FOR THREE-MONTH PERIOD

Physical Inventory as of May 1 . . . . . . $ 6,000
Purchases May through July . . . .+ 10,500
      Total merchandise handled . . . . . . └⟶ $ 16,500
Sales May through July . . . . $ 9,500
*Markdowns May through July . . . . . .+ 500
      Total . . . . └⟶ −$ 10,000
Book Inventory. . . . . $ 6,500
Physical Inventory as of July 31 . . . .− 6,400
      Merchandise shortage . . . . $ 100

*Note that the price changes—particularly markdowns—must be included in the calculation of retail inventories.

Illus. 47–3   Most merchants record inventory in terms of retail value. The procedure for finding a book inventory is shown.

If the physical inventory is smaller than book inventory, which is usually the case, the difference is a **shortage.** A shortage represents a loss of merchandise in the department or store. If the physical inventory is larger than the book inventory, the difference is an **overage.** An overage often indicates an error in the physical count.

In many stores, merchandise shortages exceed 3 percent of the store's sales; in some, the percentage is even higher. Most retail experts believe that shortages in ex-

MAJOR REASONS FOR SHORTAGES

Clerical Errors
    Failure to record all markdowns taken
    Charging goods to wrong departments
    Errors in handling records of sales and customer returns
    Failure to count part of physical stock

Physical Loss
    Internal employee theft
    Customer theft
    Breakage and damage
    Giving customers more goods than they are charged for
    Undetected shortage in receipts from vendors
    Physical shrinkage in weight or bulk of certain goods

Illus. 47–4   Almost all shortages in the retail value of an inventory are due to recording errors or physical loss.

cess of 0.5 percent indicate serious problems. While some of the reported shortages represent errors in recordkeeping or in taking inventory, a considerable proportion represents theft.

INVENTORY AT CURRENT MARKET VALUE

Merchants usually take inventory at the current retail prices and, for profit-figuring purposes, translate the total retail value to cost or **current market value.** This translation is done by determining the markup percentage on the total merchandise handled (opening inventory plus purchases) and then applying this percentage to the retail price of the inventory. For example, if the current retail inventory is $10,000 and the markup on the goods handled to date is 40 percent, the closing inventory or current market value is $6,000.

Taking inventory at cost is preferable especially in those departments or stores where the markup percentages vary considerably for SKUs. Using computerized stock records, merchants can take inventory at cost and find the total cost value simply by adding the costs of the SKUs. Some merchants also take inventory at cost by referring to codes on price tickets or to other sources of cost data. Since some of the merchandise on hand may be shopworn or out of style, it may have to be valued at less than cost. Thus, the merchandise is valued at the current market value. For example, if the cost of a lot of goods was $1,000, but the merchant estimates that goods of the same style and type and in the same condition can be obtained today for $700, he or she will value the merchandise at $700. However, if the replacement value of these goods is $1,100—$100 more than cost— the goods will be valued at cost ($1,000 in this example). The accepted rule is to value merchandise at cost or market, whichever is lower.

Summary   Merchandise represents the major investment of working capital for most retailers. Good merchandise records are essential to maintaining control over this investment. Two major merchandise records are the purchase order and the invoice. For each of these records, there are recommended procedures to assure that proper control is maintained. Inventory records are necessary if the merchant is to know how much of which goods has been received and sold, and how much remains in stock. The two methods of inventory are physical and book (or perpetual). Nearly all merchants periodically take a physical inventory of stock, and many of them also maintain a perpetual or book inventory. The general practice is to calculate inventory at cost or market value, whichever is lower.

Review

1. Describe the movement of an invoice from the receiving point to the store office.
2. Define the terms *physical inventory* and *book* or *perpetual inventory*.
3. Describe how a physical inventory is taken using inventory sheets.
4. What are the chief reasons for merchandise shortages?
5. At what level are shortages considered to be serious problems?
6. How is the current market value of an inventory determined?

Terms

The following terms were introduced in this chapter. Write a separate sentence correctly using each new term.

book inventory or perpetual   opening inventory
  inventory   overage
current market value   shortage
invoice control

Discuss

1. More and more stores are using computerized merchandise records. Is it necessary for these stores to have paper copies of purchase orders and to move paper copies of invoices through the store? Why or why not?
2. Why is it important that every purchase order be filed in the purchase-order file?
3. If a physical inventory is taken while the store is open and customers are buying merchandise, how can an accurate count be obtained?
4. Why is it necessary to determine closing inventory at cost rather than at retail only?

Problem Solving

1. The manager of a moderate-sized women's ready-to-wear store has asked your help. In recent months, several invoices have been misplaced and, as a result, payments to vendors have been late and cash discount opportunities lost. Currently, purchase orders serve as the basis for receiving, checking, and pricing operations. Invoices received in the office are set aside until a purchase order is sent up from either the receiving or the selling department indicating that goods have been received. You are to recommend to the manager ways to improve the control of purchase records.

2. You are the manager of a small feed, seed, and fertilizer business. Much of what you sell is sold in bulk; that is, when a customer wants five pounds of rabbit feed, the salesperson goes to the storeroom where feed is kept in 100-pound bags. The salesperson weighs out 5 pounds of feed in a paper bag and closes the sale. Frequently, sales are lost and customers are inconvenienced because the feed or seed they want is not on hand. How can you organize this part of your business to assure good inventory control?

3. Your physical inventory shows the following four lots of goods on hand with the original cost prices and current values as shown. What total value should be placed on these four lots?

> Lot A: cost price $720; current value $510
> Lot B: cost price $980; replacement cost $1,270
> Lot C: cost price $1,450; replacement cost $1,160
> Lot D: cost price $1,130; current value $860

4. Your six-month records show the following for men's work gloves:

> On hand 1/1 . . . . 216 pair
> Received 1/1 through 6/30 . . . . 480 pair
> Sold 1/1 through 6/30 . . . . 509 pair
> On hand 6/30 . . . . 184 pair

Do you have a shortage or an overage? How much of one do you have? If the average retail value is $3.19 per pair and the average cost is $1.69, what is your overage or shortage in retail? in cost?

CHAPTER 48

Sales and Expense Records

CHAPTER OUTCOMES

When you have mastered the information provided in this chapter, you should be able to:

1. Explain the purpose of a cash fund

2. Explain how sales registers are used in recording daily sales

3. Set up and accurately complete a proof of cash

4. Classify expenses in natural expense categories

5. Identify and calculate direct and indirect expenses

6. Describe the procedure for establishing and maintaining a petty-cash fund

7. Identify prepaid and accrued expenses

Records of sales and expenses are important for several reasons. Certainly, the retailer wants to be sure that the money taken in, as well as that paid out, is properly accounted for. The merchant also wants to use the data from sales and expense records to identify areas where adjustments need to be made, additional merchandise ordered, and cost controls initiated. The purpose of this chapter is to present basic information about recording and collecting sales data and to illustrate ways of classifying expenses that will be helpful in analyzing and controlling retail performance.

SALES RECORDS

The sales transaction is a key event in the merchandising cycle. The retailer is keenly interested not only in the dollar volume of sales but also in what is sold. Each store or department is striving for a certain level of sales. The merchant may check sales readings hourly to determine if promotions are working or if objectives are being reached. Analysis of both successes and failures and planning for the future require that adequate sales records be maintained.

Recording Cash Sales

A sales register is the principal means of recording sales data. In small businesses, it is usually the sole source of sales records. The sales register contains an adding machine that adds each sale as it is made. If the numbers on the machine are turned back to zero at the beginning of each day, the amount shown at the end of the day represents the total amount of cash sales. In stores with more than one register, the total daily sales are the sum of the readings of all registers.

Some merchants do not turn the register back to zero at the beginning of each day. Instead, they turn the register to zero on a weekly or monthly basis. The last reading of the register becomes the starting number for the next day. For instance, if a register shows $525 at the end of one day and $990 at the end of the second day, the merchant will have to subtract $525 from $990 to get the second day's sales—$465.

The amount of cash put into the register for the purposes of making change is called the **cash fund.** Some supermarket managers, for example, start each register with $100 in currency and coin to handle a day's transactions. Because of the cash fund, the amount of cash in the drawer is more than the register reading of total sales.

Recording Credit Sales

If a customer charges a purchase, the sales record of the transaction must indicate a credit sale and provide information for billing the customer. In small stores, the salesperson usually completes a sales slip, marks it as a charge, and asks the customer to sign the slip. At the end of the day, all sales slips are totaled and then filed in customer folders. At the end of the month, bills are prepared from the slips in each folder. (Customer payments are recorded in a similar manner.) In stores that have electronic sales registers tied in with computerized accounting, credit sales entered into the sales register are automatically entered on the appropriate customers' charge accounts.

At the end of the billing period, the computer prints out a statement for each customer which shows the department, merchandise classification, price of goods purchased on various days, amount paid on account, and balance due. Finance charges (interest on unpaid balances), if any, are also figured electronically and included in the amount due. Some merchants and banks have worked out systems whereby the amount of a customer's charge is automatically deducted from the customer's bank account and added to the store's account at the time of the sale.

Determining Total Sales

All businesses must determine total sales for a specific period. Without the total sales figure, other data from the store records cannot be interpreted and used for store control. The total sales for a day are determined by adding the sales register reading and credit sales, if they are not included in the sales register. This amount

Illus. 48–1 A sales register is the principal means of recording sales data.

represents gross sales. If any merchandise is returned by customers, the value of the returned goods is subtracted from the day's gross sales to obtain the amount of net sales. Net sales plus the cash fund should equal the amount of cash actually in the sales register drawer.

In some specialty stores, a sales slip is made out for every sale, even cash sales. At the end of each day, the amounts on all the sales slips are added. The total represents the gross sales for the day. When sales slips are used to record sales, the slips must be handled as though they were money. Sales slips are numbered and a sales audit is made to determine whether any sales slips are missing. A missing slip will cause the sales figures to be incorrect; therefore, all missing sales slips must be accounted for.

In large stores that have many departments and many salespeople, total store sales can be analyzed by computing the amount of sales for each department or salesperson. Some sales registers have a separate drawer for each salesperson who uses the register. These registers record the sales figures for each drawer separately. In supermarkets and hardware and variety stores, different sales register keys are used to record sales figures for each department or classification of goods.

When using the register reading to determine total sales, it is necessary to count the cash in the drawer to make sure that the amount of cash agrees with the register reading.

The procedure for checking the amount of cash against the sales register reading is called *proof of cash* or *cash-register audit*. Proof of cash involves two steps. The first is determining how much money should be in the sales register. Subtracting the last sales register reading from the current register reading gives the sales for the period. This amount, plus the beginning cash fund, is the amount the drawer should contain. The second step in proof of cash involves totaling the bills, coins, checks, and vouchers in the drawer. Results of the first and second steps should be equal. Any difference is reported as a cash shortage or a cash overage. Regular checks on cash shortages and overages is another means of business control. An example of proof of cash calculations is shown in Illustration 48–2.

Collecting Sales Data

A variety of sales registers used in retail stores have the capacity for accumulating considerable sales data. The current technology uses an electronic wand or scanner that reads the information on price tickets or UPC bars. This information is transmitted to a sales register where each item is recorded and the total sale is computed. The customer may be given a sales slip from the register that shows the name and price of every item purchased. The sales register may immediately pass the information to a computer or may hold the data in a memory unit for periodic transmittal to a computer for recording and analysis. Whatever point-of-sale electronic system is used, the sales data can be periodically sorted, calculated, and tabulated into a sales report.

The electronic and UPC systems are proving a boon to fast-moving sales operations, such as discount stores. Electronic systems reduce the training time required for cashiers, since many operations—such as special sales items, sales discounts, and

PROOF OF CASH

Current register reading	$ 4,657.00	
Last register reading	− 3,124.00	
Sales for the period		$ 1,533.00
Beginning cash		+ 65.00
Drawer must account for		$ 1,598.00

Vouchers and Receipts in Drawer

Refunds (vouchers necessary for all items)	$ 45.00	
Removal for deposit (receipts necessary)	+ 500.00	
	$ 545.00	

Cash in Drawer

Checks	$ 625.00	
Bills	392.00	
Coins	+ 35.45	
Total cash	+ 1,052.45	
Total cash, vouchers, and receipts		$1,597.45
Short		+ .55
		$1,598.00

Illus. 48–2   Study this proof-of-cash procedure carefully. Retail personnel frequently must make proofs of cash.

sales taxes—are handled automatically. Errors are dramatically reduced, and lines at the sales registers move faster. The detailed records that are available on SKUs eliminate the need for frequent physical inventories. Thus, labor, time, and money are saved. Specific means of processing sales data are described in Chapter 50.

EXPENSE RECORDS

The cash outlays and debts that come about in the operation of a business are referred to as *expenses*. Certain expenses, such as rent, utilities, and insurance, are re-

quired and recurring. Other expenses, such as office supplies, bad debt losses, and advertising, may vary considerably from month to month. Proper business control requires grouping expenses into two or more categories.

Classifying Expenses

The many different expenses involved in running a store are easier for the merchant to analyze if they are arranged into classifications. By classifying and analyzing entries in an expense record, the merchant can periodically get a report of total expenses and a breakdown by expense categories. The owner of a small store may need only a simple record of expenses. In a large store, a detailed classification of expenses is necessary for efficient operation.

Any system of classifying expenses should provide guidance to management in future business decisions. Often, a store will use several means of classification at the same time.

Natural Expense Categories. One way to classify expenses is to set up so-called **natural expense categories.** Natural categories include expenses on the same items or clusters of closely related items. For example, all expenses for managers' and buyers' travel naturally belong to a category. Likewise, loss of value (depreciation) on buildings, equipment, and fixtures represents a natural classification of expense. Stores of different sizes use different kinds and numbers of expense categories. A small store may need only six to ten categories, while a large chain store may need 30 or more categories. Following are 18 categories frequently used for expense records in department and specialty stores.

1. Payroll: salaries, wages, commissions, and bonuses
2. Employee fringe benefits: health insurance
3. Advertising: all payments for media used
4. Taxes: local, state, and federal, except income taxes
5. Supplies: for wrapping, delivery, office, and repairs
6. Services: cleaning, repair, delivery, and trash collection
7. Utilities: light, heat, water, and power
8. Unclassified: cash shortages and meal money
9. Travel: transportation, meals, and hotel bills

10. Communication: postage, telephone, faxes, and telegrams
11. Pensions: retirement allowances
12. Insurance: fire and public liability
13. Depreciation: building, equipment, and fixtures
14. Professional services: legal, accounting, and resident buying office
15. Donations: charitable, welfare, and educational
16. Bad debts: bad checks and unpaid customer charge accounts
17. Equipment rentals: sales registers, delivery trucks, and special fixtures
18. Real property rental: store building and warehouse

Interest charges incurred on borrowed money are also treated by many stores as additional items of operating expenses. Some department stores treat interest charges as deductions from income but do not classify the charges as operating expenses. Whatever the size of the business, it is important to use enough categories to provide the information needed.

Functional Expenses Categories. Large stores also classify their expenses by **functional expense categories** of the business. Functional categories include expenses associated with particular functions such as merchandising, selling, sales promotion, store operations, and control. These headings may be further divided into subcategories. For instance, in promotion, the subcategories may be print media, direct mail, radio, television, and public relations. The functional category of store operations might be subdivided into payroll, fringe benefits, supplies, utilities, and depreciation. The need for other functional divisions varies with the size and type of store.

Fixed, Semivariable, and Variable Expenses.

Another means of classifying expenses is to consider them as fixed, semivariable, or variable. **Fixed expenses** include rent, insurance premiums, taxes, and other expenses that do not change with sales volume. **Semivariable expenses,** such as advertising expenditures and charitable donations, vary somewhat according to sales volume but are more or less controlled by management policy. **Variable expenses** fluctuate almost in direct relation to sales volume. Commissions to salespeople and expenditures for supplies are examples of variable expenses.

Direct and Indirect Expenses.

Expenses that are paid out solely for the benefit of one department and are charged against that department's sales income are called **direct expenses.** Direct expenses include salaries for employees, advertising, selling supplies, and travel and communication expenses.

Indirect expenses are outlays of funds that serve the whole store. Examples are rent, heat, electricity, taxes, insurance, and payroll of nonselling departments. Thus, if a department's sales are $57,000, the cost of goods it sells is $40,000, and its direct expenses are $11,500, the department is contributing $5,500 *($57,000 − $40,000 = $17,000; $17,000 − $11,500 = $5,500)* to cover the indirect expenses and the profit of the store as a whole. Some stores allocate indirect expenses among departments. Such allocations may be made on the basis of space used (if a department uses 40 percent of the space, it may be charged 40 percent of the indirect expenses) or on sales volume (if a department produces 30 percent of the sales, it may be charged 30 percent of the indirect expenses).

Analyzing Expense Records

After expenses have been properly classified, they can be analyzed by comparing the dollar figures in each classification with figures from past records. Or, expenses may be analyzed by translating the dollar figures into a percentage of sales and comparing the percentage to that of previous periods. The latter method of analysis is preferred. Simply comparing dollar figures does not always give an accurate picture of the relationship of expenses to other aspects of the company's operation. Suppose, for example, that payroll expense was $24,800 last year and $26,280 this year. Comparing these two figures indicates that payroll expense is increasing, which may cause concern. However, suppose that last year's sales amounted to $310,000 and this year's sales amount to $360,000. The payroll expense last year was 8 percent of sales; this year it is 7.3 percent of sales. In this case, the dollar increase in payroll expense should cause no alarm.

Mishandled Expense Records

Three types of expenses often mishandled, especially by the small business owner, are petty cash expenses, delayed expenses such as depreciation and interest, and personal salary expenses. It is easy to fail to record these expenses, but every business should make a special effort to avoid overlooking them in recordkeeping procedures.

Petty-Cash Fund.

Small expenditures, such as those for an urgently needed light bulb, pencils, and postage, are paid from the **petty-cash fund.** The merchant may write a check for $50 and from this cash pay small incidental bills. When the fund becomes low, another check is cashed to restore the amount to the $50 level. A record should be maintained of the amounts and purposes for which the petty cash was spent. A petty-cash record is shown in Illustration 48–3, a similar record can be kept on a computer. Periodically, the merchant can classify these expenses along with other expenses.

Prepaid and Accrued Expenses.

Merchants must keep records of expenses that involve cash outlays that cover future obligations and expenses which are paid sometime after they occur. A **prepaid expense** would be insurance. Insurance pre-

miums are usually paid in advance for six months or a year. Thus, they are prepaid for a period. An **accrued expense** is one that accumulates but is not paid immediately. For example, a delivery truck, for which $10,000 was paid, may wear out in five years. When the truck was first purchased, the $10,000 paid was treated as an asset not as an expense. Every year, however, the truck is worth less. The amount of depreciation should be included in expenses and an appropriate amount deducted from the asset amount. After five years, the accrued expenses for the truck should be sufficient to buy a new one. Also, any taxes due during the year are expenses but may be paid on a quarterly or yearly basis. A store may spend $350 for supplies and, at the end of the year, $75 worth of supplies may still be on

PETTY CASH RECORD				
Date	For	Paid To	Cash in Fund	Cash Paid
Jan 3	Cash	Petty Cash	50 00	
Jan 6	Pencils-Felt Pens	Green's Variety		7 17
Jan 11	Order Forms	B&D Printing		10 60
Jan 17	Stamps	U.S. Postal Service		11 80
Jan 21	Newspaper	Craig Winn		4 60
Jan 29	Display Signs	Graphics, Limited		14 32
				48 49
Jan 31	Balance		1 51	
Jan 31	Cash	Petty Cash	48 49	
Jan 31	New Balance		50 00	

Illus. 48–3   Wise retailers set up petty-cash records to keep track of small incidental expenses.

hand. The expense figure for supplies is the cost of supplies used—$275. The $75 worth of supplies left is an asset.

Owner's Salary. The merchant may include as an expense a reasonable salary for herself or himself. If a salary is drawn out regularly, it should appear with other expenses in the cash payments record. If a salary is not drawn out, the undrawn salary may be included in expenses and treated as a liability (an amount owed by the store). Recording her or his salary as a business expense helps the merchant determine whether the business is providing a return in addition to a reasonable salary.

Summary

Successful merchants know the importance to business decision making of having accurate sales and expense records. In most stores, a sales register, used to store the cash fund, is used also to record sales data. Both cash and credit sales are entered in the sales register at the time of the sale; in addition, credit sales are recorded on customer-account records and mailed monthly. Almost all merchants determine total sales and a proof of cash each business day. Up-to-the-minute information about what is sold is as valuable as knowing the dollar volume of sales. Electronic register-based systems allow large amounts of sales information to be gathered, analyzed, stored, and reported with little investment of time or effort.

The expenses of operating a business must be recorded, too. A first step in control is classifying expenses into natural (related) or functional categories. Expenses also may be classified as fixed, semivariable, or variable, according to variation of the expense in relation to sales. Expenses associated with a particular department are called *direct*, while those for a whole store are called *indirect*. Expense figures have meaning when they are analyzed and compared with other figures, such as total sales. Wise merchants take extra care to keep accurate records of petty-cash expenses, prepaid and accrued expenses, and owner's salary expenses—three expenses often handled improperly.

Review

1. Explain how daily sales are determined from a sales register.
2. How do merchandise returns by customers affect the daily sales total?
3. Describe the proof-of-cash procedure.
4. List at least eight natural expense categories.
5. What is the difference between fixed and variable expenses?
6. Describe two ways of analyzing expenses after they have been grouped into classifications.

7. List three special expense records that are often carelessly handled by the small-business owner.

Terms

The following terms were introduced in this chapter. Write a separate sentence correctly using each new term.

accrued expenses   natural expense categories
cash fund   petty-cash fund
direct expenses   prepaid expenses
fixed expenses   semivariable expenses
functional expense categories   variable expenses
indirect expenses

Discuss

1. What effect will a power failure have on the selling activities of a large department store? If you were a salesperson, what would you do to complete sales transactions in the event of a power outage?
2. You are a department manager. You have four sales registers and ten salespeople. Register proof-of-cash regularly shows both shortages and overages. What action should you take to make sure that cash is properly handled and that the sales records are correct?
3. Which natural expense categories are most likely to be used by an owner of a small radio and TV business?
4. Why would a large store prefer to allocate indirect expenses among the departments?

Problem Solving

1. Develop a list of the various types of sales registers that could be used by retailers (mechanical, electronic, and electronic with optical scanners). Visit several retail stores in your community and observe the type of sales register(s) used by each. From what you have observed, which types of registers are most commonly used and which types of data are collected on each sales transaction of each register?
2. If the beginning sales register reading is $650, the cash fund is $45, and the ending sales register reading is $975, what are the sales for the period? If you have $310.35 in cash and coin and two checks and credit sales slips totaling $69.75, do you have the correct amount? If not, how much are you short or over?

3. A petty-cash fund starts with $25. The following expenses are paid: pads, $3.10; stamps, $2.40; postage due, $1.05; Girl Scout cookies, $5.60; and newspapers, $2.60. How much should remain in the petty-cash fund?

4. Visit one department of a department store. After examining the department operation, list what you consider to be the department's direct expenses and indirect expenses. Now take each expense and further classify it as fixed, semivariable, or variable. What problems did you encounter when making these classifications?

CHAPTER 49

Tax Expense Records and Financial Statements

CHAPTER OUTCOMES

When you have mastered the information provided in this chapter, you should be able to:

1. Describe each of the five most common taxes paid by retailers

2. Describe what data and calculations are necessary to prepare an income statement

3. Explain three ways to increase net income

4. Calculate net profit and pure profit for a small business

5. Describe what data and calculations are necessary to prepare a balance sheet

6. Explain why a retailer should have a records-retention schedule

Retailers must pay various kinds of taxes. **Taxes** are sums of money or fees imposed by local, state, or federal governmental units. Some taxes are paid from business income, and other taxes are collected by the retailer from customers and employees. These taxes are a source of revenue for local, state, and federal governments. According to law, taxes must be paid to the appropriate government agencies at specific times. Accurate tax records are needed by every retailer.

Records of tax expenses are also an essential part of preparing financial statements for a business. Financial statements show what is happening to a business. With records of purchases, inventories, sales, and expenses (including taxes), financial statements can be prepared that reflect the total picture of a business operation.

TAXES

Retail merchants pay various kinds of taxes. Records are necessary to assure that tax money is properly collected or calculated and then sent to the appropriate local, state, or federal agency. Only with good records on each kind of tax can the retailer have adequate control over these expenses. The most common taxes paid by retailers are income taxes, property taxes, sales taxes, payroll taxes, and special taxes.

Income Taxes

Businesses must pay a federal income tax based on their profits. In a majority of states, business owners must pay a state income tax as well, and, in recent years, a number of cities have established local income taxes. State and local taxes are usually lower than federal taxes.

Owners of corporations are actually taxed twice. The corporation's profits are taxed; then, the shareholders pay personal income taxes on dividends they receive. Persons in partnerships and sole proprietorships are taxed only once. They pay no taxes on the business earning, but owners pay personal income taxes on the money they receive from the business.

Property Taxes

Three kinds of property owned by a business person are also taxed: real estate, personal property, and intangible property. A **real-property tax** is one levied on real estate; that is, land and buildings. Local government units get most of their operating funds from real-property taxes. A **personal-property tax** often is levied on such items as furniture, merchandise, and equipment. An **intangible-property tax** is levied on the stocks, cash, and securities a business owns. Property taxes are stated in terms of mills (a monetary measure; one mill equals one tenth of a cent) or dollars for each thousand dollars of assessed valuation. (Note: The assessed valuation of property set by the local government may not be the same value as that reported by the business on its financial statements. The business reports the true value of its property investment.)

Sales Taxes

The sales tax is the largest single source of revenue for state governments. A general sales tax is paid by consumers when almost any merchandise or service is purchased at retail. The retailer is responsible for collecting these sales taxes and remitting them to the government. Most states have a general sales tax, ranging from 2 percent to 7 percent of retail prices. There may also be a general city or county sales tax, usually 1 percent to 2 percent of retail prices. Some items, such as medicine and food not consumed on the store's premises, may be exempt from the sales tax. There are, in addition, selective sales taxes that apply only to certain items such as gasoline, cigarettes, and liquor.

The excise tax is similar to the sales tax except it applies to manufacturers, wholesalers, and retailers. These businesses pay the federal government a percentage of the value of certain items sold, such as jewelry and luggage. The amount that the manufacturer, wholesaler, and retailer pays in excise tax is eventually passed on to the consumer.

Payroll Taxes

Employers pay taxes to provide employee benefits under the provisions of Old Age, Survivors, and Disability Insurance (OASDI) and the unemployment insurance programs. In some states, the employers purchase workers' compensation insurance to protect the employer should employees suffer work-related injuries. In other states, a certain percentage of the employer's payroll is paid to the state to form a workers' compensation fund from which such payments can be made.

The employer is also responsible for withholding from each employee's wages the amounts the individual must pay toward federal, state, and local income taxes and the employee's share toward social security benefits. Employees' contributions to health and medical insurance, pensions, and retirement must be collected by employers and remitted to the appropriate agencies as well.

Special Taxes

Depending on the city in which it is located, a business may pay an occupational tax. This is a tax paid for the privilege of occupying a certain location within the city. A license tax is similar to the occupational tax. Certain businesses, such as restaurants and hair styling salons, must have licenses before they can operate, and a tax must be paid when the license is obtained. There are certain other taxes that vary with the type of retailing or location.

FINANCIAL STATEMENTS

Basic financial statements take two forms. The first is the *income statement,* which measures the business earnings or losses over a period of time. The second is the *balance sheet,* which measures the worth of the business at a specific date. Financial statements can be relatively simple or exceedingly complex, depending on the nature of the business and the type of accounting system used.

The Income Statement

The **income statement**—also known as either the profit-and-loss statement or the operating statement—shows the progress of a business during a certain period of time. Statements can be prepared weekly, monthly, quarterly, or yearly. They show relationships among sales, cost of merchandise sold, expenses, and resulting profits or losses. As an example, consider the case of Bavaro's Card Shop.

Penni Bavaro, owner and manager of a card shop, prepares an income statement each month as shown in Illustration 49–1. From her sales records, Penni determines that net sales for the month of March were $7,910. She then examines the inventory records and finds that the month's opening inventory at cost was $8,790. Next, she checks the purchase records to find the amount of merchandise purchased at cost during the month. The sum of the opening inventory and net purchases during the month is the total cost of merchandise available for sale. Penni's net purchases were $3,670, so the total cost of merchandise handled is $12,460.

Penni must now determine how much merchandise is left at the end of the month; so she calculates the book inventory at retail and converts this to a cost figure. With a book inventory of $11,420 at retail and cost prices averaging 65 percent of retail, the ending inventory at cost is $7,423. Now,

BAVARO'S CARD SHOP INCOME STATEMENT FOR MONTH ENDING MARCH 31, 19--

			Percentage
Revenue from sales			
Gross sales	$ 7,990		
Returns and allowances	− 80		1.0*
Net sales	⌐———→	$ 7,910	100.0
Cost of merchandise sold			
Opening inventory on March 1		$ 8,790		
Purchases (including			
transportation)	$ 3,770		
Returns to vendors	− 100		
Net purchases	⌐———→	+3,670	
Total merchandise handled		12,460	
Closing inventory on March 31		−7,423	
Cost of merchandise sold	⌐———→	−5,037	63.7**
Gross margin.		2,873	36.3**
Operating expenses		−930	11.8**
Net income (operating profit)		1,943	24.5**

*percentage of gross sales   **percentage of net sales

Illus. 49–1 Penni Bavaro prepares an income statement such as this each month. Some firms prepare such statements weekly; others do so only quarterly or annually. Notice that to make month-to-month comparisons easier, the cost of merchandise sold, gross margin, operating expenses, and net income are expressed as percentages of net sales.

Penni subtracts the amount of the ending inventory from the total cost of merchandise available and determines that the cost of the goods sold during the month was $5,037. This figure, subtracted from the net sales figure, gives the amount of **gross margin:** $2,873.

Penni still does not know how much profit she has made. She knows that the $2,873 gross margin is not all profit because she had to pay certain operating expenses during the month. Her expense record shows that the total expenses amount to $930. The final step in preparing the income statement is to subtract the total expense figure from the gross margin figure. The resulting figure—$1,943—is Penni's **net income** and represents her earnings from operating her own business and assuming the risks involved. If the total expenses had been greater than $2,873, then, of course, Penni would have had a net loss for the period.

Importance of Figuring Net Income.
An accurate calculation of net income is important in several ways. It enables the merchant to determine how much income tax must be paid. It indicates whether the business is a success or is heading toward bankruptcy. It also helps the owner decide how much money he or she can afford to draw out of the business without impairing the operation and profit-making potential.

Perhaps the chief value of the income statement is that it shows how net income may be increased in the future. There are three basic ways to increase net income (or to decrease net loss):

1. Increase sales with only a proportionate increase in cost of merchandise sold and little or no increase in expenses.

2. Decrease cost of merchandise sold without decreasing sales—this is equivalent to realizing a larger gross margin or markup.

3. Reduce expenses.

A careful analysis of the income statements will suggest to the merchant which of these would be the best way to increase net income.

Elements in Profit.
Net profit for a period is what remains after all expenses except taxes are deducted from gross margin. Net profit before taxes is the amount used in calculating the income tax to be paid by the retail firm; that is, the net-profit-before-taxes figure indicates the amount subject to federal, state, and local income tax rates. Obviously, these income taxes vary with the firm's level of profitability. For the large firm organized as a corporation, the net profit figure is of major concern to stockholders. The net profit after taxes represents the amount available for reinvestment in the firm or for distribution to stockholders as dividends.

The small-store owner should look at profit after taxes from two points of view. First, the owner should receive a certain amount as salary for services as the manager of the business. Second, the owner should receive a fair rate of return on the amount of money invested in the business; that is, in the building, equipment, merchandise, and supplies. What the owner has invested in the business should be viewed just as though he or she had deposited the money in a bank and was earning interest on it. Thus, if banks currently paid interest on deposits at a rate of 10 percent, the retailer should seek at least a 10 percent return on what has been invested in the business. This amount of money, called *re-*

turn on investment, is the amount due the owner for the use of her or his money in the business.

When the owner is fortunate enough to earn more than a fair salary and a return on investment, the excess is what economists call *pure profit,* or the return for risks assumed. Retail businesses that are exceptionally profitable soon find competitors attempting to get a part of their market. In the long run, pure profit, when it is earned by a business, rarely exceeds 3 percent of sales.

The Balance Sheet

The balance sheet shows (1) the value of the assets owned by the business, (2) the liabilities owed by the business, and (3) the merchant's interest in the business. This third element, called *equity,* is the difference between assets and liabilities. On an ordinary balance sheet, it appears as proprietorship. For a corporation, it may appear as capital or stockholders' equity.

Assets.   The assets of a store are determined as follows. Cash includes the cash in the bank and the cash in the store, which may be in the registers and in a petty-cash fund. Government securities are United States Treasury bills owned by the store that can be turned into cash in a short time. Accounts receivable, the amount due from credit customers, is determined from the charge-account records. Merchandise inventory is determined by an actual count and is valued at cost, not retail. Prepaid assets, such as supplies, are valued at the amount paid for them. Likewise, insurance may be paid for several months ahead. As the supplies and insurance coverage are used up, the amounts used appear as expenses on the income statement. Those assets that can be turned into cash rather quickly and easily are called **current assets.**

Land, buildings, furniture, and fixtures owned by a store are **fixed assets.** The value of these assets is determined from a record of the original amount paid for them, and depreciation is subtracted from their value (except land) according to the number of years they are estimated to last. Fixed assets are listed on the balance sheet at the present-day estimated value, with the depreciation amount listed as an expense. Any long-term investments such as bonds are included in fixed assets. The sum of current assets and fixed assets represents the total value of what the business owns.

Liabilities.   After the assets have been determined and listed on the balance sheet, the merchant lists all business liabilities. The chief liabilities generally are accounts payable, notes payable, and accrued expenses payable. The value of accounts payable is obtained from a record of unpaid vendor invoices. Notes payable consist of short-term debts; that is, promissory notes that must be paid within a year. Accrued expenses payable are expenses incurred but not yet paid. For example, salaries that have been earned by salespeople but have not yet been paid by the store are liabilities. These payable items, which will be paid within 12 months in most instances, comprise the **current liabilities.** To these are added fixed liabilities, such as a mortgage or a long-term promissory note on which money was borrowed. **Fixed liabilities** are those that are paid over a number of years in the normal operation of the business. The sum of current and fixed liabilities represents the total value of what the business owes.

Proprietorship or Equity. The difference between the total assets and the total liabilities is the amount of the merchant's interest or **equity** in the business. The proprietors of small businesses must work to make sure that their equity, as a percentage of total liabilities and proprietorship, remains constant or actually increases over time.

Pat Baxter prepares a balance sheet for her store, the Adobe Shop, at the end of each year, as shown in Illustration 49–2. From her records, she determines the amount of current assets owned by the Adobe Shop. These assets include cash, government securities, accounts receivable, merchandise inventory, and prepaid insurance. The Adobe Shop also has fixed as-

Pat Baxter's Adobe Shop
Balance Sheet
December 31, 19--

Assets

Current assets:
Cash	$ 2,100
Government securities	750
Accounts receivable	3,800
Merchandise inventory	16,200
Supply inventory	800
Prepaid insurance	+ 300
Total current assets	$23,950

Fixed assets:
Building (minus depreciation)	$30,000
Furniture and fixtures (minus depreciation)	4,100
Delivery equipment (minus depreciation)	2,800
Total fixed assets	+36,900
Total assets	$60,850

Liabilities

Current liabilities:
Accounts payable	$5,500
Notes payable (short term)	2,900
Accrued expenses	+1,300
Total current liabilities	$ 9,700

Fixed liabilities:
Mortgage payable	+32,000
Total liabilities	$41,700

Proprietorship

Pat Baxter, capital	+19,150
Total liabilities and proprietorship	$60,850

Illus. 49–2 Compare this balance sheet of the Adobe Shop with the income statement of Bavaro's Card Shop. How does the balance sheet differ from the income statement? What effect would there be on this balance sheet if Pat Baxter rented or owned the store building?

sets. These include the store building, furniture and fixtures, and delivery equipment, each minus depreciation. Pat totals current assets and finds that she has $23,950. Fixed assets amount to $36,900. The total of current assets and fixed assets ($60,850) represents the total assets of the Adobe Shop.

The Adobe Shop also has liabilities. The current liabilities include accounts payable, notes payable, and accrued expenses. Pat Baxter calculates these to total $9,700. The mortgage on the Adobe Shop building is a fixed liability and amounts to $32,000. The total liabilities for the Adobe Shop is $41,700. The difference between the total assets and the total liabilities is $19,150. This figure represents Pat Baxter's equity or proprietorship in the business. Her equity consists of her original investment plus accumulated profits, minus withdrawals. Baxter's equity is 31.5 percent of the total of equity plus liabilities.

Importance of a Balance Sheet.
A **balance sheet** shows the value of the business at a specific time and supplements the income statement, which shows income and outgo over a period of time. A balance sheet is generally required by a bank from which a merchant wishes to borrow money because it shows, even better than the income statement, whether a store will be able to repay borrowed money when it is due. Comparison of balance sheets from year to year provides the merchant with critical information about which aspects of the business need attention and control.

RETAINING RECORDS

Every business has a variety of records that must be kept for legal reasons. Some must be kept only a short time simply for purposes of immediate operations. Other records are required by law to be kept for a minimum number of years for possible inspection by government agents. For example, information on employee wages and hours must be retained for three years to comply with the Fair Labor Standards Act. Payroll records, which include wage payments and deductions for federal income tax and social security, must be retained for at least four years after the tax is paid. Some state and local regulations require that payroll records be kept longer than four years. State and federal income tax returns and the records that confirm the figures on the returns should be kept at least six years. Because of the importance of records, the retailer should obtain legal help in setting a schedule of record retention that will meet local, state, and federal requirements. Records also should be protected to withstand disasters that may strike the business.

Summary   Retailers must have accurate tax records to assure that tax money is properly collected or calculated and sent to appropriate government agencies. The most common taxes paid by retailers are income taxes, property taxes, sales taxes, payroll taxes, and special taxes such as occupational taxes and license fees.

The purpose of financial statements is to show the financial condition of a business for current and future use. Basic financial statements that should be prepared by all retail businesses are the profit-and-loss statement or income statement and the balance sheet. An income statement shows the amount of sales and costs of doing business for a period and the difference between them, which is either a profit (sales exceed costs) or loss (costs exceed sales). A balance sheet shows the assets (amounts owned) and liabilities (amounts owed) at a particular time and the difference between them, which is equity. These financial statements can be relatively simple or complex, depending upon the nature and size of the business.

Review

1. List the most common taxes that must be paid by a retail firm.
2. List three forms of sales taxes.
3. What is the purpose of financial statements?
4. Why is it important for a businessperson to calculate net income?
5. List three basic ways of increasing net income.
6. Name the three major sections of a balance sheet.
7. Explain the difference between current and fixed liabilities.
8. Explain the purpose of a records-retention schedule.

Terms

The following terms were introduced in this chapter. Write a separate sentence correctly using each new term.

balance sheet	income statement
current assets	intangible-property tax
current liabilities	net income
equity	personal-property tax
fixed assets	real-property tax
fixed liabilities	taxes
gross margin	

Discuss

1. How often should an income statement be prepared for a retail store? Should a new business, such as Bavaro's Card Shop, have its income statement prepared more frequently than does a well-established firm? Why or why not?
2. Some people say that no business should be allowed to make a pure profit. Do you agree or disagree? Explain.
3. If a business has an increasing amount of sales and a sizable increase in cash, does this mean that the business has increased in financial strength?

4. Should retailers be reimbursed for collecting sales taxes for local or state government?

Problem Solving

1. Compute the net income from the following information and express it as a percentage of net sales.

Sales	$57,000
Opening inventory	20,000
Closing inventory	22,000
Purchases	40,000
Expenses.	15,000

2. Recalculate problem 1, making the following adjustments:

Returns from customers	$300
Returns to vendors	200
Transportation charges	100

3. Prepare an income statement using these figures:

Gross sales	$95,000
Returns from customers	500
Opening inventory	100,000
Purchases	50,000
Returns to vendors	1,000
Transportation charges	700
Closing inventory	83,000
Expenses.	17,000

4. Assume that, at the end of the accounting period, your business has these figures in addition to those presented in problem 3:

Cash	$10,000
Accounts receivable	17,000
Fixed assets	40,000
Accounts payable	20,000
Notes payable	5,000

Assume that the beginning capital was $114,200. Prepare a balance sheet for the past accounting period.

CHAPTER 50

Retail Information Systems

CHAPTER OUTCOMES

When you have mastered the information provided in this chapter, you should be able to:

1. Outline for a retailer the four steps necessary in processing retail reports

2. Describe the two kinds of data recorded in a retail transaction

3. Explain three ways of recording retail transactions

4. Describe five reports prepared from repetitive retail transactions

5. Describe five major applications of computers to retailing

6. Explain how retail forecasting is aided by a retail information system

Accurate and complete store records are essential for several reasons. Retailers need to account for the money that is received and used. Merchants need to know the profit or loss and the amount of taxes that must be paid. Records are needed to guide the retailer in merchandising and other management decisions. The retail buyer should be aware immediately of a sudden increase in the sale of a particular style, color, or model so that reorders can be placed and goods received while the demand is still active. To collect information on the thousands of items in the typical store and then to arrange these data quickly into useful reports is the purpose of various retail information systems discussed in this chapter.

PLANNING THE INFORMATION SYSTEM

Before any information system is established, the retailer must answer three questions. The answer to "Which data must be collected?" will influence the nature of the source document or original transaction. The answer to "Which classifications and comparisons of data are needed?" will depend on how the information is to be used by retail management, buyers, and other store workers. The answer to "How quickly must the data reports be available for use?" will help determine the equipment and procedures used in the processing of data. Answers to these three inquiries set guidelines for the type of retail information system the retailer will use for store records.

The actual processing of data for retail records involves four basic steps:

1. Recording the data about each transaction in a standard, orderly way
2. Transmitting the data to processing equipment where data are sorted and arranged
3. Analyzing the data by combining them and relating them to data already on hand
4. Reporting information, usually in tabular form, for use by store management

TRANSACTION DATA

Transactions take many forms. A **transaction** may be a sale to a customer, a customer return, a purchase order sent to a supplier, a return to a supplier, a price change, a payment made to an employee for hours worked, or a payment to a vendor on account. Even a small store has thousands of business transactions each year. Each transaction involves separate pieces of information that together make up the data necessary for store records.

Data recorded about a transaction are of two kinds: (1) **identification facts** that reveal the nature and characteristics of the transaction and (2) **quantitative facts** that indicate the number of items and values involved in the transaction. For example, the identification facts for a sale of hosiery include the brand, type, material, color, and size. The quantitative facts include the number of pairs sold and the price.

Some facts about certain transactions may be unimportant for future decision making and may require no analysis. However, most data are worthy of being recorded and analyzed, though their worth may not be obvious. The sale of a particular style and size of slacks may not seem worthy of study, but the style sold may have certain characteristics—such as material, cut, or color—common to other styles sold. If the sales of slacks are analyzed by these characteristics, important trends in customer demand may become apparent, and profitable changes in buying and selling plans may result.

RECORDING TRANSACTIONS

There are three different ways to record the data for transactions. The data can be recorded and processed manually; that is, by having a worker write out the facts of a transaction and hand sort the data. Data also can be recorded mechanically on punched cards (or punched tickets removed from items sold) and processed by punch card readers. This method of working with data is called *automated data processing* (ADP). Once widely used, ADP is giving way to the third means, which is *electronic data processing* (EDP). In EDP, data are recorded electronically and processed by a computer. An example of recording a sales transaction with each approach follows.

Manual Recording

Midori Tanaka bought two letter pads and a greeting card at Bavaro's Card Shop. The amount of the sale was $4.68 including tax. If the amount of the sale is all the information recorded, Penni Bavaro will not know which items have been sold at the end of each day or each week. Therefore, Penni writes a sales slip for each sale. The sales slip for Midori Tanaka's sale lists two letter pads (stock number 714) at $2 each; one card (stock number W-89) at $0.50; and $0.18 tax. The sale is rung up on the sales register. The original sales slip is kept in the sales register until the end of the day. The copy of the slip is given to Midori Tanaka. Every week, Penni records the information from each sales slip onto a summary sheet that serves as a weekly sales report. Because her store and the number of sales transactions are small, the manual method of recording and reporting data is feasible.

Mechanical Recording

In Burke's Hardware store, all merchandise is classified by department. Whenever an item is sold, the amount of the sale is recorded on the sales register by department number. For example, Barb Scholl sold two paint brushes and a package of light bulbs to Chi Wang. The paint brushes ($4.98 each) were rung up under department 3, which is the paint department. The package of light bulbs ($1.98) was rung up under department 6, which is the electrical department. If Chi Wang returns one of the paint brushes, Barb will refund the amount by ringing a "paid out" from department 3. The sales register will provide Barb with the amount sold in each department of the store and a total of all sales. For now, the sales-register tape serves as a record of all transactions. In the future, if Barb wants detailed information about merchandise within a department, she can ticket merchandise with a punched ticket to be removed when the item is sold. The information on these tickets can then be tabulated and reported using mechanical equipment such as punched card readers.

Electronic Recording

As Pat Baxter increased her business in the Adobe Shop, she discovered that she needed more and faster information about her merchandise. By adopting an electronic sales-register system, she was able to automatically update her inventory record at the time of each sale. For example, when Pat sold Mr. Dobbins a sport coat, she entered into the sales register the identification facts—code numbers for the color, size, style, vendor, and salesperson. Pat also keyed in the quantitative facts: the quantity sold and the price. The information was automatically transferred to a computer and both sales and inventory records were updated. Pat could check sales and inventory status by calling up this data on her computer monitor or she could, if she wished, periodically print out a hard copy. What would require many hours of manual or mechanical work was done electronically in only a few minutes.

Although more and more retailers have their own computer equipment, some retailers still find it less expensive to buy computer services from a data-processing center. Computer data-processing service centers are operated by computer manufacturers, independent firms, banks, and accounting firms. Using a data-processing center service saves the retailer the cost of equipment, installation, maintenance, and training of employees to use it.

KINDS OF RETAIL REPORTS

Modern electronic data-processing methods are well-suited for handling large numbers of repetitive transactions. Five kinds of reports, based on a large number of repetitive transactions, that are prepared and used in most stores are (1) daily sales audits, (2) purchases by credit customers that are recorded in accounts receivable, (3) inventory control (sales, purchases by the store, and inventories by classifications), (4) store personnel performance, and (5) payroll expenses.

Sales Audit

Every store audits its sales to assure that sales and receipts for sales are in agreement. If the store is departmentalized, the merchant reviews the sales slips, register readings, or other records of sale and then totals the sales for each department. A comparison is then made of the totals by checking the sales records against actual cash and credit sales totals. If the store is not departmentalized, the sales audit will cover total store sales. Also, the sales audit is used to compare current store or department performance to that of the same period last week, last month, or last year.

Accounts Receivable

When a store sells on credit, the customer's account is charged for each purchase made and is credited for payments made or goods returned. If these transactions are recorded manually, an extra copy

Illus. 50–1   The transaction, at point of sale or elsewhere in the store, is the source of data that results in important store records and reports.

of a sales slip must be prepared to use in posting the customer's account. A copy of the current customer account becomes the store's record of the status of each account. Charges to customer accounts are checked daily against the sales audit figures to determine any errors in recording.

With electronic data processing, the transaction data are sent to the computer immediately or periodically during the day or week. These data are entered automatically in each customer's account card at the same time that the store's daily charge sales are reported.

Inventory Control

Probably the greatest value that electronic data processing offers retailers is the computation of sales and inventory information by units of analysis that are smaller than the totals for each selling department.

Merchants who formerly believed that it was too much work to analyze sales for groupings smaller than a selling department can, with computers, prepare reports on sales and purchase data for each merchandise classification (SKU) by color, size, style number, vendor, and price line within each department. These data allow the merchant to reorder more accurately in the future. An example of a sales and inventory report is shown in Illustration 50–2.

Personnel Performance

As a basis for evaluating employee performance, many merchants maintain records of the sales transactions made by each salesperson. These reports provide weekly or monthly selling costs for each salesperson. The selling cost is the ratio of the salesperson's salary and commissions to her or his net sales. Sales by each salesperson in each merchandise classification and within each price line are reported. Customer returns may also be reported for each salesperson. The total sales of each salesperson for a week, a month, or a season can be obtained quickly. The weekly earnings of each salesperson can be reported, and total selling costs for each salesperson can be determined.

Nonselling and noncommission employees' production may be evaluated if productivity can be measured in terms of number of records handled, number of price tickets attached, and number of packages wrapped or delivered, for example. Analysis of such performance records may serve as a basis for assigning work or filling staff positions.

SALES AND INVENTORY SUMMARY

Department 700   Month Ending March 31, 19--

Code	Price	BOM Balance	Purchases	Sales	MU/MD	EOM Balance	Purchase to date	Sales to date	MU/MD to date
710	$8.98	$700.00	$520.00	$684.00	$42.00	$494.00	$2600.00	$3542.00	$210.00
712	10.98	1493.00	1100.00	1045.00	84.00	1464.00	3623.00	5225.00	418.00
714	13.98	1970.00	1320.00	1134.00	130.00	2026.00	6700.00	5570.00	647.00
716	19.98	2143.00	1008.00	840.00	60.00	2251.00	5030.00	4100.00	301.00
TOTALS		$6306.00	$3948.00	$3701.00	$316.00	$6235.00	$17955.00	$18437.00	$1576.00

Illus. 50–2   The sales and inventory report is invaluable in keeping stock in each classification balanced to sales. Note the extremely large closing stock that is on hand in Code 716. In Code 710, however, the closing stock seems to be quite small in relation to sales. This information would enable the buyer to adjust planned purchases to fit the needs of these two classes.

Payroll

The base pay for each employee can be entered into a computer memory. A salesperson's rate of commission and amount of sales and returns can also be entered. If a person is on an hourly rate, the regular and overtime rates may be entered along with the number of regular and overtime hours worked. The amounts to be withheld for taxes, social security, and health insurance may be entered for each employee. Purchases of merchandise to be charged against an employee's salary may be entered, too. The computer calculates each employee's take-home pay and may automatically print a payroll check. The payroll report provides department and store managers with detailed information on their salary expenses which can be compared to their planned expenses and prior years' salary expenses.

SPECIAL INFORMATION SYSTEMS

A wide variety of microcomputers, microprocessors, and minicomputers makes computer technology available to retail businesses of almost any size. With improved computer technology, retail firms have developed numerous special information systems. Five common applications are (1) retailer-wholesaler programs, (2) electronic ordering, (3) check and credit authorization, (4) mail orders, and (5) retail forecasting.

Retailer-Wholesaler Programs

As wholesalers and suppliers have begun using computers, they have influenced the many retailers with whom they do business. The coordination of data-processing programs between wholesaler and retailer has meant that even small retailers have gained the advantages of computerized recordkeeping. For example, one wholesaler offers business customers full business-records service. This service means that the wholesaler maintains a general ledger and an accounts receivable ledger for those retailers who take advantage of the service. The general ledger computer program issues monthly profit-and-loss statements, balance sheets, departmental operating statements, general ledger totals, and other related information for the retailer. The accounts receivable computer program provides the retailer with duplicate monthly statements for each customer account and an overall summary of accounts receivable.

Some retailer-wholesaler programs involve an inventory-maintenance plan. Data from sales transactions are analyzed on a regular basis (most often weekly). As the retailer's inventory on certain staple goods reaches a predetermined point, the computer automatically prints an order for the needed amount of replacement units. The retailer can set whatever stock levels seem appropriate and instruct the computer to change levels on any item to reflect changes in business activity.

A limitation to the retailer-wholesaler program is that it works only for retailers who buy almost all merchandise from a single wholesaler. For the retailer who buys from many manufacturers and wholesalers, the automatic-reorder program is not feasible.

Electronic Ordering

Some stores have computer programs that serve as reorder systems. These stores feed unit sales and purchase data into computers programmed to calculate reorder quantities. The buyer can scan the status of her or his department SKUs, make any desired adjustments, and then send the computer order to the supplier's computer in lieu of a purchase order. The supplier's computer immediately initiates assembly of the ordered merchandise. If requested, the supplier's computer prints price tickets to be attached to goods as part of the order-filling process or to be included with the shipment. Use of electronic ordering allows goods to be shipped to a store within 24 hours after an order is received.

Credit and Check Authorization

Another important use of the computer in retailing is for authorizing credit and check purchases. When a customer presents her or his charge card, the salesperson records the customer's number on the sales register or inserts the card in a machine. In either case, the information is transmitted to the computer, either in the store or at a central credit office. The computer has in its memory an up-to-date list of all referral accounts (those having a balance due that is near or over the credit limit), a record of delinquent or slow payments, and a list of cards reported stolen. If an account number is not listed as a referral account, the computer activates an audio or visual authorization of the credit transaction. If the customer's account number is listed as a referral account, the salesperson must get authorization from the credit office before charging another sale to the account.

A similar system is also used for the authorization of checks. The customer, rather than the cashier, may insert her or his check and personal check-cashing card into a machine that is linked to a computerized-banking service. On the keyboard of the machine, the customer enters a code indicating the type of check transaction. For example, the check may be for the amount of purchase only, for a specific amount over the purchase, or for a cash amount only. The customer also keys in the amount of the check. The machine either accepts or rejects the check by printing *OK* or a denial statement on the back of the check. Authorization of the check is based on the computer's examination of the customer's checking account. Check-authorization equipment, em-

Illus. 50–3   Instant check authorizations are done by customers who insert a personalized check authorization card into a card reader linked to a computerized-banking service.

ployed in many large grocery stores, speeds checkout by eliminating the check-authorization step for the cashier. It also helps to reduce the number of bad checks.

Mail Orders

A growing number of customers order merchandise by telephone. Therefore, it is not surprising that many mail-order firms are using computer communication systems. A customer anywhere in the United States may call the toll-free number of one particular firm and state her or his name, address, and charge account number and the style number, color, and quantity of the items wanted from the company's catalog. The caller's voice is translated into machine language and fed into a central computer that is connected to all of the firm's distribution points. The central computer relays the order to the distribution center that serves the particular customer's area. There, the order is filled, sometimes within minutes, and started on its way to the customer. The laborious steps of writing the order in a local office, sending it to the proper distribution point, checking the customer's credit, and preparing shipping documents are eliminated. The personnel formerly required to perform these manual operations can now be used for other jobs in the business.

Forecasting

The ability to forecast future business conditions and trends is vital to retail decision making. While a retail information system cannot actually predict the future, it can help a retailer estimate the future effects of certain decisions. Using existing data in a retail information system, the retailer can test out a variety of decisions in terms of probable future results. These decisions may be about whether to establish a new store, build a new warehouse, change brand policy, set different markup goals, or add new lines of merchandise. For example, a retailer may use a computer spreadsheet program to test the effects on monthly income statements of raising markup by 1 percent, 2.5 percent, and 3.25 percent. It may never be possible to include all of the factors that might mold the future of a retail firm, but a carefully developed retail information system provides substantial data for forecasting purposes.

Summary

Retail information systems are needed so retailers will have complete and accurate information on which to base management decisions. Data for an information system are collected each time a transaction—a sale, a return, a purchase order, a return to a supplier, a price change, a payment to a vendor, or a payment to an employee—occurs. Transactions may be recorded manually, mechanically, or electronically. Transaction data are tabulated and prepared for five common retail reports: sales audit, accounts receivable, inventory, personnel performance, and payroll.

Special information systems have been made possible by the widespread use of computers. Wholesalers now provide retailers with a variety of accounting services and data on various merchandise lines. With computers, retailers now have electronic ordering systems as well as credit- and check-authorization systems. Mail-order firms using computer communications systems are able to receive orders by phone and process orders electronically. By using the data acquired in their retail information systems, merchants can forecast the business results of certain merchandising decisions.

Review

1. Name the four basic steps in processing retail data.
2. List two kinds of facts that can be recorded about a transaction.
3. Describe three methods of recording retail transactions.
4. List the five reports based on repetitive transactions that are prepared by most retail stores.
5. How do retailers and wholesalers cooperate in computer services?
6. How is the computer used in the authorization of credit purchases?
7. How are telephone orders facilitated by the use of computers?
8. Describe how retail information systems aid retail forecasting.

Terms

The following terms were introduced in this chapter. Write a separate sentence correctly using each new term.

identification facts   transaction
quantitative facts

Discuss

1. How does a retailer know which information to record about a transaction?
2. What effect will an error by a salesperson in recording, either on a sales slip or on a sales register, have on a sales or merchandise report?
3. What retail records would be most important to the new retailer during the first year of operation?
4. If you, as a retailer, purchase most of your merchandise from one wholesaler, what advantages could there be to having a co-ordinated computer system?
5. What factors determine how frequently a retailer should have reports on sales and inventory?

Problem Solving

1. You manage a men's apparel store with a sales volume of about $1 million a year. How would you find out what electronic recording systems are available to you? How would you evaluate them?
2. Observe the sales transactions at three different stores. Determine what information is collected during each transaction at each store. What factors seem to influence the data collected at the time of a sale?
3. Using the yellow pages of the local telephone book and/or city directory for your area, develop a list of firms that offer computer services that may be used by retailers.
4. Penni Bavaro prepares a sales slip for each sales transaction. The sales slip contains the stock number of the item sold, quantity, price, and sales tax. How are these facts used in each of the following records: sales audit, accounts receivable, inventory control, and sales tax collections?

CHECKING KEY POINTS

This exercise is designed to check your understanding of material presented in Unit 8. On a separate sheet of paper, list the numbers 1 to 26. Indicate your response, *T* for true or *F* for false, for each of the following 26 statements.

1. Fixed capital is used to purchase merchandise and cover operating expenses.
2. A cash-reserve fund, as a percentage of total capital needed, should be kept as low as possible.
3. The investment in a business by the owner is called *equity capital.*
4. Trade credit is credit extended to the retailer by suppliers.
5. Lenders ask for personal and financial facts from retailers who apply for loans.
6. The procedure a store uses to keep track of invoices in process is called *invoice control.*
7. Most stores take two physical inventories a year.
8. If the book inventory is larger than the physical inventory, there is an overage.
9. If the current retail inventory is $12,000 and current markup on goods is 30 percent, the current inventory value is $3,600.
10. Most merchants value inventories at cost or market value, whichever is lower.
11. A sales register is the principal means of recording sales data.
12. A cash fund is the amount initially placed in the sales register so change can be made for sales.
13. Gross sales minus returns to vendors equals net sales.
14. Indirect expenses are those paid out solely for the benefit of one department of a store.
15. In the analysis of expense records, dollar amounts should be figured as a percentage of sales.
16. Prepaid expenses are classified as business assets.
17. The income statement measures the worth of a business at a specific date.
18. Pure profit is the excess of earnings over a fair salary and interest on investment.
19. Inventory and cash are examples of current assets.
20. Notes payable is classified as a business asset.
21. Sales taxes are paid by the consumer but collected by the retailer for the city, county, and/or state.

22. All business records must be kept for a minimum of seven years.
23. A transaction is a source of separate pieces of data that make up store records.
24. Every store audits its sales.
25. Retailer-wholesaler inventory-maintenance programs work well for nearly all retail businesses.
26. Referral credit accounts are those automatically approved for additional customer charges.

BUILDING BASIC SKILLS

Calculations

The following calculations were used in Unit 8 to demonstrate certain facts about retail merchandising. Make the calculations necessary to answer each of the questions.

1. Your physical inventory shows goods on hand with a retail value of $1,760. Your book inventory shows goods valued at $1,710 at retail and $1,026 at cost value. Average markup is 40 percent. Do you have an overage or a shortage? If so, what is the amount of it at cost?
2. The sales-register beginning reading is $1,472. The cash fund contains $75. The ending sales-register reading is $2,197. How much in cash and/or credit slips should be in the cash drawer at the close of the day? What is the amount of sales for the day?
3. Compute net income from each of the following. Express net income as a percentage of net sales.

	A	B	C
Sales	$46,900	$65,700	$91,300
Returns from customers	$ 1,100	$ 1,900	$ 2,200
Opening inventory	$17,000	$31,500	$46,100
Closing inventory	$16,500	$33,400	$42,100
Purchases	$26,300	$36,300	$46,700
Expenses	$14,000	$17,900	$24,000

4. Compute the cost of goods sold based on the following:

	A	B	C
Opening inventory	$11,700	$13,200	$15,500
Purchases	$ 7,300	$ 8,400	$ 9,100
Returns to vendors	$ 400	$ 550	$ 600
Transportation	$ 750	$ 400	$ 900
Closing inventory	$12,900	$12,300	$16,200

Working with People

Workers in retailing regularly must meet with other employees, supervisors, and customers. Mistakes in communication and misunderstandings may occur, which, in turn, lead to human-relations problems. Many successful workers solve these people problems with the four-step DICE approach described in Unit 1 (see page 78).

Read each problem situation below. Then, use the DICE approach to find a solution for each. Remember, you must first define a problem before you identify or choose a solution. Describe what you think the consequences of your chosen solution would be.

1. You and a coworker have been assigned the task of taking physical inventory in the plumbing section of a builder's hardware department. Your coworker doesn't take the task very seriously. When he counts items, he says, "About five" (there may be six or seven); when he records, he often puts a count under the wrong stock number. You tell him that the inventory must be accurate, but he says, "It doesn't make any difference; no one really cares." What is the problem and what action should you take?

2. You own and operate a small ice-cream store. You sell cones, sundaes, and bulk ice cream in 30 flavors. You employ eight part-time employees who work shifts of varying lengths; all serve and sell ice cream. The average sales transaction is about $3.20. You have just one sales register with a single cash drawer. Almost every day, your register checks out with a shortage ranging from a few cents to several dollars, always in uneven amounts such as $1.17 or $3.43. What could be causing these errors and what action should you take with the employees?

3. An elderly customer has just selected a set of towels. The merchandise ($9.98) plus tax ($0.70) totals $10.68. The customer says that because she is a senior citizen she shouldn't have to pay the tax. She offers you a $10 bill in payment for the purchase. When you ask for the additional $0.68, she loudly complains that you are ripping off the older customers. What is the problem and what action should you take?

4. The store in which you work uses a credit-authorization system. For all charge sales, the customer's credit-card number is keyed in a digital entry/print-out machine. If credit is approved, an approval number is displayed. The cashier writes the approval number on the charge slip. On three occasions, your supervisor has criticized you for not following procedure and giving credit to customers when it should have been denied. How could this have happened? What should you say to your supervisor?

Writing Skills

Communication skills, oral and written, are essential for nearly all retail jobs. Writing skills are important for communicating with workers, other business people, and the public. The clarity and precision of a statement can make the difference in the way a message will be received and understood. Prepare a written document as requested in each of the following situations.

1. You will apply for a loan at Community National Bank to capitalize a small retail business. The loan officer will require a description of your character before your loan is considered. Write a statement describing the sort of person you are. Concentrate on your character and business abilities.
2. At a recent Chamber of Commerce meeting, some local merchants were debating the issue of valuing merchandise inventory. "Value it at cost, always," one said. Others argued for valuing it at market. A few saw advantages to valuing inventory at whichever value is lower. Where do you stand on this issue? Write a short paper, including supporting arguments for your position.
3. As manager of a men's shoe store, write a policy for the petty-cash fund. Indicate how the fund will be created, what the amount of the fund will be, for what purposes the fund may be used, and the procedure to be used for replenishing the fund.
4. Using library resources (business and economics books), learn all you can about pure profit. Try to find at least two definitions of the term. Write a short explanation of the concept. Don't forget to give authors credit if you quote from their books or articles in your paper.

APPLYING YOUR KNOWLEDGE

Can You Do the Following?

1. Explain the difference between fixed capital and working capital.
2. Explain how trade credit can be used to help a business finance some portion of working capital.
3. Diagram the flow of an invoice from receiving point to payment point.
4. Explain physical inventory and perpetual inventory and how these two forms of inventory are used by retailers to control merchandise.

5. Explain how to determine whether goods should be listed at cost or at market value.
6. List ways sales data can be collected.
7. List examples of at least three possible accrued expenses of a retail store.
8. List the information necessary to prepare an income statement.
9. List the information necessary to prepare a balance sheet.
10. Name the five types of repetitive transactions that occur most frequently in retail stores. Explain the reports prepared for each.
11. Explain how computer technology can assist a retailer in ordering merchandise.
12. Explain one way that computers assist in retail decision making.

Retail Decisions

1. A person planning to start a retail business is concerned about how to obtain the capital needed to begin. What advice would you give on this concern?
2. You have planned to keep $8,000 for reserved capital. You can invest this amount in 60- and 90-day accounts and earn 7 percent interest or in three-year certificates and earn 9.5 percent interest. Which of these choices should you take? Why?
3. A merchant has just installed a computerized stock-control system with electronic registers and UPC and optical-character readers. With this improved control on perpetual inventory, the merchant is planning to do away with an annual physical inventory. What advice do you have for this merchant?
4. What identification facts should be collected when selling shoes, gloves, or shirts?
5. What potential problems exist in a store where sales records are based entirely on written sales slips?
6. Which way of classifying expenses (by natural expense categories or by functional categories) is most appropriate for an owner-operated, independent shoe store?
7. How often should a retail business prepare an income statement? Should a new business prepare such a statement more frequently than a well-established firm? Why or why not?
8. Does having an increasing amount of sales and a sizable increase in cash mean that a business has increased financial strength? Could this situation occur and the firm still have a decrease in profits? Explain.
9. What kinds of expenses are easiest to reduce by more careful management?

DEVELOPING CRITICAL-THINKING SKILLS

Retail Projects

1.   Rick Gillder is planning to start a retail business but is concerned about the amount of capital needed. Rick has $8,000 of his own money to invest; he has arranged to borrow $6,000 from a bank; and he has arranged for $3,000 in short-term trade credit. Rick has two options for his planned store. One is to lease a space in a shopping center at a monthly cost of $450. The other is to buy a building for $7,000 down and monthly payments of $325. What would be the advantages and disadvantages of each of these choices?

2.   The Redway Furniture Store is a high-volume discount store that buys from many vendors. Goods are received daily and must be quickly placed on the selling floor in the hope that they will be sold just as quickly. Mr. Redway, the owner, frequently finds that purchase orders to vendors and vendors' invoices do not agree. Also, invoices often are misplaced so that opportunities for discounts for prompt payment are often lost. Set up a purchase-order and invoice-control system for Mr. Redway to assure proper follow-up on purchase orders and invoices, as well as on the merchandise.

3.   One of your friends plans to open a luggage store. She expects to carry an inventory at retail of about $10,000 and to have annual sales of about $65,000. Outline the basic records that you recommend she set up for the store and describe the relationships among these records.

4.   Rex Kolb is the owner of a medium-sized hardware store. He regularly finds discrepancies between book inventory and physical inventory. Sometimes there are overages and other times there are shortages. List steps that might be taken to locate the cause of these overages or shortages. Arrange the steps so that those that are the most important and that are to be taken first are listed first.

5.   Using the information below, prepare the April income statement for Bavaro's Card Shop. (See Illustration 49–1, page 569.)
     Gross sales: $8,655
     Returns and allowances: $105
     Opening inventory, April 1: $7,423
     Closing inventory, April 30: $7,990
     Purchases (including transportation): $4,315
     Returns to vendors: $65
     Operating expenses: $1,280

6.   Mitzi Potasi operates a small fashion-oriented women's clothing store. Most garments are ordered in small quantities, even as single items at times. What value would a computer service be to

Mitzi in terms of monthly sales and inventory reports, semiannual income statements, and an annual balance sheet? Considering the decreasing cost of computers, should Mitzi consider buying a small computer for in-store use rather than contracting with a computer service?

Field Projects

1. Identify a retail business investment opportunity in your community. With your instructor's help, arrange to interview appropriate persons to determine what funds would be needed to buy the business. Report to your class what the capital needs would be to buy, open, and operate this business.
2. Individually or with a small group of classmates, investigate the inventory procedures used by three local retail businesses. Determine how physical inventory counts are made, how frequently they are taken, what procedures are used, and what type of reports are prepared. Based on your findings, what suggestions for improvement can you make to each firm?
3. Obtain from your instructor, school or community library, or other source the annual reports of national or community corporations. Examine the financial statements of these companies. What information is reported by all firms? What information is unique to certain firms?
4. Using the yellow pages of the local telephone book and/or city directory for your area, develop a list of firms that offer tax-preparation services that can be used by retailers.
5. Using library sources, information from your local Chamber of Commerce or city/county offices, or other sources suggested by your instructor, determine which local, state, and federal taxes or license fees must be paid by local retail merchants. What kinds of records must be maintained to keep track of the taxes to be paid?

CONTINUING PROJECTS

Developing a Career Plan

Many people have a desire to establish and operate their own businesses. Adequate resources are, of course, essential for starting a business. However, also important for success in business, is a clear understanding of one's motivation for becoming a business owner. Based on the information presented in this text, identify at least six requirements for business ownership. For each of these requirements, indicate whether you feel you meet that requirement now or possibly will in the future. Conclude your analysis with a statement as to why becoming a business owner fits or doesn't fit into your career plan.

Developing a Business Plan

Do the following for the retail store you plan to operate:

1. Prepare an analysis of the capital needs of your business; then, write a detailed plan for obtaining the funds needed to finance the business.
2. Develop a sample income statement as you hope it might be after your first year of operation.
3. Develop a sample balance sheet as it would be when you start your business and a second as it might appear after your first year of operation.
4. Describe the procedures you will use to control purchases, inventory, sales, and finances of your business.

UNIT 9
Future of Retailing

The future of retailing can be expressed in one word: change. To cope with change, successful retailers apply established research techniques to solve operation problems. These successful retailers also apply technological advances and new retailing practices to keep up with competition. Some of the most visible changes in retailing are those affecting shopping centers and malls.

Your future in retailing also will be marked by continuous change. Therefore, you should begin now to set your job expectations, find and perform well on your first retailing job, and plan for the future. To go far in the field, plan ahead. Constantly be aware of the jobs you would like to hold later. Explore those jobs and begin preparing for them.

UNIT OUTCOMES

After studying this unit and completing the activities, you should be able to:

1. Identify and explain the steps in the retailing research procedure
2. State ways in which retailers are using computer technology to meet customer needs
3. Describe key changes in retailing practices
4. Describe changes in shopping centers and malls
5. List sources of job information
6. Describe the career planning process

CHAPTER 51

Research in Retailing

CHAPTER OUTCOMES

When you have mastered the information provided in this chapter, you should be able to:

1. Define the term *retailing research*

2. Name seven ways in which retailers use retailing research to solve store problems

3. List and explain the steps in the retailing research procedure

4. Name six sources of secondary information

5. Identify three methods of gathering primary information

6. Explain the importance of research skills for a career in retailing

Ben Kimura has noticed a gradual change in the buying habits of the customers who patronize his hardware store. In the past, he could count on customers to ask for such basics as tools, nails, and paint. Now, requests for prepackaged hardware, do-it-yourself repair kits, appliances, tool and equipment rentals, and even furniture have become common. Ben wishes he could more accurately predict his customers' wants and needs. Down the street, Sonia Torres, owner of a sportswear shop, finds that a growing number of her best customers prefer high-priced, high-fashion clothing. However, Sonia has been hesitant about increasing her inventory of this merchandise in case the demand should suddenly drop. As a result, sales have been slow. Furthermore, there doesn't seem to be a clear-cut reason for the changes in her customers' buying habits.

Faced with problems similar to those of Ben and Sonia and with the increasing costs of doing business, more and more retailers are employing retailing research techniques to improve store operations. **Retailing research** is defined by the American Marketing Association as "the systematic gathering, recording, and analyzing of data about problems relating to the marketing of goods and services." This chapter tells how merchants use retailing research and presents the procedures they follow to solve marketing problems.

HOW RETAILERS USE RETAILING RESEARCH

There are those who believe that research can be conducted only in sterile laboratories by individuals in white uniforms.

This, however, is not the case. Often, research such as the type conducted by retailers is done in stores and shopping malls and even by mail and telephone. Research may be complicated or simple depending upon the problem that the retailer wants to solve. The goals of almost all retailing research are to improve customer services and to increase store profits. Retail managers have met these goals by using the results of research to solve problems in various areas. Some of the most-studied areas of retailing will be discussed.

Store Location

Decisions regarding the right place to locate a new store carry considerable risk. Retailing research usually includes an investigation of (1) competition, (2) availability of potential customers, (3) parking, (4) traffic access and flow, and (5) shopping habits.

Customers' Needs and Wants

In recent years, increased attention has been given to determining customer attitudes, buying habits, and motives. The results of this research have provided valuable information about the kinds of merchandise customers are most interested in, desired price ranges, quality of services rendered, and changes required to meet customer needs and wants.

Sales

A study of sales by any merchandise classification—such as appliances, cloth-

Illus. 51–1   Retailing research often is an effective tool in selecting the proper location for a new store. This retailer is collecting research data by means of observation.

ing, television sets, hardware items, and lawn and garden supplies—can provide valuable information about a particular store's ongoing sales performance. Research of sales usually involves a comparison of sales of specific items in the retailer's store with the sales of similar items in a previous year or with the sales performance of competitive stores. If the local retailer discovers that sales are lagging, he or she surely wants to know why. A variety of possible reasons may be identified—merchandise, personnel, service and sales techniques, customer attitudes, competition, advertising frequency—and then corrective action must be taken.

Advertising and Display

Research studies may determine which types of advertising media and merchandise displays sell the most merchandise in a specific store. For example, in one store, sales in the casual-wear shop were not satisfactory. In contrast, other merchants who were selling similar merchandise seemed to be doing very well. By researching this problem, the retailer determined that the department's displays were neither well designed nor properly located. In addition, the retailer learned that competitors were emphasizing counter displays that contained sale merchandise advertised in local newspapers. Steps were taken to improve displays and to present advertised merchandise in counter displays. As a result, sales volume immediately increased and continued at a satisfactory level.

Personnel

Locating and hiring the most qualified personnel available is a very real problem for many retailers. What are the best sources of job applicants? Which are the most effective interview methods? What criteria are most important when making employment decisions? Research can also help a retailer find solutions to employer-employee relations problems. Areas of study include training, compensation, motivation, and evaluation of store employees at all levels. Currently, some stores are studying employee promotion policies and the relationship between aptitude test scores and job success, and between working conditions and morale. Screening inventories are becoming more popular in retailing. These inventories or series of questions help predict success rates for job candidates. Some of this testing also tries to predict the honesty of job candidates.

Operations

Research in the operations area involves store layout, building maintenance, customer services, receiving and marking, and warehouse procedures. Determining the best locations for merchandise, how to improve store appearance, and effective ways to prepare, mark, and transfer needed merchandise to the sales floor are typical operations problems. The value of operations research is obvious if the research helps the retailer find ways to reduce the time and expense involved in operating the store.

Information Systems

The complexity of operating a retail store has created a growing demand for prompt and accurate data for making management decisions. Automated information systems, including computer-linked sales registers, help meet this demand in many stores. Before installing an automated information system, though, a retailer should ask questions similar to the following: Do we need an electronic information system? Should we update our present system? What kind of new equipment do we need? Where should the hardware be located? Will the updated or new system be cost effective? Retailing research can help the store manager answer such questions.

Automated information systems support managers' decisions in another way: Such systems are used in conducting research to analyze input data and print the results.

Illus. 51–2   Computer information systems can help analyze retail data gathered during the research process.

RESEARCH PROCEDURES

Regardless of the size of the business or the nature of the research problem, the retailer must follow an organized procedure to conduct retailing research. The procedure includes (1) identifying the problem, (2) organizing the study, (3) collecting the data, (4) analyzing and presenting the data, and (5) making a decision. Not all retailers take these steps in exactly the same way, but this procedure has worked well for many.

Identifying the Problem

All research must begin with a clear, written statement of the problem to be solved. "Sales are down" is certainly a retail problem, but the statement is much too broad to be researched. The retailer needs to be able to link possible causes to the problem. A specific statement follows: The problem is a 5 percent drop in Dept. G sales over the past three quarters. Now, the retailer has a definite problem and may begin the search for a solution. Phrasing the problem as a research question often is helpful. This retailer might ask questions about promotion activities in Dept. G for the past nine months, for example: Has the advertising budget for Dept. G been cut within the past nine to twelve months? Are different advertising media being used than were used nine to twelve months ago? Are in-store displays in Dept. G changed as often as they were last year? Has a change in personnel occurred in Dept. G?

Organizing the Study

A retailer may suspect that lost sales are the result of improper display methods. To be certain, the retailer must collect all available data related to current display methods so that they can be organized and analyzed. Two major types of information are valuable to the researcher. One type is referred to as **secondary information**— data that have been compiled and published. The other type, called **primary information,** are data that the researcher has gathered through her or his own efforts. Obviously, secondary information sources should be checked first to see if the data needed are already available. After all, there is little point in devoting time, money, and effort to gathering information that is already available.

Secondary Information.   Among the many important and most widely used sources of information that retailers use are the following:

1. *Company records:* sales records, invoices, customer refunds, accounting reports, and previous research records
2. *Governmental data:* Small Business Administration publications, Department of Commerce reports, and Census Bureau studies
3. *Private information services:* A. C. Nielsen Company (radio and television ratings) and Dun & Bradstreet (reports of credit and economic conditions)
4. *Libraries:* most major business publications, such as *Chain Store Age, The Wall Street Journal,* and *The Journal of Marketing*
5. *Trade associations:* retailing groups— for example, Retail Bakers Association of America, National Association of Retail Ice Cream Manufacturers, Independent Motorcycle Retailers of America, National Association of Variety Stores—that provide data related to specific problems
6. *Colleges of business:* schools and universities that provide research assistance to both small and large retail organizations at a nominal fee

Primary Information.   If, after reviewing secondary information, the retailer has not found the type of information needed (which is often the case), then primary information must be collected. In the field of retailing, sources of primary information include customers, wholesalers, competitors, employees, advertising media, and product manufacturers. In organizing the study, the retailer decides which of these primary information sources to use.

Collecting Data

A number of methods can be used to collect and record primary information. Time, money, and personnel are important factors in choosing a data collection method. Most important is assuring that the data will be accurate and useful. Common methods of data collection include the following.

Counts (observations). Counts include **traffic counts** (the number of persons passing by), **fashion counts** (the kinds of clothing people consider fashionable), and **shopping-service counts** (the types of services provided by sales personnel). People who conduct counts must know exactly what to look for. The timing of counts is also important. For example, if a retailer wants to know whether salespeople usually provide a particular shopping service, counts should be made when store traffic is average—neither light nor heavy. The same person should not conduct counts for long periods, as fatigue may cause an increase in counting errors.

Questionnaires (the most widely used method of collecting data). A questionnaire is a list of questions. Questionnaires may be mailed to selected individuals along with a request to answer the questions and return the form. Or, answers to the questions may be collected through

interviews of respondents—in person or over the telephone. Writing a questionnaire requires considerable skill; the questions should yield useful information. For the method to be effective, the retailer must question the right people. For example, catalog shoppers should not be asked about in-store displays. Also, the questionnaire must be answered by a large number of people in order for the results to be meaningful.

Consumer Panels. Some retailers organize consumer panels of typical consumers who express opinions on such topics as the retailer's merchandise, advertising methods, and customer services. Consumers on panels must have had firsthand experience in these areas and be willing to provide opinions and suggestions for improvement.

Organizing the Data

Once the data have been collected, they must be organized so they can be interpreted and reported. Organizing data involves tabulating and summarizing the information. **Tabulation** is the process of classifying data and arranging it in tables. **Summarizing** is the process of pulling together the separate pieces of data in the form of written statements. A sample data table is shown in Illustration 51–3. Tables can be arranged manually, or, in extensive research efforts, computers may be used to tabulate data. A summary of the data in Illustration 51–3 might contain these statements, for example: (1) Over one-third of the traffic (36.7 percent) uses the Spring Avenue entrance to the mall, while about half as many people (18.5 percent) use the

WASHINGTON SQUARE MALL TRAFFIC COUNT

	Day and Time							
	Monday		Wednesday		Friday			
	A.M.	P.M.	A.M.	P.M.	A.M.	P.M.	Total	Percent
Location	10–12	5–7	10–12	5–7	10–12	5–7		
Walnut Street	112	135	109	113	106	124	699	18.5
Concourse A	80	128	99	152	91	203	753	19.9
Concourse B	98	176	106	188	111	267	946	24.9
Spring Avenue	181	217	132	257	212	389	1,388	36.7
Total	471	656	446	710	520	983	3,786	100.0
Percent	41.8	58.2	38.6	61.4	34.6	65.4	100.0	

Illus. 51–3 This table shows the number of customers who entered the shopping mall at four different locations in two 2-hour periods on Monday, Wednesday, and Friday. A study of the data helps a retailer in the mall decide where to locate, where to set up displays, and when to have all salespeople working.

Walnut Street entrance. (2) The heaviest traffic (65.4 percent) occurs late in the day on Friday; the lightest traffic (34.6 percent) occurs on Friday morning. (3) Afternoon traffic on Wednesday afternoon is almost one-fourth (22.8 percent) greater than traffic on Wednesday morning.

Analyzing and Presenting the Data

Data collected are useless unless the retailer can draw conclusions from them. To tell the retailer something he or she needs to know, the data must be analyzed. Some data must be analyzed statistically in order to find the particular relationships among the seemingly different pieces of information. Other data, such as that collected by counts, may be analyzed without statistics.

Just by looking at the data table and summary in Illustration 51–3, the retailer may conclude the following: (1) traffic in the mall is heaviest through the Spring Avenue doors and lightest through the Walnut Street entrance; (2) overall, afternoon traffic is heavier than morning traffic; and (3) afternoon traffic is heavier at the end of the week than at the beginning, but morning traffic is heavier early in the week than later.

The data should be presented and explained in a written report so that those people who were not involved in conducting the research can understand the outcomes. Data may be presented in tables, bar graphs, pie charts, or other visual forms to make it easy to comprehend. The report also should contain the statement of the original problem, an explanation of how the study was conducted, and the statements of the main findings or results. A study tells the retailer some action is necessary; an action statement should end the research report.

Making a Decision

If the research procedures have been performed properly and the data analyzed correctly, the findings usually suggest action for the retailer to take. First, though, the retailer should read between the lines of the results of the study and then draw upon her or his experience and insight into the problem before making a decision to act. In other words, retailing research does not replace common sense but supplements it. If a merchant has a 60 percent chance of solving a difficult problem on the basis of experience alone, research efforts may raise the chances to 75 percent or 80 percent. Thus, retailing research is well worth the effort in many instances.

IMPORTANCE OF RESEARCH SKILLS

For the person who plans to advance in retailing, a basic understanding of research procedures and research interpretation is essential. Even if the person does not conduct the research, he or she must be able to interpret research findings reported by others. Business magazines, trade organizations, and the government produce great amounts of data that are important to retailers. To be promotable, a person is expected to be able to make accurate decisions on the basis of research findings.

Summary   Retailers use retailing research procedures to gather, record, and analyze data related to problems they wish to solve. Problems most often studied are those related to store location, customers, sales, sales promotion, personnel, and operations. To obtain the information needed to make appropriate decisions, retailers follow a certain research procedure. This procedure includes (1) identifying the problem, (2) organizing the study, (3) collecting data, (4) analyzing and presenting data, and (5) making a decision. Although an individual may not conduct research, he or she should be able to interpret data presented by others. This interpretation ability is essential to advancement in the retailing field.

Review
1. Define *retailing research*.
2. Identify seven ways in which retailers use retailing research to solve store problems.
3. Name and explain the steps in the retailing research procedure.
4. List six sources of secondary information.
5. Identify three methods of gathering primary information.
6. State the importance of research skills for a career in retailing.

Terms   The following terms were introduced in this chapter. Write a separate sentence correctly using each new term.

fashion counts	shopping-service counts
primary information	summarizing
retailing research	tabulation
secondary information	traffic counts

Discuss
1. What are the major goals of retailing research activities?
2. Why is it important to have an organized approach to retailing research?
3. How do secondary and primary information differ? Is primary information more important?
4. State five problems a retailer may have in retaining customer goodwill. Which problems are researchable and which are too broad as stated to be studied? Give reasons for your decisions.

Problem Solving
1. Obtain a copy of a completed retailing research project from a local business. Do not review the researcher's solution until you have studied the remainder of the report. Based on the informa-

tion provided, identify a course of action you would recommend to solve the problem. Compare your decision with that of the researcher.

2. You are the manager of an independently owned leather-goods store. Over a period of three months, you have noticed a decline in sales of what used to be a very popular jacket. Write a clear problem statement. Following the steps outlined in this chapter, describe how you would organize your study. Explain where and how you would obtain needed data and how you would analyze it. List some conclusions you might reach if you were actually to conduct the study.

3. Your store manager asks you to find out how many convenience stores are located within a certain area of your city. Identify three possible methods of collecting the data needed to answer your manager's question. Determine the advantages and disadvantages of each method. Choose one of the three methods and give reasons for the choice.

CHAPTER 52

Technological Advances in Retailing

CHAPTER OUTCOMES

When you have mastered the information provided in this chapter, you should be able to:

1. Name one key factor in bringing about technological changes in retailing

2. Identify three reasons retailers are seeking new ways to reach consumers

3. Name three examples of in-store merchandising technology

4. Define the term *kiosks;* explain how kiosks are used for in-store merchandising

5. State how retailers use in-home technology to sell merchandise

6. Define the term *EFTS* and give five examples of how it can be used in retailing

7. Identify two new areas in which retailers are using computer technology to make management decisions

Without a doubt, technological advances are changing the retailing industry. Almost every phase of a modern retail store's operation will be made less costly and more profitable as a result of these advances. One key factor in bringing about change has been the increased use of minicomputers, microcomputers, and other computer-linked technology. These activities have allowed retailers to develop and produce more and better business information. As a result, retail managers are able to make difficult decisions rapidly and confidently.

For example, many retailers are using computers to select store locations; design store layouts; improve merchandising and counter layouts; improve selling techniques; and order, receive, and mark merchandise. Some merchants are also using computer technology to offer customers automatic fund transfers and credit authorization as well as real-estate, health, financial, and insurance services. Still others are conducting computer-assisted research to determine the effects of color schemes, floor displays, lighting, and fixture choices on customer buying habits. Clearly, modern technology is moving the retailing industry into the twenty-first century. This chapter presents some of the success stories that are the results of this emerging technology.

TECHNOLOGY IN MERCHANDISING

Buying merchandise with the aid of a computer, while still a vision of the future for some, is today's reality for most retail customers. Although electronic merchandising is still developing, many systems are functioning with great success. Shrinking retail profits, increased competition, and fewer customers to go around are key reasons that progressive retailers are seeking new ways to reach consumers. Customers receive benefits from electronic merchandising innovations because the systems shorten the time required for a customer to make a purchase. In addition, electronic merchandising methods provide accurate and complete product information. These merchandising systems can be used in the customer's home as well as on the sales floor of the retailer's store. Some methods even make it possible to select items not available in the store. Many merchants believe that retailing technology will increase customer traffic and sales as well as reduce the costs of doing business.

In-store Technology

The combination of a computer and interactive laser video disks makes it possible for customers to view assortments of merchandise; adding a touch screen to the system allows quick, on-the-spot ordering of the viewed merchandise. Florsheim Shoes uses electronic catalogs in some of its stores to expand the number of shoe styles it can offer the public. With just a few taps on a computer screen, the hard-to-please or hard-to-fit customer can see many shoes of the right style and size not available in that particular store. With just a few more taps on the screen, shoes can be ordered and delivered directly to the customer's home.

Visual merchandise presentations with computer-ordering capacity are being used to merchandise real estate, cars, stocks and bonds, appliances, and furniture. There has even been some experimentation with the sale of furniture through the use of electronic kiosks. An **electronic kiosk** is a stand that contains both a screen display and equipment for ordering the displayed merchandise. On one kiosk a retailer can display up to 1000 full-color images of living-room, dining-room, and bedroom sets that are available from a variety of manufacturers. Thus, the customers have a wider assortment of merchandise to choose from than would be available in most furniture showrooms. The retailer also benefits be-

cause the electronic kiosk increases customer selections, eliminates the need to carry large inventories, and reduces the need for floor space to display products.

Many other uses of computer technology can be found in stores today. For example, some cosmetic manufacturers now offer computerized facials. The customer's image is projected on a screen, giving an indication of how that customer would look if certain lipstick, rouge, and eye shadow were applied. Similarly, customers can see how they would look in new clothing without actually trying on various outfits. The computer indicates needed clothing sizes and how well the clothing selected matches the customer's need for certain colors or lines. This system makes it possible for the customer to view a large variety of clothing choices in the time required to try on one or two items.

In yet another example of merchandising technology, Sears, Roebuck and Company customers who wish to purchase curtains in the store can enter into a computer the dimensions of the windows, the materials and styles of curtains desired, and the price range desired. The computer evaluates each customer's needs, calculates the price of the curtains the customer has selected, and places an order with the appropriate vendor.

Despite all of its potential, technology does not win everyone's favor. Some merchants complain that many customers resist new technology. They say customers want to be able to touch the actual merchandise. People like to pick the item up and examine it. Some retailers themselves resist change, perhaps because of possible high costs and risks involved in trying something new. However, most retailers agree that new

Illus. 52–1 Computer technology helps customers make decisions rapidly and confidently.

technologies will continue to emerge for years to come.

In-home Technology

In-home shopping systems are similar to those offered by retailers in stores. Most in-home merchandising methods rely on cable television, television shopping channels, and personal computers to provide product information, displays, and instant ordering capabilities. When a customer identifies a desired product on the home television or computer screen, he or she can enter an order for it on the home computer, which is linked by telephone to the retailer's computer system. In another example of in-home merchandising, the customer simply provides information about any product he or she wishes to purchase; model numbers, sizes, styles, and prices are typical kinds of information required. Various sources of merchandise are checked to find the product requested. If the product is available at a price satisfactory to the customer, it is ordered, billed, and shipped directly to the customer's home. Some companies that specialize in catalog sales follow similar procedures except that customer product selections are limited to those contained in the catalogs.

Will electronic in-home shopping systems, similar to in-store systems, eventually

Illus. 52-2   Many retailers use computers to provide customer services.

Illus. 52–3 Technology makes it possible for customers to shop without leaving home.

TECHNOLOGY IN CUSTOMER SERVICES

Most visible of all the customer-service technologies is equipment that transfers funds electronically, or **electronic fund-transfer systems (EFTS).** Currently, there are thousands of these electronic fund-transfer systems in operation throughout the retailing industry.

New uses for EFTS are being developed every day. Some EFTS also serve as check authorization machines. Other electronic transfers also serve as credit authorization equipment. Some merchants provide EFTS for customers who wish to make savings account deposits and withdrawals; make mortgage, insurance, or installment loan payments; pay utility bills; or invest in the stock market.

EFTS technology may eventually make it possible to shop anywhere without cash, checks, or credit cards. A national hookup of banks and retail outlets accepting one all-purpose **debit card** is a distinct possibility. Unlike credit cards, which allow payment after the purchase, debit cards would require that funds be available in the customer's bank account when the purchase is made. Money could be transferred electronically, if necessary, for the sale to be completed. This system would not only be simpler than credit sales transactions, it could reduce the time spent in checkout lines, reduce customer account handling costs, and provide customers with up-to-date records of their personal transactions. Most customers appreciate the convenience that EFTS technology offers. While some customers prefer to deal with people rather than machines, ease of use, confidentiality,

become major merchandising techniques for retailers? No one really knows for sure because an in-home system is a relatively new way to present goods and services. Convenience appears to be the most likely reason for customers to use an in-home system. Time savings and novelty also have great consumer appeal. A study by *Chain Store Age Executive* revealed, however, that consumers hesitated to use in-home systems as an alternative to store shopping. When they did shop at home, their choices were mostly limited to books, small appliances, records, and games. Many customers are quick to say, "I like to see what I'm buying" or "I prefer to go to the store and shop in person." In spite of this concern, innovative retailers believe electronic in-home shopping, similar to in-store technology, will succeed.

and accuracy are factors that almost ensure public acceptance of this technology.

TECHNOLOGY IN MANAGEMENT DECISION MAKING

Retailers rely heavily on computer technology to help make important decisions about store activities. Traditionally, tasks such as sales forecasting, buying, merchandising, and financial control took most of a manager's time. Technology reduces the amount of time these areas demand by quickly processing raw data and providing information with which decisions can be made quickly and accurately. Today, retailers are exploring the use of technology in other key areas of management responsibility. Exciting innovations are developing. Time-consuming activities such as identifying new store locations; determining effective store design; and selecting interior colors, fixtures, and lighting are now being aided by technological advances.

Selecting Store Locations

Some fast-growing chains are beginning to use computer systems to identify promising new locations. This technology saves vast amounts of time and expense formerly involved in visiting every potential site. Data that describe successful trading areas are entered into a computer. Included is information such as population sizes, consumer income and educational levels, competition, and employment trends in the trading areas under study. Computer analysis of this data results in a written description of the typical location required for a successful store. Those locations having characteristics most like the computer profile are considered seriously as future store sites, while the other locations are disregarded.

Store Design

The development of computer-graphics technology makes it possible to see different store layout ideas before actual construction of a layout begins. Store design systems are somewhat similar in operation to those systems used to create store location profiles. Instead of generating a written description, the store layout system produces a diagram of a store from the design data entered into the computer. The diagrams can be studied on the computer screen; the best designs can be printed and studied more extensively. The major advantage of a graphics system is that management can see and evaluate in advance the proposed store design. With very little physical effort, managers can study the effects of minor variations in (1) display fixture types and placement; (2) lighting; (3) wall, ceiling, and floor treatments; (4) customer traffic flow; and (5) costs of construction. A store graphics-design system can help a retailer decide which of several possible layouts is right for a particular store. For example, computers are being used to determine counter layouts. Sales performance and gross-margin figures are fed into the computer, along with product dimensions. The computer then designs the counter layout, including item locations.

Summary

Technology is having a dramatic impact on retailing. Management decisions about such concerns as store location, merchandising methods, and selling techniques are but a few of the areas influenced by technological advances. For example, to increase sales and reduce costs, some merchants are using in-store computers and interactive laser disks to sell merchandise. Customers are able to visualize, select, and order goods in the store without salesperson assistance. In-home cable television, television shopping channels, and personal computers allow consumers to view and order merchandise without actually going to the retail store. Technological advances in customer services allow the electronic transfer of funds from the customer's bank account to the retailer each time a purchase is made. As a result, no cash or checks need change hands. Computer technology can also be used to identify promising new store locations. This process is accomplished by comparing sites under consideration with ideal store location profiles developed from data fed into a computer system. Similarly, decisions about effective display and fixture placement, lighting, wall and floor treatment, and customer traffic flow can be more accurately predicted with the assistance of modern technology.

Review

1. Identify one key factor in bringing about technological changes in retailing.
2. Name three reasons retailers are seeking new ways to reach customers.
3. List three examples of in-store merchandising technology.
4. Define *kiosk;* state how kiosks are used for in-store merchandising.
5. Explain how retailers use in-home technology to sell merchandise.
6. Define *EFTS* and list five uses of EFTS in retailing.
7. Name two relatively new areas in which retailers are using computer technology to support management decisions.

Terms

The following terms were introduced in this chapter. Write a separate sentence correctly using each new term.

debit card   electronic kiosk
electronic fund-transfer system
  (EFTS)

Discuss

1. How are technological advances changing the retailing industry?
2. What are some possible disadvantages of in-store and in-home merchandising technology for customers and retailers?
3. What advantages, besides those mentioned in the chapter, does electronic fund-transfer technology offer customers? retailers?
4. What effect has the development of computer-graphics technology had on retail-store designing?

Problem Solving

1. Identify three articles in trade magazines or papers that each describe a different technological advance not discussed in this chapter. List what you believe are the advantages and disadvantages of each technique. State reasons you would or would not use such technology in your store.
2. You are employed by a large department store that has decided to offer electronic fund-transferring service to its customers. Some customers seem hesitant about using the service, and convincing them of the value of EFTS has become your responsibility. What means would you use to do this and what kinds of customer benefits would you stress?
3. You are the owner of a medium-sized furniture and carpet store. You have received a number of requests from your customers to carry additional lines of merchandise, but your store is limited in the amount of sales floor space available for additional products. Identify specific types of in-store and in-home merchandising techniques you would use to resolve your problem. Give reasons for the choices you make.

CHAPTER 53

Changing Practices in Retailing

CHAPTER OUTCOMES

When you have mastered the information provided in this chapter, you should be able to:

1. State how shopping for staple goods and specialty goods is changing

2. List and describe five kinds of innovative shopping malls

3. Describe where and why multi-use malls have grown

4. Explain how manufacturer involvement in retailing has changed

5. State how megamalls differ from other kinds of shopping malls

6. Explain the superstore concept and name examples of no-frills retailers

7. State the main reasons international retailing has been successful

Retailers are risk takers. The chance to develop a successful business depends in part on a willingness to try something different. People took chances when they started the first self-service store, discount operation, videotape-rental store, drive-through pharmacy, one-hour photo service, gardening and lawn-care service, used-carpet store, and one-stop wedding shop. Clearly, then, retailing is not for the faint of heart. Creativity, imagination, and risk taking have brought forth a steady stream of new and exciting business opportunities.

As a retail operation grows and prospers, chances increase that it could be replaced by new ventures that might perform better and at lower costs. Some retailing experts believe that shopping for staple goods such as food and clothing will become so routine as to involve more self-service and machines than personal service. Specialty items such as sporting equipment. high-fashion clothing, stereo equipment, and furniture may, on the other hand, require new methods of selling and increased personalized service to attract and retain customers. Further, experts predict dramatic changes in shopping-mall operations along with increasing standardization of store operations, products, and management procedures. This chapter explains some of the rapidly changing business practices that will usher retailing into the next century.

SHOPPING MALLS

Among the most visible changes taking place in the retail industry are those af-

fecting traditional shopping centers and malls. Innovations include (1) multi-use malls, (2) strip centers, (3) high-fashion malls, (4) manufacturers malls, and (5) mega-malls. Following is a brief description of each type of operation.

Multi-use Malls

Business developers have difficulty finding suitable locations for the construction of new malls and centers. Some even question the need to continue locating in suburban communities given the slight trend toward living in central city areas. As a result, there has been some growth in the development of downtown malls in remodeled old buildings. Unused waterfront piers, office buildings, banks, and government buildings are among prime targets for redevelopment. Many of these structures offer ideal locations because they are in heavy traffic areas. They also offer unique opportunities to develop themes or atmospheres by taking advantage of the original purpose of the mall location. Such sites usually can be purchased or leased at reasonable prices.

The key to the success of downtown shopping malls has been their multi-use design. Unlike the traditional shopping centers, the **multi-use mall** contains offices, convention centers, apartments, condominiums, and parking ramps, in addition to retail stores. One example is Bandana Square in St. Paul, Minnesota. This multi-use mall is located in a renovated repair shop for railroad cars and locomotives. In addition to housing specialty shops, offices, and restaurants, Bandana Square adjoins a large townhouse complex and a motel.

Illus. 53–1   Dramatic changes are taking place in the development of shopping malls utilizing a variety of existing buildings.

Strip Centers

A **strip center** is made up of convenience stores and built on a small site of approximately 15,000 square feet. Often, such locations are corner lots in prime commercial areas. Spaces once occupied by gasoline stations are likely choices for locating strip centers; thus, a decreasing number of gasoline stations has increased the availability of potential sites. A typical strip center contains a half dozen small stores and 15 to 20 parking spaces. It is not unusual to find a convenience store such as 7-Eleven serving as the anchor store in a strip center. Dry cleaners, copy centers, videotape stores, and other service enterprises make up the majority of other retailers located in strip centers.

The main attraction to potential strip-center tenants is location. Developers build these malls in heavily populated areas—typically older communities. Good locations are those that have a minimum of 100,000 people within a 2-mile radius and a daily traffic count of 45,000 cars. Retailers may pay rents ranging from $1 to $3 per square foot to locate in a strip center. Comparable space in a conventional shopping center ranges from $1 to $1.50. Tenants willingly pay the higher rates of strip centers because of the customer traffic that strip centers generate. Strip centers provide a valuable service—especially to urban customers who otherwise would have to travel long distances to shopping centers. Therefore, the potential for continued growth of strip centers seems certain.

High-fashion Malls

Unlike the strip center, the **high-fashion mall** offers specialty shopping with emphasis on high-fashion merchandise. Clothing, jewelry, fur, and furniture stores as well as travel agencies are likely tenants of high-fashion malls. Because the shoppers in this type of mall usually are those with high incomes, most high-fashion malls are located in or near affluent neighborhoods. Retailers know that high-income shoppers tend to seek out specialty stores where customer service and quality merchandise are emphasized. Therefore, the success of a high-fashion mall depends on attracting tenants such as Gucci and Cartier. More than other types of malls, high-fashion malls are adversely affected by changing economic conditions that reduce shoppers' spendable income.

Manufacturers Malls

In the past, manufacturer involvement in retailing was usually limited to the operation of outlets that sold factory overruns or defective merchandise. For the most part, this merchandise could not be sold through regular retail channels. To overcome this problem, some manufacturers opened their own retail stores in what is called a **manufacturers mall.** These efforts typically met with limited success because retailing was not the manufacturer's strength. Levi Strauss, for example, liquidated its chain of 70 close-out stores in 1980 to concentrate on the manufacturing process. More recent efforts by manufacturers to merchandise their own products have been directed at malls containing only manufacturer-operated outlets.

A problem for manufacturers-turned-retailers has been an inability to offer a broad assortment of merchandise to fill a store. Limited product choice has meant few customers. More important, perhaps, is the fact that manufacturers risk alienating their regular outlets—department stores—by directly competing with them in the retail market.

Megamalls

Perhaps the most innovative of all the changes taking place in mall design is the **megamall.** This concept combines retailing with entertainment or tourism in a large space. For example, Morton Plaza in San Diego opened early in 1986 with two live theaters and an art museum. Woodbine Centre in Toronto, Canada, has an indoor children's park featuring numerous rides. The West Edmonton Mall in Edmonton, Canada, has four submarines running on tracks around an indoor lake stocked with sharks. Wild birds, caged animals, carnival rides, and a skating rink are more examples of the many, many attractions at the mall or planned for future construction.

Some retailers are skeptical about combining entertainment with business, but competition dictates that new methods of attracting and holding customers be found.

Illus. 53–2   Megamalls often combine entertainment with retail services.

SUPERSTORES

A trend away from typical supermarkets and toward superstores emerged in the mid-1980s and continued into the 1990s. The **superstore** offers a much broader range of consumer products than the supermarket. Customers are able to purchase, in addition to grocery items, appliances, garden equipment, televisions, clothing, hardware, and sporting goods. To house this increased variety of products, floor space is greater than in supermarkets by 100 percent or more. Grand Bazaar's superstores in Chicago range in size from 68,000 to 89,000 square feet and have as many as 40 checkout counters in each store. Retailer interest in superstores is prompted by the potential such stores offer for greater profits. In addition, the appeals of one-stop shopping and huge parking lots should help to assure the success of superstores.

NO-FRILLS RETAILERS

A recent innovation in retailing has been the development of the **no-frills store;** that is, stores that offer minimal customer service and decor but that offer goods at low prices. Jewel T and The Atlantic and Pacific Tea Company (A&P) are examples of large chains that have turned to no-frills merchandising methods as a means of lowering operating costs. At a typical no-frills grocery store, customers pay cash, bag their own groceries, and carry them to their cars.

Bulk merchandising is another example of no-frills retailing. Bulk items are not prepackaged but are stored in bins and priced by the pound. Candy, powdered foods, nuts, and dried fruits are typical bulk items. Customers can buy in bulk simply by scooping the merchandise into a bag and having it weighed at a checkout counter.

Sometimes, these stores are referred to as *box stores* because even prepackaged merchandise is displayed in the original shipping carton rather than being unpacked and placed on shelves and display units. No-frills retail operations are not limited to the food industry. A growing number of appliance, clothing, toy, and sporting-goods dealers are turning to box-store merchandising as a means of attracting more customers.

INTERNATIONAL RETAILING

International merchandising by U.S. retailers is continuing to develop. Growing numbers of American retailers are finding new markets for their goods in other coun-

Illus. 53–3 Product recognition makes it easier for American retailers to operate in foreign countries, such as Japan.

tries. J.C. Penney, Sears, McDonalds, Holiday Inn, and KFC are just a few examples of the many retailers who have started or are planning to start operations around the world.

The success of international retailing can be attributed in part to a growing similarity in life-styles of people in different countries. As a result, customer wants and needs can more easily be satisfied with standard goods and services. The rapid development of international travel and greater use of international advertising media have heavily influenced consumer buying habits, too. As competition for American consumer dollars grows, retailers increasingly look to international markets as a way of building sales volume.

Summary
Many retailers are successful because they are willing to change their business practices. Some of the most dramatic changes have been those affecting shopping centers and malls. Multi-use malls, strip centers, high-fashion malls, manufacturers malls, and megamalls represent a trend away from the traditional shopping center. Superstores with immense floor space and a variety of goods such as appliances, garden equipment, clothing, and hardware compete with supermarkets selling a single line of merchandise. No-frills retailers offer minimal customer services and decor in exchange for lower customer prices. Growing similarity in consumer life-styles worldwide is making it easier for retailers to sell their goods in international markets where product recognition has already been established.

Review
1. Explain how shopping for staple goods and specialty goods is changing.
2. Identify five kinds of innovative shopping malls.
3. State where and why multi-use malls have grown.
4. Define *strip center* and compare strip centers to high-fashion malls.
5. State how manufacturer involvement in retailing has changed.
6. Describe how megamalls differ from other kinds of shopping malls.
7. Explain the superstore concept; describe no-frills retailers.
8. Explain the main reasons international retailing has been successful.

Terms
The following terms were introduced in this chapter. Write a separate sentence correctly using each new term.

high-fashion mall   no-frills store
manufacturers mall   strip center
megamall   superstore
multi-use mall

Discuss
1. What is meant by the statement "Retailers are risk takers"?
2. Why would retailers look to existing buildings as locations in which to operate shopping malls?
3. How are strip centers located and organized?
4. What are some advantages of no-frill stores to customers? to retailers?

Problem Solving

1. Joan Sill has operated a high-fashion women's clothing store in a strip center for two years. Lack of floor space has limited the lines of merchandise that should be carried. In addition, Joan has not been able to attract the kind of clientele she seeks. A new location must be found or the store will have to be closed. Suggest three general locations for this store. Give reasons for each choice. Select the best type of location and identify the advantages of this choice over the others.

2. You are the assistant manager in a typical supermarket operation. Because the store has not been profitable, the owner believes a new method of operation is necessary. You are sure that a no-frills approach will improve the profit picture. Try to convince the owner by pointing out various no-frills methods of operation and suggest how your examples could reduce costs and increase profits.

3. You are employed in the office of a land developer. Two years ago, your employer built a mall in a suburban location near a large metropolitan area. At that time, a trend toward central-city living was beginning, and a large downtown renovation project had begun. Currently, the mall operated by your employer is only 70 percent occupied. Would you have made a different decision about mall location? What information would you have used to make your decision? What kind of mall would you have proposed? Identify specific features of the mall you would have promoted.

CHAPTER 54

Your Future in Retailing

CHAPTER OUTCOMES

When you have mastered the information provided in this chapter, you should be able to:

1. List seven expectations potential employees may have about their jobs

2. Identify four traits most retailers prefer in the people they employ

3. Explain how interest and aptitude tests can help identify career choices

4. State how individual values may influence job choice

5. Name four sources of job information

6. Explain the importance of an updated résumé and how it can be kept current

7. Define the term *productivity* and list four ways to develop good work habits

8. Define the term *time management* and list eight time-management guidelines

Retailing can offer you a wide range of career choices. Working with a variety of customers and products is exciting and dynamic work. Thus, your first job in retailing could be the beginning of an interesting, challenging, and satisfying career. While some people may perform the same retail job for their entire lives, others hold several different positions. Still others may be employed in more than one store or work for a variety of retailing organizations. The variety in retailing careers indicates the constantly changing nature of the retailing field and the opportunities it can present. To assist you in planning your career in retailing, this chapter contains information related to (1) setting job expectations, (2) finding sources of information, (3) understanding elements of job performance, and (4) planning for advancement.

SETTING YOUR JOB EXPECTATIONS

As a potential employee, you should have certain expectations of the job you are seeking. For example, you might ask yourself, "Will the job I am considering provide personal satisfaction or a sense of accomplishment?" "How much will the job pay?" "What are the working hours?" "What type of work is involved?" "Are there opportunities for advancement?" Questions related to job location and employee benefits—health insurance, vacations, and merchandise discounts—also need to be answered. Thus, while understanding the employer's expectations is important, you should also identify your own expectations.

It is true that numerous retail jobs are available in most communities. This does not mean, however, that employers are willing to hire just anyone. On the contrary, most retailers expect that the persons they hire will demonstrate such traits as being enthusiastic about their work, wanting to be part of a team effort, valuing customers as important, and constantly seeking ways to improve personal retailing skills. They also expect that potential employees will have good educational backgrounds, be organized, display strong interpersonal and communication skills, and be self-motivated. Retail employers tend to favor those with previous experience. But persons who possess the traits listed above also have an excellent chance to be hired. That is why your first job in retailing can take on special importance. Job performance establishes a record that will follow you throughout your career. The way you perform on your first job will influence your chances for promotion within the firm or for receiving your employer's recommendation if you apply elsewhere. Your first job also provides the all-important work experience that is often a job qualification.

Job expectations can be set in various ways. Initially, you may want to talk with a career guidance counselor who can help you assess personal interests and abilities. Also, you should do a self-assessment by making two lists of job-related activities—those you would like to do and those you would prefer not to do. For example, you may like working with people but not dealing with numbers. Perhaps you would like to develop creative display ideas but not actually construct the displays. In addition to the self-assessment, the counselor may advise you to take one of several interest tests.

Such tests can reveal interests you never knew you had. If possible, the retail job you select should involve several of your high-interest activities. Keep in mind, though, that no job is perfect—every job will involve some low-interest activities.

Generally, a person is interested in those activities that he or she does well, but such is not always the case. Therefore, you need to identify not only your interests but also your aptitudes or abilities. By talking with you and reviewing your grades in school, a career counselor may be able to help you identify the types of things that you do particularly well. Also, the coun-

selor may administer one or more aptitude tests designed to point out your strengths and weaknesses.

Your **values**—personal beliefs about what is good, important, or desirable—need to be understood. The person planning a career in retailing should also learn the values of the firm and the values of those persons with whom he or she may associate. For example, an employee might believe that fair treatment of customers is important or that opportunities for advancement and recognition should be judged on individual merit. If the employer does not share these values, the employee likely will

Illus. 54–1   That first job in retailing could be important in building a career.

become uncomfortable and dissatisfied with the job.

Your interests, abilities, and values are the basis upon which you conduct your daily life or life-style. As you make life-style choices—including a career choice—you must think about the person you want to become. Who you are two years, five years, or ten years from now will be determined in part by the first job you choose.

SOURCES OF JOB INFORMATION

Once you have made a decision about the kinds of retail jobs that will best suit your needs, you should look for firms with job openings. Sometimes, openings are plentiful and employment is easy to find. However, when jobs are not easy to find, much depends on the job seeker's willingness to look for and track down leads. There are many sources that can help you locate good employment possibilities. Some of these sources are (1) friends and acquaintances, (2) help-wanted advertisements, (3) employment agencies, and (4) school career-planning and placement offices.

Friends and Acquaintances

When looking for employment, you should tell your friends and acquaintances that you are interested in a particular kind of job. They may know or learn of an opening or suggest an employer who may be interested in your qualifications. Many firms urge their employees to recommend friends who are well-qualified. Most companies value recommendations from present employees and look favorably on applicants who are referred in this manner. This is an excellent way for job seekers to identify potential employers.

Help-wanted Advertisements

The help-wanted columns of newspapers and trade magazines regularly carry job openings in the retail area. In addition, some specialized publications contain lists of job opportunities. Typical help-wanted advertisements explain what and where the job is, the qualifications needed, the salary offered, and how to apply. Some advertisements also require a letter of application and most request a personal interview with applicants. Beginners are likely to find their first jobs listed in the help-wanted columns of newspapers. Experienced workers may find positions listed in the classified columns of retail trade magazines or papers.

Illus. 54–2 Newspapers, trade magazines, and specialized employment publications list a variety of job opportunities.

Employment Agencies

Often, retail employees find positions by using the services of private or public employment agencies. In every large city, there are private agencies that, for a fee (which is sometimes paid by the employer), place both experienced and beginning store workers. Some agencies specialize in retail personnel.

The best-known public employment agency is the state bureau of employment services. Trained placement personnel help individuals find the most appropriate types of employment and schedule interviews with firms that have reported job vacancies. No fee is paid for this government service.

Career-planning and Placement Offices

For students seeking retail employment, a career-planning and placement office in high school or college is perhaps better than employment agencies. Employers regularly list their needs for new personnel with these offices. Schools that offer marketing education or cooperative retailing programs generally have a coordinator who is well-acquainted with the retail employment needs of the community. A card of introduction from the program coordinator to a retail employment manager usually assures a student a prompt and cordial employment interview. Keep in mind that it is not a good idea to apply for every retailing job turned up by these sources. Rather, you should match job information with your personal expectations.

Illus. 54–3   Career-planning and placement offices are excellent sources of employment assistance for new workers.

ELEMENTS OF JOB PERFORMANCE

Too often, people with great ability, good skills, and a sincere interest in a career fail to find new employment or to move ahead because they do not plan their time and organize their work. Most people are occasionally lax; however, habitual failure to plan and organize can cost talented persons good employment or desired promotions. Following are suggestions for planning time and increasing output so that you can use your abilities and skills to your best advantage.

Developing Work Habits

Productivity is the output or contribution of a worker to a business. Productivity results from a combination of an individual's putting forth effort, using equipment, following procedures, and responding to the work environment. Much attention is given these days to ways that managers can help employees be more productive. Ultimately, though, each worker must be sure that he or she is productive. High productivity can lead to increased income for the individual and consideration for promotions.

Development of good work habits is vital to your on-the-job productivity. You can learn ways to work better and faster by (1) watching and imitating successful and experienced workers, (2) asking questions, (3) experimenting with different procedures, and (4) practicing skills on your own or with your supervisor's help.

Managing Time

Time management is the efficient and effective use of time. A job done quickly must also be done well. Why is it then that some persons, in the same amount of time, do more work and do it better than others? Part of this variation in productivity is due to differences in skill and experience. But, in nearly every case, individuals with high productivity are those who make excellent use of their time. Seldom do they say, "I just didn't have time."

Imagine that this morning you were given $1,440 to spend. This money can be spent any way that you like for things that you believe are really important to you and your career. At the end of the day, whatever you have not spent is lost forever. Now compare this situation to the 1440 minutes that everyone has each day. You can spend those minutes any way you wish for things that you think are important. However, those minutes that you do not use wisely are gone forever.

A few simple guidelines can help you become a better time manager: (1) Set priorities; decide which activities matter most in terms of your personal and employment future. (2) Start promptly on priority work and keep at it, making decisions quickly. (3) Balance creative, planning, productive, maintenance, and leisure activities. (4) Reserve time for reading essential materials, magazines, books, and correspondence. (5) Schedule your best hours to do the most demanding work, putting the most difficult tasks first. (6) Control how you spend your time; do not give in to distractions. (7) Keep track of how you spend your time. (8) Review your record of time use regularly and eliminate those activities that you believe are not important or productive. For the person planning a career in retailing, these guidelines will help ensure effective use of each day's 1440 minutes.

PLANNING FOR ADVANCEMENT

The process of preparing, applying, and interviewing for employment is described in Chapter 17. The importance of having a well-prepared personal résumé, a neat and effective application letter, and good preparation for the job interview is emphasized in that chapter. In addition to these basics, which are necessary each time you change jobs, other matters are also important to building a career in retailing.

Your first day on a new job becomes the starting point for continually updating your personal résumé. While the résumé need not be retyped until you want to use it for a job change or promotion, you should keep it up to date. Some persons wait until they are ready to apply for a new job and then find that they have forgotten exactly when they handled an important inventory project, won a sales award, or performed activities that could be important in getting a job. Every few months, you should add to your résumé new experiences and activities—whatever will enhance your job qualifications. Then, if a résumé is needed at a

moment's notice, you have one that is current. Any workshops, training seminars, or other educational programs in which you participate should be listed on the résumé, and copies of the programs as well as certificates of completion should be retained.

Brush up on your job interviewing skills even though you may have a job. During meetings with your supervisor, you should practice your skills in listening, questioning, and persuading. If it has been some time since you changed jobs, a session with a career counselor will help you remember the subjects usually discussed during interviews. Because of your job experience, you should know what questions you want answered before accepting another job.

Illus. 54—4   Preparation for a job interview increases chances of obtaining employment and advancement.

Summary
Retailing offers many, many job opportunities. For this reason, care should be exercised when making career choices. As a potential retail employee, you should have certain job expectations. Retailers have expectations, too. They expect employees to be enthusiastic team players with good work habits who are eager to learn new skills and to serve customers. You should be aware of several sources of job information for identifying potential employment. Knowing how to develop good work habits and manage time also are important to your future in retailing. Planning for advancement should begin on the first day of employment. A current résumé is vital to career advancement.

Review
1. Name seven expectations potential employees may have about their jobs.
2. Identify four traits most retailers prefer in the people they employ.
3. State how interest and aptitude tests can help identify career choices.
4. Explain how individual values may influence job choice.
5. List four sources of job information.
6. Explain the importance of an updated résumé and how it can be kept current.
7. Define *productivity* and list four ways of developing good work habits.
8. Define *time management* and list eight time-management guidelines.

Terms
The following terms were introduced in this chapter. Write a separate sentence correctly using each new term.

productivity   values
time management

Discuss
1. How might an employee's job expectations influence progress on the job and long-term job satisfaction?
2. Why might school career-planning and placement offices be more effective sources of job information than friends or acquaintances?
3. How are productivity and time management related?
4. Why are listening, questioning, and persuading skills important in a job interview situation?

Problem Solving

1. Larry has been employed in the furniture department of Chang Imports for six months. Clearly, he is not happy with his work. When asked what his job expectations and future plans are, he can only give vague responses. As his friend, you offer to help Larry formulate a plan to identify his job expectations, interests, and abilities. What course of action should Larry follow?

2. Devise a daily log or means of keeping a written record of how you spend your time each day. Keep this record for two weeks. Analyze your activities and prepare a summary of how your time was spent. What changes, if any, should you make? Why?

3. Identify a retailing position that you would like to obtain. Make a list of what your job expectations would be for that position. Compare your list with the actual experiences of someone who has a job similar to the one you are seeking. Also, get the opinions of a store manager. What similarities or differences among expectations did you find? What conclusions can you draw?

CHAPTER 55

Planning a Future in Retailing

Perhaps one reason you have studied the material in this text has been to determine if a career in retailing is suitable for you. If your answer is "Yes, I want to be in retailing," you already know that there are many opportunities and challenges awaiting you in the marketplace. The retail employee who does a good job, works well with co-workers, and is ambitious has most of what satisfying employment requires. In addition, dynamic decision making will be essential to a successful career.

Of course, a person's first retailing job should be chosen carefully; likewise, one must choose options throughout her or his career. This chapter discusses three major factors in planning for a future in retailing: (1) establishing a sound foundation of basic skills and qualities, (2) developing a personal career plan, and (3) deciding whether to become an independent business owner.

PERFORMING ON THE JOB

The retail employee who seeks a better job, an executive position, or ownership of a business must be committed to continuous self-improvement. The employee who has good communication skills, human relations or people skills, and math skills has a foundation upon which to build additional competencies. Therefore, retail personnel should keep these basic skills sharp throughout their careers by using the skills and learning new ones. Other keys to continued advancement are responsibility, loyalty, resourcefulness, initiative, and expertise in one or more merchandising areas.

Responsibility

Willingness to accept responsibilities readily and to fulfill them successfully is a quality of a valuable employee. The beginning worker who carries out small responsibilities can expect to be given additional responsibilities and opportunities. On the other hand, people who complain about their job situations can expect to find themselves with dull jobs—or no jobs at all.

Responsibility includes willingness to help other employees at all levels. Helping newcomers to the job by giving them a fair chance to succeed is particularly important to employees who want to go places in retailing.

Loyalty

Never underestimate the importance of loyalty to your employer. As long as a worker accepts a salary from an employer, that employee owes the employer loyalty in return. However, questions can arise when an employee receives conflicting orders from different superiors. When loyalty to one person results in apparent disloyalty to another, to whom does one owe loyalty? Usually, the immediate supervisor is responsible for giving job instructions. The employee should follow those instructions in spite of different instructions from someone else.

Resourcefulness

Most employees want to perform assigned job tasks to the best of their abilities. What is more, supervisors expect employ-

Illus. 55–1   The willingness to accept job responsibility is an attitude that is important for job advancement.

ees to follow directions and to apply what is learned during the training sessions. Because supervisors and managers have many duties other than supervision, almost nothing annoys them more than repeated interruptions to answer an employee's unnecessary questions. Therefore, employees should carry out most work assignments without constantly consulting the supervisor. Store policies, of course, provide the framework within which an employee acts; therefore, learning the policies and keeping a copy of them handy is vital. In addition, employees need to be able to apply common sense and good judgment to those ar-

eas not spelled out in the store policies. Being resourceful means running the risk of being wrong. But being wrong is not totally bad if the employee learns from the mistake.

Initiative

Retail employees should never hesitate to do extra work. An ambitious salesperson, for example, may visit competing stores during free time to compare appearance, services, assortments, and values. Time spent studying store manuals and training materials is also a valuable use of time. Such activities help salespersons by giving them more confidence in themselves and their store or department. Moreover, the salesperson may acquire ideas that can be passed on tactfully to supervisors.

In every store, there are ways in which store methods and systems of operation can be improved. Store executives may be too close to the operation to realize a need for change or may be too busy to attend to it. Employees who take the trouble to study situations and suggest possible improvements usually find that their ideas receive sympathetic consideration. Some stores have a formal suggestion system. Store employees are urged to recommend changes in procedures, and prizes are awarded for the best suggestions or those put into operation.

Merchandising Expertise

Individuals seeking advancement in retailing should build and demonstrate skill in as many merchandising areas as possible. Just as in-depth product knowledge is essential to good selling, a thorough understanding of the broader areas of merchandising is essential to job advancement. Persons who move up the ladder in retailing must demonstrate not only product knowledge and selling skills but also knowledge of promotion, merchandising, buying, and financial control. The individuals who thoroughly understand one merchandising area have a foundation for expanding their competence in other areas. Therefore, you would be wise to focus on developing the main skills of your first job while acquiring knowledge of another merchandising area at the same time. With

work experience, you should continue to branch out into new areas of the retailing field. Few retail executives lack proven excellence in several areas of retailing.

PERSONAL CAREER PLANNING

People who want successful retailing careers can do a great deal to progress rapidly and directly toward that goal. **Career planning** involves three other phases besides job performance: awareness, exploration, and preparation. As soon as an individual is established in a position, he or she should begin looking for opportunities for advancement. A beginning retail employee should find out which jobs typically follow the current job so that a clear career path can be identified. After becoming aware of these positions, the employee should explore them by talking with those who are doing such work and, when possible, actually doing some of the required tasks. This strategy will help the individual determine whether he or she has the aptitude and characteristics needed. Once two or three positions have been explored and selected, the person should write a career plan.

The employee should set a career goal to be reached within the next year or two and learn exactly what types of on-the-job experiences and training will be required to achieve the goal. Requirements may include learning new skills by taking a college course or, perhaps, by assisting a supervisor in the performance of specific duties. Deadlines for meeting each requirement should be listed in the career plan. Each requirement for advancement is a rung in the career ladder. By taking the steps one at a time, the employee eventually reaches the top of the ladder. In the meantime, for the worker who has a career plan, each day's work is more challenging and exciting than it is for the one who does not.

Continuous Planning

The career planning process is continuous. Awareness of the next step is important to taking each step. When one goal is reached, another should be set. Irene James, for example, started as a stock clerk in Daniels Department Store and later moved into sales work in the hardware department. Irene did well and was eventually given additional duties as head of stock for the department. However, Irene wanted to get into buying; so she accepted a position as assistant buyer for Morris Department

Illus. 55–2 A personal career plan can be a great benefit to the person seeking advancement in retailing.

Store. After 16 months, she was promoted to buyer. Irene is now planning for another advancement to either divisional merchandise manager or to assistant manager in a small store. Notice that at each stage of Irene's career it was necessary that she not only perform the functions of her position but develop an awareness of promotional opportunities. By exploring future job opportunities, she tested her skills and prepared for the next level of work. Thus, the process—awareness, exploration, preparation, and performance—is continuous throughout a working career.

Continuing Education

The predicted rate of change in society and business over the next 20 years makes continuing education essential. It is a mistake to assume that major retail career opportunities await high-school graduates who do not continue their education through periodic full-time or part-time study. Some high school graduates do succeed in retailing without higher education. However, such success is very rare. Most individuals who lack additional education may not progress beyond supervisory positions. A few experienced executives are not college trained, but most young executives in large retail organizations hold college degrees. Today, a higher percentage of college-prepared people are seeking retailing careers than ever before. Chain stores, department stores, specialty stores, and franchised businesses are competing for the best personnel that advanced education can produce.

Therefore, to move ahead in retailing, you should plan for additional education and training. Besides subscribing to the various publications that will keep you abreast of a particular line in retailing, consider taking courses in buying, management, salesmanship, marketing, merchandising, accounting, or management-information systems that are available in most large universities. Chambers of Commerce and various retail trade associations sponsor seminars and workshops on the latest practices in the retailing industry. You should attend such sessions regularly. Most progressive retail organizations offer in-store management training programs; never pass up such good opportunities to improve yourself through education and training. Continuing education will contribute to your success in the retailing field.

Owning a Retail Business

Many persons who have highly developed retailing skills must decide whether to start their own businesses. A person who operates her or his own business is called an entrepreneur. An **entrepreneur** is an individual who organizes and manages a business and assumes the risk of failure or gains the benefit of success. Entrepreneurs are responsible for deciding all of the matters discussed in this textbook. They determine the type of business, the type of ownership, the location, the store policies, the products or services, and the prices—everything.

The decision to become an entrepreneur is an important career step. Many new businesses fail because the owners do not have enough experience in business organization and operation. In fact, over 90 percent of retail store failures can be attributed to owners' lack of management skill. Successful entrepreneurs usually are people who have developed their business skills while working for someone else. It is wise to obtain information about small business development and to study all aspects of business ownership before taking the crucial step of becoming an entrepreneur. Excellent sources of information about owning a business are the small business development centers established in many states.

Illus. 55–3 Starting a retail business is risky but a great opportunity for the individual who has management skills.

*S*ummary Decisions about career choices and requirements for future advancement require careful thought. Major factors in planning a career include (1) establishing strong basic skills and qualities, (2) developing a personal career plan, and (3) deciding whether to become an independent business owner. Keys to job advancement include computation and communication skills; being responsible, loyal, resourceful, and self-motivated; and knowing more than one merchandising area. Personal career planning is an unending cycle of awareness of new jobs, exploration, preparation, and performance. Young retailers should plan for education and training throughout their careers to move ahead in a changing field.

Review

1. Identify three major factors in planning for a future in retailing.
2. Name four characteristics of successful retail workers and explain the importance of each to advancement in the field.
3. Describe a personal career plan.
4. Name the four phases in the continuous career-planning process.
5. Identify three ways in which additional retail training and education can be obtained.
6. Define *entrepreneur*.
7. State the main reason new business owners fail.

Terms

The following terms were introduced in this chapter. Write a separate sentence correctly using each new term.

career planning   entrepreneur

Discuss

1. Why are qualities such as responsibility and loyalty as important as selling skills?
2. Could a written career plan hinder a person who aspires to a career in retailing? How?
3. Why should all new retailers plan for additional education and training?
4. Why is retailing an important part of our rapidly changing society? In what ways is it important?

Problem Solving

1. Jamie has worked hard since high school; seemingly, her hard work has paid off. Jamie, at age 20, has just been promoted to a department manager position. She sees little merit in registering for an evening class in management principles at the local university. She sees no value in developing a career plan. Can you convince Jamie to begin a career plan now?
2. Amelia Martinez has eight years of experience in retailing as a salesperson and a manager. Help her write a personal career plan that will increase her chances of success as an entrepreneur.

3. Recently, you were promoted to the position of personnel director for a large, independently owned retail department store. You have just recruited ten new management trainees. Part of their orientation to the store is a presentation to be given by you entitled "Planning for the Future." Outline the topics you will cover in your presentation.

UNIT 9 ACTIVITIES

CHECKING KEY POINTS

This exercise is designed to check your understanding of material presented in Unit 9. On a separate sheet of paper, list the numbers 1 to 20. Indicate your response, *T* for true or *F* for false, for each of the following 20 statements.

1. Retailing research is the systematic gathering, recording, and analyzing of data.
2. Kiosks do not contain computer ordering equipment.
3. Business developers have difficulty finding locations for new malls and centers.
4. No-frill stores offer maximum customer services.
5. Continuous use of basic skills is essential for good job performance and advancement.
6. Young retailers should plan for additional education and training.
7. Research is always complicated.
8. Most retailers believe that technology will increase costs and decrease sales.
9. Retailers are risk takers.
10. Retailing provides a narrow range of career opportunities.
11. It is an employee's duty to accept responsibilities not specifically assigned.
12. Locating and hiring qualified personnel is relatively easy for retailers.
13. Electronic fund-transfer systems allow customers to make purchases without using cash, checks, or credit cards.
14. Strip centers are also called *convenience centers.*
15. People with great ability do not have to plan their time.
16. Advancement in retailing seldom requires an individual to move from one retail firm to another.
17. Secondary information is data that already have been compiled and published.
18. Computer graphics make it possible to experiment with various store layouts.
19. School placement offices are good sources of information about job opportunities.
20. A résumé should always be up-to-date.

BUILDING BASIC SKILLS

Calculations

Part of your responsibility as an assistant store manager for the Sterns Department Store is to conduct retailing research. One of your recent projects was to obtain customer opinions about store services. A copy of the questionnaire filled out by 50 customers is shown below. The numbers indicate how many customers checked each response.

Check to make sure that all responses have been entered by adding the numbers recorded for each question; write the result in the TOTAL column.

STERNS DEPARTMENT STORE CUSTOMER QUESTIONNAIRE

Please indicate how you feel about each of the following statements describing Sterns Department Store. For each statement, *check* the space that best describes your level of agreement: SA = strongly agree; A = agree; N = neutral; D = disagree; SD = strongly disagree.

	SA	A	N	D	SD	TOTAL
1. Stern offers a wide choice of merchandise.	11	25	7	5	2	_____
2. Products are of a high quality.	25	15	5	3	2	_____
3. Merchandise is reasonably priced.	15	12	10	3	5	_____
4. Merchandise is easy to find.	8	10	11	10	5	_____
5. Ads are easy to read.	30	10	0	5	5	_____
6. Adequate supplies of sale merchandise are available.	23	7	10	6	4	_____
7. The atmosphere at Sterns is friendly.	30	15	5	0	0	_____
8. Employees are well trained.	28	10	6	4	2	_____
9. Parking is adequate.	5	5	12	20	3	_____
10. Sterns should locate in a mall.	10	10	4	5	15	_____

Next, analyze the results of the survey by answering the following questions. (Be prepared to give reasons for your analysis.)

1. Does Sterns offer sufficient choices of merchandise?
2. Are products of a high quality?
3. Is merchandise reasonably priced?
4. Is merchandise easy to find?
5. Are advertisements easy to read?

6. Are adequate supplies of sale merchandise available?
7. Is the atmosphere at Sterns friendly?
8. Are employees well-trained?
9. Is parking adequate?
10. Should Sterns relocate to a mall?
11. What is customers' general opinion about Sterns?
12. What changes, if any, should Sterns make?

Working with People

The future of retailing depends in large part on the people who are attracted to retail careers. New employees will be faced with a constantly changing work environment heavily influenced by high technology. Problem-solving skills, the ability to adjust to and accept innovation, and continuous training will be the rule. With this background, how would you deal with the following situations?

1. Officers of the local retail-merchants association and several local bank representatives are planning a meeting of the association membership. The purpose of this meeting will be to discuss whether to install an electronic fund-transfer system. Several of the retailers in your mall are opposed to such a system because "It won't work." How would you respond?
2. Right now, your plan is to finish school and then work toward a management position in retailing. What steps will you take to reach your career goal?
3. A business associate of yours is planning to become a partner in a new travel agency. Many of the details have been settled, but a location for the agency has not been decided. Space is available in a strip center, multi-use mall, and high-fashion mall. Which would you recommend? Why?
4. Customer complaints about the lack of merchandise on the shelves in your department have increased. You know the problem is one of time management rather than lack of merchandise; some employees waste time while marking and displaying goods. What will you do to improve this situation?
5. A retailer you know thinks a change in store location would improve business. Questioning reveals that this store operator is not sure what the problem is or how to solve it. What steps should be taken?

Writing Skills

Select one of the situations described below as the subject for a written communication. Investigate the topic presented using interviews, written materials, or other references as sources of information.

When preparing the written assignment, be sure to credit your resources for the ideas, views, explanations, or quotations you use. The assignment should be no more than two double-spaced typewritten pages.

1. It is your turn to write an article for the Chamber of Commerce newsletter. Your topic is "Shopping Malls of the Future." Prepare an outline of the items you will cover in your article.
2. You are employed in a large department store located in a major shopping center. Your task is to submit a brief report at the next managers' meeting on how in-store technology could be used to merchandise items not kept in stock. Write the report.
3. You have been asked by a high-school counselor to be a guest speaker at the annual career information days event. Your topic is "Locating Potential Jobs." Copies of your presentation will be handed out in a number of classes.
4. You have been asked to speak from in-school or on-the-job experience about the importance of responsibility, resourcefulness, and initiative at the next new-employee orientation session. Make a list of points, including examples, to share with the new employees.
5. Your marketing instructor has announced that a major class project will be to conduct a retailing research project. You are to choose a topic that is of special interest to you. The first step in the assignment is to describe how you will conduct your research. Write the plan.

APPLYING YOUR KNOWLEDGE

Can You Do the Following?

1. Describe how shopping for staple goods and specialty goods may change.
2. Identify a key problem in operating a manufacturers mall.
3. Develop a list of 12 ways in which an individual can become more productive.
4. Identify four traits that employers look for in the people they hire.
5. Explain why knowledge of promotion is important to a salesperson seeking job advancement.
6. Explain the importance of employer loyalty to a retail employee.
7. Name a key factor in bringing about technological changes in retailing.
8. Name four areas related to store location to which retailing research can be applied.
9. State a major reason for the success of international retailing.

10. Identify the main benefit of using a graphic-design system to design a store.
11. Explain the difference between secondary and primary information.
12. Explain why the first job in retailing may be the most important.
13. Identify two goals of all retailing research.
14. Identify two customer and two retailer benefits of merchandising technology.
15. Explain why some customers are hesitant about using in-home systems to purchase merchandise.
16. Explain the relationship between continuing education and success in retailing.
17. State the major advantage to retailers of a multi-use mall.
18. Explain the difference between a supermarket and a superstore.
19. Name four sources of potential retailing jobs.
20. Explain why specific problem identification is an essential part of any retailing research.

Retail Decisions

1. How could modern merchandising technology be used to sell automobiles?
2. You have been offered two jobs; both are in stockrooms of local department stores. Job A pays $4.75 an hour and involves performance review for possible promotion in six months. Job B pays $5.75 an hour and involves performance review and a possible $.10 per-hour raise in nine months. Which job will you take? Why?
3. If a customer says, "I prefer to inspect an item firsthand rather than by looking at a picture," what would be your first response?
4. The owners of a food store in your community want to convert to a box-store type of no-frills operation. List six changes that should be made to support the conversion.
5. Is "Retailing and entertainment do not mix" a valid statement? Indicate why you agree or disagree.
6. Someone you know has been out of high school almost five years. In that time she has held four retailing jobs, the last two at the same level and pay. You notice that she's stopped talking about her future in retailing. Next time you have an opportunity to discuss her career with her, you will offer friendly advice. What will it be?
7. Do you agree with the statement "Retailing research cannot, by itself, solve all of a retailer's problems"? Defend your answer.
8. What is the value of determining customer attitudes, buying habits, and motives?

DEVELOPING CRITICAL-THINKING SKILLS

Retail Projects

1. Choose a retail store that you would like to operate. Then, select three different types of malls in which you would consider locating your business. Compare the advantages and disadvantages of each mall. Select the type of mall that would be best. Provide reasons for your choice.
2. Review the guidelines for effective use of time. Next, draw a schedule of how you plan to use your time for one week. Indicate the tasks to be done, how much time each will take, and how you will measure the success of your plan. Compare your plan with the results at the end of the week you have selected.
3. To determine the current career plans of the members of your class, you have decided to prepare a questionnaire. Your questionnaire should ask at least ten questions related to the selected topic. Tabulate the responses of your classmates. Draw conclusions about their responses based on the data you have collected.
4. Prepare your personal five-year career plan.

Field Projects

1. Call upon a retailer in your area and volunteer to design a questionnaire that will survey customer attitudes about store policies, merchandise, prices, or other topics for which the retailer would like data. Tabulate the data and present it in an appropriate form to the retailer.
2. In follow-up to the activity above, provide your interpretation of what the data mean. Be prepared to tell the retailer how you arrived at your conclusions if asked to do so.
3. Identify two retailers who are currently using some form of electronic fund-transfer system or who plan to do so in the future. Ask each merchant to name the advantages and disadvantages of such systems. Ask if there are other ways in which the system could be used by these retailers to provide additional customer services.
4. Often, employers have varying opinions regarding the best source of new workers. Determine where ten retail employers in your community locate new people. What are the results? What can you conclude from the responses you have received?
5. Identify four merchants who you believe could make effective use of the new in-store merchandising technology to sell products they

currently do not stock. Discuss with each merchant her or his attitude regarding the use of free-standing, electronic display units. Are all four in favor of technology to sell merchandise? What are some comments they make in favor of the display units? against the units?

CONTINUING PROJECTS

Developing a Career Plan

In each of the previous Developing a Career Plan activities, you were asked to complete a variety of assignments. These tasks were designed to help you begin to identify potential career goals as a result of your study of a variety of retail job opportunities. Ideally, you now have set some initial career goals. However, we know that career aspirations change over time. Therefore, it is important to regularly make use of a career planning process such as the one suggested in Unit 9. This process involves the study of new job skills, awareness of possible career opportunities, exploration of those opportunities, and preparation to qualify for the new career.

The purpose of this activity is to look beyond initial goals and identify where you want your career to be in two to four years. Using your best estimate, determine (1) for whom you would like to work; (2) where you would like to live; (3) additional job skills needed; (4) formal education required; (5) and any other items you would consider personally important. Write a summary of your findings and include this information in your career-planning notebook.

Developing a Business Plan

From the facts you have learned in this unit and the study and research of other resources, add to your manual by completing the following assignments:

1. One part of your plan to operate a retail business requires that you make specific decisions about the kind of personnel you will employ. Prepare a written plan of action for recruiting personnel that provides answers to the following:
    a. Types and number of positions to be filled
    b. Personal qualifications needed
    c. Educational requirements
    d. Previous work experience (if needed)
    e. Sources for recruitment
    f. Procedures for selecting and hiring

2. To compete with similar stores, you have decided that you must find a way to attract more customers. You believe that innovative merchandising technology might be the answer. On the basis of the type of business you plan to operate, outline a plan that includes the use of:

   a. In-store technology
   b. In-home technology
   c. An electronic fund-transfer system

   Be specific about the technology you plan to use, provide reasons for your choices, and list the benefits that you and your customers will gain.

GLOSSARY

Accrued expense. Expense, such as the cost of operating a delivery truck, that accumulates but is not paid immediately.

Accuracy. Exactness; one of the three characteristics of effective communication.

Add-on. Commission or bonus for a manager based on individual performance or on store sales for the year.

Adjacent colors. Colors found next to each other on the color wheel which create the least contrast when used together.

Adjustment. Response made or action taken by a retailer to remedy a customer's complaint.

Advertising media. Forms of communication by which retailers advertise to potential customers.

Agent middleman. Intermediary who assists in the sale of goods but does not own the goods.

Aging of accounts. Process of finding out how long a merchant's accounts receivable are past due.

Annual accounts receivable turnover rate. Figure calculated by dividing a merchant's total yearly credit sales by the average amount owed each month.

Anticipation discount. Discount given on an already discounted price to buyers who pay for merchandise early.

Apron. First copy of the receiving record.

Articles of copartnership. Contract stating the important points of a partnership agreement and providing for the dissolution of the partnership in the event of the death of either partner.

Attitude. Mental position of a person with regard to a particular fact, person, or situation.

Automatic retailing. Retailing that allows the customer to immediately receive the merchandise selected after putting money in a machine, such as a soft-drink vending machine.

Average stock. Figure determined by adding the stock in inventory on the first of every month to the year-end stock and dividing this sum by 13, on the basis of retail prices, cost prices, or number of units.

Bad debt. Account due that a merchant feels will not be collected.

Bad debt loss index. Figure calculated by dividing the bad debts incurred by a store during a period by the total credit sales for that period.

Bait and switch. Unethical advertising practice of advertising an item at a remarkably low price and then trying to sell a high-priced substitute.

Balanced stock. Assortment of goods that will appeal to most customers of a retail store.

Balance sheet. Financial statement that measures the worth of a business at a specific date.

Bank credit card. Card issued by banks to approved applicants authorizing purchases on credit.

Bank credit plan. Agreement that a bank will grant a customer a certain amount of credit and charge a 1 to 1 3/4 percent monthly service fee on the unpaid balance.

Basic needs. Conditions or goods and services essential to human nature and survival.

Basic stock list. List of goods that should be in stock at all times in a retail store.

Blind check. Process by which a checker prepares a dummy invoice of goods received by a store and compares it with the original invoice.

Book inventory or **perpetual inventory.** Record of the amount of merchandise that should be on hand.

Bottom-up planning. Planning that starts with

estimating sales by merchandise classifications and then moves to estimating sales at the store level.

Broker. Agent who does not handle goods but helps sellers find buyers or buyers find sellers.

Budgeting. Process of developing the merchandising plan in terms of money.

Buyer's record. Third copy of the receiving record which goes to the buyer.

Buying plan. Plan that shows the classifications, price lines, and other important characteristics of the merchandise expected to meet customer demand.

Capacity. Customer's ability to earn money and pay bills; it is considered by creditors when determining whether to grant credit.

Capital. Machinery, tools, buildings, and money used in the production and distribution of goods and services; one of the five basic elements of an economy; also, a customer's assets that can be seized for nonpayment of bills.

Capitalism. System made up of many people investing and reinvesting capital in businesses; free-enterprise system.

Career planning. Process of devising professional long-term goals based on job performance, awareness, exploration, and preparation.

Cash discount. Percentage of reduction of the list price of an item.

Cash fund. Amount of cash put into a register for the purpose of making change.

Cash reserve fund. Money readily available to retailers to cover any unexpected expenses.

Centralized. Describes a retail function in which major decisions are made at the main office of a firm rather than by personnel in a local store.

Central wrap. Sales system in which an employee at a central location in a store performs the wrapping or bagging function.

Chain store. One of a number of similar retail stores under single ownership.

Channel of distribution. Path that merchandise takes from producer to consumer.

Character. Customer's honesty as indicated by living and past payment habits; it is considered by creditors when determining whether to grant credit.

CIA. Cash in advance; billing terms under which an immediate cash payment is required usually of new merchants or of those who have poor credit ratings.

Clarity. Lack of ambiguity; one of the three characteristics of effective communication.

Closed interior display. Interior display design that protects the merchandise on display from damage or theft.

Closed window design. Window display that uses a full background panel to completely separate the store's interior from the window display.

COD. Cash on delivery; billing terms under which goods must be paid for upon delivery at the retail store.

Code dating. System of merchandise dating whereby a letter or symbol indicates to store personnel when goods were received.

Coding. Choosing words and pictures for an advertisement to send the right message to potential customers.

Collateral. Anything of value owned by a borrower that a bank can sell to recover a loan if the loan is not repaid.

Collection agency. Organization that collects payment of delinquent accounts for merchants.

Collection percentage. Figure calculated by dividing the payments made to a merchant by credit customers during a certain period by the accounts receivable outstanding at the beginning of that period.

Commission. Compensation paid to a salesperson as a percentage of his or her individual sales over a certain period.

Commission merchant. Agent who handles the actual goods he or she sells.

Community services. Activities, such as sponsorship of art shows, undertaken by a store on behalf of the community.

Competition. Rivalry among retail businesses for customers.

Complementary colors. Colors found on opposite sides of the color wheel which are most effective in creating color contrasts.

Conscious level. Level of thinking at which customers deliberately take actions.

Consumerism. Any activity by a government, business, or private agency designed to protect customers' rights.

Control functions. Record-keeping activities that produce up-to-date information about the financial condition of a retail business.

Controlling. Making sure that all employee assignments have been carried out according to a set schedule.

Control system. Set of procedures or techniques used to obtain information for successfully operating a retail business.

Convenience goods. Items that customers buy frequently and for which they do not wish to make special shopping trips.

Convenience services. Nonmerchandise services provided for customers of a store, such as rest rooms.

Convenience store. Small retail store in a residential neighborhood that meets the needs of persons living nearby.

Cooperative advertising. Advertising for which manufacturers, suppliers, and retailers share the cost.

Corporation. Form of retail business ownership in which several people share in the ownership of a business through the purchase of stock shares.

Cost. Expense of buying goods, transporting them to the store, and preparing them, if necessary, for sale.

Current asset. A business's asset that can be turned into cash quickly and easily.

Current liability. Business expense that will be paid within 12 months in most instances.

Current market value. Cost of all goods in stock in a retail store.

Customer services. Services offered in relation to sales of tangible goods, including gift wrapping and store credit.

Debit card. Card that authorizes the immediate electronic transfer of funds from a customer's bank account to a store's at the point of sale.

DECA. An association of students that provides opportunities for its members to participate in a variety of job enrichment activities.

Deferred or **revolving account.** Credit plan under which buyers of nondurable goods may pay a small sum each month rather than the full amount of their monthly purchases.

Department store. Retail store that consists of a large number of related merchandise departments under central management.

Department wrap. Sales system in which a special employee in the department where an item was purchased performs the wrapping or bagging function.

Direct check. Process of checking goods received by a store against either the invoice or the order copy.

Directed economic system. Economy in which a person or group of persons in authority decides what and how much to produce, when and where to produce it, and for whom and for what purpose to produce it.

Direct expense. Expense, such as employee salaries, that is paid out for the benefit of one department in a store and is charged against that department's sales income.

Directing. Helping employees complete their work.

Direct-mail advertising. Advertising in which retailers send promotional items directly to prospective customers.

Direct retailing. Retailing that involves a salesperson coming to the home of the customer with either merchandise or samples, such as in door-to-door merchandising.

Discount. Reduction from the list price of an item.

Discount retailing. Approach to retailing that involves selecting low-cost locations, offering few services, operating on a cash-and-carry basis, and keeping overhead expenses to a minimum.

Discrepancy report. Report describing any irregularities in a shipment to a store, such as breakage or missing items.

Discretionary fund. Discretionary income plus the dollar amount of goods and services purchased on installment credit.

Discretionary income. Disposable personal income minus the cost of a minimum standard of living.

Display lighting. Lighting that highlights special displays in a retail store.

Display requisition. Request form sent to the display department recommending an item of merchandise for display.

Disposable personal income. Personal income minus all local, state, and federal taxes.

Dollar control method. Method of controlling the amount of stock by calculating the dollar value of forward and reserve stock at frequent intervals.

Drawing account. Account that allows salespeople in a retail store to be paid during slow-selling periods against their future commissions.

Dummy invoice. List of the actual contents of a shipment.

Dummy layout. Model of a proposed advertisement, showing the sizes and arrangement of the elements.

Economy. System of producing, distributing, and consuming goods and services in a society; conciseness, one of the three characteristics of effective communication.

Electronic fund-transfer system (EFTS). Equipment that transfers funds electronically and can be used to authorize checks, make bank account deposits and withdrawals, and invest in the stock market.

Electronic kiosk. Stand that contains both a screen to display merchandise and equipment allowing customers to order that merchandise.

Electronic media. Electronic forms of communication, such as radio and television.

Emotional appeal. Appeal to consumers that stresses the security, safety, love, beauty, social acceptance, or power that may be derived from use of a product.

Emotional need. Need to be accepted by others (to belong), to be recognized for accomplishments, to achieve personal goals, or to feel good about oneself.

Employee benefits. Extra rewards, including health insurance and retirement plans, for personnel.

Employee discount. Price reduction given to retail employees who buy goods within the store.

Employee stock-ownership plan. Special-incentive plan that gives each employee a certain number of shares of stock in the company.

End fixture. Display at the end of a merchandise aisle that features merchandise specials.

Entrepreneur. Individual who organizes and manages a business and assumes the risk of failure or gains the benefits of success.

EOM. End of month; billing terms under which the payment date is figured from the end of the month.

Equity. Difference between total assets and total liabilities.

Equity capital. Money initially invested in a business by a retailer.

Ethical behavior. Employee conduct that reflects honesty, dependability, fairness, and loyalty to oneself, the employer, and the public.

Expense. Expenditure required to operate a store; maintain a building; buy, sell, and handle merchandise; or administer or manage a business.

Expense record. Record of the amount of money a retailer has spent for goods, salaries, advertising, taxes, and all other costs of doing business.

Experienced personnel. Long-term employees who require regular retraining.

Extra dating. Billing terms under which the buyer is given a specific number of extra days in which to pay an invoice.

Factoring. Practice of selling a retailer's installment contracts, or accounts receivable, to a finance company at a discount.

Fad. Style of merchandise, art, or activity that catches the fancy of a sizable group of people, has brief popularity, and dies out quickly.

Fair risk. Customer who can be relied upon to pay credit bills but who tends to put off payments.

Fashion. Style of merchandise, art, or activity that appeals to a large number of people at a given time.

Fashion count. Primary information gathered through observation of the kinds of clothing people consider fashionable.

Fashion cycle. Sequence of steps that a style passes through on its way to becoming a fashion, including origination, rise, acceptance, mass production, decline, and abandonment.

Fashion goods. Items that are new or the latest or most popular styles.

Fashion show. Presentation of a variety of merchandise and information in an interesting and appealing manner.

Feature unit. Display used to call attention to goods that many customers would miss if the goods were displayed only in the regular department fixtures.

Final selling price. Final price charged for an item by a retailer.

Financial statement. Statement showing the status and progress of a retail business in terms of dollars and cents.

Fixed asset. A business's asset, such as land, that is difficult to turn into cash quickly.

Fixed capital. Money invested by retailers in land, buildings, store fixtures, and equipment.

Fixed expense. Expense, such as rent, that does not change with sales volume.

Fixed liability. Business expense that will be paid over a number of years.

Flat expense. Expenditure that is about the same for every article of merchandise carried by a retailer, regardless of its cost or retail price.

Floor limit. Maximum amount a customer can charge without management approval.

FOB destination. Shipping terms under which the seller is to pay all transportation costs and is to own the goods until they arrive at the store.

FOB destination, charges reversed. Shipping terms under which the seller owns the goods until they get to the store, though the buyer agrees to pay the transportation charges.

FOB factory. Shipping terms under which the buyer is to pay all transportation costs and is to own the goods from the moment they are shipped.

FOB factory, freight prepaid. Shipping terms under which the goods are owned by the buyer as soon as they are shipped, but the seller pays the freight charges.

FOB shipping point. Shipping terms under which the seller pays for transportation of the goods to a transportation company.

Formal balance. Aesthetic achieved when an imaginary line can be drawn through a display, resulting in two identical halves.

Formal organization. Retail business organization whose activities can be outlined in a chart.

Form utility. Utility added to natural resources when they are changed into usable products such as furniture, clothing, appliances, cars, and foods.

Forward stock. Merchandise maintained in the selling area of a store.

Franchise. Permission granted to an individual or group to conduct a retail business or to sell a product under the owner's name.

Franchisee. Retailer of a franchised product.

Franchisor. Person or firm that owns a franchised idea or product.

Free economic system. Economy in which the consumers of goods and services, through their decision to buy or not to buy, determine what and how much will be produced and when and where the products will be used.

Functional discount. Discount given to buyers in recognition of the functions they perform for the seller; trade discount.

Functional expense category. Classification of store expenses by particular functions, such as merchandising, selling, sales promotion, store operations, or control.

Garnishment. Court order to a debtor's employer to turn over a percentage of the debtor's wages to the creditor until a debt has been paid.

General lighting. Lighting for most retail store purposes that is almost always installed in the ceiling.

General store. Retail store that carries groceries, staple clothing items, house furnishings, nonprescription medicine, and numerous other articles for local customers.

Good risk. Customer who in the past has shown character, capacity, and capital but who is temporarily negligent in payment of credit bills.

Goods. Material items, such as a pair of shoes, a sweater, or a gallon of milk, provided by retailers for customers.

Government. Laws, regulations, taxes, and social services that influence the activities of producing, distributing, and consuming

goods and services; one of the five basic elements of an economy.

Gross domestic product (GDP). Gross national product minus the value of national companies' output produced abroad.

Gross margin. Figure calculated by subtracting the cost of goods sold by a store during a given period of time from the net sales for that period.

Gross national product (GNP). Market value of a country's total output of goods and services for one year.

High-fashion mall. Shopping complex that offers specialty shopping with emphasis on high-fashion merchandise.

Human relations. The behavior of individuals in personal contacts.

Identification facts. Data on the nature and characteristics of a transaction.

Income statement. Financial statement that measures business earnings or losses over a period of time.

Indirect expense. Expense, such as rent or heat, that serves the entire store.

Individual motive. Motive that originates within an individual, such as hunger, thirst, comfort, curiosity, or freedom from fear and danger.

Inexperienced personnel. New employees who have not had prior experience in retailing and who require training.

In fashion. Description of a particular style of merchandise, art, or activity that appeals to a large number of people.

Informal balance. Aesthetic that results when the halves of a display are not equal.

Informal organization. Retail business organization that covers the uncharted, undefined relationships of people and work.

Initial markup. Difference between the cost price and the original retail selling price of an item.

Installment plan. Agreement that the buyer of an expensive durable good will take possession of an item and make a series of payments of a stated amount for the merchandise.

Institutional advertising. Advertising that focuses on building store prestige and store acceptance over a long period of time.

Institutional display. Display designed to create goodwill among customers and the general public.

In-store retailing. Retailing that occurs in a conveniently located building.

Intangible-property tax. Tax imposed on stocks, cash, and securities.

Interior display. Display of merchandise located on the sales floor of a retail store.

Intermediary or **middleman.** Dealer who is responsible for the distribution of goods from producer to ultimate consumer.

Inventory record. Record of merchandise a retailer has in stock.

Invoice control. Procedure followed by a store to keep track of invoices in process.

Job analysis. Detailed study of a particular job that includes (1) job title; (2) location of the store where the job is performed; (3) job duties and responsibilities; (4) experience and education required; and (5) pay, hours of work, and promotion possibilities.

Job description. Summary of a job that gives an employer a clear notion of the type of employee needed and helps the applicant understand what the job entails.

Key resource. Vendor that has been found by a retailer to be most satisfactory.

Labor force. Those persons who are able to work and are either seeking work or actually working; one of the five basic elements of an economy.

Large-scale retailing. Retailing that involves more than one merchandise line; examples include the department store, variety store, supermarket, mail-order firm, and low-margin or discount store.

Layaway plan. Agreement that a buyer will make regular payments to a store until the full price of an item has been paid and only then take possession of the item.

Layout. Arrangement of the headline, illustration, copy, signature plate, and price in an advertisement.

Leader. Retail item sold at a reduced price for the purpose of increasing customer traffic.

Lease. Contract for the transfer of the use of real estate, equipment, or facilities to a second party for a specified time and rent. In a lease agreement, nonstore personnel pay a store for the right to provide store customers with a service.

Legal action. Option for retailers to force someone through court proceedings to pay a delinquent credit account.

Limited-line store. Retail store that offers a wide selection of only one kind of merchandise.

List price. Price of an item set by the manufacturer or vendor.

Loss leader. Retail item sold at less than cost.

Mail-order firm. Retail business that engages in mail-order retailing.

Mail-order retailing. Retailing that requires customers to examine and order from a catalog or advertisement describing merchandise offered by a retailer.

Maintained markup. Difference between the cost price and the final retail selling price of an item.

Management. People who decide how natural resources, capital, and labor will be used to make the greatest contribution to business and society; one of the five basic elements of an economy.

Manufacturers mall. Shopping complex that contains retail stores operated by manufacturers.

Markdown. Reduction from original retail price of an item.

Marker's record. Second copy of the receiving record which goes to the marker.

Marketing. Movement and sale of merchandise and services to consumers and business users.

Marketing Education (ME). Program that provides marketing training for high-school and post-secondary students.

Market segmentation. Process of classifying consumers in categories or segments on the basis of their personal characteristics.

Markup. Amount that a merchant adds to the cost of merchandise to determine the retail selling price.

Medium. Means by which retailers can advertise to potential customers.

Megamall. Shopping complex that combines retailing with entertainment or tourism in a large space.

Merchandise. See *Goods*.

Merchandise breadth. The number of merchandise lines carried by a retail store.

Merchandise depth. The quantity of a line of goods offered in various colors, sizes, styles, and price ranges by a retail store.

Merchandise island. Selling fixture that has an open space in the center where a salesperson is stationed to serve customers.

Merchandise manager. Employee who has the responsibility for merchandising in larger retail stores.

Merchandise mix. Variety of merchandise lines carried and the breadth and depth with which these lines are stocked in a retail store.

Merchandise plan. Plan that sets goals for each merchandise area of a retail store.

Merchandise shortage. Lost stock due to damage or theft.

Merchandising plan. Plan often expressed as a budget that reflects the various merchandise policies set for a retail store and that describes how these policies are to be carried out.

Middle line. Merchandise of the quality demanded by most customers and offered in the deepest assortment by a retailer.

Milline rate. Cost of one agate line in an advertisement adjusted to the actual number of copies circulated.

Model stock plan. Plan that helps merchants determine which price lines, sizes, colors, and current styles to carry in their main fashion lines.

Modified free-enterprise system. Capitalism limited by government regulations and social forces.

Motivate. To provide employees with a cause, need, or desire to act.

Motivated behavior. Action taken to satisfy a need or to fulfill a want.

Motive. Need or want that leads to action.

Multiple price. Price for several units of the same item carried by a retailer.

Multi-use mall. Shopping complex that contains offices, convention centers, apartments, condominiums, and parking ramps in addition to retail stores.

National brand. Class of goods made and distributed all over the country by a major manufacturer.

National income. Total earnings of workers and business owners in a nation resulting from the production of goods and services.

Natural expense category. Classification of store expenses into closely related items, such as payroll, supplies, communication, or professional services.

Natural resources. Land, minerals, water, and plant life; one of the five basic elements of an economy.

Needs. Goods and services necessary for an individual's survival or well-being.

Net income. Figure calculated by subtracting all fixed and variable expenses of a store during a given period from the gross margin for that period.

Net national product. Gross national product minus the value lost from depreciation and obsolescence.

New, experienced personnel. Employees who have had prior retailing experience with another employer but require further training.

No-frills store. Retail store that offers goods at low prices with minimal customer service and decor.

Nonpersonal selling. Selling that does not involve direct contact between the customer and the salesperson but rather uses advertising, visual merchandising, and other promotion to inform customers about merchandise and to encourage them to come into a store to buy.

Nonprice competition. Strategy to gain customers that involves offering higher quality merchandise, providing wider merchandise selections, or giving better service than other retailers.

Nonpromotional store. Retail store that stresses assortments of goods, leadership in fashion, or customer services.

Omnibus advertisement. Single advertisement that features many different merchandise items.

One-price policy. Policy that states that on any given day all customers will be charged the same amount for a certain item of merchandise.

Open dating. System of merchandise dating whereby the actual date of receipt is marked on an item and can be read by customers.

Opening inventory. Amount of inventory with which a retailer begins each period of sales.

Open interior display. Interior display design that allows customers to inspect and handle merchandise without the help of a salesperson.

Open or **regular account.** Credit plan under which a customer is billed each month for purchases made during the previous month.

Open-to-buy. Difference between the planned purchases for a period and the merchandise orders already placed for delivery by a retailer in that period.

Open window display. Window display that does not use a back panel, allowing customers to look directly into the store.

Organization. Arrangement of the activities

necessary for the successful operation of a retail business.

Original retail selling price. Price originally charged for an item by a retailer.

Overage. Amount by which the physical inventory of a store is larger than the book inventory.

Overhead. Expenditure required for operating a retail store or department.

Partnership. Form of retail business ownership in which two or more persons join together to own and manage a business.

Par value. Stated value of a stock share at the time of issuance.

Personal income. Total income of all persons from all sources.

Personality. Total of a person's thoughts, feelings, and actions.

Personal property. Anything of value that people use, buy, or sell.

Personal-property tax. Tax imposed on items such as furniture, merchandise, and equipment.

Personal selling. Selling that involves direct contact between a customer and a salesperson.

Personal shopper. Salesperson who provides individual assistance to customers who have little time to shop or need extra help in choosing merchandise.

Petty-cash fund. Fund used by a store to pay for small expenditures such as light bulbs, pencils, and postage.

Physical distribution. Process of handling, moving, and storing goods.

Physical need. One of the basic survival or safety needs, such as food, clothing, shelter, rest, or security.

Place utility. Utility added to goods when the manufacturer ships them from where they are produced to where they can be sold.

Planned purchase. Amount of retail stock to be purchased.

Planned shopping center. Facility designed

to accommodate many retail and service businesses.

Planning. Deciding in advance what needs to be done, who will do it, and when it will be accomplished.

PM (premium money). Special-incentive plan that rewards salespeople for selling specific items of merchandise.

Point-of-purchase (POP) display. Display located near merchandise or at checkout counters where purchases are made.

Policy. Rules governing a retail business operation.

Poor risk. Customer whose credit rating is barely good enough to be granted credit and who has a low credit limit.

Possession utility. Utility added to goods when a customer purchases them.

Postdating or advance dating. Billing terms under which invoices are dated after the date of shipment, giving buyers extra time for payment.

Prepaid expense. Expense, such as insurance, that covers future obligations.

Preretailing. Writing retail prices on a duplicate of a purchase order before the goods are received; process of marking items with retail prices based only on the purchase order.

Preticketing. Marking the price of or attaching the price to an item of merchandise prior to shipping.

Price. Amount of money asked by a retailer for an item as a measure of its value or worth.

Price competition. Strategy to gain customers that involves offering goods at lower prices than other retailers.

Price-line policy. Policy that states that only a few prices, or price lines, are set and then applied to many different items of merchandise.

Primary information. Data that a researcher or a research team personally has gathered.

Primary services. Services offered as independent entities, including sporting events, theatre entertainment, car washes, and dry cleaning.

Printed media. Printed forms of communication, such as newspapers, magazines, direct mail, and billboards.

Private brand. Product brand named by an intermediary such as a wholesaler or retailer.

Productivity. A worker's output or contribution to a business.

Profit. Sales income earned by a business that is in excess of the costs of providing goods and services.

Profit services. Services, such as engraving, available to customers of a store for a charge.

Profit sharing. Special-incentive plan that entitles employees to receive a portion of store profits.

Promotion. Advertising; efforts by retailers to provide information to help consumers sort through goods and services; also, relocation of an employee to a new job with more responsibility and authority.

Promotional advertising. Advertising that focuses on attracting immediate customer traffic and creating sales.

Promotional display. Display featuring merchandise for sale that can usually be evaluated through measurable sales results.

Promotional mix. Combination of messages and media that a retailer uses to communicate information about merchandise to prospective buyers.

Promotional store. Retail store that stresses sales, bargains, and price reductions.

Proportion. Correct relationship between object and space in a display.

Publicity. Nonpaid promotion by the public media of a retail business or its products and services.

Public relations. All retail business activities designed to develop and retain the goodwill of customers and the general public.

Purchase record. Record that shows which

goods have been ordered from which suppliers and at what cost to the retailer.

Quality product. Item of merchandise that is carefully constructed of excellent material.

Quantitative facts. Data on the number of items and values involved in a transaction.

Quantity discount. Discount given to a retailer who is buying unusually large quantities of merchandise.

Quota. Dollar amount that a salesperson is expected to sell in a given time period.

Quota plan. Compensation plan in which a store manager sets quotas for salespeople.

Rational appeal. Appeal to consumers that stresses the good features of a product— its fair price, its quality, and its dependability.

Real-property tax. Tax imposed on real estate.

Receiving. Taking physical possession of goods in a store.

Receiving area. Place in a store where shipments are opened, checked, and marked.

Receiving book or **receiving record.** Record of various facts about the receipt of goods at a store, such as the number of packages received, the date and time, and the vendor's name.

Receiving manager or **traffic manager.** Employee designated to handle receiving goods for a store.

Reduction. Decrease in profit resulting from markdowns, merchandise shortages, and employee discounts.

Reserve stock. Merchandise held or stored off the selling floor of a store and used to replace goods sold from the forward stock.

Résumé. Summary of a job applicant's background; personal data sheet.

Retail credit bureau. Organization that accumulates from merchants complete information about credit customers.

Retailer. Person who manages or assists in the management of a retail business.

Retailing. Process of obtaining a variety of goods and making them easily available for sale to customers.

Retailing research. Systematic gathering, recording, and analyzing of data on problems relating to the marketing of goods and services.

Retail marketing. Marketing of goods and services used by individual consumers.

Retail store. Business that provides goods and services to individual consumers.

ROG. Receipt of goods; billing terms under which the date of payment may be computed from the date goods are received by the store rather than from the date of the invoice.

Salary. Compensation for employment that is paid by the week or month.

Salary and commission plan. Compensation plan in which a salesperson receives a straight salary plus an additional amount depending on individual sales.

Salesclerk. Retail employee whose responsibilities include greeting customers, operating sales registers, and wrapping merchandise.

Sales demonstrator. Retail employee who shows customers how to use a product or service.

Salesperson. Retail employee who performs the functions of both salesclerk and sales demonstrator.

Salesperson wrap. Sales system in which a salesperson performs the wrapping or bagging function.

Sales presentation. Attempts to inform customers about products.

Sales promotion. All marketing activities such as advertising, visual merchandising, public relations, and personal selling that promote the sale of retail goods and services.

Sales record. Record of the total dollar amount of sales and the specific items that were sold by a retailer.

Sales representative. Retail employee who may be called upon to complete tasks usually performed by other sales personnel but whose primary responsibility is to sell higher priced items.

Sales transaction. Process of recording a sale and providing the customer with a proof of payment or charge.

Seasonal goods. Items, such as Halloween costumes, that are sold only during certain periods of the year.

Secondary information. Data that have been compiled and published.

Secondary wants. Conditions or goods and services not essential to human nature or survival, unlike basic needs.

Self-selection. Sales policy requiring a customer to examine merchandise samples and, after making a selection, to ask a salesclerk to get the selected article from stock.

Self-service. Sales policy requiring a customer to select items from an open display and take them to the checkout point for purchase.

Selling and shopping services. Services, such as delivery, that are associated with the selling of the merchandise carried by a store.

Semiclosed window design. Window display that uses a half-panel background to separate the store's interior from the display.

Semipromotional policy. Advertising policy that combines promotional and institutional advertising techniques.

Semipromotional store. Retail store that features merchandise assortments at regular prices with infrequent special sales or reduced prices.

Semivariable expense. Expense, such as advertising, that varies somewhat according to sales volume but is more or less controlled by management policy.

Service charge. Interest charge added to a store credit holder's monthly account balance.

Services. Special functions, such as credit, alterations, and delivery, provided by retailers for customers.

Shopping goods. Retail goods that the customer believes require careful selection.

Shopping-service count. Primary information gathered through observation of the types of services provided by sales personnel in a store.

Shopping traffic. People who pass a store site and are interested in buying.

Shortage. Amount by which the physical inventory of a store is smaller than the book inventory.

Signature plate or **logotype.** Distinctive typeface, trademark, emblem, or symbol that may help consumers identify a particular store.

Social motive. Motive, such as the need to be accepted by others, that arises from an individual's relationships with other people and objects in the environment.

Sole proprietorship. Form of retail business ownership in which only one person owns and manages a business.

Specialty store. Smaller retail store that carries a fairly broad selection of a single line of merchandise or a group of closely related goods.

Split run. Advertising practice that permits retailers to buy space in just those issues of a magazine that are circulated in their area.

Spot announcement. Radio advertising message lasting 30 to 60 seconds.

Staple or **regular goods.** Items that form the core of a retail store's merchandise offering and are carried year-round.

Stockkeeping unit (SKU). Specific classification of merchandise by kind, material, price, color, size, brand, or supplier.

Stock turn. Number of times the average stock is sold during the year.

Store design. Combination of all the physical objects of a store, both inside and outside.

Store layout. Physical arrangement of a store

to facilitate the receiving, displaying, selling, and delivering of goods.

Store policy. Rules or guidelines employees must follow in the daily operation of a retail business.

Straight-commission plan. Compensation in which a salesperson is paid only a percentage of his or her individual sales over a certain period.

Straight-salary plan. Compensation plan in which a flat amount is paid to a salesperson for the time worked and no direct attempt is made to measure individual productivity.

Strip center. Shopping complex that is made up of convenience stores and built on a small site of approximately 15,000 square feet.

Structured traffic. People, including nonshoppers, who may pass a store site en route to their destinations.

Style. Lines and characteristics of an article or activity that distinguish it from other articles or activities of the same kind.

Subconscious level. Level of thinking at which customers act on the basis of emotional urges but do not admit the real reasons for their actions.

Subleasing. Act by which one who has leased property from someone leases it to another person for a shorter term and keeps rights under the first lease.

Subletting. Act by which one who has leased property from someone rents it to another person.

Summarizing. Process of pulling together separate data in the form of written statements.

Supermarket. Large, departmentalized food store carrying a wide variety of fresh, frozen, and packaged foods as well as many home-related items.

Superstore. Retail store that offers a much broader range of consumer products than a supermarket including appliances, televisions, and sporting goods in addition to grocery items.

Supervisor. Person in a retail store who oversees the work of others.

System. Set of procedures or techniques carried out by people and/or equipment to accomplish a given purpose.

Tabulation. Process of classifying data in tables.

Target market. Potential customers of a retail store in a given advertising market.

Tax. Sum of money or fees imposed on a business by local, state, or federal government to finance their operation.

Terms of occupancy. Cost and conditions of purchasing or leasing a particular building or space.

Texture. Surface of a product or display unit; used to create contrast in displays.

Tickler file. Manual system used by retailers to keep track of delinquent credit accounts.

Time management. Systematic procedure for the efficient and effective use of time by employees.

Time utility. Utility added to goods when a retailer makes them available at the time customers want to buy.

Top-down planning. Planning that begins with establishing the overall goals for stock, sales, expenses, and other figures at the store level and then subdividing them into divisions, departments, and various other merchandise classifications.

Trade credit. Credit granted by wholesalers and other store suppliers to allow retailers to buy merchandise for resale.

Trade discount. Deduction from the list price of an item that has been set to include a retail profit margin; functional discount.

Trademark. Word, mark, symbol, device, or a combination of these that represents a brand and is limited in use to the firm that owns it.

Traffic count. Primary information gathered through observation of the number of persons passing a retail establishment.

Transaction. A procedure involved in the

daily operations of a retail business, such as a sale, a return, or a purchase.

Transfer. Relocation of an employee to another job with about the same level of responsibility.

Trial close. Comment or question a salesperson asks to lead a customer to decide to buy.

Ultimate consumer. Person who finally uses goods for personal benefit and satisfaction.

Unconscious level. Level of thinking at which customers act in certain ways but do not know the reasons for their actions.

Unit control method. Method of controlling the amount of stock that uses the number of units or items in stock rather than the dollar value.

Unit pricing. System of setting prices in terms of a standard unit, such as pounds or ounces.

Universal Product Code (UPC). Machine-readable block of thin and thick vertical lines on an item of merchandise that convey product information.

Unlimited liability. Feature of partnership requiring each partner to contribute personal assets to cover the debts of the business.

Utility. Economic value of goods that makes them useful to consumers.

Values. Personal beliefs about what is good, important, or desirable.

Variable expense. Expense, such as sales commissions, that fluctuates almost in direct relation to sales volume; expenditure that is different for each type of good carried by a retailer.

Variety store. Retail store that handles a large assortment of general merchandise, features lower-priced goods, and gives less attention to fashion, furniture, major appliances, and specialized goods.

Visual merchandising. Method of product promotion that allows customers to view merchandise firsthand in displays, descriptive signs, and the decor of a retail business.

Wage. Compensation for employment that is typically earned on an hourly basis.

Wall lighting. Lighting for the walls and other interior surfaces that is usually individually designed for a retail store.

Wants. Products or services that do more than just satisfy a need.

Warehouse control system. Method of controlling the amount of stock by preparing a control file for each separate unit of merchandise.

Wholesaler. Intermediary who buys directly from many producers or manufacturers and then sells to retailers or commercial users.

Window display. Display of merchandise designed to be viewed by potential customers outside a retail store.

Working capital. Money available to retailers to buy merchandise for resale and to cover operating expenses.

INDEX

Direct-mail advertising, 319
Direct retailing, 6
Discount, 266–68
  employee, 232
  retailing, 110
  stores, 110–11
  unit, 111
Discrepancy report, 499
Discretionary fund, 103
Discretionary income, 103
Display, 45, 599
  arrangements, 353–55
  designing, 358–66
    principles of, 362–63
  elements of, 359–62
  evaluating, 373–74
  installing, 367–77
  institutional, 374
  interior, 350–53
  lighting, 460
  planning, 369–71
  planning budget, 370
  planning calendar, 370
  point-of-purchase (POP), 351
  promotional, 374
  requesting, 369, 370
  requirements, 355, 368–69
  visual merchandising, 347–57
  window, 348–50
Disposable personal income, 103
Distribution, 90–93
  of merchandise, 87–95
  physical, 93–94
Distributive Education Clubs of
  America (DECA), 195
Document, 141, 142
Dollar-control method, 515
Drawing accounts, 169
Dummy invoice, 497
Dummy layout, 332

Economic system, elements of, 97
Economy
  community, 125–26
  measures of, 101–4
  of United States, 101–2
EFTS. *See* Electronic fund-transfer
  systems (EFTS)
Electronic advertisements, 333–34
Electronic banking, 70–71

Electronic fund-transfer systems
  (EFTS), 611
Electronic kiosk, 609
Electronic media, 44, 319–20
Electronic ordering, 582
Electronic payment systems,
  70–71
Elements of display design,
  359–62
Emotional appeal, 43
Emotional needs, 199–200
Employee
  discounts, 232
  introducing, 186
  locating and selecting, 177–88
  stock-ownership plans, 169
  theft, 519–20
  training, 189–97
Employee-benefits policy, 169–70
Employee-evaluation policy,
  170–72
Employment
  agencies, 627
  interview, 184, 185
  in retailing, 8
  seeking, 72
End displays, 351
End fixtures, 459
Enterprise, private. *See* Private
  enterprise
Enthusiasm, 200
Entrepreneur, 637
Equipment, 462–63
Equity, 572–73
Equity capital, 537
Estimating, prices, 265–66
Evaluation, of merchandise, 261
Exclusiveness, 310
Expense records, 62, 559–63
Expenses, 286
  classifying, 559–61
  planning, 236
Express company delivery service,
  471
Extraction, 89
Extra dating, 269
Eye appeal, 364–65

Factoring, 478
Factory direct store, 111

Factory outlet, 111
Fad, 246
Fair Labor Standards Act, 573
Fair risk, 483
Fashion, 309
  counts, 602
  cycle, 247
  goods, 245–47
  language of, 246–47
  studying, 246
Feature unit, 458–59
Final sales price, 277
Financial statements, 62, 568–73
Financing
  a business, 535–44
  corporate, 538
  outside, 478–80
Finishing-out, 140
Fixed assets, 571
Fixed capital, 536, 540
Fixed expenses, 561
Fixed liabilities, 571
Flat-amount lease, 140
Flat expenses, 286
Floor limit, 430
FOB destination, 269
  charges reversed, 269
FOB factory, 269
  freight prepaid, 269
FOB shipping point, 269
Forecasting, 583–84
Formal approach, 409
Formal balance, 363
Formal organization, 13–14
Forward stock, 514
Franchise
  businesses, 120–21, 146–48
  contracts, 147–48
  retail, 25–26
Free economic system, 97
Free enterprise, 96–105
  elements of, 97–101
Free on board (FOB), 269
Functional expense categories,
  560

Garnishment, 485
GDP. *See* Gross domestic product
  (GDP)
General lighting, 460

ACKNOWLEDGMENTS

COVER PHOTO   Comstock ©/ Christina Rose Mufson, Washington, D.C., Georgetown Park

UNIT 1   p. 22 (top, left), Jeff Greenberg, Photographer, Merry-Go-Round; p. 22 (top, right), Jeff Greenberg, Photographer; p. 26, Jeff Greenberg, Photographer, Bradlees; p. 27, Courtesy of International Business Machines Corporation; p. 35, © Michael Wilson; p. 47 (right), Courtesy of McAlpins, Kenwood Towne Centre; p. 53 (top, right), Thompson & Formby Inc.; p. 53 (bottom, left), Jeff Greenberg, Photographer, Merry-Go-Round; p. 54, Jeff Greenberg, Photographer, Bradlees; p. 60, Photo courtesy of Hewlett-Packard Company; p. 70, Jeff Greenberg, Photographer

UNIT 2   p. 89, John Deere & Company; p. 90, Courtesy of Chrysler Corporation; p. 99, Melvin Simon & Associates, Inc., Indianapolis, Indiana; p. 146, PIP Printing Headquarters, Los Angeles; p. 152 (left), NCR Corporation; p. 152 (right), Jeff Greenberg, Photographer

UNIT 3   p. 174 (left), Jeff Greenberg, Photographer, Bradlees; p. 174 (center), Jeff Greenberg, Photographer, Bradlees; p. 174 (bottom), Jeff Greenberg, Photographer; p. 192, Jeff Greenberg, Photographer; p. 194, Jeff Greenberg, Photographer; p. 201, Jeff Greenberg, Photographer; p. 202, Photo courtesy of Brown Group, Inc., St. Louis, Missouri; p. 211, Jeff Greenberg, Photographer

UNIT 4   p. 230, Jeff Greenberg, Photographer, Bradlees; p. 257, Jeff Greenberg, Photographer; p. 270, Jeff Greenberg, Photographer, Bradlees; p. 271, Jeff Greenberg, Photographer; p. 281, Jeff Greenberg, Photographer, Bradlees; p. 288, Jeff Greenberg, Photographer; p. 292, Photograph courtesy of Texas Instruments

UNIT 5   p. 309 (left), copyright Tiffany & Co.; p. 309 (right), Phillips Petroleum Company; p. 310, Jeff Greenberg, Photographer, A&S; p. 321 (top), Jeff Greenberg, Photographer; p. 321 (bottom, left), Jeff Greenberg, Photographer, Bradlees; p. 349 (bottom), Photo courtesy of Pier 1 Imports, Inc.; p. 352 (top), Jeff Greenberg, Photographer, A&S; p. 352 (center, left), Jeff Greenberg, Photographer, Bradlees; p. 352 (center, right), Jeff Greenberg, Photographer, Bradlees; p. 352 (bottom, left), Jeff Greenberg, Photographer, Bradlees; p. 352 (bottom, center), Jeff Greenberg, Photographer, Bradlees; p. 352 (bottom, right), Jeff Greenberg, Photographer; p. 359, Jeff Greenberg, Photographer, A&S; p. 360, Jeff Greenberg, Photographer, A&S; p. 371, Jeff Greenberg, Photographer, A&S; p. 372, Jeff Greenberg, Photographer, A&S; p. 373 (left), Jeff Greenberg, Photographer, A&S; p. 373 (right), Jeff Greenberg, Photographer, A&S

UNIT 6   p. 392, Jeff Greenberg, Photographer; p. 406, Jeff Greenberg, Photographer; p. 411, Jeff Greenberg, Photographer, Bradlees; p. 412 (all), Jeff

Greenberg, Photographer; p. 419, Jeff Greenberg, Photographer, A&S; p. 421, Jeff Greenberg, Photographer, A&S; p. 423, Jeff Greenberg, Photographer, A&S; p. 428, Jeff Greenberg, Photographer, A&S; p. 429 (all), Jeff Greenberg, Photographer; p. 433, Jeff Greenberg, Photographer; p. 438, Jeff Greenberg, Photographer, A&S

UNIT 7 p. 456, Jeff Greenberg, Photographer, Bradlees; p. 481, Jeff Greenberg, Photographer, A&S; p. 493, Jeff Greenberg, Photographer; p. 494 (both), Jeff Greenberg, Photographer; p. 504, Jeff Greenberg, Photographer; p. 510, Jeff Greenberg, Photographer, Bradlees; p. 515, Jeff Greenberg, Photographer, Bradlees; p. 520, Jeff Greenberg, Photographer, A&S

UNIT 8 p. 557, NCR Corporation; p. 583, NCR Corporation

UNIT 9 p. 599, Jeff Greenberg, Photographer; p. 600, Photograph Courtesy of Texas Instruments; p. 603, Jeff Greenberg, Photographer; p. 609, Photo courtesy of SERVICE MERCHANDISE; p. 610, Billy Grimes, Photographer; p. 617, Jeff Greenberg, Photographer; p. 619, The Postcard Factory; p. 620, International Dairy Queen, Inc.; p. 625, Jeff Greenberg, Photographer, A&S; p. 637, Jeff Greenberg, Photographer